FEARSOME FOURSOME

HEADSLAP

"Those were monumental times, times of great unrest and civil change in the United States, and Deacon's recollections in *Headslap* bring it all back to life, just like it was yesterday. I laughed and wept, thinking back on those days, days of thunder and violence on the field, in the streets of our nation, in all our hearts."

—ROSEY GRIER

"My very good friend Deacon Jones always did have a big mouth, and a ready rage for injustice on or off the football field. He could near frighten a person to death, the things he would say. . . . And now he's doing it again in his new book *Headslap,* giving the straight story of what it was like for us in the NFL. The wild times, the pain and joy, the politics, the prejudice, the drugs, the victories and the failures, and above all, the emerging triumph of the human spirit—it's all here, captured in these tales. I honestly couldn't put it down."

—LAMAR LUNDY

"He was—what?—a 14th round draft pick, out of some unknown little college. He came out of nowhere, chasing the Great American Dream and every quarterback in the league. Before he was through, he changed the game of football. I know. I had to shape the Cowboys' game plan around him and the rest of that famous front four, and so did every other coach in the league."

—TOM LANDRY

"What was it like to play against Deacon Jones? How did people feel about Attila the Hun?"

—BART STARR

"I owe everything to Deacon Jones. If it wouldn't have been for him and his lightning sack rush, I wouldn't be known today as the greatest scrambling quarterback in history."

—FRAN TARKENTON

"Deacon was the most outstanding defensive end there ever was. He gave us more trouble than anybody. Running an offense against him was like playing against the shark in *Jaws.*"

—JOHN UNITAS

HEADSLAP

The Life and Times of
DEACON JONES

John Klawitter and Deacon Jones

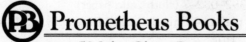 Prometheus Books

59 John Glenn Drive
Amherst, New York 14228-2197

Published 1996 by Prometheus Books

00 99 98 97 96   5 4 3 2

Library of Congress Cataloging-in-Publication Data

Klawitter, John.
    Headslap : the life and times of Deacon Jones / John Klawitter & Deacon Jones.
        p.   cm.
    Includes bibliographical references and index.
    ISBN 1–57392–082–7 (cloth : alk. paper)
    1. Football players—United States—Biography. I. Jones, Deacon, 1939–   . II. Title.
GV939.J63K53   1996
796.332'092—dc20
[B]   96–21494
                                                                                        CIP

Printed in the United States of America on acid-free paper

For my two families:

The first, Ishmeal and Mattie,
my heritage in Eatonville,
the ones who taught me faith and survival,
and then had the strength and courage to let me go.

And the second, George and Etty Allen,
who had the understanding and the love
to take me in on the other end
and encourage me along the path to glory.

Contents

Foreword

You know the cry "Dee-fense! Dee-fense!" that you hear at football games these days? Well, before David "Deacon" Jones, there was no such yell. The Deacon put the "D" in football. He was the first defensive player in the game to become a star. Before the Deacon, defensive players were as anonymous as spies. They were the unknown soldiers of football, known but to God—and the line coach.

Deacon Jones changed all that. The first time he came hurtling off the line of scrimmage slapping the helmet of the lineman trying to block him, the crowd at the L.A. Coliseum knew they were looking at something special. It was like watching a cop raid a crap game, the Lone Ranger bust up a rustling ring.

All kinds of words hit the language because of the need to keep up with this one of the Joneses. The "sack," for instance. If it was used before, Deacon popularized it and put it in the language. He was the first one to make the quarterback look like something that should be put in burlap and hauled off to the warehouse.

Deacon revolutionized the position of defensive end because he was (1) fast; and (2) unstoppable. He came into the line of scrimmage like a guy jumping through a skylight.

The title of his book is *Headslap,* and there's a story there. In Deacon's day, you could rattle the cage (or at least the helmet) of the guy trying to block you by belting him alongside the head. Deacon did this better than anyone in the game. You could hear his headslaps

9

clear up on the rim of the Coliseum. They weren't jabs. They were full left hooks, right crosses. You were glad you were only hearing them, not feeling them. They had the impact of a Jack Dempsey right, a Mike Tyson uppercut.

How devastating were they? They were so devastating that they were outlawed. Deacon got the right to the head ruled illegal. That was after offensive players complained he should at least wear six-ounce gloves.

Deacon piled up a hundred unassisted tackles a year in his good years. He sacked the quarterback twenty times a year or more, twenty-six one year, twenty-four another. He broke up the play even when he didn't get there. There wasn't a quarterback in the league who didn't hurry up his throw when he saw Deacon coming.

It's hard to imagine the impact he had on the game. Prior to Deacon, defensive linemen got drafted just higher than placekick holders. It was the view of coaching staffs that any 250-pound mastodon would do.

Deacon changed that, too. First of all, he had so much straight-ahead speed that he frequently out-sprinted backs in preseason practice. He could change direction like a fox. He was the only guy in the league Fran Tarkenton couldn't get away from.

People used to get up and go out for a hot dog or popcorn when the Rams didn't have the football. They considered the defense to be just the janitors. Get the place cleaned up for the Ram offense, the glamour part of the lineup—Bob Waterfield, Dutch Van Brocklin, Vitamin Smith, Kenny Washington, Tank Younger, Tom Harmon, Glenn Davis. Legends. Guys with the football.

Deacon got the defense equal billing. He even got his role a name. He became known far and wide as "The Secretary of Defense." It used to be said that the duty of the defensive end or tackle was to smash through the interference and arrive at the quarterback in bad humor. Deacon arrived with a smile. The quarterback wasn't smiling.

Deacon wasn't mad at anybody. He just wanted the one with the football. If he had to throw a few others out of his way—or slap them out of his way—there was nothing personal. Just business as usual.

Deacon had big help. The whole Ram front four was a mountain range of menace and muscle—Deacon, Merlin Olsen, Roosevelt Grier, and Lamar Lundy. They were so good the league appropriated a nickname that had been fastened on a lesser San Diego frontline and transferred it over to the Rams rushers. They became the "Fearsome Foursome."

They made the pass rush famous. In fact, they choreographed it. Before this fearsome foursome, linemen just took their own individual paths to the quarterback. Deacon and company perfected a series of maneuvers known as "stunts" or "loops," which had the effect of a ballet line doing *Swan Lake.* They swapped assignments at the line of scrimmage to confuse the blockers. They made a science out of rushing the passer.

Deacon Jones was to defensive football what Babe Ruth was to offensive baseball. He was a genius at it. He was like an archangel out there swooping down on the quarterback. Prior to Deacon, most defensive linemen just tried to submarine the play. They would dive at the feet of the interference and set up the stoppage for the linebacker or defensive backs. Before Deacon, linemen had to be fast only for a step or two. Deacon used to run down ball-carriers from behind. Deacon was never out of the play if he was upright. And he was always upright. He was, without question, the most intimidating force in the history of defensive football. It was a brave quarterback who ventured on Deacon's side of the field.

If all Deacon had been was a ferocious tackler and pass rusher, his reputation would have been secure, but Deacon was a spokesman for the Rams and for pro football in general. Deacon was never your churlish, you-saw-it-write-it type of postgame interviewee. Deacon was generous with his time, savvy about public relations, a spokesman for his race and a spokesman for his game. And he was most anxious that people recognize the achievements of the overlooked minority he represented—the defense.

It's safe to say Deacon was instrumental in raising significantly the pay scale for defensive players. No more $200 a game for tacklers and playbreakers. Deacon dramatized their contributions, giving them arguments at contract time. I'm not sure, but I believe it was Deacon who popularized the distribution of defensive statistics in the press box. The stat sheet tabulation of tackles, assisted tackles, rushed passes, and sacks may be another of Deacon Jones's monuments.

Deacon was a crusader against racial prejudice by the sheer weight of his personality, accomplishments, and attitude. It was impossible not to like him and impossible not to listen to him.

Deacon was not only all-pro, he was all-man. His contributions to the game and to society cannot be minimized. Growing up in the Deep South, Deacon never played against a white man until he joined the Rams in 1961. He had gone to a segregated college and led a segregated life. But the whole world was Deacon's turf, not just the hundred yards from end zone to end zone. He became a confidant of the Kennedy family, and a respected member of the political community.

He was the greatest at what he did. His achievements lit the way for generations who came after him. There was only one Deacon.

JIM MURRAY
Los Angeles Times
Syndicated columnist

Introduction

This is a history of America as much as it is a book about sports or my personal life and accomplishments. It is an attempt to record important events and the thoughts of the men who lived them. Things happened, and I was fortunate enough to be there. Of course, being Deacon Jones, I do have strong opinions on most matters, and you will hear them. However, you will also find the thoughts, ideas, and opinions of many of the people who were there. Not everyone agrees with me, and that is as it should be.

We Americans owe more than we can ever say to the Jewish people; our language, art, literature, science, and religion would be lacking without their contributions. Black Americans and Jews have traveled a parallel road of faith and suffering, and have more in common than is understood or admitted by many. I, in particular, owe a debt to the Jews, for they have taught me that underdogs may dream high dreams and accomplish much, and that history must never be forgotten.

And so, although I started as an angry young man, this book is not written in bitterness or rage, but rather with a pride in what we blacks and whites and reds and yellows and browns have accomplished together, with hope for the future, with a smile for the moments we've shared along the way, and with a touch of sadness for those who still do not understand.

DAVID DEACON JONES
October 1995

13

Acknowledgments

This book could never have been written without the patience, understanding, and long hours of research contributions by my wife, Lynn Jensen-Klawitter. And just as true, it could not have been done without the efforts, contacts, and sincere encouragement provided by Deacon's wife, Elizabeth Jones. It is not your usual, off-the-top-of-the-head sports story; we have gone to extraordinary efforts to recreate the life, the times, and the actual games themselves. A special vote of thanks is owed to the Los Angeles Rams, particularly owner Georgia Frontiere, Vice President Marshall Klein, and John Oswald, for making available their official team files and records, and to the NFL Hall of Fame in Canton, Ohio, particularly Joe Horrigan in the Research Library, for the same. Thanks to John M. Turney for his years of research and compilation of his "NFL Career Quarterback Sack Leaders." To Jason, C. R., and Matt Klawitter for putting up with my long absences ("Earth to Dad, come in, please") during the past five years. Thanks as well to the Los Angeles sports writers of the Deacon Jones era, particularly Mal Florence, Jim Murray, and Paul Zimmerman of the *Los Angeles Times,* and Bob Oates of the *Los Angeles Herald Examiner.* Also, credit is owed to writer Bill Libby, whose 1979 publication *Life in the Pit* provided a wealth of detailed information on the first decade of Deacon's career, as well as quotes from players and coaches Libby interviewed at that time, and to Bill Eppridge for helping find certain long-lost photos. Thanks also to the long list of

15

famous players, coaches, NFL officials, celebrities, and other people who agreed to be interviewed and have given their time and opinions to this enterprise; among these, the long list must include (in no particular order except that Deacon's mother comes first) Mattie Jones, Jimmy Dean, Mary Moore, G. D. Clay, Willie Jeffries, Ann Peeples, Jack Teele, Carl Eller, Etty Allen, Bruce Allen, Greg Scopitoni, Paul Zimmerman, Don Paul, Rex Paul, Jim Bowen, Pervis Atkins, Dick Bass, Bob Lilly, Y. A.Tittle, Roger Brown, Charlie Cowan, Tommy Prothro, Harland Svare, Pete Rozelle, Lamar Lundy, Merlin Olsen, Rosey Grier, Bradley Merville, Marion Motley, George Menifee, Tom Fears, Gale Sayers, Fran Tarkenton, John Unitas, Jack Patera, Alvin Hall, Ollie Matson, Elroy Hirsh, Tom Landry, Weeb Ewbanks, Roman Gabriel, Dr. Arnold Mandell, Judge Robert Baxley, Michael Klein, Bill Kilmer, Jhoon Rhee, Rene Thomas (of KLAC radio), Steve Lapin, Ray Kipp, Beth Wood, Anne Magill (these last four from the *San Diego Union*), Prof. Frederick Sontag of Pomona College, Tes Safavi, Margo Braer, and many, many others. Many books, publications, magazines and newspapers have been researched, and are cited where they have been quoted. Special thanks to Terry Henning of SYNCOM, who kindly retrieved some vital computer data just before it was lost forever in Tronland. And last but not least, I owe very much to my editors: Editor-in-chief Steven Mitchell, who asks all the right questions; Managing Editor Mark Hall; and line editor Reg Gilbert.

JOHN KLAWITTER

1

Just Another Child of the South

To know how it was, we have to go back to the beginnings, back to the Deep South, to the whoop and holler and the rebel yell, to the way it was in the fifties, after World War II but before the civil rights movement. The world has changed; you can't get there any more, not really. But if you want a small taste of history, head north out of Orlando a few miles. There's an exit there that can tumble you back into a another world, into a small black town that is hemmed in by white communities and by the last vestiges of the swamps themselves, a place that time itself seems to have forgotten. You'll be in a small patch of the Old South . . . in Eatonville, Florida, the birthplace of David Jones.

The Watermelon Lovers

It was a warm and sunny Sunday morning going on towards noon in Eatonville. The all-day affair known simply as "Sunday church" was in full swing at the whitewashed, steepled structure that was the Open Door Missionary Baptist Church. Eatonville may have lived hard Saturday night, but it was serious about Sunday church. For the kids there would be Sunday School, lunch, the BYPU (Baptist Youth Progressive Union), and then evening services. The opening service had been a long one, but now it was over and there was a brief spell for socializing.

17

David "Davey" Jones yawned as he watched the townfolks, all dressed in their Sunday go-to-meeting clothes, gathered in little clumps and bunches to talk the local talk. The year was 1950, and Davey was twelve years old. He'd come to church with Mattie, his mother, his five sisters, and his two brothers, Judson and Harold. Davey didn't mind church. The preacher gave a mighty mean sermon, and the singing was fun. Davey knew he had a good singing voice, good as any around.

Ishmeal, his dad, couldn't be there. He was "house niggering" for a white man over in Winter Park, which meant he played the roles of chauffeur, butler, fix-it man, and all-around servant—the South's answer to the outcome of the Civil War. Davey didn't feel any resentment; that was just the way things were, and he knew they were lucky his dad had the job. Davey himself worked whenever he could find a job. Mattie and Ishmeal scratched like alley cats for a living, anything to make ends meet. The whole family worked the fields in season, and odd-jobbed for the *crackers,* that is, the poor whites, in the all-white towns that surrounded Eatonville. Together they scraped in enough money to get by in the two-room shack they called home.

The lucky blacks got the house-niggering jobs. Mostly, aside from that, it was bone-hard work under the broiling Florida sun, picking beans and corn and tomatoes in the white man's fields. It was sun-up to sun-down, all for five or six bucks a day, fall into bed and sleep like you're dead—and be ready for sun-up the next morning.

Young Davey pitched watermelons until his muscles screamed. On the farmlands of central Florida, the melons are rolled in a line and as the truck drives along in the field, a pitcher on the ground throws them to a catcher in the truck. It's easy for the first three hours or so, but just about the time your muscles start to feel the toll, the day is just begun.

Standing on the church steps, Davey stretched his arms, yawning again as he looked around for the fellows he usually hung out with. He was big for his age, and strong-minded; the others, his gang of friends, looked up to him. He heard a distant rumble and saw dust down the road. Somebody comin' into town, he thought.

That in itself was odd. There were only a few rattletrap clunkers in Eatonville, and folks didn't zoom through, not ever. Eatonville had always marched to the tune of its own drum. It was off the beaten track, connected by a rutted dirt road that looped off the main highway through town; you had to go out of your way to get to Eatonville.

Davey eyed the distant vehicle closely. Nobody else even noticed it, or if they did, they didn't say. Easy to see, they were mostly caught up in the Sunday social, the young girls flirting, the older married men in a group, lighting up their unfiltered Camels and chewing over such things as prices and wages, the married women passing the details of life in their own little world.

It was a shiny new convertible, a pale yellow Plymouth. Davey could see it more clearly as it turned the corner and headed down the dusty main street. Maybe they had made a mistake—had been out for fun and made the wrong turn—but he didn't think so. He had a sudden uneasy feeling in the pit of his stomach. Still, what could be happening here in his own town on such a bright and sunny morning? He held one hand over his eyes and squinted in the bright sunlight. He could make out the people in the convertible; it looked like a load of whites—likely, high school kids from Maitland—dressed casual like they were headed to one of the lakes for a picnic. The Plymouth skidded a bit on the dusty road as it cornered and then lined up for a run through the center of town, and Davey heard a distant rebel yell.

"Look out! Car coming!"

Nobody paid him much attention. A few of the men closest to the street moved back a few steps, but everyone else was too busy to listen to a young kid yelling. And then the speeding car was right on top of them.

The car was packed with white teenagers, whooping foolishly like they were drunk or crazy. One of them stood in the back seat. He looked like a football player, with thick arms and a thick neck. The huge, red-faced cracker was holding a big green watermelon high over his head.

"Here ya go!" the thick-necked footballer yelled. "You niggers like watermelon!" He threw the melon, and it arched through the air. "Look ooout!" Davey screamed.

He saw the melon turn lazily in the air as if it were moving in *slow motion.* Luckily, most of the other church-goers saw it too, except for a group of old ladies with their heads close together, gabbing away and not paying attention. The melon crashed down on one frail old grandmother and drove her to the ground, where her head cracked on a stone. She lay motionless in the dust, bits of green rind and pink melon flesh and black seeds all around her and a seep of blood from her nose and ears.

For a moment Davey stood stunned. Wild thoughts raced through his mind. How could anyone do such a thing? Do they think black people are dogs? And then, without thinking, he threw off his coat, loosened his tie, and began to run behind the church and across the fields. He knew every inch of the Eatonville loop; when he was younger, he'd caught crawdads in the ditches and played pirates and soldiers and cowboys in the empty fields that bordered it. There was only one way back to the main road, and that car full of white trash had to take it. He ran until his side ached and he was gasping for breath, and he came to the road as the yellow car was approaching. He staggered across a ditch, ruining his pants and shoes as he went knee-deep in brackish water. He frantically waved his arms from the side of the road.

"Waa-hooo! Gonna get us a coon!" the driver whooped, stepping on the gas. Davey dove for the ditch at the side of the road. The car swerved toward him, and somebody flung an empty whiskey bottle.

"Have ya'self a drink, nigger!"

The bottle grazed his head and he found himself on his hands and knees in the scummy water. He heard laughter and the car roaring away in the distance.

That evening, the usual group of black men gathered outside Hank Steele's Pool Hall, sipping cheap whiskey, nursing beers and hawking tobacco spit into the dusty street. There was only one subject of conversation. The old lady struck by the melon was in a bad way; the doc couldn't do anything for her, and everybody could see she wasn't going to last but a few days, if that.

Davey sat on an upside-down pail on the fringe of the group of men, mulling over what had happened. He finally said, "I think we should go to Maitland."

The older men looked at him with scorn. "And whut?" one of them said. "What you gonna do, little black boy?"

Davey shook his head stubbornly, refusing to be intimidated, "We should git ourselves t'gether and tell somebody about dis!"

"Say what, fool?"

"We gotta report it. I could point out th' one what hucked the melon."

"Re-port it!" the man hooted. "Wit' who we gonna do that?"

Davey wasn't quite sure who handled such matters, "Well, with the newspaperman or a lawyer—or the police."

"Yer uncle here's a policeman. Report it to him!"

Davey's uncle looked down at his hands. True, he was the sworn constable of Eatonville. But he knew nobody outside of town cared two beans about that. He shook his head, refusing to look at the young boy, "Davey . . . it be best if we let this go . . ."

"We can't just do that! We're people, just like white folks! We're th' ones agreein'—we're lettin' them treat us like animals!"

The uncle sighed, "Davey, I don' think them kids was actually out to kill nobody. They was just headed for the lake, and on the way they thought they'd have a little fun . . ."

"I can't stand it!" the boy screamed. "That old lady is gonna die! That's murder!" His voice broke into a high tenor, and that embarrassed him. He jerked to his feet, looking around for someone to hit or something to throw. "That's murder, and they's treating us like dogs, and you all are just goin' to bury her like a dog and take it!" The black men of Eatonville looked at him or the ground, saying nothing, and Davey angrily walked away into the night.

Finally one of them shifted on his seat and sighed, "That boy's gonna cause a lotta trouble bu'fore he's through."

"See the size on him? He's gonna be a big one."

The man with the wine bottle nodded, "He's gonna need it."

"That be true enough. He could bring us all to mournin'." They turned toward the uncle, "Don't his pap give him enough of a lickin' to keep sense in him?"

The uncle shook his head, "It ain't his pap. His pap cracks him plenty, but you can't make grits out of gravel. Davey takes after his gran'paw. Now there was a mean man."

One spit out into the street, nodding out into the night in the direction Davey had gone. "Young buck best have mean to the bottom of his bones."

The man with the twisted-cap wine bottle nodded again, "Yep. He's gonna need it."

Closed Circuit

Davey was in Hank Steele's Poolroom, rattling the balls around on the best of Hank's three shabby tables. He was facing off against his favorite sucker, young Doc Smith, for ten cents a game. Doc Smith, who was gradually taking over his practice from his father, *old* Doc Smith, had come to Davey months before, asking to learn the finer points of the game, and Davey had agreed to play him for a lowly dime a game. A dime wasn't much, but, since Davey never lost, it all added up. Now, while Doc looked on, he lined up the six ball, banking the cue ball around the ten, and the six dropped into the leather side pocket with a satisfying clunk. Pool was all angles and hard nerves and cool follow-through. It was something he understood. There were other, more complicated things he could only puzzle and rage over.

Living as a teenager in Eatonville in the mid-fifties, the local history meant very little to Davey. He didn't care that it was the oldest chartered and incorporated all-black community in America, or that it existed as a small pocket of black culture and black poverty with roots going directly back to the days of slavery. Thoughts like that, true or no, were useless—they couldn't even put one thin dime in your pocket. A fine, straight pool stick, on the other hand . . . well, that was another matter.

The old black woman struck in the head by the watermelon had, as predicted, died a few weeks after she was hit. That had happened three years ago, but folks still talked about it sometimes, and when they did it was in whispered tones. Some said it truly was a shame, while others noted she was old and going to die anyway. Perhaps it was God's will, and even a blessing that she didn't linger longer than she had, death being the hard business that it was. Davey had turned it over and over in his own mind, and he didn't agree with any of it. He had become sullen and sensitized to the ways of the Deep South, to waiting at the end of the line, to stepping off the sidewalk and waiting for the whites to pass by, to sitting in the back of the bus when almost all the good seats up front were empty. It bothered him to drink from the Blacks Only water fountain, to use the dank and filthy rest rooms reserved for blacks, to sit in the mean black section of restaurants and to order food from the small carry-out window at diners that didn't allow blacks at all. Why? he would ask himself. Why do they do these things to us? And why do we stand for it?

Time to go. It was spring training season, and a bunch of the gang were going to drive an old jalopy over to Orlando to see if they could sneak into the game. Maybe they wouldn't even sneak in this time. Over the past two days, Doc Smith had more than paid for his ticket, and bought him a fat little 12-ounce bottle of Coca-Cola on the side.

Black Ball

The bat was a blur in Jackie Robinson's hands. From their bleacher seats, Davey Jones and his high-school gang heard the sharp crack and saw the ball fly over the leaping second baseman's outstretched glove into center field. The right fielder came on fast, scooped the ball on one hop and fired in to second, but Jackie hook-slid in safe to beat the tag. And then, in a move so clear they saw it even from the black section clear in the back of the bleachers, the white second baseman stepped on Jackie's hand, grinding in his cleats as he did so. Then he turned and walked away, grinning and innocently lobbing the ball to third as if to say I didn't do anything. His pose of innocence didn't matter, because the white umpire was making an obvious point of looking the other way.

Davey stood and booed as loud as he could. Sugar Man at his side yelled and waved his fists. Normally nutty and fun-loving Willie James didn't have a smile on his face now; always loyal to the cause, he stood and howled his rage. Even the two short guys, Lonnie Bellamy and Bo Bo, were on their feet, screaming for revenge.

Jackie stood and dusted off his uniform, ignoring the blood dripping from his fingers. He may have been the Georgia-born son of a sharecropper and the grandson of a slave, but he had attitude. He carried himself with an inner pride that made him untouchable. The pitcher went into his wind-up, and Jackie streaked toward third. In the stands, Davey and his friends howled with glee, "Ol' Jackie don't like second base, seems like! Noooooo, sir!"

"He sure din't stay long!"

They had an attitude, too, and they knew it—Davey, Sugar Man, Willie James (called Wee for short), Lonnie, and Bo Bo. And understanding that it wasn't wise to be African-American and different in any way in the Deep South of the 1950s, they found safety in numbers. They shared boyhood jokes, adventures, and one common dream. They all wanted to get out of Eatonville.

They had borrowed an old junker from somebody's sister and driven eight miles along the two-lane blacktop from Eatonville to Tinker Field in Orlando to see the game. It was spring training, and the Washington Senators were entertaining the Dodgers, who had come up from Vero Beach to play. Even though the Senators were the hometown team, none of the blacks rooted for them. They came to see

Jackie and the other Negroes who were just breaking into the big leagues.

This was something new, blacks playing baseball in the white man's league. Sure, there had been a few blacks who played in the 1800s, but that was old, dead history. There had always been great black ballplayers, but they had been forced to play in the old Negro Baseball League. Blacks, they said, were too undisciplined to play in the real game. Too wild and uncontrollable. They might have raw talent, but they didn't have the training and the skills for the big leagues. And anyway, the story went, who would want to see a black man play?

Jackie Robinson had broken the color line in baseball. Signed by Branch Rickey in 1945, he came up to play first base for the Brooklyn Dodgers in 1947. That year some southerners swore they would mutiny, and at least two clubs threatened to strike. Jackie answered with his bat, hitting .293, scoring 125 runs and stealing 29 bases. Soon the Cleveland Indians in the American League signed Larry Doby, and the old ban started to unravel. But the way wasn't going to be easy for blacks.

Two pitches later, Jackie was called out trying to squeeze home. The play was close, but from the bleachers it was clear he had been cheated again, and a new roar went up from the crowded black section. The few poor white folks unlucky enough to be stuck nearby in the cheap white seats eyed Davey and his gang nervously. Damn! Don't they know their place no more? That's what comes of lettin' darkies play white man's ball!

The Dodgers picked up their mitts and took to the field. The talk in Davey's small group turned to music. Davey was considered the expert, and Bo Bo asked, "Who's comin' to d' club?" Club Eaton was an all-night nightclub sprawled in the center of a big, rutted parking lot right across Kennedy Street from Davey's house. Almost all of central Florida closed at two in the morning, but Eatonville was incorporated by the sons of slaves, and one of the few ways they could show their independence was to make their own laws about when to close their bars. Since the hours of the day were filled with work, they kept the club open all night. The fun didn't start until you could hear a cricket chirp, and it didn't end until dawn. Whites wouldn't come in, but after two they might stray up to the gate to buy a bottle of whiskey, the only place for miles around where it was available. Davey somehow talked his way into running errands for the bartender, and so they let him sneak in the back door and listen to the singers.

Davey watched Jackie trot to first base and throw the ball around. He looked like he was going to be okay. "James Brown and the Famous Flames," he said without really thinking about it.

"Oh, wow—they gonna let you in?"

"Don't see why not." He always got in. He had somehow figured his way in to see them all, up close, and even talked to some of them, got to know the drummers and the musicians who did longer stints, hanging around for more than a day or so. Sam Cook had played Club Eaton. And the Jackie Wilson Review. Davey had been five feet away, listening to Smokey Robinson and the Miracles, Gladys Knight and the Pips, and Hank Ballard and the Midnighters.

"You don' like d' Flames," Bo Bo said, seeing his look.

"They okay," Davey said grudgingly.

"You don' seem all that tickled." Lonnie gave him a poke in the ribs, imitating the frown on his face.

"James Brown is great. They's all great. Best singers and bands in the world."

"Then what eatin' you, man? Why you got such a long puss?"

The frown deepened on Davey's face. "You ever wonder how come the greatest musical folk in the whole wide world end up playin' for peanuts in poor little ol' Eatonville?"

Willie James scratched his head. "Well, 'cuz it custom dat they come . . . ?"

Davey snorted in disgust. "No, Wee Willie. Don't always be the fool. It be the only place they allowed to play."

"Dat ain't so . . ." But Willie James wasn't so sure.

"Where else then? Where else?"

Davey looked angrily around him. A few of the older blacks nearby gave him warning glares, and one fat mamma gave him a dirty look and put her finger to her lips in a warning gesture. But nobody answered his question. Nobody could think of a place.

"It stinks," Davey said.

By now, the fat mamma and most of the other Negroes had moved a bit away from him, as if to say, Don't misunderstand; he ain't one of us. One or two of the whites looked like they were listening up, and—as any southern black since the grim days of slavery would tell you—that wasn't good. But Davey was started now and he didn't care. He would say his mind. The whites were outnumbered here, and they would be gone after the game. If they didn't like it, they could go sit with their own kind.

Today, we think of black singers, dancers, and musicians as part of our national heritage, but in the mid-fifties, eighty-odd years after the end of slavery, nearly all the finest and most talented black musicians could only find work by traveling the "Chitlin' Circuit," a string of smoky dives, bars, and shabby nightclub lounges throughout the South and in the black sections of Northern cities like Detroit, Chicago, and Cleveland. These musicians showed up at the Club Eaton every year or so. For many blacks, their success proved things were looking up for the brothers. But Davey, who enjoyed his church singing, had asked about it. He'd talked at length with many of the traveling musicians, and the stories of their wandering, difficult lives served to reaffirm his deepening beliefs—no matter what they did, no matter how great they were, blacks ended up playing and singing and working with and for other blacks. There simply was no way out.

Eatonville was self-sufficient, and Davey was tempted to stay there. If he wanted, he would never have to leave. He could stay with black folks and never have to deal with whites. If only he didn't hate it so, his closed little black world!

As the ninth inning wound down, it was clear the Dodgers would win. No group of white thugs armed with clubs and bricks materialized, and most of the older Negros left the bleachers feeling a sigh of relief.

The game over, Davey and his gang ran around to the small pathway where they knew the players walked to the dressing room. Running full-tilt, they rounded a corner and nearly ran over Jackie Robinson, who was signing autographs for a crowd of about a dozen blacks. They all fished around for scraps of paper, and one of them came up with a pencil stub. As the line grew shorter, Davey fell silent. There was his hero, standing not five feet away. Davey could see there was no empty brag to the man. He had his own quiet dignity, and he talked to everyone like they were full-grown and respected. As he inched closer, Davey could see the spike marks on the back of Jackie's hand.

"You hand gonna be okay?" he asked. He couldn't think of anything else to say.

"Yes," Jackie said.

"I guess y' get used to it," Davey said, hardly daring to look the man in the eye. It was more a question than a statement.

Jackie studied the tall young boy in front of him for a moment. "No, son," he answered gently. "You don't never get used to it."

"Then how——?"

Jackie smiled and put his hand on Davey's shoulder, "We got the talent. What we do is, we beat 'em on the field."

Davey nodded, feeling a stirring. Usually impatient to be moving, he stood quietly by while his buddies Lonnie and Willie James got autographs. Jackie stayed until he'd signed the last bit of paper and answered the last question. The Dodger's star first baseman didn't seem in any hurry at all. He was at home with these boys. He knew how important he was to them, and he'd thought through what his role was. He was the first, the inspirer, the fire-starter. You never knew where the sparks would fall, so the next generation could carry the flame forward. Who could be sure? He'd come from poor beginnings in nearby Georgia, himself. Maybe one of these raw Florida kids, inspired by something he said or did, would grow to make his mark in the big leagues. That was the thing, you had to be there for them all; you never knew *which* one it was going to be . . .

Davey's gang whooped and hollered, pumped by their success, as they ran for their jalopy. They'd actually talked to their greatest baseball hero! Davey followed behind, walking alone. He sat in the back seat with his feet hunched up on the tattered seat, studying each of his friends. The five of them supported each other, reinforced each other's resolve. Davey knew they were the best his generation had to offer from Eatonville. But the odds were clear enough—they weren't all going to make it out of town. They'd be lucky if any of them escaped!

One line drummed itself over and over in Davey's mind, I must beat them on the field, I must beat them on the field, I must beat them on the field. He was more determined than ever to get out of Eatonville . . . and maybe there was another way besides pool sharking.

Death of the Empress

Davey was playing tackle for Hungerford High, going both ways, as usual. They were playing Jones High, out of Orlando, another all-black team. That's all they played—other blacks—the leagues being separated. As a sweep developed around his side of the field, Davey slid into the hole and made the tackle. He went down hard and at the same time felt a helmet slam into his upper thigh. There was a stinging numbness. He jumped up and limped back to his position, wishing for the hundredth time that they had thigh pads. Hungerford, like the other black schools, wasn't much on equipment. They were lucky they had helmets, shoulder pads, shoes, and the one good game uniform. Luxuries like tape and thigh pads weren't available.

Davey looked across the line at the opposing team, now gathered in their huddle. He didn't bother to look back at his own sidelines. Coach Zip Head wouldn't take him out for a little thing like that. Zip wasn't big on resting his players. And it wasn't anything to worry about, anyway. After all, it wasn't even bleeding.

After the first week, the bruise stopped aching. It seemed to be healing, although there was a slight lump. As the months went by, the lump raised itself, becoming the size of a walnut, and then a lemon. At first Davey was proud of it. It was a war wound, a trophy earned in battle. But then his friend Bo Bo, who lost a brother to cancer, mentioned it might be *malignant*. . . . Bo Bo called it 'ligant, but Davey got the idea.

He'd been hiding it from his parents, afraid they might take it in their minds that something had to be done. But, in a small house like theirs, you couldn't hide a thing like that forever. One of his sisters saw it and told, and first thing he knew, they had him over at Doc Smith's place, and Young Doc recommended they go into the hospital in Orlando to have it removed. Davey wasn't very concerned. It was crazy to have a problem like this with football come and gone and baseball already in the air. As they left, he joked whether or not they could pay in chickens.

Bright and early the following Wednesday morning, his older brother Judson borrowed a car and drove Davey and his mom into the city to have it looked after. It was a drowsy Florida morning with a balmy wind. In short, baseball weather, and Davey wanted to be out shagging flies and swinging the bat.

The white doctor who would be doing the surgery nodded and gave the leg a serious frown. Yes, the tumor would have to be removed. He gave Davey's mom the necessary papers and directed them down a long hall to be admitted to the hospital. They didn't know exactly where, but somewhere they took a wrong turn. As they passed, they peeked in the rooms. They were all bright with new paint and well-lit. One or two of them even had television sets. The hospital looked about half-filled.

Judson grinned at him. "Things maybe not so bad, Davey. You got you a little vacation, here."

Davey's spirits lifted a bit. Maybe the unformed dread lurking in the back of his mind was a lot of foolishness. He'd been talking with an old piano player at Club Eaton. This old man had been everywhere and done everything, and Davey had been pumping him about what hospitals were like and such. At first he didn't want to say much. "I don't like hospitals. My experience, folks mostly goes in alive and comes out dead."

"Tain't so," Davey answered. "It's where you go to get fixed up."

The old black man's wrinkled face had a sad and rueful expression, "Sho' enough, if they lets you in."

"They gots to lets you in."

"Boy, you don't know nothin'. Why don't you just run along home?"

"What you talkin' 'bout? Tell me."

"Don't be a mother's fool, boy. Hospitals ain't no difference from restaurants and swimmin' pools. You black, and they don't got to let you in nowhere they don't want to."

"But if you was sick and really needed it—"

Suddenly angry, the old pianist grabbed Davey's arm. He was surprisingly strong; his hand was like a claw. "You don't know nothin', boy! Likely 'fore you was born, I used to tour with Bessie Smith."

"The—the queen of the blues?"

"*Empress* of the blues, fool." The old man looked off in the distance, remembering, and the strength seemed gone out of him, "Sweet Bess had her a voice soft as corn silk, but she could belt it too when she wanted. Ol' Bess could do it all, she was the tops, the greatest, the best there ever was . . ." For a while he didn't say anything, and Davey shifted in his chair, wondering if he should make a dash for it. But then the old man started up again. "This here was in 1937, and we was on the circuit, in Memphis. There was a terrible, terrible accident. We could only find one hospital, but it was all-white. They wouldn't admit her, and she died in the parking lot."[1]

The old man's voice quavered and then rose, "I see th' look on your black face, boy. Don't say to me it never happened. 'Cause I was there when it happened, holdin' her hand."

Davey asked no more questions. He retreated out the door, won-

---

1. The death of Bessie Smith is considered the gospel truth and a part of authentic Deep South lore by a wide range of African-Americans, particularly Southern blacks, who originally heard it the way Deacon did, through the "grapevine." There are wider references; it was told at times by John Hammond, her record producer, and popularized in literature by playwright Edward Albee. Whatever actually happened, blacks being denied crucial medical treatment in the South was relatively common; today, although many whites hold little credence in the Bessie Smith story, it is commonly believed by black people.

dering if he could pay one of his gang or maybe Judson to cut his lump off with a knife.

Now, in the Orlando hospital, Davey shook the story out of his head. Bessie died the year before he was born. Ancient history. And nothing like that was going to happen to him; after all, he was already in the hospital. He already had his papers. They found admissions at the end of the long hallway. After making them wait for about fifteen minutes, a white nurse looked up from her magazine. She was thin, with black hair and bleach-white skin. She wore blood red lipstick and red nails, which made her look white as a ghost.

"My son needs t' be admitted," Davey's mom said, "for surgery." She placed the papers on the desk in front of the nurse.

"Not here," the nurse said curtly. She put out one hand, palm forward, as if she were unwilling to touch the papers. "Negro admissions is the desk at the side door."

"How do we?" Davey started to ask.

Judson took her arm, "Come on, Mamma." He picked up the admissions papers and started back the way they'd come.

"Not that way," the nurse said. She pressed her lips together, forming a thin, bloody line across her face. "That's not the niggra section. You just git your jigaboo tails back outside and walk around to the left. You'll see the signs. You *can* read, cant'cha?"

Davey was already smoldering, and he could see his brother was struggling to stay calm.

"Come on, boys," his mother said, her voice like steel. "Come on." There was no back-talking Mama, and they followed after her.

The black section turned out to be a dismal few rooms separated from the rest of the hospital.

"Follow me," a thin Negro nurse said in a tired voice. The walls were painted a dull grey, the smell of cheap disinfectant hung heavy in the air, and the section was overcrowded to bursting. Davey, Judson, and their mother had to weave their way between beds in the hallway to get to the reception desk. The lone nurse apparently did everything. She eyed every patient as she walked past, occasionally stopping for a closer look. When they finally arrived at the reception desk, she hauled out a worn appointments book and started turning the pages. Her finger trailed down page after page, reading into the future until she finally said, "God willin', we kin take him in ten days . . ."

Davey, remembering the clean, bright rooms and all the empty beds in the white section, bit his lip until he tasted blood.

Judson looked at their mother, who gave a stern nod.

"We'll take it," Davey's brother said. "Ten days is gonna be fine."[2]

Father and Son

The afternoon's work was done, bean-picking having petered out about three. The white man who owned the field kept two blacks on to truck the crates, and let everybody else go home early. Davey pocketed his two dollars and forty cents and walked the three miles back along the dusty road toward Eatonville.

He handed over the money to his mother, who looked up from doing the wash long enough to give him a quarter from the change in the pocket of her apron for spending money. He figured his gang would still all be out working, so he headed next door to Hank Steele's. He was banging the balls around when three guys came over and sat down to watch him play. They were young bucks, maybe in their early twenties, and they were smoking and drinking beers.

"Haven't seen you guys around," Davey said, artfully snagging the eleven ball in the corner pocket.

"Naw. We from Orlando," one of them said. "Come for the club tonight." He had his hair slicked back in the Nat King Cole look, not a hint of frizz in it.

Davey sank the twelve.

"Hey. You pretty good, boy."

"Not so good."

"Maybe we play for a little fun?" The one with the slick-back asked.

Davey tried to look worried. "Maybe . . . but I don't never play just for fun." They good-naturedly tossed it back and forth for a while, finally settling on a quarter a game, and he easily ran off three wins.

By this time it was nearly dark, and a small crowd had gathered around table number three, mostly local men stopping in for a beer on their way home from the fields or their jobs house niggering for the white folks.

Davey's dad, Ishmeal, came in. If he saw his son, he didn't say anything, just took a seat at the bar and ordered a shot of whiskey. He

---

2. Over time, the tumor grew back. Deacon never allowed another doctor to touch it, and today it is still on his upper thigh, somewhere between the size of a golf ball and a lemon.

never said a lot, but he was tough the way Davey hoped to be tough. Ishmeal came of slave stock; his mother had been a slave. He'd raised his sons and daughters the old way, with harsh words, jarring head-slaps, and plenty of cane switches to the backside. In the time of bondage, the plantation time, instant obedience was demanded of a child; a moment's hesitation, a questioning look, a hint of arrogance would bring a lash across the shoulders or a bullet between the eyes. Later, in the eighty years following the Civil War, such an attitude would lead to rape, senseless beatings, or the grim procession into the woods for the hanging. Black folks who brought up their kids the old way believed Klan terror and white retribution for wrongs real or fancied were always just around the corner.

Ishmeal deeply, quietly resented it to the bottom of his bones, but he had never forgotten his place in society. Now he sat in the back of the room, nursing his single shot of whiskey and watching his son play.

Davey should have been concentrating on his game. Instead, for some odd reason he found himself remembering the Saturday when he was twelve or thirteen and he had gone with his father to pick oranges in a grove near Maitland, which was a few swamps over from Eatonville back then, in the days before they drained most of the swamps. He'd climbed up the closest tree and was pulling down oranges from the very top when he got careless and lost his balance. He tumbled down head over heels through the branches, gunny sack and all, to crash-land on the ground. He lay there in a daze, the wind knocked out of him, looking up at the first rays of early morning sunlight between the leaves.

His dad came over and got him to his feet. He dusted him off and made sure he was all right. And then he just looked at Davey. His son knew what that look meant, there was no question about it. He wasn't going to have time to think about whether he was scared or not, he was going right back up there in that tree.

Davey looked up, startled. Today's hot sun out there in the bean fields must have been too much for him, making him drowsy. He was in Hank's Poolhall, not an orange grove. By this time, they were playing for dollars. Davey had won the first, but had lost the next two games. Slick-hair was saying something. Davey knew he should have backed off and gone home, but he agreed to one game for five dollars, even though he was dead even and didn't have a dime in his pockets. It was a big mistake. The slick-haired hustler from Orlando cleared the table before Davey even had a chance at a ball. With the old, famil-

iar feeling in the pit of his stomach, Davey agreed to double or nothing. It was his break, but the balls wouldn't fall for him, and once
again the guy from Orlando ran the table.

Davey was now down ten dollars, ten dollars he didn't have. The
Orlando Three were looking more and more like thugs. They hovered
over him, they leered, they made vague threats about how he'd better
have the money or faces were going to be dented and legs broken.
Davey knew he couldn't count on Ishmeal; his dad never gave him
money. He didn't carry money. He gave it all to his wife, except for a
dollar or two for smokes and a drink with the boys. His dad always
said, "I'm gonna give you what you need. When you grow up, you
gonna get what you want." Davey sighed, "In for a dime, in for a dollar," and he doubled again.

And lost again. Slick-hair yawned, "Well, looks like we best be
gitt'n on over to the club, stake ourselves some prime seats for the
evening."

"One more game . . ."

"Naw. We gots to go."

"You *gots* to give me one chance to get even."

"We don't *gots* to do nothin', child." Slick-hair reversed his pool
cue, like it was a club. The other two black turks moved closer. Slick-
hair reared back like he was about to swing a bat, "You coughin' up
that money, or do we beats it out of you?"

Davey said nothing, and hunched over, waiting for the blow. It
never came. Unnoticed by anyone, Ishmeal had somehow moved
behind the man, and timing his move perfectly, had taken a firm grip
on his cue stick.

"Folks might not take t' a local boy getting hisself banged up by
some hustlers from way out of town," he said mildly. Davey couldn't
remember ever hearing his father say so much in one mouthful. Slick-
hair tried to pull his stick back, but Ishmeal's grip was like iron. "You
and your friends might git in a bad way before you make it back to the
main road . . . *if'n* you make it back to the main road."

"This here's a fair bet! We won that money fair and square!"

"They's some might say you slickered it," Davey's father replied.
"But I tell you what. I give you a deal. Ten dollars an' you walk away."

"Or *what,* ol' man?"

Ishmeal shrugged. Anybody didn't know him, it looked like he
didn't care, one way or the other. "Or you take your chances on gittin'
the whole twenty . . . an' gittin' out of town wit' it."

Slick-hair and his two friends looked around Hank Steele's pool hall, measuring the odds. There were nearly two dozen men facing them. "Okay, maybe we take the ten . . ." he grumbled.

Davey's father produced a wrinkled ten-dollar bill from a crease in his thin wallet, and handed it across. He gave his son a wink and a nod toward the door, and without another word, they walked out together. It was the only time Davey could ever remember Ishmeal giving him money. But he would never forget it; it was the one time when it really counted.

Zip Head's Revenge

Davey threw his helmet across the locker room. It bounced off a metal locker with a clanging sound and ended up on the floor under one of the benches. Football season was over. The year—1956— had been another winner for the Hungerford High Bobcats. Nothing unusual about that. After all, they were a powerhouse in the all-black league in Central Florida. This year, the Bobcats had clawed Altamont Springs and mauled their archrivals, Orlando's Jones High.

"Better not let coach see you fling dat 'quipment," Bo Bo said quietly.

"He say 'turn it in.' Well, I'm *turning it in!*"

"More like, flingin' it in." Bo Bo retrieved the helmet and dropped it in a hamper with the other helmets. He didn't say any more. He knew what was bothering Davey. It was the same thing that was worrying him. It was their senior year. They were all being awarded their high school football letters . . . but now the season was over, and so far, none of the five had received a single inquiry from college coaches. Without an athletic scholarship, there was no hope they were going to college. It was hard enough in those days for a black player to break into sports, but without college to develop and showcase their skills, no professional team would even know they were alive.

Davey and his gang weren't dreaming of Yale, Ohio State, or The University of Southern California. They knew they weren't going to get the call from up north. Football was a primitive and even backward experience on the high school level in the old Negro leagues. Hungerford High had no line coaches or backfield coaches, no offensive coaches or defensive coaches. They had one coach for the entire team, and Ed Clark didn't have enough time for all of them, much less for any one kid. But something was wrong. The team had done well, and there should have been a couple of offers by this time, if not from the big black schools like Grambling or Southern University or Florida A&M, at least some solid interest from the smaller all-black colleges scattered throughout the South.

"We should have heard by now," Davey muttered. "Last year, Rosie got his call from South Carolina State early in the season. We hadn't played three games. 'Member? We went out and partied it up."

"Yeah, we did." Bo Bo thought about it for a while. "You know, ol' coach don't like us none too well."

"What the hell that have to do wit' anything?" Davey flared at him. "We winnin', ain't we? We won all the big ones this year. Last year, too. Winnin' is what counts," Davey repeated stubbornly. He slouched on the bench in front of his locker, sullenly staring at the wall. "Damn that Zip Head."

Ed Clark got the name Zip Head for shaving his head when he was a big star and a Black All-American under Jake Gaither at Florida A&M. Now Ed was coaching at Hungerford High. He had a big, hairless head, wide as a melon, and it was a name that had stuck to him like horse manure through all the years since. Davey's gang hadn't really used it on him until one time when they were horsing around the showers, whooping it up. Their last game had been close, too close for the coach's liking, and he'd had them doing drills until they were ready to drop. A little name-calling was in order.

Somebody remembered Ed Clark's old nickname, and right then and there they started calling him Coach Zip Head. Of course, if you were going to use it in a derogatory way, you had to use it across the street or behind his back, else he'd like to tear your head off . . . but they suspected he knew about it, anyway. Those things always got out. Still, you couldn't be sure. He never said anything, but still, he wasn't the kind of man to be amused by a thing like that. Maybe he didn't know, or they would have heard back on it by now.

Davey finally looked up at Bo Bo, "You think he hold a grudge?"

Bo Bo nodded gravely, "Yep. That how I figure. You think on it. Here's a man, talks every week with Jake Gaither. What the one evil thing he might could do to us to be gettin' even? Why, never mention us at all."

Davey sighed, the worry lines showing on his forehead. He had been a power in the Hungerford line for the last two seasons, going both ways at tackle, and he'd played first-string power forward on the basketball team as well. His dream was to play for the Florida A&M Gaters. While it was all-black, the school was still plenty big enough to have the pro scouts stop by on their way to look over the big white schools. But Jake Gaither wasn't interested in Davey, and that had to be Ed Clark's doing. Davey reached in his locker and tossed his shoulder pads across the room. This time they landed in the hamper with the helmets.

"Ya never know. Maybe they still gonna call . . .," Bo Bo said half-heartedly.

Coach Clark walked through the room, the battered clipboard that was his trademark in his hand. As he walked by, Davey said, "Hey, Coach . . . "

"What you want, Jones?" Ed Clark looked busy and harassed. "How come I ain't gettin' no offers yet?" Davey didn't believe in beating around the bush.

The older man took Davey's pads out of the pile of helmets and placed them in the proper hamper. He shrugged, not looking at Davey, "Maybe nobody impressed wit' you, Davey."

"Couldn't be you had som'in' to do with that?"

The coach gave him an angry stare, "I don't know what you talkin' about, boy! If you done the job here, dem college coaches would a' seen it."

"I done the job for you!" Davey shouted, suddenly angry himself. "I been good enough to play both ways for two years for you! We done nothin' but winning around here! Where's the reward for dat!?"

Ed's voice took on a sarcastic note, "If th' coach of Hungerford High send in a play an' it don't work, who's the first to remark in a loud voice what a dumb thing dat was? Why, that loud and uncharitable person would be Davey Jones."

"You never sent in th' wrong play in your life of coaching?"

"Davey, I'm just demonstratin' your problem. You got a loud mouth. An' you don't got the team idea. The sideline ain't no place for second-guess an' loose talk when d' whole team's tryin' to pull together."

"Coach, maybe you don' like me personally, but we won. I won ball games for you!"

The coach looked over Davey's head, off into the distance, like he saw some distant goal, like maybe an eagle to be tamed or a mountain to be climbed, "Maybe it take more than that, Davey boy. Though it be hard for somebody like you to see it, maybe even more than what you got!"

"You sayin' I ain't got the talent?"

"No, I ain't sayin' that."

"Then what?"

The sweat had popped out on Ed's wide face. The coach shook his head like he was irritated by a fly and made a move like he was going on past, but Davey stood and grabbed his wrist. For a moment, Ed looked like he was going to take a swing, but then he thought better of it. Davey was only seventeen, but he was already four inches over six feet, and he weighed 225 pounds. The coach's face twisted with emotion, and then was still.

"Let go me, Davey," he said.

Davey let go of his wrist, and the coach brushed his arm as if it had something distasteful on it.

"Trouble follows you, boy, like black clouds over d' swamp. You think you goin' places."

"You put th' black mark on me, d'nt you?"

"You think you better than the rest us ordinary folk 'round here. You better smart up, boy. Dat ain't d' case. You got away wit' plenty around here, but nobody on a real college team want dat kind of attitude!"

"You put in the black mark on me, Ed Clark. Yes, you did," Davey repeated, this time with a note of finality in his voice.

Ed puffed an angry breath from his cheeks, "I be the coach. I don't have to answer you, boy. I don't have to say nuthin' to you. Not nothin'. Not zero. Not even zip." He grimaced and his yellow teeth flashed as he spat out the last word. And then he walked out of the locker room.

He left a long silence behind him.

"I guess he found out about his nickname," Bo Bo finally said.

Workin' Things Out with Mama

After football season, Davey starred for the Bobcats as a power forward on the basketball team. After basketball he ran track, but there wasn't much enthusiasm in him and the long, slow spring dragged into June. Almost summer, and there was still no word from even a single college coach! His mailbox was empty, and no calls came to Hank Steele's pool hall, which was the closest telephone to their house.

His friends shared the same bad luck. Lonnie and Bo Bo and even Willie were not as physically gifted, and so maybe they shouldn't have been expecting the call. But Sugar Man was tall, with big hands, and Davey was big and fast.

That spring things were grim around the Jones house. Davey started to let his grades slide, and his Mama began leaning on him.

"Where's dem books, son?" she'd say before he got in the door.

"Forgot 'em at school," he'd mumble.

"You forget 'em again, you can forget where the chair is you sit down to supper."

"Aw, Mama, school learnin' don't get you nothin'."

"You be careful wit' that kind of talk. You ain't gonna graduate."

"You don't know that, Mama."

Davey's father looked up from the table, "Don' you go smart-talkin' your Mama. You lucky you got her houndin' you every step."

"I'm gonna graduate!" he flared up stubbornly. But he didn't look Ishmeal in the eye when he said it.

"I may see Jesus come 'fore you do," his father said.

"Ishmeal," his Mama cut in, "Davey is gonna graduate."

Now he'd gotten his dad in trouble. Any way he did it, he couldn't seem to win.

"If he do," Ishmeal glowered, getting in the last word, "it gonna be close like a bitch."

As usual, Ishmeal was right. Davey barely lifted the books, and so shaved it closer than even he expected. The principal of Hungerford High, handing him his diploma on the school steps, shook his head, "You got the potential to be a really great student. You apply yourself, and you'll be somebody some day."

"I don' see the connection," Davey replied sourly, his eyes wandering over the gathered faculty to single out coach Ed Clark. "My one chance out of here was an athletics scholarship." The big man was gazing over his head, out over the distant trees as if Davey didn't exist. Davey raised his voice, "I know right now I'm not the greatest player ever in the game. But I got talent an' speed given me from God, and it be a crime not to use it." He saw Clark shuffle his feet, and he thought the coach looked uncomfortable. But Davey couldn't prove anything, and so he would say no more.

The next day the gang gathered in front of Hank Steele's.

"We got to get out of this place," Davey said for what must have been the thousandth time.

"Maybe I know a way." It was Bo Bo, who had only just arrived. "I hear tell from my cousin they's a truck leavin' for New York."

"New York City?" Davey looked at him like he was crazy.

"Naw. New York, the state of. They's lookin' fo' hands t' pick beans an' cherries."

Davey looked up with mild interest, "Nobody gets rich pickin' beans."

Willie threw in his two cents' worth, "I heard tell it be different up north. They pay money by the hour an' you got rights an' everything."

Bo Bo nodded, "We been workin' the fields since Noah floated the ark. We know the drill. What we do is, we head up north, make ourselves a little pile of money pickin' and then head for New York City to get us some big-pay jobs."

Davey nodded uncertainly. He wanted to get out of Eatonville so bad it was a taste in his mouth. Maybe it was affecting his judgment. Still, any plan was better than no plan.

"So," he asked, "when's our fruit-picker truck gonna leave?"

"Ain't much time. She pulls through town at noon today."

They talked it over some more, and while there was no new information, the more they turned it over, the warmer their enthusiasm grew. They'd work the farm stuff through the summer and fall, keeping all the money they made, because they wouldn't have to turn it over to their Mamas. And by the time the last pumpkins were rolled and the last apples knocked down from those northern trees, they'd be headed for New York City to become big-city boys. There was just time enough to run home, say their goodbyes and pick up a few personal things. They agreed to meet right where they were, in front of Hank's, just before noon. They joined hands and swore on it.

After months of rejection, their ragged little plan was a sudden and unexpected ray of hope for Davey. Still, he walked home with a heavy heart. He'd always said there was nothing he would miss about Eatonville. He'd always taken the most central thing in his life, his family, completely for granted. Now a dozen unwanted worries crept into his mind. How would his mother do without the dollars he brought back from the fields? With only three sons, and all those girls, with his older brother away in New Orleans, how were Mattie and Ishmeal going to make ends meet? His home wasn't but a few doors away, yet he shuffled and hitched along, and found a dozen reasons to pause along the way. By the time he got there, he was just about ready to drop the whole idea . . . if only he hadn't reached his hand in and taken the vow with his buddies, with Bo Bo and Wee, Lonnie, and the

Sugar Man. He was the leader. Those guys were depending on him. No way he was going to tell them, I ain't goin' cause I'm worried to tell my Mama.

She was alone, energetically sweeping the porch of their old home. She was always busy like that. Davey noticed how shabby the place looked. Somebody ought to give it a lick of paint. And his mother, who had always looked so eternal, like she was carved out of rock and would live forever, suddenly looked older than he remembered. He slouched up the steps to walk on past her, and she saw right away that something was in the wind.

"Okay, Davey—what goin' on?"

"Nothin', Mama."

He tried to push on past without getting into it, but it was no use. She blocked his path to the door.

"You ain't foolin' me a minute." She gave him that look all mothers reserve for their sons when they know they're hiding the truth, "Now, what is on your mind?"

"Mama, I'm sick to death of this place. I mean, not this house. . . Eatonville."

"I know, son, but you'll be goin' away to college soon enough."

"Mama, that dream died! Nobody out there even knows I'm alive!"

"You got to believe in yourself, Davey."

"I do, Mama. That's why I'm goin' up north where I kin' make somethin' of myself."

The frown came like thunder over her face, "We don't know nobody up north. You go up there, you git yourself lost!"

"I stay here, I'm lost!"

"You hush up! You are not goin'! You're goin' on to school!"

"You ain't listenin', Mama. I had it wit' dat. I thought this all out. We gonna work the fields an' save up an' move to New York City an' get good jobs!"

He was so full of piss and vinegar, he'd forgotten the main thing about his Mama. You didn't argue with her. All his life, she'd ruled him with the back of her hand, with the cane switch and the broom handle. It wasn't just him she treated like that. The kids all had to take it, or, as she said, "When Papa come home, he gonna kill you." And there she was, standing not three feet away from him, with the broom handle in her hands.

She gave him one fierce look and swung her broom, catching him flush across the chest. He was grown nearly full size, and still he fell halfway off the porch. That should have shown him some sense, but he got up angry, closer to swinging back at her than he'd ever been in his life.

He gritted his teeth, "Mama, you should listen to me, just this once."

She reared back and swung at him again. He ducked under the broom handle and made it inside the front door, slamming it in her face. And a few minutes later he was heading back toward Hank Steele's with a change of clothes and the few dollars in cash he'd gotten for his graduation. In a few hours, Eatonville would be part of his past.

The Sport of Pro Beanpicking

It was clear from the start that their exodus was to be followed by plague and famine. Right off, Davey had to pay $25 to the driver for gas money. That left almost nothing for food along the way, and that's where the hunger mode began, with the lot of them barely three days out of Eatonville and nowhere near the promised land.

Their ride proved to be a dented old Reo dump truck with a missing tailgate. Somebody rigged a tattered canvas tarp over the open and rusty bed, which was already overflowing with would-be field workers.

The hot Florida sun beat off the tarp, which smelled of asphalt and old wine. Davey and his friends grabbed a rusty chain and pulled themselves up. More workmen crowded in behind, cutting off any easy exit. By now, he was hoping Mattie had alerted one of his sisters, who would have run to get Ishmeal. He couldn't just walk out on his buddies, but if his dad showed up and made a case that a family with five girls needed him at home, his choice would be clear. But Ishmeal didn't arrive, and after a few minutes the starter rattled and the engine caught hold.

The old dump truck bumped and thumped out of town on weak springs and bald tires, looking like it couldn't make Orlando, much less New York. The driver didn't give it a second thought. He spat out the window and turned onto the two-lane blacktop at the end of the Eatonville loop and headed north.

The premium run up north was to fly Miami to La Guardia, non-stop in eight hours. The common shot was an overnight train with main stops in Atlanta and Washington. Or, if you were driving in a good car, say a six-month-old Hudson with plenty of juice under the hood, you could make it in two days easy. But Davey's sandwiches and

apples were gone by the third day, and with the dead battery, running
out of gas, and all the flat tires, they weren't yet out of Georgia. Davey
had more money than anybody else; he insisted they put it all together and dole it out. Even on a semistarvation diet of bread and cold
beans, they were flat broke nine days later when the old Reo limped
into Schenectady.

It was mid-morning, and they headed directly for the fields. There
was work, but it wasn't at all as promised. The deal was, fill the basket or no money. And it had to be a good basket, meaning plump, ripe
beans, no diseased beans and no leaves. The field supervisor, a skinny
white man with a beet-red face and no patience, would dump each basket and inspect it personally before making a chalk mark next to their
names scribbled on a faded chalkboard. The pay was about the same as
Florida, but they had to pay for their food and other expenses, which
took everything they made. But now it was too late. They had no
money to go home. They were trapped.

Davey and his friends bent low over the long rows of plants, careful to strip only the ready beans. It was mid-morning on a sultry
August day. Davey paused and wiped the sweat from his eyes with his
ragged red bandanna, trying not to think about his raging hunger.
Like the others, at night he wrapped an extra shirt around his shoulders and slept in the fields. There was no other way. He had to spend
all the money he made on food. They'd all tried short cuts like filling
up on raw beans, tomatoes, and corn, but it only led to stomach
cramps and worse, the dreaded fieldhand trots.

Davey's back ached and his fingertips were raw, the nails broken
and dirty and the skin cracked and bloody.

Sugar Man looked around warily from a nearby row, looking for
the supe, who was busy separating about a third of the leaves and
stems from a bad basket. Sugar Man relaxed a bit and wiped the sweat
from his own forehead with his wrist.

"We operatin' on bad information here, Davey," he said for the
hundredth time.

"Wasn't my idea in the first place," Davey grumbled. He was tired
of being blamed for everything. "Bo Bo's cousin done said this was a
salary deal. You was there."

"Yeah, but you our main guy, Davey. We don't make our move but
you say so."

Davey didn't like to hear that. "We coulda picked by the basket in
Florida, an' slept in our own beds."

"Find myself thinkin' bout Mama's Sunday fried chicken."

Davey waved his long arms, nearly spilling his basket of beans in the dirt, "Talkin' like that don't do no good."

Bo Bo pulled alongside them. The supe was still arguing about the bad basket, waving the worker away. He didn't want to pay anything, and the worker, a black-tempered hillbilly, was threatening to come back at night and beat him with a crowbar.

"Man," Bo Bo complained, "starvation jumpin' on my back. I cain't pick enough of these skinny green things t' keep food in my mouth. Whut we gonna do, Davey?"

Davey sighed and looked down at his hands, deciding to do the one thing he'd promised himself he'd never do, "I'll call back to Eatonville. If I kin borrow two hundred dollars, we kin still get to the city."

"Your Mama ain't gonna give you no two hundred dollars."

"No, but Ishmeal might. My daddy ain't never let me down. I just got to time the call right, to be sure it's him I get."

"You said you was never gonna ask them for nothin' no more."

"Bo—shut up!" Davey flared. The gang went back to picking beans in silence. They knew when Davey got that way there was no sense talking to him. And, after all, it was the only plan of action any of them had been able to figure out.

That evening after the sun set in the low hills, Davey and his gang hiked five miles up the road to use the pay phone in a rural Standard Oil gas station. Ishmeal and Mattie didn't have a phone, so he called to the Club Eaton. There was a long pause while someone ran over to his house, and then the voice came on the line, "Davey? Is that you?"

His heart sank. It was his Mama. Oh, Lord, no, he thought, she been against this from the first. Now she gonna see me crawl back to the nest. He would have hung up then and there, but Sugar Man, Lonnie, Bo Bo, and Willie James were all standing there looking at him. They were counting on him to get that money. He took a deep breath and plunged right in.

"Mama, things ain't goin' so well here. A couple of us took sick an' we needed horse-pills to stop the runs and they ain't so much money as we thought to be made here in the fields."

"You gettin' enough to eat, Davey?" Even thin like that over the phone, he could hear the worry in her voice.

"Yeah, Mama. But it take all our pickin' money to feed ourselves. We be all right once we get to the city, but we just need to get a stake to get us there."

"How much you need, son?"

He took a gulp of air, "We figure about two hundred dollars . . . "

That's when Mattie really surprised him. "Don' you worry about a thing, son," she said. "I be gettin' back to you as soon as I can."

The gang was lighthearted, walking back to the fields. Davey had spent his food money on the telephone call, but he knew a spot along the road where they could load up on green apples. They would probably give him the runs, but they would keep him going until he ate again tomorrow night.

He tried to ignore the knotted, empty feeling in his stomach, telling himself that soon he'd have the two hundred dollars, and then he'd sit down to a regular meal. But somewhere in the back of his mind, he didn't believe it. Nothing had gone right on this trip, absolutely nothing. That was the problem with his phone call to Mama. He'd called, and she'd said yes, simple as that. It had been too easy.

Divine Intervention

Mattie Jones hung up the phone and walked back across Kennedy Street to her kitchen, where the collards had bubbled and frothed a green slime over the edges of the pot and put out the gas flame. She opened the back door and carefully aired out the room before snapping a wooden match and relighting the stove, but she went about preparing supper as if in a dream, thinking about what to do. There really wasn't much of a choice. Her boy was in trouble, and he'd called her for help. Still, she was worried. If she did send that money, what were the chances she'd ever see Davey again? Wouldn't he be swallowed up in New York City, like so many of the local boys who headed up north and never were heard from again?

She gnawed the problem in her sleep that night, tossing and turning like a dog with a bone. The next morning, still troubled, she set out for the Jamisons, the white family the Jones's family worked for, and borrowed the two hundred dollars.

Two hundred dollars in the hand didn't look like much, until you realized what it represented, what it could buy. Mattie stuffed the money in her dress and made her way back to Eatonville. All that day she mulled it over in her mind, wondering if it was the right thing to do. She was busy with housework and her chores, and before she knew it, night had settled in. She couldn't talk to Ishmeal about this; he would say, The boy got to stand on his own feet now, Mattie. He made his bed, now he got to lie in it. It was a big responsibility, being a mother, and there were some decisions that had no black-and-white answers. She sighed and let herself quietly out the back screen door. She had carefully placed the $200 in a rumpled envelope in her purse. If she made her way quickly, she could be at the Western Union office in half an hour.

Meanwhile, Davey and his gang picked beans throughout the day, and then he hitchhiked a ride twenty miles to the general store and post office where Mattie had agreed to send the money. It hadn't come by the time he got there. He hung around for about an hour, but the store owner didn't seem to like it, so he headed back to the fields. Surely, he figured, it would be there the next day.

He continued this routine for a week, working the fields by day and then finding his way to the store after dark. After the seventh day, he had to admit something had gone wrong. The gang gathered under a tree at the end of a cornfield to discuss their future. The days were still warm, but now the nights were cooler, tinged with frost, and they'd begun to pick the autumn crops—apples and pears, berries and musk melons, and the pumpkins weren't far behind.

"Whut we gonna do, Davey?" Willie James asked.

"You soundin' like a stuck record, Wee," Davey replied. "I don't know what we gonna do."

"She ain't sendin' that money," Bo Bo said, belaboring the obvious.

"She said she would," Davey said stubbornly.

"Naw she didn't," Lonnie said. "She say she 'gonna take care of things,' an' 'everything gonna be all right.' Maybe this her way of takin' care of things."

"I'll go again tomorrow!" Davey exploded. "I'll get us that money! Now stop gnawin' at me about this!"

The next evening he walked right up to the store owner. Elmer Curdy was a short white man with fiery red cheeks and purple veins on his big red nose. He was bald except for puffs of white hair on each side of his ears. Davey, like most southern blacks, spoke two languages, the easy, comfortable, colorful dialect he used with other blacks, and the more formal everyman's English he used with white folks. This everyman's English was identical to the soft southern drawl used by whites and blacks alike in the South. He spoke it now to the store owner, asking the same question he'd asked every night for a week, "Sir, I'm looking for a check from Florida."

The man didn't bother to riffle through the small batch of pigeon holes behind him. "Nope, sonny. Nothing today for you."

"Are you sure?"

The man eyed Davey for a moment like he was going to be flustered. Then the look in his eyes softened, "Hey, I'd know it. Ain't but 450 people live in town. I know everything that happens around here."

"That's like my home town . . . folks all know everybody's business," Davey said, heading for the door.

"Ayeah? Where is that?"

"Eatonville, Florida."

"Never heard of it."

"Central Florida. Near Orlando."

"Ohhhh . . . Orlando . . ." The man drew out the word like there was a light bulb dawning somewhere. His eyes went to a cluttered bulletin board on the wall behind Davey . . . "You boys came up here for the crops, didn't you?"

"Well . . . yes . . ." Davey didn't see where the conversation was going. He shifted impatiently from foot to foot, eager to be back on the road. It was lots easier to catch a ride before dark, when the drivers could see what they might be getting into from a distance down the blacktop.

The store owner was eyeing him more intently now, sizing him up. He finally gave a sniff and a short nod, having made up his mind about something. "So you'll be headin' back south pretty soon now?"

"Maybe . . ." Davey said uncertainly. "We thought to maybe try New York City."

"Pffft." The white man puffed the word out like he was spitting tobacco. "Don't know what you want with that. Dirty, crowded, pack-rat city, and things are expensive in New York City; d'yuh know how expensive?"

Davey had to admit he didn't. "We thought we'd get us some good-paying jobs."

"Pay's good," the man admitted. "Fairly good . . . but it costs a fortune to live there. It's gonna cost you a hundred bucks a month for a one-room apartment in the slums. An' they got crime an' drugs an' violence like you wouldn't believe. I tell yuh, I been there, boy. It ain't no place t' be."

"Yeah. Well, I got to get back."

The man raised his hand before Davey could get out the door, "On the other hand, if you were interested in gettin' back to Florida, I just might know the way." He pointed to a card on the bulletin board. The card said Driver Wanted in big, black, block letters. "Pete Jenkins got him a place near Miami. Pete runs a drive-in out by the lake, closes down end of every summer and heads south for the winter."

"What's the deal?"

"Pete takes the train, so he'll need somebody to drive his car down. Maybe you're that somebody."

"Who pays gas?"

"Pete does."

Davey nodded half to himself, "I'll let you know tomorrow."

The gang rode back south in a souped-up 49 Ford, taking turns at the wheel and driving straight through. Davey called at about noon, leaving word that he'd be home for suppertime. He dropped off the car and hitched a ride to Eatonville, making it just before dark.

His mother had prepared a feast of pork neck, ham and collard greens, fried chicken, and mashed potatoes. She gave him a big hug and sat him down at the dinner table. She was just like a Jewish mama; you could be bleeding to death and she'd wipe the blood away and ask if you were hungry. That was all right, because that was what was on his mind, too. Davey pulled his chair up to the table and started eating. Mattie kept laying plates on the table and he kept shoveling it in.

After dinner they sat around the table and he told some stories about his summer adventures. His father listened quietly, taking in every word and nodding every now and then. His sisters laughed and teased him, and his mother interrupted a lot with questions and concerns for his safety.

Finally, he had to say it, to clear the air between them. "Mama, you didn't send the money like you was supposed to . . . me and the gang was really hurtin', starvin' so's our belt buckles was rubbing our backbones, and you never sent that money."

His mother eyed him calmly for a moment. "I was goin' to send it, son—I swear. Ask your Papa it isn't so."

Ishmeal nodded. "She borrowed it, an' she even headed for the Western Union. Didn't even ask me."

"I never got it," Davey said, worried that maybe the rural store owner in New York had taken his two hundred dollars.

"Well . . ." Mattie looked down at the table. "That 'cause I never sent it, son. I was gonna send it. I swear on the Bible. There I was, the middle of the night after I talked to you on the phone, walkin' along the road in the moonlight, headed for the Western Union, when all of a sudden, a voice came to me clear an' loud out of the dark."

"A voice?"

"A loud an' clear voice, Davey. An' it said to me out of the night sky, Mattie! Mattie Jones! Don't send it! Don't send the boy that money!'"

"Mama, what you sayin'?"

"That was the voice of the Lord, Davey. The Lord hisself tol' me not to send you that two hundred dollars!"

"Mama, I can't believe this what I'm hearin'!"

Ishmeal leaned back in his chair and crossed his arms, "Yore Mama is a religious woman, son. She believes. If the Lord talk to anybody, it gonna be her."

Davey threw his hands in the air, astounded to hear of this amazing turn of events, "I'm as religious as the next man, Mama, but fact was, I was up there in cold New York state, starvin' to death, and the Lord comin' to you at that moment was real bad timing!"

"None of us question the way of the Lord," she replied. Nobody said anything for a while. And then his father gave out a little chuckle.

Davey looked around the homely little room, surprised how glad he was to see them all. He realized for the first time what a source of strength this family was to him. His Mama finally gave him that look of hers and asked, "Well, did you learn anything?"

He nodded, looking down at his rough, callused hands with their cracked and broken fingernails before looking her straight in the eyes. "Mama," he said, "I'm going back to school."

2

College Ball, German Shepherds, and Shotguns

Today, if you know anything about football, the names of the great men of the game who come from African-American backgrounds are right at the tip of your tongue: Jerry Rice, Walter Payton, Bubba Smith, O.J. Simpson, Gale Sayers, Alan Page, Eric Dickerson. The list goes on and on. Today, nearly 70 percent of the men who play the game are black, so it's easy to forget that in the 1950s the role models were few.

Segregated baseball had the old Negro leagues to let black men blow off steam, but pro football simply didn't let black men play. Less than thirty managed to play from the turn of the century until 1933. These included Charles "Black Cyclone" Follis, the first to play pro ball, signing with the Shelby Blues in 1904. Henry "Motorcycle" McDonald played from 1911 through 1926 for the Rochester Jeffersons. Paul Robeson played end for the Akron Pros before going on to fame as a singer and actor—and to notoriety for his radical political beliefs. The few who did get to play suffered ridicule and abuse from fans, and illegal bashing on the field. And then, after Joe Lillard played for the Chicago Cardinals in 1933, no blacks played in the National Football League for the next thirteen years.

The barriers started to crumble in 1946. Cleveland Rams owner Dan Reeves wanted to move his club to the West Coast. As part of his deal, the Los Angeles Coliseum Commission insisted he give UCLA star Kenny Washington a tryout. That same year, Paul Brown, owner of the Cleveland Browns, signed Bill Willis as guard and Marion Motley as fullback.

Desegregation of the NFL would take several decades. These were still the years of overt segregation, when George Preston Marshall, owner of the Washington Redskins, declared that he would never have a black player on his team. Other owners were more discreet. In the Pro Football Hall of Fame publication, *Their Deeds and Dogged Faith*, Raymond Kemp, a black man who played for the 1933 Pittsburgh Pirates (then the name of a pro football team), was asked directly why there were no black players in the NFL between 1933 and 1945: "It was my understanding that there was a gentleman's agreement in the league that there would be no more blacks," he said. When asked if it was possible that black players with sufficient ability didn't surface during that period, he replied, "I would have to assume that because of the numerous black athletes appearing on the sports scene, some of them would have qualified to play professional football. George Preston Marshall (owner of the Washington Redskins) made a public declaration he wouldn't have a black on his team."[1]

On signing black players, Tex Schramm, perhaps a bit confused on what constitutes a "gentleman's agreement," said of those times, "I don't think there was anything that was a gentleman's agreement. You just didn't do it (sign blacks). It wasn't a thing that was done."[2]

After thirteen years of no blacks in the league whatsoever, in 1946 Dan Reeves of the L.A. Rams signed Kenny Washington and Woody Strode. A few months later, Paul Brown of the Cleveland Browns signed Ohio State guard Bill Willis and Nevada fullback Marion Motley to contracts in the new American Association Football Conference. Talking about those early years in *The Game That Was*, Motley said, "Paul Brown warned Willis and me. He said, 'Now you know that you're going to be in many scrapes. People are going to be calling you names. They're going to be nasty. But you're going to stick it out.' It was rough all right. If Willis and I had been anywhere near being hotheads, it would have been another ten years till black men got accepted in pro ball. We'd have set 'em back ten years. I still got many a cleat mark in the backs of my hands from when I would be getting up from a play and a guy would just walk over and step on my hand. I couldn't do anything

1. Mike Rather and Don R. Smith, *Their Deeds and Dogged Faith* (New York: Rutledge Books, Balsam Press, Inc., 1984), p. 220.

2. Ibid.

about it. The referees would stand there and see those men stepping on us, and they would turn their backs. The opposing players
called us nigger and all kind of names like that."

So it gradually came to pass that, through the 1950s and early
1960s, NFL teams added two, four, or at the most six blacks to their
rosters—and even then, they were mostly pushed into the low-pay-
ing grunt positions. Not much of a career path for young black kids
looking to play the game.

Lightning from a Clear Sky

Judson, Davey's older brother, had played his college ball for Xavier
College in New Orleans. Judson was built like Rocket Ishmail. He
weighed 190 pounds and was fast as greased lightning. He was a Black
All-American two years in a row, 1952 and 1953, but, feeling it was
a lost cause, he hadn't gone on to try out for the pros, and now, five
years later, he was coaching an all-black high school team in New
Orleans.

Over Christmas vacation he'd driven back to Eatonville to catch
up on the news and to share the holidays. Recent rains had left the
ground soggy, and he and Davey were talking things over as they
walked around the puddles on Hungerford High's potholed quarter-
mile track. Since Davey hadn't gotten into college for the fall season,
he'd been playing basketball with a Winterpark semipro team that
toured Florida. They played other black teams in places like Coco
Beach, Bradenton, Tampa, and Jacksonville. Davey's Eatonville friends
Lester and Roosevelt Seays also played on that team, at least before
Roosevelt left for college. They played two games a week, on Friday
and Saturday, then pooled their money and had a "little old money
meeting" in December, where they threw all the money in a pot and
the best team won. But Davey wasn't kidding himself; he'd never
become a professional athlete that way.

It was a sore spot with him that Judson, who had done so well in college, and who he looked up to as his mentor, hadn't gone on to play ball.

"But you never went on to the pros." Davey had almost not dared
to bring up the subject, and it hung between them like the ghost of
an old evil.

"Nobody wanted me, Davey. They gots to call before you can say
yes."

"You was All-American two years in a row."

"Black All-American. I didn't expect a call."

"Blacks playin' in the NFL now," Davey said stubbornly.

Judson looked over at his younger brother and sighed, "Yeah. A few. Tank Younger and Deacon Dan Towler an' the rest of them got about sixty pounds each up on me. I could eat Mama's chicken all week an' not put on sixty pounds."

"Marion Motley an' Bill Willis—"

"—got eighty pounds on me."

Davey stopped in the middle of the track and angrily threw his hands in the air. "Then what am I doin' out here, runnin' around, tacklin' shadows an' tryin to stay in shape?"

"You already got forty pounds on me, Davey. Never know, you might make it."

"I gotta get to college first."

Judson paused, not wanting to tell Davey the bad news. But the time had come, and he couldn't avoid it any longer. He looked down at his shoes and off in the distance, and then finally mumbled, "Xavier can't take you, Davey. You're plenty good enough to play for them, but it's the grades . . . Honest, I tried my best for you, but they got their rules."

Davey tried not to show how crushed he felt. Long-gone were his day-dreams of crashing through the line for big-name colleges like Ohio State, Nebraska, Oklahoma, or Notre Dame. Southern black kids went to tiny, underfunded black "vocational colleges," and played in all-black leagues against other black schools.[3] He wasn't going to be eligible for the Heisman Trophy or win any national honors. He had to accept those facts. But that wasn't what hurt the most; here he was, actually unable to get into any of the black colleges!

He scuffed angrily at the track, catching his foot in a puddle and getting wet in the process. "Folks around here is laughin' at me, Judson!" he said. "An' I'm sayin' to myself, 'What all this gonna get me?' Truth is, nothin'!"

Judson didn't know what to say, and so they both moved on in silence. They had left the track and were slowly walking along Kennedy Street, back toward the house, when they saw Roosevelt Seays running toward them, waving his arms. Rosie had been a year

---

3. As late as 1965, there were still only six black college football players in schools sanctioned by the National Collegiate Athletic Association.

ahead of Davey at Hungerford, but they had played several years together, and in that time the two of them had been the dominant Bobcat players. Old Zip Head hadn't had anything against Rosie, and he'd gone on to play his first two years of college ball in South Carolina. Now he came to a halt in front of them, panting and out of breath.

"Hey Rosie," Judson laughed, trying to make a joke even though he felt frustrated and depressed about Davey, "you supposed to be in shape, man."

"I—get—'nough of that—in season!" Rosie panted. He clapped Davey on the shoulder. "Big news, Davey—you is in, pal!"

Davey was in no mood for fooling around. "What you talkin' about, Roosevelt Seays? Don't go pullin' my chain now."

"No joke, Davey. I was in the locker room last week, just 'fore I took the bus back to Eatonville for 'cation. I overhears coach talkin' how he's lookin' long an' hard for some big, fast boys for his defense line. He's lookin', but he ain't findin', an' he's complainin' all bitter that Florida A&M an' Gramblin' an all the other biggies done gobbled up all the gravy. Naturally, I thinks right off of you, an' I pops right in there an' lays your name on the line. I tells him three or four Davey Jones stories, you know, 'bout what we done together on the Bobcats, and next thing, ol' coach is talked into it! He says *yes,* Davey!!"

Judson and Rosie were both pounding him on the back, congratulating him. Davey's mind was a blank. He didn't know what to think. He'd been down so long, he couldn't really accept the fact that something good had finally showed up on his doorstep.

"What that mean, Rosie?" he finally managed to ask, still trying to catch up on what was happening to him.

"It *mean,* fool, you're comin' wit' me to South Carolina State!"

Pure, Raw Ambition

South Carolina State is a small, all-black college just outside of Orangeburg, a midsized town located about sixty-five miles inland from Charleston. In the 1950s, most of the students who didn't live in the area used the Greyhound Bus Line to get to school in the fall, and to go home for vacations. There were usually enough kids from Central Florida heading back and forth at the same time so they were able to charter their own bus. Chartering was preferable, because they could sit anywhere instead of in the back where the ride was hot, noisy, and uncomfortable, and that's how Davey and Roosevelt first traveled to SCS in September, 1957.

Everything about college football was new and exciting for Davey. There was no downside for him. He was curious about everything, and absolutely ready to go. Still, he couldn't leave his independent nature behind, and he reacted to authority with his usual flare for making his own statement.

When they put on their pads and came out for the first drills, he noticed a huge black man barking the orders, telling everybody where to go and what to do. Half an hour later he was running laps with Rosie when this same guy yelled at him to get over and run with the linemen. Davey continued on with his friend as if he didn't hear a word.

As soon as they were out of earshot, he asked, "That ain't the coach. Who is that guy, Rosie?"

"That be Madman Mattox. Maybe you better go run with the line."

"They ain't fast enough, man."

"You don't want to mess wit' Mattox," Rosie warned.

"Why not?"

"He the team captain."

"That don't give him rights to yell at nobody."

"Yes it do."

They ran on in silence for a while. Davey finally asked, "This Madman is a fair-to-bad dude then, huh?"

Rosie shrugged, "Bad enough to take All-Conference."

Davey wasn't overly impressed. "This ain't 'zactly the Big Ten." They ran on for a little while longer. "What position he play?"

"Does who play?" Roosevelt asked, his mind having gone on to other things.

"Madman."

"Oh, Madman. He play tackle, man."

The hint of a smile came over Davey's face. "Not no more he don't."

Roosevelt didn't follow. "Why you say that, Davey?"

"I'm gonna take his job."

Roosevelt whooped it up, laughing all the way back to the other end of the field. It was crazy to think that his friend could unseat the king. Everybody else seemed to agree, for later that day, when the coach called out to ask who wanted to try out for tackle, Davey was the only player who went over and stood by Mattox. Still, in the weeks that followed, Davey went after him as if he were the enemy. The only thing that mattered in the entire world was beating the Madman. And he had resolved to do it.

Maybe challenging Mattox was a foolish thing to do, but Davey took what he saw was the only door open to him. He told himself he needed the tackle position. It wasn't personal between him and the big lineman. Mattox was simply the next obstacle in his way.

Davey gave far more weight to his athletics than his classes, which he continued to see as foolish, and a necessary evil. He told himself he was going to earn degrees in Pain and Self-Discipline. He attended classes, but he went at his daily regimen with strict intensity and a belief in himself. Roosevelt, for one, couldn't believe how serious he was. For Davey's part, he didn't understand Seays either.

"Rosie," he said, "this here's your chance *at life!* Don't make no difference what you say—I ain't never gonna see how you take it easy like the way you do!"

"Why should I do different?" his friend replied. "I'm already the star 'round here, the bright an' shinin' star, far as the eye can see." Which was true, in a way. Roosevelt Seays was doing very well as a tackle and guard with the Bulldogs.

"South Carolina State ain't the end of the world."

"Davey, you're only gonna make yourself crazy," Rosie warned.

"I'm already crazy," Davey smiled. "If you don't believe it, just ask the Madman."

Indeed, the Madman would know. Davey had come to training camp weighing 230, all of it bone and muscle. The Madman was big and strong, but Davey was nearly as strong, and much faster. By this time, he was beating Mattox in the one-on-one drills. He beat him in the pit. (That yard of territory on the field between any offensive lineman and the defensive lineman who plays against him is called the "pit.") He beat him on the outside. He beat him so soundly, he made the man deny his own name. And by the time the season started, he had the Madman's job.

Later on Mattox admitted ruefully that he never knew what hit him, but in the end, their competition was good for the whole team; the Madman moved over and played guard, and with both Mattox and Jones on the line, the Bulldogs became a force to be reckoned with.

He was new to college ball, which was faster and tougher than high school. As his freshman season progressed, Davey steadily improved his basic lineman skills, doing a better and better job on this new level. On the other hand, from what Davey could see, Rosie stayed about the same. He was a good guard and tackle, but now, in his second year, the other teams seemed to have figured out a lot of his strengths and weaknesses, and he wasn't growing to dominate at his position. Maybe he'd reached his peak as a player, but Davey didn't think so. He was fairly sure it was something else. It bothered him to see his friend bask in the glow of his college glory and not really push himself to get ahead. Rosie hadn't peaked out. No. Roosevelt Seays had found the valley of his own content, and he was going to lie in it. There is a lesson to be learned in that.

Davey and the Midget

It was rumored that spare and aloof President B.C. Turner, head of South Carolina State College, didn't like the Bulldog's football coach, Roy D. Moore, very much. Coach Moore wasn't your average pug football coach; he was a highly educated man, a motivator and a leader of young people. And while the college itself was all-black by South Carolina state law, that didn't mean it was ugly or shabby. Quite the opposite. The campus had broad and beautiful lawns, well-clipped shrubbery, and fine-looking red brick buildings.

Still, the black teachers had by and large themselves been students in black colleges who became teachers in black colleges—a closed circle that over the generations, with the lower levels of both state funding and private grants, assured that the education offered was not on a par with that offered by the big white universities or exclusive all-white private southern colleges.

SCS was a showplace for the entire state, Carolina's way of saying segregation worked, and President Turner meant to keep it that way. Running it was the plum job in black education in the South. Keeping that job, as Turner saw it, meant chin up, head down, and make no waves.

Turner was a light-skinned African-American, so light he passed for white in most circumstances. Many of the students and faculty distrusted him, seeing him as distant and aloof. It was widely whispered he was interested first and only in maintaining the status quo, in keeping South Carolina State the way it was, the showcase of black education in a modern southern society that was beginning to show cracks and signs of wear.

It was only natural that he might view Coach Moore as more of a rival than an ally. Footballers, to the president's mind, were everything he was against. They were rough, uncivilized young men and they symbolized the worst of what his people had to offer. It was said that he wanted badly to dismantle the team, but that was almost impossible. After all, the Bulldogs were winning and at the height of their popularity.

Davey Jones wasn't interested in the local campus in-fighting. He'd come to South Carolina State to play football, pure and simple. His football scholarship paid for almost everything—tuition, room, and board. The food was great, the stadium was near to brand new, and he lived in new Bethea Hall, the best dorm on campus. The only thing it didn't pay for was books, so Davey didn't buy any. He figured he could borrow enough from his classmates to get by. He wasn't interested in logic, philosophy, history, mathematics, or English, for he was still convinced that a black education would only serve to more firmly snare him in the loop that kept recycling blacks to their old hometown ghettos.

Which was why, on a beautiful spring day in 1958, he was surprised to find himself standing spellbound while several students stood on the library steps and shouted that black people had to unite against the white establishment. He listened for about ten minutes, and finally raised his voice, "Hey, brothers, you ain't making no sense here."

"Ain't making any sense here," a voice at his waist corrected. It was short, scrappy little Gilbert Zimmerman, his kinky hair close-cropped where it wasn't already balding, looking up at him through thick, wire-rimmed glasses. Zimmerman was so short everybody called him Gee-Gee the Midget. The students laughed about how he could actually scoot around during tests and borrow fellow students' papers to copy the answers, and the teacher wouldn't see him.

"I already know how to talk like a white man," Davey replied, enunciating every word clearly. "Who are they, spoutin' words like some lawyer-sharp northern niggers, gonna tell us all how to live?"

"That's just the problem, brother." The little guy squinted up at Davey. "Black people should be working together instead of fighting each other."

Davey looked down into Gee-Gee's eyes, which were swimmy

behind his coke-bottle glasses. The little pip-squeak couldn't have weighed more than a hundred pounds soaking wet. Davey said, "For a little guy, you sure got a loud mouth."

"Well, fo' a big man, you shore gots a wee one!"

That was something new, being accused of keeping his mouth shut. Davey smiled, noticing how the little guy's diction slipped when he got mad. He wondered how far he'd fly if he gave him a slap alongside the head, like Ishmeal used to give his kids when they did something bad. It wasn't a friendly smile, and Gee-Gee took a step backward, tripping and falling on his behind.

Davey pointed a big finger down at him, "It's all well and good for you to make noises about your misery, but what you're doing isn't practical. Look around you, boy, an' open your eyes! Injustice is a way of life. You ain't gonna stop it by waving your little fist in the air or passing around leaflets!"

Davey held out his hand and helped Gee-Gee up.

"We got to start somewhere!"

"Look, I can't listen to this, I gotta get to the gym." From the corner of his eye, Davey saw the campus police car moving slowly in their direction. He nodded toward the car, "Ain't there someplace you supposed to be?" All around them, the waves of students were dissolving as if by magic. By this time, the two of them were nearly alone.

The car pulled alongside and Officer Tubman, a fat, middle-aged black man stuffed like licorice Jell-O into his uniform, called out from the passenger seat, "Hey, Jones!"

Davey walked over to the side of the car, "What's up, officer?"

"We got a report of a disturbance, something about troublemakers." Davey stood still, saying nothing. He resented the way the campus pigs had just trotted over at the first sign that anybody was speaking his mind. Blacks had enough trouble as it was. If this was their college, why couldn't they say what was on their minds? The officer stared around, his sharp eyes taking in the scene and then nodding toward Gee-Gee, "You or the Midget here see anything?"

"Some kids squabblin' over basketball tickets, Chief," Davey replied, looking down at his shoes. "I settled it. Tol' 'em to make peace or I was gonna bust me some heads."

His answer seemed to satisfy the two officers. They exchanged pleasantries about next year's football team. "Bulldogs gonna win it all!" Davey told them. "You bet the farm on it!" They liked to hear that. They waved and drove off.

Davey nodded after them, looking down at his new acquaintance. "So much for you gnawin' at the white folk," he said.

Gee-Gee stood with his arms on his hips, looking up at Davey, " 'Preciate you not talkin' to the porkies."

"No problem. You try an' stay out of trouble, hear?"

"If I can ever help you in any way . . ."

"I don' need no help," Davey said, reverting to his Eatonville dialect. "I already got myself organized."

"Well, you never know." Gee-Gee fished around in one of his pockets, pulling out a crumpled leaflet which he passed across to Davey. Davey took it, and the little guy grinned and walked away, cocky as a bantam rooster. Davey stood looking after him, feeling like the lion in the old fable of the lion and the mouse. He wondered if that meant he was going to get a thorn in his paw. He looked down at the pamphlet in his hands: questions asking why blacks weren't good enough to eat, drink, and go to the bathroom with whites. It brought him up short. The same had always bothered him.

Davey read the pamphlet more carefully as he walked to Bulldog Gym. The arguments were appealing, but he wasn't totally convinced. It was a modern world, the late 1950s—yet the blacks' lot in life was only a few steps removed from the time of slavery. Punishment for stepping out of line came swiftly and was often cruel and sometimes permanent. Maybe the old fables were no longer very instructive. Maybe the modern mouse could get the modern lion in a lot of trouble.

Contact

The 1958 football season came, and once again Davey Jones played in the heat and the swampy bugs for the South Carolina State Bulldogs. He was big. He was fast and quick. (Which to a football player are not the same thing.) Because he had the talent and worked at it, he kept getting better and better. He played sixty-minute football, going both ways at tackle. Most practices, he was the first man on the field and the last to leave. In addition to offensive and defensive tackle, he played on the suicide squad[4]—the kick-off team—and was the back-up punter and point-after kicker.

---

2. The suicide squad is the defensive unit which goes in on kick-off plays, so-called because they must run at the opposing team and crash into them at top speed.

There was only one problem. He was a black kid playing on an all-black team in the all-black Southern Intercollegiate Athletic Conference. They played little-known schools, like Bethune-Cookman College in Datona Beach, Morris Brown College and Clark College in Atlanta, Benedict College in Columbia, and North Carolina A&T in Greensboro. And the pro scouts, even the savvy ones who beat the bushes for talent and who were open to the possibility of a black player, never came to see them play.

Coach Moore, his assistant Ed Martin, and even roly-poly part-time assistant William Hedgespeth said encouraging things, but most of the players just laughed off the idea of playing for the pros. "What, are you nuts?" they scoffed at Davey. "You got sky-pie on your brain, nigger chil'! Best you get in out of the cold—you got the fever again!"

Here they were, the lowest of the low, scuttering around the South to play their games. Black college teams always traveled on busses, no matter how far away the other school was, even if it was in Alabama. The traveling squad of thirty-six to forty players lived in and slept on cots in the opposing teams' gyms because no motels would accept them. There were no all-black motels except in a very few towns like Atlanta.

But Davey didn't really care. Ever since his return from his disastrous northern bean-picking excursion, he'd become cemented in his ways. When Rosie had told him he was going to join him at South Carolina State, he'd been surprised but not overwhelmed. He knew then that some day he was going to get his shot at the big leagues. All he had to do was get ready. He'd read somewhere that when Abraham Lincoln was a young man, he'd said, I will study and prepare myself, and my opportunity will come! If it was good enough for Lincoln, it was good enough for Davey!

Davey's one chance to be noticed came in October, when the Bulldogs took the bus south to play Florida A&M. The Gaters were a big-enough school for the pro scouts to sometimes give them a quick look-see on their way to Georgia State, Alabama University, or Rice.

The Florida game wasn't very big to anybody else, not even to Florida A&M. For them it was a nonconference game. The small but feisty Bulldogs were on the ticket simply because by the fourth quarter they could be counted on to run out of breath, roll over, and die in front of the mighty Gater's alumni, who were filling the stands for homecoming.

Coach Moore came up to Davey before the game. He could be spare with his words, and Davey didn't know what he wanted. The coach finally spoke, "I chewed the rag a bit with Jake Gaither last night, over a couple of beers."

Davey grinned, "You tell him we gonna whup his ass?"

"Of course I did, but after that he told me something interesting. He says the Rams have a scout here. They're lookin' at one of Jake's backs. Jake tells me the young man's a sure thing for the pros."

"Oh, yeah?" Davey's ears perked up.

"Yeah." A slight smile came to the coach's lips. "So I thought I'd line you up against him." Moore started to walk away, and then turned back to Davey. "So I think maybe you should go on out there tonight and dust his ass."

"Th-thanks, coach . . . "

"You got somethin' special, Davey. I think you can go a long way. You've worked hard and given a lot to the team. It's just my way of sayin' thanks."

It was one of those games that had the Homecoming Committee wondering who had signed on the opposing team. Homecoming games are supposed to be routs, one-way streets, big, lop-sided victories with lots of long touchdown runs to cheer about. That wasn't the way this one went down.

The tone was established on the first series. Florida A&M had the ball on their own thirty-two-yard line, second and long, and the Gaters quarterback faded back to lob the big bomb to one of his backs, who had snuck out of the backfield and was streaking for the goal line. Maybe he'd lobbed it a bit high. Maybe the ball hung in the air a bit too long. Whatever the reason, just before it settled in the receiver's outstretched arms, Davey Jones got a hand on it and swatted it away. It had to be luck, the frustrated quarterback thought to himself, looking over to his coach on the sidelines. Jake Gaither must have agreed, because he sent in the same exact play a second time. This time, Davey Jones did more than break up the play. He intercepted the ball.

The game went like that, sawing back and forth without much scoring, and with Davey Jones swarming in on almost every play. Man for man, the Gaters were a heavier team, and they had twice the players. As the second half got going, the lighter Bulldogs started to wear down and the Gaters managed to pull out in front by one touchdown, and then another. Still, Davey was a demon on both offense and defense, actually scoring a touchdown for the Bulldogs in the closing minutes of the game.

After the game, Gaither crossed the field to shake hands with the Bulldogs coach. "You gave me a little scare there, Coach Roy," he said.

"A little luck an' we'd a had ya," Moore replied.

"Yeah, but then y' probably wouldn't be seeing us next year," Gaither said with a glint in his eye. Roy Moore shrugged. There wasn't anything he could say to that.

High in the stands, Rams scout Eddie Kotal sat smoking a Chesterfield and waiting for the crowd to clear. He finally snuffed his cigarette and pulled out his notes and gave them another look. He'd doodled the name David Jones over and over until his ballpoint pen had almost gone through the paper. He fished in another pocket and found his crumpled copy of the mimeographed team roster he'd picked up from the Bulldog's bench almost as an afterthought before the game. Now he was glad he had it. Jones, who had been all over the field, was listed as weighing 240 pounds and playing both offensive and defensive tackle. Kotal began whistling softly to himself, a tuneless little sound that meant he was thinking. He'd made his reputation finding talent in out-of-the-way nooks and crannies of the sports world, but this was a new one, even for him. Defensive linemen in the NFL were generally huge, lumbering oxen, bulky, slow titans who rumbled in the way of the offense and slowed it down until the defensive backs could slash in and make the tackles. This kid reminded him of another find of his—Lamar Lundy, the young Rams defensive end—only Jones was going to get maybe even bigger and faster. Kotal rolled it over in his mind. What we got here is a big, tall lineman who's quick as a cat, fast enough both to run down backs and be a good open field tackler! The fact that Jones was black didn't bother him at all. If other teams were foolish enough to recruit whites only, that was their problem.

Of course, Kotal wouldn't say anything to Jones, or to his coach. It was one of the basics—human nature, really. Once the kids knew you were interested, their price went up, up, up! No problem. Kotal felt this was a safe little secret; no other scouts had seen the game, and it was by far the biggest match the Bulldogs would play on their schedule. The way things stood, there would be no competition for the kid's services. The Rams would get Jones at the end of the draft for next to nothing. Kotal stood and stretched, and shoved his notes back in his pocket. Then he headed for the exit, still whistling tunelessly to himself.

Minglin' wit' th' White Folk

Perhaps the most widely publicized sit-ins in the U.S. civil rights movement began on February 1, 1960, in Greensboro, North Carolina, when black students from North Carolina Agricultural & Technical College tried to buy coffee at a Woolworth lunch counter. The incidents that followed have been proclaimed the birth of the whirlwind by historians. But historians are notorious for their tendency to simplify. In truth, Greensboro was just one spark in a firestorm already raging throughout the South. One will never know how many beatings, hangings, incidents of police brutality, and other injustices large and small from this period have quietly been covered up and so lost to history.

In the fall of 1959, with his second successful college football season behind him, Davey and the other players from the Orlando area packed a few things and started thinking about Thanksgiving break: there was Lester Seays (Roosevelt's younger brother, who had joined the Bulldog's backfield), Harry "Bevo" Irvin from Hungerford High's old rival, Jones High, and a guy named Burley, whose name says it all.

It was midmorning on a pleasant autumn day. The four of them slung their duffel and gym bags over their shoulders, walked out the front gate of the college, turned left and then right at the first street light, and continued a half mile downtown to the bus station. Orangeburg was a typical rural center, a town of maybe fifteen thousand people, with a lot of farmers who had retired and moved into less physically demanding circumstances. The Orangeburg bus station was like thousands of others sprinkled throughout the rural South. It had a fairly decent cafeteria in front for whites only and a dingy little colored lunchroom in the back with three stools and no tables.

Blacks were expected to order from a little window in back and carry their burgers and shakes to their area. But with all the students being let out at once, the entire station was crowded with Negro college kids. By the time Davey and the other Florida players got there, blacks had already taken over the dining room and were using the whites-only bathroom. Davey shrugged and commandeered one of the last tables in the white area.

"Maybe they got some new rules," he smiled at Burley.

"Maybe they's too many blacks to enforce the old ones," Burley replied.

The chalkboard schedule on the wall said their Orlando charter bus would be an hour late, and it would certainly be nicer not to stand the whole time. And there wasn't another white customer in the whole place.

They ordered hamburgers, fries, and Cokes just as if they were white folks, and the whites behind the counter served them. They may have been a bit wide-eyed as they went about fixing the food, but they didn't say anything. The old ticket man gave them dirty looks from behind the thin bars of his little booth, but he didn't speak up either.

They had been sitting a few minutes when Gilbert Zimmerman sat down at an empty chair at their table. He didn't say much, but the few black people who were sitting in the white section were clearly an important event to him, and his face was animated with excitement.

"Gee-Gee, git away from the grown-ups." Bevo gave a wave of his hand, "We got footballers here." The football players formed an exclusive club; they were a brotherhood set aside from the rest of the student body.

"Naw, he's okay," Davey said. "This here is Gilbert the Great. He may be little, but he got brass balls." But even as Davey spoke, a whisper of apprehension tickled the back of his mind. It was nothing he could put his finger on, just a feeling of impending doom. Being black in a white-controlled society did that to you. Davey tried to shake the feeling away, angry with himself for letting the whites have that kind of power over him. Still, he had a peculiar flashback sensation, the sinking-heart emotion like he was back in Hank Steele's poolroom, playing the three sharks from Orlando. Where were the white folks who'd been behind the counter?

Davey's eyes flicked back and forth around the room, now sure they were enjoying the calm before the storm. By coincidence, their table was closest to the door that led to the black section. Their bags, which contained nothing of real value, were stacked outside against the wall of the station. He found himself hoping the bus would show up early. Alert the way he was, he was the first to spot the tops of the police cars slide silently past a window outside. One-two-three-four, he counted five of them.

"Police comin'," he said simply. "We better go." He rose to leave by the nearby door to the black section, but in that moment a wave of blue-shirted white men rushed in, blocking his exit. They were big-bellied, young to middle-aged, with short-cropped hair in the southern cop fashion. They carried night sticks in one hand and had their other on the pistols at their belts, like they had rehearsed exactly what to do on the way over.

The leader slammed his night stick on the nearest table. There was a crack like a pistol, and french fries and hamburger bits flew in all directions.

"Oh, man," the kid who owned the food moaned, "What you go an' do that for?"

In the fifties, you didn't get five seconds with a southern cop if you were a brother. The lead cop reared back without giving it any thought at all and leveled his night stick against the young black's head; as bad luck would have it, he caught him across the bridge of his nose, breaking it. Blood poured down the boy's face and spattered on the table like runny ketchup.

Davey's hand's gripped the hard back of the wooden chair in front of him. For one wild moment he thought to raise it and bring it crashing down on the nearest white man's head.

Gee-Gee saw the look in his eyes and put his hand over Davey's. "No," he said. "Peaceful resistance, brother. They got guns."

"We ain't talkin' 'bout this!" the cop yelled. "Now git your black asses out of here!"

The police waded in, yelling obscenities, swinging their clubs and shoving the young blacks with no mind to whether they were male or female. There was general panic as all the kids tried to get out the two doors at the same time. Most of them milled around the front door, with the police yelling and beating on their backs.

Gee-Gee stood on a chair as if he was going to make a speech. "Fellow sons and daughters of Africa!" he piped up in his squeaky voice.

Davey grabbed him like a sack of flour and threw him over his shoulder. "Not now, Gilbert! We got a chance to get out the back!" Davey, Lester, Bevo, and Burley retreated through the blacks' dining area and ran out into the daylight. As they ran, they noticed a small group of whites, frowning and standing with their arms folded, watching from across the street.

Miracle of miracles! The Orlando charter bus had shown up. And it looked like all the other buses had also arrived, lined up in a row in front of the station. Davey and his friends snagged their bags and quickly climbed on board their bus. Gee-Gee disappeared somewhere, waving once and then running off in his own direction. He didn't look afraid; he looked more like a fisherman who finally had a big one on the line. The rest of the blacks, herded by the police, found their own buses and scrambled to get their seats. As soon as the buses were fairly filled, they started to head out. Within five minutes, the last of the Greyhounds were leaving the station, carrying their loads of Negro students home for Thanksgiving.

As they headed south, the mood on the bus shifted from panic to a sort of angry excitement. The students counted their cuts and bruises and found that on their bus alone six students had some form of injury. The worst seemed to be a pretty black girl whose mouth was bloody and broken. Her front teeth were short stubs, broken off by an overzealous swing from one of the policemen. It was the end of the girl's college life—her family couldn't afford to have her teeth fixed, and she never returned.

Animated conversation held sway, everybody talking about how they had to get organized to deal with the white man. Though no one knew it at the time, the Orangeburg Movement had begun. The movement would run for nearly a decade, ending in the Orangeburg Incident, a riot that resulted in the National Guard gunning down three South Carolina State students.

For now, Davey sat in the back of the bus, feet up and arms around his knees, watching the others. He hadn't been so deeply offended since the watermelon incident on the steps of the Baptist church in Eatonville years before. He held his fist to his lips, biting hard to keep his composure. He was afraid he'd start crying and screaming at the same time. He had never wanted to hit somebody so badly in his life as those white policemen. The black thoughts swept over him in waves of emotion. It wasn't fair. It wasn't right. He wanted to murder someone.

Davey wasn't looking forward to vacation any more. He could hardly wait to get back to SCS. He wanted to talk with Gilbert. Gee-Gee the Midget would know what to do.

Water Hoses, Clubs, Spit, and Dogs

In one sense, the Orangeburg Movement was largely unpremeditated and organic, like the spring hillsides bursting into green after a long winter's rest. By the spring semester students and faculty alike had become involved. You couldn't say any one person or group was responsible. It was as if South Carolina State yawned and decided to flex its muscles. Very few participants went around spouting idealistic sentiments like social revolution or equality of the races. They operated on instinct. It was foolish and wrong to keep black people out of the white section of the bus station. It made them mad, and they were going to do something about it.

Encouraged by some of their teachers, Gilbert and the other campus activists organized a sit-in during business hours, rotating students so there was constant pressure from a small group sitting outside the Greyhound station with signs protesting its segregation policy. Someone on the faculty got in touch with civil rights lawyer Matthew Perry, who promised to do his best to get anyone out on bail within twenty-four hours after they were arrested. As the spring semester got underway, demonstrating became the "in-thing." On an afternoon when there wasn't much to do, the students would say, "Let's go down to the bus station," as they might suggest going to the beach or sunbathing by the pool after class.

The administration disapproved, but here President Turner's aloofness worked against him. He had little loyalty among the student body, and so he couldn't really do anything.

The movement may have started as a flea-itch, but the mood steadily became uglier. As the semester wore on, the student body would march downtown in large numbers with the white policemen glaring and twitching their nightsticks. By this time, Gilbert was part of a band of regulars who were everywhere, encouraging the brothers and sisters to be strong and teaching the techniques of nonviolent protest.

Davey tried to stay away, aware that his powerful six-foot-six-inch frame, quick tongue, and fiery temperament were not made for the ways of nonviolent protest. But as the numbers grew on both sides, most of the football players found themselves irresistibly drawn into the conflict.

One afternoon, they donned their best go-to-church suits and ties and joined the march downtown. It started out like a party, high-fives and lots of joking around about how they were getting out of class to take a little stroll downtown. When Rudolph Cardwell, the tackle on the other side of the line, showed up, the chant went out, "Coffee! Coffee! We call him Coffee, 'cause he grinds so fine!" and everybody whooped and cheered. All the boys from Florida were there, as well as Willie Jeffries, the team center, who would go into coaching and by 1979 become head coach of Wichita State, the first black head coach of any major university.

But the group's good spirits shrank as they left the campus gates

and started along the public street, heading for the center of Orangeburg. As Davey looked around, he decided the whole thing was a mistake. He was surprised at the size and the hostility of the white people lining the streets. Shouting at him! Waving fists at him! Spitting
at him! The training course they'd had in nonviolent tactics seemed so
far away it was like something from another planet.

Gilbert saw Davey hesitate, and tried to laugh it off. "I'm staying
by you, bro! When the water hoses blow, that'll be me hangin' onto
your leg so I don't get knocked down the street!"

It was a hot, sunny spring day, and there were a thousand blacks
marching in the streets and over twice that number of whites shouting, spitting at them from the sidewalks, and waving their little
American flags like right was on their side. Bevo was hit by a stone
and Lester had to duck an empty Coke bottle that smashed in the
street.

Davey disgustedly wiped a gob of spit from his shirtsleeve.

"Hey, Burley—this nonviolent crap is for somebody else!"

Burley nodded, daubing at the blood running down the side of
Bevo's head with his good white linen handkerchief, "You said it there,
bro—we don't get to the end of this soon, I'm gonna take some white
folks out big-time!"

They were afraid and angry at the same time. This was nothing
like the previous marches. There were hundreds of police, imported
from surrounding rural hamlets. Davey heard somebody yell, "Let
loose the dogs!" and the white folks lining the street cheered as if they
were at the greyhound race track or a cock fight. He turned in time to
see a dozen policemen chasing them with German shepherds on long
leashes. The guard dogs were snapping and pulling at their masters,
eager to tear into the nearest blacks at the back of the line, who started
pushing and shoving the people in front of them. From another corner, firemen with hoses blasted away at the crowd, and in another
moment, near panic swept the marchers. They broke ranks, milling
around aimlessly.

"They got dogs!" Davey yelled. "I don't want nothing to do with
dogs!"

"Every man fo' himself!" Lester yelled back, and they ran with the
big dogs snapping at their heels.

Everything was confusion. Gilbert was nowhere around, so Davey
took off for himself. He was running down the street when he realized
someone was shooting at them. He couldn't tell if the shots were in

the air or into the marchers, and he didn't want to know. He ran like the wind, turning left at a corner he didn't recognize, when he was blasted by a cold shock of water from a group of men operating a hose from a nearby hydrant. It was a big mistake. The men were directing marchers into a blind alley. He was trapped! Before he knew it, Davey was pinned up against a chain-link fence with the icy water smashing his body so hard it split the back of his suit. The water kept coming and he couldn't hold his breath that long. He was drowning!

Davey, Lester, Coffee, Bevo, Burley—most of the football team, and, of course, Gilbert—were arrested, along with 350 other Negroes. There were too many of them to put in the jail, so they were herded like cattle into a barbed wire pen with a high-voltage wire running around the top.

Night came on, and the spring heat quickly left the air as the temperature plunged into the low forties. Davey was freezing in his suit, which was still damp from his soaking. He sat by himself in the glaring spotlights trained on the pen, sorting out his life. After a while, Gee-Gee came and sat next to him. "This is just the start of it!" he emphasized, saying the words over and over again, almost as if he were talking to himself.

Davey finally turned to the smaller man. "Gilbert, I don't want to say you're wrong, but I have made up my mind—I can't do this no more."

Gee-Gee's eyes popped wide until he looked like a black ventriloquist's puppet, "Davey, you can't leave us now. We need men like you. Dr. King has shown us the way."

"Martin Luther King is a great man, amen to that. But I see clearly in the darkness of this night that his way is not my style. Gee-Gee, I cannot stand another person spitting in my face. I never thought I would be the kind of person to say I will die before I let that happen about anything, because I love life more than any man I know."

"What you sayin', Davey? We ain't good enough for you?"

"No. You are too good for me, little man. I cannot follow the non-violent doctrine."

"Oh, come on. It's cold and you're freezing out here. Tomorrow the sun will be shining and we'll be out of here and things will seem okay to you."

Davey stubbornly shook his head. "They's things you don't know about me, Gilbert. I come from bad stock. My daddy's the meanest man in central Florida. An' his daddy make him look like a Boy Scout."

"You got to learn the ways of peaceful demonstrations, my large friend."

"Case you ain't looked around you, Gee-Gee, we livin' a violent time here. We playin' for high stakes, an' the Klan is worse than the Mafia ever was. Those suckers will burn all our churches to the ground to keep us in line. They don't care if a black baby is screaming inside, they'll just pour more oil on the fire."

"People will say you're afraid."

Davey nodded slowly, "That they might, and them what think it can say it to my face. I got a deeper problem than what folks think of Davey Jones. I know myself. I ain't taking the spit, the dogs, the water hoses, or the clubs one more day. When it comes to it, I'll kill some-body. I'm not talking like a joke, like when a person say I'll kill you and he's really kidding around. I mean, I'll kill somebody. An' that won't do the movement or me any good."

"What you gonna do?"

"One thing, I will not become a school teacher like my Mama wants. I think life is about respect. I learned a long time ago that Joe Louis an' Jackie Robinson have more respect and success than George Washington Carver ever had, an' he practically invented the peanut. I know what I have to prove. But I'll do it my way, and that way is going to be on the football field."

It took fourteen hours for the NAACP lawyers to have the marchers released from their stockade. It seemed to Davey that Gee-Gee spent most of that time trying to convince him to stay with the movement. But Davey's mind was made up. He wasn't giving up the struggle for civil rights. He was simply picking his own battlefield.

Banished

The Orangeburg police cars drove quietly onto the lush South Carolina State campus, parking in front of President Turner's office. The police were inside for perhaps an hour, during which time the whispered word spread like wildfire along the campus grapevine until every member of the faculty and every student realized they were there and knew they had to be discussing the march, the ensuing riot, and what must be done in the aftermath. After they left, Turner called in the football coaches and the players from Florida.

Once they were all assembled in his office, he gave them a stern look. "This college," he said, "is de-emphasizing sports. In these times, it is necessary that we concentrate on what we do best—educating Negro youth to be the citizens of tomorrow. And so, I'm afraid that means we are scaling down our scholarship program."

Everyone was talking at the same time, arguing or wondering what this meant. President Turner spoke over all of them, pointing to the athletes assembled before him, "What this means," he said, "is that your scholarships are being revoked."

"You can't do this to us," Davey sputtered.

"I'm afraid you, least of all, are in a position to argue, Mr. Jones. You haven't made your grade point again, have you?" It was one of those academic questions that was really its own answer. Still, Davey felt it was unfair.

"There were times I didn't make my grades before. It didn't seem to matter, and I always pulled it up the next semester."

"Unfortunately, this time, for you, there will be no next semester. We have to make way for youths who are more serious about their studies."

Davey and his friends were walking back to their dorm in the blackest of moods when one of the coaches called to them from the distance, "Hey fellas, wait up!"

It was assistant coach William Hedgespeth. "How'd you guys like to play football for me next semester?"

It was the last thing in the world they expected to hear. Hedgespeth was only a part-time assistant, and he was the exact opposite of Coach Moore. Where the head coach was educated and intellectual, it was hard to find respect for Hedgespeth, who was fat and wore heavy, thick glasses. The image everybody had of Hedgespeth was of him driving on campus eating two pork chop sandwiches, one in each hand, and driving the car with his stomach. How could you take a man like that seriously?

Lester growled at him, "What you talkin' about, coach? You was in the meeting wit' the rest of us."

"Yeah, I was there. But there's somethin' you guys don't know—nobody knows it, cause I ain't announced it yet."

"And what might that be?"

"I been made head coach at Mississippi Vocational—an' I want to take you guys with me! All you guys!"

"What about the residency rule?" Davey asked. "We can't play for twelve months."

"Come on, man," the coach said. "Remember John Smith?" They all remembered John, who had transferred to SCS and immediately started playing for the Bulldogs. Problem was, the guy could never remember his new name. At game time, the coach would be calling for Terry Brown and finally one of the players would have to punch John and say,"Man, that's you this week!"

Davey smiled at his friends, "Witness the temporary death of David Jones!"

"What you talking about, fool?" Burley asked.

"Behold, I am now David Collier. Davey Jones has died the death, and it was painless. And yet, I am born again. Davey Collier, that is me. See how easy that was? Didn't hurt at all."

"Davey Collier. Is that so hard to get used to?"

It was done a lot in the SIAC league.

They went from gloom to disbelief to joy in a flash. Maybe he was a little weird, but Coach Hedgespeth was one of the good guys. He wanted to take the Florida boys, who had been the heart of the Bulldogs, with him to his new school. It was enough for them. They didn't stop to think what life in Mississippi, in the heart of the Deep South, would be like. Realistically, there were no other options. Here was the chance to have President Turner and the white folks of Orangeburg stew in their own juices. They would take their winning football ways somewhere else, where they were appreciated! Opportunity was knocking. They looked at each other, grinned, and quickly shook their chubby new head coach's outstretched hand.

Coach Roy D. Moore stayed one more year, to coach the Bulldogs to a 5-5 season, then left in 1960 to get his doctorate. He later successfully coached at Delaware State in Dover, and at North Carolina A&T in Greensboro.

The Orangeburg Movement continued for years as the determined students of South Carolina State fought on for their rights. Davey Jones and his friends were expelled, but they were replaced by students just as determined to carry the torch of liberty. Their courageous stand never wavered, culminating in 1968 in what is known as the "Orangeburg Incident," in which the National Guard shot and killed three students from the college.

Today, there is a monument on the South Carolina State campus bearing their names, and each year students place flowers at the base of the stone in a moving ceremony to commemorate their sacrifice in the cause of freedom.

The Road West

Davey lived at home in Eatonville and worked as a handyman for a white man, James Fownes, until September, when he packed his bags. There were five of them—Burley, Bobby, Harry "Bevo" Irvin, Lester Seays, and Davey. They left Orlando in an old Plymouth station wagon, full of hope and promise. Dwight Eisenhower was still in his last days as President of the United States, and his Vice President, Richard M. Nixon was running hard against young upstart Democrat John F. Kennedy to succeed him in an election that was only two months away.

The day was bright and sunny, and they sang along with the scratchy old radio as they went, keeping a beat on the dashboard and the seats. They sang "Only the lonely knows the way that I feel," and "They's a man in the funny papers we all know, an' he lived way back a long time ago—Alley Oop Oop Alley Oop!" and "She wore an itsy bitsy teenie weenie yellow polka dot bikini."

They sang their way across Florida's panhandle, past Pensacola and into Alabama, heading for the heart of the Old South. They were on the other side of Mobile, flying along at sixty miles an hour and arguing about Sam Cooke and whether "Chain Gang" would get into the top ten, when a telltale *flup-flup-flup* noise sounded the alert that one of their tires had blown.

Burley pulled over to the side of the road and they all got out and stretched. Sleepy cows blinked and munched and looked at them across rusty barbed-wire fences.

"Couldn't have happened five miles sooner when stations were everywhere," Bobby grumbled.

Davey unloaded all their stuff from in back and pulled out the spare. He frowned as he looked it over.

"She's bald as the eight ball," he said.

Burley shrugged, "She'll get us to the next station."

The next station wasn't exactly in a town. It was more of a small rural outpost, a green, paint-peeled combination gas station and general store in the middle of nowhere. The white man who came out eyed them grimly, but he didn't say anything. He was old and wrinkled, with bright red skin on his forehead and arms. He wasn't friendly or unfriendly.

"We need ourselves a new tire," Davey said.

"Got some," the service man replied curtly. He jerked his thumb at five or six tires in a rack on the wall. Davey selected the one next to the cheapest, figuring that with the cheapest tire came the poorest service. The man simply grunted, pulled out the tire, and got to work.

"You got a water fountain we can use?" Lester asked.

The man eyed him for a moment, and then jerked his thumb again, this time toward an old faucet sticking from the side of the wall. The faucet was right next to a door on which was painted in big, drippy black letters "Bathroom—knok furst!" As they well knew, throughout the South the bathrooms and water fountains were all marked "Colored" or "White," but in a little place like this there was clearly only one of each. One after the other, the boys from Florida all began to make use of the facilities. The man eyed them a time or two in between jacking up the car and changing the tire, but he didn't say anything.

Davey dickered with him and for two dollars extra got him to replace the bald spare with the casing from the blown tire, using the inner tube from the spare. His work seemed okay, so Davey handed across the money for the job. The minute the man had the money in his hand, something about him changed. His face grew redder and redder, like he'd been storing up all his emotions inside. He turned to Harry Irvin, who was about to take his turn in the bathroom.

"Hey, you!" he yelled.

"What, man?" Harry jumped back, wondering what the problem was.

"Gol-damn it, you git away from that bathroom! You niggers had enough time in there!"

"Hey, I didn't even go yet . . ."

"You gonna cause me some trouble here?" The old man's hands started shaking so badly he looked like he was working himself into a frenzy. "Do I gotta call the sheriff? Do I got to get my gun?"

Calling on every ounce of restraint he could muster, Davey said, "Come on, fellows. This here ol' man's goin' to get his gun." Davey motioned to the others as he edged toward the car. He gave the man a little salute, "We gots to be going now."

His calmness seemed to make the man more angry than ever. They climbed back in the old station wagon with the purple-faced white man screaming and waving his fists in the air. "Git the fuck off my lot, you dirty niggers!"

"So much for the ways of peace an' nonviolence," Davey said to nobody in particular as they drove away. They left the radio on, but the top tunes stations faded, to be replaced by Bible-belting preachers and plaintive country-western music. Nobody sang along. The boys seemed lost in their thoughts. The blacks here seemed worse off than any they'd seen in their lives. They dressed in rags, went without shoes, and stared forlornly from unpainted tarpaper shacks that all seemed to be leaning haphazardly one way or another like lives without purpose or direction.

Davey and his friends sat hunched over and quiet, and their hearts were heavy as they crossed over into Mississippi and headed north, upland and away from the gulf into the rural backwoods delta country. For his own part, Davey was uneasy. His high hopes and spirits had dissolved like wisps of smoke, and were replaced with dark and foreboding thoughts. What in the world were they getting themselves into?

A Visit from the Law

The night had the unsettling ambience that those who have lived in ancient, decayed Mississippi long enough to recognize it might call a hangin' night. It was late November and most of the leaves were brown and off the trees. There was a chill, an uneasy movement in the air, not really a breeze so much as an uncomfortable feeling that made you want to be indoors, near a fire with those you loved, behind the protection of a heavily barred oak door, particularly if your skin fell into any of the shades from tan through mahogany, a range simply lumped together in that region as black.

Just another hanging night in Mississippi . . . the fog weighed heavily on the branches of the silent pines in that same dank woods outside the town of Greenwood where a few years earlier Emmett Till had been violently abducted, beaten, shot in the head, and tossed in the Tallahatchie River with weights around his neck. Emmett Till had been visiting from Chicago and his speech impediment convinced the local whites that he was "wolf-whistlin' a white woman." Somewhere a hound dog howled a long, haunting wail that broke off in a sob, a banshee mourning-widow sound to make your heart skip a beat and your step quicken. Close by in the dark a small creature made a rustling sound, nails on wood as it scrabbled up hard bark, and then all was still again. The clouds thickened over the moon. It was a night made for secret, furtive happenings, made for dark and twisted moves that by the first light of dawn would be history already lost under the broad, trackless, leaf-carpeted forest.

Twenty miles down the lonely, two-lane blacktop from Greenwood, the same cold and uneasy night hung over the Mississippi Valley State campus. The football season was over, and school was dismissed for Thanksgiving. They'd won all their games, except for a squeaker against powerful Grambling, and an equally close one against South Carolina State when the Florida Five had to hide out instead of play.

It was ten o'clock and the campus was deserted. Davey Collier and friends, lacking the money to make it home for the turkey dinner, were sitting under a single dim light in the student union, drinking coffee, and eating huge bowls of ice cream.

The man who usually tended the student union had left an hour before, telling them to lock up when they left. That had seemed a little odd because he usually was very picky, choosing to throw the students out rather than waiting for them to leave. But they shrugged it off, figuring everybody was going home for Thanksgiving and nobody wanted to stay around the miserable little dirt-poor town of Itta Bena or the nearby campus a moment longer than necessary.

"Man, the school is empty," Davey said, lifting a shade and looking out the windows at the empty stretch of beaten-down dusty lawn that stretched away from the student union. "It makes me nervous." He came back to the table and dug for another scoop of ice cream.

"A thousand miles from home an' no money for bus fare," Burley said. "It was a sad day I ever set out for the sorry-ass state of Mississippi."

"They sure don't like us much here," Davey agreed. "Me an' Lester got stopped by the police yesterday goin' over to Clarksville in the old station wagon. One of those big, fat, greasy southern cops like they make fun of in the movies. Here I was, no brakes and my license expired. I thought it was jail time, but he wasn't interested in that. He hitches up his pants an' he says 'What you boys doin' out here?' Lester pops out, 'We're from the college an' we're goin' to see my girlfriend.' Well, that porkey smacks his fat pink lips an' shakes his head. 'No you ain't,' he says. 'You niggers get out of here. Go on, get the hell back up to your vocational school where you belong!' "

Everybody but Bevo shook their heads and muttered. Bevo couldn't take it seriously. He threw a rolled up napkin at Lester, "So, loverman, how soon you goin' back to Clarksville?"

"Not me, Bevo. Not me. Get your head blown off for a little tail. Nope. It just ain't worth it, bro."

Davey nodded, "You can take this whole damn state an' shove it."

"Terrible place to play the game," Bobby added.

"Yeah, it is that. Ain't no sticky, muggy heat like this anywhere else in the world."

"I thought Florida was bad."

"I thought South Carolina was bad. Is there anything worse than Mississippi clay?"

"Sticky when it's wet and hard as pavement when it's dry." Davey stood up and looked around the room, "You guys hear anything?"

"Yeah," Burley laughed ruefully, "I think it's the sound of somebody messin' with my girl . . . back in Orlando."

"No, serious, fool. I heard something."

Nobody had a chance to reply. There was a huge, crashing sound at one door, and then at the other. After a few seconds, the sound came again, and the doors burst inward under the impact.

"Jesus," Davey said, looking bug-eyed at the splintered remains of the doors, "And they weren't even locked."

It wasn't a laughing matter; through the open doors poured several squads of white policemen. They rushed in, waving shotguns and shining flashlights in the faces of the young blacks sitting around the table.

"Up against the wall!" they shouted. "Quick now! An' spread your legs!"

The police moved quickly, from black to black, shining their flashlights in their faces and rapidly thumbing through a set of eight-by-ten black-and-white photographs until they were satisfied they had a match. When they came to Davey, they shouted, "All right, boy, who are you?"

"M-my name is David Collier!"

"Cut that shit, boy! That ain't your god-given! Le's see some eye-dents!"

Davey handed over his driver's license. "David Jones," the man read sarcastically. "This nigger-boy don't even know his own name. Your name is Jones, boy—not Collier!" Quickly leafing through the photos, the policeman came up with one he thought matched. Hands still on the wall, Davey looked backwards over his shoulder and recognized a picture of him pinned to a cyclone fence by a stream of water. Seeing that photograph, he was amazed all over at the velocity of that stream of water. No wonder his suit had split!

"Where'd you get that snapshot?" he asked.

The man slapped him across the face, "None of your business. Turn around, nigger boy. Just face the wall."

In five minutes, the police had matched all five of them to the Orangeburg pictures. "Looks like we got the whole gang."

"You can't come right on campus and do this, man," Davey said, remembering his long talks with Elroy, "not if you are following the constitution and the laws of the United States of America."

"Well, if it ain't a nigger lawyer, tellin' a bunch a' us pore ig'orent Mississippi Delta white folks what to do!" The policeman drawled sarcastically, "I wonder if the rope fits in the same place around his neck like anybody else?"

The slow feeling of dread seeped through Davey's bones, making him feel chilly and weak. "I didn't mean nothin'," he said quietly.

"You the same smart-ass lawyer who's spreddin' these pamphlets around the dormitories?" The man pushed a pamphlet in his face. The headline on the front cover screamed, "Sons of Africa, UNITE!"

"No, that ain't me."

"We think maybe it is," the policeman said. "You-all turn around an' listen up real careful for a minute. We got you Florida agitators dead to rights. You're down here under assumed names, but you're the same pack a' troublemakers caused all the damage in South Carolina."

"We just came here to play ball," Lester said.

"You don't quite get it, do you, son? We know why you come here," another of the policemen said, prodding him in the stomach with the tip of his shotgun. "Only question left is how you gonna leave. Now some of the boys," he swept his free hand around the room to indicate the rest of the police, who were leaning on their guns, or still standing at the ready, "is all for takin' you for a quiet walk in the woods. Me, I say give you a chance. We're all agreed, we don't want your kind in Mississippi. But folks in other states ain't quite so enlightened. That's their problem. We're gonna put you on a bus to one of them states. We're even gonna buy you those tickets free, courtesy of the Greenwood police force."

"When?" Davey asked.

"You got two hours to pack your stuff. We're even gonna leave and let you do it by yourselves. But don't get any ideas about takin' off in that old junk of yours. We'll be parked up the road, here an' there. Two hours, hear?"

They all said yes, and the police backed out of the student union.

Davey heard them laughing and back-slapping as they walked away toward their squad cars. "The whole damn gang of 'em!" one of them chortled in the darkness, "Every last one of them nigger troublemakers—we got em all!"

Banished, Part Two

The boys from Florida ran back to their dorm rooms in a panic. They pulled out their battered suitcases and threw in whatever they would hold. They dumped the contents of their dresser drawers in the middle of the room and scooped up t-shirts and jeans and whatever else was closest. There would be no time to pick up suits and shirts at the cleaners. And the old junk station wagon would have to be left behind. It hurt a little to lose their wheels, but no matter; better to say it had served its purpose, and to cut their losses.

Packing took about ten minutes. After that, they gathered in Davey's room, sitting on the beds and the floor, alternately frightened and dejected.

"They got no rights to be doin' this," Bevo said for about the tenth time.

"Shut up, Bevo!" This from Lester, who looked like he was about to break out into tears.

"Oh man, oh man, oh man, what be gonna to happen to us now?" Burley moaned.

"That's the heart of our problem," Davey slowly nodded, trying to sort out his thoughts. "All the chance in the world these be the same white cops who strangled, beat, shot, an' hanged poor Emmitt Till. An' if they ain't, they're cousins."

The others stared at Davey. "What you gettin' at?" Lester finally asked.

"My daddy always said, Knowin' you're gonna be hanged clears the mind right up."

"Hanged?" Lester sputtered. "We ain't done nothin' wrong here!"

"No, but you got to admit, we in the wrong place at the wrong time."

"They can't do nothin' to us!" Burley said. His voice was loud, but there was a hollow ring to it, like he didn't believe his own words. "Emmitt was one lone nigger, but we got five here. It's too many to get rid of and be quiet about it."

"I didn't see nobody else on campus all the way over here. Did any

of you?" Davey's calm gaze was met by four blank stares. "No, you did-
n't," he continued. "Not a single student, teacher, cafeteria worker.
Not even a campus policeman. We on our own here, fellows."

Somehow Davey wasn't paralyzed by the fear he felt. Maybe that
was how his dad and his grand-dad had come by their reputations, the
baddest men around. Maybe being bad was a thing so simple as being
able to think your way out of trouble. He didn't know. He didn't have
time to think about that at the moment. Like Ishmeal always said,
Deal with your priorities in the right order. Davey had a clothesline
stretched from the window crank to the top bunk in his room. During
the season he used this line to dry his practice clothes. He spoke as he
went about unknotting the rope, "I'm not worried about bein' thrown
out of Mississippi right now. Forget that. That's long range plannin'.
What we got to worry about right now is that the only way to the bus
station in Greenwood—if they really gonna take us to the bus station—is through twenty miles of swampy forest."

"What you sayin', Davey?" Lester's eyes were wide as silver dollars.

"It's simple. If they take us all the way into Greenwood, they gonna
let us get on the bus. If they don't, we nothin' but bones in the woods."

"We ain't never gonna get through! They're gonna murder us!"
Bevo stood and headed for the door, "We gotta take off before they
come back!"

Davey dismissed his idea with a wave of his hand, "We can't out-
run guns and dogs five hundred miles through the woods. Which way
would you go? Tennessee? Alabama? We in the Deep South here, boy."

"We got to run!"

"You're just askin' to be shot down like a dog."

But fear was in the air. Now Burley stood and started toward the
door, "Maybe Bevo's right. We're gonna die anyway, why not make a
run for it?"

"Yeah, Davey," Lester chimed in, "at least we got a chance that
way."

"No chance in the woods," Davey said firmly. "They'll send a thousand Klanners after us. They love to do that stuff. That's what they live
for."

"Why don't we just kill ourselves then!" Burley exploded. "Make
it easier on 'em!"

"No, that's not what I had in mind." By this time Davey had taken
down his clothesline. He wrapped the stout cord around both hands,
with a short, two-foot segment in between. "We got to take the

chance, maybe they're gonna let us get on the bus. On the other hand, if that ain't what's really on their minds, I say we be ready to take a few white men with us."

"I don't know," Bevo said, "that put us in bad . . ."

"You already in bad over your ears, Bevo. Two seconds ago, you the one ready to make a run for it."

Lester sighed and sat back down, "What you want us to do, Davey?"

"We got to take the risk an' go along with the white cops." He pulled a huge pocket knife from his suitcase and began sawing short lengths of cord, "But there ain't no sense in not bein' prepared for the worst."

"If it come to that, I don't know I could choke somebody to death. Not even a white man." Bobby, who had been silent, spoke up for the first time.

"Right, Bobby," Bevo snorted. "White man gonna hang you in the swamp, and you get nice on us!"

"I just don't know if I can do it!" Bobby shouted.

"All right, enough!" Davey put up his hand for silence. "Bobby, if we sure they gonna kill us, you got to. Look at it like this; lots of times, you choke somebody, you actually think they dead, but they are just unconscious."

"That true?" Bobby asked uncertainly.

"True," Davey nodded. "I swear on my grandfather's grave." He stood and handed out the short lengths of cord. "Now listen up careful. Nobody does nothing unless we're sure. Then it's gonna happen real fast. The police usually put the crooks in the back of the car. An' we know white police always put the niggers in the back. So we gonna be in the back seat. Count on it. Just put the cords in your back pocket. Pull your shirts out from your pants. An' pray to Jesus they don't take the ropes away from us."

Lester let his cord dangle in front of his face. "This ain't much of a chance, Davey."

"It's not like I had a couple weeks to come up with a really great plan, Les. This is all we got; if they stop in the woods, we get 'em around the neck. If we lucky enough, we get a few guns and maybe a squad car. Then we can make a run for it."

They talked more about it, but no one had any other plan. Finally, they stood in a circle and put their hands in, just like they were ready to break from the huddle.

The police had given them two hours to pack. When they showed up a half-hour early in front of the student union, the squad cars were already waiting. There were three cars, each with two policemen.

"Throw your suitcases into the first two," Davey whispered. "We'll have to overpower them and shoot it out with the third car."

The others nodded. Davey and Lester slung their heavy suitcases in the open trunk of lead car, and Bevo, Burley, and Bobby did the same in the second.

Nobody gave them any trouble. The police were in a jovial mood. They made no secret of nipping at their flat little bottles of firewater, cheerfully clapping each other on the back and spitting tobacco juice on the threadbare campus grass. As Davey had anticipated, when the luggage was loaded they shoved the blacks in the back seat and quietly drove off the campus. Since nightfall, they hadn't seen one other person, white or black, on campus. Mississippi Valley State was completely deserted, as if in anticipation of the arrival of a deadly plague.

As soon as they were on the road, Davey took out his cord and quietly wrapped it around his fists. He motioned to Lester to do the same. "Remember," he whispered, "if they pull off the road, we've got to be quick. We've got to get them before they get out."

The one in the passenger seat, a tall southerner with grinning teeth that gave his lean face a death's head look, swung his head back at them, "Whut you whisperin', boy?"

Davey shrugged, "We was hopin' you'd put on the siren an' the red lights."

The man spat out an ugly chuckle. "No chance of that. We tryin' to run you niggers out of town without a commotion."

That wasn't what Davey wanted to hear. His heart sank as the three cars headed along the two-lane blacktop, pointing toward the deep woods. He and Lester sat forward on the edge of the back seat, leaning forward as far as they dared, with their hands down between their legs. Lester would take the skinny passenger; Davey's victim was the driver, a large, heavy-set white with a thick neck. He was chewing an enormous wad of tobacco, and Davey could see the blood pulsing in the vein on the left side of his fat neck. Would he be able to kill someone? He tried to push the thought from his mind. Survival was all that mattered now. What chance did he have? That was a safer question. The only thing he could figure was that the driver was maybe in his fifties, and looked out of shape.

They drove for fifteen minutes like that, no one saying a word, and

Davey was beginning to think they were going to make it when the skinny cop yawned and said, "Hey, Billy-boy. Pull over, would you? I got to take a piss."

"Can't hold yore beer like you used to, Farley," the driver jeered softly, grinning as he squinted into the night road ahead.

"Come on, man. Do it."

"Chief ain't gonna like it . . ." Billy flipped a thumb at the car following them.

"I clearly don't give a god-damn hoot. You want me to hose it all over your floor?"

"Okay, okay—hold yore damn fire for a minute." Billy started to slow down, aiming for a gravel pull-off area about a hundred yards in front of them.

Davey gritted his teeth and nodded to Lester. His hands gripped the cord so tightly they felt numb. God, how he dreaded this moment! No matter that this was his idea, no matter how cold he'd sounded back in his room, Davey didn't want to kill anybody. God, God, God, make it not so!

The police car behind them impatiently flicked its brights on and off. Davey could see the chief waving them on. Billy took his foot off the brake and hit the gas. "Sorry, Farley. Chief ain't gonna let you have a piss-break." Lester and Davey slumped back in their seats, their faces drenched in sweat. Farley let loose a soft string of curses, not realizing his life had just been spared.

Five minutes later, as the three-car procession quietly pulled into the tree-lined streets of Greenwood, Davey and Lester pushed their short lengths of clothes line out of sight between the seat and the seat back cushions. The five black students were pulled from the squad cars and stood shakily in the light from the Greyhound sign, happy just to be alive.

The chief himself went inside and bought their tickets. When he came back out, he held the tickets high over his head and grinned, "Five one-way tickets to Orlando, Florida." He looked each of them in the eye as he handed out the tickets, and now he wasn't smiling. "Remember, niggers, you got two choices—home or the cemetery."

"We just want to go home," Davey mumbled, reaching for his ticket.

The bus didn't show up for another half hour. Davey and his friends silently huddled together, sitting on their suitcases in front of the bus station. Nobody even bothered to see if they had a separate counter inside for black people. All they wanted to do was get on that bus.

Business settled, the police were polite in their ironic and superior way. When the battered aluminum bus finally pulled to a halt and the suitcases were all loaded and the Orlando Five finally climbed on board, they smiled and nodded their heads.

As Davey boarded, Billy, the fat cop who had been his intended victim spat a stream of tobacco juice against the side of the bus. The brown dribble ran down the dusty metal and Billy said, "Now don't you niggers never come back to Mississippi again, y'all hear?"

All right, Davey thought to himself, the anger rising to a choking fury in his throat and his eyes glazing over with hate, I never will! But he didn't say anything. He didn't even look back. So close to the edge, he didn't dare. He just reached out for the metal handrail and climbed up the steps into the bus. Store up a little extra hurt and pain, his father always used to say, sometimes it's all you got to motivate you through the bad times.

Farewell to Dear Old College Days

The deep-throated diesel engine whined as their bus plowed through the night, lumbering steadily south toward New Orleans. Except for the five of them, the bus was deserted. They stayed in back where they could stretch out on the long bench seats and catch some shuteye.

After a few hours, the bus stopped at a seedy roadside restaurant. "Ten minutes," the bus driver barked at them. Davey noticed his pale-blue eyes flicking worriedly as they passed. It didn't make any difference whether or not the man was a bigot, he was afraid of them. He wasn't armed, his pot belly and heavy jowls showed he wasn't physically fit, and he obviously wasn't very happy about escorting Negroes out of the state.

As they climbed off the bus, Davey noted two state troopers sitting in the potholed gravel parking lot in their shiny new squad car, watching them. Lester nodded, indicating he, too, saw the police. "They gonna make sure we stay on the bus."

"I got all the inspiration I need," Davey said. "The great state of Mississippi has seen the last of me forever. I swear, if I fly over in a plane, I'm gonna ask the pilot to go around."

They moved into the restaurant, where they sat on battered wooden chairs around the lone table reserved for blacks. Davey went to the telephone under the watchful eye of both the troopers and the bus driver, white men he could be sure had been given very specific instructions by the Greenwood chief of police. He made his call and then went back to his table. His coffee had come. The milk in the small pitcher on their table was sour. Rather than ask for fresh milk, he drank his coffee without it. Black and bitter, he thought. Just like me.

They climbed back on the bus and waited for the driver, who took another five minutes to talk to the troopers before he closed the doors and pulled out. It was pleasantly warm sitting over the engines, and Bobby, Burley, and Bevo were soon sleeping. Davey stayed awake, watching the trooper's car following behind them and talking to Lester.

"That B. C. Turner has mighty long arms, to send our pictures from South Carolina to Mississippi."

"How you figure it was B. C., Davey?"

"Who else? The police couldn't have traced us. We all used false names. Way I figure it, Coach Hedgespeth had to get a recommendation from ol' B. C. , so he knew where we were. He couldn't be content to whup us in football, he had to get us personal."

"They'd never beat us if we'd played."

"No question, Brother Lester. But he can't leave us play football nowhere. After all, we been expelled from South Carolina State, showplace of education in the South. If somebody else just picks up on us, that makes him the fool. He's got no choice—he got to contact Mississippi an' tell them they are harborin' a bunch of dangerous agitators."

Lester nodded, "So he contacts the porkies in Orangeburg an' they send our pictures to the porkies in Greenwood."

"Yeah. Be on the lookout for the five troublemakers from Florida. They play football, and they good. How hard is that to spot?"

"Easy. We're the best."

"That's right. An' B. C. couldn't leave it alone. He's just one of those black men who gets a little power an' uses it to keep the rest of the brothers down."

"That's too sad to think about."

Davey stared out of the window. The troopers had now left them behind. He couldn't go to sleep. It rained as the sky greyed with his last Mississippi dawn. Sheets of gauzy rain drifted across the southern farmlands, making them seem dreamlike and peaceful. The engines whined and the Greyhound churned steadily southward toward a stop in New Orleans before heading for Florida. The sky was clearing when they crossed the state line into Louisiana at the Pearl River, and the sun shone as they drove over the long stretch of highway across the east end of Lake Pontchartrain and pulled into the bus station in downtown New Orleans.

Davey smiled and yawned, "Well, I'll be seeing you, Lester. This is where I get off."

"They told us not to leave the bus until Florida."

"We're out of Mississippi now, bro. If the police want me that bad, they can come across that line and get me. My brother coaches high school football in this town. I called from down the road. He'd be upset if I didn't show up . . . as is my right as an American citizen."

"I got to see you get your bags from the driver."

Davey headed toward the front of the bus. The driver looked up at him and said, "Half hour."

"No half hour, son," Davey said. He outweighed the driver, a chubby little white man with pink cheeks and grey hair at his temples, by at least seventy pounds. He shoved his finger in the man's face, "I'm gettin' off here, an' I want my bags now." The man seemed like he was about to say something. Davey curled his hand into a fist. "You got a problem with that?"

"The state police said—"

"We ain't in that state any more. I want my bags, and you got two minutes."

The driver looked around, but he'd parked on the end of the line, and there was no help in sight. Surrounded by the five black football players, the request seemed reasonable enough. Without another word, he left his seat and walked to the side of the bus. He keyed open the side compartment and let Davey pull out his bags.

After a moment's hesitation, Burley reached in for his own suitcases, "I always heard about the fine whiskey, the fine jazz and the fine women of Bourbon Street. Maybe I'll just have a see for myself."

"That seems like a fine idea to me," Bobby said, reaching for his own bags. One by one, they all took their suitcases and walked away from the bus. They were heading down the long line of buses, toward the main terminal when they passed a trickle of passengers walking the other way.

"There's Miss Ratcliff!" Davey yelled. She taught English at Mississippi Valley State, one of those skinny, bespectacled black women who had dedicated their lives to education. He waved to her, "Miss Ratcliff, over here!"

At first, she didn't seem to recognize them, and then, once she did, she looked uncomfortable. But there was nowhere else to go unless she was to turn tail and run, and that was the last thing a woman like her was capable of doing, so she approached them warily, like a lapdog afraid of being swatted with a newspaper.

Miss Ratcliff had been a favorite teacher. She believed that the normally outgoing Davey had talent as, of all things, a speaker and a salesman, and that he could do some good things if he would just apply himself to his studies. Davey, excited at seeing his first friendly face and not immediately picking up on her hesitancy, kidded, "Heading back to State so soon? You tol' me you never went back to Itta Bena 'til the last possible moment!"

"Davey . . . I wasn't going home in the first place. I really couldn't afford this trip."

"Ohh, I'm sorry . . . somebody die in the family?"

The black teacher eyed the five of them before looking directly at him. She looked older, and somehow tired when she spoke, "You've all been expelled, haven't you?"

"Not officially. Just run out of town—but how did you know?"

"We were told to leave the campus. That's how they do these things."

"Campus administration was in on it all along, weren't they?" It wasn't really a question.

She refused to look him in the eye, "I've already said too much. You, you've got your life in front of you. I've got to go back there." She gave him a brief, unexpected hug and said goodbye in his ear, "You got talent, Davey. Remember, I believe in you." Then she picked up her frayed bag and walked past them toward her bus.

Davey watched Miss Ratcliff's small, resolute frame, knowing it would be the last time he would see her. He wondered what would happen to all of them, students and teachers alike back in dirt-poor Itta Bena, lost in the heart of the Mississippi Delta.

But then his brother Judson had come to meet him, and life was so good he stayed in New Orleans for a few months. He was working out in a local park one day in January when he heard Judson, yelling from nearly two blocks away, yelling a few words that would change Davey's life forever.

"Daaa-vid!!" he called, his deep, strong voice easily carrying the distance, "Davey Jones! Listen up, little bro! You be the chosen one! You been selected in the draft, boy! You goin' out west to play for the Los Angeles Rams!"

3

Raw Ram Rookie

In 1992 top sports agent Leigh Steinberg casually informed Deacon Jones that if he was playing today his net worth would be about $3.8 million a year. As a rookie, he'd be worth a hefty bonus over $2 million. Leigh should know. He represented the league's 1989 number-one draft choice, Troy Aikman of UCLA, for a six-year contract worth $11.2 million, and Jeff George, the 1990 Indianapolis Colts number-one draft choice, for a six-year contract worth $15 million. Aikman received a signing bonus of $2.7 million, and George received $3.5 million. We're talking real money here, their first two salary years being guaranteed. Rocket Ishmail got $6 million for two years. Of course, the early 1960s were the days before the big television contracts made the owners' profit so outrageous they were forced to start sharing the treasure.

Sign Up Time

The day looked like it was threatening rain, but neither brother thought much about it. A few big drops spattered against the windshield as Judson drove the I-10 expressway out of New Orleans toward the suburb of Kenner and the old Moisant Air Field, which was now taking on airs as New Orleans International.

"How we gonna know who he is?" Davey asked. His suit was still with the cleaners back at Itta Bena, but he'd managed to scrape together an old sport coat and a pair of pants that fit him. He worried at the neck of his new white dress shirt, loosening his brother's tie with its display of interlocking black, blue and white geese flying all over it.

"Davey, man, you gonna wear out my best tie before we gets to the airport." Judson looked up from the wheel of his 53 Ford Fairlane, "Come on, bro, settle in."

Davey frowned, "Jud, we got us a problem, here. We showin' up at an airport loaded wit' white folks gettin' on an' off airplanes. How we gonna know Eddie Kotal?"

"You should 'a asked him to wear a Rams helmet."

Davey gave his brother a sock in the arm, "That ain't funny, bro." He waved his arms, "There, there!"

"I see the exit, Davey. Tell me how a man is gonna miss a huge black and white sign in the shape of an arrow with the words New Orleans International Airport blazed across it?"

Davey sank back in his seat. After a moment his lips moved and he mumbled softly, "How we gonna know it's him?"

"We'll find him, Davey. We'll find him."

Judson found a parking spot in a wide, nearly empty, gravel-covered lot, and they sprinted easily around the water-filled potholes for the terminal, hoping to get inside before the rain started in earnest. "You got your game plan in order?"

"What?"

"Your game plan, Davey. You goin' into dealings with a white man. You got to know what you want, or you for sure ain't gonna get it."

"I thought this through, Jud. We makin' history here. Look at me—" Davey stopped in the middle of the parking lot and flung his big hands in the air. "I'm a country boy wit' the speed of light an' a head like a mule. You think I don't know that?—I know that. An' I'm about to take a step no black and maybe only a few whites in the entire state of Florida ever took! There ain't gonna be no negotiations here. No arguin' over sums of money. No grindin'. My bonus is gonna be gettin' my foot in the door. I want my name on that contract, Judson Jones. That's my game plan!"

Judson, who had been in the war, and had fought his way across Europe both with and against white men and women, eating and sleeping and sharing his daily lot with them, wasn't all that convinced. White folks were no different from black folks, it seemed to him; only difference was, they owned the store and they weren't inclined to give any of it away cheap. But he knew his brother well enough to recognize there would be no arguing over the details on this one. He sighed and nodded toward the big terminal building waiting in the distance, "Well, then, Davey . . . le's get on in there and do it."

"I just hope we can find the son of a bitch. I ain't never seen him before."

The guard at the door that led out to the runway said Eddie Kotal's plane would be there, it was just twenty minutes late because it had to fly around a patch of cumulus storm in southern Alabama. The plane finally did show up; a sleek, barracudalike Super Constellation taxiing over to the hangar through the light rain, and some men pushed a metal ladder on wheels up to its side while the four big props were still spinning red and white arcs in the misty swirl. The door opened and white folks came out on the ramp and stretched their legs before climbing down the steps. An older white man with a deeply wrinkled face, grey hair, and baggy pants got off the plane and walked directly up to them. A smile creased his face even deeper, and he stuck out his hand, "David Jones, I presume?"

"How'd you know it was me?"

"Not too many folks of your dimensions in the area." He shook Judson's hand as well, "You the family lawyer?"

"Nope. His older brother."

Eddie's face wrinkled even more, thinking on that. He was a short guy, so short he even had to look up at Judson, "Jud Jones . . . Black All-American two years. Xavier College. Right?"

"You got that right!" Jud was flattered and amazed. "How you know that?"

Eddie winked, "An old man's memory." An aging DC-3 lumbered by, kicking up misty grit around them. Eddie turned to Davey, "Lets go inside for a minute. I got about ten minutes to make my next connection."

Davey shot his brother a worried glance. Ten minutes! Maybe he wasn't going to get his name on the paper after all. Mr. Kotal didn't even have a briefcase with him. Maybe he hadn't even brought a contract! Davey was a string-ball of worries as he followed the Rams agent into the waiting room, where they huddled on the other side of the doorway, out of the direct line of the wind.

"Okay," Eddie said, raising his voice over the intermittent engine roar that still made its way through the glass doors, "this is real simple. Do you, David Jones, want to come out and play for the Rams?"

"Yes, sir, I do. I made up my decision. I already told you that on the telephone."

"Yes, you did. That's why I'm here now." Eddie fumbled through the pockets of his jacket, pulling out several fat packets. He squinted at them and finally selected one. "You were drafted in the fourteenth round. Now that's not high enough for us to offer you a bonus." He eyed Davey, the unspoken question on his lips.

"Ain't askin' for a bonus." They had to hurry this up. Passengers were starting to stream around them now, reboarding Eddie's plane.

Eddie nodded, "All right then. I see you're serious about playing for us. That's good. You'll see, the Rams really take good care of their players. We're all like family. You come through for us, and we'll never let you down."

"Sounds good to me." Davey reached for the contract, but Eddie held it back for a moment.

"We're able to offer you top pay . . . that is, for a rookie of your standing."

"Sounds great!"

Eddie still held the contract just out of his reach, "But I gotta ask you one favor."

"Sure, Mr. Kotal, anything!"

"We got a little problem here. See, you been drafted number fourteen, but I scouted you myself. I know how good you really are. So I'm recommending the Rams pay you all this money—but what if number nine or number five sees you're getting the same amount, or maybe even a little better than they're getting?"

"Bad for team morale. I can see that."

"Exactly! I knew you would! So, I'm askin' you, when matters of pay come up and the guys get to talking, just zip up your mouth and walk away. Can you promise me that?"

"You got it, Mr. Kotal!"

"Good. That way you save us all a lot of trouble." Eddie opened the contract, leafing through the pages to the back page, where he checked the numbers and then said, "Okay, then—the Rams are offering you the grand sum of $7,500 to come out and play ball with the best team in the NFL! We'll send you an airplane ticket to L.A., and pay your food and lodging during training camp! Deal?"

Davey's eyes glowed. He grasped for Eddie's hand and nearly shook it off, "Deal!"

Eddie waved the contract in the air, "Of course, if you want to read all this, you can take it and sign it and send it back to us and then we'll sign it."

"I don't have to read it," Davey said, "I'll take your word for it."

"All right, great! We'll do it right here." Eddie knelt on the floor and used his own knee as a desk to scrawl his name across two copies of the papers. He handed them to Davey, who took his ballpoint pen and signed using Judson's back. Eddie gave him one copy of the contract and stuffed the other back in his pocket. "Hey, sorry to hit-and-run like this, but I've got to get my seat or they'll take off without me." He hurriedly shook hands with Davey and Judson, and pushed his way out the door. He was ten yards away when he thought of something, "Hey! Where do we send the ticket?"

"Send it to my mother's house in Florida! You got the address?"

"Yeah! We got it! See you in L.A.!" Eddie waved and walked quickly to the plane with his thin pants legs flapping in the prop wind.

Davey and Judson watched him walk up the metal ladder and disappear in the plane before they turned away and headed back to the Ford.

"So that's how they do it in the big leagues?" Judson shook his head, "Man, that was fast."

Davey was walking on clouds, "Yeah, but I got what I wanted."

"Sure, but it didn't go down exactly like I imagined. You know, little bro, he never bought us dinner—in fact, that white man got your name on his contract an' he never even bought us a drink!"

"Say what, big bro?"

"Well, here he is, a big shot with the Los Angeles Rams professional football team an' all; least he could have done was cinched the deal with a Coke or somethin'!"

Judson burst out laughing, and the two brothers ran to the car through the light rain, laughing and slapping each other on the back all the way.

The Prophet

Judson walked into the shabby living room and threw a muddy old pair of army boots on the couch where Davey was sleeping.

"Ha-hooo, Davey!" he said. "Come on, little bro, time for your morning run!"

Davey groaned from underneath the covers. Judson waited a moment and then tipped the sofa over, sliding his brother to the floor. "Up an' at em, Davey! Your happy times is just beginnin'!"

Davey squinted up from his position on the floor, "What time is it, anyway?"

"Nearly five. I see where you been pickin' up bad habits at college, boy!"

Davey reached over and picked up one of the boots, "What's this?"

"Your new runnin' shoes. Your size. Go ahead, try 'em on. I bought 'em for you special."

"They's heavy, man."

"You did say you was going to sign with the Rams?"

"Well, yeah, but—"

"No buts. Me an' yore mama an' yore papa an' the good folks of Eatonville don't want to be embarrassed, that's all. Come on, let's go."

In twenty minutes they were running along a quiet New Orleans street. There wasn't another soul in sight other than a sleepy paperboy and a few milkmen making their early morning rounds. Davey wasn't yet fully awake, but he didn't have to squint any more, as dawn was a long way from breaking. "These boots are lead, man," he complained.

Judson grinned, running backwards alongside him, "They gonna get lighter . . . after a couple months of these two-a-days, which you are beginning at this very moment."

Davey gaped at his older brother, "Two-a-days!"

Judson nodded, and the grin disappeared from his face. He looked up at Davey, "Lil' brother, you ain't yet got the moves nor the skills of a pro baller. You ain't as big as some, and you ain't as clever as others. They is huge, an' white, an' dirty, an' mean. They got all the moves, an' worse, they don' like you, 'cause you black."

"Black got nothin' to do with it."

"Maybe. Maybe not. We see about that one."

"You think I'm too skinny?"

Judson shook his head sadly, "They think you weak like a girl, 'cause you only weigh maybe 230—"

"I'll have to persuade them out of that opinion."

"Oh, yeah. You mean with the best of 'em," Judson agreed. He'd argued half the night away before convincing Davey to give up his four-inch switchblade. "But they's some bad men in the NFL. The South don't have the corner on red-necks. No matter how bad-ass you are, they ain't just gonna let no colored boy waltz in there an' take their livin' away."

Judson led them behind a church, and then they were running on a golf course, jogging in the deep rough along a wandering creek. The boots were chafing, Davey's breath was starting to come in gasps, and his feet were dragging in the wet grass. He was running out of patience as fast as he was losing his wind, "You sayin'—I shouldn't—even try?"

"No, fool, I ain't sayin' that. But you show up at trainin' camp in the shape you in now an' about three days later they gonna ship you back to Orlando in a pine box! Pap'll come an' pick you up at the airport."

They ran on in silence for a hundred yards. Finally Judson said, "You got to rely on your weapons, Davey."

"Sounds like you think I ain't got no weapons." Davey said, still smarting from Judson's earlier appraisal.

"Bro, listen up, here. You are the fastest lineman I ever seen. The fastest. You also the quickest, which is another thing entirely. Those be your strengths. You can learn clever, you can pick up all sorts of tricks, but speed an' quick come from the Almighty."

"If I'm the fastest, why ain't I the best?"

"It ain't so simple, Davey. They got men in that league weigh 270 pounds. Lots of 'em. You can't go straight at 'em, they'll squash you like a bug. You got to learn to cut an' slash, to zig an' zag like lightning."

"I don't get it. If I'm gonna be like lightning, what am I doin' out here logging time in lead boots?"

Judson gave him an iron grin. It was easy to see why he was such a winning football coach. "You workin' on endurance, little bro. They's a rule in the pros, Davey—The fast man never lasts. That's because sooner or later—an' it's usually sooner—the speedy little man always gets hisself pounded into the ground. But I swear, you put on another fifteen pounds of muscle, and I don' care if you're black, white, green, or purple, they're gonna have to make new rules for you."

"Why's that, Jud?" Davey's breath was coming in gasps, and he could feel a sharp pain in his side.

"'Cause you gonna be a new breed, little bro."

"What new breed?"

"You gonna be the first of the big, fast linemen, boy. You gonna cut through 'em like butter, Davey. Their hands gonna grasp at air an' you're gonna dance by like they standin' still! Don' let me down here—you got a chance to be one of the greats!"

Davey dizzily followed his brother stride for stride as the first orange rays of the Louisiana dawn broke over the long hills and valleys of the lush southern golf course. He was drenched in sweat, his body ached and his feet felt like they were cased in cement buckets, but he didn't seem to mind any more. Maybe he was experiencing what athletes called their second wind. Or maybe he had caught a whiff of something else . . . Judson Jones, the former black college all-star, the big brother he idolized, had all but said he was destined for greatness!

Saying Goodbye

The full moon was sinking into Florida's New Smyrna Beach like a big orange basketball. Davey sat on a log on the beach, poking the last glow of a bonfire with a long stick. It was late June, nearly time for him to climb on an airplane and head for the unknown. And a part of him was holding back. Maybe it was his family, for he drew strength from them, and he hadn't done well without them on his bean-picking adventure to New York. Maybe there was a natural reluctance to leave the South and all he'd ever known. But he knew the heart of it was that he was leaving the Eatonville girlfriend he'd known ever since they'd been little kids. He'd always taken her for granted, until now. He glanced over at her. She was looking away at the distant curve of the bay. He admired the graceful curve of her neck, how she could look beautiful just sitting on an old log.

"Pat," he started, and then hesitated. She looked over at him, her dark eyes luminous in the moonlight. "Pat, I don't feel good about leaving you like this."

She shook her head, "We been over everything a dozen times, Dave. You got to go; I got to stay."

"Baby, why couldn't you come with me? Just answer me that."

"I know you better than anybody—'cept maybe your own mother. You ain't ready to settle down yet."

"I could settle down."

She gave him a sad smile, "Look at you. You up in the morning before the dawn, running with those big boots on. Then you go work all day for Mr. James Fownes. Then you come home an' work 'til dark, doin' all those starts an' stops an' liftin' those iron bars you bought. Mr. Fownes gives you the loan of his cabin, an' we come out here weekends an' I hardly see you, you're runnin' in the deep sand wit' those boots on, driving your knees nearly so high as to hit your chest."

"That's my survival training, baby. I got to be ready!"

"I know that, Dave. Ain't nothin' wrong with that. You ain't never played against a white man before. But see, it's more than that. You got a fire in you. You got worlds to conquer, and you gonna want to do it your own way. You get that behind you, then you gonna be ready."

He put his arm around her shoulder, "I don't want to have to leave you."

She turned away again, looking down the long, dark stretch of deserted beach, but not before he saw the tears starting. "Now look what you made me do," she said. She stood up quickly and walked away, rubbing her eyes.

He clenched his fists and blew his breath out, knowing she was right and wrong at the same time. He needed her; she provided a stability in his life. She was his first love, sweet like candy. She could be patient and tender, and tough like his mother. When he got to ranting about injustice and the way things were, there was always Pat to calm him down. Even when he'd gone away to school, it was good to know she was just a phone call and a bus ride away.

And yet, she was right. With this new plan he really wouldn't have time for her. First there was the rookie camp, bad as any Marine boot camp. And then he would be on the road much of the season. You got worlds to conquer. She was right. He had a chance at the pros. Nothing and nobody could stand in the way. And here she was, saying she was going to step aside, and it was breaking both their hearts.

She stood and pulled her sweater around her bare shoulders, "I'm going back to the cabin."

Fists clenched, Davey watched her go. For a while he stabbed with a stick at the dying remains of the fire. Then he started up running along the wide curve of the beach, his bare feet slapping the cool film of water right at the edge where it made the sand firm. He ran until he was exhausted, finally looking up to see he was miles from where he had started. The moon was settling into the water, leaving a sparkling silver pathway across the calm rollers in the bay. I'll come back for her, he thought. That's the solution. I'll come back for her.

But even as he came to this resolve, Davey had a sinking feeling in his heart. The life he knew was full of uncertainty and tough times. When you made a choice in the white man's world, it was usually a hard one, and you generally gave up something of value for it. And in driving full-bore toward his life's highest dream, wasn't he going to have to give up his most treasured things? He kicked the sand for a while, reluctant to go back. But he was cooling down and the night breeze felt sharp and uncomfortable. He started the long walk back to the cabin with that sinking feeling in his heart. At that moment he didn't think it was going to go away. Not ever.

The Escape

Davey stood with his dad in the tiny Orlando airport, waiting for the DC-3 that would shuttle him to Tampa. Ishmeal stood awkwardly at his side, twisting his hat in his hands, "Son, your mama an' your sisters wish you well. Don' misunderstand, they didn't give no party or come along. They don' want to give you no embarrassment . . . if you be comin' back."

Davey shook his head, looking out at the palm trees across the short runway. This was in the days before Disney World, and the brand-new jet 707 passenger planes couldn't land there. "You think I'm comin' back?"

Ishmeal smiled and shook his head, "Only 'cept to visit."

"You the only one in Eatonville who believes," Davey said. He looked directly into his father's eyes, "Many's the night I seen you sittin' in the stands, watchin' me practice. I bet you didn't even know I seen you up there, but I want to thank you for that."

His dad shrugged his shoulders and fished in his pockets for his crumpled pack of Camels.

"I want you to know it mean the world to me. You're my number one fan." Davey was remembering back to all the practices and all the games, in the mud and the chill and the rain when Ishmeal had showed up. He wasn't only going to miss his girlfriend when he was all the way across the country. There was this quiet man who never let him down.

A smile spread across Ishmeal's face, "Always was, son. Always was."

When the time came, Davey gave his dad a hug, walked up the shaky metal steps, and ducked inside the DC-3 numbed by his conflicting emotions. He was nervous and confident at the same time. He was headed for show-town, Los Angeles, where they made the movies, for southern California, where, so the amazing story went, they didn't treat black men like niggers. He was about to step into circles about which he had no idea—he knew he had to cling to his one dream, to play pro ball, or he would be lost.

The doors closed, the engines roared, and the aluminum plane took off down the runway. And in that moment, Davey realized a new reality. He was petrified, stark-naked afraid of flying in an airplane. It was a lucky thing he was on the aisle, so he wouldn't even accidentally look out the window at whatever was impossibly far below. Davey gripped his knees and stared at the seat back in front of him until the plane settled down on the Tampa runway.

In Tampa, they were holding Davey's jet for the next leg of his flight, so he had to run for the plane. He buckled himself into his new seat—luck of luck, it was on the aisle!—and braced himself for the takeoff.

The jet took off with a tremendous rush and a steady sound like water rapids. Once they were in the air, Davey sighed and looked around for the first time. He was sitting next to a white man. This made him tense all over again. Maybe they'd made a mistake. This could lead to big trouble. But then he looked around and saw another black man further up the aisle sitting next to a white man, too. So it was true. You didn't have to sit in the back of the big jet planes!

The man next to him was saying something. "Huh?" Davey said.

"I said, this your first plane trip?"

"Yeah. I guess it shows."

The man smiled and offered to change seats with him so he could watch the land pass by below. Davey shook his head, "I really don't want to see what's down there."

The man reached over one hand. Davey took it and shook hands. The man's hand was soft, as a pampered woman's. The man was middle-aged, with fat cheeks plumping out from a round face, "I'm J. D. Perkins. I saw you on the flight from Orlando."

"Oh, you was on that flight, too."

"I go back and forth a couple times a month. I work for Walt Disney."

"Disney buyin' up a lot of swamp land."

"Where'd you hear that?"

"You can't keep no secret about something like that. Walt Disney known as the biggest fool in Florida. My daddy says he wishes he had some underwater land to sell."

Perkins chuckled, "No, I guess not. You going to visit folks in L.A.?"

"Nope. I'm goin' to play ball for the Los Angeles Rams."

The man's eyes widened, and he gave Davey a closer look, "Wow . . . I guess you could do that. What position you going to play?"

"Anything they give me. Anything at all."

"You didn't say what your name was. I'm going to need it to keep track of you in the newspapers.

"David Jones."

"Oh, that will never do." Perkins frowned and started to say something, but the airline stewardess came by then and said they would be serving dinner. The white man did something in front of his knees, and a tray fell smoothly into place. Davey tried to follow his example, but his legs were so long, his knees seemed to get in the way. Perkins and the stewardess made a fuss, removing a bag from under the seat in front of him until they finally got the tray down on his cramped legs.

The food came, some sort of chicken, and Perkins complained, but Davey thought it was delicious. If anything, he could have eaten three or four of the little meals, but nobody else was getting seconds, and so he was afraid to ask. Perkins paid a dollar for a glass of wine with his meal. Davey would have liked some wine to settle his nerves, but a dollar was outrageous. Mama, who always prided herself on giving Davey what he needed, had only given him $5.60 to make the trip. After all, his ticket was paid for, and by Eatonville standards, that should last a week. Why should he be needin' money? He was going into money! So it was $5.60, and a big, green umbrella. Davey had protested that it never rained in California, but Mama had insisted to where Davey knew he had no choice. But seeing Perkins hand over a dollar for his little bottle of wine as casually as if he were paying a dime for a candy bar, Davey wondered for the first time if maybe he should have brought along more cash. With Harold in school and Judson trying to scratch out a living in New Orleans, Davey'd given every dime he made to Mattie. By the time he had this new worry settled down in his mind, Perkins had somehow managed to turn out the little overhead light and had fallen asleep with a newspaper over his head. So he couldn't ask him just what exactly wasn't right about the name David Jones. But it gnawed at him all the way while the pilot reported they'd crossed the Mississippi River, passed Texas, and were flying over the Grand Canyon.

The pilot banked to the left so they could get a better view. Davey clung to his seat like they were going to crash. Perkins woke with a start, snuffling like a groundhog and knocking the paper off his face and onto the floor. He blinked and looked around, "What? What's happening?"

"The pilot is showing us the Grand Canyon," Davey responded through gritted teeth.

"Oh. You want to see?" Perkins slid up the little shade and the brilliant northern Arizona light flooded in.

"No!" Davey nearly shouted. "I mean, I'd rather not."

"Right. Well, it's just a big hole in the ground, anyway."

Davey looked over at the white man. "I don't mean to be out of bounds, but I have to ask. You said something was wrong with my name."

"Oh, that!" Perkins laughed like it was nothing. "It's just that you can't be a famous ball player with such a common name."

"I'm not sure what you talking about. I'm the only David Jones I know."

"Well, sure, maybe where you come from. But there's hundreds in Los Angeles—hell, maybe even thousands. How they going to know which David Jones is you?"

Davey laughed, "Well, they'll know me by my deeds!"

"That's the spirit!" Perkins chuckled along with him, but Davey could see he wasn't convinced.

He sank back into his seat. His brow furrowed and he pursed his lips as he thought over this new problem. For a long time he even forgot he was on a plane that was just a tiny speck in the sky, impossibly far above the safe and solid ground. And then there was a loud bump and a rasping noise and Davey froze all over with a horrible icy feeling.

Perkins put a hand on his shoulder, "Don't worry, David Jones— it's just the landing gear." Even though the man had been friendly enough all the way, now Davey somehow caught the faint notion he was being laughed at. He glared at the seat back in front of him and didn't say anything. The 707 gently tilted forward and they were in their long slide down toward his new life.

The Coming of the Deacon

Los Angeles International, the airport that fit the letters "LAX" attached to Davey's battered suitcase, was a madhouse. Too many people shoved and pushed and battered at each other. In the South you were black or white, but here there was a bewildering mix of races and colors, everybody all mixed and jumbled together and no time to figure who had to get off the sidewalk for anybody to pass by. You couldn't get off the sidewalk anyway—you'd be hit by a truck or one of the darting taxis.

Davey stood against the outside of the terminal, his back against the wall, watching the endless stream of traffic. He started forward, not sure where he was going, and jumped back as a polite voice out of nowhere said, "All cars parked in the red loading zone are subject to tow. Please do not leave your vehicle in the red loading zone." It was some time later when Davey realized he was standing next to a row of little glass rooms—telephone booths! He put his bag on end inside and lifted the thick telephone book, turning quickly to the "J's". Lord, that white man on the plane was right—there were twelve and a half pages of Joneses in the phone book! Just the bodies named David Jones took up over two columns. Davey sat on his suitcase and tried to puzzle that one out.

"Hey, brother!" a voice called from the curb. He looked up to see a black cabbie leaning against a battered yellow Chevy Bel Aire. The cabbie, who was picking his teeth with what looked like the splintered wooden handle from a popsicle, nodded, "Need a cab, young feller?"

"I don't think so."

"If you don't think so, you probably do. What's the matter, don't you know where you're goin'?"

"'Course I do." Davey fished frantically in his pants pockets until he came up with a crumpled note Eddie Kotal had included with his tickets. "Sheridan West . . . it's a hotel on Wilshire."

"I know what it is and where it is, brother. Now does you want a cab to get there?"

Davey looked around, but there was nobody holding up a sign saying "Welcome, Jones!" There was nothing but the cacophony of city sounds and the bewildering jumble of busy people, all confidently headed at top speed in their own directions. "Well, how far is it?" he asked.

The cabbie crossed his arms and gave a little head gesture up the road, "Say, fifteen miles that way."

Davey threw his bag in the cab and crawled in the back seat, thinking the West Coast soul brothers were somewhat more surly than those in Florida. They pulled away from the curb with a jerk and soon were lost in the wonder of mile after mile of beige, stucco houses. It was some time before Davey noticed the meter. He was used to a cab or two in Orlando where the driver took him anywhere for a dollar or two, but here was this ticking brass counter-thing up front he hadn't noticed before and it was already saying past seven dollars. Seven dollars! He didn't even have six!

Davey tapped his foot nervously, thinking over and over the words "Run-run-run-run Runaway" from Del Shannon's pop hit. He started to whistle under his breath. Finally, he gave a big yawn and a stretch and asked, "We getting there pretty soon, huh?"

"Ways to go yet, brother, ways to go. How come you all young like you is an' in a big hurry to boot?"

"No hurry."

"Settle back then. Enjoy the smog an' the fuss. I'll get you there."

The meter read $9.50 by the time the yellow Bel Aire with crumpled fenders pulled up in front of the hotel. Davey threw his suitcase on the curb and fumbled in his pockets. He slowly counted his entire $5.60 into the man's outstretched hand. Then he turned his pockets inside out, one after the other, like he was searching for lost money.

The cabbie gave him a cold stare, "I can't believe I'm bein' stiffed by a brother."

"I-I just don't have it, man! I didn't think it was gonna cost so much."

"Well, you better cough up the rest or I'm gonna call the men in blue."

"Oh, sure, fine lot of good that will do! Have some sense here. You can't squeeze blood out of a turnip."

"That some kind of jungle saying?"

"I'm from Florida, man, and I never been here before. Look, here—take this fine new umbrella and we call it even!" Davey held out the green umbrella his mother had given him.

"Um-brella! Where you been, turnip-head? It don't never rain in California!"

Davey blew out a breath, shaking his lips at the same time, like he was getting rid of a bad taste in his mouth, "Look. This here's a brand-new, twenty-dollar umbrella, and it is all I got! Now you can call the po-lice, and you ain't gonna get nothin'!"

The cabbie inspected the umbrella, popping it open and closed. "All right, you got a deal. But here, boy—I wouldn't want you to be broke, here in the big city an' all." He flipped Davey a dime, tossed the green umbrella in his cab, and drove off.

Feeling rushed and dizzy, Davey picked up his suitcase and headed for the lobby, thinking of his mother and how she'd always said, I'm gonna give you what you need. Well, in a strange sort of way, he had needed that umbrella after all. Still puzzling over how things always seemed to work out with his mother, Davey pushed through the glass doors and found himself in the middle of his first Rams press conference. The lobby was crowded wall-to-wall with people and everyone seemed to be talking at once.

"Hey," someone said, swinging a mike in his direction, "here's another one!" For a moment, Davey felt he was being swallowed up by the bright lights. The square box cameras with their Mickey Mouse ears and wooden stick legs were glaring at him like strange creatures, the popping flash from the still cameras were like silent bombs in his face. It was all going by in incredible slow motion, and Davey felt he was out of his body, having one of those religious experiences the old ladies were always talking about at the Open Door Missionary Baptist Church, only this wasn't a dream, it was real.

Hands took his suitcase and other hands led him to a waiting bank of microphones. "Who is it?" a dozen voices asked. He looked over the sea of waiting faces, most of them white people. "Who are you?" somebody said.

And then Davey forgot he was a country boy from the Florida swamps, forgot all the doubters from Eatonville, forgot the hardships and the pain of living in the South and everything else about who he was and where he was from. He felt like he had lived his whole entire life for this one moment, to be in front of the reporters. He didn't even have to think about it. The words sprang to his mouth like they always had; that wide mouth of his that was so accustomed to getting him in and out of trouble had no problem at all launching him into his newest and greatest adventure. "My name," he said, and he heard his amplified voice reverberate in the room, and that gave him even more confidence. "My name," he repeated, "is Deacon Jones . . . and I've come to preach the gospel of winning football to the good people of Los Angeles!"

"All-riiiight!" somebody yelled, "We got us a live one!" A ripple of pleasant chortles ran through the packed room. The newly ordained Deacon didn't need any more encouragement than that. He raised his hands high, shaking them like a Bible Belt preacher bringing the promise of the Lord, "Yes, my friends, the Deacon is here to assume his rightful place in the National Football League, come to L.A. with lightning in his stride and thunder in his moves, to teach the ignorant the ways of the gridiron, to bring certainty to those uncertain how the game should be played, and above all—to serve justice to the enemies of the Los Angeles Rams!"

Then Davey waved and walked away from the mikes to a hearty round of applause. Good-natured cheering and footstamping went on for quite a while, until the next speaker got to the mike and stuttered to introduce himself. This one hesitated and lost the crowd of reporters, who went back to talking to each other and trying to catch the attention of the coaches, who were standing to one side in a small group.

"Who was that masked rider?" a sports writer from the *Los Angeles Times* asked, almost talking to himself as he scratched his head under his hatband with a yellow pencil.

"Fourteenth draft choice," his companion muttered, reading from a crumpled page he had somehow pulled from under the weight of three cameras and a film bag slung around his neck, "Jones, tackle out of South Carolina State."

"Let me see that." The reporter grabbed the press release out of his hands and studied it for a moment. "Huh. You're right. All I can say is, he better have something to back his brag."

The cameraman shrugged, "Give him a break. The guy's colorful. Gives a burnt-out hack like you something to write about."

"Screw you, Hallie. Sure he will, if he's around longer than a week. The vets hear him talk like that, they'll crush him into little pieces."

The cameraman gave a second look across the room, "Our new Deacon looks to go about six foot six in his stockings. I'd say that's gonna take some lot of crushing."

The *Times* reporter pulled his hat low over his eyes and gave Hallie the sad little smile that said he'd seen it all. "They got their ways, pallie," he said. "You know they got their ways."

Everybody Needs a Car in LA

Alvin Hall, a young black fresh out of the Marine Corps, was walking through the lobby when he heard a quiet voice ask in a deep southern accent, "Pardon me, but are you'all headed out to the Rams training camp?" Alvin turned and found himself looking squarely at the neck of one of the tallest black boys he'd ever seen in his life.

Alvin, fresh out of the service, barked back, "Yes I am, boy. Why you ask?"

"Well, sir, I was hopin' I might bum a ride."

Alvin took a closer look. "Why, you that Deacon Jones everybody talkin' about at that press conference yesterday!"

Deacon allowed as to how he was.

A wide smile broke over Alvin's face. "Why don't you just miracle your way out to Redlands?"

"Come on, man. I really need a ride."

Alvin was sorry he had taken the joke approach. This kid was dressed in a tan suit with a black tie, what looked like his Sunday best. He was so polite he looked to have Old South manners. Alvin gave him a more friendly smile, "I didn't mean nothin'. You from Alabama?"

"Naw, Florida. But I seen my fill of 'Bama. It ain't no place to be from, nor Mississippi, neither. You got a ride for me?"

Alvin shook his head, "Well, I got a old, beat-up Oldsmobile that might get us out there if you're willin' to take the chance on it."

"All right! This your bag?" Deacon picked up both suitcases, and started out the door.

Alvin caught up and led the way to the parking lot. "Here she is. The Hall Love-mobile." Alvin's love-wagon had big foam dice hung from the mirror and a Playboy bunny logo stuck to the rusty back bumper. Alvin opened the back door and David slung the luggage in.

That year midsummer lay on southern California like it always does, a heavy tan-grey mix of smog and sultry desert heat. As Davey opened the door and slid into the passenger seat, it was only nine in the morning, but the sun was already too bright. The palm leaves hung like ragged, thirsty tongues. "This ain't nothin'," Alvin commented. "By this afternoon, we can fry eggs on the sidewalk."

The Oldsmobile started up with a heavy rumble. "Rocker panels are rusty, an' she could use a paint job," Alvin said, "but she goes like the wind."

"Sounds like straight pipes," Deacon said with admiration in his voice. Those were the last days before exhaust emissions, when it was still possible to hear the wild, unmuffled sound of your own engine without getting a ticket.

"Glass-packs," Alvin smiled. "I put 'em on myself." Glass-packs were little more than hollow cans filled with fiberglass. They carboned up in about a week and gave off a delightful throaty mutter. Alvin drove east, into the glare of the sun, and as he went he talked about what it was like in the rough-and-tumble world of a Marine.

"You never went to college?"

"Naw. Four years in Uncle Sam's military; that was my education."

By ten, the roadway was a furnace and they were glad the sun had risen high enough so the car roof shielded them. Even with all the windows open they were sweating.

"Hey, son, ain't you gonna take off that jacket?"

Davey, who had been watching the city grow sparse and turn into farmland and desert, looked down in surprise. "Huh. I guess so. I forgot."

"Weather like this, an' you forgot? You must be some forgetful!"

"I come from weather like this. Worse, even." Davey had started watching the gauges, "We got far to go?"

"Ten, maybe twelve miles. You gettin' eager?"

"I guess . . . I just been noticing we runnin' a little hot, here."

"Damn!" Alvin smacked the cracked vinyl covering his dashboard, but this only served to jump the dial into the red. He instantly reached for the key and turned the engine off. The Oldsmobile glided to the side of the road. He jerked the emergency brake and hopped out onto the dirt and gravel embankment as steam began pouring from the front of the car. He popped the hood and a huge cloud of steam forced him to jump back. "Damn, damn, damn! An' me with no water can!"

Davey, who had been around junkers all his life, had worlds of experience with these matters. He rummaged through the debris on the floor in the back seat until he came up with two empty soda pop bottles. He held his hand over his eyes, shielding them from the sun, and squinted up and down the road. "Closest place is maybe a half-mile back, if we're lucky. You stay with the car. I'll go get the water." Alvin found it difficult to argue that arrangement, and Davey set out walking back along the side of the road the way they'd come.

The house, a shabby, clapboard frame with peeling yellow paint, was deserted. There was no car in the driveway, and the big dog was chained, so Davey cautiously made his way to the faucet at the side of the house and filled his bottles. He'd found an RC Cola bottle by the roadside as he'd walked back to the house, so now he had three. By the time he got back to the Oldsmobile, the heavy V-8 engine had stopped hissing. Davey poured and they both carefully watched the water disappear inside the opening on the top of the radiator. They couldn't see any level at all. Alvin shrugged, speaking in his deep sergeant's voice, "Nope. We need more."

"Yes, sir," Davey said, and he headed back up the road. The second batch was enough to get them started, but they only made about a mile or so before it boiled over again. Davey scooped the pop bottles off the floor and got out of the car. This time the nearest water was only a few blocks away.

They were now clearly on the desert, with long stretches between parcels where the daring or the foolish had built their homes and tried to scratch a little out of the land. Off and on, the hot breezes came, kicking up dust-devils and blowing grit in their eyes. They continued traveling like that, making a mile or two at a time, and finally managed to pull into the Rams Training Camp at the University of Redlands, which is about seventy miles east of Los Angles, at four o'clock in the afternoon. Davey sat underneath a huge oak tree with his back against the trunk, drinking water from one of the pop bottles. Alvin came over and sat down beside him.

"This ain't gonna be no picnic, brother."

Davey frowned, "You was tellin' me you're a tough Marine. You been through hell an' back, you tol' me. How come all the sudden you talkin' like this?"

Alvin gave him a discouraged look, "I just seen a thermometer, hangin' over there on the side of a building. It's a hundred fourteen degrees in the shade. Welcome to trainin' camp, Deacon Jones."

By the Numbers

Davey had suited up and was standing beside Alvin Hall, squinting across the dry gridiron in the early morning sunlight.

"Field looks to be more gravel than grass," Alvin commented, raising a small spurt of dust as he kicked the ground at his feet.

"Makes no difference to me. I played in the sticky Florida heat, in muggy South Carolina where the bugs is so thick you can't help but suck 'em in your nose, an' on the baked red clay fields of the Mississippi Delta where if you land wrong they take you away in a basket."

"That is mighty, but you ain't never seen nothin' like this, young Deacon Jones. I hear they gonna have us in full gear, doin' two-a-days from nine to noon, and from three to dusk."

"It don't bother me, Alvin. When men start droppin' like flies is when I just get goin'."

"We'll see 'bout that. For now, you better get over there an' do your sprints with the linemen. This here's defensive backs."

Davey smiled. "I don't do sprints with linemen. They too slow for me."

They were standing on the ten yard line. "That be so, Mister Deacon? Then catch me if you can!" Alvin, who was a defensive back, took off like a bat out of hell, streaking for the center of the field and knowing there was no lineman on earth that could keep up with him.

Davey caught him in five yards, at the fifteen yard line, and ran with him stride for stride. "When you gonna turn on the afterburner?" he asked, running easily alongside.

Alvin pulled up to a halt and gave him a sharp look. "Guess I ain't in the shape I thought I was! You sure you play line?"

"The big "D" for defense, that's me. You want to go again?"

"Naw. Let me catch my breath here a minute."

They looked back at the groups of men who were beginning to assemble around the field. "Man, they got a big team here."

A lanky black who was jogging past overheard them and pulled to a stop, "This ain't the team. This is just the rookies. Team don't report 'til next week."

Davey looked unhappily across the field, "There must be over a hundred men here! When does any of us get to play?"

The black looked him and Alvin over for a moment, "New to this, huh?" He held out his hand, "I'm Lamar Lundy. Showed up a few days early to get in some conditioning." They shook hands all around, and then slowly walked along the edge of the field together. "Here's the way it is," Lamar continued. "Out of all these guys, an' all the vets who ain't even here yet, only thirty-four of us is gonna make the team."

"Oh, man! You sure about that?"

Lamar nodded calmly, "League rules. Plus seven or eight gets on the taxi squad—spare parts when the regulars get banged up."

Alvin shot him a worried look. "Not very good odds."

Lamar shrugged, "It's worse an' better than you think. The good part is, you take a look over there an' about half of those folks ain't never gonna make the Rams. You can see 'em—too fat, too lazy, too little, too slow."

Davey didn't take his eyes off Lamar. He'd already made that observation. "So . . . what's the bad part?"

Lamar shot a quick glance around to make sure they were alone. To anybody looking on, they might have been discussing the weather. "Okay. Now one or the other of you gentlemen may have noticed the three of us are black." He didn't wait for a reply. "So, if you would have done your homework before you accepted the Rams generous offer an' got on the plane from wherever you come from, you would know that every team in the NFL has two, four, or at most, six black ballplayers, 'cept for the Washington Redskins an' a few others who don't have any."

Davey's thick eyebrows were starting to take on their thundercloud look, "What are you sayin', man?"

"Well, you wouldn't have an odd number, 'cause blacks don't room with whites. An' you won't have more than six, cause they's a quota."

Davey was suddenly furious, "Man, I can't believe it! I came here lookin' for a fair shake! I thought this was about money an' winnin'!"

Alvin raised a warning hand, "Ah, maybe tone it down a bit."

"Tone it down? I thought here at last was the one place my black skin wasn't gonna matter!"

Alvin shook his head, saying, "See ya later," as he walked away.

"Come on. Let's talk some more." Davey noticed Lamar was walking him away from the team, which was grouped down at the other end of the field. Lamar smiled at him, "I seen you give him a jumpstart an' dust his ass back there. That was pretty good."

Davey didn't say anything, still upset over what he'd heard.

"What position you goin' out for?" Lamar asked.

"Line."

"Well, that's good. Now, you want to be on this team?"

"I never wanted anything so bad in my life."

Lamar nodded. "Okay. But from what I see, you got a bad temper an' a big mouth."

Davey started to speak but then held it in.

Lamar continued, "That be enough to make me want to stay away, so I don't get caught up in it when you go down for the fall. But that ain't the way. The good book say a man got to reach out for his brother. So you listen up good, 'cause I'm only gonna read you the routine one time." Davey nodded silently.

"You go all 'round the National Football League, you don't find no blacks in skill positions. For you, that means when you doin' the drills an' Ol' Stoneface sends out the call for quarterbacks, you don't step forward. You black, child, you don't belong there. Same also, any drills for offensive guards or centers or receivers, anything where you got to handle the ball or signal responsibilities, you keep your black ass back."

"I got to use the black water fountain, too?"

Lamar sighed, "Don't be sarcastic, now. I'm tellin' the way it is. This ain't the South, but black an' white do sit at their own tables. Ain't no law; it just works out that way."

"So all this crap is still the same. It's like segregation. It's the same as segregation, it just went underground."

"So, you gonna let it overcome you?" Lamar was eyeing him calmly, but his words plainly were a challenge.

Davey glared at him. "I came here to play," he said.

"Good." Lamar said. "Then see that you do. We need a couple good linemen, particularly on offense. Fast like you are, you got a real shot there. An' you never know, Reeves might pick more than six this year, desperate the way he is for that winning combination." He waved and smiled and took off jogging around the field. Davey watched him for a moment, and then slowly nodded his head. The gauntlet had been tossed. He walked to the other end of the field and joined the big, churning group of linemen, easily the biggest group on the field. His face was set with a new determination. Offense or defense, he told himself, it makes no difference. No matter what, when the final thirty-four are counted, I am going to be there.

The Warning

Dick Bass got his back up against a tree and watched the goings-on with heavy-lidded amusement. He didn't need any of this training camp bullshit. Sure, run through the plays at maybe three-quarters speed, but let's not get ourselves mangled before the season starts. A star running back practically since grade school, he relied on his quickness and his instincts as a premier runner to get him through. The particular object of his amusement was his new roommate, the big rookie lineman who called himself "Deacon." A classy showman himself, Dick knew raw talent when he saw it. Why, the kid had gotten almost as many laughs as he had from the reporters! Dick wasn't sure he was pleased about that. But be that one way or the other, out here on the football field this Deacon was acting like a wildman. He was everywhere, going full-out on every play, blasting into people, and the regulars didn't like it. Already a couple of the guys had come up to him, giving him the off-hand word that maybe his rookie-roomie better ease up a bit. It made sense; nobody wanted to get busted and broken before the season even started. The Rams talked all that family stuff, but the truth was, pro ball was a tough racket. Once you were laid up, you were relegated to the taxi squad, if you were lucky. Most of the injured were simply dropped from the squad and forgotten.

He'd promised he'd pass the word along, so when they finally broke for lunch, he called Deacon over, "Hey, Roomie! Deak, man—over here!" Deacon hustled over like there was no tomorrow.

Dick shook his head, letting the disgust show. "No, man, I didn't mean you should sprint over . . . ah well, never mind. Sit down here for a minute, I wanna talk to you."

Deacon took a last glance over his shoulder.

"Don't worry, man—you ain't gonna miss nothing."

Dick saw the rookie's face was streaked with grime and sweat. There was a big scrape on his left forearm and his uniform had more dirt on it than Dick got on any of his in an entire season.

"What you want with me?" It was easy to see Deacon was eager to be off.

"Man, I want to talk with you. Now is that so much to ask?"

Deacon reluctantly gave up and slumped to the ground, "Okay, what?" He looked exhausted.

"I just want to know what you think you're doin' out there. The man calls Offensive linemen! and you jump in there. The man calls Defensive linemen! and you jump in there. You the first guy in line, whatever the coach needs."

"What's wrong with that?"

"They gonna think you don't know what you want."

Deacon had known his roommate for less than a week, but he already knew that witty, fast-talking Dick Bass didn't have to work for anything in camp—he already had it made with a multiyear, no-cut contract. He reminded Deacon of Rosie Seays in his prime at SCS. Bass may have made the team, but he was a party boy, and Deacon wasn't impressed. "It don't work that way," he said. "Not for the rest of us. Coaches don't care what we want. They're gonna tell us what we get."

Bass shrugged, "Yeah, maybe so . . . but you out there, going like a demon on every play."

Deacon shrugged, "I came here to kick ass."

"I'm just warnin' you, friendly-like, the vets ain't takin' friendly to it."

"Dick, what do you want me to do? There's five guys yellin' for every spot! New guys comin' in here every day! Hell, new draft choices alone, there's twenty-three guys! We got Marlin McKeever, linebacker from USC, we got Willie Hector, a guard from University of the Pacific."

"Yeah, I know him."

"We got Robert Lee Smith, a back from UCLA; Joe Scibelli, tackle from Notre Dame; Charlie Cowan, guard from New Mexico; Ernie Wright, tackle from Ohio State—"

"I know, I know . . . a lot of guys."

Deacon shook his head, "No, Dick. Not just guys—big college boys, with lots of experience an' lots of coaching under their pads!"

"Yeah, but for every one of them, there's a Zoot Simms, who's only claim to fame is that baggy suit he wears. You think he's gonna make the team? Or how about Yama Bahama, that big black from Mississippi?"

Deacon didn't say anything for a while. Finally he rubbed his face with a grubby t-shirt and said in a quieter voice, "Look, Dick, I got real problems here. . ." He hesitated before going on. "You know Vic Linskoff?"

"Yeah. Offensive line coach. You ain't kissed his ass right?"

"No, nothing like that. Two nights ago, he handed me his playbook. It was so big and fat I figured he was showing me a photo album of his kids!"

Dick waved it off, "No sweat. Standard playbook for the pros. You ought to be able to break it down into types of plays."

"Yeah, in a few weeks! Dick, any school I went to, we could write our entire playbook on the back of an A&W Root Beer menu! My schools didn't have that many plays in our entire history!"

"That's too bad."

"That ain't the half of it. So I get the offensive book, an' then las' night defensive line coach Don Paul handed me his book, and now I got another 1,500 plays to memorize!"

"So, what are you telling me, you can't get it?"

"No, Bass, I'm gonna learn those playbooks." Deacon's voice was flat and angry, "But right now, I don't know them. That means wherever I go and whatever I do, it's wrong! So what I do every play, my plan is, I always hit somebody! I hit 'em hard. I knock 'em down. The coaches like that. They a sadistic bunch of fellas. You can tell by the grin on their faces. They like that a lot."

Dick stood and yawned. "Well, as I already may have mentioned to you, the veterans do not."

"They gonna have to fend for themselves, Dick—this here is war, an' you can tell any man who chooses to replace me on that squad that he is my sworn enemy. I'll rip out his heart and drink the blood."

"You always this light-spirited?" Dick clapped his new roommate on the back and got to his feet. He walked away without waiting for an answer. As far as he was concerned, the conversation was ended. He didn't think he should worry about it. After all, he'd done his best to worn the poor dumb rookie. He wandered over toward the cafeteria, whistling a sad, off-key version of the Johnny Mercer hit "I Get A Kick Out of You." He knew he didn't have any rhythm, but it didn't bother him. Maybe Dick Bass couldn't carry a tune, but that was okay. Dick Bass could carry the old pigskin to daylight, and that was what really mattered. When he looked in the mirror and asked who was the fairest of them all, it never said anything but Dick Bass.

Mortgage on His Soul

The Rams training camp quickly segregated itself into vets and rookies, but there were other categories, groups and subgroups. There was, as always, the automatic black-white line. The draft picks tended to hang out together, with the top five or so sticking to each other like glue. The other rookies were divided into those who had been invited but not drafted, and those on the bottom of the pecking order who showed up by themselves, sorry hopefuls like Flu Ella, a black who took a cab from San Luis Obisbo for a tryout. Flu had no shoes of his own, so he borrowed a pair of star Ollie Matson's high-tops. Everybody warned Ollie, but he was a soft touch from the word go, always trying to help a brother make the big leap into the NFL. Flu tried on that pair of high-tops, but they felt uncomfortable, so the moment Ollie left the locker room he cut the tops off and taped over the cut edges. Flu was gone in a week, and Ollie was left with those ruined shoes.

In that respect it was like a circus, with new people showing up every day to try out for the same few positions. The competition just motivated Deacon to hustle more, to stay in the coaches' faces. Dick Bass hadn't said anything more about him backing off, but he noticed an attitude from some of the vets. Ollie, of course, was Ollie, the most big-hearted man on the team and unwilling to give any man static. Lamar Lundy was as friendly as ever, full of tips on the field, but even he seemed cool and distant anywhere else. The rest of them, Deacon had decided, could bear careful watching. There had been a time or two when he was gang-tackled, buried in the bottom of the pile on what had started out as an ordinary sweep, and he'd been up-ended by a few cheap shots to the knees. After one of those, Lamar had taken him aside and advised he wear shorter cleats, to reduce the possibility of his shoe sticking in the turf on a hit. "Keep those knees churnin'," Lamar advised. "Once you plant, your knees are vulnerable."

On his own, Deacon learned when he went down to curl into a ball. That way his hands and feet wouldn't be accidentally stepped on. He had more bruises on his back, but he figured bruises would always heal.

A favorite lunch-time conversation for Marlin McKeever and some of the other draft picks centered around salary. These talks were like a poker game, with a lot of bluff and very little substance. Deacon could see they'd been spooked by the recruiters. Since he doubted anybody was talking real numbers, he clammed up and walked away when the money talk started, just like he'd promised when he signed. It was toughest to do when he was halfway through his meal. He wasn't going to leave steak and potatoes for any man.

"Jones, Jones, Jones."

He looked up and saw it was McKeever, standing there with his empty tray.

"What, Marlin?"

"Some of us boys," Marlin nodded back to where his draft-pick buddies were still finishing up their pie and ice cream, "were wondering what they offer a guy by the time it gets to fifteen or sixteen."

"I was fourteen," Deacon said, "an' no hard feelings but it ain't none of your business."

"Oh, come on, Deacon. Nobody else is within earshot. You tell me your offer, I'll tell you mine. Why not?"

Deacon smiled, "Well, for one thing, I wouldn't want to embarrass you. When I signed, Eddie Kotal tol' me I was gettin' as much as anybody else."

"Eddie told you that?" Marlin set down his tray and straddled a chair, chuckling like that was the biggest joke he'd ever heard, "Eddie tells that to everybody. That's S.O.P. for him."

"S.O.P.?"

"Standard Operating Procedure. That's how they get you to sign. Fact is, I'll tell you something I haven't told anybody." He raised his right hand, "Swear to God, I'm getting twelve-five. Twelve thousand five hundred. There, I told you."

Deacon shook his head, "I'd still rather not say."

"Look, it don't mean nothing anyway. None of us are going to get paid anything unless we make the team."

Deacon's brows knit together. "I don't want to talk about it." He slammed his fork on his plate, jerked to his feet, and walked away.

Marlin's voice followed after him, "Were you at least smart enough to get round-trip airfare back to wherever it was you came from?"

By the time Deacon reached the door, he was practically running. No pay unless he made the team? He felt like he'd been struck by a bolt of lightning. Eddie Kotal hadn't said anything about that. He jogged across the campus toward his dorm, oblivious to the fact that he had an offensive line meeting in twenty minutes.

If what Marlin had said was true, he was in a pack of trouble. Back in Eatonville, Deacon had been an instant local hero. Nobody'd ever questioned that contract. He'd waved it in Hank Steele's and there was cheering and free beers all around. But that wasn't his biggest problem. He'd also taken it to Orlando and waved it in front of a white banker, who had loaned him the money to buy Mattie and Ishmeal a new house of their own. Deacon figured it was payback time now that he could do something for them.

That white banker hadn't noticed any fine print saying he wouldn't get the money, and he should have known, if anybody—hell, he was a banker and a rich white man, to boot. Deacon remembered how impressed the man had been. In fact, he'd gone right from the first page, where it said "Los Angeles Rams" and "David Jones", to the last page, where it said "$7,500." They'd signed off on that loan and celebrated with two small glasses of bourbon from a bottle in the cherry-wood cabinet behind the banker's wide oak desk.

By the time Deacon reached his dorm, he was sprinting. He raced down the hall and threw open his door. Bass, as usual, was out somewhere, probably picnicking with some summer-course chicks under an orange tree in the groves surrounding the university. Deacon pulled his suitcase from under the bottom bunk and popped it open, throwing shirts and socks as he burrowed for that contract. He tried to remain calm, taking the time to lie on his back on his bunk and smoothing the pages open, reading every line for the first time, slowly forming the legal phrases with his lips, even though his hands shook and his heart was thumping in his chest. There it was, on the second-last page: "This agreement is contingent upon the player remaining a member of the team through the first game of the season."

Deacon's heart sank like a stone. So it was true! And the rest was probably true as well—Marlin and twelve other draft choices were getting paid more than he was. He didn't feel so twisted up about that part, but he had trusted Eddie Kotal, and Eddie had not been straight with him. They had shaken hands and talked family. Deacon folded the contract and slapped it against his hand. What to do, what to do?

After a few minutes he felt calmer. Accept. You had to accept and go on. He climbed off the bed and stretched his sore muscles. He carefully slid the contract back where it had been, replaced his clothes and slid his suitcase back under his bed. It was a bitter lesson, but life was full of bitter lessons. Why should he be surprised? He scooped up his notebooks and hurried back down the hall to his meeting. Coach Lindskog could be pissy when a player was late. The little print in his contract was no big deal, he told himself, it just made the stakes a little higher.

Con Men

Trainer George Menifee folded his lanky frame on the dented golf cart and leaned back to keep his eyes out of the fierce sunlight. George, affectionately called "Mother" by the players because of his ongoing concern for their health, had spotted an opportunity that had nothing to do with his usual bandages, pills, rubdowns, or ice bags. The afternoon practice session was over, and he was watching Deacon Jones running the forty-yard wind sprints. Head Coach Waterfield had dictated that the team run a dozen forties after every practice, the last six for time.

Deacon, as usual, had refused to run his sprints with the linemen, and was running with the backs. Every lap he finished toward the front of the middle of the pack. What particularly interested Mother was that he ran the last lap as fast as the first, with no particular strain. Mother tapped a pencil against his teeth and reviewed the times he'd jotted on the clipboard. What if, he thought to himself, what if, as he suspected, this rookie Deacon Jones was actually dogging it? That brought up another batch of interesting possibilities. In the first place, why would he hang back? He was brash and outspoken. Why would he care about hurting the feelings of the running backs? On the other hand, the rumor was going around that the kid from the Florida swamps handled himself well in the late-night poker games that managed to spring up around the dorms.

The last of the forties chalked up, most of the team headed for the showers. Mother knew Deacon would hang around for kicking practice. He waited another few seconds and then called to his assistant, "Hey Joe. Run over and get me Willie Hector." Willie was a fifth-round draft choice from Pacific College. He was a speedster, a little light at 220 pounds, but because he was black and they didn't know where else to put him, they were trying him out at tackle. Dick Bass had also gone to Pacific, and he and Willie hung out. Mother knew that Dick, who prided himself on his speed, wouldn't race Willie one-on-one, and Willie had joked to him about it in public. Mother found that very interesting.

Willie came trotting over, "What's up, Mother?"

"Willie! There's talk you're the fastest lineman on the squad."

Willie frowned and then grinned at the trainer. "Mother, I am not the fastest lineman, I'm the fastest man in the Rams camp." He pulled off his helmet and started to saunter away.

"Willie, I know you're fast, but I think you're kidding yourself."

Willie turned around. "Say what, Mother? You gonna take me on?"

"Nooo . . . I was thinkin' more of young Deacon over there."

"Swamp boy? You want me to run against a big, hulking farm boy?"

Mother grinned, "I don't think you can beat him."

Willie made a deprecating sound, looking at Menifee's assistant. "Hey Joe—you think I can take Swamp Boy?"

"I don't know, Willie . . ."

"What is this, a conspiracy? Look, fellows, there's no upside here for me. I win, I get nothing. I lose, I been beat by Swamp Boy."

"He ever hear you call him that?"

Willie gave them a sly grin, " 'Course not. That boy got a temper like an evil wind."

Mother yawned like he didn't care one way or the other. "Tell you what, Mister Hector—I'll bet you fifty dollars you can't take him."

Willie eyed him more closely. "You serious?"

"Forty yards. Fifty dollars." Mother dug in his pocket. "I've got it right here."

"Don't go away—you stand right there on that spot, Mother. I think I be right back to take that off of you!" Willie waved a hand and sprinted for the locker room.

Mother waited until he was out of range and then walked over to where Deacon was shagging balls for the regular punters. "Hey, Jones—how much you weigh?"

Deacon caught a punt and heaved it back toward the fifty-yard line.

Without taking his eye off the punters, who were lining up the next kick, he said, "Right now? Maybe 240. Tomorrow morning, 245."

Mother nodded like he was satisfied. "Getting enough water."

Deacon drifted to the left a little and got under the next punt. He spoke without looking over at Menifee. "Seen you over there with Willie Hector. What kind of trouble you tryin' to stir up, Mother?"

"You're sharper than you look, Deacon."

"Sharp enough. I seen you settin' up a race or two yesterday. What I want to know—what's in it for me?"

Mother saw no reason to hold back. "He'll do it for fifty. I'll bankroll you. You win, we split. Either way, you can't lose . . . You think you can take him?"

Deacon looked him squarely in the eyes. "Twenty-five dollars is a lot of money to me right now. I think I could beat the devil to daylight for twenty-five dollars."

Mother nodded, "Okay, then. Wander over when Hector comes back.

Willie trotted back with a fistful of money, all singles and fives. Mother counted out fifty dollars of his own and put it in the same pile on top of the golf cart, and put an empty Budweiser bottle on it so it wouldn't blow away in the evening Santa Anas, which were starting to kick up.

Deacon snagged his last ball and wandered over to where they were standing. Time for Deacon-the-actor to pull the old humble-pie routine. He scuffed the ground and looked appropriately hang-dog, like he didn't have anything to say, or maybe was too tired for idle chitchat. No use letting Willie think he was ready. He noticed that Willie had taken off his pads and changed to lighter running shoes, but he didn't say anything about that, either.

"Okay," Mother said, "Joe down there is standing on the forty. You both ready?"

Willie got down in a sprinter's stance, but Deacon just stood there, arms hanging at his sides. He didn't even take his helmet off. "Ready, set—go!"

Out of the gate, Willie thought he had at least three steps, but when he looked over, Deacon was even with him, matching him stride for stride. It's the damn shoes! Willie thought to himself, I can't get a bite on this turf! They were neck-and-neck all the way, but Deacon lunged forward with the last step and clearly won by a half a yard.

"Damn it!" Willie said as they walked back, "That wasn't really a fair shot—I should have worn my spikes like you got on!"

The man Willie Hector had called Swamp Boy shrugged, but he didn't say anything. Deacon figured if Willie believed what he said, he'd probably want to race in a day or two so he could get his fifty dollars back. Willie seemed to have a little money saved up. If they handled it just right, maybe he'd even go for a hundred.

Deacon smiled to himself. Mother Menifee was a good man to know. There were lots of running backs and receivers hanging around who would be delighted to test their speed against a big, clunky lineman. Lord, with any luck, on a good afternoon they might split a couple of hundred between them!

Deacon and George cleaned up over the next three or four years, until nobody would run against him for money. Even after that, spring training always found a hot-shot rookie or two eager to be parted from their money. Deacon was the fastest man in the Rams organization for seven years, from the time he entered training camp through the 1967 season. Avoiding major leg and knee injuries throughout his career, he was still one of the quickest defensive linemen off the ball when he retired from the NFL in 1974.

Meeting People and Making Friends

As Deacon was doing his warmups on the edge of the dusty practice field, he was briefly joined by Lamar Lundy. This was a surprise; the quiet Lamar generally kept to himself, and the vets rarely talked to the rookies.

"Deacon," he started, "you know, it be the tradition of the Rams that the rookie supposed to fetch for the established player from time to time."

Deacon was stretching out his legs, and when Lamar's shadow fell across him, he lay back on the grass, gazing at the deep blue of the late afternoon sky, "What, Lamar, you forget your jock strap?"

Lamar looked stung, but he managed to bite back whatever he was going to say. "Look, rookie, I didn't come over here to start no quarrel."

"Okay. Sorry. What do you want?"

"It just that I have observed you are buildin' a stack of vets who don't take kindly to your personality. I think you should—"

Deacon interrupted him, "They gonna have to learn to live with that."

"Deacon, it be the tradition of the Rams—"

"Lamar, don't you start in on me wit' that tradition crap! My family may have hid in the brush an' the weeds of the South to survive, but we ain't did no fetch for no man since the war—the Civil War, that is."

Alvin Hall, who had been half-listening to the conversation from a short distance away, gave up his ham-string stretches and wandered over. "Cousin Deacon here causin' trouble again?"

"Obvious, you wasn't there." Lamar didn't see anything amusing. "We had us a couple kegs in the cafeteria last Saturday night. Some of the crackers was comin' around like you know they always do, demandin' the rooks chug entire pitchers of beer. Well, they brought their big pitcher over to wise-crack Deacon here an' he looks up from his playbook an' tells 'em they can pour it up their butts an' seal it with a cork!"

Alvin's laughter was spontaneous. "Deak, you are a crazy man!"

"Hey, a man can't study the plays when he's all woozy on beer."

"Then you shouldn't a been to the party."

"I got as much right as the next man to be there. I had me a glass or two of that free beer, too. But I done it at my own pace."

Lamar shook his head, looking around to make sure he wasn't becoming the center of attention. "You got to be a little careful, Deacon. If those people don't like you, they can give you a hundred thousand problems a minute. They could set you up and demolish you physically. I been here; I know. Ever since time began, it always been that the rookies wait until the vets have cleared the locker room. The rookie carry the vet's bags, always. The rookie sing his old college song, when they ask. The rookie go fetch another piece of pie wit' vanilla ice cream on top, when they need it."

"That is true," Alvin agreed, "or they just make you look bad in front of the white man."

Deacon's frown deepened, and his thick brows knit until they made a single dark line across his forehead. "I'm sorry, brothers, but I never caught on how to smooth those sort of things over. I'm a maverick, I'm different. I try not to offend people, but that's about as far as I go. If it's red, I say it's red."

"Red-necks is what you got to worry about," Lamar said.

"I tell you, fellas," Deacon said, "I ain't ready to repent. Those folks already don't like me. I got the word from my roommate. So I don't see where kissin' up is gonna' do me one bit of good."

"You best tone it down some," Lamar warned. "At least 'til you make the final cut."

"You know, Lamar, I ain't never played against a white man before in my life. But I am truly findin' it interesting. I love those one-on-ones. None of this I'm white and you're black in a man-to-man drill. You hit 'em hard, they go down just like anybody else. I love that. . . an' it is my continued vow to kick butt every day, every play, in every way."

"I think this gentlemen here maybe got a point," Alvin said. "Maybe you should tone it down a little bit."

Deacon smiled, but there wasn't much warmth in it. "Good friends, you know God's truth is that I was born with a mouth. I was not an easy child to raise. Now how do you expect a person such as I— born with the bark on, so to speak—to act around those shapeless jack-asses?"

"Well, don' say I didn't try," Lamar sighed. "See you around." He gave them a wave and began to trot around the edge of the field. He ran for thirty yards or so, then picked up his pace until he was fairly flying.

Alvin watched him speed around the field, "That Lundy got his-self some wheels."

Deacon smiled his bittersweet smile, "Yeah, he does. But, you know, Good Hosen, that boy's afraid to take me on for fifty bucks . . . An' you know what that tell you." Alvin, who had already been burned in the lil' ol' money race with Deacon, did know.

Going After Brews

It was ten at night, still an hour or two until curfew, and as Deacon walked back to his room, knots of players were standing around in the halls, jawing about the day. It had been a pretty good day. Deacon was keeping his resolution, every time off the ball, he hit somebody. He went full-out, 110 percent on every play. He'd made his usual hatful of mistakes, but at least he did it kicking somebody's ass. He carried his two playbooks with him everywhere he went. The day before, he'd sprained his ankle, but he seemed okay this morning. And, amazing-ly, Don Paul had talked about him to the newspapers! Someone showed him the clipping from the *L.A. Times,* "Jones has the reactions of a Night Train Lane, and he sometimes beats Willie Hector in the sprints. Willie Hector was supposed to be the fastest man on the squad, but he has lost several forty-yard wind sprints to Jones." As he made his way up the steps to the third floor, a group of eight or nine vets stepped out of the door which led to the second floor hallway and stopped him, "Hey, rookie—your turn to get the beers."

Deacon shook his head. "Hey, man, I'm tired." Every night they picked one rookie to sneak out after curfew for two cases of beers.

"Naw, naw, naw, pal," their big-name linebacker said. "It's your turn." This was trouble. The blacks whispered this white boy was the biggest redneck on the Rams.

Deacon looked them over for a moment, but he knew he didn't really have a choice; they were mostly white, but there were a few blacks sprinkled in. He was the rookie, and he had to give some token behavior, admit his rookie status, or they would never accept him. "Okay," he said, passing his thick playbooks across to Dick Bass. "How do I do it?"

"It's easy, Deak," Dick grinned. Deacon had learned not to trust that smile, but he didn't know anybody else well enough to look to them for advice. He and Dick Bass couldn't have been further from the opposite sides of the tracks. Dick, who described himself as a "gentle-man of color," was well-educated, polished and sophisticated. He came from northern California, where he'd been a famous and sought-after high school and college star. He made sure Deacon knew he'd turned down a forty-thousand-dollar contract to play baseball for the Milwau-kee Brewers. He said he'd turned down all that money to get a college education. The story went on. In 1958, as a college junior at the University of Pacific, Dick was the number-one NFL draft choice. So, while the new Deacon was clawing his way on board, Dick had already made the team. He was in the second year of a no-cut, no-trade con-tract. If the Rams weren't willing to give him a new contract, he was confident some other team would, and so he could afford to coast along and party it up.

The linebacker pushed a handful of singles into Davey's hand and gave him an evil smile. "Make it Schlitz, rookie. An' try to get back here before mornin'."

Dick put an arm around Deacon's broad shoulders and led him back to the steps. "A piece of cake, roomie. You got an hour 'til lock-out. You got to sneak downstairs past the man, make your way out the side door an' across the lawn. Be sure to prop open that side door. Take the college road across the main road an' the railroad tracks, about a half mile, an' you'll come to a little grocery store. Two cases of Schlitz, Deak."

The second floor was easy, because that's where the vets had their rooms. But as Deacon quietly made his way along the first floor, he was passing the coaches' rooms. He could hear film projectors, and heavy voices, and some of the rooms had open doors. Somehow he managed to tip-toe past all the doors without being discovered. He found a wooden wedge under the stairwell, tightly wedged the door open and slipped out into the night.

The California summer nights are chilly in Redlands, which in the 1960s was a campus and a small town surrounded by a huge irrigated citrus orchard and endless miles of desert.

Bad for him, the campus was lit by a full moon that night. Deacon scurried from oak tree to oak tree, hoping he was somewhat hidden by shadows. He made his way offcampus, ducking off the road whenever a car approached.

The manager of the liquor store saw him coming. "How many cases you want?" he asked.

"Two Schlitz. How'd you know?" Deacon asked.

"It's the same thing every night."

They were two dollars short, so Deacon added in his own money. He walked back along the road with a case under each arm. He had made his way across campus and was approaching the dormitory when his heart sank. Somebody had turned the outside lights on! When he'd left, the campus was bathed in moonlight, but there were plenty of thick oaks and bushes, and he had been able to slip through the shadows. Now spotlights glared from the corners of his dorm. It was bright as day.

Deacon squinted into the harsh light, studying the lawn in front of him. It had a few hilly rolls, and maybe if he could crawl to a corner of the building through one of the shallow gullies, he might be able to make the side door without being detected. He got down on all fours, and did the Marine crawl on his belly, pushing one case in front of him and dragging the other behind. It was hard work, and the beers slowed him down. Fifty yards took nearly a half hour, but he finally made the side of the building without being detected. He paused for a moment to catch his wind. He realized he had to make his way through the bushes underneath the open coaches' windows. After fifteen more minutes of near-panic, he passed them all and rounded the corner to the side door—only to find it locked!

Certain that somebody wanted him caught, he stopped to figure out what he had to do next. The side door he had wedged open was locked; there was no other choice, he had to go past the windows again. All he needed was to get caught. He could get thrown out of camp for breaking curfew. All for hitting hard and giving no ground. Deacon was shaking with fury. He forced himself to stop again. The way he felt, he was sure to mess up. He had to collect himself. It was five minutes before he was breathing easily again. Then, sweaty and grimy, he made his way back under the windows. He could hear defensive coach Don Paul arguing with Old Stonyface about something. He didn't wait to find out what it was about. The main door was still open, and he once again quietly made his way past the open doors where the coaches were busily deciding all their futures. Luck was with him, and he made his way again undiscovered. Once he got to the end stairwell, he took the steps three at a time, and a contingency of vets met him on the second floor.

"All right, Deacon!" they cheered. "You done good, rookie!"

One second they were all standing there, clapping him on the back, and the next thing he knew, they had disappeared into somebody's room with the booty and slammed the door behind them. Deacon was standing alone in the hallway, hot and dirty and thinking how great a beer would taste about then. But the two cases of beer were gone. That's the way it was. Rookies weren't invited to drink with the vets. Rookies fetched the beers.

Ram Klan

At lunch, Jon Arnett had been telling some old "Rastus" jokes, the punch-lines centering around the huge loins and ignorance of the blacks involved. That evening, Dick Bass relayed the ones he could remember to his roommate. Deacon, who was lying on his bunk trying to memorize a series of sweep formations, couldn't find anything funny in any of the jokes, and they had argued.

"Those aren't jokes, they are racial slurs," Deacon complained, marking his place in the playbook with his finger while he talked.

"Deak, you're prickly like a cactus. You take offense at everything."

"Maybe that's so, Dick. But you don't get serious about anything. White man offends you, an' you call it a joke an' brush it off by makin' another joke. You know the difference between right and wrong, but then you go and make fun of your own people."

That in turn got Bass a little irritated. He found it annoying the way this guy from the swamps of Florida could get him going. "Deacon, those jokes are no different from dago jokes or pollack jokes or hebe jokes. You got to lighten up, bro."

Deacon held out the back of his hand, pointing to his skin, "This ain't never going to lighten up. The difference is, I'm proud of who I am!"

"You sayin' I'm not?"

"Dick Bass, you be one of the whitest black men I ever met. You talk like 'em, you walk like 'em, an' half the time you dress like an English country gentleman."

"That's manners and taste in clothes, which I have acquired through my associations with a wide variety of people."

Deacon shook his head. "I ain't buyin' it, bro. You'd join 'em in a second if they'd let you. When they invent the miracle bleach, you gonna be the first poor nigger takin' the bath."

Those were fighting words, but Dick wasn't a fighter. He lived by his fast feet and his fast wits. He wasn't about to take on a man who was taller by a foot and carried fifty pounds more muscle. "You dumb Southern hick, you don't know what you're talkin' about! You got to get yourself a sense of humor!" Before Deacon could say anything to that, Dick huffed off, slamming the door behind him.

Deacon shrugged, his attention drifting back to his playbook. Nobody was going to change Dick Bass, and he didn't know why he'd wasted his breath.

The next day the Deacon was even more zealous than usual in teaching the gospel of the hard hit to his fellow teammates. Training camp was more than half over, and now empty lockers were becoming more and more obvious as the first cuts were made. He recognized he had to separate love of sports as fun from his current task, which was to get a job, make the team. All day long he talked to himself in his mind, *It's a business now, Davey, you've got to be ready, you've got to hit on every play.*

At noon, he and Alvin Hall walked together to the locker room. Alvin looked over at him as they cut across one end of the dusty gridiron. "Deak—what you gonna do if they cut you?"

"They ain't gonna cut me, Good Hosen." Deacon called him by the nickname he'd picked up in training camp.

"What if they do?"

A light smile played over Deacon's sweat-streaked face, "Hosen, I came here to camp with my own uniform. I don't care if they cut me, I'll still play. They are gonna have to kill me an' bury my still an' silent body—an' on dark an' stormy nights, you'll hear a scratch-scratch-scratch sound."

"A scratch sound?"

"Yeah. That would be my fingers clawin' from the inside of the box. All I got to say, they better bury me deep." Deacon winked at Alvin, and went to his own locker.

After dinner that evening, when Deacon returned to the dormitory, the hallway on the second floor was oddly deserted. He was one of the few rookies on the second floor, because he roomed with Bass. Usually the veterans were spilling out in the halls, talking over the day. Doors were open, radios blaring pop tunes, and banter was running from room to room. Tonight was different. The doors were all closed, and everything was quiet.

That made Deacon uneasy. Maybe he was missing an important meeting. He ran the day's schedule through his mind. Nothing he could think of. Well, he planned on studying the ever-present playbooks anyway, so he didn't really mind. He actually liked it. He wouldn't have to put up with joke-a-minute Bass.

He'd just settled down on his bed when there was a terrific banging on the door. He jumped a mile.

A deep, muffled voice from the other side of the door roared, "Jones! Open up! We know you're in there!"

There was no way he was going to open that door. Pranksters! he thought. Probably want me for the beer run. But then there was a key in the door. Somebody had a key, it had to be Bass was in on it, whatever the gag was this time.

The door was flung wide open, and in marched half the team, covered in white bed sheets like the Klan! They had holes cut in the sheets for their eyes, and they crowded into the room to surround him.

It was one of those jokes that hadn't really been thought through. The vets thought they would come storming in, they'd whoop it up a little, pretending to be Klanners, and they'd all have a good laugh. It didn't turn out the way they'd thought.

Deacon just stood there, with beads of sweat forming all over his face. He looked thunderstruck, and he only said two words, in a sort-of soft voice that trailed away. "Oh, Lord. . . " was all he said.

The fun slowly went out of the room, like a sagging hot air balloon. One look at their fellow-player and it was clear that this was inappropriate. Deacon looked like he was stunned, or worse, had seen a ghost. He didn't move a muscle; he didn't say a word.

Deacon's first thought was, *Don't tear anybody's head off, it's just your teammates.* But crowding that notion was another terrifying thought: *Wait a minute, you don't know if there are Klanners actually on your team.* His mind was a jumble. *They're ignorant as shoes. They don't know how cruel this is. How could they really know what the Klan means to a black from the Deep South?*

Deacon couldn't go along with the joke, not even for a minute. He stood his ground, and by his silence and his defiant attitude said, No, you aren't going to put me in this situation!

The first rounds of hoots and jeers died away. The roomful of men milled around for a bit in their white sheets, trying to whip up their former enthusiasm, but Deacon just stood there, tall and furious, fists clenched, eyes glaring, until they finally began to trickle away. Whatever else might come to pass, Deacon knew instantly he was finished rooming with Bass.

Nobody took their hoods off, ironically like real Klanners, not wanting to be identified as part of what had taken place. They just shuffled out of the room, leaving Deacon alone. It was ten minutes before he stopped shaking, and then he threw on an old jacket, and walked quickly off the campus, heading down a deserted two-lane blacktop away from town.

Hours later, Deacon found himself running through the orange groves. He stopped, bone-tired, and sat with his back to one of the trees. It was foolish running at night over rough ground. He could easily snap an ankle. He put his head back against the tree and tried to think. No matter what any of them really believe, this is not a joke. They are trying to attack my mind, he told himself. At first he railed at pro football, which would allow such a thing to happen. But then he changed his mind. The NFL wasn't to blame; the National Football League was just a reflection of the times, cold-blooded, angry, antagonistic times sweeping across America. Everywhere young black men like him turned, they heard in one way or another, Hey, nigger, you can't do that. Hey, nigger, you're less than a man. Deacon had been told that all his life, and he'd resented it all his life. Now a crack of opportunity had opened for black players, and the whites were going to hold him out with every weapon at their disposal. They're testing your will to believe in yourself, Ishmeal's voice whispered in his ear, but hang on, son, 'cause me an' your mother didn't raise no quitters.

At that moment the hardening process set in. He'd just been given another headslap, the kind he'd been getting all his life. He stood, one black man alone in the middle of acres of orange trees and raised his fist to the star-filled sky. "Screw you all!" he shouted out loud, "Every last one of you bedsheet-cowards! You won't stop me! Nobody will stop me!" There was no answer but the cold light from the hard stars above and the chill from the night wind.

Deacon started to walk the long miles back to the university, but once more the voice whispered in his mind, You're gonna be angry when you get back there, Davey boy. The secret now is to channel that anger.

By the time Deacon returned to the dormitory, it was past curfew. He walked in the front door, past a group of veterans and coaches talking in the lobby. Nobody said anything about his lateness, and he didn't say anything either. He was thinking how good it was going to be to get a good night's rest, and then suit up in the morning and hit somebody.

The days passed in a mindless whirl of scrimmages. Deacon moved his game up to the next level of intensity. The more chances he had to inflict pain, the better he liked it. The scrimmages were constant, one long haze of mean pounding and pain and hitting, and when he was tired of hitting, he went out and hit some more.

Talking about those early days, when he first met Deacon, Dick Bass said, "He'd play offense without a break, and then he'd switch over and play defense. I had my contract, and training camp was like a country club for me. I'd look over and see Deacon and say to myself, 'Where'd this guy come from with all this energy?'"

Today Bass readily admits he was one of the pranksters, "Sure, I was one of the guys under the white sheets. But don't think we were all that insensitive. It wasn't actually premeditated. I was a magnet for that kind of stuff, for jokes and fun." But the grin fades and Bass grows reflective, thinking back to the moment they came storming into Deacon's room wearing their white sheets with the holes cut out for their eyes to see through. "It certainly didn't turn out the way we thought. If I'd have known how he was going to react in that moment, I'd have never done it. But done is done, and you can't ever take it back."

Dodging the Turk

Tommy the Terrible Turk was a gawky kid, barely a teenager. He had straw-colored hair and blue eyes. Though most of them could have snapped him with two fingers, the players feared him as much as any man alive. Tommy was the son of one of the assistant coaches, and when he came with his guileless grin and poked a finger at you it was the Finger of Death. He'd raise his deadly hand and say something innocent like, "Hey, the coach wants to see you—and, oh yeah, bring your playbook." Whoever it was, once Tommy had fingered him, there would be an empty locker and a deserted bunk, and the doomed player was never seen again. Every NFL team has a Turk or two in training camp, and nobody knows how they got their name. Every team has the same problems, and the Turk is a simple answer to a difficult situation. With a rotating mob of over a hundred contesting players in camp at any one time, each day some of them have to be let go, or the food bills alone would get out of hand, to say nothing of the meetings and the drills. By the first game of the regular season, the squad had to be at 34, not 134. Even the lowest assistant coaches didn't have the time to chase down players who hadn't made the cut, elusive players who didn't want to be found. That's where Tommy came in.

It was the week before the first exhibition game, and the Rams had started to cut in earnest. Deacon and Good Hosen were trying to forget about that. They were having breakfast with some other black rookies while Brutus, a huge, good-natured black, regaled them with stories of the hard times he'd endured in the semi-pro league. Brutus suddenly stopped in midsentence, took his plate full of eggs and dumped it on Deacon's.

"Hey, man, I got enough already!" Davey protested. But Brutus had slipped down on all fours behind their chairs and was scrambling for the back door, which led to the kitchen.

Five seconds later, Tommy pushed his way through the front door and sauntered into the room. If he'd come right over to their table, he could have nailed Brutus's hands and feet to the floor, but Tommy had a puppy-dog crush on a serving girl about five years his senior, so he made a small detour through the line to snag a fresh orange and say a few words to promote his innocent, schoolboy lust. By the time Tommy made his way to the tables, Deacon was still staring at the huge mound of scrambled eggs on his tray, but Brutus was long gone.

The kid was throwing his orange from hand to hand like it was part of a juggling act. "Anybody seen the Brute?"

"Brutus? Uh-uh, no . . ."

"He *was* here but he gone."

Tommy scratched his head. "Dad's gonna be pissed."

Ollie Matson came over, carrying a huge tray of food in one hand, and caught the end of the conversation. "Shouldn't use a word like 'pissed,' Tommy," he warned. "You just a kid yet."

"Yeah, well, my dad uses it all the time."

"Well, den, maybe it's okay." Ollie was the one veteran who didn't mind sitting with the rookies. The Rams had traded eleven players to get him, and he figured he'd sit wherever he wanted.

Tommy wandered away, looking around the room, as though a six-foot-five-inch fellow black as the ace of spades could be hiding behind a glass door or inside a flower pot. Of course, with Brutus, he just might be. Whether it was luck or cleverness, the huge black man had somehow managed to be out or invisible whenever the Turk came calling, and he'd been hanging on by his fingertips for weeks.

Deacon moved over to make room for Ollie. "Brutus just avoided the jaws of death one more time."

Good Hosen nodded. "Last week I seen him hide in the shower room, wrapped in plastic curtains. Nothin' showin' but his huge ebony size fourteen feet."

"Ain't nothin'," Ollie said. "I seen players hop into lockers an' sleep under their beds an' even in the trunks of their cars, just to dodge the Turk. Makes no difference; he gets 'em all in the end."

"You can run, but you cannot hide."

Ollie looked over at Deacon's plate, "You gonna eat all those eggs?"

"No, I'm not going to eat all these eggs!"

Ollie took the plate and added it to his own. "Shouldn't take more than you can eat. Young country boy like you ought to know that."

Two nights before their first exhibition game, Deacon was standing in front of the mirror in the john, reading his playbook after lights out when he heard snoring coming from one of the stalls.

"Hey, Brutus—that you? You okay to come out now."

"Whut time is it?"

"Close to midnight, bro."

Brutus came shuffling out, ran the cold water and sloshed a few handfuls on his face. "Just a few more days," he said, shaking his huge head like a big black mastiff.

"Why you doin' this, Brutus? You know they gonna catch you."

He gave Davey a gentle smile. He had a scar running from the corner of his lip to his ear, and his ear on the other side was twisted and torn. "You know, I could have played in the pros, Mister Deacon Jones.

No, honest, I could have. I played eight years for Hollywood. Eight years of semi-pro—white men batterin' at my knees, redneck spit an' pilin' on."

Davey shook his head, "I know about the spit."

Brutus pointed to his ear. "Battle scar. Helmet came off an' a hungry Italian bit me. Hangin' by a flap of skin, an' the trainer sewed it back on in the locker with a big sewing needle we used to fix our uniforms. I swear to Jesus it be true."

Brutus ran a finger across the scar on his face. "Farm boy from Iowa stomped me. No face guard then, just that little bitty leather helmet. Cleat caught in my mouth, ripped me some."

"Maybe it's time to hang 'em up, get out while you can still walk."

"I cain't do that. I tell you what I want. I want to outlast the cut long enough so's just one time in my life I can run through that tunnel at the Coliseum and out into the daylight an' the green playing field. My boy'll be in the stands an' he'll see his daddy is a real football player, an' then I could know my life is—"

They were interrupted by somebody pushing in through the door. It was Tommy The Terrible Turk. He was eating an apple and he had a ratty *Playboy* rolled up under one arm. "Oh," he said, looking embarrassed like he was surprised anybody was up at this hour. "There you are, Brutus. Ahhh—Dad wants to see you."

Brutus looked frantically around, but there was no place to run or hide. No matter the circumstances, that was just the luck of the draw, and he was caught fair and square.

Deacon gave the Turk a stern look. "Tommy, you tellin' us that your father is still awake, right here and now at this hour of the night, waitin' down there in his office for Brutus to stop by?"

"Well, no . . . but he was an hour ago, and he will be, first thing tomorrow." Tommy seemed to collect his wits. He pointed his finger at Brutus. "That's it, first thing tomorrow, you be there." He threw his half-eaten apple at the waste can. It missed, bouncing into the corner. Not bothering to retrieve it, Tommy turned and stumbled his way out of the bathroom.

Brutus looked like he'd been stabbed in the heart.

"Come on, bro. You can dodge him one more day," Deacon said.

"Naaw. That ain't how they play this game. I been caught, Deacon. Tomorrow morning, I gots to go see the man."

"Okay, then. Tell them how you feel. They'll let you stay just for the game."

"I don't think so, Deak. The NFL got less heart than you'll find wit' the meanest hookers in Vegas."

"You gotta give it a try, Brutus. For your boy."

Bright and early the next morning, Brutus went in and pitched his case hard as he could, but in the end his self-forecast proved right. After all the pain and uncertainty, after all the one-on-ones, the endless skull sessions, the late night cramming, the hours of running and hitting under the burning sun, Brutus was cut the day before the first exhibition game. The team was down to sixty players, and Brutus, the black giant who wanted more than anything else in the world to live his dream—not even to play, just to stand one time on the field of battle with the best in football—Brutus was gone.

But Deacon Jones, who had come to Los Angeles to teach the gospel of the quick move and the hard hit, was still very much a member of the squad. He went about inflicting pain and learning his craft, and he didn't go out of his way to avoid the Turk. Instead, he glared at him whenever they met, silently daring him to raise his witching finger.

4

Waterfield's Reign

Owner Dan Reeves brought his Cleveland Rams to the West Coast in 1946, and over the next ten years they became a team to be reckoned with. They won a divisional title in 1949, tied for conference title in 1950 and 1952, won the conference title in 1955, and won the world title in 1951.

Winning is always good, but Los Angeles fans became too used to winning, and the Rams management was not successful at developing the deep and abiding fan loyalty they would need to carry them through a bitter losing streak. So the momentum was lost, and the winning tradition all but forgotten.

By the late 1950s, with season after season of lackluster football, attendance had dropped and the Rams management began to curse the fans of southern California and wonder if they had made a mistake in moving there. And in the interest of pro football, the great lie was spread. Word quietly went out from Rams management to the reporters and sports writers that maybe, just maybe, there was too much to do in Los Angeles, with the nearby beaches and mountains, and all the fine weather. With the Dodgers playing championship baseball. With the competition from Disneyland, Knott's Berry Farm, and the Wax Museum. Just maybe, it was the fans' fault . . . those fickle southern California fans.

When the accusing fingers did point closer to home, the handy scapegoat was the coach; under Reeves, the Rams head coaching position had always been a revolving door. But a few insiders—

older sports writers, team management people who refused to be quoted and the players who had to live through those times—were shaking their heads. Dan Reeves himself had a heavy hand in everything that went on with the Rams, from drafting to trades to actual play-calling on the field. And, as important as anything, his tight fist controlled the team wallet.

After a 2-10 season in 1959, some major show of concern, some drastic action was required. Coach Sid Gillman "resigned," and general manager Pete Rozelle left to become the NFL commis-sioner, but by now the losing had run on long enough that blame had to placed in other quarters. The next logical culprits were the players. As one of his last acts before he left, Rozelle traded away a fourth of the team to acquire one man—the great back Ollie Matson, then a seven-year veteran, from the Chicago Cardinals. In an attempt to return to the golden days of yesteryear, Gillman and Rozelle were replaced by heroic Rams players from the glory days of the early 1950s—quarterback Bob Waterfield, already a legend in southern California, became the coach, and the great receiver Elroy "Crazylegs" Hirsh became the new general manager. It was nearly a clean sweep, with only one possible problem to dim the glowing horizon—Reeves continued to operate as he always had. After all, he owned the Rams; it wasn't the players', the coaches', the reporters', or even the fans' team—it was his team. And he could play the game any way he wanted.

Nervous Time

When the Rams took the field for the first exhibition game of the season, Brutus may not have been there, but Deacon Jones walked out onto the field and raised his fists to the roaring crowd for him. "For you, Brutus," he whispered. "An' for that kid of yours." He hadn't talked to the man since he was cut. The poor fellow had packed his bags in shame and left in the dead of night. So Brutus would never know that the gesture was for him. Maybe others might think it was a useless gesture, but Deacon didn't care. This was his chosen arena, his field of dreams. To Deacon, this level grass field with its clearly defined white chalk marks would always be the place where grudges and debts were paid, where a primitive sort of gladiator justice was dealt and where honor and comradeship counted for everything.

That day, Deacon started at offensive tackle. He was shifted back and forth from offense to defense, moved from tackle to guard to end, and flopped from side to side. He didn't care where they put him, he hit harder than ever, flinging his body into every play with all-out abandon. Now there was little time left to impress the coaches. It was to be a critical few weeks in Deacon's life, and there would be no letting up, not even for a second.

In the quiet of his own room, Deacon had read the fine print in his contract over and over again. It was as crystal clear as a lawyer could make it. He could start in all the exhibition games and still not make the team. Hell, he could star in them and still end up driving somebody's car back to Florida for the gas money. Call that motivation, he said to himself. I will not fail.

In that first exhibition game, the Rams crushed the lowly Washington Redskins, 26-7. The fans and reporters were pleased, but not particularly impressed, for Washington was the doormat of the league. Midweek after that game, the excitement of the Coliseum was just a memory. The team was back at Redlands, running through the seemingly endless drills under the blistering sun.

Deacon eyed the other men on the practice field as he did his wind sprints with Ollie Matson. Dick Bass, who had been giving an interview in the shade of his favorite carob tree, walked over to join them, calling out in his best imitation-English dialect, "What-ho, chaps. How goes the training?"

Ollie gave him a huge grin., "You are one lazy 'chap,' Dick Bass! Some day your wicked, slothful ways gonna catch up with you!" In the days since Deacon moved out of Dick's room he hadn't had much to say to him, but his cool attitude toward the cocky running back seemed to have no effect whatsoever. Nothing offended Bass, certainly not anything a rookie might think about him. He grinned at Deacon. "I hear tell you been challenging some of the slower backs around here to foot races, an' I just wanted to ask, my good man, aren't you sort of like the moose who thought he was a race horse?"

Bass was two or three inches shy of six feet, and weighed around two hundred pounds. He was lightning quick, a nifty open-field runner, and hard to bring down once he got going. But Deacon knew he had an edge; like most of the players he'd raced, Bass couldn't imagine someone his size having any speed. Deacon looked at him for a long moment before answering. "Make no mistake, Bass. I'm the fastest man on the Rams. Faster than you, faster than Ol' Man Ollie here, faster than anybody. Pull out fifty bucks an' I'll take you on right now."

"Let me think on that a minute." Bass picked a few blades of grass and let them drop like he was studying the wind. That was the way he was; he never took anything seriously, he never answered a question directly, and you never could tell what he was going to do next. He put a hand on Ollie's shoulder and tossed his head in the direction of the other players, who were grouped in their various drills around the field, "You notice anything weird lately, Coach?" The blacks all called Ollie "Coach," out of their respect and admiration for the man.

"Yeah, they ain't caught on what a loafer you are," Ollie laughed.

"No, serious, Ol. Look at 'em! Waterfield got to cut down to four —or at the very most, six—persons of color before the regular season. But I gaze around us at the hue and tone of the folks who remain in this training camp, and I am truly amazed."

Deacon gave him a somber stare. "With that no-cut contract in your back pocket, you can afford to be amazed. Folks like me are just plain scared to death."

Ollie kicked at a loose clod of dried grass. "It don't add up, that's for sure. Bass an' me take two spots . . . that leave room for two or at the most four more." Bass shrugged, clearly feeling that, while the situation was interesting, it wasn't his problem, "Ol' Stonyface an' his merry men gonna have to throw out a dozen chocolate cookies in the next couple of weeks, or they gonna make history in the NFL in a way they will live to regret!"

"Why's that?"

"First owners' meeting he goes to, they'll stone him to death. Nobody loves a nigger-lover."

Deacon frowned and turned to set up for his next wind sprint. "That's what's great about you, Dick. You the very heart of compassion."

Bass clapped Davey on the back. "Come on, young Deak—check again. Maybe you counted wrong."

Davey should have known better; he looked in the direction Bass pointed, and by the time he turned around again, Bass was streaking for the distant sideline, too far ahead for him to catch up. At lunch Bass would claim Jones, the upstart rookie, had challenged the Great Dick Bass, and had been sorely beaten. He'd pick a moment when Ollie was out washing his Cadillac or something, and it wouldn't do any good for Deacon to try and contradict him. "Hey, Rook—all's fair in the NFL," Dick would say. "What did you think this was, some sweetheart sport like track n' field?"

Fifty Bucks a Game

In the summer and fall of 1961, the Rams were scheduled to play five exhibition games before the regular season. After the second game, in which they tied the powerful New York Giants 17-17, Deacon and Lamar Lundy happened to be walking out of the locker room at the same time.

Lamar had served his rookie time in 1959, and Davey thought he'd take advantage of the moment to ask him some questions, "Lamar, I was wonderin'. Is it just me, or are we all only getting paid fifty dollars apiece for these games?"

"Everybody get paid the same."

"Lamar, I wanted to be a pro ever since I was a young pup wraslin' gaters in the swamps of Florida. But I didn't know pros just gave it away like this."

Lamar nodded and continued walking, saying nothing. He'd played his college ball at Purdue, but he was born and raised in central Indiana, in the heart of Klan country. If there was an educated Negro anywhere in the world who knew how to maintain his inner pride and yet keep the peace, he felt he was that man.

Deacon walked faster to catch up and kept on talking, "I mean, don't you believe fifty dollars is hard money for all that runnin' an' hittin' an' bein' stomped on?"

Lamar stopped and put his hand on Deacon's chest. Then he stepped back and raised his finger like a scolding preacher. "Look, Jones, I like you," he said. "I ain't got nothin' against you. An' I think you got the potential to be a great ball player. But it don't do no good to go scuffin' against the ones who pay you. Don't do it around me, an' don't ask me to do it."

"I was just askin'—"

"I know what you was 'just askin' '! I don' want to talk about it! I been here two full seasons. Chances are, I'm gonna make this team again. Lord knows, they need my help—an' I don' want my chances messed up 'cause I was rabble-rousin' with a rookie, who chances are, ain't gonna be around in another two weeks!" Lamar started to walk away, then paused for a moment. "Nothin' personal . . . hear?" he said, without turning around. He started walking again without waiting for an answer.

Deacon watched him go without saying anything more. He walked alone to the team bus, slung his gear in the compartment on the side and climbed on board for the trip back to Redlands. The only seat still open was next to Lundy. He managed to hold his peace until they were well out of the city. He pretended to doze, but his thoughts kept itching like dandruff under his skull. Finally he couldn't stand it any longer. He said quietly, "Lamar, fifty dollars a game for a professional football player is downright criminal! Hell, I could make fifty dollars in one good afternoon at Hank Steele's pool hall. I once made fifty dollars in a pick-me-up basketball game."

Lamar sighed. After a long pause, during which he looked around to double-check whether any coaches or any of their stoolies were within hearing range, he whispered, "Everybody know it a disgrace, Deacon Jones, so just shut your mouth about it!"

Deacon found himself whispering back, as if they were two conspirators. "Football ain't like no other sport, Lamar! One unlucky hit an' you busted up for life! And why are we whisperin'?"

"I'm the veteran. I know that, already. An' we are whisperin' to prevent you from gettin' your ass booted out of football."

But Deacon was rolling now, and not to be denied. "The fans don't care that it ain't the real season yet, they're already payin' real money for tickets an' hot dogs an' beers an' programs. The owners are making a fortune on these games, an' we gettin' a miserable, stinkin' lousy fifty bucks!"

Lamar put his fingers to his lips. "Lordy, Deacon, hold it down!" He gave another wide-eyed look around the bus, and then hunched down in his seat to be sure his low whisper wouldn't be overheard. "Get this, Deacon Jones, an' listen up sharp to what I say, 'cause I'm only gonna talk about this one time: What do the owners own? The owners own us! That's why they call them owners! We got no cards to play, Deacon. We got no union, no organization, no order."

"We could get it all if we hung together." Deacon smiled to himself, thinking of his early campus protest days and how he was starting to talk like Gee-Gee the Midget. You can take the man out of the protest, but you can't take the protest out of the man. But Lamar wasn't buying any of it. He was going to need a lot of work.

"No way, brother," Lundy whispered. "The owners got a monopoly, handed out on a silver plate by the government of the United States of America. We players get whatever they want to give us. We got no choice."

"Scraps from the table, again." Deacon was thinking back to his life in Eatonville.

His words seemed to agitate Lamar further. "You can't look at it that way, Deacon! You too young to be talkin' this way! You gonna go an' jeopardize your whole career! You get on the wrong side, there's nowhere else to go. Say you are lucky enough to get on this team. Just get Mister Dan Reeves pissed one time, an' no other owner in this league will touch you. It don't matter if you're the greatest player since Jim Thorpe."

"I'm not lookin' to cause trouble, Lamar. I'm just talking about where we are in all this. A man's got to be free to talk about his rights."

Lamar shook his head vigorously. "Not you. An' not around here. You're in the NFL, son. You open your mouth an' you got three strikes against you. Automatic, you out before you start."

Deacon angrily shook his head. "You talkin' crazy, Lamar. What three strikes?"

"One an' two, you're black. An' three, you're a troublemaker, if they say so. All Reeves or Waterfield or any one of their assistants got to do is say the word an' nobody else in the NFL will touch you! An' the NFL is the only game in town." Lamar pulled a thick book from the bag under his seat. Deacon saw it was the Bible. Lamar took his religion as seriously as he took his football, so the conversation was nine-tenths over. Lamar read for a moment and then looked back up, "I opened the good book, and what would you guess is the first thing I see here?"

"Blessed are the meek?"

"No, Deacon. 'In God is my salvation and my glory.' Do you know what that means?"

"Yes, I do, Lamar. It means you are reading Psalms."

Deacon sighed and stared at his hands bunched on his lap before him, thinking about what he'd gotten himself into. He'd tried to talk about these things with other players and had the same results. They all knew they were being taken advantage of; yet, to a man, they shut their mouths and refused to go after what was rightfully theirs. He'd driven himself to his limits to prove he was as good on the field as the best white ball players; now he was starting to realize there were issues beyond white or black that affected them all. He knew what Gee-Gee the Midget would say: White ball players, black ball players, I don't see the difference—you folks are all niggers around here.

Welcome to the Rams

For the players who remained on the Rams roster, the final marathon weeks before the first regular season game were filled with an awful tension. Since their last exhibition game would be played in Minnesota, and they were traveling directly on to Baltimore for the season opener, the final cuts would have to be made by the middle of the week before the Vikings game.

Deacon Jones walked around that week like a soldier in shellshock. To come so close, and to be cut in the final moments was unthinkable. Yet it was happening all around him. He wondered what it would be like to finally be accepted, the one great moment when they would call the team together and say You guys are it. You're the 1961 Rams. We've picked you to lead us to victory! Would there be champagne, a big cake, reporters? Would Stoneface Bob finally get up and make a speech? Or maybe it would be quiet and individual, the various assistant coaches coming around to the rooms to shake each player's hand and welcome them on board.

Actually, nothing like that happened. In fact, nothing at all happened. The coaches had said the final cuts had to be made by the Tuesday night before the game. When Deacon went to bed late Tuesday evening, falling asleep while memorizing his playbook, Tommy the Terrible Turk still hadn't come. Wednesday morning dawned, and thirty-four players came down to breakfast and looked at each other across the tables in the cafeteria. Nobody in authority said anything, and after eating, the players ran out to their morning drills. Strictly business as usual.

But Deacon knew, as did all the others, that something monumental had happened. For him, it was a moment of absolute joy and relief. The white banker in Orlando wasn't going to get his hands on the new home he'd bought for his mother and father. He wasn't going to have to slink back to Eatonville in disgrace. He was still a hero in Hank Steele's pool hall, the Eatonville Lounge, Hungerford High School and the Open Door Baptist Church. He was a member of the NFL! He had made the team!

On a personal level, this was a tremendous accomplishment. And yet, something of a wider significance had happened to the Rams in the past few days, something with far-reaching implications for Negroes who wanted to play professional football. The team was down to the required thirty-four players—but the blacks who would have been cut in earlier years were still on the team!

That night, the black players gathered at a local bar to celebrate their good fortune, toasting each other with beers until long into the night. It was a moment to remember, and one of the rare times Deacon took a break from his playbooks. The color barriers in the NFL may not have tumbled like the walls of Jerico, but now there was a big crack in them. Of the eleven rookies who made the Rams squad, eight were black. Counting the taxi squad (seven players over the thirty-four on the regular squad), the Rams had fourteen blacks for the 1961 playing season. They were Duane Allen, Pervis Atkins, John Baker, Dick Bass, Charlie Cowan, Alvin "Good Hosen" Hall, Willie Hector, Deacon Jones, Elbert Kimbrow, John "Bulldog" Kinnison, Lamar Lundy, Ollie Matson, Frank Williams, and Tom Wilson.

Traditionally, on the night after the final cuts, curfew was a bit relaxed, and so they were still gathered around a table in the back of the bar as the hour grew late. They drank to each other, the coaches, and even the trainers. They toasted the departed players, their fallen comrades who had tried and failed, and even "Pooch," the mongrel dog who lived somewhere in the orange groves and strayed on the field during practice.

Alvin finally raised his glass for one last toast, "How about one for good old Dan Reeves?"

Deacon put his glass down and stared. "I don't know about that one, Good Hosen. It ain't like the man was motivated by his conscience."

Dick Bass laughed. "More likely by his wallet. Where else would he find such a premier group of football gentlemen at such an excellent price?"

Deacon nodded, but he didn't smile. You could see around the table they were thinking about it. Even Lamar had put his glass down. They all knew the old stories about Reeves. He'd been forced to make football history once before, by the Los Angeles Coliseum Commission, when he wanted to move west from Cleveland. The commission said, sure, come on out, but while you're at it, give black ballplayer Kenny Washington a fair shot at making the team. Deacon was thinking back to the time a few years before when he was in Alabama on the road to Mississippi Valley State. He remembered the old white man who had changed their tire, smiling and being nice until he had the money in his hand. Then he had turned on them like a rattlesnake. They always treat you nice until they get what they want.

Deacon stood. "Fellas, this is a great night for all of us. But let's don't forget what happened here. The Rams been in terrible trouble the past few years. They have fallen upon losing ways, and in desperation have called upon us to be their salvation." After each phrase, voices muttered from around the table, saying amen and tha's right, brother. Deacon continued, "We all earned the right to be here. But that ain't exactly why we are here. Stung by his money-need, this white man has allowed us to climb on board the back of the NFL bus. An' that means our troubles aren't finished, they is just begun!"

Ollie stood and clapped a big hand on Deacon's back. "All of what the Deacon says is true. He means, an' he is right, that when the hot sun comes up tomorrow, we must perform or we will be no longer on the NFL bus, we'll be on the first bus home! However, for the moment, the important thing is, all of us are here!" He picked up Deacon's glass and gave it to him, and then raised his own, "The Lord say we must be of generous heart. So, it don't matter why he done it. Here's to Dan Reeves, an' to all of us in this room! Together, we just made football history!"

To a man, the blacks in the room all rose and gave a ringing toast. "To Dan Reeves! To the Rams! To a winning season!" It was a brief, rousing moment in the middle of what would be one of the longest losing spells in Rams history, a losing streak then in its sixth year that would go on for an incredible five years longer . . . and the beginning of the strangely mixed bag of joy and pain that playing in the NFL in the early 1960s—as blacks on a losing team—would bring to their lives.

Deacon was quiet as Alvin Hall drove them through the darkness of early morning in his rumbling Olds 98, heading back for their dormitory. Good Hosen's radiator problem had been "sort of" fixed, and, though the engine ran hot, the chilly desert night air kept the needle out of the red. Deacon was thinking about Eddie Kotal and how he'd signed his contract all in a rush at the airport in New Orleans. The Rams are going to be your new family, Eddie had promised, in that hurried meeting which now seemed to have taken place in a time so long ago it belonged to a different age. Deacon smiled a sad and sleepy smile, still feeling puzzled and empty over the lack of even the smallest welcoming gesture to the players who had finally made the team. It's a strange family that takes such care of its children, is the thought that kept running through his mind.

Over the years, the "unofficial exclusion" policy practiced on blacks has been denied by coaches, owners, and NFL officials alike. Even today, their usual reaction is to stonewall, to vigorously deny that it ever happened. But occasionally, in a loose moment, perhaps over a drink in a bar or some other casual situation, there are cracks in the ice. Lamar Lundy remembers Harland Svare, who coached for the Giants, the Rams and the Chargers, once telling him, "The number of blacks was held down to four to control the possibility of unrest and dissent breaking out." Harland does not remember this. For his part, Svare earnestly believes that, due to inferior training in college (because they played in black schools with inferior athletic programs), blacks were not ready to play in the NFL. Deacon agrees to some extent with Svare, and has said many times that this was a factor; but he strongly disagrees that this is the entire story. Deacon believes that blacks being excluded was also the result of a general feeling throughout the league that black ballplayers wouldn't generate enough interest to draw the fans out to see them play.

Few others have been willing to discuss the reasons behind the lack of black ball players in the NFL for all those decades. However, Elroy "Crazylegs" Hirsh, interviewed thirty years later, has shed some light on the situation by talking about his experiences in breaking the color barriers in 1961. As Rams general manager, Hirsh was a member of the inner sanctum and privy to much that went on behind the tightly closed doors of the L.A. team's management and the even more secretive NFL. Hirsh said, "Rams owner, Dan Reeves, may have been the first to break the four-blacks-to-a-team rule . . . come to think of it, he probably was. But, believe me, he caught a lot of guff and flak from the other owners around the league for that one!"

Expect the Unexpected

Gene Brito was a big part of Deacon's problem, an obstacle in getting to where he wanted to be. Gene was a tough, accomplished veteran lineman. The Rams had acquired him from the Redskins, and he was solid at defensive end. No one on the team had a more secure lock on their position than Gene Brito did at left end. The other defensive end, Lamar Lundy, was young, lanky, and fast. He'd put together two excellent years, and was just coming unto his own. Lamar would also be difficult to unseat.

Davey wanted to play defense. He felt his true love and greatest strengths were on defense, and Don Paul, the defensive line coach, liked him. At 245 pounds, the coaches hesitated to put him in at guard or tackle; defensive end, however, where his speed and quickness could be used to their maximum, might just be the perfect position. But Deacon couldn't afford to get into a battle for either of their spots, because they were really good and he didn't have the pro techniques, the skills he would need to unseat them. At that time he was so green he never even taped his ankles. He had never gotten that kind of attention in high school or college. Deacon saw Ollie Matson having his ankles taped and asked, "Hey, man—why you do that?" Deacon thought it was some kind of ritual. So he concentrated on the offensive line, where it looked like he was going to grab a starting position.

Late in the exhibition season, after the final cuts had been made, the team took the plane to Minnesota. They beat the Vikings to close out their exhibition season with two wins, two losses and a tie. In spite of this win, there was a restless shuffle, and the reporters and fans were beginning to mutter unpleasant things. The Ram's sputtering, on-again off-again performance clearly hadn't won their hearts or their minds. As the regular season approached, *Los Angeles Herald Examiner* sportswriter Bob Oates summed it up a few days before the opening game:

A defeat here [in the opening game of the season] will tend to confirm suspicions that Bob Waterfield's second annual production is as bad as it often looked in the exhibition season. The Rams are already an emotional item in Los Angeles before the air went in the first ball or the first whistle. The Rams have made too many trades, too many enemies and too few touchdowns to get out of this with their rompers intact unless they win. There is no other way now to bottle the horde of critics. In the language of football, the critics of the Rams have finally jelled.

It was the season opener, 1961. Gloomy clouds hung over Baltimore Stadium. Deacon stood at the fifty-yard line, wearing Rams blue and white. The rabid Baltimore fans hissed and booed when their names were read, but he didn't care. He was swept away as his fantasy became real for the first time. He had begun his dream, his life as the thunder-bringer, the great Deacon Jones. The color, the noise, the excitement that radiated from the fans thrilled him. Deacon looked and saw nothing but a multicolored horizon of pure energy all around him. He could separate the sounds. The yelling crowd was a white noise, but within that noise were the other voices, the linemen yelling plays, the deep backs yelling the coverage, the linebackers yelling their defensive calls, the quarterback barking out the plays. Then the linemen, listening for the signals. The world in tension, Hut 1, Hut 2! And the release, as if shot from a bow and again the mighty roars and groans from the crowd, reacting as if an organic part of the teams on the field. Deacon knew his sacrifices were valid. He had made the right choices along the way, and there was nowhere else he would rather be.

Reeves's and Waterfield's team was almost totally revamped from the previous season. Deacon was starting in the tackle position formerly occupied by Charley Bradshaw. The quarterback was the rifle-armed Zeke Bratkowski, who had been traded from the Chicago Bears for Rams quarterback Billy Wade. The lineup was so heavily revised that Jon Arnett was practically the only veteran playing in his accustomed position. It is no wonder the scribes and fans had their doubts.

There was one other player missing as the Colts game got underway. Gene Brito did not suit up. At the beginning of the training camp, Gene had seemed a sure bet to keep his position, but halfway through he left for a battery of medical tests. No one knew it at the time, but he would never return to play for any team. He had contracted a rare disease, myasthenia gravis. Years later, the same deadly affliction would strike Lamar Lundy. (Benefitting from advanced treatment, Lamar's disease is in remission, and he is today alive and well.)

Defensive line coach Don Paul was giving big John Baker a shot at Brito's position. John was fast for a three-hundred-pounder, but as the game progressed, Deacon could see he wasn't nearly quick enough to rush the Colts' quarterback, the nimble and tricky Johnny Unitas. Unitas, who was then in his prime, used the pocket to perfection. With his quick release, he was never in danger the entire game. Deacon nodded to himself. He wasn't gloating over Brito's bad fortune—he felt that nagging concern all players have for a fallen brother—and he didn't wish John any bad luck, either. But he could see the Rams were having trouble at left end. Before the week was out, he would have to have a serious chat with Don Paul.

The Losing Trail

The Rams opener proved to be a nail-biting turf-banger, with the Colts pulling the win out in the last quarter, 27-24. The Baltimore team was a major power in the league, perennially the team to beat. They'd been the champions in 1958, and a contender in 1959 and 1960. But there was no consolation in that, and the Monday *L.A. Times* sports section headlined, "RAMS MUFF CHANCES." The "muffs" referred to were two field-goal attempts that place-kicker Danny Villanueva missed from inside the thirty-yard line, and a Tom Wilson fumble at the Colt twenty-two that gave the brilliant Unitas all the chance he needed to win the game. It was the big one that got away, and after the game, Coach Waterfield could not hide his exasperation. "There is no excuse," he said, "for a kicker of Villanueva's ability to miss two field goals from twenty-eight and twenty-five yards."

Backfield Coach Hamp Pool was irritated as well, as a special "Lonesome End" play he'd hoped to use was disallowed by the referees. On this trick play, the Rams had planned to use three of their fleet receivers—Carroll Dale, Duane Allen, and Red Phillips—on pass patterns that would start one step from the sidelines. The idea was to spread the Colts' defense so that hard-throwing Bratkowski could zip the ball past their relatively slow defensive backs. But the Colts complained it was illegal, and the officials sided with them, ruling the Rams' receivers had to start five yards in from the sidelines. The Rams reverted to a predictable two runs and a pass offense that the Colts were able to contain.

The players could have taken pride in the fact that they had come so close to beating the mighty Colts; instead, cringing under the public tongue-lashing from their coaches, they slunk back to Los Angeles for their season home-opener, only to be beaten in another squeaker, this time to the hated Chicago Bears. It was ex-Ram cast-off Billy Wade who ran and passed the Chicagoans to a 21-17 victory before fifty-three thousand frustrated Los Angelinos.

This time the headline ran "Wade's Bear-Hug Ruins Rams". The reporters made a big deal out of "The Wade Trade". Dan Reeves came under heavy fire for his trading ways. Owners all over the league liked to see Dan Reeves coming. He had a good eye for the college draft, but he was also impatient. He generally gave up on his picks after two or three years, just before they reached their prime, and most of the NFL teams had one or two ex-Rams in their starting lineup.

Deacon, given a chance on defense, opened some eyes when he ran down the Bears' speedy Willie Galimore from behind. But again it was a Ram error that made the difference in a close game, and Rams fullback Tom Wilson was chided by the Times for "coughing up his customary fumble."

The following week, the Rams won in the Coliseum against Pittsburgh, 24-14. Ollie Matson won it by sprinting sixty-five yards with a pass from Frank Ryan, who had replaced Bratkowski. The Los Angeles press remained unimpressed. *Times* reporter Mal Florence, routinely grim from a decade of losing campaigns, reported casually the next day that "until Matson cut loose, it was a grubby, dull tug-of-war."

Spirits were low as the Rams headed north to San Francisco, where the 49ers used three quarterbacks—John Brodie, Bill Kilmer and Bobby Waters—and a ruthless shotgun offense to rack up an incredible 531 yards. The Rams had been beaten in two close games, but until this game their opponents hadn't found the team's real weakness, an inexperienced defensive backfield. The San Francisco squad found it; they revved up five long touchdown marches of 81, 80, 80, 77 and 96 yards, to amass a 35-0 shutout. Coach Waterfield bitterly blamed the loss on a lack of aggressive play by his men.

It was about this time that Deacon Jones, more preoccupied with winning his starting position at defensive end than anything else, began to notice the angry muttering among the veterans.

The Monday after the game, he walked into the shower room to overhear one surly vet angrily talking over the hiss of the showers. "I see Ol' Stonyface done another good job of laying the blame."

Deacon looked around, surprised to see the vet was talking to him. Vets didn't do that much with rookies, and this guy was white to boot. Deacon figured maybe it was a trap to get him talking out of turn about the coaches.

"I didn't read it," he mumbled, turning on his own shower. "Been reading the playbooks, takes up all my time."

Another vet spoke up from the other side of the shower room, ignoring Deacon as if he wasn't there. "Well, I read it! Damn that Stoneface! Now we ain't playin' aggressive! He blames the whole team! An' he ignores the fact that it was the San Francisco passers picking us apart. As if he and Reeves didn't trade away our whole defensive backfield!"

Everybody in the shower seemed to have an opinion. Somebody else piped up. "Before that, he told 'em 'No excuse for a fumble.' You know, he's right—but then, why don't he make us do more running drills?"

"Yeah. Same-same for Danny. 'No excuse for a bad kick,' coach tells the press. But you don't see him shaggin' Danny's butt out there after practice, gettin' him to do a little extra work on his kicking."

Deacon grabbed his towel and headed for his locker. Before he left, he turned back and said, "Hey, look—we all could use some work. Next time it could happen to any of us."

Nobody said anything. Everybody was suddenly busy, soaping up, with their head under the showers.

Deacon turned to see assistant coach Hamp Pool standing behind him. Hands on his hips, Hamp eyed him like he was the plague. "So now we got a rookie tellin' us how to fix things."

"Every man has an opinion, Hamp," Deacon said, pushing past and walking away from the man before he got into a full-blown argument. Bad enough Hamp had heard him say anything. The coaching staff was already trying to build a case against the popular Ollie Matson as antimanagement, what they called a "locker-room lawyer," a troublemaker. Now he would be tossed in the pot with Ollie.

Waterfield had a lot of problems, and they weren't just brought on by losing. As Deacon toweled himself off, he remembered Ed Clark back at Hungerford High. The Bobcats had been a winning team, and yet the coach had been unpopular with the players. It was hard to be a good coach. Some people seemed to have what it took and some didn't. It was as if Waterfield didn't know how to do the little important things right, the things that united a team rather than letting it drift apart. Just because of the way he was and what he did and didn't do, he built a barrier between himself and his players, and they responded with mistrust and by calling him "Stoneface." Ol' Stoneface just stood there throughout the day, glaring at the team or staring off into space. Bob's assistant coaches did most of the communicating, and, from what Deacon had experienced, they did it by yelling and screaming. They really laid on the pressure: if the players could throw, kick, and carry the ball while they were yelled at, they could perform in the real game when the heat was on and thousands of fans were yelling at them. It was a common way of coaching, but Deacon didn't think it worked: their methods reduced the players' confidence rather than building them up.

The way Waterfield talked to the newspapers was a bad sign. It was as if he didn't understand—or didn't care—that, come Monday morning, his players would all be reading the sports page. Maybe he figured that publicly flogging them would do some good. Whatever Waterfield's strengths were, building team spirit wasn't one of them.

Sitting at his locker, Deacon smiled his bittersweet smile. He'd hardly opened his mouth at all back there in the shower room, and

Hamp Pool was surely going to spread the word that he was rabble-rousing. Bad timing, again! Deacon chided himself, Nobody really care what you think, Deacon Jones. Be more like Lamar Lundy. Just go out there and play ball. And, Lord, try to keep your big mouth shut!

Bad Toe

When you're one and four, things are bad, but it's also still early in the season. There's still a chance, still some time to turn it around. The game that took away that faint hope and sank the Rams' 1961 season took place on a gloomy Sunday afternoon in Detroit. Now desperate to find the winning magic that had eluded him so far in his coaching career, Waterfield was rotating Zeke (Brat) Bratkowski and Frank Ryan on every series, alternately jerking them after the Rams stalled and were forced to punt.

The fans, the press, and the players could see that it didn't matter which quarterback was in there; the quarterback wasn't the problem. The Rams couldn't get a drive going because their offensive line wasn't holding. Not to take anything away from the Detroit defensive line, which excelled in the bruising "black and blue" division, week after week taking on defensive powerhouses like the Chicago Bears and the Green Bay Packers. They were one of the best in the pros, and that day the Los Angeles offensive players couldn't hold their charging line out of the backfield. So Waterfield's two unfortunate flingers, Brat and Ryan, spent most of the afternoon hucking desperate "Hail Mary" passes and fleeing from the outstretched arms of the Lion defenders.

Exasperated sports writer Bob Oates described what it looked like from the stands for his *L.A. Examiner* readers: "If they had any offense . . . if they had any clever surprise plays . . . but the offense here was the same old thing, a mixture of prayer passes and hopeless runs. There are no screen passes in the Rams book and the draw play has been forgotten."

Remember, except for the drubbing they took in San Francisco, the Rams had been in every ball game right up until the final seconds. And here in Tiger Stadium, despite the lack of offensive punch, Deacon and the rest of the Rams defensive line were once again keeping them close. In the waning moments of the fourth quarter, the Lions were winning by only one point, 14-13.

And then, just when it was time to hang up their cleats in defeat until next week, the Rams defense held one more time, forcing the Lions to turn over the ball. And finally, impossibly, the Rams offense caught fire. For this one brief series, their line firmed, their runners and receivers managed to hang on to the ball, and the Rams marched it down the field. After several first downs, they had the ball on the Lions' twenty-one yard line. From the sidelines, Deacon and the defense were screaming themselves hoarse, encouraging their teammates onward. But here the Rams drive gave out one last gasp and stalled. Rams ball, fourth down, with the ball at the fourteen. Waterfield called in Villa-nueva to kick the easy three-pointer and give the Rams the victory. While everybody in the stadium looked on, the ill-fated little kicker adjusted his thin shoulder pads and ran out on the field.

On the sideline, Deacon wrung his hands, thinking of all the times he had stayed on the practice field, long after the rest of the team had gone to the showers, to practice his own kicking. He'd kicked in high school and college, and fancied himself a backup kicker, even though it was beyond his wildest dreams that they would ever put him in a real game. He would have felt more comfortable now if Villanueva had been out there all those evenings, getting twenty or thirty extra boots along with him.

Deacon wasn't alone. The whole team was nervous, and the coaching staff was beside itself, chewing tobacco, spitting, grabbing their charts like there was no tomorrow—after all, the guy had already blown the season opener by missing two easy kicks! If there were an altar for football, these grizzled veterans would have burned incense, old socks, and jock straps and begged Oh, Lucky Goddess of the Grid-iron, be with us for one lousy, stinking kick!

L.A. Times sportswriter Paul Zimmerman describes what happened next: "Richter's center-pass back for the kick was perfect. Ryan placed it well at the 21. Villanueva seemed to raise his head as he booted the ball, and it squirted a couple of yards to the left of the standards."

Standing on the sidelines, Deacon shook his head in disgust. He'd seen the snap down, the blockers hold, and yet Danny had found some way to blow that kick! And it was his own damn fault! Danny never seemed to miss in practices, so he probably thought he was okay. But his real problem was that he didn't take enough kicks. By this time, Deacon realized that everybody on the team had the same problem. There was enormous talent, but nobody on Waterfield's teams worked hard enough at the basics to stand out at what they did. Deacon him-self had spent the entire training camp knocking himself out from morning to night. But he could see now that almost no one else had the level of intensity that he did. The training schedule assumed that, once you made the team, you knew your craft. They ran plays, but they didn't emphasize the basics. They didn't emphasize special team plays. And, to Deacon's mind, they didn't do enough of anything. A few hours in the morning and a few hours in the afternoon weren't enough, even for professional ball players, if they wanted to play flawless football. That was why runners fumbled, receivers dropped sure passes, and kickers booted wide.

Deacon snapped out of his gloom to realize Alvin Hall was screaming in his ear, "How can that little bean-head go nine for nine in the exhibition season and blow it in the games when it counts?"

Deacon threw his helmet on the ground, his vow of silence forgotten, yelling, "God *damn* it!" He caught himself before he said anything more, grinding his teeth and going over to retrieve his helmet, which had rolled right next to Waterfield.

That's how it came to be that Deacon was standing next to the head coach when Danny trotted off the field. He would never forget what happened next down there on the sidelines after that botched kick. As the distraught kicker was walking back to the bench with his head hung low, Bob Waterfield reached out and patted his butt and said in front of the entire team, "That's okay, Danny."

It was easy to see what Waterfield meant; he was trying to make Danny feel a little better for muffing an easy kick with the game on the line. When Deacon heard that, his mind screamed, No! No! No! He knew in that moment that Waterfield just didn't get it. He was the Rams' coach, their physical, mental, and spiritual leader. And it definitely was not okay, Danny. We're here for only one reason, and that's to win, and you just blew a gimme kick and the ball game, and it isn't okay by a long shot!

After the game, the Rams' head coach was philosophical about Danny's performance when he met with the reporters, who, of course, all wanted to know what was going on with their kicker, "It happened to me once," Waterfield said. "He feels bad enough as it is. After all, he's human. Only I wish in this case he wasn't quite that human."

Waterfield may not have realized it, but his attitude was affecting the whole team in a negative way. He didn't drive his team to their limits, and he found ways to shrug it off and pass blame when they lost. These were among his biggest failures as a coach. In the words of George Allen, one of the winningest coaches of all time, from his book

Strategies for Winning, "I believe in winning. To encourage anything less is to tolerate losing." As a player, Waterfield had been nothing but a winner. As a coach, he was nothing but a loser.

The Incident at the Taft Hotel

Deacon tumbled off the plane at La Guardia, stiff and numb as always from sitting rigid throughout the long and difficult flight from the West Coast. The weather was bad, and the New York traffic worse than usual. Of course, Deacon didn't know what usual was like, this being his first trip to the city. From what he saw of the beeping, bleeping madness on the way in from the airport, he was glad his youthful odyssey had ended in a bean patch rather than Harlem. Had he and his high school chums actually made it into New York, they would have been swallowed up in a moment!

Deacon had been rooming with Lamar Lundy for some weeks, and so they took a cab together to the Taft Hotel, where the Rams were putting the team up for their game with the Giants. They checked in at the lobby, dog-tired from traveling cross-country and cross-town, and dragged their own bags up to their room. Deacon threw open the door and looked around. "Whoo, Lamar. This is the wrong place— looks like we got the janitor's closet by mistake!"

These were the days before teams in the NFL allowed black players to room with whites. If you were a black player with a white friend on the team, you couldn't room with him. It wasn't allowed. Blacks had to room with blacks, which is why NFL teams in those years tended to carry an even number of black players, if they had any at all. The first black and white roommates in the NFL were Jerry Kramer and Willie Davis of the Packers, and that wouldn't happen until 1967.

Lamar crowded in past Deacon to have a look. The two men and their luggage took up whatever space in the room wasn't occupied by two single beds, which were crammed wall-to-wall with just enough space between them to get to the tiny washroom. A steady drip came from both the sink and the boxlike shower, and there was a puddle of water oozing from the base of the john. Lamar shrugged and settled on the nearest bunk. "We best make the best of it, Deak. We ain't gonna get nothin' else."

"Why they treat us like this?"

"My rookie year we played an exhibition game against the Redskins down in Mobile. I think we had four blacks on the team at the time, an' we couldn't even get a hotel room. We ended up roomin' across the tracks with a black minister from one of the local churches."

Deacon was peering around the little bathroom. "Man, I hope there's no roaches in here. I hate anything that crawls."

"I thought you was from the swamps."

"That's why I hate 'em, man." Deacon was about to lower his six foot six inches onto his own bunk, which was about a foot shorter than he was, when somebody knocked loud enough to blow their door down.

Voices from outside the door yelled, "Hey, Deak! Lamar! You guys in there?"

Deacon recognized Dick Bass and Pervis Atkins and threw open the door. "Sorry we can't invite you in, brothers. We're gonna have to sleep with our feet out the windows ourselves."

Pervis pushed his way past Deacon. "Just as I thought!" he exclaimed angrily. "Just as I thought! Look at this, Dick!"

There was no way Dick could fit in the room, but he did manage to poke his head in. He shook his head. "The person of the colored persuasion is done in by the white man again"

"What you talking about?" Deacon was tired and hungry. "We don't have time for any Dick Bass foolishness!"

"Come out here, rookie, where we can talk this over."

Deacon came, more than half ready to light into Bass, with Lamar right behind, ready to grab him if things got out of hand. "Okay, Dick. What's goin' on?"

Pervis got between Bass and Deacon and held up both hands. "Just listen for a moment, Deacon. Listen up. This is serious stuff."

"It better be"

"Listen up!" Pervis's tone was enough for Deacon. He nodded, and Pervis continued, "Dick and I came up to our room ten minutes ago. We's drag-ass tired from the long plane ride, just like you guys. We turn on the light, and the roaches run for cover. We pull back the shade to look at the view—after all, this is the town of Babe Ruth an' Mickey Mantle, an' we're lookin' for some class here—an' all we see is another window eight feet away! An' I swear, our room's smaller than yours, an' we got this sweaty radiator in between our bunks, which is saggy an' small as yours. The bathroom is a slum!"

"Look at ours," Lamar said. "Welcome to de neighborhood."

"Yes, my dear colored friends," Bass said, "but that is not all. We couldn't stay in there. There wasn't enough air for two grown men. So we wandered down the hall. An' guess what? Jon Arnett has not just a big room, but a really nice suite! This being curious to us, Jon being white the way he is, and all, we went on a little exploration."

Pervis nodded, "That's right. Now Les Richter an' Eddie Meador was kicked back in their big suite, watchin' television."

"They got television sets?"

"Yes, sir, Swamp Rookie. That white boy defensive back Charley Britt has a really nice room. However, those unfortunate black fellas, Duane Allen an' Charlie Cowan, have themselves one of these really bad little closet rooms."

Deacon felt an icy chill settling over him. "We got to do something about this," he said. "I didn't come to the National Football League to be treated like a second citizen." Deacon had picked up the term "second citizen" at South Carolina State. It meant the rulers of the country treated you like slaves in your own land. Gee-Gee the Midget used to say it all the time. We got to stand up! We ain't gonna be second citizens in our own land!

"Now Deacon," Lamar warned. But even as he spoke, he was filled with misgivings. Lamar had seen the ranting, angry Deacon Jones, but this was something different. This was a man who wasn't going to be talked out of whatever he decided to do. Even Dick Bass pulled back, for once out of wise-cracks.

"What you want to do?"

"First, let's check every room, to be sure we're not making this up." The Rams team occupied the entire floor, so it was easy. Deacon started down the hall, banging on doors and looking in all the rooms, and as he went, the group of angry blacks and a few curious whites followed after him. By the time he reached the end of the hall, he was sure they were right. The whites had the good rooms. It couldn't be a coincidence.

"Okay, he said. "Now we go down to the lobby."

"What good will that do?" Dick Bass asked.

"As you would say, Bass, 'We gentlemen of color will inquire as to how such a thing could be.' " Without waiting for a reply, Deacon turned and started toward the elevator with the more adventurous half of the blacks trailing after him.

Six or seven blacks trooped into the lobby, and Deacon and Dick walked up to the check-in desk and rang the bell. After three or four rings, a middle-aged white lady came out. She was wearing a tweed wool dress and looked harassed, like she didn't have time for them. "What is it?" she said through pursed lips.

"How were we assigned our rooms?" Deacon asked.

"Is that all you want? How in God's name should I know?" the woman said, turning to leave.

"Wait a minute!" Dick's voice rose. "We're not at all through!"

"I have more to do than—"

Deacon's voice rose, "Lady, we're not askin' for the world here. If you can't be civil, just give us Elroy Hirsh's room number. Elroy will handle it."

The lady fussed around behind the desk and found a printed list, which she threw across the counter at him. "Young man, I simply do not have time for this! Here—look it up, yourself!"

Deacon handed the list to Pervis, whose eyes narrowed as he studied the list. "Exactly what is this?" Pervis asked the woman, who was retreating through a door behind her desk into another room.

"Can't you read?" The woman turned back and nearly spit the words at him. "That's the list we got from your office in L.A.!"

Pervis showed the list to Dick, pointing out his name on the list and the asterisk behind it, "Look, my good man of color. You've been fingered." He held up the list and pointed out the asterisks behind every black player on the team.

Bass took the list and carefully studied it for a moment. He took on the airs of an offended English lord. "As have we all," he sniffed. "You will notice," he pointed out in his best Sherlock Holmes voice, "the asterisks are typed by the same typewriter that typed out the list. Therefore, someone in Rams management let the hotel know who the blacks are!" Dick sometimes used that voice to be funny, but this time he was deadly serious.

"Just like the Old South," Lamar whispered, "they got us marked for colored rooms!"

"We got the bottom end of the Ram again," Pervis agreed. "Important thing is, what we gonna do about it?"

Deacon smiled, thinking how he had now come full circle from his stand in Orangeburg. "I think it's time to hold a sit-down strike."

"What?" Lamar was nearly shouting. "You gone crazy, Deacon? We can't do that!"

"We can if we stick together. There's enough of us. The blacks on this team don't play, the Rams won't even be able to field a team. Even if they do, the press will go nuts with it!"

There's no telling what would have happened if matters had gone on untended another five minutes or more. But the woman behind the counter, recognizing she had blundered in placing the list in the black players' hands, had been busy on the phone and had been able to alert Elroy Hirsh, who came running down the stairs into the lobby.

Elroy was all apologies. There had been some mistake, some foolish typing error. It wasn't official Rams policy. It was some foolish hotel clerk at the Taft. Matters would be instantly remedied. He saw to it that the rooms were changed at once. There was some muttering, but the group went off to relay the news to the other brothers and to move their bags to their new rooms, which all were large suites with big beds and television sets.

So, thanks to some quick thinking and instant action on the part of the Rams' general manager, the black players got good rooms and showed up on the field the next day to take on the Giants . . . and the first racial protest strike to threaten the National Football League was averted.

Elroy Hirsh, now living in Wisconsin, had this to say about the incident: "I saw it myself. There were asterisks after the names of all the black players. I couldn't believe that—that wasn't America! It was so unjust. I don't know how it happened. I was sure nobody in our organization did that."

Looking back, Deacon feels it was a rare moment in racial relations within the NFL. "You have to be a little amused. Those people are 100 percent denial, even today, even after being caught red-handed. Truth is that someone in the Rams office did it. And we caught them at it. Once we found out and confronted them, they dropped it."

Pervis Atkins and Dick Bass also remember the Taft Hotel incident as critically important in their battle to open up the NFL to Negroes. Pervis commented in 1991, "Black players had to put up with salary discrepancies, player preferences on the part of the coaching staffs, dirty playing on the field, and slurs and insults on and off the field—but it was done quiet and clever. This incident forced the NFL owners to take a look at one of their discriminatory practices and then to shift their ways."

Deacon sums up his feelings: "People tend to be too harsh on the NFL. You have to remember professional football was a reflection of the times. And something more—they were in untried waters. Nobody had mixed blacks and whites on a team before.

There were lots of people back then who believed it couldn't be done. But step by step and push by push we blacks and whites did it together, and looking back, there's a lot to be proud of. Looking back, you see professional sports—football, baseball, and basketball—has done as much for the harmony of the people of the United States as has all the civil rights legislation of the 1960s. And I'm proud to have been a part of it."

Love Thy Enemies

The problem with Y. A. Tittle began that Sunday afternoon at Yankee Stadium. Tittle, probably the best drop-back quarterback in the league—with the exception, possibly, of Johnny Unitas—was in great midseason form, and the Giants looked for an easy win over the hapless Rams.

Deacon took to the field in an emotional uproar, still furious about the treatment the black players had been given at the Taft Hotel. On the first play from scrimmage, he was a little late in getting to the line, and so he lined up off-center on his man. He wouldn't be able to get a good, direct hit, but maybe he could hit him from the side, like a billiard ball. If he was lucky and the play ran the other way, maybe nobody would even notice. Any way you looked at it, it wasn't a great way to start the game.

But Deacon had no time to worry about it. The Giants snapped the ball and Tittle dropped back in the pocket to pass. At this same time, Deacon bounced off the man assigned to block him and found himself in the backfield! Surprised at this turn of events, he hesitated for a split-second, just long enough for the New York halfback to cut him down from the side, nearly an illegal block, but the referee's whistle didn't blow, and so Deacon got up and knocked a lump of sod out of his shoulder pads.

Deacon played the rest of the series in a fury, angry at the illegal block, angry at himself for lining up wrong, just angry at the world. The Rams finally held, forcing the Giants to punt, and he walked over to the bench, thoroughly disgusted with himself.

"Hey, Jones, come over 'ere!" It was Don Paul, his defensive line coach.

"Sorry, coach. I know I lined up wrong."

"What you talking about?"

"That first play . . ."

"Jones, that first play was the play you lined up right. Look who you're playing against. I know you think you're strong as a bull, but so does he. The only problem is, he weighs thirty pounds more than you do. You ain't gonna move him."

"I gotta move him, coach."

"Deacon, you gotta get around him! Think back how you did it that first time." Don winked and yelled for one of his guards, already on to the next problem. That was why he was the best coach on the Rams. He knew how to fix things midstream, and he gave you the answers, but he didn't shove them down your throat.

To nobody's surprise, the Ram offense didn't move the ball, and Deacon was quickly back in, lined up against his man. The guy was a grizzled vet, and he knew all the tricks. First play from scrimmage, he managed to smash an elbow into Deacon's helmet. Deacon went down like he was stoned. He wasn't hurt, but his head rang like a bell. The Giant lineman grinned at him. He was a big, ugly white guy. His two front teeth were missing, he needed a shave, and his belly hung slightly over his pants.

What had Don Paul said? Deacon couldn't remember. All he could think to do was to line up off-center on the guy. He saw the snap out of the corner of his eye and shot forward. Again, he bounced off the lineman's shoulder and was in the backfield! This time, the Giants ran a sweep to the opposite side of the field and the play was over before he could get to it. Deacon walked back to the line, head down, thinking it over. His opponent was thinking about it, too. "Lucky move, rookie," he said.

Deacon didn't reply, too busy trying to take in what he'd learned. On that play, the lineman had seemed incredibly slow. Were they always that slow? Deacon lined up again, this time dead center. The Giant across the line smiled. At the snap, Deacon hung back for a fraction of a second until the man committed. He was in full lunge when Deacon cut sideways, slapped his shoulder, and was around him. His speed and that shoulder slap was all he needed; his opponent was on the ground. And there was Tittle before him in the pocket, and again the cup held. The pass dropped incomplete, and this time, as Deacon walked back to the line, he saw the Giants's quarterback looking over at his side of the line. Maybe Deacon's rush had helped put on a little pressure. The next play was a broken play, the fullback recovering his own fumble at the line, and the Giants had to kick away. Deacon came off the field thinking how much fun football could be when things were going your way. He was almost hoping Bratkowski would throw another of his interceptions so he could get back out there and hit somebody.

The Rams quarterback didn't have to do that. The Giants easily stopped the L.A. offense, three plays and a punt, and Deacon was on the field again. By now it was the second quarter, and Tittle had his guys moving. But these guys didn't get to be pros by being stupid. The big Giants lineman had adjusted to Deacon's little hesitation and hitch-to-the-outside move, and Deacon wasn't getting through any more. What if, Deacon thought to himself, instead of hesitating, I went right for the outside on the snap? The Giants settled into their stance, and this time, when the center hiked the ball, Deacon went at once. His opponent was frozen and Deacon was past without touching him! And this time, Deacon was so early he got past the startled halfback as well! He was in on Tittle like thunder, tackling the great man just as his arm came forward. The Giants quarterback managed to get the ball off, but it fell five yards in front of the receiver, who was in the clear and streaking for the goal line. Deacon would get a "Quarterback Hurry" for that one!

Deacon hit Tittle so hard the quarterback's helmet flew off. He was amazed. The famous Y. A. Tittle was only human; he went down just like anybody else! Deacon picked up the helmet. It was his first close look at the Giants quarterback. The great Tittle was a thin, wiry white man, and it looked like years in the helmet had rubbed most of his hair away.

"So that's why they call you the bald eagle," Deacon said, the words popping out before he even thought about it.

"Just what the league needs," Tittle snarled, "another smart-mouth rookie." Deacon tossed him his helmet. "Thought we ought to get to know each other—since I'm gonna be seein' you all day."

"Only in your dreams, rookie."

"My dreams, your nightmares, baldie."

Tittle's face reddened, and for a moment it looked like he might do something unwise, but the referee pushed Deacon and pointed him back to his own line.

The game went like that. Deacon was faster, so whenever the man across from him guessed wrong, he was able to break through the line and put pressure on the passing game. On the next Giants offensive series, Deacon combined with Lamar Lundy to dump Tittle for a twenty-yard loss. Back then the term sack hadn't been invented, and the press called it a "quarterback dropped behind the line for a loss." Deacon made sure the referee was looking the other way and said a few words to "Old Baldy." What the quarterback said back was unprintable.

In the third quarter, with the Giants first and ten on the Rams twenty-two, Deacon broke through to smear Tittle again, this time back on the thirty-two. Some more words were passed back and forth, and one of the Giants tried to shove Deacon. He was watching for something like that, and he made an exaggerated dodge sure to catch the referee's eye. By now he had half the Giants offense thinking murderous thoughts. That was all right. It kept them from concentrating on their moves.

The Rams were actually winning in the fourth quarter when the Giants forty-one-year-old quarterback, Charley Conerly, came off the bench and threw two touchdown passes to pull the game out of the fire.

The Rams lost 24-14, but a photograph of young number 75 giving Tittle a shot across his head ended up in national syndication. And Deacon made sure Tittle got a copy, air mail special delivery. Why? He was remembering something Ishmeal had told him once, a long time before. Son, it don't matter what a man's profession, whether he gonna be a preacher, a warrior or a judge. There are three kinds of enemies you make in life—personal, business, and on the field of battle. Of these, the ones you love to hate the most are always on the battlefield. From the first, Deacon wanted there to be no question about it. His sworn enemies were rival quarterbacks. He understood that the psychology of battle was as important as his actual physical moves on the field. If they knew he was coming, they were already worried.

Still, over the long haul, sending that photo would prove to be a mistake. They never forgive or forget in the NFL, and Tittle would wait five years to get his revenge on the young defensive end who had turned his afternoon a little ugly, and then had the audacity to crow about it.

Waterfield's Woes

The Rams limped home to the Coliseum, where their offense laid down, rolled over, and played dead in a rematch against the Lions . . . except for Jon Arnett's thrilling 105-yard kickoff return. It was wasted, though, because that was the only Los Angeles touchdown.

By now poor old Bob Waterfield was doing his best to distance himself from what he must have seen as a loose bunch of shirkers, misfits, and malcontents. Football scribes were calling them the F-Troop of the NFL (making reference to a popular TV comedy of that time about a group of incompetent soldiers stationed in the western frontier), the gang who couldn't play straight, the eleven stooges of the gridiron. Waterfield told the reporters who were starting to swarm him like pesky gnats after the games, "We didn't want to hit anybody, offensively or defensively. That's the whole story. You can't win if you can't hit." Waterfield would have done better distancing himself from the reporters, who were no longer buying what he was selling. *Times* writer Bob Oates wondered why forty-nine thousand Californians had even bothered to come out to watch "a hapless Ram squad that has won only five of its last twenty-seven outings over three seasons." Not convinced by Waterfield's excuses, Oates continued, "The team showed the unhappy crowd the same old offense."

The next week, halfway through the season, Ram team spirit revived a little when they beat the last-place Minnesota Vikings to escape from the conference cellar. However, the irrepressible Norm Van Brocklin, then in his rookie year as the Vikings coach, wisecracked, "The only thing worse than the Ram defense Sunday was the Viking defense. Unfortunately for us, we were playing them at the time." Van Brocklin, who had alternated at quarterback with Waterfield in their playing days, was another coach who could not bring himself to blame the offense for defeat. Wins were the result of running, passing, and catching. Losses were caused by bad defense.

And then the San Francisco 49ers, who had destroyed them earlier in the season with their shotgun offense, came back to town. The Rams still had the same slow and inexperienced defensive backs, and the same stodgy offense. But this time, a new weapon showed itself. Young, raw Deacon Jones provided an inspiration for the entire defensive line, and they were able to claw their way into the rival backfield before the 49er quarterbacks could set up. The Rams gained their revenge, winning 17-7, and Deacon impressed *Times* writer Mal Florence, who reported on the Monday after the game, "The 49ers showed early-season shotgun form on their first series, passing to the Ram 34, but Deacon Jones smothered Kilmer for a twelve yard loss to end the threat and set the tenor for the first half. San Francisco spent the rest of the first half in its own back yard as Jones, Urban Henry and John LoVetere indiscriminately whacked Kilmer, Brodie, Waters, and J. D. Smith for frightful losses."

Young and inexperienced as he was with the ways of NFL coaches and the press, Deacon found Waterfield's handling of the press upsetting. When the team lost, their coach had quotes for the press, but when they won, he was strangely silent about the heroics of his young rookie defensive end and the rest of the defensive line which had pulled the team to victory. Deacon himself began to see that Waterfield, an offensive giant in his playing days and still partial to the offense, couldn't bring himself to congratulate the defense for a victory. And the man would go to his death before saying anything nice about a rookie.

Deacon thought about it on the plane east. He had a lot of time for thinking. He sat rigid as a statue, never looking out the window, arms gripping the arm rests at his side as if that might help keep the frame square and the wings up. The Rams were three and six and heading back for a crucial three-game swing through the Midwest with games against Green Bay, Chicago, and Minnesota. Air travel was slow and inconvenient; the flight took twelve hours, and Deacon was nearly deaf from the engine noise when they stumbled off the plane.

The Rams took a bus to the University of Wisconsin, their headquarters for these three games, and on November 19 the team lost to a tough, aggressive Green Bay team, 35-17, on a humid, overcast day. After the game, Waterfield had the reasons for the defeat at the tip of his tongue, ready for the reporters. He blamed the loss on his defensive line! Not the defensive backfield that Bart had picked apart all day. Not the offensive line that had allowed the Packers to stream in on the Rams quarterbacks. Not his receivers or backs who dropped the ball with dependable regularity. The way Waterfield saw it, his team hadn't put an adequate rush on Bart Starr, the Green Bay passer. "I don't think we ever touched Starr," he said.

Davey read about his coach's remarks in the papers, and snorted, "He must have been watching some other game." He felt he was living in an episode of the "Twilight Zone"; both he and Urban Henry had been called for fifteen-yard penalties for roughing the passer in that game! How do you get a major penalty for roughing the passer without touching him?

Green Bay protected their star quarterback better than anyone in professional football. When someone did manage to break through, if the play was close, the referees would be inclined call a penalty, the line of reasoning being since the Green Bay offensive line is so good, it had to be a foul. Led by Deacon, Waterfield's linemen had broken through to rough up Starr twice, unprecedented that entire year—yet Waterfield publicly blamed them for the defeat!

With their coach kicking whoever was visible at the moment, team morale reeled as the Rams aimed for their next game, against the Chicago Bears. The players' general mood was one of bleak despair, and the sportswriters had long since written the Rams off as a lost cause. Los Angeles was a big-league town, filled with talented writers, all loaded and eager to shoot the Ram in the butt. The angles they took ranged from frustration to anger, from an "I give up" attitude to spoofing astonishment. Jim Murray of the *Times,* amused by so much disaster on one team, wrote the following classic lines the day after the game:

> When the old pro Dynamite Page told me last week the Rams were planning to use the shotgun Sunday, I thought for one terrible minute he meant on themselves. On the other hand, the way these guys are going it would probably jam. I really feel sorry for Ye Olde Rams these days. Nothing they do turns out right. When some teams run out on the field in front of a crowd, they cheer. Other teams, they boo. With the Rams, they just laugh. They really ought to come out in one of those break-away clown cars. You know, the ones that sputter and backfire in the middle of the circus ring, the doors fly open and out pours an endless stream of guys with flour on their pants, lipstick on their noses, in baggy pants and pointed hats.

More than anything, this was the stuff that sent Bob Waterfield into his silent rages. They couldn't be talking like this, printing things like this in the papers, making clown jokes, about him! He wanted nothing to do with this team of buffoons—this millstone around his neck!

Battling Bob

Bob Waterfield walked to his temporary office on the campus of the University of Wisconsin with the thunderclouds around his head, same as they'd been for the last few years. He prided himself that he'd always been able to keep his feelings to himself. His image of leadership was to be the strong, silent type, firmly at the reins. But he was finding it far more difficult to hold that pose as a coach, particularly now that the Rams' long losing streak was showing no signs of coming to an end. At least here in the Midwest he wouldn't have so many reporters swarming around. He sighed and settled his six-foot-two frame into the sagging chair behind his desk. At 210 pounds, he was only ten pounds over his playing weight. Greying, but still strikingly handsome, the head coach of the L.A. Rams studied the small pile of messages on his desk and then reached for the half-empty bottle of bourbon under the paper clippings in his bottom drawer. Murray's piece about the circus clown Rams fell from the messy overflow of papers to the floor. Bob crumpled it in a ball and threw it in the waste can. How had he ever managed to fall this low?

Battling Bob Waterfield had always been a winner. A college All-American at UCLA in 1942, he served in World War II and joined the Rams in 1944 for what was then an astounding $7,500 contract. Known as a brilliant field general and a pinpoint precision passer, his cool, unemotional leadership on the field had led the then Cleveland Rams to a divisional championship in 1945, when he was only a rookie.

Waterfield had been tremendously popular in southern California, and when the Rams moved west, this popularity skyrocketed, elevating him to the status of demigod and local legend. It was a position he had earned. Waterfield was not only a brilliant passer, he also proved to be a dangerous runner, and an excellent punter and place kicker. As if that weren't enough, during the first four years of his professional career, Waterfield played defense as well, and earned twenty career pass interceptions. Elroy "Crazylegs" Hirsh, one of his favorite receivers, when asked about Waterfield in a telephone interview in 1994, said simply of him, "Bob Waterfield is the best football player I've ever seen."

Waterfield's last five playing seasons were somewhat dimmed in that he had to share time with another brilliant passer, Norm Van Brocklin. Waterfield played the first and third quarters, Van Brocklin the second and fourth. Still, every year Waterfield played the Rams had a winning record. During his reign, the team won three divisional titles, tied for another, and captured NFL championships in 1945 and 1951.

Waterfield had retired at the height of his career, in 1952. No one was sure why, and he never said. The speculation was that Waterfield was frustrated with having to share his quarterbacking chores with Van Brocklin. Sid Gilman's resignation after the disastrous 2-10 season in 1959 left the door open for the head coaching job, and Waterfield took it. Now, barely a year and a half later, he was regretting the move. Waterfield was finding that playing was one thing, coaching something entirely different.

Back in Waterfield's playing days, the players played and the coaches coached. Now Waterfield had to worry about runners and receivers who couldn't hang onto the ball and seemed to think it was the coach's fault. He tried to treat his men like grownups, yet he had the nagging suspicion that they slacked off behind his back. They should be driven to greatness, as he once was, to perfecting their craft on their own. They were veterans, they were professionals. They seemed to do well enough in practice, yet they were disasters on the field. And then there was the fistful of blacks on his team—whatever had convinced Reeves to take them on? Desperation. It had to be desperation. Whatever, the way they hung together had the assistant coaches worried; nobody could figure out what they wanted, but whatever it was, it was more than they had, and it wasn't good for team unity. And to make his day complete, Jones, his loud-mouthed rookie, was popping off to the press again! Just what he needed, somebody to bait the Bears! Clever old Pappa Bear George Halas was a master at using scraps of nonsense like that to fire up his men and turn the day ugly. As if he didn't have enough trouble already.

Waterfield rummaged in the half-empty waste can, looking for the article he'd thrown away. He'd read it a dozen times in the past few days, and he still couldn't believe it. A clown team . . . they were saying Bob Waterfield coached a clown team! He snorted in disgust. They hadn't seen anything yet—the Rams still had to play three really tough games—Chicago, Baltimore, and Green Bay. Plus, they would have to get past unpredictable Van Brocklin's Vikings. Would this long, terrible season never end?

Waterfield eyed the bourbon on his desk. Soon the assistant coaches would show up and they could all have a drink together. They'd better hurry, or they were going to have to send out for their own bottle.

Bear Claws

Even with the Bears record at 5-5 for the season and the divisional championship looking like it was going to Vince Lombardi's Packers, pigskin talk was in the air around the Windy City. Bear rookie tight end Mike Ditka was news. Billy Wade, traded from the Rams, was news. Legendary Bear owner and coach George Halas's every word was news. Even the sensational Rams rookie, Deacon Jones, was news. The reporters flocked around, paying Deacon more attention than he usually got in his own town. Chicago was like that, a hard-nosed football town that loved to serve its heroes and villains straight up on the sports page.

Naturally, Davey's new alter-ego, The Deacon, loved it. "What are we gonna do?" he asked. His eyes went wide in mock-amazement and the wide, bittersweet grin spread across his face as he looked down at the sea of reporters in front of him. "We gonna kick the Bears' ass, both singly and collectively!" On the road, Jones was one of those guys you loved to hate, and the local press never failed to eat it up. From the time he got off the plane, from his first game in the NFL, Deacon was always ready with a quotable quote. This time, all that talking showed up in the *Chicago Tribune* and the *Chicago Sun Times,* in the homes of fans all across Chicagoland, and pasted to the lockers of individual Bear players. By game time, Wrigley stadium was filled with rabid Bear fans, merrily howling their rage over the snowflakes and the national anthem. Deacon realized, as he walked through the tunnel and along the narrow ramp past hundreds of taunting fans, that Chicago was indeed a different sort of a football place, a den where referees routinely picked up the rolls of toilet paper and the occasional beer bottle so play could resume.

The Bears took the kick for a short run-back. On the first play of the game from scrimmage, the Bears weak side went into a tight formation, and they brought Johnny Morris, their little All-Pro flanker in tight, right next to the offensive tackle on the weak side. This looked like a double tight end situation (with two tight ends going out for a pass), but it was not—it was actually a special running play, with both offensive ends blocking Deacon.

Regardless of what the Monday morning quarterbacks believe, many, if not all, NFL games are won by actively searching out, uncovering, and exploiting weakness. It is part of the greatness and unpredictability of the game that these weaknesses often pass unnoticed by fans, players, rival scouts, rival coaches, and (of course) owners. And, one of the joys of football remains the fact that, in attempting to take advantage of an opponent's perceived weakness, the attacking team is generally vulnerable at some other point. If you set up the long pass, you're vulnerable to the blitz, and so on.

Now George Halas knew Reeves and Waterfield were stinging from all the bad press they'd been getting for trading away Billy

Wade. Billy was a good thrower, and he had badly stung the Rams with his passing game since he'd become a Bear. George figured the Rams would be looking for a passing attack, so he reverted to a running game.

In reviewing the Rams' defenses, the Bears' grizzled old coach decided their best point of attack was the Rams' inexperienced rookie defensive end. By nullifying Deacon's speed off the ball, they hoped to open holes in the weak side. Johnny Morris wasn't very large, and he wasn't a good blocker, but he knew how to get in the way. So Deacon was effectively double-teamed, with the big offensive tackle blocking him from coming straight in, and Johnny keeping him from going around.

This play worked, and so George naturally tried it again. And it worked again. In fact, it worked throughout the entire first half. The Bears kept running over Deacon's position, gaining big yardage each time. The defensive backs had to shift over to plug the hole, and, of course, that left room for Wade to start up his passing attack.

By half time, as Deacon walked back down the ramp to the shabby visitor locker rooms, he was frustrated and boiling with anger. He was double-teamed, and couldn't do anything about it! Kick the Bears' ass, indeed! The Bears were making him eat his own words! Deacon turned the corner, and ran into the entire team, which had been assembled by Waterfield. He was surprised, because this was far from the ordinary. At half time the Rams usually broke up into individual meetings, with the assistant coaches taking the offensive line, the defensive line, the offensive backfield, the receivers, and so on into separate huddles to make the necessary adjustments. But the entire team was sitting on the benches and on the floor, in a semicircle around Bob Waterfield. And every man in the room was looking at him.

"There you are," the head coach started, his voice soft, and yet shaking with emotion. "We've all been waiting for you." His voice started to rise. "I just want to know, where a guy like you, a kid out of the goddam swamps, gets off coming up here to the big time *and telling us all how to do* our business?" There are some questions that are not meant to be answered. Deacon just stood, thunder-struck, staring at the spectacle. Here was his head coach, the man who hadn't said two words to him in almost a year, the man who never showed emotion, hopping up and down like a crazed baboon. Waterfield's face was red, the veins standing out on his head, and by now he was yelling, "You lousy, no-good, rotten rookie! You empty-headed, pea-brained, foolish, ignorant son-of-a-bitch! You dirty, stupid, foolish, worthless brag-gart!"

The yelling went on, and on, and on, through the entire half-time intermission. Waterfield didn't say anything to anyone else, and he didn't say anything constructive. He just yelled and called Deacon names while the team and the coaching staff looked sheepishly at the floor or off into space.

The endless ragging was finally over, only because one of the assistants ran down the ramp and warned them they had to get back on the field. Deacon walked toward the locker room, shaking from humiliation and rage. He was ready to quit, just walk away from it all. But as he started to take off his shoes, he was joined by Don Paul.

Don sat beside him, not saying anything for a moment, and looking the other way as Deacon wiped the tears from his eyes.

"I can't go back out there, Don." Deacon said. "That man humiliated me in front of the whole team."

Don shook his head, still not looking directly at him, "We got a game to play, Deak."

"I can't play for him."

"I think you can. In fact, that's the only thing you can do. You can show him out there on the field. You can show them all." Those words struck a chord in Deacon's memory. He saw himself a young teenager outside Tanker Field in Orlando, when the great Jackie Robinson had said much the same thing. Deacon paused, thinking about it, then shook his head.

"But Don, Stoneface is right—I stink out there."

"That's why I'm here, Deacon. Let's talk about it a little."

"They got me stopped dead in my tracks."

Don gave him a wry smile. "You're forgetting that Johnny Morris is a baby bear. He probably only weighs 170 soaking wet."

"Yeah, but . . ."

"Listen to me, Deacon." Don shook his shoulder, "I want you to forget your normal blocking assignment for a play or two."

"You what? Stonyface'll kill me!"

"No he won't. I'll handle that end of it." Don Paul smiled with a hawklike intensity, "Little Johnny Morris is a very valuable asset to the Chicago Bears organization. I think they will go to some length not to see him pounded into the turf, which is exactly what you will be doing."

"I will?"

"Right. Here's the deal. You wait until the offensive line sets. You start to get into your set, then crab one little half-step to the outside. That should put you right on our Johnny-boy, shouldn't it?" Don gave Deacon a wink and an encouraging pat on the shoulder, and left him to his thoughts. "You got about thirty seconds to get those shoes on," he said as he walked out of the locker room.

The first time the Bears got the ball, they came at Deacon with the same formation. But now, he knew what to do. He waited for them to set, and then he moved a foot to the outside, just one bare, crabbed half-step. He looked across the line and saw he was head-to-head with Johnny. He could see by the whites of his eyes that the poor little guy saw it coming. The Bear center snapped the ball and Deacon accelerated into Johnny like one of those dragster hotrods, full of rage and frustration and itching to hit somebody hard. He had at least seventy pounds on the baby Bear, and they didn't pay Johnny to stop freight trains with that lightweight frame of his.

Halas ran that play twice more, and each time Deacon charged right over Morris, who was having trouble getting back to his feet. He was starting to stagger around like he didn't know what planet he was on. One look at his dazed baby Bear, and Hallas knew they had to shift back to their regular formation or they were going to have to send Johnny home to his family in a packing crate. The Bears shifted back on the next play, and Deacon was in the backfield on the snap, chasing Billy Wade like there was no tomorrow. Freed to work his magic, the Rams rookie came alive, cutting through the Bears' line time after time to disrupt Wade's timing and break up the play. The Bears went into a tailspin, and the Rams were actually ahead by three points late in the fourth quarter. Still, football is a team sport, and Deacon and the Rams' defensive line—try as they might—couldn't do it all by themselves. The Rams' defensive backfield was notoriously weak, and Halas knew it. Time to switch tactics. Reverting to his passing game, he directed his Bears down the field for what turned out to be the winning score.

By the end of the game, Waterfield had regained his usual public composure. He cordially greeted the press with praise for ex-Ram Billy Wade, who had snatched the victory from his Rams by picking apart his secondary. He had nothing at all to say about his half-time outburst, and studiously ignored any mention of the heroic efforts of his own team.

Shortsighted

On the afternoon Deacon and the rest of the Rams took the field against the Vikings, the weather was 46 degrees and drizzling. There was no sign it was to be one of the wildest games of Deacon's career. In those days, the Vikings played in Metropolitan Stadium in Minneapolis, a stadium open on the ends. When the harsh winds blew down from Canada and the Arctic, ruffling the short, stiff hairs of whatever miserable brown lumps of grass still clung to that gridiron, the older players started thinking of retirement and career changes and the younger ones of trades to Miami or San Diego. They saw themselves sitting by the warm fire with a big goblet of brandy and Ralph the Dog resting his chin on their feet.

This day wasn't freezing, but it was cold, wet, and miserable. The game was wild from the opening kick. It was scrambling quarterback Fran Tarkenton pitted against a Los Angeles defensive line that was determined to get to him before he could launch his passes. Fran was only in his first year, but he was already a young legend. It was the Vikings first year in the league—and in their first game ever, Fran had come off the bench to pass and run for five touchdowns, stunning the Chicago Bears in what many called the upset of the decade.

In the weeks since then, Fran had been responsible for turning the pro game topsy-turvy and promoting a major controversy; before Tarkenton, when a quarterback scrambled, it was for his life. Scrambling didn't win games, it was a desperation move to save broken plays. But Fran was a special breed all to himself. While not particularly fast, he was agile as a cat, and lightning quick. Fran weighed only 185, but he was as difficult to tackle as a greased pig. When the normal pocket protection broke down, Fran was just getting started, dodging and darting all over the field. Some coaches said he was just a flash in the pan; others saw him as the wave of the future. Ironically, his own coach, Norm Van Brocklin, had strong reservations about his style, and played him only because he had no other real alternative. He felt Fran deviated too quickly from the Vikings game plan.

Deacon, arguably in the best shape of anyone on the field, was in the Viking quarterback's face the entire day, doing his best to hurry Frantic Fran's throws. He had four tackles and nine assists on the day, and by half time, even with the Vikings in the lead, he was well on his way to becoming Van Brocklin's least favorite person.

Norm was the polar opposite of Bob Waterfield. Where Bob was cool and poised, Norm was emotional, temperamental, and unpredictable. The two had formed an uneasy alliance as star quarterbacks on the Rams in the early 1950s, and now here they were, rival coaches, playing to stay out of the league cellar.

As the first series warmed up, players on both sides of the line got into a little pushing and shoving. The referees shivered, wiped the fog off their glasses and seemed inclined to let the game play rather than calling penalties on every infraction, which in this kind of contest could be a mistake. Calling penalties keeps games in control, but it also makes them considerably longer. The refs might have been thinking that since the weather was foul and it was a game of no importance, they might as well get it out of the way as soon as possible. The league will deny it, but that happened back then. Maybe it even happens today. Referees are human, just like anyone else. Problem was, in no time at all emotions were running high on both sides of the ball, and things were getting rough.

As the clock wound down to half time, Deacon managed to break past his man and race into the Viking backfield. The Vikes were running a play to the far side, but Deacon had found that, if the blocking held for a moment or two, he was sometimes fast enough to rotate across the field and catch up with the runner. So, instead of giving up on the play, he crossed the width of the gridiron, running on a diagonal as he streaked after Minnesota halfback Tommy Mason. The offense wasn't expecting him; he was literally coming in from behind the play, like a kamikaze pilot streaking out of the sun. For a moment, it looked like Tommy had a clear path down the sidelines, but then Deacon's intercept angle converged on the runner. The Ram rookie hit the ball-carrier like a dark avenger; Tommy flew ass-over-teakettle and they both tumbled out of bounds at the Minnesota forty-nine.

Deacon looked up to find himself in the middle of the Vikings bench. All he saw was the white-stocking legs of the home squad. He was surrounded by the entire Minnesota team. Not only that, florid-faced Norm Van Brocklin himself was staring down at him. The man was livid, red with anger. He pointed a finger in Deacon's face and yelled, "We're gonna git you, nigger!"

Deacon slowly got to his feet, shrugging his shoulder pads back into position. The slow, dull red anger started, but even young and sassy as he was, he wasn't about to get into a shouting match with crusty Norm with thirty Vikings standing around.

"Only a fool poke a hornet nest with a stick," he said quietly.

"What's that—country wisdom?" Norm snorted.

"Calling me 'nigger' is short-sighted, fool. Next few years, we're going to see each other a lot."

One of the Vikings pushed him, but Deacon had already turned away and was headed back on the field.

As the second half began, the referees lost control of the game. Even though by this time his team was nursing a big lead, the tempestuous Van Brocklin was irked by a call and stormed out on the field in a childish display of temper. The Vikings coach put on the worst tantrum seen in professional football since the heyday of George Halas. After that, almost every play ended in a brawl, fists flying after the whistle on every series until the end of the game.

Safe in the locker room after the rowdyness had subsided, the Rams head coach took the lofty ground. "That's just Norm," Bob said, "and actually, I think he's mellowed." *Times* writer Mal Florence was disgusted, "Sandlot football, Viking style, sent the Rams floundering to a humiliating 42-21 defeat Sunday in Metropolitan Stadium." Columnist Jim Murray took the gloomy approach, "The way I feel right now, I don't even want to know who beat the Rams this time."

But the thoughts of Deacon Jones were going far beyond a single win or loss. Usually, he'd be in the thick of the reporters, giving out his quotable quotes. Not this time. He sat alone in a far corner of the locker room, plotting revenge. Maybe Norm thought he could use racism to get Deacon's mind off the game. Maybe it was just another trick up his sleeve. And maybe not. Whatever it was, it wasn't very smart on Norm's part. For Deacon had chosen the gridiron as his field of battle. One-on-one in the pit, skin color, race, or creed didn't matter. And it was on the gridiron—that lush green field of trumpets, honor, and bravery—that Norm and his team would be punished.

After that, Deacon would never have to worry about getting up for a game against the Vikings. And in the years to come, many a Minnesota lineman, forced to play across from a cold and fierce Deacon Jones, came to regret Norm's rash remark without ever knowing what he'd said or why. Some years later, at the height of his career, Deacon dragged himself out of his sick-bed to play one of the best games any defensive lineman ever played against Minnesota, crushing them and single-handedly destroying their playoff hopes. All because Crazy Norm, like so many white people in that era, didn't stop to think before he blurted out the word nigger.

Salt Lake Brews

"Yeah, but Don, you ain't the chug champ any more. Now we got a rookie chug champ."

Don Paul sat in the back of the plane, taking the ribbing from the vets who were slouched in the seats around him. Don smiled, "Maybe he's the new champ, but I made him earn his title."

"What—did you buy him another round?"

Don didn't say anything. He was remembering how he'd made Deacon run laps around the track at the University of Wisconsin. It was one of those cold mornings when the rain coated the trees in a sheet of ice. The rest of the Rams were all snug in their beds, but Deacon was sloshing around the track, learning his lesson. Don had told him he thought he was slowing down and needed a little midseason sharpening. But he was sure his prize rookie got the real lesson. Don't ever beat the coach at anything, least of all, not in public! Now, on the slow plane ride back to L.A., it seemed like that chugalug contest was the most fun they'd had on the entire trip. Don was a great beer drinker, and he took a macho pride in the championship. He felt fairly confident he'd win a rematch, now that his young rookie knew what was at stake.

The Rams had lost all three games on their Midwest swing. Better to try to forget for a while, and all this talk of beer contests was getting Don thirsty.

The veterans started to talk over their raging thirst and what to do about it. As usual, they came up with the rookie solution. "What do you say we get one of the rooks to get off in Salt Lake City and pick us up some brews?"

"No rookie's that dumb. Salt Lake's a dry town."

"Bet I can get our new chug-champ to do it."

"Five says you can't!"

So one of the vets heaved himself up and wandered down the aisle until he found Deacon, who was engaged with Lamar Lundy in an argument about God's intent in writing the Bible. The turboprop plane wavered and its nose dipped as he leaned his arm on Deacon's head rest, "Comin' in to Salt Lake City, Deak. We're takin' up a collection. Hows about you hop off an' get us a few cases of suds?"

Deacon's gaze was not friendly, "Last time I done that, I nearly got thrown out of trainin' camp—an' I didn't even get a single swallow or word of thanks for my trouble." The vet wasn't at all perturbed by

Deacon's attitude. He figured, if he wanted, all he had to do was say
Do it.

Another vet joined in, waving a fist full of dollar bills, "Tol' you
he couldn't do it, man!"

Deacon glared at him, "What you mean, couldn't do it?"

"Almost impossible to find liquor in Salt Lake City. Mormons
frown on the practice."

"I can find it if any man can."

"Side bet, a hundred bucks says you can't!"

"You're on, sucker."

Deacon would have a half-hour while the plane refueled. He ran
down the metal steps and sprinted across the tarmac toward the airport terminal. One thing bothered him; there was hardly a single
black anywhere, even doing the menial jobs. This was pure white
bread country. He stood for a moment in front of the terminal, squinting in the light of the midday Utah sun. There was a long line of cab-
bies, and luck of the gambling man!, one of them was a withered old
black man! Deacon ran quickly to the cab and hopped inside, "Brother, I need four cases of beer in twenty minutes!"

The old man's skin was wrinkled like light brown parchment.
"Son," he said, "you come to the wrong state. This here town is dry as
a bone."

"Gotta be a place. Gotta be a way."

"There always is . . . but can you pay?"

Deacon waved the bills in his face, "We gotta do it—now!"

The old man carefully backed out of the line and drove off pon-
derously and slowly.

"What you got, a school bus or a steamship, here? I mean, can't
you move this thing?"

The old man looked back over the edge of the seat at Deacon. They
were going so slow he didn't have to stop or pull over to do it, "Son,
they is anti-negroid around here, which is they fancy way of sayin they
don't like us niggers. We don't observe the speed limit, we ain't never
gonna git there at all."

They drove on for five endless minutes, and the cabbie finally
pulled over and left Davey off in the middle of a run-down residential
section of town.

"You sure this is the place?"

The old man waved his encouragement, "Jist go around the back,
sonny. Steps lead down to the basement. I be waitin' fo' you here."

A big woman with hazel eyes and dark cherry skin peered out of a rusty screen door in answer to Deacon's frantic knock. After five minutes haggling, he managed to buy her entire stock—two cases of mixed brands of warm beer at the outrageous price of a dollar a bottle. He raced for the cab and the driver putted him back to the airport at the same maddening pace.

The moment they got there, Deacon threw ten dollars on the seat and was out and running before the cab pulled to a complete stop. He skidded and skipped his way through the crowded airport lobby, weighed down by the two cases of beer, and ran out on the tarmac just in time to catch a last glimpse of the stewardess closing the door from the inside. The metal stairs had already been pulled back, and the pilot gunned the left engines, causing the plane to start a small semicircle toward the runway.

"You can't go out there, sir!" a stewardess yelled at him.

"Call back that plane or I'm gonna chase it down the runway! An' I'm just fast enough to catch it, too!" Deacon yelled back. He didn't say what he'd do once he caught it. He hadn't thought that part through; but his threat was enough, and the stewardess contacted the pilot, who cut the engines and waited for the steps so Deacon could board the plane.

Deacon ran up the steps, his boot heels clanging on the metal stairs—and wished he'd missed the plane. Standing there with a face like fury was Bob Waterfield. He was a by-the-numbers guy, and with the team's horrible losing record, there were no extenuating circumstances, nothing that could excuse a rookie—much less this rookie—for showing up late.

Waterfield gave him his second public raking over the coals, making it clear that of all the many stupid and dumb rookies he'd hated over his long career, Deacon Jones was at the top of the list. He finished by screaming, "You're gonna pay a dollar for every minute this plane is late past our scheduled arrival time in Los Angeles!" Then Waterfield turned to Don Paul, "Can't you keep your people in line? What kind of an example are you, anyway?"

With no other choice, Don Paul moved in front of his boss and began to yell at Deacon. He yelled for a few minutes after Waterfield retreated to his own seat, but by now he had winked and shown Deacon that he didn't really mean it. Finally he said, "Well, at least you got the beer."

Don took both cases and retreated to his seat in back, where the vets gathered around and started drinking. Deacon returned to sit next to Lamar. The plane took off, winging them southwest over the mountains toward L.A. After a half-hour, Lamar looked up from his bible, "By any chance did you have the wisdom to slip a few of those beers in your pockets for us before you got on the plane?"

"Shut your mouth, Lamar," Deacon said. He was in a foul mood. He'd never wanted a beer so badly in his life. He'd made a hundred dollars, but the plane had lost forty minutes in Salt Lake City, and was now bucking serious headwinds. Chances were, with his silly dollar-a-minute penalty, he was going to be in the red before they taxied in to the terminal at LAX. It was an unjust fine, considering the circumstances, but Waterfield was going to insist he pay it. That was just the way he was.

They Only Respect Winning

With two more games to play and a terrible 3-9 record, the Los Angeles Rams took the field against the powerful Baltimore Colts. It was perfect football weather, sunny and 68 degrees with a light breeze blowing across the Coliseum, and the Rams had nothing to lose.

Deacon, Les Richter, and Lindon Crow relentlessly hounded the Baltimore quarterbacks the entire game. Deacon was nearly unstoppable, getting to Johnny Unitas once for a big loss and completing five key tackles. It is a rare day when defense alone wins ball games. But for once the Rams offense came alive, and with the offense and the defense pulling together, the Rams won a stunning upset victory, 34-17. Stunning, indeed: for once, Waterfield was jolted into silence, and had nothing bad to say about his own men.

The following Sunday, the Packers showed up at the same place. By now, Deacon had the basics of his slashing style of attack in place. He had a lot to learn, but he was proving effective against slower and heavier linemen. Early in the first quarter, Vince Lombardi tested his running game against Deacon's side of the line, and Deacon continually stuffed the plays for little or no gain. On a running play around the opposite end of the field from his position, Deacon somehow managed to thread his way laterally across the entire field to tackle fullback Jim Taylor after a gain of six yards. This was something new for the NFL, a lineman who could catch and tackle a great running back from behind, and Lombardi cogitated the matter on the sidelines for a moment or two before going to his passing attack.

There was nothing left to the season, so Deacon decided to go for broke. In the second quarter, with Green Bay in a third-and-eleven situation on their own forty-three, he guessed pass, juked his man by faking one way and going the other, and broke into the backfield. It was the type of thing he would become famous for, one of those maneuvers that leave coaches gasping—if he'd guessed wrong, there was nobody between Jim Taylor and the goal line. But when he looked up, there was Bart Starr dead ahead in his sights, pulling his passing arm down and hugging the ball like a teddy bear. Deacon roared in like a freight train and slammed him to the ground. That was news, because in those days nobody got through to Bart Starr. It was almost a rule in the NFL. Yet here he was. It was a jarring tackle, and Starr was so surprised he coughed up the ball. Deacon scrambled across him and picked it up on the Green Bay thirty-five, carrying it for a ten yard return to the twenty-five before he was tackled.

The rest of the day was colored in personal glory for the young defensive end. Playing on the suicide squad, he tackled Green Bay back Herb Adderly on a return. He got through to Starr again in the third quarter, causing him to fumble a second time. Packer offensive tackle Norm Masters managed to recover the fumble, picking the ball off in midair, but they still suffered a five yard loss.

Deacon was, as always, emotional, waving his arms from the sidelines and cheering his teammates on. His total involvement in the game seemed to pick up the entire team. Dick Bass was brilliant, scoring two touchdowns on long runs. The defensive unit rose to the occasion again and again, stopping the Packers' dangerous passing attack on key third-down situations, particularly in the third quarter. But, for all that, the Rams couldn't pull out the victory. They wasted several scoring opportunities late in the game, and Starr managed to connect through the weak L.A. secondary for one last rally, winning 24-17 in the final moments.

And, after that great game and all of the team's heroic efforts, Bob Waterfield looked on the gentlemen from the press with his great, mournful stare and told them the real problem was that his players lacked the enthusiasm and the drive it took to win.

The truth was, except for the San Francisco blowout early in the season and the wild sandlot game in Minnesota, the Rams had been in every game until the final minutes. It had been a season of heartbreakers, with fumbles, interceptions, blown field goal attempts and missed assignments in the team's weak defensive backfield accounting for the losses. But the coach no longer respected them; he had soured on them as a team. They were impostors masquerading in Rams blue and white. Waterfield's real Rams had faded into history, taking their trophies and their stack of wins with them. The reporters joked about them, and all but the true-blue hard-core fans had turned their backs on the team. How could they look for respect from any other team in the league? And worse, how could the players find respect for themselves? Football is a team sport, but if the players didn't respect themselves as individuals, their talent and their passion for the game would wither. Their path seemed dark and gloomy, and with no light at the end of the road.

At the end of the 1961 season came the usual banquet. Ye Olde Rams Club convened to pass out the yearly accolades for best this or that, and Deacon Jones was voted Rams Rookie of the Year, beating out number one draft choice Marlin McKeever and twelve other draft choices selected before him.

Deacon and the other winners donated their awards to a fund for the dying Gene Brito. Ram Rookie of the Year honors meant the world to Deacon personally, but he didn't get much national recognition out of it. "It wasn't the same back then; you didn't get the coverage you do today. I'd had only one game where I was seen nationally, and I'd played well, but the Green Bay Packers were featured in that game. Of course, I did make national coverage with the syndicated photo of me smacking Y. A. Tittle."

Deacon Jones had arrived to teach the gospel of football, and he had shown that he was in the big leagues to stay. But the owners gave nothing away in those days; the players had no bargaining power; Deacon was on his way to becoming famous . . . but, getting rich would be another story. Deacon's one-year contract was renewed for a second year, and the Rams sensational Rookie of the Year came to terms with management for $12,500. To make ends meet, he spent the off-season selling vacuum cleaners door-to-door in L.A.

The Vote

The week before the 1962 season began, the black boys who played for the Rams were hoisting brews and knocking down the pins at a bowling alley on Beverly Boulevard. That's just the way it was in the early

1960s; the whites went somewhere by themselves to drink beers and relax, and so did the blacks.

There were a few dollars on the game, enough to keep Deacon mildly interested, but there was a bigger game in town, and they all knew it. Tomorrow was the vote for team captain, and history looked to be made, because Ollie Matson had enough votes in the bag to become the first black team captain ever in the NFL.

In between slinging the ball down the alley and watching the skirts, the men all muttered and argued. They calculated the odds on the backs of placemats and old score cards. There were thirteen or fourteen black players in the bowling alley on that night, and they swore to a man to vote for Ollie. It should be more than enough. With the black vote and the crossover whites who had also promised their vote, it looked to be Ollie by a landslide. They rolled their final frames, Deacon picked up his money, and they went home.

The next morning they gathered in the old Rams headquarters over on Pico Boulevard. Deacon hung back at the door, studying the crowd. It was a habit he'd picked up from his growing-up years. Always know what you walkin' into, his daddy had warned. Most of the blacks were in a jovial mood. There was a lot of back slapping, high-fives, and general tomfoolery. Some of this spilled over into the whites, but there was a small, quiet group, maybe five or six players and two or three assistant coaches, who sat in an isolated pocket. This group included Jon Arnett, who seemed the favorite among the whites. They didn't seem happy at all, and for good reason—from the hoot and holler going on around the room, Deacon could see the white vote was going to be split among four or five players. Judging by the players who were loudly promoting their favorites, Ollie was going to pick up a significant chunk of white votes, probably as many as Arnett, and the rest of the white vote would be scattered around the room.

Waterfield showed up, and after a short conference with some of the coaches and white players, handed out slips of paper and pencils. After a few minutes, he walked around collecting the names in a hat.

The blacks started chanting, "Count the vote! Count the vote! Count the vote!" and "Oll-ie! Oll-ie! Oll-ie!"

Arnett threw his hands in the air and said angrily, "Well, he's got to have quiet to do this!"

Waterfield started toward the door, heading for the next room with the hatful of votes.

"He should count it here, in front of us!" Deacon said, loud enough to be overheard.

Waterfield paused and gave him a withering stare, "You don't trust me?" Without waiting for an answer, he continued out the room, followed by several of the assistant coaches.

They were gone five minutes, long enough for nervous jokes to pass around the room about how long it took an NFL coach to count to ten. Long enough for Deacon to curse himself for opening his mouth. Long enough for the people in the next room to decide on what they were going to do.

The coaches returned and Waterfield held a hand up for silence.

"It's Jon Arnett by a landslide!" he said.

There were one or two cheers, but most of the room was filled with low and uncertain conversation. The blacks were all cursing under their breath and asking each other Which of us miserable black dogs didn't vote like we swore? They glared at each other, and then they took their own count. Hamp Pool came over and tried to break the group up, hurrying them on to other meetings, but three or four of the blacks just looked at him, and he scurried away with a worried look on his face. The blacks were in a surly mood, and there was none of the usual joking. They asked for a show of hands. What dog hadn't voted for Ollie? There was a long pause, and finally one hesitant arm went in the air. It was Ollie, and he said in a sheepish voice, "Well, you ain't supposed to vote for yourself, are you?"

Still, even without his vote, Ollie should have won by three or four votes at least. A few of the white players came over to see what was going on, and some of them had voted for Ollie as well. Pretty soon, nearly everyone on the team wanted a recount. They sent a few representatives, black and white, over to Waterfield, but he just waved them off with an irritated glance, "Hell," he said, "don't be spoilsports—the voting's over! Arnett won. Now let's go have a beer and celebrate his victory."

The Rams silently trooped out of the building after their coaches, each man lost in his own thoughts. It wasn't an auspicious start to the new season.

In 1994, Ollie Matson talked about how amazed he was at the time. "What they did was most unusual. Every place I'd ever been, and even with the Rams before that, the voting had always been left to the players. But this time, the coaches controlled the functions of the voting, and then left the room to count the votes. And when they came back with the choice of Arnett, almost all the players, white and black, were truly upset. You could hear whites saying to one another, 'Hey, I didn't vote for him, I voted for Ollie!' It was a bad move and it really hurt the team."

Also interviewed in 1994, Pervis Atkins clearly remembered that moment, "Oh, yeah, it really happened. There was Jon Arnett and Red Phillips splitting the white vote, and all the blacks had agreed to vote for Ollie Matson. Ollie was a nice guy, but innocent—he once bought a new Cadillac and didn't know how to get the top down for six months. And Ollie did vote for Jon Arnett. Still, we had thirteen guaranteed votes, and that should have been enough. The coaches left the room with the votes and counted and came back, and Jon Arnett was declared the winner. There was a big stink, and we demanded a recount, but the coaches said no."

It was the last time the Rams would be able to fix the election. A few years later, Jon was traded to Chicago and Lamar Lundy was chosen the first black captain of the Rams. And Deacon became captain after Lamar retired in 1969.

Bonus Baby Blues

In 1962 the Rams switched their training camp from the desert heat of Redlands to the desert heat of Chapman College in the city of Orange. If there was any difference in the climate, it had to be marginal, and after a day on the hot battlefields of football, a big, foamy pitcher of ice-cold beer seemed worth more than all the gold in Fort Knox. Though a keg or two might be shared on weekends, for the average every-day, it was drinking with your own kind, and the blacks used to hurry after practice to Me & Ed's Pizza Parlor, one of the few places they were welcome for a few brews before dinner.

Late one afternoon, Deacon convinced Ollie Matson to drive his big Cadillac in that general direction so they could wet their whistles. The two of them, plus Alvin "Good Hosen" Hall and Lamar Lundy piled onto the plush leather seats. Ollie pushed a button to let the convertible top down as they were wheeling out of the driveway, and they were on the road, happy as kings to be away from the sweat and the pain for a while. At least, Deacon was happy; Lamar had a few concerns over Deacon's recent behavior. "Deacon," he started, "you know, it be the tradition of the Rams, that the player don't talk salary in front of the man, particularly not the black player."

Deacon was leaning, head back against the tan seatback, gazing at the deep blue of the late afternoon sky. "Lamar, don't you start in on me. I just wanted to know what the white rookies was makin'."

Alvin grinned and looked back from his spot in the passenger's seat, "Cousin Deacon causin' trouble again?"

"Obvious, you wasn't there, Good Hosen." Lamar didn't see anything amusing, "We had us a couple kegs in the cafeteria last Saturday night. Some of the crackers were comin' around like you know they always do, demandin' the rooks chug entire pitchers of beer. Deak here sidles up to big white farmboy, Merlin from Utah, an' asks if it be true he got a $100,000 bonus!"

Alvin's laughter was spontaneous, "Deak, you are a crazy man!"

Ollie kept his eyes on the road ahead, but he didn't look happy, "What he say?"

"Oh, Muley admitted it, all right." The bittersweet smile played across Deacon's features for a moment. "He was real proud of it. It be more than his daddy ever made."

"It be more than I'm makin' right now," Ollie said. "Don' get me wrong, fellows, I ain't complainin'."

"Eatin' off the back end of the Ram again," Alvin said.

Ollie half-turned in his seat, "Us out here on the Rams ain't the only ones t' get the big screw." He turned and swerved the car back in his own lane as Deacon yelled, "Do the drivin', Ollie! We all can see you ain't upset!"

"Okay, okay" Ollie said, his good nature returning. "I just wanted to tell what happened to Johnny Sample, acquaintance of mine, plays cornerback for the Pittsburgh Steelers. He tol' me a story about what happened a couple months ago when he was tryin to negotiate his own contract. Last season he made $14,000, an' he had a fantastic year. He had nine interceptions, he was All-League, an' All-Pro, an so he was askin' fo' a raise to $22,000. That sound fair, don't it? But Art Rooney—he the owner of the Steelers—he laugh at that, he says 'I give you $15,500.' Well, Sample refuses, which you gotta know took iron balls right there, 'cause a black man is half off the team anyway. It comes to Rooney won't talk to him no more, he sends him to coach Buddy Parker to get some sense talked into his wooden nigger head. Now Rooney is a legendary cheapskate, an' so Sample don't think much of his problem, he is still thinkin' all he's dealin' wit' here is Rooney's tight wallet. So he sticks to his guns wit' Parker, insistin' he had a great year in 1961, an' spellin' out all the reasons he deserves the raise. Ol' Buddy Parker cuts him short in midsentence when he says, 'I know you had a great year, Sample. But black athletes just don' deserve pay like that, an' we ain't gonna pay it!'"

Deacon spoke up again, "Did you fellas know our other white rookie also got a $100,000 bonus?"

"No shit? Roman Gabriel? How'd you find that out?"

"Asked him. He didn't make no bones about it."

"It ain't easy to do the same job alongside a man makin' ten times what you are, that's for sure." Lamar sighed. Nobody else said anything for a few minutes.

Deacon looked at the unfamiliar highway around them, "Ollie, where the hell are we? Did you get us lost again?"

"Ahh, I must have missed the turn-off, fellas. Don't worry, we somewhere in Orange County."

"Yeah, Ollie, we somewhere on earth, too," Lamar said. "Pull in that gas station—right there!"

Ollie swung the big car in a sweeping, dusty U-turn and they pulled into the service station in a billowy cloud of dust. It was an older no-name station, one of those crumbling stucco southern California places that mixed repairs, groceries, and two pumps out front. They waited thirty seconds, but nobody came out of the building. And suddenly, like a scene from a Keystone Cops movie, black-and-white police cars pulled up in front and back of them, and they were surrounded by four officers with their guns drawn.

"Everybody, hands in the air!" one of the policemen shouted.

"Don't see how they could get any higher," Deacon muttered. "What's goin' on, officers?"

"Keep your hands up an' climb out of there!"

It wasn't easy, but they somehow managed to pile out of the car with their hands in the air. A wizened old man came out of the station, cackling, "Got 'em! Congratulations, officers—you got 'em!"

The officers looked at each other, at the old man, and at the four Negroes. Almost as one man, they put their guns away. The policemen who had first yelled now asked quietly, "You guys got any I.D.?"

Lamar pulled out his wallet, "We all from the Rams camp. We lookin' for this local pizza place."

The officer took one look, pursed his lips, and then handed Lamar's wallet back to him. He blew out a breath, turning so the old man couldn't see what he was saying, "Sorry about this. The old geezer over there got all excited when you pulled in and thought he was being robbed by four black giants. Said it was some sort of gang from L.A. He called you in, and we were just down the street."

The policeman gave them directions, and Ollie swung the big car around, heading back the way they'd come. By now, dusk was settling over Orange County, one of those sunsets that made the land dark while the sky is lit up with fingers of red and gold. Ollie flicked on his lights, and Alvin fiddled with the radio, finding one country-western station after another.

"Lots of rednecks here in southern California," Deacon commented to no one in particular.

"I'm surprised you didn't mouth off at the po-lice," Alvin said.

Deacon shook his head, "Uh-uh-uh, not me. Nor Lamar, either. He's from southern Indiana—heartland home of the Klan, you can look it up in the travel guide. Where we come from, the upholders of the law shoot first an' talk later. These southern California officers of the law were downright courteous, to my mind." They traveled in silence for a few more miles.

Alvin finally gave up on the radio. He looked over at the driver, "Ollie, fess up—you got us lost again!"

Deacon spotted a big neon sign up the road, "Yellow Rose Bar. Pull in, Ollie, before we die of thirst."

Matson wheeled his big car into the wide and nearly deserted gravel parking lot, and once again dust flew in the air. The four of them silently marched into the place, which proved to be full of nearly empty tables. The bartender hitched his suspenders, pushed back his ten-gallon hat on his bald head and eyed them gravely from the other side of a long bar. One end of the huge room had a raised platform for a band, but the music in the place came from a juke box. Guitars twanged and Marty Robbins wailed about brown-eyed Spanish girls and death in the afternoon.

"Round of beers," Deacon said, throwing a five-dollar bill on the bar. The bartender didn't say anything as he served them. The four of them drank their beer in one swig, and turned, elbows and back to the bar, to look around the room. Three or four of the tables here and there were spotted with men wearing shit-kicker boots and blue jeans. Everyone had stopped whatever they were doing and was looking at them.

"Funny crowd," Deacon said. "I'm beginnin' to realize where every redneck who ever left the South ended up."

"Maybe we better go," Lamar said quietly.

Ollie nodded, "Yeah, come on, Deak." As they headed for the door, Ollie looked back and said in an offhand way, "Well, see you later."

"Like hell you will," the bartender said.

Deacon half-turned, like he was about to start something. Lamar took his arm on one side, and Ollie on the other. "Come on, Deak," Lamar implored, "le's just get out of here."

"Yeah, come on," Ollie said, "We already had us enough entertainment out of Orange County fo' one evening."

Deacon nodded and slowly unclenched his fists. Leaving probably was a great idea; as they headed for the door, they passed the reinforcements, a few more truckloads of cowboys coming in for a night of brews and hee-haws. Outside, the air was fresh and cool. Stars shone in the night sky over the parking lot, and the deeply potholed lot itself was starting to take on pickup trucks and an assortment of beat-up Dodges, Chevies, and Fords. Off in the distance, Mt. Waterman showed its jagged black tooth against a blue-black sky. The four Rams quietly climbed back in Ollie's car.

"Training camp's that way," Alvin said, pointing to the dying glow to the west. "Maybe we can still catch us some dinner." Ollie started the big V-8 and pulled the long white Cadillac back onto the road.

Lem Barney, Detroit's great defensive back, played for eleven years in the late 1960s and in the 1970s. Lem, who broke the "roommates color barrier" on the Lions in 1969 when he and white player Mike Wegner roomed together, said of the salary disparities that existed in the NFL, "I started playing six years after Deak came into the league. Of course, I knew him through his antics, and his intimidating, ominous, daring style of play. By the late 1960s, NFL management was no longer so blatant as to come right out and tell you you weren't worth as much. We black players on the Lions were aware our white counterparts were making more. There would be a white guy at the same position, or a white guy who wasn't getting as much time on the field—but in the negotiating procedures, you knew you weren't in his financial category, and there was nothing you could do about it. Management was getting more polished; that translates to say the discrimination was going underground."

Uplift

By the time the Rams team left Tiger Stadium and showed up at Detroit Metro to take the long, long journey home, they had played five regular season games, and lost them all. True, they had been close, hard-fought, bitter games, but in the end the result was always the same. Last-minute fumbles, interceptions, and lapses in the Rams secondary; one way or another, Los Angeles managed to self-destruct, and was saddled with another defeat.

Their red-eye flight had been delayed by fog, and the plane would be at least an hour late, so the entire team spread out in the bar/cafeteria at the airport, nursing drinks gotten from one side of the big room and chewing the warmed-over eggs and pizza served all hours of the night and day on the other side. The blacks huddled together at a few corner tables, sipping beers and trying to look invisible to the coaching staff, which was belly-up to the bar and showing their dangerous loud and aggressive mood. It was blame time, again, and the coaching staff of the Rams didn't take blame, they gave it.

Outside, illuminated by huge spotlights, passenger planes whined and grumbled through the drifting fog. Inside, in one of the few booths near the bar, Waterfield was having a long, unhappy conversation with his gorgeous wife, Jane Russell, and every now and then their argument peaked over the general hub-bub in the room. Jane Russell wasn't just Waterfield's wife; she was a movie star celebrity in the middle of a long and lustrous career (She would star in twenty-five movies over four decades, from 1943 to 1983. Russell burst on the public scene with her sultry role in her first movie, Howard Hughes's *The Outlaw,* where she appeared wearing what the movie marketing people claimed was a "super uplift" brassiere, a device supposedly designed by Hughes himself to highlight her considerable bosom.) Russell was no shrinking violet on-screen or in real life. A dark-haired beauty with flashing eyes and a tart and clever tongue, she was well-liked by the Ram coaches, the players and their wives for her wit and her no-airs attitude.

Hollywood promoted Jane Russell as a good-bad woman, that is, a rough-talking woman of worldly ways who, underneath her brusk exterior, was actually a lady possessing strong moral values and a heart of gold. Roles in her range could include that of the tough, two-fisted hard-liquor drinker. It was a case of life imitating art. In her autobiography, she cites numerous instances, some of them funny and some sad, where she drank a great deal. For instance, she talks freely about an affair she had with a man she dubs "Lance," in 1957 when she was working on "The Fuzzy Pink Nightgown," a box-office flop and the one film that Bob Waterfield, who was then her husband, produced. "It had been a truly beautiful relationship, " Russell writes of her relationship with Lance. "Yet, because we were drunk, I'm sure, we did the one thing I'd sworn I would never do. We went to bed."[1] Later in her book, she talked about the years after she divorced Waterfield, how alcohol became a real problem, and how she fought and, after enormous difficulties, overcame it. "There was nothing to hold me together but memories. And drinking. I was doing a great deal of that and everyone was going crazy trying to keep me away from it. Drinking and staring at walls were all I was interested in doing."

Waterfield and Russell were busy, strong-willed people with careers that tended to pull them apart. Their relationship was stormy, with the fireworks occasionally spilling uncomfortably out into the public view. There had been incidents, near-brawls and the like, that were not in keeping with Waterfield's "golden boy" sports hero image of yesteryear. Russell describes one of the more serious of their public quarrels, which took place in 1952,

> When *The Las Vegas Story* [a movie in which she starred] came out, it was to open in Vegas, naturally. The night before, Robert [Bob Waterfield, then her husband], Bob Kelly (sports announcer), Hamp Pool (Ram coach), Ozzie Lang (Schlitz beer representative), John Sanders (Ram coach), Don Paul (Ram center), and their wives, all drove up. I'd been working a lot and really missed Robert, but he wasn't content to just be with me . . . I was feeling sorry for myself. We were all drinking a lot, and at dinner he said something nasty and I ran my fork down his face, leaving four little red lines. He didn't do anything, but tears of humiliation formed in his eyes. Everyone watched in silence. When we got home he went to the mirror and looked at his face. I came up behind him and said, "Honey, I'm so sorry." He just turned and slapped me. I fell back, but stupid me, I didn't stay there. I was mad as hell. He had never slapped me before. I said, "Oh, I'm sure you can hit harder than that," so he did. I got up as many times as I could, and finally, when the room was spinning, I said, "You poor fool, you don't have any idea what you've just done." He left without a word.

---

1. *Jane Russell: My Path and My Detours* (New York: Franklin Watts, Inc, 1985), p. 176.

In a following passage, Russell tells how sorry Waterfield was afterward for his behavior, and she blames the alcohol, "I had decided it was because we were drinking. If we hadn't both been loaded, it would never have happened."[2]

As the night dragged on in the cafeteria at Detroit Metro, Waterfield and Russell continued their argument. From a table across the room, Dick Bass smiled his wicked smile and lifted his drink. "To beautiful, sharp-tongued ladies," he said softly. "Sure takes Bob's mind off the game, don't she?" Deacon had noticed that, while Dick Bass practiced speaking the king's English, his dialogue with his fellows slid back and forth between perfect diction and the expressive, lilting black-to-black patois and the joshing, informal slang of the players in general. Anybody probably could do that, if they had an ear for it, and listened. Deacon himself had gotten away with sounding like a white man on the telephone, just for fun, or when he needed information or something that might be resented coming from a black man. He wondered if Dick even knew he talked like that.

They were watching Jane go at Bob out of the corners of their eyes, turning every now and then, making it look casual like they were really studying the clock or the interesting old lady scooping milky eggs behind the cafe counter. That is, all of them except Dick Bass; raised in liberal Northern California, his reflexes were more those of a white man, and he just boldly stared right at them.

"Remind me never to take you home to Florida," Deacon said.

"Or anywhere between Texas and Georgia," Lamar added. "You'll be dead an' buried before we can get you back on the plane."

Dick waved them off with a scoffing, backhand gesture worthy of an English dandy, "This is the sexy sixties, my friends. Age of opportunity for the gentleman of color."

While the others hooted Bass, Ollie shook his head sadly, still thinking about the game. "You fellas stop to realize that Bratkowski an' Miller only completed four passes all afternoon?"

Deacon grinned, "Yeah, if you're only counting members of our own team."

"Sure puts pressure on the run," Ollie observed unhappily.

Bass snorted, "Hell, nobody runs against the Lions."

"Can you believe those lineup shifts? Moving Les Richter to center and Marlin McKeever an' Merlin Olsen to offensive guards was the thinkin' of a desperate man."

---

2. *Jane Russell: My Path and My Detours,* p.123, 124.

"Where was our fabulous rookie QB, anyway?" Bass asked in a voice nearly loud enough to be heard in Cleveland. "There's the $100,000 question!"

If Waterfield weren't so preoccupied with his domestic problems, he would surely have had an answer of some kind. Actually, Waterfield's stubborn refusal to play rookie quarterback Roman Gabriel was on everybody's mind. Reporters filled the papers with their theories, and rumors and gossip were everywhere.

Alvin Hall mournfully looked into his half-empty beer mug. "Stoneface ain't gonna let him play. He thinks there's only one kind of passer—touch passer, like he was. Gabe's a cannon out there. Hell, he'll knock you over with that ball."

Ollie nodded, "That be true enough. The young man could learn to back off on the heat. But that come with time."

Bass shook his head. "No. That comes with experience, my dear friend Ollie. And he's not ever going to get any, long as Bob is the boss." Bass's grin took on a wicked light, "Now me—I think its all that personal stuff, myself."

Lamar shot him a warning glance, "Bass, you gonna get hung by the neck until dead, talkin' that way. It don't matter we in Detroit, L.A., or Mobile, Alabama, Bob'll find a way to get a rope around one of them palm trees an' your neck an' do it hisself!"

Deacon nodded, "He'll hang you from the arch in the Coliseum." Again, Bass waved them off with a toss of his hand.

Bob was a handsome man, tall and athletic, and growing old gracefully in a grey-templed, noble sort of way. In another life, he could have easily played an aging leading man. Roman Gabriel was also a good-looking fellow. A ladies man from the word go, he took for granted that women would fall for him, and they usually did. Gabe was the young stud on the block, and outgoing and personable as Waterfield's wife was, Russell and Gabe had developed an easy, bantering relationship that Bob couldn't possibly have ignored. It looked innocent enough—after all, Jane was friendly with everyone—but to a lot of the guys on the team it looked like Waterfield thought she was using the young quarterback to bait him.

"Easy, easy, Lamar." Bass put both hands in the air, as if he was pushing away evil. "I didn't say they were engaged in intimacies, though the flesh is weak, as the Bible says, and they well may be. My point is, Bob thinks they are. And that means hell will freeze before he hands that boy the football."

Ollie looked around the table, "What did Stoneface tell the press after the game? I couldn't bear to stay."

Deacon shrugged, "Same old thing. We didn't want the win bad enough. I was right there. He didn't care I heard what he said or not."

Lamar looked downcast. "We been playin' our hearts out. Deacon here nails Milt Plum for a fifteen yard loss, blocks a field goal, and the both of us are in the Lions backfield all afternoon, an' he tells the reporters that kind of crap! Man, I wish so bad they'd trade me somewhere!"

The intercom squawk bleated out their flight number, and they wearily picked up their hand luggage and made their way to the plane. It was well after midnight by the time they took off; even flying the new 707 nonstop to L.A., dawn would be breaking by the time they landed.

For some reason, seating was all screwed up, and Waterfield, Russell and the coaching staff ended up in the very back of the plane. They were all so emotionally drained that nobody bothered to fix things, to give the players the worse seats where things were a little more cramped and the engine howl a constant in your ears. Even though it was dark, and the shades were pulled over the little round windows, Deacon had made sure Lamar got the window seat. He was sitting on the aisle, and Bob and Jane were sitting a few seats behind him, and every once in a while he could overhear them bitching at each other.

Deacon couldn't sleep, and he started to think back, mentally ticking off the season. Their first game, against Baltimore, he had come out with the slogan Kill Johnny Unitas. That day, he, Lamar, John LoVetere, Merlin Olson, and the Rams linebackers had made the great quarterback miserable. It had started so beautifully! He personally had tackled Unitas in the first quarter, averting a huge gainer on a QB keeper. He dropped Unitas three times behind the line that day. He also deflected Tom Gilburg's fourth-down punt and made a critical tackle when fullback Mark Smolinski tried to sneak through on a draw play. And they said he could only play the pass! If you were quick enough, you could play everything! In the fourth quarter, the Rams were winning, 27-16. But the Colts scored one touchdown, and then Rams fullback Art Perkins fumbled on the twenty-seven! All he had to do was hang on to that football, and they would have won the game. Still, even after that, it was close like a bitch. On fourth down—the Colts' last chance—Unitas eluded the entire charging Rams front line to throw a touchdown to Jimmy Orr. Final score, Colts 30, Rams 27.

As usual, Waterfield spent no time praising his team's efforts. He told the press after the game that it was "the most disappointing loss in his coaching career."

After that heartbreaker, the Rams played the Bears in their home-opener at the Coliseum. The temperature was 101; Deacon remembered how he and Lamar drank a lot of lemonade and went after Bear quarterback Billy Wade. Kill Billy Wade! They harassed him the entire game, forcing him out of his timing, and Deacon twice caught him behind the line for losses. But in the end a Bratkowski fumble and an interception on a poorly thrown pass led to the Bears' win, 24-23. Surrounded by reporters in the Rams locker room, Waterfield had said, "It's pretty bleak."

"Let's talk about the bright side," one reporter suggested.

"I don't see anything pleasing," Waterfield replied. "Nothing at all."

The reporters described how, in the other locker room, old George Halas smiled like the cat who'd just eaten the canary. "There's nothing wrong with the Rams," he declared, his ancient, crafty face ruddy with victory. "This is the best Ram team I've seen in ten years."

The following week, they lost to Dallas, 27-17. *L.A. Times* writer Mal Florence said of the game, "In the city of futility, no one is more futile than the Rams." Waterfield, on the other hand, went out of his way to praise the Cowboys defense. Pressed on whether he planned any radical changes, he replied, "We have to do something, but right now I don't know what it will be."

The week after that, they flew to Washington, D.C. The Redskins, usually a doormat for the rest of the league, used Norm Snead's long-range passing attack to take advantage of the Rams weak secondary, and won 20-14. By this time, the Rams co-owners were becoming restless with the leadership of Dan Reeves. Disgruntled Ed Pauley made his comments available to the press: "It's a game I think we should have won instead of lost." Waterfield, now surrounded by reporters, insisted Bratkowski was still his number one quarterback. Pressed as to why he chose to send in Ron Miller rather than Roman Gabriel, the coach curtly replied, "Did you see Gabriel warming up? He couldn't hit anything."

And now, the game they'd played earlier today. After all the sweat and glory, Lions 13, Rams 10. Deacon knew his defensive line was holding the opposing teams close. Week after week, they were putting in their Herculean effort. But they were getting no credit for all their efforts, particularly from their boss. Put it out of your mind, boy. The hour is late and you are tired. He leaned back in his seat and tried to rest, even though his six-foot-six inch frame was bunched up against the lowered seat back in front of him. He slept on and off, and finally woke when the wheels were lowered with a heavy clunk and locked down for their landing.

The landing at LAX was uneventful, and they taxied across the runway and came to a halt before the terminal. Everyone stretched and yawned. The doors finally opened, and, disconnected and half-asleep, they started to stagger off the plane. After the coaches passed, Deacon stood in the aisle trying to get the kinks out of his back.

"Pardon me," a sleepy voice behind him slurred. It was Jane, half-standing and hanging on to the seat behind him. Deacon caught a momentary thrill of fear, just a little jolt, that black men from the South always feel in moments like that. It passed quickly as he remembered where he was. The NFL. California. Things were different here. A little different, at least.

"Oh, sorry, Mrs. Waterfield," he said, stepping back out of the aisle and bending half over to avoid hitting his head on the overhead baggage compartment. "You kin go past."

But Jane couldn't go past. Feet splayed like a mule, she took one step and tumbled on her face in the aisle. She laughed to herself and tried to get up, singing some song he'd heard her singing in the bar back in Detroit. Deacon reached for his luggage, trying to ignore her. When she got like this, Waterfield and one of his assistants usually escorted her off the plane. Or sometimes some of the white boy veteran players would do the deed. But Waterfield must have been too angry or disgusted to remember, or maybe he was wondering what to do with the rest of his career, now that he was enmeshed in losing football. Deacon looked around, but the compartment in front of them was empty, everyone else already having left the plane.

"Oh, God, Lamar—You got to help me here!"

But Lamar was turned the other way, like he was busy with his luggage. He'd been fooling with that luggage since Jane spoke up, and if he had to, he was prepared to work on it until the work crew came to clean up the plane.

It was one of the hardest decisions of Deacon's life. He knew dozens—hundreds of stories of black men who were silently and swiftly murdered for just looking the wrong way at a white woman. Poor, confused Till dead for wolf-whistlin' a white woman, when all it was was a speech defect! The old, cruel images played in his mind like horror movies. But, on the other hand, his Mama had raised him to respect all women, white or black. He'd grown up having to take care of his five sisters at home. He knew what was expected of him.

In spite of Lamar's low, warning, "No, no, no, Deacon. I wouldn't do that, man.", Deacon bent over and lifted her to her feet. After that, he felt committed to taking care of her, but he didn't know what else to do. In her present state she was more like jello, all giggling and jiggling, but absolutely not capable of maneuvering by herself.

"Bring my bag," he said to Lamar, tossing it to him before he could say yes or no.

Then Deacon reached down and picked Jane up, and started down the aisle. Jane had her arms around his neck.

"Take me behind the barn, Clevis," she said softly. "You're so strong." Bombed out of her mind, she was playing a scene from one of those sensational plantation romances, where the white southern belle has an affair with the huge black slave. Deacon was tempted to drop her right there. He couldn't see where he was going, and so they weren't making much progress down the aisle. His slow passage was interrupted by a rough voice. "Hey, Jones, what you doin' with my wife?"

Deacon's blood ran cold. It was Stoneface, himself. Visions of murder and death swam before Deacon's eyes and ran riot in his brain. "I— I'm just tryin' to get her off the plane, coach. I wasn't sure anybody was comin' back for her."

By now, she was limp as a rag, and snoring to boot. It was the snoring that probably saved his life.

"Hand her over," Waterfield said. Deacon did so, and found himself looking straight into his coach's face which, as he reached to take her, was only about a foot away. Deacon could see the man's jaw was still set like granite—but there was a world of pain in his bloodshot eyes. "Don't ever say anything to anyone about this," Waterfield warned him in a soft, whispery voice that seemed filled with cloaked fury and sadness at the same time.

"I won't," Deacon was about to promise. But Old Stoneface didn't want to hear anything from him. He'd already turned away with his wife and was heading off the plane.

Predictor Dick

On the Monday morning after the seventh Rams loss in eight games, the players moved around the locker room like zombies. On their own side of the room, the black players wandered about glumly and tried not to think about the period of anger and recrimination that was nearly upon them.

"Blame and shame time, fellas," Ollie said, trying to make light of what was to come. "Let's go, we got to suit up!"

"Oh, man, man, man, trade me now," Alvin Hall muttered from his corner, "so I don't have to hear all that yellin' an' screamin'.'"

"You ain't gonna get traded," Pervis Atkins said. "Waterfield is."

"You don't know that," Deacon said. "Reeves ain't that smart."

"Gentlemen, it's a sure bet," Dick Bass chimed in. "Fan discontent mounts, ticket sales slump, and the situation clearly cannot last. What do you do? Shoot the coach, naturally."

"Better him than us," Lamar said. "Maybe we get somebody good."

Dick shook his head sadly, like it was all settled and he knew all about it, "Eat your heart out, Hoosier-boy. No real professional leader of men would come here to be slave-coach under the hard whiplash of Mister Daniel Reeves. How many coaches has he used up since he came to L.A.?"

"Don't forget, Reeves has four co-owners to fight with."

"Sure, but Reeves always pulls the strings. How many coaches, I ask?"

Ollie, somewhat of a team historian by reason of having been in the league longer than anyone, started counting on his fingers, "Snyder lasted the first year, 1947, I believe . . . Shaughnessy was here in 1948 an' '49 . . . Stydahar lasted two . . . Hamp Pool, three . . . an' then Sid Gilman, a whole five years!"

"Reeves always stuck with Waterfield so far," Deacon protested. He'd come to think of Old Stoneface as a permanent fixture in his professional career. "The man is a proven loser—nine wins against twenty-three losses, an' he's still here."

"No, Deacon. Even a stubborn fool like Reeves has to see the light sometime. And that 'sometime' is when it shines through the hole in his worn-out old pocket book." Dick seemed utterly confident.

"If no good coach will take the job, who's he gonna get, then?"

Dick smiled, "One of Waterfield's lackeys, of course."

Deacon pulled his shoulder pads on over his head and looked at Dick. The natty little running back was still dressed in his English tweed suit, leaning against a corner locker. He didn't seem to care that he would be late on the field. That no-cut contract of his covered a lot of ground. "Okay, Dick," Deacon said, "since you know so much about this—who's gonna get it?"

Dick smiled as if he'd been waiting for the opportunity, "Now boys, we all know it's been neck an' neck between Hamp an' Harland." Hamp Pool was the offensive coach, Harland Svare the defensive coach. "And it is my belief that Suave Svare, who has to see Hamp as his biggest rival, has finally managed to turn the tables and get the knife in the Old Swamp Foxes back! I, Dick Bass, therefore personally predict our new head coach will be none other than Harland Svare!"

"Harland?" The room exploded in a round of derisive catcalls and laughter. "Harland ain't no older than Ollie, here! He don't know shit from Shinola! He's just barely an assistant coach! You a sharp dresser, Bass—but you sure as hell can't tell the future!" Lamar was the only one who took the idea seriously, "Well, it do make a kind of sense, if it had to be one of the assistant coaches. After all, defense keeps us in most our games." True or not, the blacks who played offense naturally hooted that one down.

Dick stretched, immensely proud of himself, and held his hands up for quiet. "Well, then, good fellows, you don't believe me! But just answer me this one question—how come the Suave Swede is over there right now?" Dick jerked one thumb in the general direction of the Rams offices, "He's subbing for Waterfield at the Monday morning meeting with the football writers!" Dick bowed like a gracious potentate and wandered off to check his mustachio in the mirror and then suit up at his own pace. He didn't seem to care that he'd left behind a room full of disbelief and wonder. If anything, he was pleased. Couldn't the boys have figured out that one by themselves? Apparently not, apparently not.

One by one and in small clumps, the players finished dressing and ran out on the practice field. There was still no official announcement, but something was clearly up; Waterfield was nowhere in sight, nor was Svare. The few assistant coaches who did show their faces on the field were subdued and involved in quiet conversations with each other. It was an oddly quiet practice session, run by the numbers almost as if the players didn't exist. There was nobody screaming at the defensive line and the receivers, nobody howling at Miller to put more steam on the ball and Gabriel to put less, and—most telling of all—no yelling about the team's performance in the previous Sunday's game, a bitter defensive struggle against the Lions in which the Rams were limited to twenty-two yards rushing, Bratkowski lost forty-seven yards attempting to pass, and the L.A. team lost by a final score of 12-3. The mood was somber, coaches and players all looking inward and calculating the possibilities and what change might mean for each of them personally.

Deacon did his warmup laps with Ollie and Dick. Bass, supremely confident, kept explaining why it had to be Svare. "Look, fellows—he's the perfect choice. He'll come cheap, and Dan likes cheap. And he's inexperienced, so Dan can bend him to his will. Little Danny likes to be the boss."

Deacon shook his head, "Dick, I'm just a simple country boy from Florida, willing to buy almost any story—but you can't convince me of what you're preaching today."

"Why not, Swamp Boy?"

"I'm sorry, Slick Richard—It's just too totally far-fetched and absurd. After all, there's a hundred assistant coaches in the league with more experience. Proven winners, too."

"I didn't say he's the best man, Deak. He's just in the right place at the right time."

"Uh-uh, Dick. I'm not buying it." Deacon ran stride for stride with the two running backs, absolutely convinced that Bass was the worst predictor in the world. But life in the NFL could be terribly strange; unfortunately for Deacon Jones and the entire Rams team, Dick Bass had never been more right about anything in his entire life.

Harland Svare was younger than many of his players. He didn't have the experience or the know-how for the job, but who can blame him? It's hard for any player to make that leap to the ranks of the coaches. Interviewed recently at his sports physical fitness and rehabilitation clinic in San Diego, Svare's young-old face broke into a smile, and his eyes twinkled, "I couldn't wait to do it! Looking back, I can see that I was grossly inexperienced—but back then, what an opportunity!"

Today, Svare insists all the supposed intrigue among Waterfield's assistant coaches was "rumors and idle locker room talk from players who had nothing better to do." The real truth, he insists, was a lot less interesting. "When Waterfield left, no one else was available at the moment, and Reeves simply hired me as interim head coach."

It was a logical choice, assuming Reeves and the other owners were going to limit their search to the L.A. staff. Svare was young and untried as a head coach, but he had a reputation for toughness and he'd tasted victory as a player and assistant coach on the New York squad; and he was in good company as the fourth New York Giant-trained coach active in the league at that time, the other three being Vince Lombardi, Tom Landry, and Allie Sherman.

Here Come Harland

As a young linebacker out of Washington State, Harland "Swede" Svare had been the Rams seventeenth round draft pick in 1953. He was traded to the Giants after the 1954 season, where he'd played linebacker on the great Giants teams of the late 1950s. In 1960, Tom Landry, who was then the Giants defensive coach, took Svare, Andy Robustelli, and Jimmy Patten and made them player-coaches. In 1961, when Allie Sherman took over as head coach of the Giants, Svare was told he could either become full-time defensive coordinator or go back to playing linebacker. Svare was only thirty, and he wanted to play some more. On the other hand, he realized that a very rare opportunity was knocking, so he reluctantly hung up his spikes for the chalkboard and the sideline earphones.

Svare's job lasted one year, and, after a loss to Green Bay and an argument with Sherman (the Packers crushed the Giants 37-0 in the NFL championship game in subfreezing Wisconsin weather), Svare went back to L.A., where he lived during the off-season. At the start of the 1962 season, he was walking across a parking lot in L.A. when he ran into defensive coach Don Paul; he hemmed and hawed around a bit, and finally got to the part where he was out of a job. Paul was overjoyed with the serendipity of the moment. He said he himself was quitting as defensive coach to concentrate on his booming restaurant business (Paul had opened The Ram's Horn in the San Fernando Valley some years before, and things were going very well for him), and asked Svare if he'd like to take over his spot with the Rams.

While a lucky moment, it was not all that outlandish to consider Svare for the slot. After all, under his command the Giants defense had gone 10-3-1 and gone all the way to the championship game. If the brutal winter weather, which was particularly suited to Green Bay, had been different, they might even have walked off with the NFL crown.

Svare said yes to Don Paul and the Rams, and as defensive coach, was instrumental in snagging bonus rookie Merlin Olsen, who could

also play offense, for his defensive line. This may not have paid immediate dividends in the win-loss column, but over the years it would be
of enormous significance to the team.

Svare's coaching resume clearly wasn't extensive. At the time of
Waterfield's resignation (or dismissal, depending on who you talk to),
he had been player-coach and then defensive coach for one year with
the Giants, and then defensive coach for eight games with the Rams.

On that fateful Tuesday, the morning after he had handled the regular day-after-game press conference for Waterfield, Svare was pulling
his car into the Rams parking lot and saw Waterfield heading the
other way. The young defensive coach brought his car to a stop and
stuck his head out the window.

"Hey, Bob! Where are you going? We're supposed to be starting
practice."

"I'm going pheasant hunting," Waterfield replied, "and if you
have any sense, you'll come with me." Bob eyed Svare for a moment,
shrugged, and drove on without another word.

Svare turned down the hunting invitation; instead, at the youthful
age of thirty-one, he accepted the offer to become head coach of the
Rams. The *Los Angeles Times* commented, "Svare is acclaimed by all for
molding a respectable Ram defense in the light of a 1-7 record." The
papers generally recorded the grim details; Svare was taking over the
most challenging job in the league, the Rams having lost thirty-two
of their last forty-two games. Bob Oates, writing for the *Herald Examiner,* tried hard to put the new appointment in a positive light:

> A man named Harland Svare stood up at a Rams meeting today and
> said, "This team can win." Svare, an assistant coach for less than
> three years in New York and Los Angeles, outlined a new all-day
> program of meetings and practices for a squad that has been work-
> ing from 11 to 3 and he began implementing it with a revised staff.
> Two new player-coaches, London Crow and Les Richter, have taken
> charge of the defense, with Jim David moving to a role as player-
> scout. Hampton Pool and line coach Vic Lindskog remain with the
> other platoon, Pool as offensive coach.

Citing the long list of close games the Rams had lost, Oates went on
to eulogize the outgoing coach, and to allude to the pressures of coaching for the Rams

Waterfield will live in the memory of the Rams as their most popular player and most unlucky coach. When Waterfield succeeded
Gilman in 1960, he said he thought it would take five years to
rebuild the Rams. This year's series of near-misses would seem to
indicate the club was on this game plan. But in Los Angeles, few
coaches are allowed five years. Some have been given only five
months.

So the press, which had been hounding Reeves to make some big
changes, backed off at least temporarily; Svare would have his chance
to prove he was a good head coach. Now all that remained to be seen
was whether he could rally the team around him and lead them on to
winning football.

*In her autobiography, Jane Russell talks about Waterfield leaving
the Rams, "In 1962 in New York State at a dinner theater where I
was doing Bells Are Ringing, he (Waterfield) called and said,
'Honey, do you care if I quit?' He'd been having a terrible time
coaching. There were five owners and only two would speak to
each other. He had to get five okays to make any decision. It was
killing him."*

*"I answered, 'Hell no. Come back here with Edith and me. We'll
go to New York, the two of us, and have a blast seeing the shows
on Broadway. He did, just like that. When the press asked him what
kind of a coach he thought he'd been, he gave the typical Waterfield answer. 'Losing,' he said. He resigned in November . . . 'for the
good of the team' and came East the next night."[3]*

*Deacon remembers that Waterfield took his dismissal from pro-
fessional football hard. "Bob couldn't accept any sort of life away
from football. He was born and bred a local hero, a college and
pro football quarterback genius, married a famous movie star,
moved on to coach the mighty Rams. But in later life, he couldn't
live up to the expectations the good people of Southern California
had placed on him, and it all came crashing down. He drank
whiskey up and down Ventura Boulevard in the San Fernando Valley. The life of fame can do that to you . . . Lord knows it did enough
to me." Deacon frowns for a moment, and then a thought softens
the harsh lines on his face. "But I tell you, there was a time, Bob
Waterfield could really throw that football. No one can ever take
that away from him."*

Jane Russell talks about Waterfield's life after football, "He

---

3. *Jane Russell: My Path and My Detours*, p. 210.

rediscovered pool. He had been dropping by that neighborhood bar for years and had never picked up a cue, but suddenly he started playing and everyone wanted to play him. It became his life. Every morning, from the minute he awoke until 2:00 A.M. he was at the Barrel, except for dinner. He'd come home then, eat, and ask me to go back with him. I did try a few times, but it was not for me. The guys were all decent enough, but the conversation never left football or pool."[4]

Bob Waterfield and Jane Russell were divorced in 1966. He died in 1983 at the age of 62. Russell is, at this printing, still alive. She is widely recognized for her work as a great actress. Less widely known is her life-long dedication to the WAIF organization, which she helped found in the 1940s, and which has helped over 40,000 orphaned children to find homes with adoptive parents. Through it all, Russell has been, in real life, a good-bad woman with a heart of gold.

4. *Jane Russell: My Path and My Detours*, p. 215.

5

Learning the Game

There were five games left in the 1962 season, and, under young Harland Svare, the team lost four and tied one. Svare would coach twelve games before winning his first for the Rams. In his three and a half years as the L.A. head coach—in fact, in his entire career as a head coach—he would never have a winning season.

The Rams long losing streak would continue, but things were vastly changed for the players. As Svare had told the press the day he took the reins, the country club days were over. Under Bob Waterfield, the Rams had reported on weekdays at a leisurely eleven o'clock in the morning. Their workdays were short, consisting of one ninety-minute practice followed by a meeting. Svare knew the Rams were making mistakes and muffing a lot of plays due to lack of practice. To correct that, he blew the whistle at 9:30 in the morning and insisted on a full day of football. Every practice day there was at least one tough, two-hour workout and two meetings. Some days, there were a lot more.

As the seemingly endless losing season waned into late November, the days between games grew harsher. Svare, always a believer of full-contact practices, of hitting and hitting until the team "got it right," continued a relentless and rigorous schedule, and his practice sessions got longer and longer.

Screamers

The press went into the customary honeymoon period with the Rams new head coach. They reported him as open and agreeable, a pleasant switch from Waterfield, who could be curt and aloof. Noting his stylish attire, they soon dubbed him the "suave Swede." But the Rams players quickly found there was another side to their young coach. Almost immediately, they dropped the "suave" and just called him "Swede."

If Deacon Jones had wanted to impress his new boss, he started off well enough with five solo tackles against Johnny Unitas and the powerful Colts. The papers, less interested in individual effort than in the end result, chortled, "New Coach, Old Rams, Same Old Story," and recorded how several missed scoring opportunities had ruined Svare's debut. But the defense had accounted well for itself, and Svare was quoted with what would become his lifelong theme, "Hard work to improve our execution and sustain our attack is the only solution."

But the following week, John Brodie and the San Francisco 49ers showed up with a new strategy meant to take advantage of Deacon's speed and turn his strength into a weakness. Billy Kilmer, who later found success as a quarterback, was then an exciting running back with San Francisco. Kilmer, interviewed by telephone in 1993, explains San Francisco's strategy: "Deacon was the fastest defensive lineman we'd ever seen. His pure speed set him apart. But this was in Deacon's raw youth as a lineman, and he didn't have all his tricks down, so we were able to trap him behind our line, because he was so fast."

There were a lot of things to learn in the NFL, and reading the play was one of the most important. Deacon was beating his man on nearly every play, but San Francisco was calculating the hole he left, trapping him in the backfield, and running over the position he'd vacated. Although Svare didn't say much for the press, the following Tuesday he announced a full-contact scrimmage.

The players were amazed; nobody in the NFL scrimmaged during the season, it was too dangerous. There was too much chance the regulars would be injured. There was nothing subtle about Svare. He ran the same double-team block against Deacon for an hour, over and over again. After the third or fourth time the same running play came at him, the young defensive end got the idea; Svare was punishing him for his play in the San Francisco game. Since the Swede didn't call anything else, Deacon found it easy to jam the play up solid, time after time. But after the tenth time the play ran, both the offense and the defense began to look at each other, wondering what the idea was. It was not only physically gruelling, the session had drifted from instruction into mindless vengeance. If this kept on, somebody was certain to get hurt.

Not that Svare and Hamp Pool weren't doing their best to communicate. Where Waterfield had been silent as a stone, Svare and Pool were both ranting screamers. As the single-play scrimmage continued, they poured invective on both sides of the line until the players were jumpy as cats.

After twenty-odd repetitions of the same play, Deacon uncurled and pulled himself out from under the pile of Rams and looked over at Lamar, "Hey, Lamar, what they yellin' at you about?"

"I can't even tell any more, Deak. They just yellin' to be heard."

Deacon shot him a worried look. "Swede's threatening he's gonna trade me."

"Trade you? That'll be the day. The fans will lynch him, first."

"Still, he's sayin' it."

"Kinda makes you lonesome for old Stoneface." Lamar glanced over to see if Svare was looking and quickly went back to his side of the line. The blacks all knew the coaches didn't like it when they spent too much time talking to each other on the field. It made them uneasy, like maybe they were plotting a revolution.

As the same play came up time after time, Deacon went into his survival mode. He practiced more than stopping the play; he made sure to pick up his feet, to keep them pumping, and to roll into a ball after the tackle, when the weight of the play came crashing down on him. After all, he had come to play in the big leagues, and nothing was going to stop him. If Swede is that intent on grinding down his own players, he thought to himself, I'm going to be the last rock to go.

It was bruising and dangerous on the practice field, and the coaching staff filled the air with recriminations and abuse, but the players were certain this particular madness could only go on for a fairly brief period in their lives. As Dick Bass, who was still living in the glory of his earlier predictions, told them, "Not to worry, gentlemen. Mister Daniel Reeves is a smart fellow. In no time at all, he'll catch on to how bad Swede is and hire somebody who knows what he's doing. It's a sure bet!"

Looking back, Deacon feels the seemingly endless scrimmaging was good for him personally. "I knew I was behind on my techniques. Fortunately for me, I didn't get injured while learning my craft in those long sessions. I perfected my game, and to this day I owe Harland for that. But that's the selfish approach. Football's a team sport, and in that light, I think what he did was negative; those cruel practices beat the hell out of most of our players, especially our receivers and our running backs."

Interviewed recently at his highly successful training and rehabilitation center near San Diego, Svare strongly disagrees, feeling the good outweighed the bad. "I did run the hell out of them. I may have been just a kid myself, but I realized if we were going to compete, we had to be in shape. And contact is what football is all about. You can't run a play at half-speed, or tell a player to hit somebody gently."

The argument between contact and the noncontact coaches is not a new one. But Deacon feels Svare was extreme, even for a believer in the contact method of practice. Deacon remembers, "Harland's modus operandi won him few friends. Most of the players felt he simply wanted to unleash as much pain on us as possible. And he openly admitted that he scrimmaged to punish us for losing." This is, of course, a common attitude shared by coaches of football squads from high school through college and on into the pros. Game films are viewed the morning after the game, and in the week which follows, various types of "conditioning" are handed out, depending on the number of missed tackles, blown assignments, and so on.

Shotgun Wedding

The Rams were flying back from the Midwest after tying Minnesota and losing to Green Bay and Chicago. The players were playing cards, sleeping, or reading the tattered magazines, teasing each other, and making passes at the pretty stewardesses to pass the time. Back then jet air travel was in its infancy and stewardesses didn't have strong unions; they were generally young and friendly rather than hard-bitten and leathery like old railroad conductors.

Everyone was drinking beers and hitting on the stewardesses, and it was a game. They all were aware Rams middle-linebacker Les Richter had started out flirting with a stewardess and ended up marrying her.

As usual, Deacon was sitting on the aisle, having no intention of looking out the window. At first it was hard for him to forget he came from Florida. He kept remembering you could be hung for looking at a white woman. But the girls were pretty, and they included him in the banter, and somewhere after the first few beers, he started to convince himself that maybe, just maybe, things were different now. He was Deacon Jones, up-and-coming superstar. He lived in free-living, free-loving California. Surely, power had its privileges. After a while, he found himself going along with it. In fact, he was soon one of the ringleaders in the general horseplay. And yes, the particular stewardess in the thick of things was a white girl—of course she was white, in those days a black stewardess was rarer than the pork in a can of pork and beans.

It all seemed innocent enough. She didn't seem to mind. In fact, she seemed downright flattered. It was Lamar, as ever in the window seat next to him, who gave him the warning sign, "Deak. Don't look now, but Les Richter is sitting behind us, an' he definitely is not pleased at your behavior."

Deacon turned around to look directly into Les giving him the bad eye. "Hey, Les, what's wrong?" he asked.

"Nothing," Les replied, giving him a long, glaring stare before he went back to reading the magazine on his lap.

Deacon jostled Lamar, "What's wrong wit' the white boy?"

Lamar shook his head, "He got the craziness." Deacon knew what that meant. All some whites had to do was see a black having fun with a white woman and they conjured up images of rape and white slavery.

Deacon knew it wasn't fair, but he couldn't help himself. At that point, the fun went out of it for him. He wandered down the aisle away from the white-girl action and got himself involved in a card game. But it wasn't over.

Early the next week, Elroy Hirsh called him into the front office. Hirsh was the Rams general manager at that time, having replaced Pete Rozelle in 1960 when Rozelle went on to league things. Elroy had retired from a career as the legendary "Crazy Legs" Hirsh, the great Ram receiver of the early 1950s, but Deacon could see right away he didn't want to chew the fat over the fantastic moves he'd made in old football games.

"David, you're starting to be an embarrassment to yourself and the team."

Deacon was thunderstruck. He stood there silently, mouth open, while Hirsh listed a number of incidents in which various team members had been drinking and boisterous in public. Hirsh had a reputation as a diplomatic general manager—he had to be fast on his feet to stay at his job with a handful of millionaire co-owners bickering for control of the Rams—but dealing with black players was something new for everybody in the league. If Hirsh had any idea how his comments would be received, he certainly wouldn't have proceeded. And Deacon, coming from his own heritage, certainly was going to be no help to him. He stood still as a statue. He felt Hirsh's words were throwing him right back down into the Florida dirt. It was like a big slap on the side of his head, only Crazy Legs wasn't his daddy, and had no right to be speaking to him so! But Crazy Legs was the white boss, and so for once young Deacon's tongue was tied.

Still, everything Hirsh said was incendiary. Everything. And with every sentence, he dug himself in deeper.

"If you want to play in the NFL, you have to live up to certain standards."

And all Deacon could think was, Why don't he talk to the white boys that way?

"You've got a great future ahead of you; don't let your early success ruin you."

And Deacon was thinking, I got here through grit and determination. I don't need Crazy Legs to be telling me this.

"You've convinced us here that you're serious about your career. You should think seriously about settling down."

And Deacon's inner voice was shouting, Did he talk this way to the white players who were also flirting on the plane?

"What I think you should do—and I know I'm not alone on this—is find a nice girl and get married!"

If Deacon was ever going to lose his cool in the NFL, it was at that moment. It took every ounce of his fiber to stand there, saying nothing, doing nothing, while the voice within him roared, You mean a nice nigrah girl, don't you Crazy Legs? You're saying white girls are off limits to black boys, right?

And yet, in that darkest of moments, mad and confused and upset as he was, Deacon didn't forget how far his sacrifices and self-discipline had already carried him. The general manager of the Rams wasn't discussing a business arrangement to huck some watermelons for a few dollars a day, drinking out of the hose around the side instead of the water fountain in front, or picking up the fried chicken at the little side-window—he was talking about playing the game, the one thing Deacon had wanted to do ever since he was a kid. This was the way he'd chosen to show he was a man, equal to any in the world. He had made it into the selected ranks of the NFL. He was a starter. He was a pro. He had dedicated his life to it. And nothing and nobody was going to take it away from him.

So, instead of busting Crazy Legs in the face, which was the first thought that came to his mind, Deacon held his tongue and temper and managed to get out of the room without being thrown out of organized football. He stormed out of the office, got away from the Rams' camp, walked alone for hours at night, trying to think it through. And finally, out of the shame, humiliation, and stinging despair of what he took to be Elroy Hirsh's racial insults came a new resolve, a new dedication, or perhaps simply a hardening of his old resolution. Nobody was going to cheat him out of his chosen career! Nobody!

Interviewed recently about this controversial incident, Elroy Hirsh remembers trying to convince Deacon to settle down, but he has a different recollection about exactly what he said, "It wasn't anything like I was forcing him to do anything. At first, when some of these guys got to the big leagues, they couldn't handle it. I'd seen it before. They'd go wild and throw it all away. Deacon was probably the fastest big man I'd ever seen. He also had a chip on his shoulder a mile wide. He had a surly side. He was in the big town, in L.A for the first time. He had a great career in front of him. I wanted him to have that career, to enjoy it."

Dick Bass comments on what happened to Deacon: "When Deak came into town, he was a green kid from the Deep South, and he didn't know how far a man like Hirsh could and would go. I can believe Hirsh pressured him about personal things which were none of his business, because the nearly-same thing happened to me. The year of the World's Fair in New York, I flew back there for an appearance on the Giants coach's TV show—the 'Allie Sherman Show.' Things really clicked and I ended up doing a variety of appearances around the town.

Well, one night, I went to see Miles Davis at a club. Terry Gibbs was there—Terry and I had a rivalry over a pretty little girl, but this night, she wasn't there, so Terry said, 'You see anything you like?' Well, I looked around the club and there was this really classy woman sitting alone with a drink in her hand. To make a long story short, Terry introduced us, and I spent four wild days and nights with Ava Gardner. You can't party in New York City by yourself, and somebody must have heard about it and passed it on to the Rams. Well, no sooner did I get back to L.A. when Elroy Hirsh called me in

*his office and the first words out of his mouth were, 'You DOG, you,'
in that half-joking tone some men use when they want to compli-
ment you and still bring up a difficult subject.*

*"Now, I was born and raised in northern California, and Hirsh
wasn't a good enough friend to be even bringing up the subject.
He was the general manager of the Rams. I knew the law, and I
knew my rights. I was an adult. Ava most certainly was of age and
knew her mind. I'd done nothing wrong, bad or illegal. It truly was
my own business, thank you, Hirsh, but butt out, fella. And, unlike
Deacon, I had my no-cut, no-trade contract. I was playing great
ball, and if the Rams did insist on trading me, I would be in demand
elsewhere. And so I figured I knew how far Hirsh could go with me.
I gave him fire for fire; I laughed, my way of saying believe it if you
want, but I'm not going to talk about it. I just tossed it off, water off
my back, and since he couldn't figure out a way to challenge me,
nothing ever came of it."*

*Elroy Hirsh also remembers talking to Dick Bass, but he remem-
bers talking with Dick about his New York fling in a harmless, joking
way. Dick wasn't tall, and Ava was. Hirsh says, "I remember slyly
referring to Bass's height—or lack of it—by asking him 'Who put you
up to it?'!"*

Starting Out

Deacon was heading east across New Mexico in the used, dark blue
Thunderbird he'd bought in L.A. They'd held the wedding in
Phoenix, because Iretha wanted it there. It had been all right, he
guessed. Running back Tom Wilson had come with him, and that was
good for a few laughs before the ceremony. The champagne after had
made him sleepy, and they'd lost a few hours taking pictures and gabbing, when all he wanted was to be on the road.

It had been late afternoon by the time they got all Iretha's luggage
in the car and strapped to the roof; still, the Arizona summer sun was
fierce, and so naturally his air conditioner died a few miles out of town.
Iretha turned sulky in the heat, pouting at him like he ought to be
able to fix anything. Deacon had had the idea at the back of his mind
that Iretha had a fiery temper, but since she'd always been nice to him
during their whirlwind courtship, he hadn't given it a second thought.
Now, alone in the car with her, he realized they were two very strong
and very different personalities, and he was going to have to watch

what he said. No sweat, he thought, my daddy always watched what he said around my mama.

On Route 66 passing through Gallup, the long summer light turned orange and stretched away to the West, lighting the flat tops of the buttes in front of him into fiery red curtains. Fleecy purple clouds drifted across a blue-black sky by the time they got to Albuquerque, but as they had started late, Deacon thought they'd put some miles on before finding a place to stop for the night. Iretha had found some jingle-jangle country-western music that he hated, but at least he didn't have to listen to her whining.

By midnight they were barreling through western Texas with the window on Deacon's side open as much as he dared to let in the cool desert breeze. Iretha had complained earlier that the wind was messing her hair, so he'd only gradually let the one window down after she'd fallen into a restless sleep. Thank God for small favors, at least she wasn't nattering him about the heat any more.

Deacon sighed and tried to put the past few months in perspective. Since Svare had taken over, the season had been a disaster. Deacon personally had played well in most of the games, and he, Lamar, and Merlin had terrorized their share of quarterbacks. But Svare was showing an interest in "fixing" Deacon's play—his stance, his slash-and-burn method of attack, his strategy, his attitude—and Deacon resented it. He liked the practice and the repetitions, but resented the feeling that he was being tinkered with, the subject of an experiment.

After the jolting interview with Hirsh, Deacon had had no friendly moments with the Rams general manager. Hirsh had had his say, and that was that. No matter what Crazy Legs' intentions were, Deacon took them to be serious as a heart attack. The Rams had dealt him his cards; now it was up to him. For a while Deacon had thought about Pat, his old girlfriend from Florida. It was too bad, but he'd never been good at writing. He'd dedicated his time to the team, and in the process, he'd let that relationship drift.

That left the local girls. Until now, Deacon had been young and free-spirited. Dedicated to the game, he'd hardly had time to sow any wild oats. His mind wasn't even in the marrying direction. But with Crazy Legs' advice heavy on his mind, he took a good, hard second look at what was available. And Iretha—gorgeous, hot-tempered and sufficiently black—happened to be in the right place at the right time.

Lamar had said something to him once during his brief madcap courtship days about watching out for the women who wanted to live the life of glamour they visualized as coming along with marrying an NFL player. They're everywhere, Lamar had said. You got to watch out. Good, old, patient, level-headed Lamar!

At three in the morning, Deacon was bone-tired and wishing he had stopped in Albuquerque, where they might have found a motel that accepted blacks. Now there wouldn't be anything until Houston, which was out of the way, or his brother's place in New Orleans. He looked over at Iretha, who was snoring like a trucker. He was amazed that such a slight person could make such a loud noise.

"Iretha, honey, you think you could maybe drive for a hour or two so I could get some sleep?"

She snorted and snuffled and turned away from him so she faced the window, trying to burrow deeper into the pillow.

"Iretha." He tried again. "It's the middle of the night. I need you to drive for a bit, honey."

She yawned and stretched and squinted first out at the flat, barren blackness surrounding the road, and then at him. "Where are we, honey?"

"Middle of nowhere, babes, middle of nowhere. You got to drive so I can get some sleep."

"Uh-uh," she said, her lips forming the pout that had been cute only a few days ago. "Don't you know anything, Deacon Jones? The woman don't drive. That why she have the man to do it for her."

He thought she was joking, "Come on, Iretha. I'm tired here."

"What?" she replied, her irritation obvious. "I ain't drivin' your big ol' car in the middle of nothing. I'm tired, too. People supposed to sleep at night. What if I drive it off the road or somethin'?"

"But Iretha, we got a problem here."

"No, you got a problem. We married, Deacon Jones. You got to take care of me, now." She turned her back to him and settled her head back on the pillow.

He choked back his anger and the notion that he should leave her out here with all her luggage in the middle of the dusty sagebrush, the rocks and the coyotes. His parents had made a go of it in spite of their strong temperaments. No matter what the odds, why couldn't he do the same? His mother was married to his daddy for life—how could it possibly be any different for him?

He drove on east through the star-studded night, heading for Florida to show off his bride to Mama and the rest of his fans in Eatonville. Iretha was a short little scrapper of a woman, but she was built, as the saying went, like a brick shithouse, and the boys would like that.

The west Texas road stretched endlessly away before him, a long series of low, rolling hills now showing their jet black shoulders under the deep grey sky that announced the coming dawn. He rubbed his eyes and cast a glance over at Iretha's quiet form resting next to him, oblivious to his world. For the first time the realization of what he'd done came over him, flooding his mind with worry and uncertainty. She was right about one thing, the man got to do for the woman. He sighed and gripped the wheel a little tighter. It was going to be a long, long journey.

The View from the Back of the Ram

It was during the off-season, just after the holidays and the NFL championship game, in the middle of that dull time before spring practice, and Pervis Atkins was throwing one of his famous parties. In those days, the Rams all partied hard, and Deacon Jones was learning to be right in there with the best of them. Hard alcohol was an important part of the American way of life. Folks drank if they were happy, if they were sad, if they were a success, if they were a failure. You drank because you were a man, and because you were a man, you had to drink. Popular movies and novels all promoted the image of the hard-drinking good guy; cowboys pulled into dusty bars and drank their whiskey neat, explorers toasted their adventures with brandy, soldiers had a brave pull at the bottle before bullets and arrows and spears were extracted from their bodies, even the kamikazes had their snort of fermented cherry juice before lifting off into the rising sun. It was the honorable thing to do.

Pervis had most of the black players and their wives scattered around his patio while he blackened some burgers and dogs on the barbecue. Dick Bass and two or three of his latest female conquests were hanging around. Charlie Cowan was trying to get Pervis's record player to play on the outdoor speakers. Alvin, Lamar, and a few of Pervis's show-business friends were playing poker. Ollie and his wife Mary and Deacon and Iretha were there. Pervis had invented a new drink he called the Icelander, guaranteed to get folks friendly and mixing. It was a big Mason jar filled half with Tanqueray gin and half with vodka.

Before long, the men had separated out and were talking football, leaving the women to their own chatter. And, without the pressure from the rednecks on the team to hold them back, it was not the general range of conversation you might hear anywhere else.

"His youth stick out like a sore dick," Deacon was saying. "One thing—he talks more than Bob," Alvin Hall said.

"Hell, Good Hosen, the sphinx of Egypt talks more than Bob!"

"I just wish he would back off on the yelling and the screaming," Ollie said.

"The poor bloke has a problem," Bass added with an aristocratic sniff. "You have to see his side. He finds it impossible to banter and joke around because he is endeavoring to be a leader in spite of his tender years. And he is not, by nature, a diplomat." Bass was in fine form, having showed up in a tan gabardine hunting jacket and a scarlet silk ascot.

"That he ain't," Deacon agreed. "Send him to Russia an' the Cold War be hot in five minutes! And I have never seen any man, even in the Deep South, strip a black man in a public meeting the way he do. He laid the whip on Ollie a few times this past season. I was sure I saw blood flow."

Ollie nodded, "It ain't just me. It's all the brothers."

Bass shook his head, "Miss a block? You are going to be humiliated. Let a man slip by? Get ready for the dog poop. Drop the football? Slit your own wrist before Swede gets to it."

Alvin Hall waved his half-eaten hamburger in the air. "That what he does is just for us bubbas. You notice he don't lay it on Richter or Arnett or Olsen or any them other cracker white boys the way he do us."

"He's always threatening he's gonna trade me!" Deacon snorted in disgust, "Man, it's comin' to where I wish he would!"

"He got us all thinkin' we're hangin' on to the Ram by a thread!"

Ollie held a hand up for silence. "I'll tell you boys a trade story. Week before our last game, Harland come by lookin' all important an' says, 'Ollie, I'm thinkin' we're gonna trade you.'"

The other blacks scoffed and made light of it, "That's like trading away the team!" "Never happen, Ollie, never happen!" "No way, Coach!"

"Well, he said it. An' I looks him back right in the eye an' says, 'That may be your thought, but you can't do that, Mr. Svare.'

"'I don't see why not,' he says, gettin' all huffy-like, kind of like a big, pink toad.

"'Well den, you better go have a look at my contract,' I says, 'payin' particular attention to the part where it says "No cut, no trade." '"

"I'll wager that got his proverbial goat," Bass said.

"Oh, yeah, it did," Ollie's smile grew wider. "Swede don't like it when somebody else know something he don't. He got all excited an' upset, like. But, bein' Swede, he tried to hide it. 'Well, I wasn't aware of that,' he says in a gruff sort of a voice, tryin' to pretend he old enough to be my daddy.

"'But, I tell you what,' I says, real friendly like. 'I might not mind a trade, say, if it was to Detroit. I hear that Wilson's a pretty good coach, knows his stuff an' all.' After that, he nods and goes away. Later that afternoon, I see him talking and waving his arms around in a corner of the field with Crazy Legs and Dapper Dan [Reeves]." Ollie gave Deacon a big clap on the back. "The moral of the story, Deak, is that you've got to learn to separate Harland-the-screamer from Harland-the-coach-boy. In your case, he's absolutely not going to trade you. Reeves an' Hirsh wouldn't let him. You the future of the Rams. Me, he might trade. I'm the past."

Pervis wandered by with big jugs of gin and vodka, refilling Icelanders. "Oh, talkin' about our favorite Swede, huh?

"How you feel about him switching you from running back to tight end, Pervis?" somebody asked. Atkins had beefed up as best he could, but he maxed out at only about 220, and they all could see he was getting pounded to pieces at that position. Svare was having him run against Ollie, which was like a fly running into the side of a boxcar.

"Yes, Mr. Pervis Atkins," Bass quizzed, "Tell us, how do you feel about a move that's gonna take five years off your career?"

"Off his life, more like," somebody added.

Pervis gave Bass a grim look and shot back, "How'd you feel when you flunked your intelligence test a second time?"

Bass tossed it off. "Swede's no more prejudiced than any other coach in the league. He's just a little less intelligent." The circle of men enjoyed that one, and Bass had to wait until the laughter subsided. Intelligence was something Harland Svare said he valued very much, and he'd run around giving IQ tests to prove it. The white players resented it because it brought up the notion they were dumb jocks, and the black players hated it because they felt Svare wanted to prove to himself they weren't really just monkeys out of the jungle. A few days after Svare had insisted they take the tests, the news spread throughout the squad that Bass, whether through his own stubbornness or lack of ability, had scored lower than any of them. Bass was naturally embarrassed, but Svare was absolutely unwilling to believe the results. Dick Bass was witty and urbane, and had better diction and a larger vocabulary than anyone on the team, or any coach, for that matter. After Bass took it a second time and still did no better, Svare had quietly dropped the testing.

Remembering those tests, Deacon was quick to anger. "You ask Swede what he looks for in a player and he uses the word intelligence. White men did the same thing to us back in South Carolina and Mississippi! They all say that same crap to paint the brother in the corner as talented but stupid! The problem here is—Who's measuring the intelligence? Who's the so-called self-appointed intelligence picker?"

Lamar, who had been quietly nursing a beer, spoke. "Now see, you good folks have done gone an' riled up the Deacon. Now we're gonna hear it."

"Naw, I'm through," Deacon said. "Gonna go get me another Icelander."

Lamar's worried look followed him as he walked away. Deacon was selling Volkswagen bugs in the off-season, to make ends meet. He had put on weight in the past two months—too much weight, to Lamar's way of thinking. And he had already put away two Mason jars; with a third in him, it would take two or three stout volunteers to pile him in his T-bird so Iretha could drive him home. Iretha wouldn't like that. She liked to be driven and pampered and waited on. Lamar shook his head, thinking, marriage sure makes some folks unhappy.

When interviewed in 1992, Harland Svare had a rosier recollection of the way things were. "We didn't really have a black problem on the Rams, none that I was aware of, and as the head coach, I would have been aware of it. It was my policy, and the policy of the coaches who worked under me, to treat everybody fairly and alike."

Today, Lamar Lundy remembers the early 1960s in the Rams locker room. "The correction time, when the coaching staff went over plays from the previous game, was very negative on the black players. Maybe the coaches themselves didn't feel it, maybe they had a blindness to their own attitudes, but we blacks all experienced it. The hostility, the tone of voice, the verbal way of correction, was all a lot rougher on the blacks. You had to accept it. There was no other way. In the thirteen years I played pro ball, I never played under even an assistant black coach. They were all white. And, of them all, the Svare staff was about the worst when it came to dealing with blacks."

Svare replies, "I tried to be fair to them all. Ball players take a lot of attention. You get close to them and you end up knowing every-thing about them. In some ways, they are like sensitive kids. Sure, maybe I was stern sometimes, but there were plenty of times when they needed it, and I did my best to look out for them."

Looking back after thirty years, Deacon tries to see the staff's inadequacies in broader terms. "You have to remember, the NFL was adjusting, it was changing, it was opening the doors to blacks for the first time. Perhaps the system dictated that Harland and his coaches have the kind of attitude they did toward blacks—thirty-year-old Harland, lucky by anybody's standards to be in his job, wasn't going to stick his neck out and change the system. And, of course, he's for-gotten all this by now, if he ever understood any of it in the first place."

Asked recently what he had always looked for, first and foremost, in the draft or in a trade, Svare promptly replied, "I always looked for intelligence in a ballplayer. You can have two men of equal physical ability, but intelligent play is what wins ball games." After all this time, he expressed surprise to hear that the blacks on his team had resent-ed his IQ tests and his use of the word intelligence.

Looking back, Svare's many threats to trade Deacon can be seen as bluffs, perhaps attempts to establish his authority over the rising young star. When asked recently if the Rams would have trad-ed Deacon back in the early sixties, Elroy Hirsh replied, "Never! I myself would have been fired the next day! The fans would have had me hung! Deacon was one of our most popular players in an era when we didn't really have many."

The Trouble with Ollie

A few days after spring training began, Deacon came in to find Ollie cleaning out his locker.

"You don't like the company no more?" he asked.

"I been traded, Deak." Ollie grinned at him, "Goin' to the Lions."

"No, man. You can't do that!" Ollie was more than the Rams superstar, he was an inspiration to all the young black players. He gave unsparingly of his time to teach them the tricks of the trade.

"It's done, brother. I'm gone already."

Deacon had heard Ollie talk about being traded before, but now that it had come to pass, he couldn't believe it. "Why? Why would they even want to trade their top player?"

"Well, you know they haven't been using me around here to my full potential. The Lions will put me back in the backfield where I belong. Not that I minded playing tight end for a change, but everybody know that be an odd place to put a star running back who can also block and catch the ball out of the backfield. It means I only get to contribute about a third of what I might be able to for the team."

Ollie sat on the bench and flexed his huge shoulder muscles like he was working out a cramp. He eyed Deacon for a few moments before he spoke. "There's something else . . . Reeves told me I'm a clubhouse lawyer."

"He say that to you?"

"Those very words. He say I been branded a troublemaker since the vote last year."

"The vote they stole!"

"I've been accused of agitation, of stirring things up here and there. I'm bad for the team."

"Did he give specific examples?"

"Nope. Everything was very general, but you know it don't take much to stain a player, and they put the bad mark there." Ollie paused a moment, thinking back on the past few years. "You know, Deak, I came to the team with a great deal of prestige, an' I always tried to tell you players to be the best you could be, for the fans. It's hard to see how that could be mistaken for group agitation."

"So it was that lousy, stinking vote for team captain!"

Ollie shook his head, "It goes back further than that, Deak. I heard the whispers since I been here. I know what it's all about."

"What?"

"The crackers say I'm to blame for all the losing going on around here."

Deacon looked around for a helmet to slam, but the room had been cleaned up neat as a pin, "What fool come up with that notion?"

Ollie lay back on the bench, and, grabbing it overhead with his hands, started to do leg lifts, doing them as effortlessly as if he was walking, "They gots to blame somebody, Deak, at least in their own minds. I'm a good choice. See, Ol' Crazy Legs wasn't here when I came. The eleven-for-one trade was made by Pete Rozelle, so there's nobody here to defend it."

"How can they blame you for that?"

"They blame all us blacks."

"What?" Deacon was almost beside himself. He stormed around, waving his hands in the air. "What is this you're telling me, Ollie?"

"I know what I'm sayin' ain't logical . . . let me try to explain, anyway, cause the way they think makes a sort of sense if you be a redneck on a loser team. Now, in the trade to get me, Reeves an' Rozelle gave away seven good men, from both the offense and defense. I know 'em by heart: four tackles—Ken Panfil, Frank Fuller, Art Hauser, an' Glenn Holtzman—end John Tracey, fullback Larry Hickman, an' halfback Don Brown. In addition to that, they gave away a second-round draft pick in 1959, an' a player to be named later. Maybe it would have worked, but the white players the Rams used to plug the holes left by that trade didn't work out. That's one reason so many blacks made the team in 1961."

"Yeah, but—"

Ollie smiled, "Now hold on. Listen to the rest of it. When you boys all made the team, there was a lot of fear an' resentment runnin' around in the redneck section of the white crowd, which, as you know, includes most of the coaching staff. I mean, a lot of the white players took it okay, but those redneck boys was goin' crazy with fear; here their sacred Rams was with two or three times as many blacks as any other team in the NFL—what was gonna happen next, an *all-black* Rams team? An' believe me, it didn't help matters none, us comin' so close to winnin' the team captain thing a year later. They couldn't let that happen, why, there'd be niggers runnin' the Los Angeles Rams!

So we forced 'em into the big lie, an' they picked the redneck from USC. But their own scheme backfired—they cheat and give Arnett the team, an' the team loses. Now who they gonna blame?" Ollie heaved himself off the bench and went back to cleaning out his locker. "They's nobody left but the bubbas, brother. An' so the only thing they can do is trade the big black troublemaking ringleader away. That might buy 'em another year or two, until—"

"Until somebody figures out they can't coach."

Ollie shrugged. "Winnin' ain't the only thing around here, Deacon Jones. It ain't about winnin' with the Los Angeles Rams."

"No player worth a nickel would ever agree to that."

"We ain't talkin' players here, we talkin' management. They'll tell you you're family around here, Deak, but don't you ever forget it: they don't care about your feelings, your reputation, or your career. All management interested in is power."

Ollie finished cleaning out his locker and did the rounds, saying his goodbyes. The young black ballplayers were all as stunned as Deacon. The whites were happy for him or sad to see him go, depending on who they were. But they all wished him well, and the big man headed out the door.

Ollie Matson talks about being shifted to tight end: "It wasn't all Waterfield. I found his assistant, Hamp Pool, to be another difficult, do-as-I-say type guy. He would be abrasive if you didn't do it his way without question. He was very innovative with the "x's" and "o's," but he ran into problems getting his little chalkboard letters to execute on the playing field, when he tried to squeeze the actual talent to fit with his ideas. Bob went along with it, but it was originally Hamp's idea to change me to a tight end. They saw in the game films that I was a very good blocker. I learned that by taking extra practice and blocking with the linemen, and I always wore big pads. But as a tight end, my contributions were limited to blocking and pass-catching. In the backfield, I could do many things: pass-catch, block, run, and decoy. Hamp didn't play my strengths. He put his own ideas above winning. Of course, Svare just wanted me traded."

Raw Meat

The Rams gathered for their 1963 spring training once again in the desert heat at Chapman college in Orange County. Svare made it clear from his first meeting that nobody was safe. The veterans were given no preference over the rookies. Anybody who didn't perform, if they were worth anything at all, was up on the trading block. The vets naturally grumbled; once you proved yourself at any position, it was yours until a younger, stronger, faster man took it away. At least, that's the way it had always been. But Svare wasn't in a listening mode; last year's team had won only one game, and he was determined to make a difference. There was going to be bruising contact, long hours, and whoever came out of the pit alive had the job.

Lamar and Deacon were stretching in the morning sunlight, waiting for the coaching staff to show up on the field. They were still in their first few weeks of spring training. The two were rooming together, and it was clear to Lamar that his roommate had beefed up in the off-season. Ever the diplomat, Lamar was having trouble finding the right words to say his mind. He finally blurted out "Uh, Deak—how much more you weigh than last year?"

Deacon looked over at him, his eyes narrowed to slits. After a long pause, he said, "Fifty pounds."

"What's the idea?"

Deacon gave him another of those long looks that seemed to say more than words ever could. Lamar could read unhappiness there, and a sullen anger. He finally answered, "Last year I was the fastest big man in the game. This year, I aim to be the fastest, biggest man in football." Deacon saw the skeptical expression on Lamar's face and shrugged. "I thought I'd give it a try. Man goes with what he's got, you know?"

Lamar nodded slowly, "Yeah, I guess. Hey, here come the Bass Daily Trumpet."

Bass sauntered up to them, eyeing the area around the practice field with disdain. "I miss those big oak trees we had at Redlands. Nothing cool like that deep oak shade." Nobody said anything, and Bass sighed and reached down to touch his toes, a casual tribute to the art of warming up, "Where are the Boy Scouts?" That was Bass's name for the coaching staff.

Deacon couldn't help being amused. They'd had their differences, but he admired Bass's style. "Probably studying the playbooks."

Bass grinned, "Dick and Jane Play Football. Remember when Swede promised the press he would surround himself with the most talented assistant coaches in the business? His very words, 'the most talented.'"

"Yeah. We remember." Nobody said anything for a while. Deacon couldn't stand the silence. "They *better* be brilliant, 'cause they sure are *untested.* I got a high school coach back in Eatonville who knows more about the game."

"Surely, Swamp Boy, you don't think our youthful general is going to risk overshadowing himself with experienced help. He just got rid of his last real rival."

Deacon grinned, his voice rich with humor, "Hamp Pool, elevated to scouting."

"This be the swinging sixties. Make way for the youth movement." Bass did a dance step as he talked. As usual, he screwed it up. Deacon and Lamar looked at each other, but neither said anything. They didn't have to. Dick Bass couldn't dance his way out of a paper bag, and they were both thinking He soaked up so much of the white man's sophistication, the poor bro done lost his own natural rhythm. Lamar, always the kind one, raised one sympathetic fist in the air, "Amen, brother. Power to the people."

On the surface they could joke about their new coaching staff, but they all knew this was serious business. The Rams would be facing teams led by successful coaches like clever George Halas and tough-guy Vince Lombardi, men who had surrounded themselves with the most talented and experienced assistants they could find. Svare, on the other hand, had hired five player-coaches to be his assistants, and it was the talk of the camp, at least among the veterans who thought they'd seen it all, until now.

Bass nodded, "Baby coaches all, out to play in the Rams sandbox. It's like a cruel joke. I mean, are we a professional team, or what?"

"Players, yes." Deacon was stretching, holding on to his toes. "I'm starting to believe Ollie had the right idea."

"What," Lamar asked, "go to Detroit?"

"Naw. Ollie say that—players an' coaches—we're all alike to Mister Daniel Reeves. He run the butcher shop, an' we all just raw meat on the shelf."

Bass took one look at Deacon's girth, and his eyes widened like he was seeing him for the first time. "Hey, Fat Boy. Talk about meat—you still claim you can keep up with me?"

Deacon gave him his slit-eyed challenge look, "Mother Menifee will hold your money, boy. Only let's do it after practice so you don't embarrass yourself." Deacon thought he could beat him, but he didn't really want to race with his extra weight. He also knew Bass wouldn't call his bluff. Bass had more to lose than he did.

"You're on!" Bass wandered away, seeking, as always, the deeper shade. Deacon knew he wouldn't see him for the rest of the day.

Lamar looked at Deacon, but he was gazing off into the distance. If he was concerned about doing forty yards against the Rams fleet running back, or about anything else, he didn't show it.

Retaining Harland Svare as his head coach had to be one of Dan Reeves's all-time controversial decisions, as the Rams had yet to win a single game under Svare's leadership. The Rams owner had recently regained complete control of the team by purchasing the interests of his partners, who had often disagreed with his auto-cratic methods and decisions. Soon Reeves would recoup his cash outlay by selling 49 percent of his interest to seven new limited part-ners, including singing-cowboy-turned-entrepreneur Gene Autry. These new partners would have far less power to question Reeves's decisions. Retaining Harland as the head coach was entirely Reeves's decision. It can be argued (and probably was) that a fresh new look, new ideas, and bright young faces on the coach-

ing staff were just what the Rams needed to pull them out of their tailspin. Today, only the grim win-loss record of the next few years remains to show what a bonehead idea it really was.

Each of "Swede's neophytes," as Bass called them, had only a year or two of experience; they were young would-be coaches Svare had worked and played with on the Giants, or their friends. There was Don Heinrich, the new quarterback and running back coach (Heinrich had once been the backup quarterback on the Giants and a player-coach for a year or two in Dallas); Jack Patera, defensive line coach (no prior experience, recommended by Heinrich, with whom he had played in Dallas in 1960-61); Bob Schnelker, tight end and receiver's coach (player-coach for a year or two with the Giants); Ray Weitecha, offensive line coach (former Giant center); and Linden Crow, defensive back coach (no previous coaching experience before functioning as player-coach with the Rams). For all of them it was the chance of a lifetime, and some of these young coaches, in later years and for other teams, would prove to be decent coaches.

Fearsome Foursome

Harland Svare leaned back in his chair. From his office he could hear the faint noises of the camp coming to life. There was a rattle of metal doors from the locker rooms, the distant sound of somebody telling a story, the smell of coffee in the air. To Svare, training camps were all pretty much the same. A little over ten years before he'd been a rookie with the Giants in a camp that looked and felt and resonated just about like this one. Smell of witchhazel and rookies singing old school fight songs in the showers. Drills and yelling and the crash of helmets. Spring training.

Svare's mind went back to those earlier days and he found himself thinking about the Giants. He'd played on a world championship team in the fifties, on the same team with Sam Huff and Rosey Grier. He'd even played in the famous game of 1958 against Baltimore, one of the first nationally televised games, when Alan "The Horse" Ameche scored a winning touchdown in overtime to beat the Colts. That was a game for the ages!

Svare turned over in his mind the elements of those great New York teams of yesteryear, looking for points of similarity and difference with his current Rams. He had a gift for this sort of analysis, and he treasured his few moments alone when he was free to let his mind roam over the endless possibilities and combinations that might make up his own winning team. The single constant that kept coming back to him was "D"—the Big "D"—as in "Defense." And, in the heart of the defense, the Giants had always featured an awesome front four.

The 4-3 defense was in wide use throughout the league. What if he were to build the Rams front four into something awesome? Why not? The way he saw it, he was already over halfway there. The vets didn't know it, Svare having them sweat for their jobs, but he had already made some key decisions. Lamar Lundy would play right end because he had height and containment ability. Jones at left end was young and raw, but the kid had speed and could penetrate.

And Svare already had the third member of his "awesome foursome." When Merlin Olson first showed up with the Rams, Hamp Pool had snared the huge farm boy and penciled him in to play offense. But Svare had yelled and kicked up a fuss until he got Olson switched over to defensive tackle. Merlin himself had taken some convincing. No problem. In scrimmaging, Svare had switched him over to play on the side of the line directly against Deacon. It never was any fun to go against Jones, who practiced every down as hard as he played. Olsen was tough, but he wasn't dumb, and after a few weeks of that kind of punishment he gratefully switched over to defense. Now in his second year, the kid from Mormon country seemed to be coming along nicely. He couldn't penetrate like Jones, but he was quick, and strong as a horse, and he had good lateral moves.

Okay, that was three out of four. Thinking to himself that morning, Svare let his imagination run free. If he could have anybody in the world, who would he want for that fourth man? Easy. It would have to be massive Rosey Grier, who he already knew from his playing days in New York. Rosey was an older player, perhaps with only three or four more years left in him, but he had always possessed great penetrating ability, surprising in a big man. He was a proven winner, and he had that vital something Harland needed in the worst way—experience. Now how the hell could he pry the world's premier interior lineman away from the Giants? Svare knew Allie Sherman wanted to put his own stamp on the New York team, and that generally meant change was in the wind. Then too, Allie had been unhappy with Rosey's perennial weight problems. Harland wondered if Rosey had been into the pork chops over the off-season months. A smile came over his face and he reached for the phone.

Svare's first few calls were to old friends, Giants assistants he knew, and they talked general chit-chat about how spring training was going. Svare didn't even have to ask; Rosey's weight was the talk of the camp. Once again, the big man was up way over three hundred pounds. Allie had called him a giant bowling ball and said if he got any bigger they were just going to call the plays and roll him down the field.

Young Svare took a deep breath and called Allie. Sherman was indeed an unhappy man, and in the next few minutes the Rams head coach was able to trade defensive tackle John LoVetere for the great Rosey Grier. It was the deal of his lifetime, and the start of the most celebrated front four of all time, the Rams mighty Fearsome Foursome.

Svare set down the phone with mixed feelings of elation and resolve. Far from being over, his team building had just begun. Svare tapped his fingers on the desktop, remembering the personal habits of the legendary defensive players from his own playing days. Those guys had never really been in shape! Men like Gino Marchetti, Andy Robustelli, Dick Modzelewski, and Tom Scott, great as they were, would be winded by the third quarter, and running on empty before the end of the game. How much better those old-timers might have played if they had been in shape!

Svare had his foursome. Now it was time to run the hell out of them.

Harland Svare pulled off the trade of the century when he brought Grier to the Rams, creating the nucleus for a defense that lived long after he was gone and thrived after even the original players were gone, continuing to terrorize the league for over two decades. Young Svare came by his belief in a strong defense naturally, having been a successful linebacker with the Giants, and there playing on one of the greatest defensive teams of his era. Ollie Matson, who played against him, remembers him as "one hard-nosed player. You know what they say about Swedes—stubborn and relentless. That was Harland; the kind of guy who would come after you."

Hard-nosed as he was as a player, Svare would prove an equally tough disciplinarian as a coach. He continued his regimen of conditioning into the exhibition season, scrimmaging his team the Wednesday following every loss. These were long, brutal scrimmages to pay for the sins of Sunday. No Rams player from the team of 1963 will ever forget the scrimmage he held after their exhibition loss to Cleveland. Deacon recalls, "We did 112 plays in the 100 degree heat at Chapman College, playing the equivalent of two complete back-to-back games. That was the day Rosey Grier passed out twice because of the heat. And then, on Saturday, five of us Rams down-linemen returned to that same field to execute 108 more plays!

"NFL teams no longer scrimmage that way, and most of them didn't back then; the NFL Players Association, weak as it always has been, finally got the guts to push through some rules against it, recognizing it doesn't make sense, grinding down your own players against each other when you should be concentrating on next week's game. But back then, it was Harland's way."

Svare was not alone. And playing hard in hot weather was favored by coaches in the NFL long after Svare retired as a coach. Rob Huizenga, a doctor for the Raider's team during the 1980s, talks of practicing in extreme heat in his book You're Okay, It's Just a Bruise, *"Other coaches did allow water but were under the misconception that practicing in outrageously hot and humid conditions somehow prepared a team for the hot games in the early fall. The problem is that when a player's body temperature heats up too much, because of either an inability to expel heat in the hot humid conditions or an insufficient intake of water or both, then the muscle function goes down. And if your muscles are complaining, it's going to be hard to get in good shape or practice technical skills like blocking and catching. Plus, hyperthermia, with muscle, kidney, and brain damage, is always a risk."*

The Miracle

In their fourth exhibition game of the 1963 season, the Rams took on the Cleveland Browns. By this time, Deacon was once again the starting left end, and was working on his new straight-ahead techniques. He wasn't making the daring behind-the-scenes plays so much any more, but he was plugging his side of the line and getting his share of tackles. Even weighing 285, Deacon was still quick as a cat; but now, using the extra weight, he felt he could also bulldoze his man at the line instead of having to trick him with his old slash and burn techniques.

The Rams played a short series and were forced to punt. The kick was a good one and the Browns were pinned deep in their own end zone.

On the snap Deacon gambled run and slipped past his man into the Cleveland backfield. He was on the immortal running back Jim Brown so fast the man barely had the ball, and as he brought him crashing to the turf the ball popped loose. Deacon saw the ball spinning crazily on the five yard line. He scrambled to his feet and dove for it.

He managed to scoop it in his arms, but after that he didn't have time to recover, to tuck himself into a ball before disaster struck. Strength, after all, may be what gets a player into the game, but quickness is what keeps him out of the hospital.

There was that awful moment of stillness and then the entire Browns team came thundering down on top of him. Still hanging on to the ball, he caught the full force in the back and he went down under a tangled pile of bodies. He didn't lose consciousness, but time seemed out of joint. It took forever for the pile to unscramble itself and crawl off him. And that's when the fear set in—He couldn't move his legs!

One of the coaches was looking down at him like he was a slab of beef. Somebody was waving for Mother Menifee, and some other players came out and slung Deacon's arms over their shoulders and carried him off the field, his legs dragging behind him like limp celery stalks.

Stretched out behind the bench, he looked up at the sky and his teammate's legs and realized the stunning end that had come to his career. All his pain and driving determination for nothing! All the years of dedication and sacrifice, only to end up a cripple!

Somebody was talking. He heard the low mumble of George Menifee's encouraging voice in his ear. How long had it been? Five minutes? Ten minutes? Time itself was a blur. Out there on the field they were already in the second quarter. But wait . . . there was a tingling in his legs, in one of them, at least. Deacon tried with all his might—there, his left leg twitched! In modern times, he would have been strapped to a board and carried off to the hospital to be kept under observation for a week. But in the 1960s the game didn't feature such niceties. Deacon was on his back behind the water cooler and the first aid kit, and it was sink or swim.

Deacon's mind wandered. He thought back to his childhood, to being dipped in the lake at baptism, submerged in the God of Isaac and Jacob, swallowed up by the love of the God of Israel, the God of his race, the God of his mother Mattie. Mattie, Mattie, Mattie, Deacon called over space and time, Mama, don't God owe you no miracles for all your hard work an' time put in? Deacon's head was spinning and he knew he was thinking crazy thoughts, but Lord, if there ever was a time for miracles. Deacon prayed or babbled, not even knowing what he was saying as he strained every nerve for some small sign from on high. It came to him, crystal clear—not a sign, but the hard-shell knowledge of what it was that he had to do. It wasn't a voice or anything melodramatic. It was a feeling of calm resolve, the simple idea that all his efforts could not have been for nothing—could not, would not, have been for nothing. He couldn't accept it. Deacon gritted his teeth for an all-or-nothing effort.

"Get me on my feet, Mother," he muttered.

"Deacon, no. . . we've sent for the ambulance."

Deacon looked around and saw the Rams offense was on the field. "Lamar," he called. "Lamar, come over here. An' say a prayer, bro."

Lamar had been hovering nearby, not wanting to intrude, but so nervous he was actually wringing his hands for his friend.

"Okay, Lamar," Deacon directed. "Let's get the show on the road."

Between the two of them, Lamar and Mother got him upright.

"All right. Now I'm going to walk," Deacon said quietly. And somehow, he did, taking two quick half-steps before he fell forward, flat on his face. He cried, the tears falling in the grass. He couldn't get up. "Again, fellows. Come on, Lord," he called out loud. "Kill me or cure me." The second time he made four steps before tripping over a helmet and sprawling on the grass. By now his teammates were giving him the strained, furtive pitying looks players reserve for the injured. "Come on, Lamar. Get me up."

Call it luck, grit, or foolishness, but by half-time, Deacon's back was a mass of pain and his lower body was a million pins and needles from his waist to his toes—but Deacon Jones was walking under his own power.

When the team went under the stands for half-time, Deacon stayed on the sidelines, at first painfully jogging and then gradually lengthening his stride until he was sprinting at nearly full speed. The trainer gave him a couple of pain pills, and when the team came back for the second half, Deacon put on his game face and walked over to Svare.

"I'm ready, Swede."

Svare found his recovery hard to believe. "You sure you want to go back in there?"

Deacon gave him a bleak stare, "Justice must be served."

It was a language Svare understood. He didn't say anything, just nodding once, and a brief moment of understanding flashed between them. The two men shared the same harsh gladiator's code, and in that moment a bond of respect was forged that would last their lives, no matter what other differences might come between them.

On the first play from scrimmage, Deacon lunged across the line and gave Monty Clark a hard left forearm to the helmet. He'd had his forearms taped until they were hard as plaster casts. Monty, playing right offensive tackle, went down like he'd been hit by a brick, and came up looking for the whistle. But the referees had been looking somewhere else, and so he grumbled and went back to his huddle. On the next play Deacon juked with his left and gave Monty a right, again across the helmet. Again Monty went under, but this time he managed to get a hand on his rival's chest and pull him down with him.

"What the hell you doing, Jones?" he growled, wiping the blood from his face.

"Didn't want you boys to think I went soft or anything."

"Damn it, I wasn't even in on that play!"

"I don't care, Monty. You're the guy who got to pay for it. I'd like to punish every Brown personally, but you know this is a team sport!"

Thirty years later, Deacon reflects on that moment with a wry sense of amusement. "Monty paid for that tackle for the rest of his career, every time we played the Browns, and it wasn't even his fault. But that's the way it is in the NFL—you can't show weakness or they will devour you."

Bye, Bye, Daddio

It was after dinner, but they still had a half hour before the meetings started. A group of the black Rams was gathered over coffee in the cafeteria. One of the assistant coaches ambled by at just the wrong time to overhear somebody mention something about a player's union. The assistant coach paused and backed up, slopping some coffee on his shoes as he did so.

"I thought we got rid of Ollie Matson," he said, looking pointedly at Deacon.

"Yeah, you the fools," Deacon agreed.

The man's face reddened. He was white, of course. There were no black assistant coaches on the Rams. "We're trying to promote team unity around here, Mr. Jones."

"The masters on the plantation always say that to the slaves. We got to pull the plow together now."

"Is that how you think we treat you?" The guy was really starting to lose it. Deacon had a sudden thought. Swede should give his assistants his precious intelligence test. That way, they'd be at least as smart as the players.

"Calm down, coach," Bass said. "We were just discussing the sad fate of poor Alex Karras and his buddy Paul Hornung." Karras, the Lions star lineman, and Hornung, the great Packer man-of-all-seasons, had been suspended for betting on NFL games. The assistant coach was like a bull in the ring, eager to charge after the next target. "What about it?" he yelled in a voice loud enough to address a convention. "Those bums got what they deserved! Like Rozelle said, NFL football players must be above suspicion."

Deacon couldn't believe it, "An' you're tellin' us you never bet on a game? Not even a lousy five-spot with your buddies?"

"Maybe you forgot." Bass pointed a finger at the coach's big gut, which hung over his belt, "Back in your playing days, before you acquired that growth, you probably felt different."

"I never did!" The man tried to suck it up while he radiated rage like a blast of heat.

"The point here," Deacon said, remembering his long conversations with Gee-Gee the Midget, "is not whether you gambled or not. The point is that Rozelle is making up the laws as he goes along." He saw Bass was staring at him, nodding in agreement, but surprised at this coming from the Swamp Boy. "There was no law against players gambling until Pete invented it, like some king or emperor," Deacon continued. "If we had a union, they could be pointing these things out to the American people. Of course, the owners don't want that."

"Or their lackeys." somebody at the table muttered loud enough so everybody heard.

The coach snorted and glared around the table, but nobody said anything more. He was finally about to leave when Lamar rushed in breathlessly, "You boys heard? Big Daddy's dead!"

"What?" The table erupted in disbelief. Big Daddy Lipscomb, the huge black All-Star defensive tackle who had been released for a song by the Rams, was playing for Pittsburgh, and was in the height of his career.

"Heroin overdose, the papers say!" Lamar passed over the sports page, and it quickly went around the table. "Says he'd been drunk at the time and was shootin' up on dope!"

A wave of angry response ran around the table.

"That don't make no sense a-tall!"

"No, no, man!"

"Dope an' booze don't mix!"

Although they'd ignored him, the coach was still standing there, his great belly hanging in the morning sunlight while the coffee was growing lukewarm in his cup. "See," he said. "You players are just children. You don't need a union, you need mothers to take care of you."

Deacon quietly looked up at him, "Big Daddy had a lot of friends at this table. You better move along, fat man, before you get yourself hurt."

The blood drained from the man's face and he quickly moved on, muttering something about how they hadn't heard the last from him. Deacon watched him go and then said to nobody in particular, "I met Lips my rookie year. I hung around with him at the Pro Bowl. That man drank his whiskey right out of the bottle, and he could consume an awesome amount . . . but you never seen a man with a more gentle spirit, or one so willin' to help a man when he was down."

"All that," Lamar agreed, "but he was too trusting. He carried all the money he had in his pocket. He figured no man would ever take him on."

Deacon shook his head and tossed the paper on the table, "I don't believe what they say here. Big Daddy loved alcohol too much to do heroin."

"The two don't mix no-how. You never see a man with both habits."

"Paper say somebody dumped him out of a car in front of the hospital. Left him on the sidewalk."

"Sounds like murder to me."

Deacon got up and left the table, wanting to be by himself. He walked slowly along the tree-lined sidewalks while the sun turned reddish orange and settled through the smog and behind the western horizon out into the darkening Pacific Ocean where he could not see. Big Daddy was gone. It was hard to believe. Some men seemed bigger than life, like they were carved out of a mountain . . . and now he was gone. The sidewalk dipped and Deacon walked out of the slanting sunlight into a small park already filled with shade. He sat on a bench and mused over the way things were; here he'd struggled and scratched and fought to trade away his life as an underdog in the Deep South for a new life as an underdog in the NFL. Well, at least he had a life. Big Daddy had been left with nothing. He looked around at the trees and the bushes, all spring-green and flowery, their pastel colors muted in the oncoming darkness. It was a good place to mourn a friend.

Big Daddy Lipscomb hadn't been known to use drugs, and a closer examination of the facts led investigators and close friends to believe he'd probably been injected with the fatal dose by people intent on robbing him.

Johnny Sample, the Steelers player who roomed with Big Daddy, said in his book Confessions of a Dirty Ballplayer, *"The people with him must have eventually got him to his car after he got so drunk he couldn't move or after he passed out, and they had taken whatever money he had. And just to make sure he didn't wake up too soon, they shot him with narcotics and drove him to the hospital, pulled him out of the car onto the sidewalk where they left him. It was supposed to appear that he had overdosed himself and had tried to make it to the hospital. But I'm certain that the narcotics wasn't self-inflicted. All three injection marks were in his right arm and there were no other marks anywhere else on his body. Now Big Daddy was right-handed, so logically he would have used his right arm in giving the shots. That means the injection marks should have been in the left arm. But they weren't."*[1]

Deacon still feels strongly that professional football should have mustered its resources and done more to bring the real situation to light. "There is overwhelming evidence to indicate Big Daddy was robbed and shot up with dope, and died from an overdose. That's murder where I come from, even if they hadn't really meant to kill him. Maybe we couldn't expect the NFL to do anything, but we players should have gotten our union to hire the right people and open an independent investigation. After all, we're supposed to take care of our own. The murderers have never been apprehended, which is one thing—but Big Daddy's name is tarnished forever when he could have been exonerated by a panel of his peers."

Farm Boy Meets Swamp Boy

When Deacon came in from practice, he was even later than usual. He'd found that sweet spot and had been kicking field goals from thirty and forty yards out. He said he'd stay until he missed, and that had

---

1. Johnny Sample, *Confessions of a Dirty Ballplayer* (New York, Dell Publishing, 1970), pp. 91, 92.

turned out to be seventeen kicks later. By that time the ballboys were ready to revolt so he hurried and shanked one to the right and they all left the field happy.

By the time he got to the locker room, everybody had finished up in the shower room. It being Friday night with no game on Sunday, most of the team members were getting dressed up and slapping the hair tonic on their heads for a night on the town in Orange County. For the blacks that meant pitchers of beer and pizza at Me & Ed's, one of the few places they felt they were welcome. As Deacon rounded the corner to his locker, he thought he saw Merlin Olsen, the big white boy who played next to him on the line, moving quickly away from his locker.

"Hey, Muley—what you doin' in my locker?"

Merlin turned toward him, looking guilty as sin, and flung his arms wide, "Hey, nothing. I was just walking past."

"Look to me like you have to do a big U-turn to walk past my locker, it bein' in the corner an' all."

"Well, that's how it was." Merlin sounded offended. He was big as a country outhouse, with a genuine western drawl to boot, and grievance played on him about as sincere as it would on a bull elephant.

Deacon looked around the room, "Was this guy in my locker?" Everybody just looked at their hands or the floor and shook their heads like they didn't know. "Lamar, was this guy in my locker?"

Lamar mumbled, "I didn't see nothin'."

Deacon figured Merlin had always been the bully on the block back in his tiny home town in the sticks, the kind of guy you waded into and he folded because he wasn't used to real trouble. "You lucky my brother took my pig-sticker away a couple years ago, white boy, or right now it would be stickin' in you!"

Merlin flushed, "Now hold on. Who you callin' a pig?"

"I ain't callin' nobody a pig! You went in my locker, man!" Deacon balled his big fists and moved to where his chin was inches from Merlin's. "Where I come from, that's a major offense! A man's got to defend what's his, an' he don't expect his teammates to be stealin' from him!"

The color on Merlin's face progressed into bright crimson, "But I wasn't stealing anything!" He looked around the room for support, but, again, nobody was saying anything. And Merlin realized that, by fate or coincidence, he was the only white man left in the locker room.

"Well, I say you was!"

Deacon slammed open his locker and started to check his things, looking first in his wallet and then in his shoes where he'd hid one of his new watches. He'd won big money in a poker game, and had been the laugh of the camp when he went out and bought six watches. Bass had led the laughter when Deacon proudly displayed them all on one arm at dinner the other night. But the chuckles had died quickly enough when he explained he just wanted to show them what he'd bought with their money. But this stealing thing was no laughing matter. Olsen could go buy his own watch—hell, with the bonus money he got, he could buy a store full of watches and rings and what- ever the hell he wanted!

"Look." It was Olsen talking behind him. At that moment, Deacon was angry enough to turn around and give him a fist to the face. In fact, that's just what he was going to do. He balanced himself for the attack, gauging how much space was between them.

"Look," Olsen continued behind him, "I'm sorry. I didn't realize you'd get so mad. I just needed to borrow something, that's all. See, I didn't know you were so . . . territorial."

Deacon slowly turned and looked at the big white tackle, sudden understanding breaking over him. He didn't even stop to wonder what it could possibly have been that the white boy wanted to borrow. That wasn't important any more. Deacon asked, "Playin' up there in Mormon country, you didn't meet a lot of black boys, did you?"

"Not many. We don't have black people where I come from. At least, they're pretty rare. So this is just a little new to me."

"Oh." Deacon was remembering the first year he'd played in the NFL and the bewilderment and anxiety he'd felt, going up against white players for the first time. Here was Olsen, this Mormon kid right off the farm, playing the line with a Deacon, a Rosey, and a Lamar. "Okay, I kin see that," he muttered.

But at that moment, just when Deacon was softening, he reached into the pocket of his jacket, hanging up inside the locker, for a pack of chewing gum he was sure he'd left there, and came up with some- thing soft, warm, squirming and—alive! It was a huge, monster rat! Deacon's eyes bugged like saucers, and he threw the evil thing in the air and jumped on the bench behind him.

"Yikes!", he yelled. "It's a filthy rat!"

The room burst into laughter. Suddenly it seemed like the entire team was back in the room. Merlin chased the rat and caught it, hold- ing it captive in one giant hand while he stroked it's back. "Naw, look, Deak—it's only a harmless laboratory rat!"

"Git it away from me! I hate rats!"

By now his teammates were howling with glee. Deacon's obvious horror and everything he said delighted them. "What, Swamp Boy," Bass yelled, "you're always tellin' us about the Florida wilderness. How come you can't even stand a cute little mouse?"

"I been there—that's why I can't stand 'em! I hate bugs an' spiders an' snakes of all description! I don't want 'em near me, man! Get that stinkin' rat out of here!"

The crowd gradually dwindled, still chuckling about Deacon's horror over a harmless little rodent. For his part, Deacon brooded alone while he threw off his soiled clothing and took his shower. If that was Muley Olsen's idea of a joke, he was going to set race relations back twenty years! Still, in the isolation of the steaming shower room, he couldn't help a small, rueful smile. He'd get that damn white boy back if it took him the rest of his life!

Today, Deacon readily admits the joke was on him for most of his playing career, "That first time in the locker room, I really should have popped him one in the face, because after that, he was always playing those farm-boy tricks on me. I'd open my locker and there would be a big, black plastic spider dangling on a string, or a life-size rubber swamp snake from Disneyland coiled up to spring on me . . . frogs or toads would hop out, there'd be a mouse in my shoe or something else just as evil. That was Merlin's idea of a joke. They should have called him Merlin the Merciless. The only thing that saved his life was what he'd told me about us being the first blacks he'd ever played ball with. He made me recognize that, coming from two totally different parts of the world, we still shared some things in common. And that opened my mind to see his true greatness—his athletic ability and his drive to be the best. We had a lot in common, but I just had to grow as a person to where I could admit it. Ended up, I was proud to play alongside Merlin, though I never could appreciate his weird sense of humor."

For his part, to this day Merlin Olsen doesn't have a remorseful bone in his body about any of his farm-boy pranks. "You've got this huge defensive end, six foot six inches of total badness, willing to take on anybody in the NFL with his moves and his loud mouth, and the guy turns out to be deathly afraid of God's little creatures of the woods and the forest. I'm sorry, but that's funny!"

Tinkering with Greatness I

Perhaps if he hadn't been so tired, Deacon wouldn't have been suckered
into another of their late night Bible arguments. Lamar liked to apply
the Bible's teachings to everyday living. And, while Deacon didn't run
around quoting it, in his time he'd won a prize or two for Bible knowledge at the Open Door Missionary Baptist Sunday School. The trouble
started because Lamar took Jesus' saying from Matthew 22:21, "Render
therefore unto Caesar the things that are Caesar's; and unto God the
things that are God's" and translated "Caesar" to mean anybody in
authority. That, of course, meant that it said right in the Bible that a
player should obey his coaches, absolutely and without question, or at
least more than Deacon did. Deacon, in turn, argued that it was a political teaching, meant only for emperors and other heads of state. In the
heat of the debate, Lamar had told Deacon that the root of his problem
was that he personally didn't pay homage enough to those in power.

Deacon had turned to the wall in sullen fury and refused further
debate, but Lamar's ideas had enough of an influence on him so that
the next day on the practice field he decided to try a small experiment.
He picked a time when Svare was alone and walked up to the coach.
"Wonder if you got a moment for me," he said.

"Sure," Swede said, trying hard not to show his surprise.

"Been havin' a little trouble gettin' off the ball. Wonder if you
spotted anything." Deacon figured Svare was smart enough, knowing
he was still forty pounds over his last year's playing weight, to simply
tell him to drop another twenty pounds.

But it was a rare day that Svare's surly young defensive star asked
any coach on the staff for anything, and Svare decided to make the
most of it. "Well . . . I have noticed a thing or two. We're about to run
a series here. I'll watch your stance, and we'll talk."

They ran a running play, with Deacon facing off against offensive
tackle Frank Varrichione. Svare studied Deacon's motions, and then
asked to see the play again. Brows knitted and hand cupping his chin,
Svare concentrated on the vectors, the angles, the complicated formu-
la involved as potential energy became kinetic energy and players
flung themselves at each other. Svare was good at this sort of thing. He
could abstract himself from the blood and guts of the moment and figure other options and better ways. He was confident he knew how to
fix things.

After the play ran the second time, he called Deacon over. "I've got

it, Jones. A couple of things. You're a little knock-kneed, and you're trying to get your legs underneath yourself. When you're in your stance,
your fingers are still moving. That means you're not forward enough.
Tell you what—instead of your fingertips, put your first knuckles down.
That will force your body forward maybe just enough. Try it."

Deacon did, and on the next play he went past Frank so fast he
couldn't believe it. Svare nodded, satisfied, and there was a gleam in
his eyes, "Okay. You get in that stance, and don't leave it."

Deacon nodded and went back to his practice. It did feel better. It
wasn't much to go past Varrichione, who was slow as a cow, but maybe
Svare had something. Every little inch counted in the game. Deacon
shrugged, wondering if maybe Lamar was right and there were
rewards associated with giving Caesar his due.

The trouble didn't develop immediately, it happened when
Deacon had all but forgotten his attempt to render unto Swede the
things that were Swede's. It was three or four practice sessions later
when Svare called him over again. Deacon walked to the coach's side
with a sinking heart. By now Lamar's sermon was as cold on his heart
as yesterday's pea soup. His spirit of cooperation had disappeared. Still,
he had to see what the Swede wanted. Svare gave him the same steely
eyed squint as he had before and said, "Think I've spotted something
else, Jones. Something major."

"What's that, Swede?"

"I think you're driving off the wrong foot. I think your natural
stance would be to switch to exactly opposite of what you're doing."

"But . . ."

Swede cut him off, clearly having the bit between his teeth and
wanting to run with it. "No buts, Jones. You normally put your right
hand to the ground and your left foot forward. Do it the other way."

"But Swede—the way I do it, I use my power into the tackle.
That's who I face off against on mostly every play. You got me aimin'
my power at the tight end, who's usually workin' a pass pattern. I
don't see him come in on me but three or four times the entire game!"

Swede, who had been signing off some forms and only half-listening, looked up and was surprised to see Deacon still there, "Jones.
Don't argue. It's your big problem—attitude. Just do it. I was right
before, and I'm right on this!"

So Deacon went through the exhibition season and into the first
games of the regular season firing off his opposite foot at the snap. Not
that the two were necessarily connected, but the Rams continued their

tailspin, following a weak 2-3 preseason record with a 23-2 loss to the Lions. The two points against Detroit were scored by the defense; rookie quarterback Terry Baker and Zeke Bratkowski between them could muster no offense at all. Roman Gabriel had been set aside as a "slow starter," and didn't get into the game until it was too late to make any difference.

The Rams weaknesses were clear; the offensive line wasn't holding, and the defensive backfield was leaky as a sieve. But the Tuesday after the loss, Svare punished the entire team with one of his scrimmages. It didn't do anything for morale, and seemed to do even less for the team's mechanics. The following week they lost to Washington, 37-14. After the game, Svare told the press, "We just let them push us around the field, beat us up, in the second half. They outhit us, punched big holes in our line. We were real bad. We didn't play smart defense, so we didn't get a chance to play offense." What Svare couldn't see was that he was wearing the players out with his midweek scrimmages, and what he neglected to say was that every time the Rams did go on offense, it was three futile tries and a punt.

The paralyzed and steadily failing Gene Brito watched the Rams-Redskins game from a wheelchair on the sidelines. Gene, who had played for the Redskins before he came to the Rams, and who was respected by both teams, was awarded the game ball by the victorious Redskins. Deacon watched the ceremony from his own sideline, his mind a jumble of mixed emotions. He couldn't help but remember how he'd taken over Gene's position in training camp three years before. He wondered what Gene would say to Svare's command that he fire off the ball from the wrong foot. Of course, Brito was a white guy, and had established himself as the best in his position. He probably wouldn't have listened to Harland in the first place!

The Rams traveled to Cleveland for their first away game of the 1963 season. They took to the field in a light but steady rain with the temperature in the low fifties. Still punishing the Browns for the paralyzing play that almost ended his career, Deacon had his first good day of the season. In spite of coming off the ball wrong, he amassed four tackles and a swarm of assists. In the second quarter he smashed through the line along with linebacker Jack Pardee and threw Frank Ryan for a huge twenty-two yard loss. A few plays later, Deacon came through solo and threw Ryan for another six. They held the powerful Browns to twenty points. But the Rams offense scored only six, and the team lost its third game of the season.

By now, with a long string of losses in his cap, Svare was experimenting with more than Deacon's stance. He was willing to try anything. Determined to unlock his offense, he benched Hydrogen Ball Baker and alternated Bratkowski and Gabriel on every play throughout the game. While this alternating quarterback system, which had been tried out before by Tom Landry and the Cowboys, enabled the Rams coaching staff to call all the plays from the bench, it did nothing for the rotating quarterbacks' sense of timing or for their self-confidence. Still, when interviewed after the game, Svare thought he saw positive signs: "Offensive backfield coach Don Heinrich called every play and I think he did a fine job." Svare felt the Rams' inability to score was becoming psychological. "It's like making a three-foot putt in golf. You know it's easy, but when you start missing them, you begin to wonder when you'll ever make it."

The sad season rolled on, the Rams losing on Green Bay's Lambeau field and to Chicago in the Coliseum. The Bears beat them 52-14, seemingly a terrible day for the Rams defense, but *all but seven* of the Bears points were the direct or indirect result of Ram fumbles, pass interceptions and penalties. Still, Swede stubbornly stuck to his rotating quarterback offense.

Svare may not have been talking about it, but the reporters noted that, in spite of the big score the Bears rolled up against them, the Rams' front four were superb. The men from the press also noted that, as they walked up to Svare and owner Dan Reeves, the two looked like they were waiting for their execution. Svare remarked, "I don't know how we will do the quarterbacks against the Vikings next Sunday. It's a week-to-week proposition."

"Day to day," Dan Reeves added sadly, "hour to hour."

And Svare responded to the losses the only way he knew; he called another of his notorious midseason scrimmages to punish the team for losing. And he stopped by every once in a while in practice, just to let Deacon know he was still checking how his new stance was progressing.

Deacon sadly shakes his head looking back on those grim times: "We were their kindergarten and their grade school, we were their education and their excuse when things went wrong. Notice how their thinking went: the offense wasn't clicking, so blame the quarterbacks and call the plays yourself. When the offense still doesn't score, blame the defense for not holding. After all these years, I still feel sorry for the L.A. fans, who didn't really have a chance to see what was going on behind the scenes and who had to put up with all the losses."

Don Paul, who had "discovered" Deacon in his rookie training camp, said when interviewed in 1993 at his office in Woodland Hills, "I never saw such raw talent in my life. When Harland took over my job, I advised him, 'Make Deacon work hard, but don't give him any rules to follow. You tell a normal guy to always block and close the hole. But Deacon has genius on the field. He'll go around, then block and close the hole.' When you have a great player like Deacon, you just don't mess him up. You let him do it his way. That's what I told him. And then, when Harland became head coach, I was announcing the games, and we used to have dinner together the night before the games. He'd tell me the game plan and some of the signals to make my job easier in the booth. My advice to Swede on Deacon was this: I told him, 'You are not going to teach Deacon a thing more about being a defensive end. If I were you, I'd try him at fullback. He's got great hands, and he's the biggest, fastest man I've ever seen.' But Harland never listened to me on that one."

Tinkering with Greatness II

After five games, the Rams had five losses, and Deacon had tackled quarterbacks behind the line only twice. He was getting his share of tackles and plugging up his side of the line, but his bulked-up size was a definite disadvantage in the fourth quarter, when carrying that extra weight was like strapping on a bowling ball. And the new stance was giving him fits.

Deacon quietly went to assistant coach Jack Patera and explained his problem. Jack listened patiently and then drew him aside where no one else could hear them. "Look, Deacon. Nobody's very happy with anyone around here these days. In case you haven't noticed, whole careers go by between Ram wins. My best advice to you is, hunker down and cover your ass."

"But Jack—I know I'm doing things wrong, and it's hurting me. The opposition has spotted what I'm doing. Hell, they can see it from the other bench. And next week, our next opponents get the game films. They're going to exploit my weakness until I fix it! But Swede won't let me fix it!"

"You could be wrong, you know. You could be dead wrong and Swede could be right. After all, you're just as stubborn as he is."

"Damn it, it's not about who's the most stubborn! Everybody in the stadium sees it!"

Jack shook his head, "I'm telling you, Deacon. The head coach says do something, you do it!"

These matters, which may seem long ago and far away—of minor concern in the modern world—are still deadly serious to those who were involved. Harland Svare, who has over the years developed many of his theories into one of the most advanced and forward-thinking sports rehabilitation clinics in the world, disagrees with Deacon to this day, becoming irate at the notion that he might, out of the millions of decisions he made at the helm of the Rams and the Chargers, have made this one coaching mistake. Interviewed by this writer recently in San Diego, Svare declared emphatically, "Deacon's full of shit if he thinks I screwed him up in any way! I helped him, for God's sake! And he admitted it at the time. And years later, when he came to the San Diego Chargers, he came to me again, complaining his stance didn't seem right. He'd picked up some bad habits, but when I got his weight back on his first knuckles, we cleared that up. And he thanked me for it at the time!"

Deacon admits Svare did help with his idea to get his weight a bit more forward—and was a help until he got that idea to shift his feet. And when Svare recently told Patera that Deacon held them responsible for shifting his stance to the wrong foot, Patera commented gruffly, "Deacon may have forgotten more about football than we ever taught him!" But when asked directly if he and Svare actually had tried to change Deacon's stance and what the results were, Patera replied, "That was nearly thirty years ago. I can't remember specifically if we did or didn't, or if so, what." That was three decades ago . . . but Jack, not Deacon, seems to have the memory problem.

The Schnelker Offense

Since offense wasn't Svare's area of expertise, he gave his assistant Bob Schnelker a great deal of latitude. The coaching staff was always looking for new ideas, and Schnelker generally came up with a trick play or razzle-dazzle formation early in the game. But as soon as the trick failed and the dazzle fizzed, the Rams reverted to the dull, grind-it-out offense that was as predictable to opposing teams and coaches as it was to the fans and the press.

Stung by the team's mounting losses, Svare declared a temporary end to the quarterback wars by naming Roman Gabriel starting quarterback, and the Rams began to respond. In the sixth game, Svare's "awesome foursome" began to show their extraordinary strength; playing in the Coliseum, they harassed the Vikings so intensely that their vaunted passing game couldn't get going. In the second quarter, Deacon beat his man, got his hands high and blocked a field goal attempt. That blocked field goal proved to be the difference in the game, and the Rams won their first game of the season 27-24. Times writer Mal Florence, perhaps not realizing that Swede punished the Rams after every loss, wrote, "Svare had 'punished' his troops with an unprecedented scrimmage this week and the Rams responded with a courageous victory, winning a game that could easily have been lost because of their own errors and Tarkenton's evasive tactics." Describing what it was like to play against the elusive Viking quarterback, Florence continued that, "Tarkenton ran an exhausted Ram end, Deacon Jones, into the ground before he speared Brown with a seven yard touchdown pass that actually traveled forty yards in the air." At that point, the Vikings had gone ahead 24-14. But Gabriel, who went all the way, refused to give up, and led the Rams to a come-from-behind victory.

It was a sweet and memorable win, for this was Harland Svare's first victory ever as an NFL coach. Svare declared, "I'm going to stick with Gabe all the way now." He smiled, unabashed to let the world know about his carrot-and-stick approach to football. "There won't be a Tuesday scrimmage this week . . . not this week."

The Rams also beat the 49ers the following week; Roman hit fifteen of twenty-five pass attempts, with two touchdown passes and no interceptions. Svare attributed the hard-throwing quarterback's success to the fact that he was now releasing the ball faster, and on the long bombs he was "pulling the string" rather than "going with his blazer," techniques that it seemed he thought obvious to the world Svare's coaching staff had taught him. But in Minnesota the following week, two Ram fumbles set up unearned Viking touchdowns, and the Vikings won 21-13. In Chicago, the Bears beat the Rams 6-0 in another of those famous defensive struggles. Roman Gabriel's nose was broken, and Svare told the reporters his team had played their best defense of the year. "We really came to play. We were just harassed by the Bear's defense." He didn't say anything about the lead-bottomed Schnelker offense. There wasn't really anything to say.

Svare would stick with Schnelker while losing year after year in Los Angeles, and he brought him along after that for his five losing seasons in San Diego with the Chargers. As Deacon comments with a deadpan note of gravity, "There are some in this world who would call that loyalty . . . I'd consider it more a fatal attraction."

After all these years, Roman Gabriel comments on Schnelker, "Personality-wise, he coached by screaming, cussing and hollering at people. In practice, one of us quarterbacks would just barely get the ball and be dropping back, and he'd already be screaming, 'Throw it to so-and-so, throw it, you dummy!' Then, if you'd throw it somewhere else and it fell incomplete, he'd scream 'God damn it, I told you so!' He'd do the same to the receivers, yelling at them before the ball even got to them, or if the play was broken up and the ball didn't come their way, he'd say, 'It don't matter, you were gonna miss it anyway!'"

The Birth of the Stunt

After their bitter defeat at the hands of the Bears, Deacon still had thrown quarterbacks for a loss behind the line only twice the entire year. In the opening moments before the Detroit game he decided to shift his feet back to his old stance. He had more than given Caesar his due, and it had cost him dearly. Now he was going to take back what was his.

The first quarter, Deacon swarmed all over the field. He was in on almost every play, juking his man one way and cutting back the other way with lightning speed into the backfield to harass Lions quarterback Earl Morrall. Merlin Olsen, playing next to him on the line, was quick to notice, "Hey, Deak! I see you went back to your old stance!"

The front four was standing in a row behind the ball, glaring across the line at the Detroit offense the way Svare had taught them. That was the thing about Swede. You never knew when he was going to come up with a really good idea, and this was one of his best. In the old days, the defense used to rest on one knee, waiting for the offensive huddle to break up. Harland figured out the psychology of the relationship between offense and defense. If his "awesome front four" was to have the presence he wanted, they had to be standing there with snarls on their faces, waiting to punish the offense, eager to get on with the next play so they could crash through and destroy the quarterback or crush the runner.

Deacon looked over at Merlin, "What I got to lose? Swede say he's gonna trade my ass anyway, once the season's over. I'm doing it the right way from now on."

Olsen cast a quick glance back to their bench, "You're gonna be okay unless you mess up. Then they're gonna flay your hide."

Deacon shrugged, "I'm gonna play it like I see it. If I miss a tackle or get ridden out on a play, I'll take my lumps in the Tuesday review meeting. I learned my lesson, man. So long as I get to the quarterback, what can they say?"

This was revolutionary thinking for that age. Deacon was announcing that he intended to take unheard-of risks on a regular basis. The old style defensive players were big and slow. The philosophy in using them was to plug holes. They might lose a few yards on every play, but if they could keep the opposing team from making ten yards in three plays, their team would get the ball back. But Deacon was the first of the big, fast defensive linemen. His new style relied on his speed and quickness. By gambling on the flow of the play, if he guessed right, he could catch runners and passers behind the line of play and throw them for losses. This was for the fans to watch, and came to be very popular. Of course, if he guessed wrong, the results could be disastrous. Deacon will admit he single-handedly lost a game or two early in his career; but as he matured, he came to dominate the game as few players have ever done.

"Way to go, Deak. That's my man," Olsen grinned. "As long as you're in a gambling mood, you want to try something?"

"Yeah, sure. What?"

"I've got an idea. On the snap, you wait a half-beat and I'll come across and smear your guy. They won't be expecting it and that should cut you free."

Deacon caught on immediately. The evil light came to his eyes, "Sort of an intentional mistake."

"Yeah. A pre-thought-out stunt."

"Swede's gonna have a heart attack."

"If it works, he won't even know what happened. If it doesn't, we say we missed our assignments."

Deacon gave one brief nod, "I like it."

Morrall led the Lions out of the huddle, hurrying because they'd taken more time than usual in the huddle. On the snap, Deacon hung back and big number 74 lurched past him, slamming into his man. There was a huge hole, and both he and Merlin raced in to tackle Morrall for a big loss!

Olsen got up and winked at him, "Don't say anything, Deak. We'll work on it some more, like a secret weapon."

Deacon had a great day. He batted down one of Morrall's passes, knocking his arm aside for an incomplete pass, what the scorers list as a "QB hurry." He was credited with three solo tackles and numerous assists, and another sack on Morrall with Rosey, and the Rams won 28-21.

After the game Deacon took his shower with complete satisfaction. Thinking back on it, two important things had happened that day. First, he untinkered what the tinkering Svare had done to his stance, and second, Merlin helped him see the possibilities of premeditated stunting on the line. Before this time stunts had proved sporadically effective. Usually an accident and the result of a missed blocking assignment, they would in the future become one of the many weapons in the Fearsome Foursome's arsenal, and would gradually be put into widespread use throughout the league.

In this game, Gabriel hit Carroll Dale with three touchdown bombs. In spite of this performance, the next week Dan Reeves told reporters he was eagerly looking forward to the college draft because he was "looking for linemen, defensive backs, and quarterbacks."

Today, Gabriel thinks it was the long shadow of Waterfield that continued to haunt him. "After Bob gave up the head coaching job, he kept in close touch with Dan. He still scouted for the Rams, and he told Reeves 'the answer to the Rams, quarterback problem' was first Terry Baker, and later, Bill Munson." This hurt the Rams in the long term because Reeves continued to use his high draft choices to load up on quarterbacks, instead of rebuilding his two obvious weaknesses—the Rams offensive line and defensive backfield.

The Business of Football

It was late November, a grey, overcast day in southern California, and the Rams were practicing at their customary in-season training facility in the San Fernando Valley. After one of those endless series of running the same play to get it right, Deacon noticed the coaches were ignoring the players. Instead of calling in another play or simply waving their hands to run the same one over, they were caught together in a tense little knot on the sidelines. It was odd, because they weren't into their usual yelling or screaming with everybody trying to out-shout the others in panicked enthusiasm. Their attitude was strangely quiet, even somber.

Somebody died was the first thing that flashed through Deacon's mind. He, Merlin, Rosey, and Lamar were standing in their customary clump at the line. Watching the coaches gathered quietly together, they all had similar thoughts.

"Maybe Swede's got his can fired."

"Oh, Mama," Rosey said. "Too good to be true." Rosey, one of the quickest men in football for the first ten yards off the ball, had been waging guerrilla war since he had gotten to the Rams in an attempt to avoid any conditioning and distance training. Taking up the chal-lenge as something personal, Svare had him running a mile for time every day along with the rest of the squad. Rosey would push his huge bulk along fast enough to get around the first turn of the track, far enough from the starting line so the coaches wouldn't come after him, and then he'd slow down to a walk.

"Maybe Reeves died," Deacon wondered. "Or sold the team."

"More wishful thinking," Lamar said. "He'll die before he sells the team."

They didn't have the heart of the matter, but they were right—it was something important. Svare gathered the team in the center of the field, and what he said next stunned them and changed their lives for-ever. No one was saying a word, but he raised both hands for silence. It was an awkward gesture, and Deacon had the sudden memory of an old black preacher on a long-ago Palm Sunday morning raising his hands in sorrow over the death of Christ. Without knowing why, he dreaded Svare's next words.

"The President of the United States, John F. Kennedy, has been assassinated in Dallas . . ."

Sounds of shock and dismay ran around the group. Rosey, who had worked directly with Kennedy, gave a choked sob and started crying, unabashed at his grief. Deacon, like many blacks, saw the young President as the best hope of the next generation, the best chance Americans had to live together in peace and harmony.

Svare raised his voice over the group, "That's the end of practice. Go home and be with your families. I really doubt we'll have a game this weekend. Be on standby, and we'll give you a call later today or tomorrow." It was already Friday. The team straggled off the field, showered, and left in silence. There wasn't a man on the squad who thought there was a chance they would play on Sunday.

The second unbelievable call came Saturday morning. Deacon was out washing his car in the carport when Iretha called down from an open window, and he ran up to grab the telephone.

It was Lamar. "The owners just held a meeting and decided to play the games scheduled this Sunday."

Deacon was dumbstruck, "But . . . the President's dead . . . the nation's declared a national day of mourning!"

So it was that on Sunday, November 24, the day Jack Ruby killed Lee Harvey Oswald, the powerful Baltimore Colts and Johnny Unitas came to town. Nobody on either team wanted to play, but what were they going to do? There was no union to speak for the players. No one came to the locker rooms and asked for their opinion. They sat around in their uniforms, waiting for some last-minute cancellation.

"The owners could push the whole schedule back a week," Deacon said to nobody in particular.

"Yeah. I suppose it is a bother, you know, changing stadium dates and moving games around for the whole league."

"They could just drop one game from the schedule."

"Heresy, friend Deacon," Dick Bass said. "Imagine the money they would lose."

One of the assistant coaches came by with the rumor that there might be a sit-down protest at the fifty-yard line, and another brought the news that the game would now be played with stern-faced, uniformed policemen ringing the stands.

Both teams played as if in a trance. For the record, the Rams upset the visitors 17-16, but nobody cared, and after the game the fans shuffled silently out of the stadium while the players went back to their locker rooms like zombies.

In his sports column, Jim Murray noted that horse racing great Willie Shoemaker, who stands four foot eleven inches and refused to race on that day for $75,000, stood taller than Pete Rozelle, who at six foot one inch insisted pro football go on as scheduled. In some of the most moving lines ever to appear on a sports page, Murray summed up his feelings and those of many Americans in his *Los Angeles Times* column of November 24, 1963:

The drums are rolling in the background. A body is being carried up the Capitol steps on a TV screen. A wife and a daughter—

mine— are weeping as a band plays "Hail to the Chief" and I could go on but this blamed fool typewriter never would work with water in the keys. And why is it the mind is empty when the heart is full, the fingers dry when the eyes are brimming?

That night Deacon walked the streets of West L.A., near where he lived, trying to find some reason why he should respect the NFL owners' decision. Try as he might, he wasn't able to think of a thing. He thought about the morality of the things he'd done as a kid. It was one thing to skip church on Sunday when the sun was warm and the fish were biting. But to fail to pay homage when some member of the family, somebody like a father or a grandmother, had died . . . that was an outrage against the nature of what people were supposed to be. How much greater was the sin of disrespect when the dead person was the head of the country!

The Monday after the game, in an effort to muffle the hue and cry that went up, owner Dan Reeves was quoted in the L.A. newspapers, "If we offended anybody, we apologize, but there can be no disrespect to President Kennedy's memory when none was intended." Deacon smiles sadly, shaking his head slowly from side to side, "That was Dan, the Money Man, in his true form. That's one time his PR department couldn't cover his greedy butt. What Reeves said to excuse his own and the other NFL owners' greed was awful. It was like a man telling you, 'I'm going to kick your dog, steal your horse, burn down your house and have my way with your woman—an' I'll tell you when to be insulted.' After all, nobody was asking the owners to cancel the games, just postpone them for our national day of mourning out of respect for President John F. Kennedy."

Pete Rozelle retired several years ago after serving as NFL league commissioner for nearly thirty years. In those years pro football went from a collection of small but profitable city franchises to the booming mega-business it is today. Reached by phone at his home in southern California, in January of 1996, he remembered "taking a lot of criticism for playing those games."

His problem, he said, was compounded by the day of the week President Kennedy was killed. "Planes were to go in the air for (carrying the players to) the away games," Rozelle said.

He had to make a quick decision, and an important one; unlike baseball or hockey, each team in pro football only played a dozen games a season. To cancel the games would represent a substan-

tial drop in income for the year. To postpone them would involve a tangle of stadium commitments, ticket refunds and rescheduling.

With the nation in shock and his own uncertainty about what to do in a situation without precedent, Rozelle says he decided to seek advice. "I called Pierre Sallinger, who was an aide to the President, as well as a close confidant and friend of the Kennedy family. Pierre said that plans for the funeral were still uncertain, but that the President had always been an enormous fan of football and would probably want the games to go on. So we decided to go ahead and play the games."

Upon hearing Rozelle's comments, Deacon replied, "If that's what really happened, it was never communicated to the Ram players. We were just told to get out there and play, business as usual. Even after all these years, you've got to question their motivation. In our society, if you want to pay respect, you halt what you are doing; you don't find some excuse to go on as if nothing happened."

Playing during the period of national grief wasn't Reeves's only questionable call that year. At the end of the 1963 season, undaunted by the 5-9 record, or by Svare's abysmal overall record of five wins, fourteen losses, and a tie, Reeves announced that he was asking Svare back for 1964. Deacon comments, "Men like that deserve what they get. Foolish Dan Reeves made his own bed, and he was going to have to lie in it. The only problem was, he made that bad decision for all of us, and it had a negative affect on my life, my teammates' lives, and the hopes and aspirations of every Ram fan in the world."

6

Svare's Chance

In all, Harland Svare's reign as head coach of the Rams endured for three and a half years, from the day Bob Waterfield went bird hunting through the 1965 season, when the fans and sports writers finally had enough and began hanging him in effigy. Although it is safe to say he wanted to win as badly as any man, and that he drove the team through countless hours of serious practice, and that he tried a variety of rosters, formations, trick plays and the like, in the end Svare failed to find the winning combination that takes a team on to victory week after week and in the end wins league and world championships. In his first year, 1962, Svare coached the last six games of the season for five losses and a tie. In 1963, his team went 5-9. In 1964 they were 5-7-2. And in 1965 they were 4-10.

Of course, no coach wins or loses all by himself. His staff, the assistants he hires, and the players he is or isn't blessed with all play a role. A good owner over him, and a little bit of luck never hurt. Football's the kind of game where one unlucky bounce can cost a game, a title, and even a career. And don't forget that owner. The head coach's relationship with the team's owner can be a major factor in building a winning football team, and Dan Reeves, who had dedicated enormous amounts of energy to the Rams, liked to be involved.

Even with the many personal recollections of the time and all that has been written about the Rams of the period, no one can fully understand the reasons why Svare's total record amounted to a meager fourteen wins against thirty-one losses and three ties. While he couldn't turn the Rams into winners, Svare's legacy is the development of the Fearsome Foursome—to this day the most famous front line ever to play the game.

Sharpening the Blade

On December 29, 1963, the Chicago Bears beat Y. A. Tittle and the Giants 14-0 in frigid Wrigley Field for the NFL championship. One week later, on January 5, the Chargers defeated the Boston Patriots 51-10 in sunny San Diego to win the AFL Championship. Once again, the Rams spent their holiday watching television. While they munched chip dip and downed margaritas under the palm trees other teams went to the playoffs. Since the Super Bowl hadn't yet been invented, the two league championships marked the official end of the professional football season.

In Deacon's mind, it was also the beginning of the 1964 season. After watching the San Diego game, he'd been awake most of the night, tossing and turning until Iretha grumbled at him to lie still or sleep on the floor. He'd put a foot to her back and unceremoniously pushed her over the edge of the bed, and she'd crawled back in without saying anything more.

Now, at one minute to five, Deacon heard the click the alarm clock made just before going off. He quickly reached over and shut it off. No sense riling Iretha more than she already was. He sighed and heaved himself up to sit on the edge of the bed, wishing he hadn't had that final celebratory bottle of whiskey with his friends the night before.

"Jones," Iretha whined, "it's the middle of the night."

"None of your mind," he said.

"I'll give you a piece of my mind," she fumed.

Deacon managed to hold his silence, getting up and going over to the chair where he'd set out his jogging outfit the night before. He went to the bathroom, and nearly fell asleep while sitting on the toilet. After five minutes, a leg cramp woke him up, and he quickly pulled on his sweats. He picked up his keys and headed for the door. His boots! He'd forgotten his old army boots! He rummaged around in the darkness on the floor of his closet until he found them.

"Davey Jones, what are you doin'?" Iretha's voice carried from the bed. For a little thing, not weighing much over 105 pounds, she sure

packed a lot of temper. But now, dressed and on his way out, Deacon
could ignore her.

"Nothin' that concerns you, babes," he said, keeping his voice
level. In another moment he had his hands on both shoes and an extra
pair of socks, and was heading out the door.

The sky overhead was matte black, the heavy clouds dragging low
with the threat of rain. The air was chill and misty, and when Deacon
exhaled, small puffs of steam came from his mouth.

His faithful Thunderbird turned over on the first try, and the big
V-8 engine pulled him west on Manchester Blvd. to the 405 freeway.
The traffic was surprisingly light, and after five minutes on the 405 he
turned west on the Santa Monica Freeway, getting off before the bridge
turned it into the Pacific Coast Highway. He parked on the street near
the pier and, slipping through a hole in the cyclone fence, jogged
down to where the calm, outgoing tide was slapping the sand and the
logs underneath the pier itself.

Deacon thought about his previous year as he did his warmups.
The experiment with his weight had been a miserable failure; the extra
forty pounds, which he'd carried the entire season, had taken away
some of his quick; carrying it had left him out of gas in the fourth
quarter. Never again! he vowed to himself. I'll report to spring training weighing 245, not 290!

Deacon stretched and strained, making mental notes of the flab
that had to come off. The weight wasn't the only thing. By now, he
could admit to himself that his marriage to the little fireball wasn't
going well. He had to block that out. He couldn't let her get to him,
even if he had to push her entirely out of his personal and private life.
The minute she got him angry, he'd start eating again, and that was
bad. He had to be in control of his own body, if he was to reach his
goal, now redefined and reaffirmed . . . to be among the best that ever
played the game . . . to be the best that ever played his position in the
NFL . . . to get there, Deacon was going to work harder than ever
before. He looked around under the dark pier, suddenly feeling lonely
and small. What was he doing out here in the middle of the night? He
tried to conjure up the steady determination of his father, the calm
spirituality of his mother, the fierceness of his wicked grandfather, and
the steady encouragement of his older brother. Deacon thought about
the idle hangers-on in Eatonville, who wouldn't care one way or another, and of all the high school, college and would-be pro players who
had now fallen by the wayside. Deacon knew he'd wasted a year play-

ing the game on sheer talent, and he'd somehow gotten away with it. But that couldn't continue. It was time to get back to the basics, time to regain his edge.

It was still dark as Deacon moved out from under the pier. A light, cold drizzle played on his face as he headed north, jogging in the wet sand. He ran in the early morning, in the predawn darkness, with the salt breeze in his face and the cold wind in his hair. He ran for miles, only stopping when the sandy strand became too narrow and the waves crashed in front of him against a wall of rocks that the construction engineers had rolled down from the highway. He watched a pair of surfers dodging in and out between rocks in the breakers, and saw a pair of graceful pelicans swooping down to beak some fish. He jogged up a pathway to the highway, still heading north toward Malibu. The season of hope had begun.

Conditioning became Deacon's daily ritual, his early-morning way of life. He blasted his way through the loose dry sand, accelerating away from the water, his powerful legs churning like pistons, still wearing the heavy combat boots his brother had loaned him years before. He laced the boots around his neck and ran knee-deep in the icy surf. He practiced his stance, his starts, his acceleration. He strapped five-pound weights around each ankle. A tall and powerful young man with a scowl on his face, he passed without seeing the bleached-blond surfers and the romantic couples, the scattered early morning beach bums and the cleanup crews who turned to stare as he ran by.

Deacon was strong enough to break blocks, fast enough to over-take fleet backs, quick enough to escape blockers trying to protect a passer. He had the graceful quickness of a halfback. He was a daring open-field tackler. He'd been a fool to change the basics that had gotten him to this point! Quickness was the thing, and as he ran he felt the poetry in his own motion. A blocker comes at me full blast, and he gets nothing but air! Deacon felt a superb confidence:No one and nothing can stop me. Not the best players in the NFL.

As the weeks went by, Deacon fell into his old patterns and habits: the ritual of hard, determined conditioning that he'd used in college and during his first years in the pros. The extra weight slid off, at first reluctantly, and then more easily, almost as if it were meant to go. Deacon found himself quietly saying no to the extra drink, to the extra helpings of food on his plate. By March, he was down to his fighting weight of 245 pounds.

The other black pros who lived in Los Angeles laid off a few months, and then started up their personal training programs in March. A group of them met over at Dorsey High, where Rams and other players who lived in the Los Angeles area would work out together. Deacon would finish up at the beach at nine, shower at home and then go over to Dorsey, where he'd lie under a tree and watch the others make their moves and listen to their stories. He never told anyone about his intense conditioning program, and he soon got the reputation for never doing a bit of training. The guys teased him for being a lazy lout, and warned that he was going to lose his starting role with the team. Deacon would just smile from under the shade of his tree, that bittersweet gambler's smile flickering across his lips, and say nothing in reply. It was going to be one hell of a season!

The Bite of the Show Biz Bug

Dick Bass, who delighted in imitating European show business personalities of the time who spoke cultured or accented English and had captured the public fancy—characters like the Pink Panther or Hobbs of British Intelligence—was flowering as a local personality and a syndicated radio talk show host. Bass was generally known as the team comic, and his antics with the Rams were on their way to becoming legendary. He once showed up to MC the Rams black tie Christmas party in a colonial khaki outfit, riding a rented elephant and accompanied by two little white boys wearing loin cloths. He had a natural flair, and his urbane and sophisticated manner—generally unexpected in a person of color—was beginning to open opportunities for him beyond his life on the football field.

Bass and Pervis Atkins had a black network talk radio show called "Bass & Atkins" that they recorded on Washington Blvd. After a lot of joking about whether or not the Florida Swamp Boy would swallow his tongue on the air, they invited Deacon to appear on the show. These were years of change, as the civil rights movement was finally making some headway for blacks. Bass and Atkins were proud that they had more than a fluff show. They did rely on Bass's comedic abilities and his way of imitating the voices of famous personalities, but they also had a sense of being on the cutting edge of social change, and they got into serious topics of concern to blacks. Bass's quick mind could handle a spoof about a bus full of whites and how they selected which ones would sit in the back, or a scene where a black man sitting in a restaurant argues the sex of the fly in his soup with a haughty white waiter.

When the show with Deacon's debut began, Bass and Atkins introduced him up front, doing a brief and complimentary bio on how he loved to "kill" quarterbacks and how he and the other three members of the Rams front line were dominating the league, making sure to point out that three of the Rams up-and-coming front four were black men. Then talk turned to the subject for the show, which was a semi-joking discussion on whether or not a black man would ever get his face on a cereal box. At that time, it was taken for granted in both the white and the black community that blacks were simply excluded. Some cereals featured "average American families" or a stereotyped member of the family, "the mother" or "the cute son or daughter" enjoying a bowl of the cereal. Black models and personalities were not used for this purpose, supposedly for economic reasons, that is, since whites made up nearly 90 percent of the population, they would have no interest in buying a cereal with a black person's face on it. Wheaties was a little different, in that the box featured pictures of the greatest sports champions and their statistics. If a black was ever going to get his picture on a cereal box, it would be here.

In 1960, Atkins said, Rafer Johnson had beat out C. K. Yang in the Olympic decathlon, and suddenly the decathlon was seen as a big deal in the advertising world, and it seemed logical that makers of Wheaties, the "Breakfast of Champions," might want to put the American decathlon champion on the Wheaties cereal box. Bass chimed in to point out on the air for his black listeners across the country that the problems were monumental, "We all know poor Rafer is a gentleman of color."

Deacon nodded, and Pervis said, "It must not have seemed right to have a black man looking across the breakfast table at you from the cereal box, that is, if you a decent white lady."

Bass did a little kid voice, "Mama, Mama, there's a black man in the kitchen!" He switched to a cool, aristocratic woman's voice, "Well, dear, tell him to take out the trash!"

They all laughed, and Pervis said, "Ex-act-ly!"

Deacon nodded again, but before he could say anything, Bass chimed back in, "So the good Wheaties folks sat around and thought and thought and thought, and finally one of their top thinkers slapped his hand on his knee and said (here Dick used his imitation Professor

Higgins English voice), 'I've *gaught* it! I really think I've *gaught* it! We'll use that Mathias chap!' Here, everybody stood up together and said, 'Who?' 'Bob Mathias', the ad chap says, 'the white bloke who won it back before that—that *gentleman of color*.' "[1]

Pervis cut in, "*Right!* So they all whooped for Wheaties and cheered for Cheerios and went back a decade or so and revitalized Bob Mathias, the white boy who won it back before Rafer, and they put *him* on the box."

"Right," Pervis added. "So, if you're a black athlete like me and Dick and our guest the Deacon here, you can talk about getting your face on the cereal box, but don't start counting that money, brother, because the only way it's gonna get there is if your own dear mama pastes it on!"

"That's right, Pervis," Bass said. "Promotional money, we find, is extremely limited for gentlemen of color, such as we. Do you find yourself getting calls to do fried chicken commercials back in Florida, Deacon?"

"Huh? Uhh, no, I don't." The question took Deacon by surprise. He was liking the way the banter went back and forth between his two acquaintances, and hadn't expected them to call on him at that moment.

"There, you see," Bass picked up smoothly, "Promotion money is extremely limited for blacks."

"I do manage to get a few personal appearances around town."

"Uh-huh," Atkins agreed. "Grocery store openings and the like, generally when they are in the black neighborhoods, and maybe sing a song or two in front of the yahoos at the county fair."

Deacon started to mention he'd recently been guest singer at a church function, but they'd been over this material before the show and Bass rode right in on him, "There is no such thing as a person of color doing a national promotion or a national television commercial or a national radio commercial."

"They tell us the South will not buy from a black," Pervis added. "Who is the 'they' I am referring to?"

"Our agents!" Bass said in his deepest, most conspiratorial voice. "And they should know, because they the ones doing the hiring and the firing!"

The show went on like that, Bass and Atkins batting the chatter

---

1. Bob Mathias won the Olympic Decathlon in 1948 and repeated in 1952. In 1956 it was won by American Milt Campbell. Rafer Johnson won it in 1960.

back and forth and Deacon rising to the bait every now and then, generally a beat or two late, after the other two were already off and running. They asked Deacon, as part of the final wrap, if he was discouraged, or if he felt he might find a place as a black entertainer in show business. "Well," he replied truthfully, "I sang in the choir when I was a boy, and nobody ever could keep my mouth shut, whether it was a story, bet, or dare. So I guess that makes me a natural!"

Deacon's openness, and the unexpected nature of his answer delighted Bass, who was still laughing when Atkins signed off the show. All in all, Bass and Atkins felt the show had quite a bit of snap, and they asked Deacon if he'd come back some time and do it again.

Thinking back to that show, Deacon says, "I know I was pretty awful, but being on the show felt right for me. I knew right away that here was something I was going to have to explore, outside of football."

Dick Bass also remembers. "That was the young Deacon Jones, the kid who couldn't stick three words together without tripping on his tongue. And yet, I heard him give a motivational speech recently in front of a crowd of thousands, and he was awesome, just awesome! Back when he started out, none of us could see he had that talent. He just believed in himself, and once he set out to do a thing, he never looked back."

Welcome Back, Deacon Jones

The 1964 season began under sunny skies and crisp sixty-five- degree weather in Pitt Stadium, on Sunday, September 13. It was a day when the Rams played near-perfect defensive football.

As the game began, Deacon could feel—he *knew*—he was in the best shape of his life. There were a thousand fine points to the game, movements and judgments he realized the fans never saw from the stands. At moments like these his awareness seemed to grant him a sixth sense. All the training, the endless hours of willing repetition and fierce practice led to this, to being able to concentrate. He seemed to see nothing and yet he was aware of everything. He could see the fingers of his opponent, the offensive tackle across the line. The fingers wiggled and waved a bit, revealing it was a pass play. He didn't bother to juke, roaring past the man to harass Steeler's veteran quarterback

Ed Brown. He nearly got Brown, too, the quarterback just managing to get the ball off for an incompletion before Deacon and Rosey burst on him like heavy water over a dam. On getting up, Deacon gave Brown's helmet an affectionate pat. "Get you next time," he said.

On the very next play, Deacon saw that the offensive tackle's weight was forward on his hand. They're gonna run, he thought. And he could see by the way the weight was on the hand the direction the tackle intended to block him! On the snap, Deacon gave a hitch in that direction, shifted gears and was in high speed past the man before he was off his knuckles. The next play, he saw the man's eyes flicker, again showing where the play was going to run!

It was a great day to play football! It was the day football became fun again. Deacon could tell from the quarterback's eyes where the pass would fly. He could feel the quick count by the way the quarterback walked up to the center. Deacon concentrated a different sense, and his ear picked his individual signal out of the sound of sixty thousand roaring Pittsburgh fans.

It's barely a second before the opposing quarterback snaps the ball. Deacon's peripheral vision sees the ball out of the corner of his eye. But he doesn't leave on the ball. He leaves on movement. He leaves when anything out of context moves! He lets the normal shift and the normal motions happen. He doesn't worry about these things. Anything else moves, and he is gone! If his man breathes wrong, he is up and off that ball.

Pretty soon, Deacon's got his man jumpy. He's thinking about protecting Ed Brown. He's thinking about the last time Deacon beat him. He's been reading the newspapers; he knows what an animal Deacon Jones is, because Deacon told his hometown reporters just what he was going to do to him, and they had the bad sense to print it. Deacon's man is going to jump all right, and he does when Deacon yells, Hut!, mixing it right in with Ed Brown's "Ready—Set—2—83!" Offsides, against the Steelers offensive tackle! Deacon smiles as he walks forward five yards. He's got his man responding to him, and that means the guy's timing is off. It's all about intimidation, Deacon thinks to himself. Next thing, this dude is going to miss his audibles. And, before the quarter is over, he does.

The Rams had entered the season with another quarterback controversy. As he had promised late the year before, Dan Reeves went to the college draft and selected Utah State's star quarterback, Bill Munson. Zeke Bratkowski had been traded to the Packers, but that still left Terry Baker, Roman Gabriel, and the new guy all vying for the position. Svare had benched Baker early on for throwing slow-as-a-blimp "hydrogen balls," and Gabriel had broken his ankle, so Munson was coming in with the chance of a lifetime.

The Rams had also developed a more effective offensive line, consisting of Joe Wendryhoski, Joe Scibelli, Don Chuy, and Frank Varrichione. They'd gone 3-2 in the exhibition season, but nobody was impressed, as the teams they'd beaten were weak sisters. But the team's other longstanding weakness, the defensive secondary, was still with them. They'd patched it up with two rookie starters, but it looked to be a problem all season. But not for this first game against the Steelers; this time the Rams could do nothing wrong. The defense actually stole five passes, with Lindon Crow, Jerry Richardson, Jack Pardee, Eddie Meador, and Lamar Lundy each getting one.

The Rams defense held the Steelers to fourteen points. With the exception of one eighty-three yard offensive surge, all the points scored by the Rams came as a result of the relentless pressure their defense put on Ed Brown.

The Rams were leading 19-7 early in the third quarter when the game turned on one brilliant defensive maneuver. Deacon, his personal game plan working so well that he was freezing his man with a simple hitch of his shoulders, went through the line like smoke and arrived in time to break up a bit of razzle-dazzle. As *L.A. Times* sports writer Mal Florence described the action, "Flanker Gary Ballman, trying to throw a southpaw pass from his goal line after taking a handoff from Brown, was rapped by the Deacon as he let loose. The dead-duck pass was picked off by Lundy on the fourteen and he lumbered in for the score and an eventual 26-7 lead."

Deacon knew Gary never should have thrown that pass. Of course, the poor man was caught between the 'gater an' the water moccasin— if he hadn't let it fly, Deacon would have gotten him for two points and the touchback!

After the game, there was an unusually giddy feeling in the Rams' camp; Svare winked for the reporters and chortled, "Say, we're tied for first place, aren't we?" The news media, snake bitten themselves so many times over the years, nervously pointed out that the Rams were still having trouble punching the ball into the end zone. But, with only one game played, the reporters were already talking about Deacon Jones making his bid for All-Pro.

Brief Visions of Glory

Nursing his broken ankle from the bench, Roman Gabriel had plenty of time to meditate on the wayward direction his life seemed to be taking. In the second game of the season, the Rams home opener against the Lions, Svare had put in a tricky double-quarterback formation. He inserted Terry Baker in the lineup along with Munson, positioning Baker near the sideline behind three Rams linemen. The "first" quarterback, Munson, took the snap from center and pitched the ball to the "second" quarterback, Baker, whose option was then to run or throw. The play was called back on penalties (as often happens on trick plays, due to the multiplied possibilities for error), and the Rams retreated to their more conventional and dull form of attack, two predictable runs followed by a desperation pass.

Still, rookie Bill Munson looked good throughout; the Rams were in the driver's seat in the fourth quarter with a 17-10 lead when a string of penalties pushed them back and finally forced them to turn over the ball. Lions quarterback Milt Plum had been ineffective all day; now he was replaced by Earl Morrall, who engineered a drive to tie the score. The Rams had one last chance, but rookie kicker Bruce Gossett's fifty-one-yard field goal was blocked with four seconds to play. Svare said he was satisfied. His team had come to play ball, and if it hadn't been for a couple of calls, they would have won the game.

The Rams won their third game, too, against the Vikings. Still looking for offensive punch, Svare switched Terry Baker from quarterback to halfback, and the second-year man responded with 114 yards rushing and receiving. Munson started at quarterback and was again effective. But the game ball really belonged to the Rams defensive line. John Hall, writing in the *L.A. Times,* described the game: "The front four of Rosey Grier, Deacon Jones, Lamar Lundy, and Merlin Olsen were at their pulverizing best, especially the Deacon. He settled some old scores with Minnesota's scrambling quarterback, Fran Tarkenton, being principally responsible for debiting Francis with thirty-nine yards lost attempting to pass."

By now, Roman's ankle was 95 percent recovered, but his old job wasn't waiting for him. The mighty Colts were next on the schedule, but Svare declared he was going to stick with Munson. It was an aerial duel between Munson and Unitas. Munson completed eighteen of thirty-two for 256 yards and one touchdown, but Unitas was able to pick on Rams rookie cornerback Jerry Richardson, throwing three long touchdown passes to ex-Ram Jimmy Orr. And left-footed Lue Michaels, also an ex-Ram, kicked five point-after conversions.

The Rams front four applied good pressure, spending the afternoon chasing Unitas out of the pocket, but the Colts had seen the game films and learned well what the Lions had found out about the Rams: if you had a few good receivers and a quarterback with a quick release, the L.A. team could be had. Baltimore's coach, Don Shula, admitting that Grier, Olsen, Jones, and Lundy had put the squeeze on Unitas, said, "They're a real tough club, one of the toughest."

Svare shrugged the loss off, "We played a real good game today, but Unitas killed us with the bomb."

Cliff Livingston, the Rams' veteran linebacker, admitted that his bunch needed some work, "We made some mistakes, but we'll correct them. We'll be better."

Livingston must have read the wrong fortune cookie, because the next Sunday Billy Wade and the Chicago Bears destroyed the Rams with the short pass. Gambling that they could get to Wade early in the game, Svare ordered his team to come with a full blitz. Wade was forced to release before he was ready, but he still found flanker Johnny Morris and tight end Mike Ditka all alone in the Ram secondary. Wade's passing success and Munson's four early interceptions had the game over by halftime.

Meanwhile, Roman Gabriel pitched from the sidelines and waited his chance. Gabriel was making progress under the tutelage of assistant coach Don Heinrich, and even in defeat he was attracting attention. Svare put him in and he gained 300 yards in the second half against the Bears. Chicago defensive coordinator George Allen commented, "This guy should be starting somewhere!"

The following Sunday, Gabriel got his first start of the season, burying the 49ers, 42-14. He threw rookie receiving star Bucky Pope four touchdown passes in the first half. Svare shook up the Rams secondary, sitting down player-coach Linden Crow in favor of rookie safety Bobby Smith, playing Andy Von Sonn over veteran Jack Pardee at linebacker, and putting Aaron Martin in at cornerback. This youthful and enthusiastic secondary picked off seven San Francisco passes for a Rams record. Jerry Richardson stole three, Martin two, and Bobby Smith returned one ninety-seven yards for a touchdown.

And the next week, the Rams pulled the upset of the year with an incredible comeback. Down 17-0 early on, they were able to turn things around and beat Green Bay, 27-17. The game started badly for the Los Angeles team, with three lost fumbles and two interceptions. The score would have been worse, but in the first quarter, after the Pack had moved to the Rams two yard line, Bart Starr fumbled to Deacon Jones. Deacon jumped on the ball, and that ended the Green Bay drive. Les Josephson scored for the Rams on a fifty-three-yard run, and Bucky Pope hooked onto a fifty-five-yard touchdown pass from Gabriel with another of his "amazing" catches.

The Rams defense took over in the second half, snuffing out every Green Bay scoring attempt. On five successive plays in the third quarter, Jones, Olsen, Grier, and Lundy threw Bart Starr for losses. Starr, who had enjoyed tremendous protection in previous outings against everybody in the league, was thrown for losses six times in the game, losing fifty-one yards in the process. It was the best performance any defensive line had ever achieved against the Packers in the club's history. Vince Lombardi said, "We have been beating ourselves this year, but not today. Today we were licked."

The victory over Lombardi and the semilegendary Packers was one of the high points of Harland Svare's coaching career. When it was all over, Ram safety Eddie Meador tossed the Rams head coach the game ball, saying, "This is for the greatest coach in the National Football League."

The following day, Bud Furillo commented in his "Steam Room" column in the *Herald Examiner,* "It doesn't seem possible, but Svare's whiz kids are in a contending position for the Western Division title. Not even the Rams' amazing coach dreamed they would have a contender this year. That Rams defense, led by the Gruesome Foursome, ruined the sale of Lombardi's book *Run to Daylight.* The Packers only ran into white shirts."

The championship dreams lasted seven days. Then the Lions came to town. Figuring they needed a few seconds to evade the Rams front four while their receivers got clear, they rolled Milt Plum out most of the afternoon. They also ran a double-wing, shotgun formation, with quarterback Plum standing three paces back from his customary position directly behind the center and taking the long snap like a single wing tailback. Plum was on target with his passes, and Lions receivers Terry Barr, Gail Cogdill, and Jim Gibbons played like All-Pros. The Rams' fresh young secondary, put to the test, simply didn't have the experience to contain them.

Bitterly disappointed and unable to conceal his feelings, Svare blurted out to the crowd of reporters, "We knew we had to stop their passing and we didn't. All we were doing was chasing, making tackles—after they had the ball. We were two steps behind the ball. We had people around the receivers, but nobody around the ball." When he was reminded of the inexperience of his rookie secondary, Svare angrily shook his head, "I can get high school kids to cover better than that. If it's too much for them, I'll get someone else. They're NFL players. I'm not going to sit and watch it."

The Rams won next week, 20-10, over the Philadelphia Eagles. But the week after that, the Bears put out their fire, using ex-Rams Rudi Bukich, Jon Arnett, and Joe Marconi. Bukich took advantage of the Rams' soft secondary with a flurry of short, accurate passes. On some plays, the crafty Halas went to a triple flanker setup, flooding a zone with receivers. When the Rams started looking for the pass, Bukich would slip the ball to Arnett, who had a combined total of 143 yards rushing, receiving, and returning kicks.

By now, Svare had gone back to alternating his quarterbacks in a desperate attempt to find the old winning magic. Nothing seemed to work. The blitzing Colts dumped Gabriel and Munson for losses totalling 102 yards. Then, in 6-degree weather in Minnesota, the Rams turned the ball over five times on fumbles and interceptions, losing again. Bill Munson ended up with three frost-bitten toes and a long line of stitches in his throwing arm. Still, he started the following week in the team's loss to the 49ers. Svare blamed the receivers for the loss: "Our receiving has deteriorated in the last month. No one can do anything right. They don't get open and they're running bad patterns." He added, "You can say I'm looking forward to seeing Jack Snow." Snow, an All-American receiver from Notre Dame, had just signed his rookie contract with the Rams.

In the final game of the season, the Rams put on a fierce defensive battle against Green Bay. They led at half-time 21-7. Deacon and Merlin led the defense to turn back three major Packer drives, stopping them cold at the Rams twenty-three, six, and three yard line. Deacon was out to do it all; he tackled Starr so hard in the second quarter the ball popped out and he recovered for the Rams on Green Bay's nineteen.

The front four never faltered, throwing Starr for losses six times. In the third quarter, Green Bay's Jim Taylor burst through for sixty-seven yards to the Rams' eight—but his great run went for nothing as Deacon almost single-handedly started the Packers offense running in reverse.

With under thirteen minutes left in the game, the Rams held a 24-10 lead. But once again the offense couldn't hang onto the ball in the fading minutes of the game, and the great Starr, taking advantage of every Ram mistake, managed to score twice and pull out a 24-24 tie.

Owner Dan Reeves, indicating that Harland Svare was in no trouble at all, told the papers, "I was very pleased with the season. We made an awful lot of progress."

And Roman Gabriel, tired of the yelling, the belittling and the blame-placing, just wanted to be traded.

Deacon smiles his slow, bittersweet smile, remembering how Svare handled victory and defeat. "We players couldn't help but notice how, when Harland explained things to the press, our defeats were the result of 'the team not coming to play' or 'the team not executing' or 'the team not having the desire to win'. . . but our wins always sprang from some little bit of magic he thought up."

Deacon remembers Svare's outburst to the press after the Rams lost to the Lions, and the effect it had on the team: "That was a unique moment for the reporters. No more of this 'suave Sven, the dapper dresser' stuff. They got a chance to witness the real Harland Svare, the hypercritical, blameful Svare that we players had to live with every day. It's easy to cheer your guys on when you're winning—but that was a difficult loss for all of us. It would have been bad enough if he'd restricted his punishment to the scrimmages, but to take his case like that to the public . . . it was a time to be healing, not blaming, and if I had to pick one moment when the 1964 season went sour, that would be it."

Interviewed by phone in 1992, Roman Gabriel commented on the continuing quarterback controversy, "The Packers asked for me first (when the Rams traded away Bratkowski), but Reeves wouldn't let me go. I have no idea why, since they weren't giving me the chance to play. The only reason Terry Baker, Bill Munson, and I could tolerate the situation was we became friends. We were three individuals working on our careers, and we knew it would be better if we helped each other. The Rams system was terrible on a quarterback's self-confidence; we were all getting beat up mentally, but at least we stuck together. You can go back to the newspapers of that day and you'll never see anything negative said by any of us. It was interesting, though, how Harland's staff would lie to you. I was told at the beginning of the year that whoever played best in the preseason would get the starting job. But at that same time, when rookie receiver Bucky Pope was deciding whether or not to come to the Rams or jump to the American Football League, Schnelker told him that Bill Munson was the starting quarterback. At least, that's what Bucky told me."

Writing in the L.A. Times, columnist Sid Ziff brought up another sore point, noting Dan Reeves's habit of drafting, training, and then trading away superior ballplayers. It was enough to send Ram fans into screams of frustration, "watching ex-Rams quarterback Frank Ryan cream the New York Giants 52-20, hurling five touchdowns, running for another, completing twelve of thirteen passes to lead the Cleveland Browns to their division title. Frank Ryan, like Bill Wade and so many others, came into his own after he left the Rams. . . The guys can go over at other places, but not here. It makes you wonder what is wrong with Ram thinking."

Fame, If Not Fortune

The hot white light beat down unmercifully, from every direction, and Deacon couldn't remember when he'd been so overheated. This had to be hell on earth!

"Move over, Muley," he growled.

"No room, Deacon," Olsen growled back.

"Quiet, you guys," Rosey said from a few inches away in the back seat. Lamar sighed, but his sigh said as much as their grumbling. Circumstances were trying even his patience.

"Settle down, everybody," the cool, detached voice of the director carried inside the car.

"Easy for him to say," Deacon whispered, "he only wearin' a T-shirt."

"Camera rolling," the cameraman said.

"Sound rolling," the soundman said.

There was a significant pause, and then the director barked, "Annnnnnnnd—Action!"

Merlin opened the door and dashed out of the car toward the camera, followed closely by Deacon. But in his haste to keep the proper timing, Deacon caught one foot and sprawled gracelessly on the cement floor of the stage.

"Cut, cut, *Cut*!" came the voice of the director, managing to sound infinitely patient and utterly superior at the same time. "People, resume your places."

"Mark slate," the assistant director said.

One of the countless unnamed helpers on the stage took a piece of chalk from his pocket and replaced the number 33 with the number 34.

"All right, now, settle down, people," the director said.

It seemed that a famous British motor company was coming out with "an improved version" of its popular imported MGB sports car. The rumbly little machine had always been a two seater. But, yielding to the demands of modern society and its research department, the company had extended the roof line and taken away most of the rear trunk to squeeze another seat in back and so create the world's first MGB four seater. In Europe, where road and rally racing is a real sport and sportsters were only supposed to have two bucket seats, this was sacrilege, but the company's pipe-puffing researchers swore that the savages in the American colonies were calling for such innovations.

So the company had created the four seater, and though its own style department cringed at the ungainly look of the machine, now it had to get the word out to the American public. How could the company best explain that it had taken the untamed fun of the open road and packaged it for the entire family? The company's bright young American advertising agency had worried over the problem and come up with a solution. They would find four of the biggest men around and pack them into the car. If these fellows could ride in the MGB four seater, so could pop, mom, and the two kiddies! The creative team had hit on the idea of using the Rams Fearsome Foursome. You're not going to find anyone bigger! The only problem was that they hadn't done a commercial before. They wouldn't be recognizable outside their uniforms! No problem—they would wear their uniforms!

Perhaps the agency creatives hadn't realized how big the members of the Foursome really were, or bothered to calculate how bulky they would be in their uniforms cramped into that tiny space. The storyboards made it look easy, the four of them grinning happily as they bounced out of the tiny sportster and dashed off to play in their game. But capturing the same action on film was proving very difficult. The director, talking about his reputation and integrity in the advertising business, insisted the action had to be filmed in a single, continuous take to prove that the four of them actually were in the car at one time.

Patient Merlin crawled back in the car without saying a word. And Deacon, Rosey, and Lamar weren't going to say anything. After all, they were making history. They were actually doing the impossible. After all the negative comments from their agents, they were the first blacks they knew of who were actually doing a national promotion! In this sense, the Foursome was doing something that none of them could have accomplished separately. Working together brought results both on and off the playing field.

For Deacon, this was only one of the rewards for his season. No matter how you looked at it, he'd played a terrific year's worth of football. He had dropped his weight, shifted back to his old stance on the line, and regained his edge. He was once again the mighty Deacon Jones, the quarterback killer from the Deep South, come to the green pastures of the NFL to serve justice! He had twenty-two sacks—not so many as he would have later in his career, but already tying the "NFL Individual Season Sack Record," which as of 1995 refuses to recognize sacks made by any of the great players who played before 1982, even though their records can be validated by official team statistics.

Deacon was voted the Rams "Player of the Year" by the Southern California Writer's Association. As Al Wolf said in the *L.A. Times,* he made "the scribes look good by playing a great game at defensive end. He gave Starr particular fits." The Ye Old Rams, the club's "alumni" organization, were still not inclined to name a black defensive lineman their "Player of the Year." They gave that award to safetyman Eddie Meador, naming Deacon "Rams Defensive Lineman of the Year."

And Deacon finally went to his first Pro Bowl. That year the winners were paid $500, the losers got half that. Deacon didn't have to travel far to get to the game. In those days, the Pro Bowl was played in Los Angeles. (In 1972, it moved to Dallas, and later, to Hawaii.) Deacon would end up playing in the Pro Bowl as a representative of both leagues, for many years on the National League side when he was with the Rams, and then on the American League side after he was traded to the Chargers. But nothing beat the thrill of that first Pro Bowl game back in 1964. Deacon's determination and hard work were paying off. After years of preparation, he was actually living his dream. He was proving what he had set out to do—that he was a man, the equal of any man in the world at his chosen profession.

And now, jammed next to Merlin Olsen in the front seat of the tiny MGB, Deacon realized that he didn't care how long it took to get the commercial finished. They would do it over and over again until they got it right. Deacon found something appealing about that. Show business wasn't that much different from football! Once again he felt the faint stirring he'd enjoyed when he was on Dick Bass and Pervis Atkins' show. This show biz stuff was something he could do!

The shoot dragged on through the long afternoon. Their pads hooked onto each other and they couldn't get out of the car. Rosey caught a leg cramp and staggered rather than ran. Their smiles were too "pasty and forced." Their sweat ran in buckets and the sympathetic film crew handed in towels through the open windows. But the Foursome endured, and in the end the director got his shot and history was made.

Deacon remembers his first Pro Bowl game: "I felt like a king—Gino Marchetti, Willie Davis, and me at left end. I just walked around with my eyes wide. Just being there was fantastic. Lombardi was the coach—in all, he coached me three times in the Pro Bowl, so I got to know him pretty well. This is how it was—you had one week of intense preparation, and then you played the game. Some coaches and players treated the ProBowl like fluff, like the reward for a season well done, but Lombardi would have none of that. He was intense, and he hated to lose at anything . . . my kind of guy, I could see that right away.

"I also saw right away that color made no difference to Lombardi. He had a rough Marine drill sergeant way about him, and he treated all his players the same—crappy—and they loved him for it. Win, just win. Herb Adderly, Willie Wood, and Willie Davis all had a high regard for him, and, when it was over, so did I."

The Marked Man

Standing on the sidelines during practice for the Pro Bowl game—one of those odd moments, a lull in the action, when the ever-active, always-hyper, Lombardi has a moment off—Lombardi looks around and finds himself standing next to Deacon Jones.

"Jones," he says. "Come here."

He takes Jones by the arm, and they walk a few paces away from the sideline, "You got to Starr a few times this season, didn't you?"

Lombardi's piercing glance goes right through Deacon, and he doesn't know what to say. He realizes he doesn't have to say anything. It isn't really a question.

"A couple," he agrees, looking at this man, this rival coach who is already a legend in the NFL for his fierce determination and his winning ways.

Lombardi nods back and a smile twitches one corner of his mouth. "You got unbelievable quick off the ball. Nobody in the league can touch you right now. But what about next year?"

"What you mean, Coach?" Deacon is thinking to himself how odd it is that he can call this man "Coach" like it's his proper name, when the word sticks in his throat on his own playing field, and 'Swede' is what comes out instead.

Lombardi pokes a finger in his chest, illustrating his point. "It's simple. You convinced us this year, Jones. You got our attention. Now we gotta adjust. That's what makes this game so great. By next year, you're not going to get through any more. You're the marked man, pal."

"So, what do I do?"

"That's just it. I can't tell you. Nobody can tell you. It's like new turf, you know? If there is a way, you gotta figure it out yourself. If you can't, we gotcha!"

The offensive line coach called for Lombardi's attention; he gave Deacon his brilliant, aggressive, wicked smile, and turned his attention to the rest of the team.

If anybody else had said it, Deacon would have just passed it off, buried the poor guy in a volley of lip-jazz about how devastating he was going to be next year. But this was Vince Lombardi throwing down the gauntlet. Lombardi the consummate coach, the leader of men, the innovative thinker. After the Pro Bowl was history and his private training for the 1965 season began, Deacon could think of little else.

He pounded through his early morning drills at the beach with extra fervor. He never really got out of shape after the season, but now he burned to put that extra edge on his quick, to get even faster than before. And still, as he went through his preparations for the coming season, a feeling of dread hung over him. Nothing he could do would really be enough. They were going to double-team him, maybe even triple-team him. That would leave another man open on the line, and that was good for the Fearsome Foursome . . . but what about him? His lifelong pursuit to develop his own greatness wouldn't let him relax. He became more moody than usual, refusing to talk to Iretha for days. There had to be something he could do, something he was forgetting.

Deacon reviewed his moves endlessly, his jukes, and his slips. He and Merlin could work on their trick plays, their stunts. Execution was everything. They could pick up some ground there. Maybe the Foursome could do a total line stunt—just the thought of it made the bittersweet grin come to his face. That would give Harland a heart attack, for sure!

And there were ways to play off two men. With his speed, if he got the angle, they both had to be backing up. One step on them, and no man alive could keep him out. Still, it was two men, and that was more sheer physical weight to get around, and a play only took a few seconds. There were going to be times when he was too late. Deacon needed some new weapon, some element of surprise.

A surprising answer began to come to him in April while he was watching a television sports rerun of the Muhammad Ali—Sonny Liston fight, which had taken place in Miami a little over a year before.[2] It had been a spectacular fight, and the promoters were using it to stir up interest for the rematch, which would be held in May. Because of his lightning-like, slashing attack and the colorful way he handled the press, some of the sports writers were comparing Deacon to Ali, calling him "The Muhammad Ali of football." So Deacon already had more than a passing interest in the fighter. There was Ali on the TV. He used to be simple Cassius Clay, the uneducated southern black boy. Now he was dancing around Liston like a pit bull after a tired old horse. A dejected Liston claimed an injury to his arm and failed to answer the bell for the seventh round, and it was all over. That started Deacon thinking: Just exactly what made Ali so great? Of course, there were many answers—the devastating jabs, his grace, his speed, his quick. There hadn't been a fighter like Ali since the great Joe Louis. Now, when you thought about boxing, there were similarities to playing the line in football . . . there was only a finite number of moves a boxer could make, and the same was true for a lineman. Another similarity was that the defense could use the hands.

They were interviewing Ali, who looked like he'd barely broken a sweat. Then the show replayed highlights from the fight, which had taken place in Miami. Again and again Deacon watched Muhammad easily slip inside his foe and deliver his unbelievably fast combinations, right-left-right, and then dance away while poor Liston stag-

---

2. February 25, 1964, Muhammad Ali (then still using his given name, Cassius Clay) defeated Sonny Liston by a technical knockout in the seventh round. Ali beat Liston in the rematch, held on May 25, 1965, by a knockout in the first round.

gered and reeled. This held Deacon's interest, and he wasn't really sure why. Ali, of course, had great execution. All fighters learned how to throw combination punches; it was a part of their arsenal. Ali excelled because he did the ordinary better than anybody else.

The fight had only gone seven rounds. Of course, that was a long fight for Ali. Some of his opponents didn't last through the first round. Deacon switched off the TV set and slipped into his sweats.

"Where you goin', Jones?" Iretha asked.

"Out, babes—out," he said.

"What about supper?"

Deacon knew Iretha would make a really big deal out of this if he let her. But supper was never a big deal; Iretha rarely cooked. They just selected from a long list of carry-out places, some of which delivered, some not.

"Order what you want, babes," he said. "I've got some thinking to do."

Deacon drove down to the beach and began to jog along the sand. He couldn't get Ali's performance out of his mind. There was a key in there, somewhere . . . What were the similarities? Of course, the obvious one—defensive linemen could use their hands. They couldn't punch, but they could slap. Nothing new there, either. The headslap had been used for years. Gino Marchetti was one of the best at it.

But the inside story on the headslap was that it slowed down the man using it. Sure, it could ring the clock of the guy across the line, but the defensive man had to take time to deliver the blow, and by then the play was usually past him. But did that necessarily have to be so? A shiver ran down Deacon's back. He was starting to see the idea. He was as fast, in his own way, as Muhammad Ali. Suppose he could develop his headslap to the point where he could deliver it on the move as part of his forward motion? Maybe he would lose a fraction of his quick, and maybe not. Even if he did, he might gain something on his opponents that would enable him to slip past. And what about the combination headslap? Nobody in the league had ever been fast enough to even think about that one.

Totally wrapped up in his new idea, Deacon got down in his stance in the sand and tried a few practice moves, lunging forward and slapping air. It became an extra part of his daily regimen, and the few people enjoying the beach that wind-swept February didn't really pay much attention. After all, this was California, and if a young black man chose to leap out of a crouch, mutter deprecating comments and swing at nothing, that was his own business.

For his part, Deacon was in seventh heaven. There was much to be done, but he'd found the direction his next steps toward greatness would take. And for that, ironically, he would always have rival coach Vince Lombardi to thank.

"Football is a game of moves, a game of edges," Deacon says, "I aimed to create a weakness; I would slant, go for the angles. That way, even against two men, it wouldn't be a Mexican stand-off. With my quickness, I'd make a move. The guy setting up across from me goes for it, but he's already beat. Now he's got to move backwards. That's when I take him on. I'll go outside or reverse and cut inside.

"Just as the players jumped on weakness, Lombardi brought my attention to the fact that they concentrated on success; in the years to come, I would find myself double-teamed and triple-teamed, and I had to be able to do something about it."

Interviewed by phone in 1992, Bob Lilly, the Dallas Cowboy's great defensive tackle and end, said he'd had the same problems. "I had twenty or twenty-one sacks in 1966 or 1967," he said, "but the next year the league figured they had to stop me, so I got double-teamed and didn't get nearly so many. Harvey Martin had a good year in 1978 and got twenty-two sacks, which I think is the Cowboy record. George Andrie had twenty or twenty-one in, I think, 1966. You can measure Deacon's greatness by the fact that, year after year, they double-teamed him and he still got through for his sacks—Deacon Jones is definitely the greatest pass rusher of all time."

Green Bay's great quarterback, Bart Starr, said, "As great an offensive blocker as Forrest Gregg has been, we had to give him a helper, doubling up on Deacon, trying to stop him by constantly harassing him. There were times we stopped blocking the tight end on him because he couldn't catch up to him before he'd have to clip him. You don't clip a Deacon Jones."[3]

When interviewed by phone in 1992, Hall of Fame quarterback Y. A. Tittle still vividly remembered Deacon's headslap. "That left hook of Deacon's gave the opposing lineman a temporary stun. With his speed and that headslap, he became the most dominating pass rusher of my seventeen years in the game."

3. Bill Libby, *Life in the Pit*.

Southern Ways in Southern California

Back in Orangeburg, Deacon had been expelled from South Carolina State and had made a conscious decision to leave the activist side of the civil rights movement to make his mark in the sports world. But all the time Deacon was fighting his battle for equality in the NFL, the other struggle, the one in the streets, continued. In fact, by 1965 it had grown in intensity to where it once again came around to affect Deacon's life.

By now Deacon accepted that he had to excel just to be treated as an equal in the NFL. But he also realized that most blacks couldn't do what he was doing; ordinary, decent, God-fearing American citizens with good skills and a good work ethic, these people felt trapped and cheated. They had no outlet, no way to work toward the goal of equality, except to protest in the streets. That was why, with a force driven by generations of frustration, the civil rights movement grew steadily more vocal and physical in both the South and the industrial cities of the North until protests, lunch counter demonstrations, and acts of violence and bloodshed seemed to be everywhere. The Nation of Islam leader, Malcolm X was assassinated in February of 1965. Then, the Rev. James Reeb was beaten to death in Selma, Alabama. Hoping to put out the fires and restore some sense of justice and order, President Johnson requested sweeping voting rights legislation in a television address to a joint session of Congress. Dr. Martin Luther King led a five-day civil rights march from Selma to Montgomery, Alabama. Then civil rights worker Viola Gregg Liuzzo was shot and killed in Selma by the Ku Klux Klan.

That year there was escalating war in Vietnam and civil rights strife at home—but the AFL and the NFL still played football. When Deacon worried he might be taken in the military draft, the Rams management told him, "Don't sweat it, we've got it taken care of." In fact, spring training camp started as it always did under Harland Svare. Outside in the real world an uneasy spring wore into a long, hot summer, and an ugly mood seemed to hang over the land like a dark and angry thunder cloud. But in their enclosed world of training camp, hearty breakfasts, lunches, and dinners hit the table with regularity and the players were in bed by curfew time.

Deacon practiced his moves and topped off his conditioning. The regulars were wary of his speed, but he and George Menifee managed to pick up a few bucks running the forty-yard dash against the new guys. Deacon had left the civil rights movement years before; he had no idea, as he prepared for the coming season, that now it was about to catch up with him again.

This was Deacon's fifth campaign as a starter for Los Angeles. By now he had learned to read the team that was being molded around him, and he knew he wasn't going to get much help from the defensive secondary behind him. Instead of trading for experience to beef up the defensive backfield, Dan Reeves had gone back to his old tricks and dipped into the draft. He'd come up with a handful of promising rookies—defensive back Clancy Williams from Washington State, and linebackers Fred Brown from Miami University, Michael Strofolino from Villanova, Doug Woodlief from Memphis State, and Ron Caveness from the University of Arkansas. They also had second-year man Jerry Richardson from West Texas State (after 1965, the Rams' management would give up on Richardson, as they had so many others, trading him to the Atlanta Falcons).

This meant there would be almost entirely green men in the defensive secondary, putting additional pressure on the front four. And worse, this spring Lamar Lundy and Rosey Grier weren't making it through Svare's grueling preseason scrimmages. As the exhibition season drew nearer, it looked like both of them would be playing hurt, when they could suit up at all.

Then, on August 11, a white policeman stopped a black driver suspected of being drunk in Watts, a run-down black ghetto area of Los Angeles, and the week-long riots were underway. Before it was over, thirty-five people would be dead, hundreds injured, and $200 million worth of damage would be suffered in the black section of town. The Rams continued their practice schedule; after all, the season opener was only about a month away and they had to be ready.

The riots escalated. Finally, on Saturday afternoon, August 14, Svare broke a brief workout with the news that the players were to go home from training camp that night. As he told the reporters, "Some of the players were worried about their families." In minutes, the entire team had stripped, showered, and peeled rubber out of the camp.

Deacon left in his new brown Cadillac. He and Iretha lived in Baldwin Hills, in an area "just up the hill" from some of the worst rioting. Maybe they didn't have the best of marriages, but she was his responsibility, and he was worried about her. He tried to stay close to the speed limit, because he knew a black man in these times couldn't be too careful.

He was driving slowly up Crenshaw Blv., awed by the blocks of shattered windows and still-smoldering ruins. Gaping at the mayhem and destruction around him, Deacon was at the roadblock before he knew it. It was a makeshift roadblock, not enough to stop a tank, but adequate for cars. There were ordinary crumpled cars pushed across the street, blocking all but one lane. A jeep narrowed the final lane, and white boys in olive drab uniforms were sprinkled behind the road-block, pointing their rifles in his direction.

"Where you goin', buddy?" one of the National Guardsmen said. He was just a freckle-faced kid, but he had his mean look on, and he poked his assault rifle in the front window of the Cadillac, inches from Deacon's face.

Deacon felt the blood turn to ice in his veins. He'd been in similar situations in the South a time or two; but this was an angry teenage kid with a semiautomatic rifle! The kid was white and scared, and Deacon could see there wasn't much keeping him from making a bloody mess of things.

"Now just take it easy, son," he said.

"I asked you a question, nigger!" the soldier flared.

Deacon sighed. At that moment, he'd rather have had a potbellied southern redneck cop sticking a gun in his face than this raw and unstable recruit.

Deacon put his hands in the air. "It doesn't do no good to call names. I got every right to be here. I live here, just up the hill." He gestured mildly with one arm.

"You got any I.D.?"

"Course I do." Deacon lowered one hand to reach in his pocket.

"Keep your hands in the air!" the frightened young guardsman said, practically slamming him in the face with the rifle.

"Well, now, I thought you wanted to see my I.D."

"Where'd you git this fancy car?"

"I bought it, son. I play football for the Rams." The senseless con-versation was starting to get to Deacon. He wasn't back home in the South. He was in California, where a black man was supposed to have rights. "Look, I'm Deacon Jones. I play defensive end for the Rams. I live in Baldwin Hills. I got every right to drive through here!"

The kid looked dangerously unstable, "You ain't got no rights unless I say so!"

One of the other guardsmen wandered over, "Ah, let him go, Charley. You can't play God out here."

"He probably stole this car off the lot down the street!"

"If he did, he saved it from getting trashed. The cops will sort it out later."

Deacon put his car in gear and began to slide around the two guardsmen and past the jeep.

"Stop or I'll blow your head off!"

By this time, most of the guardsmen were gathered around the Cadillac. One of them looked in the open window and said, "Hey, that is Deacon Jones! I'd know him anywhere! Hi, Mr. Jones!" The kid waved, and Deacon had the insane notion that if he'd had a pencil he'd be giving out autographs.

The second guardsman took the rifle by the barrel and pulled it aside. He waved Deacon through with a flip of his hand.

"You crazy man!" the first guardsman screamed. "Get your hand off my fucking weapon!"

While they were arguing over whether to hold him or shoot him, Deacon wasted no time maneuvering through the roadblock and accelerating down Crenshaw toward Baldwin Hills. When he got to his home, Iretha was curled up on the sofa, eating potato chips and sipping a crushed ice drink while she watched the riots on TV.

"Hey, babes," he said, his voice shaking a bit. "What's happenin'?"

"Crazy fool niggers makin' a mess o' Watts," she replied. "What you doin' home, Jones?"

He looked around the room, half expecting to see smashed windows and smoke billowing from the back rooms. There was nothing. Wherever the riots were, they weren't on his block.

"Swede let us go for the night."

"Oh," she shrugged, turning back to the television set.

He looked down at his hands, which were trembling slightly from his ordeal, and wondered if there was any of the good brandy left. Sure he was in training, but if ever there was an exception, this was it.

Thinking back to the Rams 1965 spring training, Deacon says, "Lamar and Rosey weren't as young as Merlin and myself. You can beat a young dog, and maybe he'll come back and get in the pit for you . . . but flesh and muscle can only take so much punishment, and then it starts to give way. When those two guys started to come up lame, that was just so much more pressure on Muley and me."

Of that grim night when he almost didn't make it through the Watts riots, Deacon remembers: "It seemed like eternity on earth before the barrel of that gun pointed in another direction. I could see my whole life flashing in front of my eyes. Thank God somebody in that group of kiddie-soldiers finally recognized me. I was one of the few who got through. I heard later they were turning everybody else back. God only knows if they actually shot anybody. If they did, I don't think you'd ever hear about it. That's all they needed in this country, for the National Guard to be accused of murdering innocent blacks in the streets. We would have had bloody revolution right there."

Swamp Boy's Revenge

With the onset of spring training Merlin turned into Merlin the Merciless. Preying on Deacon's fear of spiders and snakes, it seemed like every other day the farm boy from Utah had another trick up his sleeve. Deacon would open his locker and a rubber python would spring out. He shoved his foot down in one of his fine new boots to find out he was sharing it with a newly squashed frog.

The childish tricks continued unabated as the uneasy summer wore on, almost as if Olsen—like the rest of the NFL—had no idea what was going on in America. The *Los Angeles Times* Charity Game, due to be played in the Coliseum the night of Sunday, August 15, was called off Sunday morning. Otis Chandler, publisher of the *Times,* announced the game would be postponed until Tuesday "in the interest of public safety." Not a bad idea, considering the stadium wasn't all that far from the heart of the riots. The next day Deacon found a horde of plastic wiggly worms in his locker. The locker had been locked, so somebody must have pushed them through the slotted air vents on top.

By Tuesday night the eight o'clock curfew in the troubled areas had been lifted, but Gov. Pat Brown asked parents to keep their children off the streets and everyone to limit their travel. Fire-bombings and "minor sniping" were reported in locations as scattered as Pasadena, Pacoima, Venice and downtown L.A.

On the other hand, many Californians saw it as a media event. There were major traffic jams all over Watts. Not content to see it on television, sightseers jammed in bumper-to-bumper, driving through the tattered and burned sections of Watts. And the night of the Times Charity game, the police had to stand guard on the overpasses that cross over the Harbor Freeway to keep the people of the inner city from throwing bricks and pipes down on the cars below, streaming in from outlying areas headed for the Coliseum. There was NFL football on tap, and the Los Angelinos weren't going to let a little riot stop them.

The show went on, and 31,579 fans—an enormous crowd, under the circumstances—gathered to watch the Rams beat the Cowboys 9-0 on three Bruce Gossett field goals. It was a tough game. Deacon looked up from the field and it looked to him like there were more National Guardsmen and policemen there than fans. Nobody down on the field was concentrating on the game. If you were from L.A., particularly if you were a black player, you were wondering if your house was still standing. And if you were a white player on either team, you were just worried about getting out of the stadium in one piece.

Bill Munson started, and Roman Gabriel substituted, but neither could sustain a drive. The best thing that could be said for the evening was that everybody got out with their skins intact . . . except second-year receiver Bucky Pope, who sprained his knee. (This injury would be aggravated as the season continued, and the young star would never again regain his first-year speed and effectiveness.)

As the game wore down, Deacon noticed that Merlin was nervous. This was interesting; the big, cheery farm boy had never showed himself to be afraid of anything. Late in the fourth quarter, he looked over at Merlin as they stood on the line waiting for the Cowboys to break from their huddle.

"Hey, Farm Boy, what's shakin'?"

Merlin was looking wide-eyed at the stands. "We should never have played this game. I just don't want to get a bullet between my eyes."

Deacon grinned, hands on his hips as he eyed the crowd in the stands. "That don't happen 'cept only in Westerns. Black guys don't shoot that good. Like as not, you'll get it in the guts, or maybe get your big toe shot off."

"Thanks a lot . . ."

"Hey, just jokin', Muley. Can't you take a joke?"

Merlin gave him a black look and by that time the Cowboys were walking up to the line so it was back to business. The rest of the game went that way, Deacon imagining that he saw the glint of rifles and sawed-off shotguns in the end zone "where they stuffed all the blacks," and wondering out loud what it felt like to get shot. "They say you never even know the one with your name on it," he told Merlin.

"Cut the fooling around, Deak," Merlin told him. "This isn't the time for it."

Surprisingly, that particular game, and the game of professional football in general, probably did its bit to help quell the rioting and begin to heal the wounds that were tearing the city apart. There is much good that a football franchise can bring to a city. Men who ordinarily would spit on each other's shoes or hide behind closed doors with guns in hand can still come down to the stadium and cheer and shout and hoist their beers together in common cause for the home team. That remains one of the most important things about football— at its best—in our society today. It can bring people together, uniting a city in a common cause.

But this game sure was hard on the players. It finally wound to its conclusion, and Merlin ran for the locker room with Deacon jogging along side him, taking care to point out that an ordinary person had ten pints or so of blood in him, and chances were, it wouldn't all run out before they could get some more pumped in.

Yes, the Rams played while Watts burned. And maybe it seems inappropriate that Deacon finally got one back at Merlin the country boy in that most distressed of times. But it's important to remember that true humanitarian progress is never made by the big, nebulous thing called society, but by individuals. Though you'll never read about it in the history books, thousands of individual acts of friendship and understanding between the races were what actually prevented the riots in Los Angeles, Miami, New York, and Detroit from breaking into full-scale bloody revolution all across the United States. And so it is not surprising that a black man from Florida and a white man from Utah chose that time and a little humor to strengthen a friendship that still exists today.

Merlin Olsen, waiting to go on the Roy Firestone Show with the three other members of the Fearsome Foursome more than twenty-five years after the fact, remembers how Deacon got even that night in the Coliseum. "Our game was played on Tuesday more to settle things down in L.A. than for any other reason, and it was really hard for any of the players to get their minds on football. I think we all were worried about being shot at from the stands. And then, after the game, we were worried about getting to our cars in the parking lot and getting out of there. I know it did bother me, and, as we were walking away from the locker room, I poured my heart out to the other members of the Foursome. 'If there is any trouble,' I said, 'I am counting on you guys. Remember, I'm your soul broth-er.' And I'll never forget, David gave me that evil grin of his and said, 'You're on your own, Whitey.'"

Lem Barney, interviewed by phone from Detroit where he makes his home, noted the positive effect the NFL has had in Detroit, where he played his football. "There have been times when I personally have thought not only our Detroit Lions, but also our Tigers, our Redwings, and our Pistons were the best things we blacks shared with the whites. Those teams go a long way to hold-ing this city together, because we can all share with pride in their achievements."

Playing Hurt

Battered and banged up by the rigors of a Harland Svare spring train-ing, the Rams still managed a respectable 3-2 exhibition season. The first game of the regular season was played in muggy eighty-five-degree weather in Tiger Stadium. The Rams' offense managed to push the ball into Lions territory only three times.

The Rams' defense kept the team in the game until the fourth quarter, when they only trailed 3-0. At that, the front four was play-ing hurt. Svare had been forced to move tackle Merlin Olsen to defen-sive right end, to replace the injured Lamar Lundy. It wasn't a pretty game. As if they were in a conspiracy against their own teammates, Ram runners fumbled three times while they were just running with the ball, without ever being touched by an opposing player. The offen-sive line got pushed around by Detroit tackles Alex Karras and Roger Brown, and the secondary gave away undeserved completions to Milt Plum.

After the game Svare was outspoken in his criticism of the team, and on Monday Mal Florence of the *Times* reported, "If the Rams felt they didn't get a sufficient workout Sunday, this will be attended to on Tuesday. Harland, who referred to the collapse of his team as 'inexcus-able,' has scheduled a game-type scrimmage in San Fernando as a dis-ciplinary measure. This is not unprecedented for Svare, but NFL teams rarely engage in stimulating contact sessions once the league season gets underway."

That Tuesday, the players sat around on the playing field waiting for the coaches to arrive. Over half of the starters seemed to be nursing aches, sprains, bruises, or injuries of one type or another. Deacon and Lamar found a place away from the rest of the team and started to stretch it out. Deacon watched him gingerly try his sprained leg: "Lamar, this team is already in disarray, bandaged, and banged up like a cripple. What the hell is Swede trying to prove, anyway?" Lamar just shook his head, biting his lips at the pain.

Deacon continued, "Nobody—but nobody—holds scrimmages like this for losing."

"He say that again?"

"It was in the papers. We're being punished for losing. Only me, he told personal—I'm being punished for not overcoming a double-team block."

Lamar gave him an unbelieving stare. "They use two men to block you out, freeing up somebody else on the line, and Harland punishes you for it?"

Deacon nodded, his narrowed eyes looking at the smog- blanketed hills to the north. "Ain't gonna be fun out here. We already got more than our share of injuries from Swede's bash'em-up training camp. Now here he is, instead of getting us ready for next Sunday, sending us out to bruise and batter each other some more as a punishment for our sins!"

"Your quick the only thing keepin' you out of the hospital." Deacon's quickness not only enabled him to get in on plays and make tackles, it also helped him roll into a ball to protect himself at the end of a play, just before the pile of players came down on him.

"Amen to that, brother. I'll always prefer to be the hitter rather than the hitee." Deacon saw Lamar was limping badly. "Why don't you sit this one out, bro?"

Lamar shook his head, and Deacon could see the worry there. "I sit this one out, I may never be back."

In those days, there was no such thing as orthoscopic surgery. Major knee surgery involved up to four huge, six-inch scars, and rehabilitation was a lot more primitive than it is today.

"One injury is all it takes. The old career is over."

Deacon nodded, "Every time they snap the ball, it's the dance with death." He stood and gave a slight motion with his head, "Well, Lamar, here they come."

The scrimmage was long and brutal. Svare ran the double-team block at Deacon for a full forty-five minutes. When Deacon didn't evade the block, the defensive coach screamed at him; when he did evade it, the offensive coach screamed at the men double-teaming him. The ball was snapped and the wall of bodies came at him again and again. After each play, he'd pull himself out of the pile of tangled arms and legs and look over at Swede as if to say *What the hell's your problem? Are you crazy, man?* Deacon wasn't the only one who resented the practice-for-punishment. In fact, the entire team resented it with an animosity that only aggravated their injuries.

"It's like hell on earth," one of the guys on the offensive line across from Deacon grumbled.

Deacon gave him a curt nod. *This is a turning point,* he thought to himself. He could feel it. One game into the season, and the entire team was going sour.

The following Sunday, crafty old George Halas brought his Bears to L.A. Svare's midweek punishment scrimmage didn't seem to have any positive effect. On Monday, the day after the game, *L.A. Times* columnist Sid Ziff recorded the action: "Their reputation was in shreds in the first half. They were so inept people were laughing at them. They were listening to the Dodgers on their transistors and cheering Don Drysdale but booing coach Harland Svare for not switching his quarterback."

Once again, the Rams defense kept the team in the ball game until the offense finally came alive. The Rams scored twenty-one points in the final quarter to win, 30-28.

After the game, Dan Reeves said, "I'm numb. I have no feeling. I'm not kidding. I'm numb." The speculation had been mounting that he would make a coaching change. Now it looked like the heat was off, at least for a while.

Svare ecstatically declared that the Rams win was "my biggest thrill ever." Little did Svare or Reeves know that the spectacular come-from-behind win would be one of the few reasons to celebrate during the season. With a patched and battered squad on the field, another of the high points of the year was the superstar play of the team's defensive left end, the seemingly indestructible Deacon Jones.

In the third game of the season, against Minnesota, Rosey and Lamar made only token appearances, leaving Deacon and Merlin to chase Fran Tarkenton all over the field. Between the two of them they kept it close, but Minnesota finally won by a field goal.

"There were inexcusable errors," Svare said after the game. He didn't mention the fact that the team, already hammered and limping, was staggered with eleven Ram players injured or re-injured during the game, with five of them sent to the hospital. The injured were Ken Imam (sprained neck), Ed Meador (bruised shoulder), Cliff Livingston (severe right knee sprain), Tony Guillory (neck strain), Jack Snow (contusion on the calf), Rosey Grier (foot sprain), Joe Scibelli (twisted ankle), Tim Powell (ankle sprain), and Marlin McKeever (bruised ear). Then there were those like Bucky Pope, who hadn't even suited up due to earlier injuries, and Lamar Lundy, who would be questionable all season. Team physician Dr. John Perry sighed, "The whole team is going to the hospital with a six-pack."

Afraid of being replaced and cut from the team, individual Rams played hurt. They weren't the only players to do it in the NFL, and, in fact, it is still a common practice today. Deacon remembers, "If the bone wasn't sticking out through the flesh, you'd be better to suck it up and drag your ass back out there on the field. There simply was no other way, if you came to play the game of football. We had no job security, no union, and the NFL was the only game in town."

Mike Hull, a fullback and tight end who played with Chicago and Washington, talks almost casually about playing hurt in George Allen's book Strategies for Winning[4], "In 1974 I had pinched a nerve in my neck, paralyzed my left arm, broken my nose, and generally wiped myself out on a tackle in the Philly game. We were going to play the Cowboys the next week. I was in traction for a couple of days and feeling was coming back to my arm. I returned to practice with a brace on my neck, face guard altered to protect my nose . . . I played in the game. And although I was strapped together like a mummy, I managed to do something significant."

The Bottle of Pain Pills

The injured Rams patched themselves together as best they could and took to the field in Chicago the next Sunday. It was a sunny, smogless 60-degree day in ivy-covered Wrigley field, a perfect day for football, but the Rams could do no right. They gave up three fumbles, dropped

---

4. George Allen, *Strategies for Winning* (New York: McGraw-Hill Publishing Company, 1990), p. 73.

passes, and waved at others instead of pulling them in. Worse, veteran cornerman Aaron Martin broke his arm, adding his name to the
long list of the walking wounded at the sidelines or replaced by the
taxi squad, the group of seven substitutes who were allowed to practice with the team while not being part of the thirty-four regulars.

As the Rams headed for the dressing room, the jeering Bear fans
cursed and shouted obscenities from the other side of a screened catwalk. Deacon ducked his head and prayed no Coke bottle would come
flying his way. He decided it wasn't as bad as the Orangeburg demonstrations. The Chicagoans were just as close and crazy, but nobody was
spitting, and there were no German shepherds or water hoses.

By now, the Rams trainers and doctors were using every trick
known in the NFL to keep their players on the field. During the
games, they deadened the pain of major muscle damage with injections of novocaine and xylocain. They taped the linemen so they could
play with broken bones, with their arms, wrists or hands in casts. The
players routinely took the field with broken fingers; that was easy, the
trainers simply taped the broken ones to the sound ones. They entered
their field of battle doped up with pain pills, numbed by injections,
and wrapped like mummies.

All these practices were common throughout the league. It wasn't
a question of legality, or of the league giving permission—no matter
what spectators thrill to in the stands, on the field it is a little war, and
in the locker rooms the players are repaired and sent back out to battle with all the medical, surgical and pharmaceutical skills learned
over a century of playing the game. Deacon was playing in the critical
transition period when football was becoming a big-money sport.
Once television broadcast of games on a regular basis enabled professional football to take on a national status, difficult questions raised by
the common use among some players of pain pills, pain shots, recre-
ational drugs and strength-producing hormones would have to be
addressed by the league commissioner. Still, promoting new rules and
change could be a sticky problem, for the commissioner himself was
elected by the owners. And no one in the league wanted to admit that
over the generations they had turned a blind eye to these practices.

When, in the early seventies it became apparent that the NFL was
going to have to do something about drugs or risk governmental inter-
vention, the league was forced to move into an area which had hither-
to been considered individual team business. Gene Klein, owner of the
San Diego Chargers, is unique in that he openly voiced his frustration

with the problem of drugs: "We [Charger's management] did our best to investigate every rumor, to prevent the distribution of drugs, to educate our players, to offer help, but after a while I realized that there was really nothing I could do that would make a difference. My mama didn't raise me to be a cop."[5]

The shots, the pain pills and the taping of broken bones was all part of the game to Deacon. If that's what it took to stay in professional football, he accepted it with the same grim determination he displayed through all the contact drills and practice scrimmages. He never pulled back on any play, from the first practice drill to the last hit of the season. Though he'd been lucky to avoid a major injury thus far, his body was a mass of bruises and pain throughout the season. Deacon relied on pain pills to keep him going as much as anyone on the team.

The most common pain pills were aspirin and amphetamines. Aspirin, the old reliable home remedy against illness of all types, was popular for its anti-inflammatory properties. Amphetamines were equally as common. The drug had been invented by the U.S. Army in World War II as a "bravery" pill, to give to the men before they went into battle. Soldiers returning from Europe and Asia brought them back. By the time Deacon got to the NFL in the early 1960s, there was relief available throughout the league. In those days, pharmaceutical drugs commonly available through prescriptions were sometimes available as samples. Everyone wanted to support the home team, and there were a dozen ways a handful of well-meaning physicians and local sales representatives and other employees of legitimate companies tried to give their boys the fighting edge. Locker rooms had their special bottle, sitting in full view on the training table with the salt tablets, the aspirins, the tape, and the witchhazel. Some teams had two bottles, one with reds and one with the greenies—the uppers and the downers—and some had rows of bottles, all the colors of the rainbow.

In the Rams locker room there was only one big, taped bottle with every pill thrown in together—red ones, white ones, yellow ones, black ones, little blue triangular ones. There wasn't a man on the Rams, from the owner, head coach, trainers, and players on down to the ball boys who didn't know about that bottle. It was no big secret or scandal. It wasn't even a hidden practice, though almost all deny or seem to have forgotten about it today. Deacon recalls that Waterfield had been a

---

5. Gene Klein and David Fisher, *First Down and a Billion* (New York: William Morrow & Company, 1987), p. 263.

player, and Harland Svare as well, and they never acted like there was anything extraordinary about the Rams "rainbow bottle." That little dispensary was part of the pro football way of life, and it was provided by the team. It was the normal thing in and around the locker room. You had your cleated shoes, jock strap, pads, uniform, and helmet— and your pain pills. You taped your ankles and other injuries, rubbed black under your eyes, took an injection to deaden the effects of any serious muscle tears, and took your pills to get ready for the pain you knew was coming. Did amphetamines improve performance? Probably not. On the other hand, they weren't as dangerous as the steroids that were to come into fashion in the seventies and eighties, or as habit-forming and dehabilitating as cocaine, which became the drug of choice in the years after use of amphetamines gradually waned or went underground. Of course, pain is pain, and where there's a need, the product will be successful. Deacon is sure the habit never did die out; Deacon says that, based on his discussions with active players around the league (who wish to remain anonymous), the players themselves estimate use of amphetamines is currently at around 50 percent.

Medical experts think amphetamines helped less and in different ways than today's over-the-counter muscle relaxants and inflammation reducers, which you will find in every NFL locker in the land. Amphetamines make you feel better, when, in fact, you may be in no shape to play at all. Other evidence suggests that amphetamines decrease performance: in the short term, the side effects include a warped view of reality and a bad sense of timing; in the long run, as the players build up resistance to the drug, it takes larger and larger dosages to have an effect.

Pain pills could blunt the pain of injury, but they weren't going to be enough to put the beat-up Rams in the win column. Although Deacon and Merlin continued to play outstanding football on the line, the following week the team lost their fifth game of the season to the San Francisco 49ers, 45-21. In this game, three of the 49ers' first four scores were set up by the Rams with a fumble, a fizzled punt, and a pass interception. Jack Snow muffed three catches, and with nobody on the offensive line doing his job but Charlie Cowan, Munson was sacked five times and forced to hurry almost every pass.

After the game, Mal Florence noted in the L.A. Times that the Fearsome Foursome, riddled by injuries, wasn't up to its usual game. Svare, perhaps ground down from anger to disgust, said, "It was the longest day I've ever spent. How long did it take to play the game, ten hours?"

Dan Reeves echoed, "It was an evil day. A day without a redeeming feature."

Some things can't be cured, not even with a huge bottle filled with all the colors of the rainbow.

Deacon breaks the player's unwritten code to talk about how widespread the acceptance of amphetamine use was in the NFL in those days: "Our trainers brought the amphetamines and other drugs into the locker room by the carton. They didn't do that on their own. They were simply Rams employees, doing their job for the good of the team." Maybe it was a simpler age; although these drugs were legally only to be prescribed by a physician and distributed by a pharmacist, back then a wide range of the society from overstressed businessmen and depressed ladies to celebrities like Elvis took amphetamines—common thinking of the times was that they were good for you. "Many of them were manufactured by top pharmaceutical companies, and handed out by our trainers and team doctors for a wide variety of ailments. And, of course, amphetamines got you racing, so you needed different pills—say, Quaaludes—to calm you down after the game. Amphetamines and 'Ludes' were everywhere, and I don't know any veterans who didn't take them. All the big names at the time used them, though since the league—starting in the early seventies—put a stigma on them and made the players the bad guys, lots of retired players who want to preserve their reputations and sign autographs for little kids play dumb to the whole issue."

It is Deacon's contention that, while the common use of amphetamines was no secret to coaches and owners throughout the league, nothing was done until newspaper exposés brought about unpleasant publicity in the early seventies. Why? Because, Deacon says, professional football is about winning, "And all is fair in love and war." Gene Klein seems to bear out this line of thinking in his book. Talking about his experiences as owner of the Chargers in the late seventies and early eighties, he says, "When we had evidence that a player was using drugs, we got rid of him. We didn't get rid of him because we had evidence he was using drugs—certainly not—but because we didn't feel he was a very good football player. However, if the user was a star, or superstar, we learned to live with his problem. Was that hypocritical? Of course it was. But we weren't going to be the only team in pro football to strictly enforce drug regulations. The result of that policy probably would have been a drugfree, losing football team. And fans, the people who buy tickets, aren't interested in curing drug addiction; they are simply concerned about the final score. It's much easier to be idealistic about the drug problem if you don't have fifty thousand seats to fill every Sunday. I became a pragmatist.[6]

When interviewed by this writer in 1991 and 1992, Lamar Lundy seconded Deacon's comments. "When it comes to amphetamines, about 99 percent of everybody took them! Nobody's interested in digging up old dirt, or dragging their comrades-in-battle through the mud, and I'm not going to open my mouth and name names. But you go on yourself right now, and you think the name of any pro who played in that era on any NFL team; chances are 99 percent he put his hand regular in that bottle! A & A—amphetamines and aspirin—were our pain pills. We knew we were going into battle, and that we were going to get beaten and bashed, and our bodies would ache. Heck, our bodies still ached from the previous week!"

Pervis Atkins talked to this writer in 1991 about the first time he took pain pills. "I swallowed some of the blue triangles, and the first half went by like ZIP! ZIP! ZIP! Well, it got to be halftime and the rest of the team was heading for the locker room, and there I was, sitting on the bench, nodding off to sleep!"

Deacon remembers Pervis sitting on that bench. "The whole team enjoyed a good laugh over it. Pervis had just come to understand one of the bad side-effects of uppers—you had to take enough to keep from crashing before the end of the game!"

In his book First Down and a Billion, *Gene Klein talks about the NFL's continuing difficulties in controlling substance abuse in the seventies and eighties, "The league did have a drug program. It didn't work, but it was a program. It was basically an educational program. Once, for example, Carl Eller, the great Vikings lineman whose life was almost destroyed by cocaine addiction, spoke to the team. On another occasion an ex-FBI agent working in the league office gave a powerful lecture about the physical and legal consequences of drug abuse. Unfortunately, at a cocktail party after the lecture, he got drunk and fell into the salad bar."[7]*

---

6. Gene Klein and David Fisher, *First Down and a Billion* (New York: William Morrow & Company, 1987), p. 263.

7. Ibid.

Svare's Woes

In their next two games, the sixth and seventh of their fourteen game season, the Rams lost to the Colts and then the Lions. They had one win and six losses, and the critics began sharpening the knives in earnest. They may have been brutal before, but now they went looking for targets.

One disgusted writer said, "They made more mistakes than the Italian army." Sid Ziff commented in his column in the *L.A. Times*:

> It's getting so you can write these Ram stories in advance. It's always safe to lead off by saying, "The Rams messed up another one today." They should have been playing "Drop the Handkerchief" Sunday, not football. They fumbled the ball seven times and gave the game to the Detroit Lions.
>
> Trailing 14-0 in the third quarter, the Rams finally made a first down passing. "Quit pouring it on, Svare," thundered a sarcastic fan.

The situation was getting out of hand for Svare. Facing the reporters after the game, the Rams youthful head coach threw up his hands in despair: "If I start benching every man who fumbles, we wouldn't have enough left to field an offensive unit. My eyes have gotten old watching the mistakes. There's no easy way to explain it."

Deacon, always good for some statement about how he was going to tear out his opponent's heart, how he was going to stomp his rival into the dirt, or how many times he would bury the opposing quarterback, was silent when the reporters asked him what was wrong with his own team. They were all in it together, he felt, and it didn't do any good to go casting the blame. As for his strong opinions about Svare and the coaching staff, he also kept those to himself. Svare had enough problems of his own, without hearing it from a player. Deacon knew Swede was in a swamp of trouble. So he heckled his rivals and bantered with the press, but he held his peace with his own team. Sometimes he talked about the good he saw, such as sparks of improvement in the defensive backfield, or Gabriel having a good afternoon.

And the losing streak continued. In Minnesota the Rams lost their sixth straight, 24-13. The Monday following Sunday's game, Bob Oates commented in the *Herald Examiner* that if the Rams' offensive line "had played as eagerly as David Jones, who was the outstanding athlete on the field, the Rams could have won." Oates continued in tongue-in-cheek fashion: "The Rams, as you know, are always looking for a new way to lose. In Minnesota, they were hardly unrewarded. Here, enthusiastically, they committed suicide."

After this game, Svare finally spoke openly about one of the team's major problems. "I was unhappy with our pass protection, otherwise we would have won."

Deacon was awarded a Golden Helmet, a Los Angeles award, as the Southland's pro player of the week for his outstanding play in the game. Deacon's comments when accepting the award show that he was adding some sophistication to the quick wit that had been his trademark since he made his rookie announcement that the Deacon had come to town to teach the gospel of football. He graciously accepted the award, and in turn thanked the team in general and the Fearsome Foursome for enabling him to make the plays and to perform at high levels on the field.

Nice words, but they weren't helping win games. The Rams moved on to Green Bay, where they fumbled away the game and lost in the last seconds, 6-3. In the next day's *L.A. Times,* Mal Florence was beside himself: "Just like the drunk who said that the last step was a dilly after he fell down the elevator shaft, the Rams last mistake was the one which hurt the most." Florence praised the Rams defensive line even in defeat: "You couldn't find a more determined defensive end than Deacon Jones Sunday, while his Front Four friends, Merlin Olsen, Lamar Lundy and Rosey Grier were at the peak of their games."

In the fading seconds of the game, Deacon almost preserved the tie for the Rams. He talked to Florence about it in the locker room after the game: "Because Chandler (the field goal kicker) was so close to the goal posts, he had to kick the ball almost straight up. As it was, I just barely missed it. If he had kicked from farther out, I would have had it sure."

"We really put it together today," Svare agreed. In a sour sort of way, he continued, "When you play defense like that, you should win . . . but we're still defeating ourselves—fumbles, penalties."

Rosey Grier had the last word: "We couldn't get a break if we tried to buy one." But the great Rosey was wrong. They were about to get a break. Unfortunately, it wasn't going to be a good one.

Playing San Francisco at Kezar Stadium in one of those rugged north-south grudge matches, Bill Munson was hammered to the ground in what looked like a late hit. He suffered ligament and cartilage damage to his right knee. Munson, who had been the starter,

Deacon flanked by his parents, Ishmeal and Mattie, at their Eatonville, Florida, home in 1964.

Deacon's older brother, Judson Jones, in 1960.

Deacon with former L.A. Rams teammate Dick Bass at an event at the Hollywood Center Studios, Hollywood, Calif., in 1988.

The "Fearsome Foursome"—from left to right, Lamar Lundy, Roosevelt Grier, Merlin Olsen, and Deacon Jones—together at a charity fundraiser for Myasthenia Gravis in 1971. (photo courtesy Irv Antler)

From left to right, Johnny Unitas, Deacon Jones, and event promoter Jack Mark on the Super Bowl Cruise in 1987.

Deacon performing at the Ragdoll Supper Club in Los Angeles in 1970.

From left to right, Tom Shropshire, Sr., Vice President of Miller Brewing; comedian Redd Foxx; and Deacon at the Black Achievement Awards banquet in 1978. At the time Deacon was a spokesperson for Miller. (Willie Dooley, Sunset Photo Service)

Deacon in hot pursuit of Baltimore Colts quarterback Earl Morrall in 1968. (© Dave Bass, NFL Photos)

The last play of the last regular-season game of Deacon's career in 1974. Joe Theisman holds as Deacon success-fully completes his one and only point-after-touchdown attempt. (© NFL Photos)

A long way from a poor town in Florida: Deacon at his induction ceremony at the Professional Football Hall of Fame, Canton, Ohio, in 1980.

would be out for the rest of the season. Roman Gabriel came off the bench and nearly engineered a win, only to have San Francisco score in the last six seconds to take the victory by three points.

Like most of the players of that team, Deacon thinks at least a good part of their miserable offensive play can be explained simply: "At last it can be told. The Rams coaching staff, to a man, had an attitude that made the players uncertain about their own talent. They wouldn't stand up for you. Everything that went wrong was always the players' fault. We saw it with the quarterbacks, who got blamed and jerked in and out like silly puppets whenever anything went wrong. You felt sorry for them. All the yelling, particularly Bob Schnelker's, made Bill and Gabe tense up just before they heaved the ball, and made the receivers tighten up when they went for the grab. Our coaches were prophets of doom, and after a while, you know, it's self-fulfilling. Not that we were perfect—but we were professionals, and they whipped and scolded us like kids, and bad kids at that!*

"But don't look to Harland and his merry band of screamers for all the blame. After ten losing years in a row, Dan Reeves should have been learning that pro ball had progressed beyond the point where even top-pick rookies could take the field and expect to play effectively with veterans. Of course, he never did. He believed exclusively in the youth movement until the day he died. He'd take on great kids, give them a few years experience, and then lose patience and deal them away just as they learned the tools of their trade. As for Harland, one of his great learning experiences had to be that his awesome Fearsome Foursome couldn't carry the entire team, not even when we were healthy. The Rams only had two solid veterans in their secondary. There was Jack Pardee behind me, our left linebacker. Jack was an All-Pro, and so we were steady there. And Eddie Meador was excellent at free safety. Clancy Williams was only a rookie with a lot to learn, and Jerry Richardson was still green. The rest was like a sieve, and our coverage constantly broke down. This ought to have been obvious; it wasn't going to do the Foursome any good to rush a scrambler like Fran Tarkenton if he was going to find open men in the secondary. Dan loved to come down on the sidelines, and man, there were times when I would have loved to walk over there and grab him by the ears. Can you see it, this huge, crazed black guy trying to shake some sense into the little, runty owner of the Rams, 'Come on, Daniel, we need some help, for God's sake, give us a few experi-

*enced men here! You should have the picture by now; after all,
you've had us down and out for a decade. You must be doing
something wrong! Trade away a few of those top draft choices
you're stacking like cord wood every winter for coming in at the
bottom of the league!' "*

The Penalty for Success

After Munson's injury, the San Francisco game deteriorated into a
brawl. It was one of those dissatisfying games the outcome of which
is decided largely by the officials. It was a problem in Deacon's time,
just as it continues to be a problem today. Fans in general don't realize how difficult it is to referee the complex game of football in a fair
and impartial manner. And there is the human factor to consider; just
as in baseball, where nearsighted umpires are legendary, in football
certain referees have always been notorious in the inner circle for calling bad games, for letting the game get out of control, and for sloppy
play calling.

Whatever the reason, on the 49ers' winning drive, on what may
have been the deciding play of the game, Deacon was accused of a face
mask penalty. He and Merlin had risen to the challenge and had combined to stop the San Francisco drive dead in its tracks. The play was
over and the players were getting up and walking back to their sides
of the line when the yellow flag came fluttering down. It was what the
players term a "tickey-tack" or a "chicken-shit" call. It was just one
bad call, but this one decided a ball game. And when set alongside
other calls that had gone against Deacon throughout the season, it
added up to a real problem for the Rams' star defensive end.

In defense of the referees, and the game in general, it must be said
that Deacon was breaking new ground. The refs really didn't know
how to react. There had never been a defensive player on the line who
employed speed and strength with such devastating results. Defense
had always been the necessary evil, the dull, boring guys who came in
until the offense could get back out there. Deacon Jones, with the help
of Merlin Olsen, was changing all that. In some games, he broke
through the line and was in the offensive backfield more often than
not. Some series, he put pressure on the quarterback on every play.
Rival teams were now switching their offenses to the quick pass, to get
the ball off before Deacon got there, and to the shotgun, which before

this time had been used mostly on third-and-long situations, so Deacon would have longer to run to get to the quarterback. Teams rotated their running game to run to the opposite side of the field, and even then Deacon sometimes chased down and tackled the back from behind. Film clips record the legendary Deacon Jones slipping his man and threading his way laterally through the entire opposing team to make a tackle on the far side of the field, twenty, thirty, or even forty yards away from where he had assumed his stance. Football, notoriously a team sport, particularly on defense where the players were supposed to be faceless gladiators in the trenches, was taken by surprise. History shows the inner circles did not adjust well to one man—and a black man at that—revolutionizing the sport. There is, of course, no written evidence, but the officials had to have been alerted, and had to have talked this new factor out among themselves, because Deacon Jones became the object of intense scrutiny. This guy must be jumping the gun. Unwilling to believe their own eyes, the referees often called Deacon offside after the fact, figuring nobody could get into the backfield with the regularity he did.

True, with his gambling, quick-off-the-line, style of attack, there were times when Deacon guessed wrong, particularly in his first few years in the league. There is embarrassing footage of him in the backfield, grinning at the rival quarterback, and the ball is still in the center's hands. But those are obvious mistakes. The bad calls he got at the line during his entire career were judgment calls based on the notion that nobody could move that fast, therefore he must have been offsides. In time, the better, more independent-minded referees learned not to make this call against Deacon. They looked too foolish as the age of stop-motion and freeze-frame came to football, often preserving what really happened and re-running the play for the fans on television.

Then too, Deacon was assuming a certain notoriety. Deacon's head-slap was causing rival linemen to complain, and it was obviously one of his most successful weapons, but the officials couldn't do anything about it. Defensive linemen had always been allowed to use their hands at the line, and the headslap had been around for years, indeed it was available to any defensive lineman who wanted to use it. It was just that Deacon had refined it into a method of attack that, along with his quick, made him practically impossible to stop.

Rival quarterbacks, accustomed to protection from their offensive line that would see them through entire games without the rude touch of an enemy lineman, were being unceremoniously dumped on their butts with alarming regularity. This was the year Lombardi and other rival coaches had shifted their offenses to compensate, and Deacon Jones was still getting through with a regularity that was astonishing. Rams fans lauded his greatness. Others around the league—coaches and players as well as fans—were disgusted their own local heroes couldn't stop Deacon, and often complained there had to be something illegal about his moves.

It was one thing when a lineman complained he'd had his bells rung with a slap across the helmet. It was another when the quarterback made the same complaint. A good quarterback was the franchise. Quarterbacks like Unitas, Starr, and Brody were the engines that powered their teams. They couldn't be knocked around like so many sacks. And here was a guy who openly declared his that intent, his goal, his reason for existence was to "kill quarterbacks!"

As the year wore on, Deacon and his fellow members of the Fearsome Foursome noticed a sobering statistic—an increasing number of questionable calls in the backfield. When roaring in on a quarterback who was dropping back to pass, the defensive man was taught to get his hands high, to block the pass attempt. Whether the quarterback got the pass off or not, the defensive player's hands had to come down, to help him make the tackle. And woe be to any member of the Foursome, should their hands brush the quarterback's helmet on the way down! It would be an instant "facemasking" call, a referee's call for hanging on to and pulling the face mask that was accompanied by a fifteen yard penalty.

The bad call in San Francisco seemed to the Rams' defensive players to so clearly indicate a pattern of discrimination against them that they spoke out publicly about it. Today, with the players' union behind them, a decision to speak out would be taken for granted. But in the NFL at that time, very few coaches or players took their case to the press and the public. To name just a few, black player Johnny Sample, who had tried to speak his mind, was branded as a troublemaker, and describes in detail how and why he was blackballed from the NFL in his book *Confessions of a Dirty Ballplayer.* Ollie Matson had had his difficulties. Players were taught to hunker down and be quiet or get out of the game.

It was commonly believed that the pressure to keep quiet came from the very top, from Pete Rozelle, the commissioner, and the message was that the referee's word was law. Paul Zimmerman, sports editor of the *L.A. Times,* noted in an article on November 10, 1965, that

Rozelle had dictated that football coaches (much less the players) should not criticize game officials in public, a decree that Zimmerman thought infringed on the right of free speech.

On the other hand, Deacon had spoken his mind since he was a little black kid in Eatonville. Injustice was injustice, whatever the level; the commissioner of football could be just as wrong as a car full of drunken, watermelon-heaving white teenagers. After the game with San Francisco, Deacon stood angrily in the locker room and told the reporters, "It was an unjust call. I didn't even touch his mask. My hand went right across his face as I was reaching for the ball." Referring to an earlier face-masking call against him that had contributed to the team's loss to Baltimore a few weeks earlier, Deacon added, "The officials seemed to follow us across the country."

Merlin Olsen agreed, feeling the flag was thrown as an obvious afterthought: "The official was reaching for the ball when he dropped the handkerchief. The play was dead. Even if Deak had touched the mask, it wouldn't have made any difference. The play was over and (the players were) getting up."

About his headslap, Deacon says, "My father's father was a bad man. He kicked pure ass, he was the meanest man I ever met . . . and I think sometimes I take after my grandfather. I have a mean streak, and in my business I needed it or I never would have made it. Pro football is, after all, a pain-giving game. My headslap gave pain, it made you not want to hold me at the line, which is the one illegal move offensive linemen get away with over and over in every game, today more than ever. My headslap was the right hand of Joe Frazier and Muhammad Ali rolled into one. Imagine this poor lineman who has to play alongside me. His coach has told him he's got to get inside and grab my jersey and hang on every play so the ref doesn't see him. And so what does he get? Every twenty-five seconds or so, another play comes along, and I lay a thunderous right hand alongside his head until I've got him ringing inside that helmet like a bell. Then I lay my speed on him at the same time. Pretty soon, I've got him trying to hold and duck. It's hard to block a man when you've got your eyes closed, and there were times when I could see that sucker close his eyes so bad you couldn't squeeze in a dime!

"The quickness of hand was everything, that and the hand-foot coordination. In the NFL—as in the rest of life—imitation is the sincerest form of flattery. Everybody playing my position at the time

tried to use the headslap. Some of them were better than others, but it was a physical skill that required strength, coordination, and timing. Like a jab in boxing, everybody can do it, but with different degrees of excellence. I'd be down in the three-point stance, coming up, going forward, and my right hand was up alongside my opponent's head before he could get his hand on my shirt to commit holding, the foul he knew he could get away with. That headslap was an attention-getter, all right. It made you know the Deacon was here, and he was going to be here the rest of the afternoon. If you were playing against me, you had to deal with it. The only problem was, you couldn't. With the headslap, I was unstoppable. And when they saw what was happening, everybody in the league started using it."

Roman Holiday

It was early evening by the time Deacon came off the practice field. At that time, late in the season, darkness came early, and he'd stopped kicking when he could no longer see the crossbar. A few guys were still banging locker doors, and somebody was singing the Beatles' "It's been a hard day's night, an' I been workin'. . . like a dog!" badly off-key in the showers.

As Deacon walked to his own locker, he saw Roman Gabriel sitting over the whirlpool with his ankle in the icy water, and a bag of ice strapped around the elbow of his throwing arm.

"Hi, Gabe," he said in passing.

"Hey, Deak."

Deacon paused. Gabriel was a good ol' boy, a southern white, but he'd always seemed fair with the players, regardless of their color. Deacon had heard him talk to the press in glowing terms about black player Charlie Cowan, one of his few effective offensive linemen. So Deacon figured, even though he was a quarterback and a white boy, he couldn't be all bad.

"Yeah, " Deacon said, "what's up?"

"You hear Harland's activating Ron Smith?"

"Yeah." The bittersweet smile came to Deacon's lips, and there was a sympathetic look in his eye. "The rookie from Richmond gets his shot. I was there when Swede was tellin' the press."

Gabe shook his head and looked into the swirling water, "It sure don't do much for a fellow's self-confidence."

Deacon dropped his helmet in a corner and sat on a nearby bench. What the hell, take a little time. Iretha would order in some ribs for supper, and they'd be warm in the oven whenever he got there. Deacon's uniform was caked with dirt and green-stained grime. He began peeling the thick strips of tape from his forearms. "Well, Gabe, you can't look to Swede for buildin' a man up. He's young hisself. He ain't thought it all through, if you know what I mean."

Roman nodded, "You . . . you had some troubles with Swede a year or two back, didn't you?"

"Yeah. The M- - - - - F- - - - - kept tryin' to fix my stance."

"That's Harland. Always trying to give me the quick fix. Throw faster, throw slower, throw harder, throw softer. I wish it was that easy." He shifted the ice bag on his arm. "What did you do?"

Deacon sighed, leaning back against the wall so the sweat didn't drip in his eyes, "The first lesson I learned was the most important one—it wasn't Swede's fault."

"How you figure?"

"It was my fault. I let him talk me out of what I do best, out of what got me to the big leagues. That made me the main fool. And I know I was right, because when I went back to the basics, things started to get better right away for me. See, Gabe, I had nothing to lose. Swede was always hollering' that they was gonna trade my ass, anyway . . . like you, I guess."

"Wish they would trade me."

Deacon was silent for a moment: "You played a hell of a game last week. You just about pulled it out for us."

"Thanks. Do you honestly think I should go back to my old game?"

"I don't know that much about quarterbacking. But I'll tell you one thing. I do think you gotta get more deaf-eared out there, Gabe. Take your receivers out and buy 'em a beer. Tell 'em they got to ignore all that yellin' an' screamin'. That ain't coachin', in my book. That's just first-class dumbness."

"Does it look that bad?"

Deacon rolled his eyes, "Lord, I'm surprised you ever throw on target, or that they ever catch it!"

"Sometimes it feels like they want us to screw up."

Deacon shrugged, "Can't let it get to ya. You been here what, four years now? Far as I'm concerned, you been gettin' better and better—in spite of Schnelker an' all his screamers. You got the touch, man, and you got good receivers. I don't think there's another quarterback in the league can compare, 'cept maybe Johnny U. An' I'll tell ya something. Reeves ain't gonna let Swede start rookie Smith next week. The press would have his hide. They're gonna start you, babes. An' I say you give 'em something to remember you by!"

"The Pack will be tough."

Deacon smiled his slow smile again, "I tell you somethin', Gabe. The Foursome is gonna *dominate.* I absolutely *guarantee* we'll get you the ball. You just heave the sucker, pal. Give Lombardi fits; make a little history out there." He groaned as he reached for his helmet. "This late in the season, I got aches on my aches, an' bruises on my bruises." And then he was gone, making his way back to his own locker.

Gabriel sat with his ankle in the whirlpool, heartened by the conversation and surprised it had come from their star defensive end. He'd always thought of Jones as a grimly determined loner. He was buoyed by the high praise. Deacon Jones thought he was as good as Johnny Unitas! Odd how a few comments like that at just the right time could make a fellow's day!

The following Sunday, Gabriel went out there and completed fifteen of twenty-eight passes for 258 yards and a totally unexpected 21-10 win over Green Bay. As Deacon had promised, the Foursome mauled the Green Bay offense and got him the ball, and Gabriel went on to make the most of it. If Svare hadn't expected it, neither had the press, and the next day Florence of the Times was quick to tell the tale in glowing terms: "Roman Gabriel, who has been shrouded in cobwebs on an obscure part of the bench for more than two-thirds of the season, stepped out of the shadows to provide the Rams with leadership befitting a John Unitas."

The papers pointed out that Gabriel had called a sound game, and had faked and hidden the ball like a wizard. They also recorded that Deacon and the other members of the front four were in All-Pro form. Whenever the Packers tried to get a drive going, Deacon or Rosey was there to make the critical third-down tackle. And Lamar batted down three Bart Starr passes, while Merlin swatted another two for an unofficial NFL record of five deflected passes. Deacon caught Bratkowski, the Green Bay quarterback subbing for Starr, in the end zone for a two-point safety.

After the game, Deacon just smiled and told the press to go talk to Gabriel. "It's Gabe's game, he's the man." The Rams quarterback, finding an audience for his concerns, said, "I don't consider myself a second string quarterback." He added that he expected to be traded after the season, "The Rams don't consider me good enough for number one, and they think I'm too good for number two."

Svare, measuring his praise, admitted some of the success in the game was due to Gabriel, and the rest to running back Willie Brown, who had gained about thirty yards in the game. Svare said, also in measured terms, that he was happy with Deacon Jones: "He is probably playing as well as any defensive end in the league. And he's been playing that way for a month."

It was weak applause for Roman, who'd just torn apart the mighty Green Bay Packers, and for Deacon Jones, the man who was tearing up the Western Conference. Deacon was well on his way to another incredible year: eighteen sacks, twenty-nine quarterback hurries, and sixty-eight solo tackles. The only person who had ever had more sacks was Deacon Jones, in the previous year, when he'd had twenty-two.

Though the season, for all practical purposes, was over, Gabriel and the Fearsome Foursome weren't through yet—Gabriel still had plenty to prove, and the Foursome was just naturally surly. In the next game, in St. Louis, they again made sure he had the ball, and the quarterback racked up 360 combined yards for a 27-3 victory. After the game, the Cardinals quarterback, Charley Johnson, said of the charging Rams front line, "I tried to slow them down with screen and slip passes and draws, but that didn't bother them one bit. They just kept coming and coming. You know they're going to get you, but you don't want it to happen on a critical down."

On to Cleveland, where the Rams held the world champion Browns, the best rushing team in the NFL, to forty yards total rushing. The next day Florence reported that the great Jim Brown "never knew what or who hit him. One time it would be Merlin Olsen, then Lamar Lundy, then Deacon Jones, and Rosey Grier." Cleveland head coach Blanton Collier, licking his wounds in the locker room after the game, said, "Let in the press, but for goodness sake, keep out that front four!"

Roman Gabriel credited his offensive line, who gave him superb protection, for giving him time to set up and pick his targets. Gabriel was fun to watch, setting up five scoring bombs with fakes and double-fakes.

"The entire team," Svare said, "played better than any other time since I became the Ram coach in '62." Asked to explain the Rams, comeback, Svare responded, "At the first of the year—after the second game—I think it was injuries that hurt us. At one time, we had to use five rookies on defense. They're still making mistakes, but they're keeping them at a minimum."

Of his future with the Rams, Svare said, "To be honest about it, we have been so busy with the draft that Dan and I haven't had a chance to sit down and talk about it." At this time, Reeves was in New York at an NFL owner's meeting, and was unavailable for comment.

In the final game of the season, against powerful Baltimore, the Rams secondary again caved in. Gabriel, who was sixteen of thirty for 233 passing yards, nearly pulled off a victory. He had his last-minute pass intercepted by Bob Boyd. The Colts retained possession as time ran out, and won the game, 20-17. After the game, Boyd told reporters, "I think I actually fumbled the ball when I hit the ground." He quickly changed his mind to a chorus of boos from his teammates. "Well, I guess I didn't fumble after all," he smiled.

Strengthened by the respect of his teammates, and by the terrific statistics in the games he'd gotten to play in, Gabriel spoke to reporters: "There are three choices. I can come back or ask to be traded or quit football. If I don't have a chance to play next year, I'll ask the Rams to trade me or I'll quit. I've let the Rams know how I feel. They tell me they want me back. But there is no assurance I'll play."

The 1965 campaign was over. The Rams had settled into a dismal seventh place with four wins and ten losses. Green Bay won the Western Division and went on to beat Cleveland for the world championship, with ex-Ram quarterback Zeke Bratkowski piloting the Packers over ex-Ram quarterback Frank Ryan of the Browns.

Deacon can only shake his head when questioned about Harland's reluctance to praise his own players, "Some men don't recognize when history is being made on their front porch. There had never been, since the NFL first started playing on midwestern corn fields, a defensive player who was destroying the opposition the way I was. And yet, that's all Harland could say about me. The truth is, I was breaking entirely new ground, bringing excitement to the defensive line. Maybe he didn't know how excited he was supposed to be. Or maybe it was something else; in those days, coaches who were in the owner's pocket thought twice before saying anything that might come back to bite the owner in the wallet at contract time."

At the end of the season, Svare refused to discuss who had won the starting quarterback position—Bill Munson, who had led the Rams through seven of their eight-game losing streak, or

Roman Gabriel, who had turned the team around with his leadership and brilliant play in the last four games.

"We're not going to have number one anything," Svare told the reporters. "That would be my policy. I won't name anybody number one, and that includes Deacon Jones. We will let the players decide by their training camp showing next summer."

If Svare still had any support among the players, he was losing it quickly. Deacon remembers that early, stubborn-minded Harland Svare: "He got better at motivating his players later on, when he did learn at least the basics, but during his stint with Los Angeles, young Harland was an absolute zero. With comments like that, he undermined the confidence of his most talented players. And worse—he pissed them off! If you've earned the right, as an NFL veteran and a starter, to be number one in your position, the new rookie has got to earn his place. The new man has got to knock you off. But here was Harland telling everybody we were all just dogs at the bowl. It would have cost him nothing to praise and reward performance, but he didn't understand the concept."

Dog Ball

Football is, generally speaking, a team sport. But this old truism breaks down when a lineman, particularly a defensive lineman, gets his hands on the football. At that moment, something wonderful happens. Three-hundred-pound sumo wrestlers with feet of clay hear distant trumpets and believe they can fly. They seem stuck in slow motion, these jelly-belly giants, and grown men jerk to their feet and wave their fists and gape in amazement from the stands and from their couches across the nation. The earth shakes as the man with the ball thunders ham-handed along the hashmarks, fulfilling the destiny fate and the risky roll of the ball have thrust upon him. He is unstoppable. Of course, he generally gets a few yards upfield and fumbles, is stripped, or buried under a swarm of rival tacklers. Still, for a defensive lineman, it's a goosebump thrill to carry that ball, and the dream of a lifetime to take it all the way in for a score.

The dogball madness even overcame level-headed Merlin Olsen in 1965, in the third from the last game of the season, while they were playing the Cardinals in St. Louis. The Foursome had Charley Johnson peddling backward on nearly every play, and they were putting his face in the grass with a regularity alarming to the local fans. On a play that even to this day lives in infamy, Lamar Lundy crashed through the line and belted Johnson, who fumbled on the Rams eighteen-yard line. Merlin picked up the ball, and in the words of *L.A. Times* writer Florence, "took off like a wounded water buffalo." Escorted by Deacon, Merlin huffed and puffed his way fifty-nine yards before he was forced out of bounds by flanker Bobby Joe Conrad. His was a long, long run—a *legendary* run—for a lineman.

In the locker room after the game, Merlin grinned and joked about it. "Little Bobby Joe was the only man fast enough to catch me," he told the reporters with a twinkle in his eye.

Deacon, standing next to Merlin, looked the other way and then quietly slipped in the direction of his own locker. Merlin was the man of the hour, and he wasn't going to spoil his moment of glory with the reporters. But the true story, the one the press never heard, was quite different.

As Deacon trotted alongside the chugging Merlin, he asked him over and over again to lateral the ball. He knew stubborn Muley Olsen was quick on the line, but he wasn't fast, and there was no chance he was going to make it all the way, no chance at all. In fact, Merlin was running so slow that Deacon was running sideways and backwards just to block for him.

He pleaded as he ran, "Farm Boy, they catchin' up on us here!" Still Merlin charged on like a wayward bull. "Please, Muley, pass me the ball, I'll take it all the way, I'll take it in for you!"

But Merlin just put his head down and plowed ahead. He never would give up that ball, even though the Cardinals were thundering right behind him.

The Rams won 27-3, so it didn't really matter that Deacon was right and Merlin was driven out of bounds, thus blowing the scoring chance—except that those chances are very rare for a defensive lineman.

Scoring touchdowns wasn't what Deacon's game was about. There was no scoring in the pit, the gladiator's arena where he was the undisputed star. They were the pit bulls. They scuffled with one another to settle whether they were going to allow the glamour guys score the touchdowns. Deacon's touchdowns were tackles. When he went flashing in on a passer and threw him for a loss, it was as spectacular as a long run or a long pass. And when the man said *Tackle by Deacon Jones!* it was like scoring a touchdown. It was music to Deacon's ears.

The Rams' official team records show that Deacon Jones is by far pro football's all-time leading sacker, a record that stands like a monument head and shoulders above anyone who ever played the game. But sure-handed and lightning fast as he was, Deacon never scored a touchdown in his fourteen years in professional football. That's just the way the dogball bounces.

Interviewed in 1994 while waiting for an appearance on the "Roy Firestone Show", Merlin Olsen remembered his "moose is loose" moment in St. Louis, and tried to turn the tables, poking fun at his old-time comrade-in-arms: "Deak, if you'd blocked for me like you were supposed to, instead of jawing the whole way down the field, I would have scored!"

"Not in your wildest dreams, Farm Boy. The whole Cardinals team was right behind Bobby Joe, and every one of them was faster than you. Great as I was, I couldn't block eleven men!"

"You were talking so much that you couldn't even block one little bitty man who was half your size!"

"You know in your heart you should have passed me the ball."

A smile spreads across Merlin's face, so familiar from his television roles, and he drawls softly, "There was no way I was going to give Deacon that ball. He had plenty of chances to score on his own. A defensive lineman only gets a few chances in a lifetime to run the ball. You think I was going to give that up?"

It's an amusing image, these two All-Pros, weighing over five hundred pounds between them, arguing like sandlot kids as they sprinted for the Cardinals goal line.

Roy's assistant director beckons, and they are about to go on the show. The slow, bittersweet smile lights Deacon's face, and he just has time to get in the last word. "Merlin, you was chuggin' along so slow you were passed by the entire Cardinals team, an' one old lady usin' a cane . . ."

Merlin wants to say something back, but the red light winks on and the video director points a silent finger. They're on the air.

The Mad Drafter Finally Picks a Winner

There may be places where losing is tolerated, where the local folk are just glad to have a team and will cheer them on even in their lowest times, but Los Angeles has never been one of them. The sun worshippers of southern California view sports as entertainment; losing isn't worth watching when there are so many other things to do. Attention easily strays to the beaches, the mountains, year-round golf and tennis, Disneyland, Knott's Berry Farm, Magic Mountain, the studio tours.

In the ten years following their move from Cleveland, Dan Reeve's Rams had been consistent winners, taking the divisional title four times and the playoff championships once. Back then, the fans enjoyed the play of great stars, the "Bull Elephant" backfield, quarterbacks Norm "The Dutchman" Van Brocklin and "Buckets" Bob Waterfield, and receivers Tom Fears and Elroy "Crazy Legs" Hirsh. But competition in the league stiffened, and the ten biblical fat years were followed by ten lean; from 1955 to 1965 the Rams lost eighty-two, won forty-three, and tied four. The team finished in sixth place four times and in seventh twice. Needless to say, the mood of the fans ranged from dispirited to disgusted. The sports writers wound up their wits and brought out the sharp tools of their trade, and attendance sagged to new lows.

In a way Deacon was lucky. After five years of playing on a losing ball team, he was a bright spot, a rallying point. The fans cheered him, loving his brash outbursts and proclamations, and the fact that he lived up to his outrageous promises with his deeds on the playing field. In 1965, he'd had such a terrific year that the Ye Olde Rams Club finally voted him the Rams Most Valuable Player. That year the Rams sent four players to the Western Division of the Pro Bowl— Deacon, Merlin, Tommy McDonald, and Eddie Meador. Los Angeles loved their defense, particularly the Fearsome Foursome, but that affection was no substitute for winning ball games.

As the season wound down, the newspapers noted that the mad drafter, Dan Reeves, was once again trying to cure his team's ills through the draft. He picked Mike Garrett, the seventh Heisman Trophy winner he'd selected over the years since he brought the club to Los Angeles in 1946. Los Angeles was already plump with running backs, and Garrett, the Rams number two pick in that draft, would choose to play in the American Football Conference for Kansas City and a lot more money. The Rams number one pick of that year went unheralded at that time, but tackle Tom Mack of Michigan would be a force on the Rams offensive line for over a decade to come.

Reeves now had full control of the Rams, but his team still wasn't winning. There was only one man left to blame. Still, Reeves must have been uncertain about what to do, because through the first weeks of December he remained uncharacteristically silent. On December 19, Morton Moss wrote in the *Los Angeles Herald-Examiner* that Reeves would only say there would be "no immediate announcement" on the destiny of the coaching staff headed by Harland Svare.

Finally, on December 22, Reeves read a prepared statement to the press, announcing, "It has been decided not to renew" Svare's contract for 1966. Reeves added that, although there was no replacement, "we have several persons in mind." The general feeling seemed to be that Reeves had little choice, considering Svare's glaring lack of experience, and his inability to bring the Rams out of their ten-year slump. The reporters tried to be polite about it, giving the Rams owner the same good press he'd always enjoyed. The following day, December 23, Bob Oates wrote in the *Herald Examiner*, "Never has there been less friction at the departure time for a Ram coach. The only thing that dictated the action was his record—and even there, the organization holds him only partly responsible."

During the last five games of 1964 and the first ten of 1965, the Rams won only once. In the last two seasons Svare's record against Western Division teams was 5-24. But, outrageous as it sounds, Svare was already rumored to be in the running for several other head coaching jobs around the league. He spoke to the reporters as if he hadn't personally had much to do with the losing. "I'm very disappointed that we couldn't win more football games. I have no regrets about the experience. I thoroughly enjoyed it . . . I have no plans. This was a bit sudden."

Herald Examiner columnist Mel Durslag saw the Rams continuing predicament as typically pathetic, and for that reason amusing.

> When the L.A. Rams dispatched Sid Gillman as coach at the end of the 1959 season, Daniel Reeves, president, was asked about a successor. "We're going to take a shower," said Dan. The shower led to a bath, which the Rams have been taking ever since. Encamped in a sweet location in which 7.5 million are goofy for pro football, the team hasn't been able to raise a gallop.

Sports writer Morton Moss, also of the *Herald Examiner*, was less complimentary, if just as amused.

> Svare charmed everybody off his feet except the employees of rival teams. You couldn't help liking him and they couldn't help licking him. Dan Reeves could only blame a poor record on the weather, nuclear fallout, smog, housemaid's knee and barber's itch so long.

Then, after three and a half years, it had to be so long. Roman Gabriel, entombed on the bench through eight straight losses, was resurrected by Svare when Bill Munson was cast from the premises with a scrambled knee. Three ensuing victories merely suggested the horrifying thought that the Rams had started the wrong quarterback for ten games.

Old-time Rams cognoscenti recognized that, while Svare had not been the positive factor he set out to be, the problem went a lot deeper than the coach. After all, management's record for retaining coaches was as grim as the won-lost record; since moving to Los Angeles twenty years before, the team had had eight coaching regimes. In other words, Dan Reeves had already fingered eight coaches as the reason his team wasn't winning. Dan's plan was to muffle this sort of criticism by hiring a local hero, John McKay, who was the successful football coach of the University of Southern California. But this scheme soon went awry; after a few days of mulling over the uncertainties of life as head coach of the Rams, McKay turned down the job, which reportedly would have paid him over six times what he was making as a college coach. Reeves hadn't figured he'd be that smart.

These were very busy times for Dan Reeves, high-pressure times filled with the need to make expensive and far-reaching decisions. It was the first age of big money in football; Commissioner Pete Rozelle had just negotiated the biggest broadcast contract ever with CBS, a two-year deal worth over $37 million. The NFL and the AFL had not yet merged, and were going on "berserk shopping sprees," shelling out $700,000 for Texas linebacker Tommy Nobis and $625,000 for Jim Grabowski, a fullback from Illinois. About the same time that McKay turned down the Rams head coaching post, Reeves refused to pay a big price for his top draft choice, Mike Garrett, and so lost him to Kansas City.

At the same time that players—even young draft choices—were proving to be expensive, Reeves was caught in his coaching dilemma, which was really a problem of his own making. He'd hired Svare because he felt he could get along with him and the young coach would take orders. But Svare, in turn, had hired assistants who were also young and inexperienced. Now with Svare gone no one on the staff stood out as an acceptable choice. While they may not all have been laughable, they would seem so to the fans and reporters.

None of the small circle of friends who over the years had been Reeves' drinking buddies wanted the job or was right for it. He'd already used up prime choice Bob Waterfield, and some of the others were leery of the responsibility. Reeves probably should have admitted to his own desire to be hands-on and in charge of all facets of his club, and should have hired an old reliable retread recommended (and fired by) one of the other owners, somebody willing to roll over and take his orders without question. But after McKay turned down the job, Reeves went in another direction; he began what the reporters soon dubbed the "Great Manhunt." Confounding experts and close friends alike, Reeves began interviewing men of experience who were truly capable of doing a good job for his team.

By January 6 of the new year, Reeves had narrowed the field to (as the reporters called them) a handful of "brave men." In alphabetical order, they were George Allen, defensive coach of the Chicago Bears; Paul Brown, legendary coach of the Cleveland Browns; Sid Gillman of San Diego (head coach of the Rams before Waterfield); Buddy Parker, formerly of Detroit and Pittsburgh; and George Wilson, until that year head coach of Detroit.

At this time, to make Reeves's decision a little more difficult, Rozelle came out with another of his arbitrary dictates, passing the word that he would not "authorize" the defection of any head coach from one NFL team to another without the consent of both clubs involved. This meant living legend and proven winner Vince Lombardi was off the list. But Reeves had been known to fly in the face of authority before, and Rozelle hadn't said anything about assistant coaches.

A few days later, the papers reported that Buddy Parker was offered and turned down the job, as had Bobby Layne. Cornered by over a decade of losses, by this series of turn-downs from qualified men, by Rozelle's proclamation that he couldn't hire somebody else's head coach, and by the amused scorn of the awakened public and the press, Dan Reeves made a decision he would regret for the rest of his days. He offered the job to absolutely the right man—a strong-willed and experienced assistant coach who knew how to win and was totally dedicated to getting his team to the top of the heap—George Allen from Chicago. Good for Los Angeles and the fans. Bad for Reeves, who was more interested in being in control than he was in winning.

Deacon remembers what it was like to play for the Rams before George Allen showed up. "It took all your pride just to show up on Sunday, suck it up, and keep going. When you win, you can laugh off the hurts. When you lose, the inside hurt is as bad as the outside hurt. And I don't care how good you are, there is no way you are going to feel good when your team is losing. And losing. And losing. Wherever you go, people ask you, 'What's wrong with the team?' And what can you tell them, "We're bad ballplayers?" Hell, you know you're not a bad ballplayer. And you know some of the others aren't. But, still, you're losing. And so, wherever you go, you get no respect."

7

The Deacon Comes of Age

George Allen's background was simple enough. He'd won nine athletic letters in high school. He was an average receiver at Michigan. At the time he was attending college, he was earning only $34 a month, courtesy of the G.I. Bill; yet he offered to pay Fritz Crysler, the Michigan head coach, the entire $34 as a contribution to the department if he could get on the staff. The department didn't take his money, but the offer got their attention, and they made him a counter-offer—he could be the freshman football coach if he'd coach wrestling as well.

Allen soon moved on to the head coach position at tiny Morningside College in Iowa, and then to Whittier College in California. The Rams, at that time, held spring training at nearby Chapman College in Orange County. Allen made the connection, and after one season as an assistant coach for the L.A. team, he became the defensive coach for George Halas's Chicago Bears. With the Bears, he installed a tough zone pass defense that allowed a stingy average of only ten points per game. While he can't be credited with inventing the zone, Allen brought it into the modern football era. With their "advanced" zone, the Bears soon were as notorious as they had been in previous decades, when defense was their main claim to fame. George Allen became known in the inner circles of football as the innovator behind those gruff and growling keepers of the goal line.

Allen was full of innovations, many of which were beyond notoriously cheap "Pappa Bear" Halas's inclination. Finally, after seven years with the Bears, the blossoming young assistant coach was becoming impatient. He wrote out a long, enthusiastic "White Paper," a blueprint for team and management improvement. This paper, studded with common sense, bright ideas, and proposals that were going to cost somebody a lot of money, probably came as an unpleasant surprise to Halas, who hadn't requested it, and who was known as one of the stingiest owners in football. Whatever his reasons, the Bears owner gave the Allen White Paper very little attention, putting off talking about it and eventually failing to get back to his eager young assistant.

That was when George Allen started to worry in earnest about his future with the Bears. He was the obvious heir to the coaching job, but with Halas retreating from earlier hints that he might retire as head coach, disillusion was setting in; and so, after serving three years of a five-year contract, Allen was ready to listen when Dan Reeves called to feel him out about the job in Los Angeles. Allen spoke to Halas, who had heard about the "Great Manhunt," and who was apparently willing to gamble that with the big names who had thrown their hat in the ring, his assistant coach wouldn't have much chance for the job. Allen later declared, "Mr. Halas gave me permission to talk with the Rams about the job." Both he and Reeves took the position that Halas had given him the right to walk away from his old contract with the Bears and to negotiate freely with the Rams.

Halas lost his gamble. But he wasn't going to let his apprentice go without a fight. Interviewed in 1993, the Bears' great running back, Gale Sayers, remembers what happened next: "George Allen was a fine coach and a great motivator. His problem was, he had a contract with Halas with two years left to go on it, and 'The Old Man' wanted to hold him to it. In those days, if you were a player or a coach, you didn't break a contract—particularly not with 'The Grand Old Man of Football.' It just wasn't done, because the league could freeze you out and there was nowhere else to go. It became pretty messy when Halas wouldn't let him go. Halas got angry and accused Dan Reeves of raiding tactics."

Halas lashed out heatedly, taking his case to the fans via the press: "I am shocked that the Los Angeles Rams and their president, Dan Reeves, would attempt to pirate our coaching staff. The Rams were told Allen's legal and binding contract with the Bears had two years to go and we expected him to fulfill the terms of the agreement. In seven and a half years with the Bears, George Allen has been an integral part of our coaching staff. The Rams utter dis-

regard and contempt for legal obligations present a serious challenge not only to the Bears but to the entire structure of the NFL."

Halas was clearly appealing to the league to take action in his favor. But two things worked against him. First, over the years, his haughty, abrasive attitude and legendary "dirty tricks", that is, shady and clever maneuvers in the grey area of league rule legality which had won him many a ball game, had also won him many enemies among the league's owners. And second, Reeves, realizing the way the NFL worked and not wanting to leave his chances with the commissioner, had already bypassed Pete Rozelle. Hell, Rozelle had worked as general manager for the Rams! So, instead of asking for permission, which would have opened the door for Rozelle to dictate in favor of the status quo, Reeves made his choice without him. After all, Rozelle had only declared head coaches couldn't be hired without the consent of the old team. George Allen was only an assistant coach.

Herald-Examiner *writer Bob Oates felt Reeves had made the right moves for success: "If Reeves had quietly gone to Rozelle, he'd have lost. He won by seizing the initiative—audaciously hiring Allen in public." Sports writer Bud Furillo pointed out the obvious— that principle is a matter of expediency in the NFL: "Pete Rozelle had a contract as general manager of the Rams when Halas and others started the move to make him the NFL commissioner. Reeves didn't stand up and scream that Halas and the others were 'tampering' with his general manager."*

So Allen broke his contract with the Bears and boldly agreed to terms of a new five-year contract with Reeves. But that wasn't the end of the story; the stubborn, aging Halas, already a legend for practically single-handedly creating the NFL, promptly hauled them both into court. Reeves was indignant and righteous in his own cause, as quoted by Bob Oates, "We acted properly in this matter all the way and followed all the rules. It is hard to believe Halas would stand in the way of an assistant coach moving up to head coach. How can we have a league if head coaches prohibit the advancement of their best men?"[1]

Halas was awarded the sum of $1 as a symbolic gesture, indicating that the suit was seen as more of a grudge match than a case with any real merit. Allen was granted his freedom, but Halas would petulantly hold the grudge and brand his assistant as an overly ambitious ingrate.

From that time on, George Allen was a rebel, an outsider, and

---

1. Bob Oates, *Herald-Examiner,* January 10, 1966.

an outcast from the NFL's Good Old Boy's Club. Even though Halas was unpopular with his fellow owners, distrusted and hated for his own record of so-called dirty tricks and bitterly envied for his winning record, he was a charter member of the club. But now, Old George Halas had inadvertently unleashed a brilliant disciple on the league, a Young George who not only had memorized the Old Man's tricks, but who had his own innovative ideas about how the game was to be played.

Dan Reeves, the maverick who had escaped from Cleveland and moved west, and then built his early success by breaking the league taboos against blacks, had scored another coup. This made many of the owners uneasy. The competition was already fierce; wins were hard enough to come by in the NFL.

The Word Is Father to the Deed

Deacon wheeled his black Thunderbird into the Rams new spring training camp in Fullerton. He unhinged himself from the car and stretched in the early morning light, towering nearly seven feet in his bushy afro and expensive, high-heeled boots. It was April, which in southern California meant *hot* and *muggy,* just the way he liked it. His secret morning sessions at the beach had continued, and he'd been working on some fakes and some new variations of the headslap, so he felt he had a few new things to show the league. He strutted into the locker room, feeling every inch the big, bold, and bad five-year veteran of the football wars. He lowered his shades, and the first thing to meet his wondering eyes was a huge poster on the wall headlined "PROFILE OF A CHAMPION." Under the headline were listed attributes—qualities like "Ambition," "Coachableness," "Aggression," and "Leadership."

Deacon stood before the poster, turning the words over in his mind. Half of him, the cool half that snapped off fancy lines for the press, wanted to say What is this shit, man?, and walk on. But there was something appealing about the notion that a champion could be defined. It was enough to start a man thinking. After all, it was what he always wanted, to be the winner, the top dog, the champion. Other notions stirred at the back of his mind. Somebody—whoever had put up this poster—was talking champion here. Champion meant championship, meant the golden crown was somehow attainable, meant that the persons reading it might somehow possess the capabilities to make themselves champions. He stood silently before the poster, taking it in and glad that none of the other guys were around. He could hear the kidding now. Ol' Deak's learning how to read. What's the matter, Deak, the words too big for you?

Below the good attributes, on the bottom half of the poster, was the "PROFILE OF AN ALSO-RAN", a listing of bad personal habits like "No Drive," "Know-It-All," "Mouse," "Follower," "Watcher," and "Corner-cutter." Again, the first thing to flash through Deacon's brain was, Is this guy serious? Deacon was twenty-eight years old, in the young prime of his career. Was this any way to talk to grown ups?

Just then somebody did come by. It was Lamar, who as team captain, had come to camp early for meetings with the new coach. Lamar clapped him on the back, "Deacon! Good to see you, man!"

Deacon nodded and pounded him in turn, the way old comrades do. When things settled down, Lamar nodded to the poster, "Sure gets your attention, don't it?"

Deacon shrugged, "Yeah, I guess."

"It's powerful stuff, Deacon! The rewards of hard work shall be ours! It could come right out of the Bible."

The slow, bittersweet smile rippled across Deacon's face, "Lamar, I been through five miserable losing years with some of the worst leadership ever to disgrace the league. I'm not quite sure I'm ready to be won over with a slogan."

"Ain't sayin' won over, but the man does know how to get your attention!"

"George Allen put this up?"

Lamar nodded, his eyes sparkling with humor. "Look behind you."

Deacon turned and saw a huge, hand-lettered poster on the wall: "Is what I am doing—or about to do—going to get us closer to our goal, winning?"

"Lamar, what is all this?"

"You ain't seen nothin' yet, Deacon."

Lamar led him to a big room filled with heavy, menacing-looking machines and bulky free weights. "We got our own weight room now!"

Deacon whistled softly between his teeth. Some of the guys had bought their own weights using their own money, and they were generally passed around the locker room, but no other team in the league had their own dedicated weight room!

Deacon followed Lamar to the locker room, and the neat, home-made signs were everywhere. "Ask yourself:" the one over Deacon's personal locker read, "What do you really want to accomplish?" Deacon sat on the bench and slowly read the room. The next sign to reach his eyes stunned him—"What you do during the rest of the year determines how you will play during the regular season." George Allen knew Deacon's deepest secret, that he trained just as hard off-season as he did during the regular season! You had to respect a man who'd thought that one through.

Another sign read, "Try not to do too many things at once; know what you want, the #1 thing today and tomorrow. Persevere and get it done. Too often we make things more complicated than they really are." The man made sense, and the simple posters had an appeal that was hard to explain. Deacon recognized that in all his experience in sports, at Hungerford High, in college, and later as a professional, none of his coaches had ever reached out in this way to the players. It was a lot to think about, more than he could digest in a brief look-see. But Deacon saw immediately that there was a logic here that said you were an equal, a man and a winner, all this combined with a morality that was nearly biblical.

Lamar sat nearby, not saying anything while Deacon took it in.

"Just words, Lamar," Deacon finally said. But Lamar knew him well enough to catch the uncertainty in his voice.

"The word be the father to the deed, my friend. You know the good book say so."

Deacon grinned, the devil-may-care attitude coming back to him. He liked to bait Lamar on the Bible, "I am the word, Lamar. That's what I tell all the reporters."

Lamar wouldn't make a joke of it. "No, Deacon," he said seriously, "You are the deed come real."

"Come on, let's go get a beer before I get all choked up." Deacon took a last look around the room. The sign over the door leading to the practice field had a particular urgency: "If not us, who? If not now, when?"

"Tacked most of them up hisself," Lamar said, answering his unspoken question.

"Boy . . . things sure gonna be different around here." "Yes, they are," Lamar nodded, "Yes, they are!"

Deacon remembers his first impressions of George Allen: "George was a twelve-month football man; he didn't believe in anything called an 'off-season.' During January and February of 1966 he called together the Rams 'solid citizens,' the men he saw as team leaders. Our team captain Lamar Lundy represented the line. Defensive back Eddie Meador. Our All-Pro linebacker Jack Pardee. He had them meet in small groups to discuss their problems and what they could do about them.

"George was a man who believed in meetings. Some of them were long, some of them were short, and some of them were meetings to talk about having meetings. He was concerned down to the smallest details. 'Little things,' he stressed over and over again, 'are what win or lose ball games.'

"And while he talked a lot, he listened even more. George was a fanatic for asking questions. It was interesting, even amazing, because as the training camp commenced, we players could see many of our suggestions actually being implemented! With Harland, we'd had no team concept, no feeling that we were contributing, that we were respected. This was something totally new for us players, to be treated as adults, equals, and to have our ideas seriously considered. George let us understand that we were contributing, we were respected, we were a vital part of the unit. We felt almost joyful, like we were coming up for air after having our heads held under water for years."

A Student of the Game

After all those years of losses, the fans and sports writers living in southern California were disenchanted with their home team. They spoofed and joked about the Rams, and laughed at the jibes the writers took in the sports pages. So it goes without saying that the attitude of the masses toward the new coach was somewhat less than enthusiastic. The southern Californians had adopted a wait-and-see attitude, and for good reason.

None of this seemed to faze Allen. He took the job in the center of a swirling controversy. No matter what Rozelle or the rest of the league thought, the deed was done. Unconcerned that he was no longer a member of the club, or that a skeptical city awaited him, Allen got on a plane and headed west to find a new home for his family and take up the reins of the L.A. team.

On Allen's arrival, one wag remarked to Reeves, "I see that we've traded in a bright young defensive coach for a bright young defensive coach."

"The main difference between them," said Reeves, "is that George has had eighteen years of coaching experience, nine as a head coach, eight on defense and ten on offense." To this day, this moment is seen by many as the high point of the relationship between the owner and his new coach. Reeves and Allen had entirely different views of the coach's role on the team, of how and why the game was played, and, indeed, different values as human beings. Their relationship would be sparked with disagreement and bitter animosity. But all that was yet to come. Meeting the L.A. press for the first time, Allen quietly listed his goal as "the championship." He seemed to get on well with the reporters, who recorded that he was a soft-spoken, courteous football student who held a master's degree and had written four books on the subject.

The new coach had his first major argument with Reeves over the old Rams training facilities. There were many ways to shake a team out of a losing lethargy, and Allen appears to have thought of most of them. He insisted the old training camp was second-rate, and belonged to "losers." The move, of course, would cost money. Reeves gave in, but not until after an acrimonious debate.

Allen immediately switched the spring training from Chapman College to brand-new dorms and facilities at Cal State Fullerton, and made arrangements for new training quarters at Blair Field in Long Beach for the Rams winter quarters. The facilities were state of the art for the time. It was a good psychological move—the team was going to have a completely new start.

At one of their first meetings, Allen assembled the entire team and spoke about his expectations: "I'm afraid some of you are going to be disappointed," he said. "I'm just as much a fitness freak as your last coach." A chorus of groans and boos went up from the players. With the old coach, such a display would have provoked outrage; Allen just smiled and continued. "But there is a major difference. I expect you to be in top physical shape—we can't be winners unless you are—but you can get there through running and using the weights. Don't get me wrong—we will have drills and drills and drills. But those drills are to perfect your moves and your timing, to put an edge on every aspect of your game. You will be challenged to be your best. The only way you get fine gold is by hammering it. You have to work hard. You have to believe in yourselves. You are here for only one purpose, *to mold yourselves into champions!*"

Hands went up around the room and someone asked the big question—would there be contact drills? Allen smiled and looked at the playbook in front of him on the desk. "They tell me," he said, "that this playbook is twice as thick as anybody's in the league, except Tom Landry's. Now I don't believe in ordinary contact drills. Sure, we'll do a few, but I want to keep them to a bare minimum. The purpose of a full-contact scrimmage is not to fight for your position; the true purpose must be to perfect your skills. What I thought we might do instead of banging away at each other for the next few months"—here his eyes sparkled from under his bushy eyebrows—"is find out whether Tom's playbook is any better than mine. So what I've done is challenge the Cowboys to a couple of practice sessions over the course of our spring training, and a few with our good neighbors to the south, the Chargers. What do you think?" There was a moment's hesitation, and then the room was filled with thunderous applause. Allen knew his players; in one fell swoop, he'd made contact drills competitive and fun again. It was one thing to grind down your own teammates, and quite another to challenge a rival team. Beating the Cowboys on an isolated practice field somewhere in Thousand Oaks, California, meant bragging rights and pride and a sense of contest.

When things died down a bit, Allen held up a hand for attention. "Most of you in this room are veterans. You are professional ballplayers. You know who you are. With rare exception, those of you who have earned a starting position in years gone by,"— here his intense look swept the room and everyone caught a piece of that stare—"have that position which you worked so hard to gain. The rest of you"— here his gaze again covered the room—"are all part of the same team. We are not a team without you. We cannot win without you. And that is what this is all about. Victory. Winning. Championship. Being the champions!" Again cheering broke out. The meeting was turning into a pep rally.

Allen held up his hand for quiet. "We're a team," he said. "The teams that are *really teams* are doing the winning in this league. That means I'm asking you for *unity,* for *team play,* for *individual sacrifice* for the good of the team! I'm going to say it so often that you're going to that think it and I am both absolutely obnoxious—but you've *got* to believe it!"

"Another thing—attention to detail. The little things win or lose ball games, as well as the big. How many times do special teams—both offense and defense—win or lose ball games for you? That's why I want you to consider it an honor if you get on one of those teams. Our punt team, our suicide squad, our point- after specialists . . . you guys are going to be on the field *actually about one quarter of the plays!* That's why I'm hiring a special teams coach whose sole responsibility is in this area. Sure, nobody does it. Sure, today it may seem revolutionary. But, I guarantee you, once they see the results we're going to get, everybody's going to do it!'"

In the weeks to come, the four-hour-long two-a-days were punctuated with long meetings. The talks went on and on, half football and half Bible-Belt tent revival. Oddly enough, nobody in the room seemed to tire of it, and as the days passed they actually did begin to believe in themselves and the team. A strange sense of expectancy hung over the camp. It gathered seemingly out of nowhere. It was on the field and in the meetings, in the mess hall and in the rooms with them at night, a sense of excitement and coming thunder.

Deacon remembers George Allen: "He went to the beat of his own drum, he was a different kind of leader. In some ways he was far ahead of his time. Many of his ideas, taken for granted today, were innovations in the mid-sixties. The advanced zone defense, which truly defined the defensive player's areas of individual responsibility, Allen first formulated with the Bears. This refinement changed pass defense throughout the league. He was the first to hire a special teams coach. He was also the first to construct two practice fields, one regular grass and one astroturf, so the team could prepare for their next game. He was the first to build a dedicated training facility, a private practice complex of fields, weights, training, locker and meeting rooms designed for and devoted to winning."

When recently interviewed the great Ram running back Dick Bass revealed that he had also become an Allen fan: "George was a coach, where Waterfield and Svare were just organizers. Harland was a linebacker who thought he knew the game. George knew the game when he came in. He took what Harland had spliced together, kept the strengths and threw out the weaknesses, added some players, molded their spirits and their teamwork, and turned the Rams into a winner."

Roman Gabriel talks about the difference between Svare and Allen practice sessions: "Harland's camp had a lot of banging and hitting. He did physically work you hard. But Allen's camp was like basic training in the army. Allen challenged you both physically and mentally. He hammered away at his winning ethic. We players were winners. But our responsibility was to work hard. Believe, just believe in yourself! Concentrate on the one, single purpose—winning the championship! We had eighteen or nineteen days in a *row of two-a-day's, and each session was nearly four hours in length. And the rest of the time was filled with meetings. We players were getting $50 a week for spring training, and we were working from ten in the morning to eleven at night, and at eleven-fifteen, the lights went out."*

Gabriel continues, "George's way to condition you was quite a shock to the system. He absolutely took nothing for granted. Every detail was gone over, and drilled time and again. We'd do drills—pass protection. I'd practice three-step drop-back, five-step drop-back, seven-step drop-back, screens . . . every day we were on the field forty-five minutes before actual practice, and we'd spend that time doing drills before practice actually started."

Allen's drills were specifically designed to sharpen each player's skills. Punter Jon Kilgore felt that Allen's methods turned his kicking around. "I give the credit to Coach Allen," he told reporters after several successful games. "Kicking two days a week under pressure has helped me keep my timing down."

Lamar Lundy remembers that first training camp: "George Allen came in and he fought for us, and we all knew it. We'd played for Reeves, and we knew how he operated. It didn't take us long to recognize that George was looking out for us. The food got better, and the equipment was all top of the line."

Rival coach Tom Landry, whose Cowboys ran their training camp fifty miles or so up the 101 freeway from Fullerton in Thousand Oaks, recently said of Allen, "George was a master psychologist, a tremendous motivator of his players, a man who always managed somehow to get the most out of his squad."

Trader George

George Allen's first player personnel move was to extinguish the quarterback controversies that had been smoldering throughout the Waterfield and Svare regimes. By the time the Rams new coach got off the plane in Los Angeles, Roman Gabriel had for all intents and purposes left the team with no intention of ever coming back. Reeves still had Munson, and he had drafted another young quarterback, so the Rams owner seemed content to sit back and let Gabriel go to the American Football League. Allen would have none of it. He flew back to the southeast to personally convince Gabriel that the Rams were his future, and that he was the number one quarterback. He must have

been extraordinarily persuasive, because Gabriel returned to the fold
for a lot less than he was being offered by the AFL.

Allen was only a few months on the job, and already there was
trouble in paradise. It was rumored that he had made promises to
Gabriel without first gaining owner Dan Reeves's permission. If true,
this was only the tip of the iceberg. Reeves had always liked to exercise tight control; his money, his team, meant everything to him. Now
he was beginning to see he'd hired a monster, a man who would make
expensive decisions in the interest of winning ball games without giving it a second thought—and worse, without even giving him a call to
talk it over.

Had Reeves taken the time to consider the facts before hiring
Allen, he would have found some key elements of his new coach's philosophy of building a winner were diametrically opposed to his own.
Reeves strongly believed in strengthening his team through the college
draft. In fact, he was one of the original owners who'd developed the
college draft as a way to keep the steady stream of inexpensive, talented
young players flowing into the league. He was constantly building for
the future. He used the trading system to dump off players in whom
he'd lost confidence, loading up a strong hand of first- and second-
round draft picks for the coming season. There were advantages to this
method, not the least of which was that, when practiced leaguewide, it
kept the players under the owners' heel, holding down the player salary
costs. No veteran player was going to get too uppity when he knew
there was a young kid breathing down his neck for his job.

Before the coming of Allen, Reeves had supervised the scouting
and acted as his own general manager, often reducing Elroy Hirsh to
little more than his assistant. Perhaps Reeves didn't realize how strong
Allen would be. From the moment he took over, Allen began to do
things his own way.

Allen's strategy was nearly the opposite of Reeves's: he valued
experience and veterans, and he believed in trading draft picks for men
who'd already been seasoned in the pros. His basic philosophy was to
swap youthful down-the-road potential for here-and-now experience.
To put it bluntly, in his years with the Rams Allen traded away future
draft choices and younger players for veterans. He carried a wealth of
statistics, practical knowledge, and just plain scuttlebutt about almost
every player in the league around in his head, and so he was ready to
move almost instantly when he smelled a trade favorable to the Rams.
He was an old-fashioned trader in the sense that he carried much infor-

mation at his fingertips, making verbal deals with the paperwork to follow, and in his career he was embarrassed a time or two for trading a player or a draft spot more than once.

When Munson expressed his unhappiness, Allen traded him without a moment's hesitation. A year later, when Grier was hurt, he went out and got Roger Brown. Trading draft picks for experience may seem like a common practice today, but very few in the NFL did it at that time, and nobody did it with the audacity, the quick decision-making, or the success of George Allen.

Another of Allen's early moves that alienated his boss was the renegotiation of linebacker Jack Pardee's contract without consulting Reeves. Jack was a big star, but the Rams owner felt he was asking too much money, and was willing to let him retire rather than pay anything near what he was worth. Allen studied the 1965 films. He saw the Rams pass coverage was breaking down and the team was getting killed in the backfield. The Fearsome Foursome couldn't do it all; coverage and the rush had to go hand-in-hand. Defensive back Clancy Williams was only a second-year man, and so if there was one man in the defensive backfield the Rams couldn't afford to lose, it was Pardee. Allen acted quickly and decisively on his belief, convincing Pardee that it was way too soon to retire. Pardee stayed for a lot more money, and Reeves was furious. The ripples went through the entire training camp; and every player had some idea of what had happened. *Allen had gone to the mat with Reeves over a player's salary and come up a winner!* Reeves may have been steaming, but the Rams new horse trader was just getting warmed up. He had inherited some good players: the Fearsome Foursome; linebacker Jack Pardee; defensive backs Ed Meador and Clancy Williams; offensive linemen Charlie Cowan, Joe Carollo, and Joe Scibelli; receiver Jack Snow; quarterback Roman Gabriel; and running backs Dick Bass and Les Josephson. But that wasn't going to be enough to win the championship. Allen needed more.

The quarterback controversy was settled, and Pardee had donned his cleats, but Allen felt there was much yet to be done. He'd seen the films over and over. There was no kidding himself or anyone else: the offense sputtered, and there were all those holes in the defensive backfield, plain as the nose on your face. Trader George immediately bolstered the offense by trading away a second-round draft pick, a lineman named Arndt, and a taxi squad quarterback to Vince Lombardi for halfback Tom Moore, who in 1966 would break the Rams record for most receptions (sixty) by a halfback.

Then, with a series of deft trades, Allen acquired Bill George, Maxie Baughan, Myron Pottios, and defensive back Irv Cross, all defensive veterans to complement his fierce front four. It was enough to make Reeves's head spin. When the Bears cut Bill George, who'd played linebacker, offensive guard, and defensive tackle for the Chicago team for fourteen years, Allen signed him as a free agent. He got six-year veteran linebacker Maxie Baughan from the Eagles and five-year veteran linebacker Myron Pottios from the Steelers. Realizing the secondary still had some weak spots, Allen brought in another experienced defensive back, five-year veteran defensive back Irv Cross from Philadelphia.

All this player-swapping—much of it for Reeves's horde of coveted draft picks, had the Rams owner beside himself, but there wasn't really anything he could do. His team was coming off of ten losing seasons during which they'd failed miserably by doing things his way, and Allen was in the first months of his multi-year contract. The bit was clearly in Trader George's teeth. Win or lose, it was going to be one hell of a season.

Roman Gabriel talks about the time George Allen convinced him to stay with the team: "In 1965, after Bill Munson finally was forced to the sidelines with his frost-bitten toes, I took over and we turned things around and won three out of four games. I thought I'd finally earned the starting position, and then Reeves drafted yet another quarterback—Billy Guy Anderson out of Tulsa! I asked Svare what was up, and he was unwilling to commit to me. That's when I told Dan Reeves I wanted to be traded to Atlanta. He wouldn't commit to naming me as the starter, and so I left for my home on the East Coast pretty sure that I wouldn't be coming back. I was driving cross-country when I found out George Allen had been hired. At this time, I'd already left the Rams in my mind. In fact, I'd signed a contract with the AFL—I was going to play with the Oakland Raiders. They offered me $400,000 over four years, big money for those days. They gave me a $100,000 check, and I was carrying it around, uncashed, in my pocket. Well, George Allen came to my home, the first time any coach had seen fit to do that. He told me we were going to build a winner, and I was his man, I was going to be his quarterback. He fought with Reeves to get my contract up to $40,000 a year. It was nowhere near what the Raiders were offering, but George got to me in another way. He said, 'You don't want the fans in southern California to think you can't play. Show them your stuff first—and then you can go if you want to.' That really got to me. I knew then that it wasn't the money. I had to prove myself, and George was giving me the opportunity to play. That's why I say he's a completely different coach than anyone I had ever met, or ever met after."

Deacon comments on the trade versus draft situation as it exists today: "Since George's teams were always contenders and were almost always in post-season play, and yet he never won the Super Bowl, people who don't like him—and there are plenty out there—will say 'George's approach can get you to the play-offs, but it can't get you a Super Bowl ring.' That's about as foolish as a man can talk, considering you've got to get to the playoffs to still be in the hunt!

"Trader George made as many enemies for his sharp dealings as for any other reason . . . he always seemed to get the better of the bargain, and rival owners and coaches were at a loss to explain to each other and to the hometown fans why they had let this or that player go, and now he was doing so beautifully for the Rams. After all those years of the various owners and coaches around the league taking advantage of poor Dan Reeves, the shoe was suddenly on the other foot, and they didn't like the pinch at all!"

Spring Scrimmage

The Rams piled into yellow buses and drove up to Cal Lutheran College in Thousand Oaks, where, after warming up and tossing around the usual jokes with the Cowboys, the scrimmage set out in earnest. There was Landry the perfectionist on one side of the field, wearing slacks and that snappy pork-pie hat on his head and with that big, fat playbook always at his side. And on the other side of the field there was Allen the perfectionist, in slacks and a polo shirt and an L.A. Rams hat, with his own big, fat playbook for instant reference.

It wasn't a real game, or anything resembling it. The coaches agreed they would alternate series, each side doing twenty offensive plays, nobody really keeping an official score, but everybody playing a sort of friendly grudge match while the bugs got ironed out of their moves.

Allen flipped a quarter and won the toss, so he ran twenty option plays, Gabriel fanning out to the right or left and passing or handing off to one of the backs. When Landry's turn came he worked on his shotgun and his short passes, Dandy Don Meredith alternating long strikes to Bullet Bob Hayes down the sidelines and short tosses over the middle to his halfback. The morning went by quickly, and they broke for lunch, the Rams players eager to see what kind of chow their friends from Texas enjoyed.

The second session began in the early afternoon. Landry started worrying over some running plays. Deacon and Merlin, standing at the line with their customary scowls on their faces, could see him in a huddle of assistants at the sidelines, fussing over some pages in his playbook, "He looks like a real nit-picky guy," Merlin said.

Deacon shook his head, kicking the grass with his cleats, "You don't want to play in Texas anyway, Farm Boy. Not if you a black dude."

"Why's that?"

"They segregated bad as Mississippi. Ask any black player."

"Naaaa." Merlin thought he was kidding.

Deacon shrugged, "Not the *Cowboys,* fool—the whole damn *state!* Ask Lundy."

Rosey moved closer, "Hey, Deak—Tommy-boy's lookin' your direction. Get ready."

"I was *born* ready, Fat Man."

"This the quickest fat you ever gonna see, Swamp Boy." Rosey smiled like a three-hundred-pound black cat about to eat a canary. Rosey had one of those personalities that was impossible to put down. He lived on his own plane, walked to his own drum, heard his own whispers in the breeze. Make love, be happy. This was, of course, in the time of the Sexy Sixties, before Rosey developed a serious preoccupation with religion and became a minister.

Landry finished his serious conversations and arm-wavings with Meredith and the Cowboys came to the line. As Rosey predicted, Dandy Don handed off to Dan Reeves, who came around Deacon's side. But Deacon had already slipped past Dallas right tackle Ralph Neely, and grabbed Reeves around the waist to neatly stop the play in the backfield before it could get to the line, much less gather any momentum.

Landry frowned and shook his head, calling Meredith back over for another chat. There was more talk from Landry, who was pointing across the field as if he could demonstrate positions, moves and mistakes with the motions of his hands. Rosey grinned, "Comin' your way again, Deak!"

"Let 'em come, Fat Man—I got all day an' nothin' else to do."

As they lined up, Deacon said, "Give you them pictures of your wife for 20 bucks, Ralph."

Ralph had just enough time to say, "What pictures?" before Deacon's thunderous headslap rattled him on the left side of his helmet. He was by the second-year man like smoke, dropping Reeves just as he took the handoff from the quarterback.

By now Landry looked a little red-faced and he called the line over to have a conversation.

Merlin grinned at Deacon, "That Landry's a real perfectionist, ain't he?"

Deacon was looking back at his own sideline, where Allen gave him an approving nod and turned away, trying hard to keep the grin on his face from being too obvious. Deacon muttered to Merlin, "Let's stunt him."

This time Neely was frozen like an old stump as Olsen and Jones cut around him and jointly drove Reeves to the ground. Deacon rolled back to his feet and found himself five feet from Landry, who had come halfway across the field to make sure his instructions were followed. He gave the Dallas coach his bitter-sweet grin. Landry didn't say anything. He just glared and fumed. Over on the Rams sideline, Allen was hiding the smile on his face with his hand.

Landry ran that play seven more times, and each time Deacon found a way to stop it dead. The Cowboys' coach finally gave up and switched over to a passing series on Lamar Lundy's side of the line.

Deacon would never forget that May day, with the lacy white clouds drifting across the deep blue sky over the rolling green hills of Thousand Oaks. It was the day scrimmaging started to be fun again.

Deacon remembers how the black mood, born of years of loss, blame and neglect, began to lift from the Rams: "We players immediately recognized we were being instructed and guided rather than harangued and threatened. You can tell when you're improving, and under the encouragement of George and his staff, and that constant hammering away of his that we had to live up to our true potential for greatness, we all started to feel we were getting better. George was so enthusiastic that it was contagious!

Respect

George Allen was a lightning rod, attracting strong positive and negative feelings everywhere he went. In his days with the Bears, even while earning the wrath of old Pappa Bear Halas, the players loved him and hated to see him go. He'd gained the reputation of being a player's coach. He stood up for the players during their contract negotiations with "Old Stingy" in the days before lawyers and agents, when the owners were tyrants fortified by an act of Congress and nobody else would dare open their mouths. Allen defended his players from the press, and more—he had an empathy for them in their day-to-day problems. When Allen left Chicago, a few of the Bear players even dared risk the Old Man's fury to publicly wish him well. The great Doug Atkins bluntly summed it up for his Bear teammates, "It's hard to coach for Halas and it's hard to play for him. I'm glad George Allen is getting away from him."

George was the meaning of the word "intense." In his book *Life in the Pit,* sportswriter Bill Libby describes Allen from those first days with the Rams. "He was married, and he and his wife, Etty, had four children. A straight soul, who seldom drank anything stronger than milk, and never used profanity, he was devoted to his family, but he would not let this devotion interfere with his work. During the season, Allen moved into a motel near the Ram practice field in Long Beach so he did not have to go home every night. He neglected everything else and concentrated on football. Yet, in spite of his dedication to the game, his style wasn't hard-edged or militant; rather, it was softened by a boyish enthusiasm. He never forgot football was a game, and games were meant to be *played.*"

When Allen came to Los Angeles, the black players soon realized that when it came to racial issues he was like Vince Lombardi—no matter what color you were, so long as you were willing to dedicate soul and body to the goal of winning, you were an equal on his team.

Still, Deacon held his own opinions. Never one to let the group make up his mind for him or to jump on a bandwagon, he was slow to come around to the new coach. Deacon liked what he saw, but he'd been snake-bitten too many times. He was energetic and high-spirited on the field, as always, but as to where his deep allegiance lay, it was first with the Foursome, and then with this family called the Rams. Deacon liked the slogans, the drive, and determination in the man, and the way he talked to the players. But his high hopes had been dashed many times before, and he'd finally come not to expect very much from a coach. Deacon told himself he didn't know enough about Allen, and with that he adopted a wait-and-see attitude.

One midweek afternoon toward the end of spring training, as the workday was almost over and the sun settling toward the western horizon, Deacon was preparing to boot some field goals when Bruce Allen, the coach's son, shyly came up and asked if he could shag balls. Bruce was about ten or twelve at the time, and of Allen's children, he was the one who most loved to hang around the camp.

Deacon grinned and waved him down toward the goal posts, where one of the young assistants was stationed. For the next half hour, Bruce ran around fetching balls, happy as a clam. But as the sun sank out of sight and darkness started to come on, Deacon noticed he seemed to be getting nervous.

"Hey, Bruce—you afraid of the dark?"

"No. I—I forgot something . . . sir, do you mind if I go now?"

"No, course not," Deacon said, charmed at the young boy's courteous manners. Bruce ran off and Deacon kicked another dozen or so before it got so dark he couldn't see the goalposts.

After that, he did a few extra wind-sprints before deciding to call it a day. The light was still on in George's office. That didn't surprise Deacon. The Rams were working harder than ever before, but they didn't seem to mind—how could you complain when Allen was a bigger workaholic than any of them? He was there before everybody came, and he was there after everybody left. George often worked so late that it didn't make any sense to go home. He slept in the dorms and often saw his wife only on weekends.

As Deacon walked past Allen's office, he saw Allen's kids were still in there. Allen was giving them a lecture in that soft-yet-firm, reaching-out manner of his—the same way he talked to the players. He was talking about "the morality of the situation."

Deacon stopped and overheard what he was saying. "Now Bruce, you know you kids have the run of the camp. I want you here. I like you here. But you have to remember. You have a responsibility to do your schoolwork, and your chores at home for your mother."

"But I was helping the kickers," Bruce tried to argue.

"Yes, and that's good," George said patiently. "But I expect you to live up to your responsibilities first. You never saw Doug Atkins shirking his responsibility! You don't see Lamar Lundy or Deacon Jones shirking their responsibilities! Those players work hard, and that's how they get to be the best! You take after them, and you're on the right track!"

Allen went on to say more about a man living up to his responsibilities, but Deacon heard none of it. He moved on toward the locker room in a pleasant daze. What a turn-around from all the ugly recriminations, all the bullying and the mean-spirited threats of being traded!

Even as he was stunned by what he had heard, Deacon knew in that instant, clear to the center of his heart, that George Allen respected him as a human being. Lord, he'd recommended him—big bad Deacon Jones, black as an ace of spades and standing nearly seven feet tall in his Afro and high heel boots—as a role model to his kids! Even though he'd heard it himself, Deacon could only half-believe it. He stood in the locker room looking at his dusty, dirty, sweat-streaked form in one of the full-length mirrors. There he was, a big-mouthed, surly black defensive end with the speed of lightning and a thunderous headslap, a huge, bushy-haired party animal who could drink a quart of vodka and work it off the next morning, being held up to the light as someone special that Allen's kids should look up to!

Allen had seen something in Deacon that longed to be recognized. Neither man recognized it at the time, but a fierce bond had been struck, and from that moment on Deacon was ready to die for Allen on the football field.

Allen concentrated on winning, and insisted his team do the same. From time to time, problems between blacks and whites would crop up on the team, but Allen managed to keep them to a minimum. Several years after Allen had left the Rams, Jack Pardee mentioned an incident which had occurred in Buffalo. Running back Willie Ellison had missed a few blocks, causing Roman Gabriel to be hit. According to Pardee, "Roman ran him off the field. Roman then criticized Ellison in print for blowing his assignments. Several of the other blacks didn't like that. Deacon Jones for one, felt strong that way. Ellison didn't start any more after that, and the whole time coach Allen was getting burned."[2] Allen knew how distractive and divisive racial squabbles could be on a team, and he wouldn't allow this incident to get blown out of proportion. He brought the subject up at the Rams team meetings, it was determined, though Gabriel shouldn't have run Ellison off the field, his being angry didn't have anything to do with the color of Ellison's skin. The incident fizzled, and the Rams got back to playing football.

Other teams were not so fortunate. Dave Meggyesy talks about the long running feud between blacks and whites on the St. Louis Cardinals, "I was first introduced to racism on the team in my rookie year, 1962; room assignments, wings of the dormitory, and the dining hall were all segregated. . . . The Cardinals had a strong southern clique, out and out

2. *Los Angeles Times*, February 12, 1972.

rednecks who were the team leaders, including such guys as Sonny Randle, Bill Koman, Irv Goode, Joe Robb, Don Owens, and Ken Grey. Robb and Koman were the most vitriolic. Long before things came to the surface in 1967, Koman would continually tell me and anyone who'd listen that niggers were generally too dumb to play pro football, that pro clubs were giving niggers a break by having them around, and so on."[3]

Deacon talks about his affection for George Allen, the man he still calls "Coach" as if there is only one true coach in the world, "It wasn't just me; the rest of the blacks saw the same things that I saw. Coach never once talked about our intelligence. He took that for granted. After all, this wasn't the quantum theory of the universe or even brain surgery. Coach felt that you were intelligent enough to play the game if you were drafted into the pros. He took it for granted. He looked for a vital something else in his players, and that something was motivation."

George Allen's wife laughs as she remembers their courtship: "I honestly believe that, if he hadn't met me during the off-season, he would never even have noticed me.

Allen's son Bruce fondly looks back, "Dad had a boyishness, an almost innocent enthusiasm. To the day he died, in a sense, he was a kid. He could look at the prize in a Cracker Jack box and say, 'Say, will you look at that!' That was the way he was about everything. All us kids always hung around the camp; we were welcome, it was our life. He had time enough for all of us, and yet you knew it, in the center of his everything was football. He brought his enthusiasm to the game, and his teams caught fire."

In 1967, Dave Meggyesy was interviewed by Jack Olsen from Sport Illustrated, *who was doing research for a five part series about the black athlete. Meggyesy says, "I told him about the unconscious racism of the coaches and about the practice throughout the NFL of letting blacks play only in certain positions (Very few blacks hold positions which are popularly thought to require a great deal of intelligence rather than a great deal of strength—such as linebacker, offensive guard and quarterback). In our talk, I helped Olsen develop his thesis about the prevalence of stacking[4] and racism throughout the National Football League."[5]*

3. Dave Meggyesy, *Out of Their League,* Ramparts Press, 1970, p.193.

4. Stacking is a spring training practice reportedly in use by some NFL teams in the early 1960s to limit the numbers of blacks on a team. The blacks were only allowed to compete for certain positions, and hence "stacked" against each other in competition for those jobs which were open to them.

5. Dave Meggyesy, *Out of Their League,* Ramparts, 1970, p.197.

Wins Go in the Win Column

As the regular season approached, George Allen said the Rams were this far—indicating with his fingers a space of a half inch—from being a winner.

The team turned in a respectable three wins and two losses in the exhibition games. They beat Cleveland 16-6, lost to Dallas 20-10, lost to Minnesota 24-10, beat St. Louis 32-14, and shut out San Francisco 29-0. Allen complimented the team, claiming they had reached their objective, a 3-2 pre-season. But had he really plugged the weaknesses that had plagued them for over a decade? The pundits didn't think so; they picked Green Bay, the Baltimore Colts, and the Chicago Bears to be the contenders in the race for the western title. The *L.A. Times* predicted in the week before the season opener on September 11, under the title "NFL 1966 Contenders," that ". . . the Rams may not improve to any great degree over their 1965 record."

If anyone was taking serious note in the rival camps, they would have seen that the L.A. team gave up only twenty-four points in its worst loss. The team beat or hung tough against the solid teams, and handily beat the weak ones. The Rams were going to be a different animal from now on, far more difficult to defeat. But at that moment in space and time, probably the only man who really believed it was George Allen.

The Rams had a tough schedule: the Packers, the Colts, the Bears, the Lions, and the Vikings—maybe the only soft spot they'd find would be the off-again, on-again 49ers, and the season opener on Saturday, September 3, against the expansion team Atlanta Falcons in Georgia.

Before the game, Allen gathered the team around him in the locker room and spoke in his soft, confident manner. "Fellas, the press is calling us the favorites. That's nice; we do have a good team. But we also have a problem here. This is the first game Atlanta will ever play. To us, it's a game, and an important one, because it's our opener, and we want to get off on the winning track. But to Atlanta, this is *history.* Those boys are ready to die to win. They're going to fight you tooth and nail, every inch of the way. And the only way you're going to win it is to earn it!"

It was, as Allen predicted, a bitter day in the trenches. The Falcons fought like madmen, and the Fearsome Foursome had their hands full the entire afternoon. But when it was over, the Rams retired to their locker room with a coveted victory in their hands. The history books would record it a Rams win by a score of 19 to 14.

They cheered and whooped in the showers. Their joy at winning was a thing to behold. A heavy weight seemed lifted from their shoulders, a fog from around their personalities. You'd have thought they'd won the title. "Look out Chicago Bears!" Deacon chortled for the reporters, "next week I'm going hunting, and I'm gonna get me some bear meat!" George Allen smiled and complimented his players, and then, in the best tradition of his old mentor, George Halas, he complimented rival coach Norm Hecker and his team, "who fought like tigers to win this historic game for Atlanta."

Not everyone was so happy. Losing Atlanta end coach Tom Fears had been a Los Angeles legend as a receiver for the Rams, and so he had the ear of the southern California press. He bitterly complained to the sportswriters that George Allen had won only by pumping a discharged Atlanta player for secrets. Fears obviously felt cheated; he angrily claimed his team had figured out a way to attack the Rams "prevent" defense, a defense specifically designed to prevent "long bomb" pass plays. The Rams, he told the eager reporters, had used this defense frequently in certain situations in the preseason, but they didn't use it as much in the Atlanta game. Fears didn't reveal how he had acquired such specific information on the Rams "prevent" defense in the first place. Instead, he went on to charge Allen with secretly meeting and grilling released Falcon kicker Bob Jencks, about the Atlanta game plans. Making it sound furtive and somehow immoral, he alleged that a clandestine meeting had taken place Wednesday night in the Rams camp, and then Allen, armed with the top-secret Falcon data, changed his defensive game plan on Thursday.

A laughing Allen denied the charges: "If we'd known what they were doing, we'd have done better. Jencks did visit us, but he spent the time with Bill George, a former [Bears] teammate."

That wasn't enough to satisfy Fears, who went on to cry to Mal Florence of the *L.A. Times,* "If he needs something like that to beat us, I wish him luck the rest of the way. It's funny they had a secret practice session on Thursday. It's a typical Chicago Bears trick."

These were interesting allegations that were guaranteed to stir up fans in both camps. Distrust and suspicion of this kind was common in the NFL in those days, and, in point of fact, it exists to the present. Most pro football executives of the era were paranoid about Halas, convinced that the long-entrenched coach had an agent in every rival football camp. It was only natural that they would accuse the Old Man's right-hand man of the same tricks, although, if the truth were to be owned up to, no one in the league was above skullduggery and spying.

In retrospect, the Atlanta outrage is amusing, and the press coverage somewhat naive. After all, where *had* the righteous Tom Fears and his Falcons learned so much about the Ram's "prevent" defense in the first place that they could figure out an incredible secret plan they were counting on to stop it? Well, Deacon remembers that toward the end of the exhibition season, the Rams had let go rookie flanker Bob Sherlag, who had come to camp fresh out of Memphis State. As Deacon tells the story, the Falcons picked Sherlag up, picked his brains about his old team, and not too long thereafter gave him a release and let him go his own way. George Allen didn't say anything about that to the press, even though it might have gone a long way toward silencing his critics back in Los Angeles, who called it "a tainted victory" because the Rams "couldn't put the Falcons away." Allen was well aware that the good old boys in the league were out to get him, and he was never one to ever let the enemy know exactly what he did and didn't know. His critics could say what they wanted, and Fears could cry in his beer all night; the Rams had the victory, and, so far as Allen was concerned, it was business as usual. For the record, he smiled and said, "We'll win them any way we can." And then he proceeded to the dressing room where he congratulated Roman Gabriel on the victory. Gabriel grinned back, full of hope for the future, and said, "This is the type of game we used to lose. Now we win it."

A win goes in the win column; it's that simple. But, as the hand-lettered poster on the wall behind Allen's desk in his office suggested, in the NFL winning never comes easy. The sign said, "You must *reach beyond* your abilities, recognize that no talent, without hard work, can make you a winner. You must be *honest* with yourself—and with others . . . there is no easy way to success."

Deacon scoffs when he remembers Tom Fears's allegations: "They all did it, and they still do; they called it scouting when they did it, and spying when somebody did it to them. Landry did it. Stram did it. We did it. Everybody did it. Halas got away with more than anybody ever did, maybe because he came first and got to invent lots of the rules of engagement. There was reason to be concerned when you played him. He even tapped the phones on our bench! Another case comes to mind, just one of a dozen I could think of.

When Carl Sweetan left for the New Orleans Saints after the 1970 season, the rumor was he stole his copy of our playbook, that's the huge playbook George developed—and the New Orleans Saints bought the Rams playbook even though he didn't make the squad! The better your information, one more little piece in the puzzle for Sunday afternoon. On the Rams, our chief spy—uh, scout— was Ed Boynton."

Bruce Allen comments, "There are a hundred things, and, no matter how sanctimonious they get about it, every team in the league knew and used some of them. For instance, Halas always put the band behind the rival team's bench, so they had trouble with their signal calling. And when visiting teams got to Chicago, somehow the spotter's headsets never worked, so they couldn't talk to the coaches on the sidelines. Dad never went as far as selling seats on his opponent's benches on the sidelines, like Halas did, but in his own way he went beyond The Old Man. Dad learned motivation on his own. He learned to inspire his teams in ways Halas never dreamed of."

Special Treatment

The following Friday night the Rams opened some eyes in the Coliseum by overpowering the Chicago Bears in what had to be one of the great grudge matches of all time. If it's any measure of the hurt feelings involved, the game featured eleven penalties in the first half. The fireworks also included an eighty-four-yard touchdown pass from Gabriel to Jack Snow, and a spectacular, twisting touchdown run from the Bears' Gale Sayers. The Bears were winning at half-time, 17–14, but the Fearsome Foursome, led by Deacon, held the Chicago team scoreless in the second half, while the Rams offense ignited with heads-up play and thrilling long bombs.

One play stood out: Gabriel faded back and passed to Tommy McDonald, but the ball popped out of the usually sure-handed flanker's grasp. Snow alertly stayed with the ball, managing to acrobatically pick the fumble off in midair and continue the play. In the old regime, it was the sort of play that the receivers, strung tight from the verbal abuse they were getting from the coaches on the sidelines, would have dropped. As Gabriel had said the week before, the Rams were now playing with confidence, and winning games they once would have lost.

The following Sunday the Rams met the Packers in Green Bay. It was a crisp, sunny Indian Summer day at Lambeau Field. Vince Lombardi's Packers, known for their flawless play, fumbled five times, and the Fearsome Foursome held Jim Taylor to forty-two yards rushing, but the Rams still couldn't pull off the win. Green Bay, feared league-wide for its running game, unlimbered a surprise passing attack, and took the victory, 24-13.

The L.A. critics, who had been waiting in the wings, descended with a howl. Sid Ziff, writing in the *L.A. Times,* chortled,

> The Ram offense Sunday was the poorest excuse for an imaginative attack since General Grant fought the Battle of the Wilderness. There was no deception, no cunning, no surprises. Meanwhile, the Rams front four was playing sensational football. Merlin Olsen and David Jones were never better. They all but parted Starr from his scalp. They forced enough fumbles and stopped enough drives to win five football games.

After the game, George Allen showed another important difference between his regime and the past when he told reporters the blame rested squarely on his own shoulders. "I thought we could run on them and we couldn't. Roman Gabriel was under heavy pressure all day and just didn't have a chance."

The Rams, down 17-0, hadn't folded. Instead they came back in the third quarter to make it 17-13. Bart Starr, who had been relentlessly hounded by Deacon and Merlin for three quarters, barely connected in the final period for the last score.

After the game, Deacon was exhausted both mentally and physically. Each member of the team felt about the same way. They had let down themselves, George, and the L.A. fans. George Allen had made winning such a high priority in their lives that losing stung like never before. The reporters crowded around Deacon in the locker room, as they always did, and he gave them their quotable quote for the week. "We took it away from them six times," he said. "I thought six would be enough. We had discussed it before the game. We felt that if we could take it away five times, we would win the game. Starr's the one who beat us. Unless you get to him early and rattle him and put the leather to him, he'll whip you. I'll say this, Green Bay is tough—but we are better! We just didn't take it to them today. We gave them seventeen points, and it was too much." With that, Deacon turned to the showers to wash off some of the grime and bruising pain gathered in his afternoon's labor.

Vince Lombardi told the same reporters, "We were lucky to come out alive. The Rams front four is the best in football." What he didn't say, but what every coach in the league now recognized, was that, to beat the Los Angeles team, you had to design a strategy to nullify the efforts of the Fearsome Foursome.

The chastened Rams returned home to play San Francisco on October 1 in another Friday night game. The 49ers had lots of talent—quarterback John Brodie, a good line, punishing runners in Ken Willard and John David Crow, and fine wide receivers in Bernie Casey and Dave Parks. But it was to be a Rams night. The 49ers weren't able to contain the Foursome, and Dick Bass ran wild, scoring three touchdowns and becoming the club's all-time rushing leader. In seven seasons with the club, the plucky, 195-pound fullback rushed for 3,494 yards, overtaking the old record set by an earlier incarnation of the Deacon—Dan Towler, who played from 1950 through 1955.

The next Sunday, the weather was a mild seventy-four degrees in Tiger Stadium, and the stubborn Detroit Lions lay in wait. Deacon was "raging around the field in All-Pro fashion," and that afternoon the Rams defense was responsible for *eight* takeovers! Dick Bass was again unstoppable with a total 137 yards, and L.A. won 14-7.

Coach Allen's defensive unit had taken the ball from the opposition a total of sixteen times in the last three games. The Rams offense had managed to blunt the Lions' two great defensive linemen, Roger Brown and Alex Karras. Joe Scibelli was a match for Karras, but the real surprise was Tom Mack, who managed to keep Brown away from Roman Gabriel. Deacon told the reporters after the game, "That's really something for a rookie to draw Brown on his first starting assignment, and then handle him."

Deacon again gave reporters their quote of the week when he commented on the last interception of the game, forced by himself and Eddie Meador. "Eddie was tugging on [Milt] Plum's ankles and I was on top. Plum turned around quickly and I was coming in so fast I actually kissed him. I guess you could call it the kiss of death."

The end result was that Los Angeles moved into a first place tie with Green Bay. Allen addressed his squad: "We beat a tough team in their own backyard. The Rams are back and on their way. This Ram team has spirit similar to the 1963 world championship Bear team."

L.A Times sports writer Mal Florence saw reason for optimism:

Los Angeles has variously been called a Dodger town, Laker town, Trojan town and Bruin town. Today, for the first time in eleven years it is a Ram town again. You have to go back to 1955—the last year in which they won a divisional title—to locate a time when the Rams (4-1) were playing .800 ball at this juncture of the season.

It was at this point, with a bright future before them, with everything to gain and everything to lose, that the Rams once again began to unravel. They traveled to Minneapolis, where on Sunday, October 16, they were torn apart by the Vikings, 35-7. Florence now had to write a report far less hopeful than his previous week's: "The Rams couldn't move the ball against what was thought to be a mediocre Viking defense, nor could they stop frantic Francis Tarkenton from making the big plays." After the game, Coach Norm Van Brocklin explained that his attack had been designed as a "planned rollout" rather than a "scramble." "The Rams are just too strong up front," Van Brocklin added. "We had to do this. We had a rookie tackle (Doug Davis) on Deacon Jones, and we wanted to get away from him."

It was a bitter, puzzling defeat for George Allen, who mused, "You build, build, build, and then this happens. It makes you wonder. There was not any one thing they did. We just didn't play football. I didn't think we could get beat like that, but I guess we'll have to live with it."

Gabriel had nine completions for twenty-two attempts, for an anemic 125 yards, but Allen insisted he was sticking with him. "We win as a team and lose as a team," he said. There was some conjecture the defensive unit lost heart after stopping the Vikings three times in the first quarter, only to have the offense give the ball right back to the enemy. In the locker room, a disgusted Deacon Jones told reporters: "We're not used to playing as a winner. But we better get used to it. People are pointing for us now." As a final dismal footnote to the game, some partisan Viking turned the hot water off in the visitor's locker room, and the Rams had to shower with icy water coming from the hot water taps. It was a subtle point well made—the old George Halas icy water trick pulled on his young disciple.

The grim road trip continued with the Rams traveling to Chicago, where Gale Sayers ran all over Wrigley Field, accounting for 241 total yards rushing, receiving, and returning kicks. Sayers was directly or indirectly responsible for all of Chicago's seventeen points. The Rams defense, led by Deacon, held the Bears scoreless in the second half. Mal

Florence noted that, "David Jones has never played a better game at defensive end, and his front four buddies were in good form, too." But the damage had been done, and the Rams offense couldn't overcome the deficit, losing 17-10.

By now, disappointment raged in southern California, and everyone thought they knew what was wrong with the sagging Rams. The general feeling among the press was that the entire Rams offense was at fault. Their attack was so predictable that opponents were able to study their habits and adjust to them. George Allen stuck up for his individual players, while admitting that they hadn't played well as a team. "We just didn't cash in on our opportunities," he said in the locker room after the game. "Also, the Bears have a defense that would make any offense look bad. Gabe has done a good job this year. You can't blame the quarterback for everything."

Old Pappa Bear, George Halas, gave the press a sly smile after the game, "Did I want to get revenge on the Rams and George Allen? We don't go after revenge in this league." But for the second week in a row, when the Rams players turned on the water in the showers, nothing came out but an icy spray.

Back in the Coliseum, the Rams met Baltimore in sweltering eighty-five degree heat. Johnny Unitas was thirteen of twenty-two for 252 yards, to give him the all-time passing yardage record—28,375 yards, besting the great Y. A. Tittle's old mark of 28,339. Dick Bass fumbled twice, the Rams missed two field goals, and were intercepted three times. The Colts won 17-3.

Deacon spent the day in a head-to-head confrontation with the Colt's great tackle, Jim Parker, the kind of classic battle that fans and reporters alike love to witness. Each man had his moments. Deacon would get through on one play, and then Parker would hold him out on the next. Florence reported it like a heavyweight boxing championship between equally matched fighters. "The verdict was a draw. Observers believe Jim Parker won the first half on points, Deacon Jones the second. On our card, we gave Deacon a split decision."

In the locker room after the game, someone muttered to Deacon, "With a little luck L.A. would have won."

"Only if Unitas was handcuffed," Deacon growled back.

The trend was now clear; opposing teams were beating the Rams by shifting their entire game strategy to negate the powerful rush of the Rams front four, particularly that of Deacon Jones. This put the pressure on the Rams offense, which was not delivering.

Columnist Sid Ziff sadly reported that while the Rams had won the battles, they had "lost another war." Sid went on,

> The Rams were trying to grind it out while the Colts went for the bomb. The Rams led in first downs 21-13 and controlled the ball most of the game. "But we had the points on the board," the winning coach Don Shula pointed out. It looks like a long, hard winter again, folks, but at least the Rams are trying.[6]

After the game, Baltimore coach Don Shula revealed that his team had used the same thinking as earlier Ram rivals. "The Colts decided in advance that against the Rams front four they were not going to grind anything out. So we set up our first bomb in our locker room just before the game."

Johnny Unitas had his own comment about the Fearsome Foursome for the L.A. sportswriters. "They're so tough you have to come up with something different to beat 'em. They're so big it's like throwing from the bottom of a barrel. You have to throw from under your armpits sometimes. I thought we would have a few more completions, but you have to give them some credit."[7]

Dirty Tricks

The homefield advantage in football can be considerable. Young, fast teams with good knees prefer hard, natural surfaces with short grass, or (sometimes) artificial turf. A slower team will like a slower field, and will do anything they can to get the field working their way. For teams living in the northern cities of the Midwest and East, this could mean long grass, wetting the field, or, weather permitting, having the field as hard and icy as possible without clearly revealing they've "slicked the table top."

In Chicago's Wrigley field, Halas always saw to it that the grass was set for his defensive mob. In Texas, Landry came to mold his team around the characteristics of astroturf, that fast but unforgiving artificial surface that has given many a rug burn and twisted ankle. But of them all, no team over the years was more blatant than the San Francisco 49ers when it came to slopping up the turf. In those days before

---

6. Sid Ziff, *Los Angeles Times,* October 31, 1966.
7. Ibid.

Candlestick Park, San Francisco played in muddy, soggy Kezar Stadium, on a field that was consistently more like a plowed field in spring than a pro football gridiron. Kezar often entertained high school and college games on Friday night and Saturday afternoon. That meant major portions of the center of the field had to be re-sodded before Sunday's NFL game. And if the rains of autumn wouldn't conspire to turn Kezar into a bog, some loyal groundskeeper could be counted on to hit the sprinklers at about midnight, where they wouldn't be discovered until dawn.

By the time the disheartened Rams walked out onto the field at Kezar, the 49ers had it ready for them. It was the Kezar Classic, the Annual Mudbowl. The conditions favored the heavy "mudder" type running backs, and speedy little Dick Bass could gain only seven yards net on seven carries the entire day.

Deacon took to the field in a grim humor. The Rams had lost three in a row, and now were 4-4 for the season. For Deacon, it was to be a bitter day. In football, they never forget. One's battlefield enemies always try to return old favors. In Deacon's rookie year, he'd given Y. A. Tittle a shot that ended up being printed in newspapers across the country. Maybe Deacon, even in the spirit of his rookie joy, shouldn't have sent Tittle a copy of that picture with a few remarks on it. Now it was five years later, and Tittle was an offensive coach with the 49ers. And Tittle had come up with a special play to get his old antagonist out of the game.

The field was muck and mud from sideline to sideline. On the 49ers first offensive series, Tittle put tight end John David Crow wide and in motion, and then had Crow come in and crack-back block Deacon, who went spinning ass-over-teakettle into the mud. This play, illegal as it is in league play, isn't whistled much by the officials, simply because they aren't looking for it. By common consent, most teams don't use the tactic, because the crack-back, which catches the victim's knees from the back and side, is the most damaging block there is. On a dirty block like that, the man who is attacked is often severely injured; one or both of his knees fold like butter and they drive him off in one of those helmet-scooters and after reconstructive knee surgery and two years in rehab he maybe tries for a comeback.

This time, Deacon was lucky; since the Bears had tried a similar tactic on him in his rookie years, he always wore short cleats that wouldn't stick. And the loose new sod of Kezar also saved him, giving away where a firmer surface would have hooked his cleats while the driving force of John David Crow would have snapped the tendons in his knees like spaghetti. Still, Deacon found himself on his back with clumps of wet dirt flying and his feet in the air kicking whatever part of Crow he could get to, to serve him what justice he could.

Deacon stood and shook himself, digging a big clod of mud from inside his helmet with one finger and knowing he'd gotten off lucky. Merlin came over. "You okay, David?"

"Bastards crack-blocked me."

"Maybe just an accident?"

Deacon glared across the line at John David Crow, who was retreating to the 49er huddle. "I don't believe in accidents," he said.

On the next play the 49ers called a draw, and John David Crow again circled in and crack-blocked Deacon from behind. This time Deacon was ready. The moment he sensed Crow bearing down on him from behind, he curled into a ball and got his feet kicking toward Crow's face. Crow caught some cleats in his helmet before he came crashing down on Deacon and they both went rolling in the loose sod.

Deacon got to his feet spitting mud and grass. Without a moment's hesitation, he marched across the line and past the entire startled 49ers team to stare into Brodie's eyes.

"John," he said, "you tell Tittle I can't get to him right now, but I can sure get to you! Tittle calls a crack-back on me one more time, and I'm going to break through and snap your scrawny neck—an' you know I can do it!"

Brodie didn't say anything, just looked at Deacon with his eyes a little wide. There was some pushing and shoving, and harsh words were said as Deacon made his way back to his side of the line. But Brodie didn't call that play any more.

This was a team the Rams had demolished a few weeks before, but with the field a mudbowl, the Rams strengths were effectively neutralized and neither team could take a commanding lead. In the third quarter, Deacon intercepted a John Brodie toss behind the line. He went up to block the pass, and it bounced straight up off his hands. When it came down he grabbed it. By this time, he was dog-tired. Still, he took off for the distant goal line. After twenty yards, his lungs were burning and the hash marks seemed to crawl by under his feet. Still, he sped for the Rams goal line. After running fifty yards, the last possible defender, San Francisco offensive receiver Bernie Casey caught him. Deacon was hauled down on the 49ers twenty-eight yard line. There the Rams blew another scoring opportunity, going on to lose the game, 21-13.

After the game, Deacon walked off the field in a rage. Instead of going with his own teammates, he made his way to the 49ers' locker room and stormed up to head coach Jack Christiansen, who was celebrating with a crowd of San Francisco players.

"Crack-blocking me was a chickenshit thing to do!" He yelled angrily.

"Hey, peace, love an' brotherhood," somebody said, giving Deacon the peace sign.

"Take that V an' stick it up your ass! I got a right to be angry! I hit a lot of people in my life, some of them so hard their bells are still ringing—but I always hit them in front!"

Boos and hisses went up from the assembled players.

"If the only way you can win is by sloppin' down the field, so be it," Deacon said. "But don't anybody ever crack-block me again. It could be your death warrant!"

They booed and hissed Deacon some more, but nobody laid a hand on him as he made his way from the room.

When Deacon got back to the visitor's locker room, he was still furious, but he didn't take his case to the press. The player's code, the code of the gladiator, dictated that he take care of his own problems. From that time on, John David Crow would retire from the Rams games with an extra batch of lumps and bruises, his head ringing from the famous headslap.

Instead of talking about the crack-blocks, Deacon exploded to Charles Maher of the *L.A. Times* about the field itself. "That field was like a hog pen! It was no place to play defensive football. I don't know why they don't find someplace else to play here. Sure, it rained before the game. But if there had been that amount of rain before a game in the Coliseum, we wouldn't have had nearly that much trouble. I don't know whether it's the drainage or what. But this field is just no good. A muddy field bothers defensive linemen much more than it does offensive linemen. The defense has to shoot right in there. The offense can just stand there. On a field like this, the defense just can't get any traction. But that's still no excuse. We should have won the ball game. They had no business getting three touchdowns on us."

It was faithful Lamar who finally dragged Deacon away from the reporters. "Owners don' like to read about their sins in the papers," he said simply. "They don't like nothin' makes 'em look bad." Deacon followed along to the steaming showers without another word. Better to get there before they turned the hot water off, and he'd said all he intended, anyway.

Still, muddy field or no, the pattern was clear; the Rams defense was keeping them in games, but the offense wasn't scoring enough to win. In fact, they hadn't scored two touchdowns in any game since winning over Detroit five games before. In wet and muddy Kezar, two dropped passes frustrated Roman Gabriel drives and meant the difference between victory and defeat. Mal Florence seemed to have his finger on the problem when he told Ram fans, "It seems obvious now that the Rams, who rely on a ball control, grind-it-out offense, must have perfect execution if they are to succeed with this offensive design. However, they do not have such execution."

Now that his playing days are behind him, Deacon looks back on the crack-block incident. "Tittle is really not that bad a guy—he just felt he owed me one for that shot I gave him when I was a rookie, and if it would help win the game, well, why not? I know all this is true—as I tell it to you—because in 1986 I was in a big charity tennis tournament with Tittle in San Diego, and he admitted it over the mike in front of a thousand people. I guess it was funny by then, sort-of an old war story. But back at the time of the incident, I was a constant menace to Brodie. Tittle was trying to get me out of the game so he'd have some chance to win. You have to respect that, if you understand the alleycat ways of survival in the pros. It wasn't the way I personally conducted my affairs, but I can understand it. And I had to threaten Brodie and go after Tittle and Brodie. If you do not know how to serve justice in this business, you'll get your ass kicked week in and week out. You don't take your case to the press, you take it direct to your foes. They had to know that if they tried business in the dirty way with me, I was just fool enough to come after them, and just great enough to make it stick."

Different people remember different parts of what happened, but nobody denies the basic story. John Brodie talks about that game: "We had John David Crow cracking back on him. Deacon was getting madder and madder. Crow came back to the huddle and said, "John, if it's all the same to you, I'd just as soon line up on the other side the next couple of plays."

Ken Willard, the San Francisco fullback, commented, "We were hoping the mud would mess up people like Deacon Jones and Merlin Olsen. And it did. But the Ram defense was also messed up by the 49er offense."

Deacon smiles his knowing, bittersweet smile. "They're talking pretty lightly about a series of plays that could have destroyed me physically and ruined my career. I still had my best years ahead of me, my years of domination in the league, and it all could have been destroyed with one blown knee—on a play designed to snap the cartilage and rip the tendons, leaving you twisting in agony on the ground. But that's life in the NFL, playing the game with the big boys."

George the Believer

As the season wore on, the days became shorter, and Deacon found himself finishing his extra wind-sprints in nearly total darkness. The Tuesday after their loss in the Kezar mudbowl, he came in to find Allen sitting alone in his office.

"Hey, Coach," he said, standing in the doorway. "How's it goin'?" Only then did he notice that Allen was on the phone.

"Deacon, come in. I've been meaning to talk to you." Allen waved him in and pointed to a chair. He put his hand over the phone so the person on the other end of the line couldn't hear them talk, "I'm waiting for Christiansen."

"Talkin' to the 49ers' coach?"

"Sure. I make a point to call the opposing coach after every game—talk about strategy, how it went, were they just lucky on such or so play, or was it a plan—you'd be surprised how much you can learn that way."

"Do all the coaches talk to you?"

Allen smiled, almost to himself, as if Deacon had hit on a personal problem, "Well, noooo . . . less likely after they lose than after they win—but that doesn't stop me from calling them. The more successful the coach, the more likely they are to give me a few minutes of their time. Landry and Lombardi, for instance, they're not afraid of anything. They take my calls, and they probably learn as much from me as I learn from them. Who knows, maybe even more . . . but it doesn't matter—the truth is, we all end up smarter; we know more about football."

Deacon set his helmet on the floor and slumped into a chair, "What do they have to fear?"

"Oh, you know—that I'm going to steal their secrets."

"Football's nine-tenths execution, anyway. That's what you're always telling us."

"That's right, Deacon. But that other one-tenth can kill you."

"What did you want to talk with me about?" Deacon knew from experience that Allen never criticized the players in front of each other, so he'd probably done something wrong.

Allen grinned at him. "Did you really charge on into the 49ers' locker room after the game?"

"Sure I did, Coach! They were crack-blocking me!"

"You're going to be a legend, if you live long enough." Allen's grin broke into a broad smile.

"Justice must be served," Deacon said, the old motto coming easily to his lips.

Allen held up his hand for silence and put the phone to his ear, listening to somebody on the other end. "Okay," he said quietly into the phone, and then gently set the receiver back on its cradle. "Seems like Jack doesn't want to talk about his victory."

"How do you personally feel about the game, Coach?"

Allen nodded and leaned back in his chair, looking at the sign on his wall that read "If not us, Who? If not now, When?" "That's a good question, Deacon," he finally said. "We knew they'd throw the mud at us, and I'm not surprised that Tittle would set up a crack-block. They've done it before. But, as to us losing, I'm honestly stunned. We should have handled everything they dished out to us. Individually and as a team, we're much better than they are." He shook his head emphatically and waved his hands as if there was no rational explanation for the loss. "This team is so much better than we've played to date!"

"I got my own theory."

Allen gave him his quick, intense look, "Let's hear it."

"We've been blamed for so much over the years . . . maybe now, even though things has gotten so much better . . . maybe it's just hard for us to gel as a team."

Allen nodded and sighed, "It certainly could be that. I tell you, Deacon, this team is a team of winners. I know it sounds crazy, but we are less than an inch away from being champions. This far away!" George held up his fingers in his characteristic gesture.

"Coach, right now, we're four and five. You probably the only man in the country who still believes that."

"Don't I know it! And just in case I have a memory lapse, the local sports scribes are making sure I don't forget." Allen held up a handful of newspaper clippings, and began reading. "Bob Oates over at the Herald-Examiner feels our losing streak is 'due to variations on the same themes of misfortune and a punchless offense.' Let me read you a little of this: 'There is an ill-starred something about the Ram team that brings out the finest in the other side's stars. Simultaneously, the Rams offense has had the same difficulties in the clutch for four weeks—dropped passes, a few missed blocks and field goals, unsuccessful play calling, damaging fouls, ill timed throws and other broken plays.' "[8]

The Rams coach pawed through the clippings on his desk, "Actually, that's a tame one. Bud Furillo hoots us in his Steam Room column . . . talks about 'The Miracle in the Mud of Kezar.' Get this: 'A two week vigil by the professional football fans in Los Angeles resulted in another miracle when a touchdown was produced by the Rams on television from San Francisco yesterday. All it took for the Rams to score six points at once, followed by a lightning-like seventh, was fourteen days, eight quarters of football and 2500 miles.' "[9]

The Rams coach continued, "I'd think this Furillo was actually a very witty guy if I wasn't the coach of the L.A. Rams. The guy goes on to speculate it's supposed to rain and so we might miraculously produce another touchdown this weekend against the Giants." He crumpled all the clippings and threw them in his waste can. "But the funny writer-man is in for a big surprise, Deacon. In fact, they're all in for a big surprise."

"What's that, Coach?"

"I tell you—this team still has its spirit intact, Deacon! And from here on in, they're going to play like winners! I see signs of it everywhere. I wouldn't want to be a Giant this weekend, oh no—because we are going to destroy them!"

Deacon looked at the light in his coach's eyes. Madman or prophet, he thought to himself, this man believes in us like no one else. He believes like we don't even believe in ourselves. First, last, and only, he's our true believer!

"I'll tell the guys how you feel," Deacon said, picking up his helmet and turning to go to the showers.

"Oh, they know," the coach smiled. "But you can tell them anyway. It never hurts to tell them again."

That Sunday, the Rams offense performed one of the most incredible turn-arounds in football history, rolling up 572 combined rushing

---

8. Bob Oates, *Herald Examiner,* November 7, 1966.
9. Bud Furillo, "The Steam Room," *Herald-Examiner,* November 7, 1966.

and passing yards and gaining thirty-eight first downs for a new NFL record (the old record of thirty-seven first downs had been set by Green Bay in a win over Philadelphia in 1962). Gabriel was brilliant, completing twenty-four of thirty-five for 298 yards and two touchdowns, and scoring two more touchdowns on tricky, one-yard quarterback sneaks.

Meanwhile, the Rams defense, lead by Deacon, limited New York to forty-seven yards rushing and 103 total yards. They harassed the Giants' starting quarterback, Gary Wood, so successfully that he couldn't complete a pass in six tries.

Stung by their humiliating loss (the final score was 55-14) the Giants felt the Rams had unjustly "piled on the score." George Allen replied, "The past four weeks we have been humiliated and downtrodden. There has been so much criticism of our offense. Cartoons and everything else you could think of. Today our offensive players especially were emotionally ready to play a good football game. And this was our best game this year by far." About the high score, he added, "We decided to go for the record. We don't like to rub the score in on anyone, especially on (Giants' coach) Allie Sherman. But because of all the humiliation we'd gone through the offense was hungry for points. I want you to be sure to put that in, about Sherman, because we didn't want to humiliate him."

By way of response, Sherman flared up with a hint of the strong feelings the good old boys of the NFL felt for George Allen. "I know George very well . . . but a professional never thinks about whether he likes another coach. He either respects him or he doesn't. But let's not get into that."

The Rest of the Season

The Rams were five and five, with virtually no chance for the title (the Packers were eight and two at that point), and only a very slim chance for the "runner-up" bowl. It was time for the players to give up the dream of greatness, to hunker down, crawl back to their locker rooms to lick their wounds and start thinking about next season much as they had in years gone by. Yet, this year, the Rams were walking to the tune of a different drummer; it was at this unlikely juncture, when winning didn't seem to matter to anyone else but themselves, that the team finally gelled as Allen had predicted.

Rain came down in buckets all across southern California on Sunday, November 20. It started to fall in the second period of the Rams-Vikings game, and continued throughout the contest. It was a day when Deacon and the Fearsome Foursome exacted their toll from their old nemesis, scrambling Fran Tarkenton. As Mal Florence described the action, "Deacon Jones, Merlin Olsen, Lamar Lundy, Maxie Baughan and Rosey Grier, who were raging around the field in All-Pro style, paid back an old debt to Tarkenton. They whacked him hard and often, spilling him five times for losses of forty yards. Tarkenton, who had almost personally defeated the Rams in seven of eleven previous meetings, completed only one pass for eight yards."

Down on the field, the Fearsome Foursome was unstoppable. Everybody tasted blood, and was after a piece of Tarkenton, and every stunt Deacon and Merlin tried seemed to work for them. Bruce Gossett scored four field goals, and the defense had a big part in the victory as the Rams scored on a fumble recovery for a touchdown, and a safety. Viking coach Norm Van Brocklin said, "Their defensive line beat us to death." George Allen called it "a great team victory." After the game, Deacon stood at the sidelines, reluctant to leave the field. Why should it end? Why did it ever have to end!

The next week, Coach Allen led the team into Baltimore Memorial Stadium, where they played before a sellout crowd of over sixty thousand screaming partisans. The Rams defense led them to a 23-7 win, their first win in twelve years in Baltimore. On a key play, Deacon rushed Unitas, who hit him in the helmet with the ball while trying desperately to unload it. The ball flew high in the air and was picked off by Rams Clancy Williams, who rambled thirty-two yards for the touchdown. Allen told the press, "My only regret is that we didn't shut them out. There's no question now that the Rams are back and back to stay."

The following week, the awakened L.A. team crushed the Detroit Lions on a drizzly Sunday afternoon in the Coliseum, 23-3. Dick Bass set up the offense's only three points with a nifty fifty-yard run. The Rams defense had three interceptions that were converted into scores.

The Lions attempted the tried-and-true strategy of puncturing the L.A. defensive umbrella with short, fast passes from their rookie quarterback Karl Sweetan. It worked for a while, but the Lions problem was that Trader George had plugged the infamous holes in the Rams backfield with some proven veterans. When linebacker Jack Pardee picked off a pass, and safetyman Chuck Lamson was able to steal two, the Lions throwers had to think a little bit before letting loose of the ball. And that gave the Rams front line the split-second difference they needed to get after Sweetan like hounds after a young fox.

After the game, walking off the field toward their respective lockers, Sweetan passed Deacon and then turned and stuck his tongue out at him. Kid-stuff, maybe, but it was a public gesture, and the reporters asked him about it later. "It was my tribute to Deacon," Sweetan said, a big grin splashing across his face. "I waited until he turned his back before I did it."

Deacon, who had deflected several of Sweetan's passes, and trapped him for his only loss behind the line when he was attempting to pass, was all seriousness, talking about Sweetan as a young enemy who had earned a measure of respect. "He gets rid of that ball real quick," Deacon told *L.A. Times* reporter Mal Florence, "We put a lot of pressure on him, but he stood his ground."[10] Deacon knew all about rookies taunting the grizzled professionals; he'd come a long way from the raw recruit who had teased Y. A. Tittle and lived to regret it.

With an eight and five record and assured of their first winning season in over a decade, the Rams looked forward to their last regular season game against the mighty Packers. Green Bay had already cinched the title for the Western Conference, but if the Rams could find some way to beat them, they would play in the "runner-up" bowl in Miami, a contest held in those days between the second-place teams in each conference, before the NFL smartened up and allowed wild card teams.

The Rams offense slipped early, with a fumble and an interception in the first quarter. On the most damaging of these mistakes, Marlin McKeever fumbled to Green Bay after catching a Roman Gabriel toss on the Packer five-yard line. These lapses changed the momentum of the game, and Bratkowski scored on three long bombs.

Victory was now impossible. No one ever came from that far back to defeat the Packers. But George Allen and his newborn Rams didn't seem to understand that. Pulling out all the stops, they put their offense on full throttle. Punter John Kilgore threw a fourth-down pass to sustain a Rams seventy-seven-yard touchdown drive. And then, on another offensive series, Gabriel uncharacteristically rolled out of the pocket to his left and threw against the grain to Steve Heckerd for fifty yards. The Rams scored a touchdown on the next play.

Although the Rams were the first club to score twenty-three

---

10. Mal Florence, *Los Angeles Times,* December 5, 1966.

points against the Packers that year, they were still five shy of the win. Inspired by Vince Lombardi, the Packers played vicious, rough football throughout the afternoon. The Rams list of walking wounded included Ed Meador, Tom Moore, Ken Imam, Maxie Baughn, Bill George, Don Chuy, Charlie Cowan, Merlin Olsen, Jack Snow, and Marlin McKeever. Still, they refused to go down without a fight, opting for a last-minute onsides kick to give the Rams offense one last chance. But the kick failed, the Packers had the ball, and the Rams defeat was assured.

To a man, the team took the defeat hard. They had been driven by George Allen to believe they could succeed. Victory had been close . . . so very close. Columnist Sid Ziff recorded the mood of the players:

> It was a little like the end of the world or the suicide ward in the county hospital in the Ram club house. Everyone was bitterly disappointed and showed it. "I expected to win," admitted coach George Allen sadly. So did the players and they had enough chances. They had five good scoring opportunities in the first half and were unable to score a touchdown.[11]

Although Deacon and the rest of the Rams had played a brilliant second half, completely stopping the Packers while the Rams attempted their impossible dream comeback, Deacon disgustedly blamed himself. "We were just plain bad defensively," he told the reporters.

George Allen accepted the defeat head on. "We had a lot of enthusiasm because we wanted to go to Miami (for the runner-up bowl), but we weren't good enough." The L.A. coach had worked an incredible turnaround. But his success made him even more of an outsider to the club owners, who were the ones who voted for NFL coach of the year. Sid Ziff noted in the L.A. Times sports section that, "Tom Landry of the Dallas Cowboys, with a big lead in votes, has been named NFL coach of the year, an honor we believe belongs to Allen. Landry had seven years to build a winner. Allen did it in one. Allen did the greatest job of rebuilding a pro club since Lombardi moved to Green Bay."[12]

For the record books, the Rams (8-6) came in third behind the Packers (12-2) and the Colts (9-5). After his brilliant coaching year, Allen received only four votes. Perennially everybody's favorite, Vince

---

11. Sid Ziff, *Los Angeles Times*, December 19, 1966.
12. Ibid.

Lombardi got four, Charley Winner of St. Louis received nine (the Cardinals placed fourth in the Eastern Conference with an 8-5-1 record), and Landry swept the field with nineteen votes (the Cowboys coming in first in the Eastern Conference with a 10-3-1 record).

In the voting that went on at Ye Olde Rams Club, Dick Bass was named the Rams MVP for achieving the second thousand-plus yards season of his career. And Deacon Jones repeated as the team's top defensive player.

Asked what he would be doing in the off-season, true believer George Allen paused, oddly struck by the idea. "I haven't given it any thought," he replied. "I thought we were going to Miami."

Today, Deacon still argues that Allen was the only real contender for the coveted coach-of-the-year award in 1966. "This may sound old-fashioned, but pride is what makes a champion. Pride, and teamwork. Anyone who has ever excelled will tell you that. When you've got pride, you don't like to lose nothing! Winners hate to lose. And George Allen was a winner. He turned our team around the first year he took over. He lived up to his motto on the wall, "The future is now!" His enemies wouldn't give him the prize, but they can never take his accomplishments away from him.

"Don't get me wrong, Landry was a good man. From everything I've said about coaches like Waterfield and Svare, and have yet to say about Tommy Prothro, you may have the notion that I don't respect them as a breed. That would not be true. There were a lot of excellent coaches in those days. Pittsburgh's Buddy Parker was known as a brilliant strategist, though not particularly good with his players. Weeb Ewbank was laid back, and expected his men to do their work. Norm Van Brocklin was considered crusty and experienced, though I always thought that while he was football-smart, he was also an erratic, pop-off sort of guy. George Allen was a proud, headstrong man, a great motivator who put winning first on his agenda and dedicated his life to becoming a master craftsman at the game. Tom Landry was very much like Lombardi in the important qualities which make a superior leader. His drive and intensity were second to none. He wasn't as tough talking or as loud as Lombardi, or as good a trader as Allen, but he got the job done in fine order.

"There was one difference, and in my mind, that made George an even better coach than Vince or Tom. Lombardi said "Do it my way or do it somewhere else." Landry had the same "Do it my way" attitude. Your suggestions didn't really matter to him. On the

other hand, George would listen to anything that might help him win. He would explore the possibilities, and his genius lay in finding that thread in all the hay, that golden key that opened the door to the winning.

"Of this small sample, you may notice one other thing—the winning coaches are the ones who did it mostly their way, the ones least compatible with the owners."

That's Entertainment

It was the Rams' first winning season in living memory (for most Los Angelinos), and the team was in demand for all sorts of parties and social affairs. With the off-season, "party hearty" became the buzzword of the day. Deacon grimly hung on to his early-morning training ritual at the beach. It was tough, but Deacon had learned his lesson well. Like the sign over George Allen's desk said, "You must consider winning as essential as eating and sleeping. You must consider success the heartbeat of life."

The Foursome followed up their MG commercial with a Honda motorbike spot. Honda was about to convince America that bikes were fun and belonged to a broader crowd than the Hell's Angels, and win an entire market away from Harley-Davidson. The Fearsome Ones zoomed around doing tight circles in full uniform on the little motorbikes, and if history wasn't made, at least nobody fell off their bike and got hurt.

By 1965, Dick Bass and Rosey Grier had started running a nightclub in the San Fernando Valley called The Locker Room, and they had the Fearsome Foursome come and sing. Rosey had talent, and a guitar to go along with it, and was adept at songs like "Up on the Roof." Merlin had the deepest voice, and Lamar and Deacon started in by adding the fill.

A year later, the four of them were sitting on a darkened sound stage rented by Capitol Records, wearing headsets just like the professional singers, cutting a 45 rpm disk. They'd already done six or seven takes.

Rosey pointed an accusing finger at Deacon, "You singin' flat again."

"Not me, fat boy. You must have flat ears today."

"You not hittin' these notes!" Rosey jabbed his enormous forefinger at the sheets in front of him.

"Lucky I can even see 'em, lookin' around you the way I got to."

Rosey glared and turned to the engineer on the other side of the plate glass. "Playback," he demanded.

Deacon could see Iretha curled up on the couch behind the engineer. There was fruit and sandwiches and cold beer, but he could tell by her pouting look that the thrill and glamour of cutting a record were long gone for her. He blanked it from his mind as he did so many of the things about Iretha these days. He'd made his deal with the devil, and he'd stick with it, but damn, sometimes it was hard! The girl didn't understand that to be good at anything took practice, constant practice—and practice took time.

The instrumental had been recorded on two tracks, with the guitars and the percussion instruments separated from the rest. After a brief garble of sound, their own voices played back at them in the earphones. It was the Foursome's first record, "Fly in the Buttermilk." Rosey stopped the song at the offending moment, and had the engineer play it over and over.

Deacon clicked the talk-mike in front of him. "Hey, you out there—is that me or the fat boy?"

"Ahhhhh," the engineer hesitated. He was a middle-aged beatnik, a pot-bellied white guy with balding reddish hair and a bushy beard who liked his grass strong and his arguments short. "I really can't tell."

This being before Rosey "caught religion like the flu," as the rest of the Foursome saw it, the big man let loose a string of profanities that would have been enough to clear a room of lesser men. Deacon eyed him calmly. "Was you a fat baby?"

"Huh?"

"Was you a fat little kid? There's a theory of science that if a child is raised fat, he got all sorts of aggressions when he grows up, you know, from bein' put on by all the other kids—"

"I was *not* born *fat*! Now let's do this song, and let's get it right!"

The bickering continued throughout the session, mostly Rosey getting on Deacon's case and Deacon laying into him about his amazing girth. After a few more takes, the engineer declared it was "good as it was gonna get," and they started in on the flip side, "Stranded in the Jungle."

It was well past midnight before they were ready for the final mix. Iretha had left hours before, pushed to well past her limit. The man from Capitol Records sent for a limousine to drive her home, and that mollified her to some extent. The wife of the famous star drives home in a stretch limo. Deacon, tired of her whining, wasn't unhappy to see her go.

Merlin had left for home right after the singing was finished, grumbling that he would be happy to hear the finished product the next day. Rosey and the engineer sat in the booth, arguing about every detail as they ran bit by bit through the pre-mix before trying a mix.

Deacon sat in a huge, soft white beanbag chair, staring at a Peter Max poster enhanced with purple light, listening to the endless round of debates and the snatches of music from the next room. Lamar had his eyes closed and was stretched out on a zebra skin couch, his long legs draped over one end and his head scrunched against the other arm rest.

"Lamar," Deacon said finally, reaching with one hand to the bottom of a huge bowl that had been filled with salted nuts, "you think I sing flat?"

There was a long pause. "Well . . . not all the time."

Deacon didn't say anything for a while, letting it soak in. "What are we, Lamar?"

Lamar grunted and opened one eye. "We're mortal men, David Jones. Mortal men, like the Bible say, with one brief span before we greets our Maker."

"No. Not that. What are we, Lamar?"

Lamar sighed, closing his one eye and settling back down on the couch, "We football players, Deacon. Like you always sayin', we the biggest, baddest, meanest, roughest—"

"Lamar, you missin' the point!"

His friend groaned and straightened somewhat on the black-and-white stripes, "Okay, what is we, Deacon?"

"Of course, we are football players."

"I said so."

"But what are football players?"

"I don't know, Deacon," Lamar said, knowing his friend was going to tell him whether he wanted to know or not. "What are football players?"

"Football players are entertainers. That's why the fans love me so much when I kill the quarterback. When I tell 'em what I'm gonna do, and then go out and do it. I make a story out of the game. "Can the Deacon plant Unitas in the dirt?" I put drama on the gridiron. "Fourth and three—the 49ers have to go for it—the ball is snapped—here comes the Deacon!"

The speakers went into an extended squawk, the rewind of the selected take of "Fly in the Buttermilk," and then the mixed version played over the speakers.

"Not bad," Lamar said as the last reverb died away.

Deacon shook his head. "It's terrible, Lamar. Terrible. I could handle a tune better than that when I was in Sunday School. If we wasn't the Foursome, there's nobody in the cotton-picking world would listen to that song."

"That's the way of the world, my friend."

"It don't have to be that way."

"Nothing we can do about it."

Deacon frowned but he didn't say any more, and Lamar was soon snoring on the couch. Deacon listened through the long mix of "Stranded in the Jungle" without saying another word. His mind was a jumble of mixed emotions. There was something about the music business that got into your blood! He loved being in front of the mike almost as much as he loved football! Sure, he was untrained now, but he'd had greater odds against him when he decided to conquer the NFL. The key to it was to entertain, and he'd never had any problems there. Just turn on the spotlight, and he could dazzle any crowd! He had an edge, he was a member of the Foursome, he was Deacon Jones, the controversial and charismatic locker room conversationalist, a joy in the hearts of reporters and Rams fans across the land. The next step up, entertaining a crowd in a nightclub, now that was a goal worth working toward! Still, he was going to have to take his act to a higher level—a man would be a fool to attempt a public career on the stage without getting the best training he could. After all, where would he be on the gridiron without Don Paul, Harland Svare, George Allen, and all the other coaches who had taught him his moves? On the other hand, he couldn't talk about this with the guys—they'd laugh him off the team! Swamp Boy learns how to sing!

He'd overheard Dick Bass talking about a voice teacher. That was it, without telling anybody he would quietly begin taking voice and singing lessons. Why should it be impossible? Like Mama always used to say back in the bad old days in Eatonville, Ain't nothin' you can't do, once you set your mind to it.

Dick Bass, starring in the limelight since his early high school playing days, had a knack for showmanship. With his radio show, his bubbling, quirky sense of humor and outlandish antics, he and Rosey Grier led the way for blacks on the team who were interested in par-

*laying their fame on the gridiron into roles as celebrities. Bass never
failed to amuse the press or the rest of his teammates. Deacon
remembers, "He was always impersonating Hobbs of British Intelligence, an English explorer in the darkest jungle, or a U.N. delegate
from some god-awful backward country. He'd show up for spring
training or a banquet wearing one eye-glass and a fortune in English
tweeds, or maybe a flower-print sarong he got from Pier One."*

*Bass's impersonations impressed everybody, except maybe
Rosey Grier. "Dick sounds like an Englishman," Rosey thoughtfully
remarked to L.A Times columnist Jim Murray, "If you imagine an
Englishman eating a chicken."*

The Right Foot

It was 1967. It was George Allen's second year as head coach of the
Rams and Deacon's seventh campaign in the NFL. Spring training
went smoothly and the Los Angeles Rams completed the first
unbeaten preseason in their twenty-two-year history. Along the way,
they defeated Dallas (the Eastern Conference champs), Cleveland (the
runner-up), and Kansas City, (the AFC champs).

Forty-niner coach Jack Christiansen told Mal Florence, "The Rams
have as strong a defensive team as I've seen and championships are usually won with defense."[13]

But, with the exhibition win over Kansas City, a huge hole
appeared in L.A.'s massive front four. Rosey Grier, never one to strain
himself in warmups, tore his Achilles tendon. In years past, the Rams
would have contented themselves with a backup player, maybe somebody off the taxi squad. But not George "The Future Is Now" Allen.
Flying in the face of everything tight-fisted owner Dan Reeves believed
in, he went out and traded away the uncertain future for seven-year veteran Roger Brown of Detroit, then at the height of his career. And
when the Rams season opener against the New Orleans Saints took
place in front of eighty thousand frenzied people in the Sugar Bowl, the
L.A. team was ready. They won 27-13 despite a partisan crowd Allen
described as noisier than Baltimore's. There were several pushing and
shoving confrontations, and, in the understatement of the new season,
Allen said both teams were "extremely emotional."[14]

---

13. Mal Florence, *Los Angeles Times,* September 11, 1967.
14. Mal Florence, *Los Angeles Times,* September 18, 1967.

Saints quarterback Billy Kilmer ducked and dodged the Rams throughout the first half, as Deacon and Lamar took inside routes to get to him. At half time, New Orleans put on a lavish show, featuring musician Al Hirt and a huge hot air balloon. But the balloon couldn't get off the ground in the near ninety-degree heat. Allen shifted his strategy at half time, having Deacon and Lamar charge to the outside, and after that the Saints offense couldn't get off the ground either.

Of Billy Kilmer, Deacon told the reporters, "I've never known a man to get rid of the ball so fast. I was on top of him every play but he'd still get his pass away." He smiled, reflecting on earlier years and other situations. "It wasn't one of our better games, and we know it. But when you can still win while not playing your best game, that's the mark of a good team."[15]

The next week, playing the Vikings in their Friday night home opener, the Rams won easily, 39-3. Deacon gave the Rams two points when he tackled Minnesota quarterback Joe Kapp in the end zone for a safety. Minnesota failed to make a yard rushing in the first half, and didn't get into Rams territory at all until the second half. The following Sunday, October 1, the Rams clashed with Dallas in the Cotton Bowl, in what was billed as a classic matchup, the NFL's best offensive team (the Cowboys) against the NFL's best defensive team. But the Rams showed all the offensive punch as Roman Gabriel engineered three long marches on the ground while Don Meredith was frustrated by the Rams defense, notably by Deacon Jones. Rams win, 35-13. Mal Florence noted: "Jones, who singlehandedly destroyed a Dallas threat in the first period, took charge again in the third quarter. He trailed an end run to nail Reeves for a seven-yard loss and set up a second-and-seventeen situation for Meredith at the Cowboy fourteen. Forced to pass, Meredith unloaded to Lance Rentzel, but the ball was tipped by the receiver and defender Irv Cross. Meador picked it off and stepped thirty yards down the sideline for a save."[16]

Various critics who had been critical of Roman Gabriel now pulled in their claws. Charles Maher, writing for the L.A. Times, said, "The fact is that Gabriel is looking better and better. Or to put it another way, the people who wrote him off as a plumber are looking worse and worse."

Cowboys coach Tom Landry was less impressed by Gabriel and the

15. Mal Florence, *Los Angeles Times*, September 18, 1967.
16. Mal Florence, *Los Angeles Times*, October 2, 1967.

Rams than he was distressed by his own team's poor showing. "We didn't have any offense, any defense, any kicking game," he said.

Two days before the game, Cowboy president Tex Schramm had charged that the Rams had a "spy" at the Dallas practice field, continuing the owner's long-time resentment against Allen. The Rams denied the charge, though in private many wondered what Tex was talking about, since every team in the league constantly and actively did their best to find out what their next week's rival was up to. Allen dismissed the charges as ridiculous, and would say of the victory only, "This one puts us over the hump!"[17]

Landry, refusing to go along with Schramm's game, wondered publicly how much a "spy" could accomplish watching practices. "If we lose," he said the Friday before the game, "this will be no excuse." But the Rams looked very good against Dallas, and this tended to put weight behind Schramm's contention that foul deeds had been perpetrated.

Deacon told the reporters after the game that the win had less to do with secret knowledge and more with football strategy. "What we did was take away their long bomb—the bomb to Bob Hayes. That's a big part of their attack. We did it with a big rush and double-coverage on Hayes."[18]

The Rams defense had put in another wrinkle for the Cowboys game, something that made it seem like they indeed had a flock of spies in Dallas. Landry ran the most complicated offense in the league, and to combat the Cowboys' dizzying effect on their defense, Allen had assigned veteran defense man Maxie Baughan to call signals in the game. There wasn't time to look back to the bench for advice; Baughan's assignment was to read the Cowboy's offensive set in a split second, decide on a counter-formation for his defense, and relay it to his teammates. This Baughan did with consistent success, and the Rams defense was regularly in position to snuff the Cowboys' charges. Considering the huge roar going up from the home crowd in the Cotton Bowl, Baughan must have had leather lungs. As he explained to the reporters who crowded around him after the game, "I called about five defensive plays in the huddle. The rest of the time I called audibles (positioning the defense after seeing how Dallas lined up). We had a simple game plan. It took us only about three days to learn it. We were running around like chickens with our heads cut off trying to get

17. Charles Maher, *Los Angeles Times,* October 2, 1967.
18. Ibid.

the thing down. Dallas has so many formations—and variations of formations."

Deacon admitted that small innovation was the key to their winning in Dallas. "Baughan did an absolutely marvelous job of calling defensive signals and we capitalized on it. He had us in the right formation almost every time. It was amazing."[19]

Indeed, it was amazing. To Schramm's disgust, Allen had found a way to out-fox the great Tom Landry. And three games into the season the Rams were 3-0.

Over a quarter of a century later Rayfield Wright, an offensive tackle and tight end out of Ft. Valley State, is talking to a crowd at the All-Time Black College All-Stars banquet in Baltimore. Rayfield remembers the 1967 Cowboys-Rams game for his own personal reasons, as clearly as if he's just come off the field. As a Dallas rookie, he'd been moved up to start for the Cowboys, and was playing in the third game of the season and one of the first games of his career. And, as fate would have it, he was playing across the line from Deacon Jones. As he tells it, "Now, you got to understand, I'm six foot seven, and my playing weight is 254. In my whole life, nobody ever, ever messes with Rayfield. I mess people, I don't get messed. So, our first offensive play of the game, I get down in my stance, I line up against the great Deacon Jones, an' the man talks to me, his voice all full of friendly concern. He says to me, 'Hey, Boy—does your mamma know you here?' I tell you I was froze, my feet stuck to the ground. Nobody talks to Rayfield that way! An' in that moment the center snap the ball an' Deacon goes flyin' by me like smoke!" The audience laughs, loving the tale of how the sly Deacon tricked yet another rookie. But here and there, throughout the crowd, the great players who had to face off against him in the good old days nod to themselves and smile ruefully. They each have a story or two to tell about Deacon Jones. If it wasn't his lightning speed, his moves, or the famous headslap, the man would juke you with a one-liner!

The Chip on Their Shoulders

Potato chips, crunch, crunch!
We'll have the 49'ers for lunch!

19. Charles Maher, *Los Angeles Times,* October 2, 1967.

The Rams looked enthusiastically forward toward their fourth win in a row. In practice the week before the 49ers game, they whooped and hollered and the "Potato Chips Ditty" became their war cry.

Deacon was at the absolute peak of his career. It was a rare day when a team was able to stop him for an entire game. Rival teams shifted their offense to compensate for him; still, on plays when they were able to hold him off with two or three offensive men, the shift made the Rams defense that much more effective, enabling other players to make the big play. By now, Deacon knew everyone in the league was after him. He had developed his speed and quickness to their limits. No one got off the ball faster than he did. His headslap, integrated into his charge, had become a refined boxing maneuver. He and Merlin Olsen had increased their unpredictability with the stunt, that is, a maneuver that has you lining up on one man and then trading assignments at the last minute and hitting another man. And when the entire front four decided to stunt together, it was a sight for the eyes, the entire front line slanting in from unexpected directions, and the offensive line picking up whomever they could. Deacon attacked opposing teams with a fury; he went at them tooth, nail—and tongue. "Lip jazz," he called it. Deacon got better and better at taunting his opponents. The Fearsome Foursome caught a lot of extra fury from the opposing linemen. Merlin couldn't understand it. He'd say, "Those guys are coming at us like fury! They're playing way over their heads. Deacon, why don't you just shut up?"

Deacon would grin at him, "They can't keep it up the whole game, Farm Boy."

"But meanwhile they're beatin' us up!"

"Are you scared, Merlin? A big guy like you—scared?"

Merlin wouldn't say anything to that. He would glower and go back to his position, and on the next snap he would come boiling off his point and like as not roll over two or three players and stop an offensive drive dead in its tracks.

Deacon would nod his pleasure, and when they were back at the line, standing there and glaring across no-man's land the way Svare had taught them, he would say, "See, we don't care, Merlin. 'Cause we are the best!"

Now, on an autumn Thursday as they prepared for their coming game with San Francisco, he gleefully chimed in with the rest,

Potato chips, crunch, crunch!
We'll have the 49'ers for lunch!

Lip jazz was his personal way of getting up for the game, of being able to drive through the pain of the hits he knew were coming. When he told the San Francisco reporters he was going to get five hits on Brodie, he knew they'd print it. Seeing his words in print, he knew he had to live up to them. Sure, it might inspire the rival team to play their best, but as a true professional what more could you ask for on a Sunday afternoon than the best playing their best?

All that having been said, there are times when a skilled motivator can use circumstances to raise the entire level of team play, and in such moments, even the least successful of teams can rise like dogs having their day. Was it a spy who spread the word or just a reporter? It didn't really matter, but somehow the word got out. The San Francisco 49ers have never liked their cousins to the south, and nobody likes to be compared to a potato chip. Jack Christiansen handed the offending news clipping around the locker room and the 49ers poured out on the playing field breathing fire.

Perhaps taken aback by the intensity of the game early on, Rams offensive blunders allowed San Francisco to take the lead. Meanwhile, quarterback John Brodie could do no wrong. His offensive line, determined to show they were not potato chips, and would not go over with a crunch, were managing to hold out the Fearsome Foursome just long enough for Brodie to get his passes away. By half time, the score stood at 20-0.

In the third quarter, the Fearsome Foursome, stung by their inability to get to Brodie, raised their own game to a higher level, managing to snuff San Francisco's offense. Meanwhile, Gabriel managed three touchdown drives for twenty-one points. And then the Rams got a field goal.

Leading 24-20 in the fourth quarter, and with the 49ers pinned second and ten deep in their own territory, the defense gambled with the blitz. The game could have been over in one play. But again, the 49ers line held just long enough for Brodie to get his passes away. After two long gainers, San Francisco's spirits revived and they drove for a touchdown. And with six minutes left, they snuffed a conservative Rams drive and managed to hold their hated rivals away from a score. It was San Francisco, 27-24.

After the game, Allen responded to the howls from his critics, who felt the Rams had reverted to "safe" football at just the wrong time. "Gabe called what he thought was correct. What if he had thrown the ball and it had been picked off? We'd been moving the ball well on the ground. Anyway, I had told them at halftime not to try and get rich on one play."[20]

For his own part, Deacon was disgusted. They hadn't gotten to Brodie once all afternoon. Merlin's dire predictions had finally come true; they had taunted their rivals into victory. Was that enough to make him change his style of attack, to give up lip jazz in exchange for a quieter lifestyle? Hardly. He got where he was by speaking his mind, and it wasn't likely he would change now. The 49ers had gotten the upper hand early. The Rams had fought back and narrowly missed the victory. The season was young, and the Rams were three and one. They were winners. The future was now. You didn't switch what got you to this point. All they would have to do was play flawless ball for the rest of the season.

Deacon talks about his methods of psychological warfare. "I don't recommend my style for everybody. Don't say it unless you are going to do it. I had my opponents afraid of what I was about, but I backed my noise up with my performance. To raise my level of play to the next higher elevation, I turned my participation in the game into a media thing. I got a thrill out of telling the enemy what I was going to do. 'Hey, sucker—I'm going to get five on you today!'

"All that lip jazz was necessary for my own survival. I gave 110 percent on every play. That meant on Monday when I was hurting from yesterday's game, I needed to create the work ethic that would build my edge for my next opponent. So I would start to let it be known what the Deacon was going to do next Sunday.

"All week long I'd hit the press with the 'I'm going to tear his head off' routine. That meant that at game time when Sunday rolled around, I had to come through. And that's when the time for all the yelling and fuss and commotion was gone. That's when I turned into the cold-blooded killer of quarterbacks that I really was. I was in the game, mentally and physically. Executing, probing for weaknesses, looking, trying to find some way to beat my opponent's ass. I knew his weakness might just surface on one play, and that would win the game for us, if I could just spot that weakness.

"I'd made the threats all week—now it was make-good time. There was nothing emotional about it. Oh, if I knew you'd had a fight with your wife last week, I might mention it . . . but that's about as personal as I'd get with the enemy."

---

20. Mal Florence, *Los Angeles Times,* October 9, 1967.

When asked about the Potato Chip Incident, the old reflex action kicks in, and Deacon is reluctant to admit another person or another team ever got the edge over him. "No," he replies, "The 'Crunch Crunch' chant didn't have anything to do with our losing that game. We were flat defensively, and we take the fall for that. Our offense was terrible, particularly in the first half, and we also take the responsibility for that." In such situations, you never let the other man know he got the upper hand, not even twenty-five years after the fact.

On Kissing Your Sister—Twice in a Row

With Baltimore leading 24-14 in the final quarter, with sixty thousand screaming Ram-haters packing Memorial Stadium, time winding down and nowhere else to go, the Rams scored ten points in three minutes to tie the game. After that, George Allen ordered his team into a conservative mode, and they ended the game in a 24-24 tie. When criticized for not letting it all hang out in a do-or-die attempt to win, George Allen would only say, "A tie can't hurt us. We play them again, and if we wind up in a tie for first, we'll win the division by beating them."[21]

Roman Gabriel said of his last offensive series, "They were in a zone defense and protecting against deep passes. They expected us to throw, and we thought we could pick up a first down by running."

Neither the Rams coach nor their quarterback alluded to the fact that the referee's calls had been running against them all day, with 121 yards chalked up against the L.A. team. It may well have been for this reason that Allen chose to play it safe. After all, there was far more than the outcome of a single game in question; they were playing for big stakes here, in one sense, for all the marbles. With no "wild card" picks, each game was a must win for the division leaders. And here in Baltimore, one more bad call by the officials could hand the Colts the win and the division title on a silver platter before the season was half over.

For Deacon, this was history repeating itself; two years before, he had been cited for three face mask infractions in this same stadium. Now, in this game, he, Lamar Lundy and Rams defensive back Claude Crabb seemed singled out by the officials. Is it any wonder George Allen chose to preserve the tie?

---

21. Mal Florence, *Los Angeles Times*, October 16, 1967.

Still, after the game no one was willing to talk about the officiating—except Deacon Jones.

"It always seems to happen here," he said to the reporters after the game, choosing his words carefully as he picked his way through the verbal minefield. After all, there was a league mandate that no player or coach was ever to second-guess or question an official's decision, much less his competence. "I'm distressed," Deacon went on, "because I believe the officials protect Unitas. If you get even close to him, it's a flag. They have got their hands right on their hip pockets. We had to let up on Unitas because of this. You do things you normally wouldn't do."[22]

On one play, Deacon threw Lennie Moore for a two yard loss, but an official determined that he had caressed Lennie's face mask.

"I had him around the neck," Deacon told the reporters, who asked about the play. "I didn't touch his mask."

A few plays later, Irv Cross was called for pass interference. Then Lamar Lundy was charged with a fifteen-yard penalty for face-masking Unitas. Lamar, who had frowned and shook his head while Deacon talked to the press, refused to comment on his own penalty. Instead, he took Deacon by the arm and quietly drew him away from the sports writers toward their lockers.

"You know it ain't gonna do a bit of good, 'cept get the owners riled up at you," he said as they left.

In the other camp, Unitas automatically told the press the same thing he always said when asked about a face-mask infraction. "He nearly yanked my head off."

Were the officials zeroing in on the Rams defense, and if so, why? Studying the game film, it looks like they were, but there is no way to know why. One thing is certain; in the entire season before the Rams game, Unitas had been so well protected by his offensive line and the officials that he'd been thrown for only one loss. In this game, not counting the plays called back because of face-masking, the Rams managed to get to Unitas three times. Those three plays, however, clearly and obviously ended in clean tackles and so the officials didn't dare throw their yellow flags.

In Washington the following week, still playing cautiously to avoid penalties from the quick-flagging refs, the Rams allowed quick-releasing Sonny Jurgensen to hit fleet Charley Taylor, Jerry Smith, and

---

22. Mal Florence, *Los Angeles Times,* October 16, 1967.

Bobby Mitchell with long bombs. Jurgensen completed eighteen of forty-one for 337 yards and four touchdowns.

After the game, Coach Otto Graham attributed the tie—considered a moral victory for the weak Redskins—to a psychological ploy on his part. The week before, the Fearsome Foursome had been featured in a *Life* magazine article. Graham said, "I took that article and pasted it on our bulletin board. Football is 90 percent motivation. If you can get your people to go out there and really hit people, you're going to win."

For his part, George Allen was disappointed. "A tie," he said, "is never satisfactory when you think you are the better team."[23] The Ram's fans, always quick to show their displeasure, heartily agreed. As *L.A. Times* writer John Hall put it, "The Rams fans are back again—with very free and loud advice."[24]

Saturday evenings, after their final practice before Sunday's game, Allen always held a meeting that was half game preparation and half Baptist revival. The Saturday after their tie with the Redskins, he gathered his team in the dank and shabby locker room assigned to them under Wrigley stadium to talk about the coming Bears game. As usual, after discussing the game plan and as many details of the coming game as he could think of, Allen threw the floor open to the players. One by one, they talked about their concern with the officiating, until Allen held up his hands and stood. "Fellas, I don't blame anybody on this team for the bulk of the penalties we've been drawing. Maybe, in a sport obsessed by offense, you can make a case that somebody is out to get us. But we'll never prove it. We all know that there's a lot that goes on behind the scenes that the fans and even the sports writers never figure out. That's just the way the game is played. But we can't dwell on that. It would just drive us all crazy. Wasted energy. We're winners, fellas. Winners. And winners don't fuss away their time and attention on the wrong thing." He paused. "What are we?"

"Winners!" a few voices in the crowd said.

"What are we?" He asked more insistently.

"Winners!!" they all roared.

"That's right. We take our lumps and get ready as best we can for the next game. I think we made a mistake in Baltimore, and we carried it over to Washington. Now, it's my fault as much as yours; I should have figured this out sooner. The way I see it, we got hesitant.

23. Mal Florence, *Los Angeles Times,* October 23, 1967.
24. John Hall, *Los Angeles Times,* October 23, 1967.

They got us to stop playing our game. Remember: Winners always do what they do best. They play their own game!" Allen paused and cocked his head to one side, "And what are we?"

"Winners!!!" The words rocked the room.

"Do you know what that means?"

"No, what?" they shouted.

"It means you fellas get back to hitting hard, and damn the consequences! We've got the best team in the league, and if it takes eleven Bears on the field and all the referees in Chicago to stop us, so be it!"

George hardly ever swore, and his mild "damn" had a riveting effect. His players stood to a man and raised their fists, and their cheers filled the small room. George gave a brief nod and a grim smile. They were definitely ready for whatever the Bears and Old Man Halas could throw at them.

Bruce Allen talks about his dad, the leader of men. "He learned motivation on his own. It was his idea to have a cake on Thursday after practice, to celebrate the coming victory! And he would have an awards session on Tuesday after a victory, where he might give out twenty-five incentive prizes. He lived the game of football, and that love was infectious."

Deacon fondly remembers the "George Allen Tuesday Evening Awards Ceremonies." "They really were fun, but there was a serious edge, too. If you didn't get an award, you knew you really hadn't played well. There would be TV sets and stereos for knocking the quarterback out of the game. If it was Roger Staubach of the hated Cowboys, you might get both a color TV and a stereo. But it wasn't the money. After all, for the most part we're talking about things like clock radios, and dinner for two, and maybe a pair of shoes for the guy who ran and hustled the best. What was important was the public recognition in front of your peers that you'd done an outstanding piece of work."

Jamming the Counts

The Rams won on a rainy, murky day in Chicago. They won on a halfback option play where Gabriel handed off to Tommy Mason who threw a fifty-one-yard touchdown pass to Bernie Casey. It didn't set well in Chicago with the fans, who booed and threw beer bottles from the screened-off catwalk as the L.A. team walked by. The fans hissed and jeered the Rams, but they set up a cheer for their head coach. "We want you back, George!"[25]

It was a sloppy grudge match, with five Rams fumbles offset by two Bear fumbles and three interceptions. The Rams' eighty-four yards in penalties was offset by seventy yards for the Bears. The difference may have been the Rams improved running game, paced by Les Josephson, Dick Bass, and Tommy Mason. The victory in Chicago was sweet, and nobody complained about the officiating as they climbed on a plane and headed west.

The Rams, the team everybody in the league loved to hate, next played their old rivals, the 49ers, in a repeat match. This time there were no Potato Chip chants to buoy up the San Francisco team; the Rams came away winners in a game dominated by the Fearsome Foursome and the rest of the L.A. defense.

Deacon talked about the win after the game. "We didn't play our type of game in the first half. We were playing a reading defense, standing and waiting. In the second half, we came off the ball fast and went after them. I think we rattled Brodie. He's a good quarterback, but he doesn't like to get hit. He was just trying to get rid of the ball."[26]

On a key play in the fourth quarter, with the game close and on the line, Deacon hurried Brodie, forcing him to throw a wobbly pass that was intercepted by Maxie Baughan. This put the Rams in position for a game-clenching field goal. Deacon then forced Brodie to fumble and lose the ball as the 49ers tried to mount a final drive.

But the game brought on another controversy. San Francisco coach Jack Christiansen accused George Allen of an old defensive ploy that he claimed was a dirty trick. He accused Allen of ordering the "jamming" of 49er offensive signals. Jamming is calling signals against the opponent's count at the line of scrimmage to throw off their timing. It is an extremely grey area, as both offense and defense have the right to call signals at the same time, and it is difficult for the referees to spot. With the roar of the crowd, the offense and defense calling signals, and the quarterback barking out the play, it takes training and discipline to sort out which signal is your own. Allen and Baughan, the defensive signal caller, denied the charge, but once again the bitter scent of hate and envy was in the air. Allen said, "If they said we were jamming, they're incorrect. We have audibles on defense, just like every team does. And they have nothing to do with the other team's offen-

---

25. Mal Florence, *Los Angeles Times,* October 30, 1967.
26. Mal Florence, *Los Angeles Times,* November 6, 1967.

sive cadence." Baughan agreed, "I wasn't jamming anything. I was calling audibles. If they were running a quick count, then they'd have some excuse for making comments like that. But they weren't, so I don't think they have any gripe."[27]

Christiansen's team had been called for three illegal procedures and three offside penalties. He blamed it all on the Rams: "The Rams were jamming our counts. It's against the rules; it's illegal, causing us to jump. I protested to the officials but I got about as far as the other protests in the world seem to be getting today—nowhere."[28]

Upon further questioning by the reporters, the 49ers coach said some revealing things about how a large segment of the coaches regarded George Allen. The *L.A. Times* recorded the following comment: "He learned it from Halas," snapped Christiansen. "Or maybe he taught it to Halas."[29]

The question of jamming was an old one. Allen had been an assistant to Halas in 1960, the year before Deacon signed on with the Rams. In a controversial game played that year, Rams coach Bob Waterfield accused Bears linebacker Bill George of jamming his team's counts. Waterfield criticized both the game officials and Halas, and drew a $500 fine from the NFL office for speaking his mind.

Asked about the jamming, Brodie didn't give his own head coach much support. "I didn't really notice it," he said. "I don't pay attention to things like that—that's the referee's job."

The following Wednesday after practice, Deacon poked his head in Allen's office. He and Allen, as usual, were two of the last Rams still in the locker room.

"Am I botherin' you, Coach?"

Allen set aside a pile of papers on his desk and smiled, "No, of course not." Indicating the statistics he'd been going over, he said, "I am more and more convinced that one of the most important statistics in football is the ratio of giveaways to takeaways. And, do you know, some coaches around the league don't even keep track of them?"

Deacon knew Allen kept track of everything. He took nothing for

---

27. A quick count is a signal which is rushed or shortened to get the play started before the defense is really ready for the ball to be snapped. Maxie's point is that the auditory signal becomes very important on a quick count. The offensive line is more tense than usual, poised to release their stance and fling themselves across the line on that verbal signal, and so any "jamming" of the signals could cause confusion, an early release, and the attendant five yard penalty for being off-sides.

28. Dwight Chapin, *Los Angeles Times,* November 6, 1967.

29. Ibid.

granted. Allen felt that moves that a player took for granted, moves they thought they'd perfected in high school, still had to be practiced and perfected. He put in fumble drills, drills that no running back in America liked. He did it to every back who fumbled the ball. He'd form two rows of linemen, and the back would have to run through there while everyone tried to strip the ball and hit him with arm dummies.

Allen turned his bright, intense stare on his star defensive end. "What can I do for you, Deacon?"

Deacon took the seat Allen indicated, and set his helmet down. "I been thinking on all this talk about us jamming the counts." George nodded, listening, while Deacon continued. "Now I been around seven years, Coach, an' in all that time it seems to me everybody tries to step on everybody's count." Allen nodded again. "But I read what you told the press, and you didn't say anything about that. You just denied it all."

Allen smiled. "And you want to know why."

"Well, yes, sir."

"Good question. There's not really a simple answer. First, you'll notice the good teams, the disciplined teams are the ones who successfully jam the counts on teams that aren't quite that good, not quite that well disciplined. A team like Green Bay jams the counts as a matter of course. The refs up in Green Bay are used to the Packers barking like that. The Packers are proven winners. To call jamming on them now would mean the officials have been ignoring an illegal 'dirty trick' for decades. We both know they can't admit that.

"Of course, we don't complain about teams jamming our counts. Even good teams have a hard time jamming us, because we *train* for it. Our offensive players know what to listen for, how to pick their own signals out of the roar of the crowd and everything going on down on the field. What Christiansen is admitting, even though he doesn't know it, is that he hasn't trained his team to be successful in this area."

Deacon grinned. "But you didn't say any of that to the press."

"And have our next opponent that much more prepared? Christiansen's already done enough damage, and he knows it. I hear you're a good poker player, Deacon, so I'm sure you understand. Then, too, no coach in the league would admit to jamming—after all, it is illegal."

"Even if everybody does it."

"Yes, but with different degrees of effectiveness." Allen mused to himself for a moment, and then leaned back in his chair. "This is a great game, Deacon. Maybe the greatest game in the world. Better than poker, better than chess, even. There's so much to know, so much to learn! I'm still learning every day. Any one of a thousand circumstances can win a ball game, and at least half of them are outside the rules! Look at a few of the obvious ones. When the 49ers forced us to play in the Kezar mud-pit a year or two ago, that wasn't in any rule book, and yet they nullified our tremendous defensive superiority and our excellent passing game and were eventually able to beat us. You've got to give them credit for that. When the crowds in Dallas and Chicago and Baltimore yell so loud we can't call an audible, we are put at a real disadvantage. Yet they get away with it. How many games a year do you think the screaming fans win for them? One of the reasons we are competitive with them is that we practice for it, knowing they're going to pull that one on us. We do our best to get the playing field as level as possible."

"So dirty tricks are okay?"

"Not a *real* dirty trick like a punch after the whistle or a crack-block where some player is sure to get hurt. But look at all the other things. Every offensive man in football knows he has to hold the Fearsome Foursome whenever he can. Lombardi or Landry would be foolish to instruct their men any other way. There is a good percentage in holding Deacon Jones. Chances are, the refs won't even see it, much less call it. And if Forrest Gregg is able to illegally but successfully hold you out on a critical play by grabbing your jersey and pulling you down, if he's not caught at it, and if Starr is able to heave a winning toss into the end zone, why, the Packers win, whether we complain about it in the sports pages or not. That's the other half of the game of football, the part nobody can or will really talk about to the reporters. Losers who find excuses are billed as complainers, while winners are, well, just winners!"

"Seems to me like they trying to take away the taste of our win."

"That's right, Deacon, they are. But they can't. You earned the game ball last Sunday. You earned it. We all earned the victory. Christiansen and the rest of them would love to take that away from us, to turn us sour by denying our win, to weaken us for next week. In the NFL, they'll use anything they can against us, on or off the field. They'll try to get at me. Or you. Or anybody on our team. They'll try to cause a split between players, between player and coach, even between coach and team owner. It's not personal; that's just pro football."

"I think a lot of stuff they say against you is personal."

Allen looked at the sign on his wall which read, "To be successful, you must win. To win, you must *work hard*." "We have to stay focused,

Deacon. We can't let them throw us off. We have to prove we are champions. We can do that, can't we?"

"Yes, sir!"

Deacon left Allen's office the way he always did, filled with fire and determination. Was there ever in the entire history of the game another coach like George Allen?

Deacon thinks back to the campaign of 1967: "For a while that year, our rivals actually had thrown us off our game. The Fearsome Foursome was so successful and devastating and the teams we played complained so bitterly that they had the refs convinced we were cheating at every turn. To be so dominating, the line of thinking went, we had to be doing something wrong. We were cast as the bullies, the bad guys. Instead of concentrating on fair officiating, the men in the striped suits were ready with the yellow flag every time we charged across the line, every time we made a tackle. And that, in turn, got us hesitating and cost us several wins."

"Of course, our drive for the championship itself was determined by the condition of the field as much as the rules of the game. We played our first playoff game in Green Bay on a treacherous, slippery field. I was double-teamed by Forrest Gregg and Marv Fleming, but the real secret was that they nullified my—all of our—speed and quickness with the playing conditions. Sure, nobody can change the weather, but to this day, I'd really like to know if the weather alone beat us or just exactly how they prepared that field. But, as George would say, if he were alive today: 'We can't make an excuse for that. It was just another aspect of the game, and we should have found a way to overcome it.' "

The Winning Trail

The Rams beat Philadelphia in a game so one-sided the high point was the still-injured Rosey Grier's halftime show, which was reported in the sports section the next day as a "polished singing performance." The low point, at least for Deacon, was Eagles offensive tackle Bob Brown, who was playing across the line from him. Deacon had played Brown twice before: in 1964, when the big tackle was a rookie, and in a preseason game the following year. In both games Deacon had "dusted his ass," as they say, and so this year Brown decided to do something about it. When they got down into their stance, he gave

Deacon a peculiar grin. Deacon figured he'd slap the grin right off his face, so coming off the snap, he led with his thunderous left, the way he often did. He sent Brown reeling, and got through to pressure Norm Snead, the Eagles' quarterback, but on returning to the line, Deacon noticed his hand was bleeding. On the next play, he gave Brown another headslap, and again took another deep gash in the palm of his hand. Bob had filed the extra chin strap snap on the side of his helmet to a razor sharpness. At the end of the series, Deacon went to the sidelines and had his hand taped, but nothing worked. The knife-like metal jutting out from Bob's helmet cut right through gloves, tape, anything.

Deacon gritted his teeth and swung away. If he gave even an inch, next week everyone in the league would have their helmets sharpened. Led by Jones, the Rams' front four harassed Norm Snead all day, and, with the Rams leading 26-10 in the fourth quarter, Allen went for the first down in a fourth and one situation from his own twenty-two. Owner Dan Reeves, who had been quiet in public of late, chided him for that one, but, since the Rams made the first down, he couldn't really say anything. After the game, Deacon didn't say anything about Brown's knife trick to the press. He hid his bloody hand behind his back and complimented the Fearsome Foursome on another job well done.

The following week the Rams scored twenty-four points in the fourth quarter to put the Falcons away. The defense led the charge, setting up the first two touchdowns as the Fearsome Foursome crushed every Atlanta attempt at offense. Atlanta had never liked George Allen, and when Norm Hector was asked if he was angry that the Rams "poured it on late in the game with a trick play," the Falcons head coach responded coldly, "They run the plays they want to run."[30]

Playing in Atlanta could be treacherous; the field was still set up for baseball, and where the infield met the grass of the outfield, the footing was dangerous. On one of the first plays of the game, Deacon tore some ligaments in the arch of his right foot, his push-off foot. He managed to stay in and play the game, but he was in great pain, and he was sure it showed on the game films. That was bad, because everybody in the league would see those films, and know he was hurting.

They played the Lions four days later, Thanksgiving in Detroit. Deacon had his foot taped as best he could and started the game. On

---

30. Mal Florence, *Los Angeles Times,* November 20, 1967.

the first play from scrimmage, Charley Bradshaw, the Lions' offensive tackle playing opposite Deacon, managed to step on his foot. Bradshaw grinned and ground his cleats into Deacon's foot. Deacon gritted his teeth and went off the field. On the sidelines, the trainers took him behind the bench and threw a blanket over his leg; the doctor gave him a huge shot directly into the top of his foot. The pain was incredible for the first thirty seconds or so. After that, Deacon's entire foot felt numb, like a block of wood. Deacon tested it, and to his surprise he could accelerate on it. He nodded to Allen and went back in to serve justice on Bradshaw and the Lions.

The Rams defense was the story again, holding the NFL's leading ground-gaining team to ninety-two yards and seven points. Gabriel had the offense rolling, and they won, 31-7. In beating the Lions they became the first Rams team in the club's history to avoid defeat on the road for an entire season. By playing on his injured foot, Deacon strained it to the point where it would bother him off and on for the rest of his career. But his slashing play convinced Charley Bradshaw and the rest of the league that nothing serious was wrong with him. Of course, Deacon was careful that the press never got wind of it. By now he knew he couldn't show any weakness, or the wolves would circle and quickly take him down.

The following Sunday, Deacon was back in top form as the Rams whipped the Falcons in a repeat performance. Mal Florence described the action for the *L.A. Times*: "If the Rams offense stuttered at times, it was immaterial in the final analysis as Allen's defensive assassins had control of the game."

The Rams were now 9-1-2, but in terms of the championship, their season was only beginning. In the days before the wild card teams could go to the playoffs, the Rams were in the same division with mighty Green Bay and powerful Baltimore, the toughest teams in the league. They would have to beat the Packers and the Colts once just to get to the playoffs, and then beat the Packers again for the right to play in the championship game.

George Allen, getting his troops ready, told the press, "We've got to do it ourselves. We don't need anybody else. It's our job."[31]

But, the following Saturday, December 9 in the Coliseum before a sellout crowd of over seventy-six thousand screaming fans, it looked like they weren't going to get the job done. With fifty-four seconds remain-

---

31. John Hall, *Los Angeles Times,* December 4, 1967.

ing, Green Bay had the ball and a 24-20 lead. All the Packers had to do was punt the ball deep into Rams territory, and hold them off for one series. Green Bay went into their kicking formation and on the snap Allen sent his special punt-blocking team across the line in a nine-man rush. It was a play you don't see much in a game, but Allen's special teams practiced it all the time. Now Allen's attention to detail was to have its reward; Green Bay's line faltered and then caved in, and the Rams came streaming through, angling for the punter, with Tony Guillory and Deacon Jones closest to the ball. Guillory got his body in front of the football and both men managed to avoid roughing the kicker. The Rams took over deep in Green Bay territory. A few plays later, the Rams scored to take the lead, 27-24. Still, the Packers, who had been the 1966 NFL world champions, tried to mount one more comeback. But the chance for a last-second miracle was snuffed out by Deacon Jones, who buried Starr for a seven-yard loss on his own thirty-four yard line. Deacon, who used the sack to celebrate his twenty-ninth birthday, said, "He put a fake on me the likes of which Tarkenton never did. Whew, I feel like I had twenty birthdays today. Look at these grey hairs!"[32]

Was this the greatest Ram victory of all time? John Hall of the *Times* put the question to Dan Reeves. The Rams owner, who was winning more but seemed to be enjoying it less, thought for a moment and started to say something about "a time in the forties when Bob Waterfield trailed Green Bay by twenty-four points going into the final quarter." But then Reeves stopped. "There'll never be a greater win than this one," he decided.[33]

Since the Rams first game at Baltimore earlier in the season ended in a 24-24 tie, the playoff rules of the day dictated that the team scoring the most points against the other would be the winner of the Coastal Division. In 1967, there were four divisions in the National Football League, the Capitol and the Century Divisions in the Eastern Conference and the Central and Coastal Divisions in the Western Conference. The Packers had already won in the Central Division. The Rams had to get past Johnny Unitas and the Colts to play the Green Bay team for the NFL championship and the right to play the winners of the upstart American Football League in Super Bowl II.[34]

32. Mal Florence, *Los Angeles Times,* December 10, 1967.

33. John Hall, *Los Angeles Times,* December 10, 1967.

34. The NFL reluctantly recognized the AFL; the two leagues were finally united in 1966 for financial reasons. The bidding war for players' services was costing both sides a fortune, and could not continue. As a result, fans everywhere benefited, with more teams and a "grand championship" game which came to be known as the Super Bowl.

In the second quarter of the Colts game, with the Rams leading 10-7, Deacon featured in what Charles Maher of the *Times* described as "the biggest play of the biggest game the Rams have played in more than a decade." The Colts had the ball and were charging deep into L.A. territory. With a second and six from the L.A. twenty-seven, Unitas dropped back to pass. He spotted his primary receiver Lenny Moore in the clear on the right side and cocked his arm. At that moment, Deacon hit him and managed to grab one leg, jerking him off-balance as he brought his arm back. In another fraction of a second, the rest of the Rams defense caught up and somebody else slammed into Unitas as he brought his arm forward, still doggedly determined to hit Moore. But the ball floated and was intercepted by Eddy Meador, who returned it to the Rams nineteen. So, instead of trailing 14-10, the Rams scored and extended their lead to 17-7. Momentum swung to the Rams.[35] In the last half, their defense gave Unitas such a powerful rush that the Colts could only score one field goal. Gabriel was eighteen of twenty-two for three touchdowns. Unitas was spilled for losses seven times and completed only one touchdown pass. He was nineteen of thirty-one, with two interceptions. To date he had been caught behind the line a total of only eighteen times in thirteen games.[36]

After the game, Deacon talked about the play that turned the tide in the Rams favor: "I made my usual charge outside. They were down near our twenty, so I figured it was going to be a quick pass. I had to make a fast move. I got by my man, and there was Unitas. I couldn't really hit him the way I wanted to. I had just gotten around my man and I wasn't going full speed. When I hit Unitas, I started sliding down him. But I did manage to hold on to one leg. I was turning his leg, doing everything I could to get him down. Now, of course, I'm happy I didn't get him down."

Unitas remarked, "I was on the way down. I should never have thrown it. It was my fault."

Commenting on the seven quarterback sacks engineered by the Rams in that game, Deacon said, "It wasn't the work of the front four alone. It's not any one part of the defense that allows you to get to the quarterback. You have to have good coverage as well as a strong rush. With good coverage, you force the quarterback to stop and pump before he throws. In my own case, I sometimes have three guys to beat before I get to the passer. And I need every second our defensive backs

35. Charles Maher, *Los Angeles Times,* December 18, 1967.
36. Paul Zimmerman, *Los Angeles Times,* December 18, 1967.

can give me by staying with their men. Today we got great coverage. Today was really the first time we put our defense, our offense, and our kicking game together. We knew when we finally did, somebody was going to pay for it."[37]

Allen smiled. "It's the greatest victory in Rams history," he said. The team had won the Coastal Division, and it should have been a time for celebration. But even as he spoke, Allen seemed a little distracted. It was easy to see he was already looking forward to the play-off game against Green Bay.

Two years later, Bob Brown joined the Rams and became part of the offensive line. Deacon showed him the scars on his hand, and Bob admitted he'd filed his helmet down in an attempt to nullify the headslap. Today, the circular scars are still plainly visible on the palm of Deacon's left hand.

When Deacon injured his right foot, Jerry Glanville, later to be the head coach of the Atlanta Falcons, was a scout for the Rams. He remembers being on the sidelines when Deacon took the shot. "The trainers threw a blanket over Deacon's leg, and when the team doctor stuck that big horse needle in the top of his foot and squeezed in the painkiller, the pain was so intense he gave out a horrible scream. It was only the roar of the tens of thousands of fans in the stadium that kept him from being overheard. A few minutes later, and he was back in the game."

Deacon shrugs, thinking about Bradshaw's motivation: "Bradshaw had been my teammate, early in his career. But that didn't stop him from stepping on my foot to get me out of the game. He figured, if he could get the world's premier pass rusher and killer of quarterbacks out of the game, why not? That's what it's like in professional football, in the game the fans never see and the reporters never report. It's trench warfare—gladiator-style combat—and your enemies will do anything they can get away with to get you out of the game. When I think about it, it makes my fourteen years in the game without a major injury seem like a miracle. Mattie Jones, back there in Eatonville, must have loaded up on the prayers to get me through."

37. Charles Maher, *Los Angeles Times*, December 18, 1967.

Spiked

The way Vince Lombardi explained it after the game, it was an entirely logical decision to run the ball into the sharp teeth of the league's second-best defense against the run. "We double-teamed Jones and took him out," Green Bay's legendary coach added. He didn't say anything about the playing field.

The game, played on a frigid day in Milwaukee, went to the Packers 28-7, and the Rams' dreams of a championship evaporated like the steam from their breath in the cold air. Early on, with the Rams leading 7-0, Rams linebacker Jack Pardee came in too strong as rookie Packer halfback Travis Williams cut inside. Rams cornerback Clancy Williams came in, too, to cover Carroll Dale, so he was out of the play. Travis simply outran the rest, ninety-six yards off right tackle to score. Much of the day went like that.

The victory seemed easy, the way Forrest Gregg, the eleven-year Packer veteran assigned to Deacon, explained it. "My man was Deacon Jones. I had the Deacon stuck in my mind all week until the picture was burning there." The implication is that drive and personal determination wins out over all. Gregg didn't say anything about the field, either, though it had been slick as glass.

Talking about their win in a *Sports Illustrated* article by Tex Maule, Packer linebacker Ray Nitschke went a little further, painting Deacon as the sucker to the Packers' unique and special strategy. "The key was taking care of Deacon Jones, who had been a menace all day when the Rams beat us. We set out to whip Deacon Jones and that's just what we did. The Packers ran at Jones, double-teaming him on sweeps, until he was so conscious of the run that he hesitated on his pass rush. The rest of the Ram defense was wondering what had happened to Jones and why he wasn't getting in on the passer and they began to hesitate and wait until they were being whipped as badly as Jones was." Nitschke also avoided any reference to the playing conditions.[38]

It was strange that the Packers should be so brilliantly successful against Deacon with maneuvers other teams had tried for years without much success at all, with the possible exception of the 49ers on a muddy field in San Francisco. After all, Deacon was double-teamed as a matter of course on nearly every play of every game with every team. Still, in the NFL, winners give reasons and losers give excuses.

---

38. Tex Maule, *Sports Illustrated,* January, 1968, also referenced in Bill Libby, *Life in the Pit,* page 107.

But what really happened in that critical postseason game, now all but lost in football history, where the temperature dropped from twenty degrees at the opening kickoff to eight degrees at the final gun? The game film shows that the Rams offensive line could not keep the Packers away from Gabriel, who was thrown five times for long losses. Meanwhile, the Packer blockers were able to hold out the Fearsome Foursome and the other Rams rushers. The theory of that day, advanced by L.A. sports writers, was that the Rams, used to playing in more temperate climates, had choked in the Wisconsin chill.

Jim Murray wrote in the *Times*:

> The Rams didn't need a football to play Green Bay in Milwaukee, they needed a St. Bernard. The Rams were frozen so solid by the second half that if they turned up on your front lawn you would put a stovepipe hat and coal buttons on them. Guys who come from a climate where summer is a season where your sled occasionally hits a rock can block and tackle—and pass—better in fourteen degree weather than guys to whom winter is a time when you only have to mow the lawn twice a week, or when you can't go swimming at night.[39]

If Green Bay or the NFL had been all that interested in fairness, they could have moved the game from icy Milwaukee Stadium to Lambeau Field, where Lombardi had installed a heating system of electrical wires under the gridiron, and where the Packers played most of their games, anyway. The system, still in use today, drives the frost out of the ground and is capable of maintaining decent playing conditions in fairly cold weather.[40]

Later, when he heard all the Packer crowing about how they'd duped him to win the game, Deacon reflected that they were about half-right. "The problem I couldn't handle in Milwaukee was rushing the passer against double-team blocking on a field that was frozen like ice. I couldn't get myself going fast enough on the ice to get them before they set up their blocks. The ice under my feet took away my quickness off the ball and gave the blockers the edge. Normally, I go with my legs spread.

---

39. Jim Murray, *Los Angeles Times,* December 24, 1967.

40. Todd Eidelbeck, a groundskeeper for the Packers, confirmed in 1992 that the system is capable of keeping the field in excellent condition in all but the worst of circumstances. Had they played at Lambeau, normal turf conditions might have prevailed throughout the game, in spite of a sharp temperature drop that occurred, with the ground retaining its warmth. However, that would not have been in the Packer's best interest.

On a slippery field, I had to keep my legs together in order to keep my balance. I could have beaten Gregg that way, but not Gregg *and* Fleming. Most of our team had the same problem; we burned other teams with our speed at the line. We came up off the ball like lightning, we were a quick team. Players who rely on speed play the game on their toes. But you had to play flat-footed in Green Bay or you'd fall flat on your face. We never did get used to it, and that cost us the game."

Flying back to Los Angeles, the players were silent, each member of the team lost in his own thoughts. Allen was sitting alone near the back of the plane, staring out the window when Deacon dropped by.

"Sorry," Deacon said, taking the seat next to his coach for a moment. There was really nothing he could say that was important or made any sense.

Allen sighed and nodded slightly. "Thanks, Deacon," he said. "You did your best. You all did your best."

"We didn't play like champions. We don't deserve the brass ring."

"No, Deacon, you played like real winners. You are winners in my heart. Of all the teams I've coached and will coach, I'll never forget this team." Allen paused. "You men really turned it around this year." He looked at the neat line of notes he'd been penciling on a yellow legal pad on his lap. "If you include the preseason games, this team is 17-2-2. When we win the runner-up bowl, we will be 18-2-2, the most successful from a won/loss standpoint in Rams history—since the beginning of the franchise."

"But we lost when it counted, Coach."

Allen nodded. "That's true. You've got to get to the big one to play in the big one. Still, you are champions, and I think I personally let you all down."

"No. Can't be. How do you figure?"

"I wouldn't be a bit surprised if Lombardi had somebody hose down that field last week. Or maybe they just didn't cover it, didn't protect it from the elements and let it get that way. That sure suited their purposes. They're much slower than we are, particularly at the line, and they know it. We already proved we can beat them on a regular playing surface. So they got nature to become their ally. We had to play eleven Packers and Old Man Winter."

"How can that be your fault, Coach? Man can't fight the weather."

"The shoes could have saved us," George sighed. "Damn!—I should have paid more attention to the shoes!" It was one of the few times Deacon heard Allen use anything stronger than "darn."

"Hell, what do you mean, the shoes? We had three pair each, Coach." At one of their endless meetings, when discussing the possibilities of playing in the Midwest in December, they had reviewed the matter of shoes, and decided on three pairs per player—sneakers with sucker-type grippers on their rubber soles, regular cleated shoes, and a special shoe with cleats which were little more than short metal spikes.

"I know," Allen nodded. "And under normal conditions that would have been enough. But the championship of the world was at stake here. We should have asked ourselves, 'How far will the Packers go to win the championship?' In other words, 'What options are available to them?' We know we're playing on their field. 'What might they do to nullify our advantage in speed and quickness?' We should have figured that gridiron would be like a skating rink. With the temperature near zero anyway, nobody would question it. The spikes on those special shoes we made up were too short, and there weren't enough of them. I know it, now. We could have invented something with longer spikes, kept our edge and won the game for sure."

"You know the refs wouldn't have let us wear 'em. We were pushing the regulations as it was."

"They were so cold, they might not have noticed."

"Still wasn't your fault, Coach."

"No, Deacon." George's eyes were bleak. "When we fail, I fail. I should have thought of something. Still, we are the better team. We are the best team in football, and we're going to prove it on a decent, normal, regular playing field in Miami."

Deacon wandered off to find his seat and nurse his own disappointment over the devastating defeat. He and George both knew that, no matter what the reasons, a loss is a loss is a loss.

Some teams of that era took the runner-up bowl lightly. But in the days that followed, George Allen worked the Rams twice a day, just as in the regular season. By Sunday, January 7, when L.A. took the field against the powerful Cleveland Browns, Allen had his team ready, and they easily crushed the Browns, 30-6. The committee sponsoring the game decided to give two Most Valuable Player awards. Gabriel won the game's MVP award for offense, and Deacon won the MVP for defense as he turned in one of the most devastating performances ever by a player in a professional football game, piling up an amazing six quarterback sacks and eighteen unassisted tackles. For good measure, he threw in a blocked field goal, a blocked extra point attempt, and a forced quarterback fumble!

Deacon achieved an honor never before posted by a lineman as he finished a close second to Johnny Unitas in the voting for Most Valuable Player in the NFL. He won the league's Most Valuable Defensive Player, and the Most Valuable Player in the playoff bowl.

It was one of the years he dominated the league. The incredible Deacon Jones was on his way to legendary status by amassing one hundred unassisted tackles and twenty-six sacks in the regular season, records that still stand today. Deacon tried to put aside his disappointment and get ready for another season. After all, win, lose, or draw, he had come to play the game.

And finally they couldn't keep the honor from him—George Allen was named Coach of the Year.

To the few who knew, Allen and Jones had both proven their point: The Rams were the best team in football and Deacon Jones was the greatest defensive player there ever was. But it all felt so hollow. Their dreams of the coveted championship had been spiked by the Packers in Wisconsin.

Even today, many professional football players, who know first-hand all the insider's dirt about the game and how hard it is for an interior lineman to make an unassisted tackle, believe it impossible for a defensive end to make a hundred unassisted tackles in a single season. Fortunately for history and Deacon's reputation, George Allen insisted his staff keep meticulous records. As for Deacon's twenty-six regular-season sacks (in fourteen games), no one else to this day has come close, even though the regular season is now sixteen games. They didn't even come close when the "In The Grasp"[41] rule made sacks much easier. When you add the sacks Deacon got in the two postseason games he played in 1967, his sack total for sixteen games in one year is an incredible thirty-two. Deacon's sack records are official Los Angeles Rams statistics. It should be simple; NFL records are derived from official team statistics. Yet, the NFL, at various times claiming it is too much trouble and that the information is not available, has yet to sanction Deacon Jones's great sack records, which tower head and shoulders above those of any other player who ever played the game.

---

41. This rule, put into effect to protect quarterbacks, allowed referees to call a quarterback down when he was ruled to be "in the grasp" of the man (or men) tackling him. According to the old rules, the quarterback had to be tackled to the ground before he was called down. Sacks were easier to come by with the "In-The-Grasp" rule. Deacon calculates that if it had been in effect when he played, he would have had twice as many sacks.

Deacon will never be able to forget the team's postseason game against the Packers. "The irony of it! All his life, George Allen is reviled by envious coaches for his dirty tricks, and nobody even says a word when we play the great Lombardi on a field iced down like glass! Of course, the fans knew the weather controlled the outcome of that game, and if you were from L.A., you felt cheated.

"You might ask yourself, why were the Packers, with their 9-4-1 regular season record, awarded the home-field advantage over the Rams, with their 11-1-2 record? After all, if they'd never had the home-field advantage, Green Bay wouldn't have been able to put us on ice. The answer is that, in those days, the rules favored the previous season's champion. If you won the previous year, you got the home-field advantage for the next year's postseason games! Easy to see, a rule like that favored the building of dynasties. That was the year we were beating everybody—if we'd played the Packers on a normal playing field, we'd probably have beaten them, and gone on to beat the Cowboys. Instead, the Pack went on to beat the Cowboys on Lambeau Field in thirteen below zero weather and fifteen-mile-an-hour winds—weather so cold even Lombardi's underground heaters couldn't keep up—to become the NFL champs yet another year, and then went on to whip the Oakland Raiders in Super Bowl II. That meant they would get the home-field advantage for the next year! It was so obvious an injustice that the league finally changed the rules. But that didn't help us much. You see, we lost in Milwaukee in 1967; forget the reasons and the excuses, that's the way the game was played and that's the way it goes in the record books. You don't complain about it. You do your best and whatever the outcome, you suck it up and go forward."

One other memory sticks in Deacon's mind. A few weeks later, on January 27, 1968, the towns of Orlando and Eatonville held a massive celebration and parade and declared the day "Deacon Jones Day." Deacon Jones, who less than a decade before had left Florida in a cloud of uncertain dreams returned to the cheers and adulation of those he'd left behind.

Jack's Bro

The other members of the Fearsome Foursome weren't interested in singing lessons. With his light tenor voice, Rosey figured he already had it made, it being hard to improve on the gifts God had already granted him. Lamar felt he was about as good as he was going to get. And Merlin reasoned there was enough evidence already on tape that his future career probably lay in other directions.

But being his own man had never stopped Deacon, and after a year of singing lessons, he felt confident enough to go out and look for a band. He found nine black musicians who were going nowhere. To Deacon, they seemed a little lazy, but they were talented and had a bluesy, funky sound when they all played together, which wasn't most of the time. They called themselves WAR, and they felt practice was mostly a waste of time. Determined to straighten them out, Deacon paid for session time and got them on a fairly decent rehearsal schedule. After a few months, he hooked up his first gig, as they say in show business, and opened a modest show at the Rag Doll Supper Club in the San Fernando Valley. The show seemed to go over well enough, and after it was over, Deacon came over to a table crowded with cheering, jeering teammates. He'd made sure to introduce his football friends to the crowd, the booze was flowing, and so it was a happy, jostling moment.

Rosey held up a hand. "Deacon, I was real impressed by what you did here tonight. Serious. An' I wondered, do you have any time, it bein' the off season an' all?"

Deacon turned a chair around backwards and sat at the table, "Well, I'm doing appearances for Schlitz beer. I got two weeks here at the Rag Doll, an' then I'm moving to the Bill of Fare club over in the Crenshaw shopping center. Why? What you have in mind, Plump One?"

"Well, presidential election's comin' up this fall," Rosey's voice trailed off and he looked into his drink.

Deacon shook his head, "I sort of lost my interest in politics when they killed Jack."

Rosey nodded and looked him squarely in the eye, "His brother's runnin', you know. He's going to announce." A few days before, longshot outsider Eugene McCarthy, a free-thinking liberal senator from Minnesota, had won the New Hampshire Democratic primary, beating out incumbent President Lyndon Johnson. The American people, frustrated and confused over the Vietnam war, were ready for a change and it looked like the race for the Democratic nomination would be wide open.

Deacon shook his head again, frowning into the new drink one of the waitresses placed in front of his half-finished old one. "Rosey, I don't want to get involved. Last time it hurt too much."

"Bobby's like Jack. Every bit like. He's somebody to believe in. He *cares* for us, Deak. He wants all Americans to get a fair shake."

"I was in the movement in 1960. I remember the dogs an' the spit an' the water hoses."

"I know that, Deacon," Rosey said earnestly. "That's why I'm askin'."

"What exactly are you asking?"

"Bobby needs a couple of us, men he can trust, to stay close, to make sure what happened to Jack doesn't happen to him. We already got a couple good ones—Rafer Johnson, for one. We travel around with the campaign, we meet people as the celebrities we are, we smile and convince them to vote right. But our other job, our main job, we stay close to Bobby."

"To tell the truth, Rosey, I consider most politicians liars and cheaters."

"Bobby's different, Deacon. I swear it on the Bible."

The Bible was serious business for Rosey, and so his comment demanded respect. Still, Deacon hesitated, "He's as good as Jack?"

"He can make a difference, Deak—I swear it."

"I don't know."

"Just come and meet him. I've got you invited to his place."

Several days later, Deacon got a personal letter from Robert F. Kennedy, asking for his support. He still wasn't convinced, but he took an airplane back east with Rosey to meet Jack Kennedy's kid brother.

On the plane, while Deacon sat stiff as a board, studiously avoiding any glance out the window, Rosey hammered away at him. "No black man is going to be elected President of these United States, Deacon. Not in our time. The best we can do is find a sympathetic white man, someone who cares for all races. Bobby is like that. You'll see. You'll see."

They did a tour, a junket, in the D.C. area, stopping at all the ghetto and poor areas that politicians usually avoided. Deacon was impressed with Bobby's sincerity and his concern. He felt, traveling close to Kennedy, he was able to see him close up and for real. Bobby Kennedy had a deep-rooted concern. He was for real. He could make a difference.

They had dinner with Bobby and his family at his home in McLean, Virginia, a few miles northwest of the capital. It was very casual, nothing like he'd expected. After dinner, Rosey played the guitar and they all sang "Up on the Roof" and "We Shall Overcome." Deacon found himself playing with the Kennedy kids, and Bobby and his wife Ethel struck him as good parents and decent people. Bobby talked for a few minutes about his aims, his goals for America in the coming years. He wasn't preaching, and what he said made sense to Deacon. He felt stirred, like he was in a moment in history. This wasn't the earth-shaking fury that had made him join the movement as a college kid. He felt genuinely moved, and convinced there was something he could do.

Later that evening, Rosey and Deacon went for a walk. "Well," Rosey asked, "are you in?"

"He really is like Jack," Deacon said.

"So, the dream lives."

Deacon presented his huge hand and Rosey met it with his own meaty paw. "Yeah. I'm in."

For his part, Rosey felt very good about it. He'd signed up the quickest man in the world, a protector with lightning reflexes and a headslap good as any boxer. He'd enlisted four or five like Deacon so far, athletes and true believers who would die before they would let anything happen to their man. This all on top of the regular Secret Service protection. It should be enough, even in an uncertain world. They might not win the election, but at least Bobby would be safe.

In his book Life in the Pit, *Deacon talked to writer Bill Libby about meeting Bobby for the campaign in Indiana. "He came walking into the room from the dentist's office where he had to have some teeth fixed up. 'A soul brother pulled me off the car,' he smiled, patting his swollen lips. It made us laugh and loosened us up. Maybe he wasn't a brother, but he was a soul brother. I said, 'This is the guy for me.' "[42]*

As time went on, Deacon became an intense and passionate believer: "I spoke for him. I listened to him and liked what he said and passed it on. I don't believe he was all talk. He had programs which would have helped, and a feeling for the needs of people which would have made him push these programs."

The task of protecting Bobby Kennedy was a physical one, and nearly impossible from the start. "One of my jobs was to hold him in the car when we'd drive down the street past the people. I couldn't believe those people. Huge crowds which felt something for him the people seldom feel for a public figure. They tried to

---

42. Bill Libby, *Life in the Pit,* p.122.

touch him, grab him, pull him to them, pull his clothes off. I'd hold him around the waist. Rosey would hold me around the knees. We'd form a human chain to keep Bobby in the car. He'd reach out to the people as he drove past and you wouldn't believe how hard they'd pull at him. Rosey and I are big men, but it took all our might just to hold him in the car. And it got awful hard hanging on to him, us all bent up and crouching in those cars for an hour at a time. But someone had to do it.[43]

Nancy

It was just another wild party, something Deacon had fallen into as a result of his regular weekly poker gathering. Bill Elliot was one of their regular poker buddies, and he was also Dionne Warwick's husband and so one week they held it over at Bill and Dionne's house, only the party was lots bigger than the usual affair—poker plus a band and milling crowds and dancing and drinking and all the wildness of the times mixed in.

Dick Bass, who loved to party heartily even better than he loved a good poker game, was there, and a few other Rams. Deacon had just signed a manager, Al Ross. Ross was wandering around, drink in hand, trying to line up some new clients. Deacon wasn't quite sure how he'd fallen in with Al. Somehow, with his interest in singing, his renewed involvement in the civil rights movement, and an expanding laundry list of personal commitments and television appearances, there was too much to do, and Al had popped up at just the right time. Al was a whirlwind; he ran All-Pro Management, and he was handling the financial affairs of football greats like Jim Marshall, Allan Page, Carl Eller, and basketball's Rick Barry.

Deacon had turned over his financial affairs to Al. Al was a real go-getter, and had the reputation of being an aggressive attorney. The new relationship was enough to make Deacon's head swim. He'd already invested in a few apartment buildings, but that was nothing. Within a few weeks after signing up with All-Pro, he and Al were planning their own recording company, music publishing house, and show business management team, and were planning to open a supper club at the corner of Stocker and LaBrea in Baldwin Hills.

The poker game was over, at least for the moment, and the patio

43. Bill Libby, *Life in the Pit*, p. 123.

was crowded with dancers. Deacon stood by the piano, nursing a drink and talking to Dick Bass, who was looking over the milling crowd of the famous, the near-famous, the Playboy bunnies, and the beautiful wannabees as they danced feverishly on the crowded floor.

By this time, the Deacon's gridiron exploits had been flashed across the nation for a number of years. With the Rams making the playoffs, his colorful and slashing style of defense was in vogue, and he was becoming a household word. Throaty-voiced Mama Cass Elliott, appearing on the Johnny Carson show, told a story about meeting Deacon in Las Vegas. "You know Deacon Jones?" she asked. "You must know Deacon Jones. The football player. Why, he is football." She laughed her deep, hearty laugh, and Johnny and Ed nodded and chuckled encouragingly. "He was at a crap table in Vegas, rolling the dice. When he won, he didn't say a word, just raked in the chips. But when he lost, every time he lost, he said, 'The Lord is punishing me for my evil.'" Mama Cass's story brought down the house. Ed, particularly, couldn't stop laughing about it. It had been very good for the show. And very good for the growing legend of Deacon Jones.

Dick Bass was interested, as usual, in the ladies and already had a pair under his wing. "Nice set of lungs over there, Deak," he said, motioning across the room to where an abundantly endowed white girl with flying, bleached-blond hair was attracting a lot of attention with her wild gyrations. "Come on, man, get in the action."

Deacon shrugged. He was tired, and when he was tired, he got to thinking, and thinking took him out of the party mode. He wasn't particularly proud that women came easily or that he got out on the wild side while he was still married to Iretha. He wanted, sometimes desperately, to find the same kind of relationship with his wife that his mother and father had shared. But they didn't have any children. They never seemed on the same wavelength, and as Deacon's reputation grew, they were drifting farther and farther apart. During the season, he might see Iretha only once or twice a week, coming home with a batch of dirty laundry, throwing together a clean suitcase or two and driving off again. Deacon saw that Iretha had what she wanted— plenty of money to get through the days until he showed up again.

Iretha showed up at the football games, usually just before the first half was over, dressed to the nines in something new (Lord forbid she should ever wear the same thing twice in a fourteen-game season) and embarrassing him the way she lorded it over the other wives as the wife of the great Deacon Jones. Oddly enough, he thought at the time,

George and Ettie Allen never seemed to notice the way she "put on the act" around them. George, particularly, honestly seemed to like her. This made Deacon think it had to be something in himself, some old anger that wouldn't allow him to let down his guard and genuinely face their problems.

He shrugged now, looking over at his old friend Bass with a lovely woman on each arm. Bass never openly questioned the adversary relationship Deacon had developed with his wife, though he couldn't figure out why the man allowed it to continue if he was really as unhappy as he seemed. Men and women were born to love, to marry, to fall out of love, as naturally as the changing of the seasons. Why didn't the man move on? Old relationships were old baggage, and an unwanted wife was a heavy crate to drag around one's life. But Deacon never said why.

"I don't know," Deacon said. "I don't feel interested tonight."

"The great Deacon Jones, not interested? You got the fever, Swamp Boy?"

Deacon, drained from a day of rehearsing with his unruly band, was only half-aware of what he was saying. "Unlike you, King Richard, the deeds and mighty legends of which I am proudest take place on the football field, not under satin sheets with two or three ladies."

Deacon couldn't stop thinking about his last disastrous session with his band. Half the musicians had shown up late, and half said they had to leave early. Lonnie Jordan, the keyboardist, had tried to avoid an argument. He was probably the most serious about his career, and besides, Deacon was letting him live free in one of his apartment buildings. "Pappa Dee" Allen, the percussionist, was surly, but at least the "Big D," as he was sometimes known, seemed ready to play all afternoon and into the night. Drummer Harold Brown had some sort of fishy excuse for showing up two hours late, and the only white guy, bass player Peter Rosen, looked distant and glassy-eyed, like he might or might not come back from a bad trip.

Deacon had hoped to get them excited about some new vocals he'd laid out real money to buy, but Rosen fell asleep while he was talking, before he even had a chance to pass the music sheets around.

You don't understand the team concept, Deacon had yelled. Big D had yawned and told him that was great for physical sports, but this was art, man, and Deacon had gone crazy and told them all to find somebody else stupid enough to pay their way.

Deacon started out of his reverie, aware that Bass was talking again.

"Then why is it, Deak, that when you're with a woman at a party, you're the most jealous, possessive bastard in the world?"

Deacon didn't like to talk about his personal life with anybody, much less the glib Bass, but he'd gone too far to turn back now. "Two reasons. First, when I am with a woman, she is with me. That's the rule."

Bass dropped easily into the patois of the southern black. "That be true enough, bro. You brings a girl to a party, nobody ever even know her name. She be yo' woman, sho enough, but dat be an insult to us, yo friends."

"Because of the second reason. Friends or not, you guys are animals. A man must protect that which is his own."

"You sayin' we don' respect women, Deacon Jones?"

"Truer words were never spoke."

"And you do?" A cloud came over Bass's features. He liked to think of himself as a gentleman. "The way you treat Iretha and all?"

Bass had gone too far, and he knew it. The words hung in the air like a dark, threatening cloud between them, but only for a moment and then Deacon jabbed his finger down into the shorter man's chest and spoke slowly, clearly pronouncing every word. "My wife has given me much for which to be grateful. For instance, she has taught me the true meaning of the words eternal hell. And yes, I tomcat on her at every turn. But she my wife, Richard. I don't want to talk against her. An' I don't want to talk about her."

In what he saw as the long and grim years of his marriage, Deacon had formed relationships with a variety of women, and Bass knew it— hell, everybody on the team knew it. Iretha herself had to be a fool not to at least suspect. Not thousands of relationships, for sure, but enough so that, as Deacon said to himself, the spoils of victory were not foolishly cast aside.

There were, on the low end of the scale, casual moments with the type of women who just wanted to see what it was like to climb in bed with a famous person. Deacon didn't really get to know them very well. Curiosity satisfied, they could get on with the rest of their lives. Generally speaking, ladies who were looking for this sort of experience got what they wanted from him. And, the way he saw it, he did, too, from them. It was an even exchange, and most everybody was the happier for it.

It wasn't what the poets call "real" love. On the other hand, it wasn't something he was ashamed of, either. Or necessarily bragged about. After all, he was married, at least in name.

Bass twisted his hands in the air and shrugged. He took on the persona of a colonial Indian walla as he said in broken English, "Veddy good, sir, veddy good. Deacon-Sir no likee female of the magnificent lungs. Perhaps Deacon-Sir suffer curse of the limp rod. Surely, some enemy has done this?"

Deacon sighed and turned away. Sometimes Bass was like a one of those tiny flies that bite and won't go away. He headed back to the bar and was standing in line when a throaty voice at his shoulder said, "How's the band going?"

He turned round, startled. "How'd you hear about that?" He was looking down at a beautiful, mahogany-colored lady. Gorgeous, simply gorgeous!

"Ain't much I don' know about the music business, honey," she laughed. "Everybody in town know you tryin' to whip some team spirit into that no-count bunch of boozin', dopin' *Negro* musicians. How *is* it going, if you don't mind my askin'?"

"Not so good," he found himself admitting. "I never met such a bunch of lazy bastards in my life. An' they want to call themselves WAR. The name should stand for 'We Are Restin.' I pay for the sessions. I pay them to show up. Then they come in late, if they show up at all. They lie around with their hangovers, and we're lucky to get anything done."

She frowned and shook her head. "Some people never get it."

"Oh, they got it, all right. I gave them the boot earlier today."

"Good. You want to get to the top, it's hard work. You don' want to hang around people who don't work as hard as you do."

He eyed her more closely, liking what he heard. "That's exactly the way I feel."

And then Bill Elliot was at their side. "I see you've already met."

"Well, not *formally*," Deacon said. "We're just waiting for a drink together."

"Allow me." Bill did a courteous bow. "Nancy Wilson, the fabulous Deacon Jones. Deacon Jones, the fantabulous Nancy Wilson, queen of popular jazz."

For some reason, they hit it off from the start. It was a lot of things. There was the physical attraction, and they were both superstars at the height of their careers. But there was something more than that. Deacon would always come back to the words "work ethic." Each saw in the other that drive and determination to be the best. They were kindred spirits, and they knew it.

Deacon shakes his head ruefully, the bittersweet smile coming once again to his lips, "You can ask Pervis Atkins or Dick Bass and they'll confirm it. I didn't go around broadcasting my exploits. To this day, they couldn't tell you the names of more than two or three girls I dated in all those years, if that many. The girls were black and white and brown and yellow. Some were more famous than others.

"Sometimes the relationships lasted a night, sometimes a few weeks or whenever I'd get into town, and sometimes longer. So it can put things out of proportion to talk about my relationship with any one lady, no matter how famous she was back then, or is to this day. Yet it is the one rumor that persists. I'll be between takes on a talk show with the mike dead and the host will get a certain light in his eyes and ask me about it, or I'll be on the eighteenth green of some big charity event and with the game on the line and me lining up my putt, one of the guys I'm playing against will amble over with his hands in his pockets and, figuring he can throw off my concentration, he'll say, 'Gosh, is it true that you and Nancy . . . ?'

"About WAR, they'd been around doin' local gigs for years before I got to them, doin' nothing much and going nowhere. In the early sixties, they were the rhythm section of a black L.A. band called Nite Shift. When I left, people said I was a fool, because some day they were going to make it big. I knew those guys had real talent, but I just couldn't stand anybody who didn't go all-out for success. After me, they got 'discovered' by music producer Jerry Goldstein who teamed them up with Eric Burdon, the English vocalist who'd been with the Animals, and they still went nowhere. Eric was on board for about a year, and then he couldn't take it any more and left. Some time after that, WAR figured a few things out and started to work their way up the charts as 'black funk.' They ended up with some gold records on their wall, probably their most famous hits were 'Slippin into Darkness' and 'The World Is a Ghetto.' Their big LPs were "All Day Music" in 1971, "The World Is a Ghetto" in 1972, and "Why Can't We Be Friends?" in 1975. It may sound strange, but when I think of WAR, I think of all the athletes I've met who had real talent and yet never made the top honors because they didn't give it their all. Sure, WAR eventually made the musical big leagues and a pile of money, but they could have been big like the Beatles or the Rolling Stones. Sad for me, but when they finally did make their little mark in rock 'n' roll and all that money it was long after I stopped supporting their lazy butts, and so I never got a dime out of my investment."

Death of the Dream

"Well, with Martin dead . . ." Deacon could hear the blacks talking in the seat behind him. The voice trailed off, the way they all did when they thought about what might happen now that their greatest leader was gone. *With Martin dead,* the words reverberated in Deacon's mind. It was late, and he was too tired to think clearly. On the trail with Bobby, the long hours of endless vigilance were taking their toll. Life after Martin was uncertain and grey. It was hard to think about bald-faced political murder happening in the land of Washington and Lincoln, the land of the free and home of the brave. *If they killed Martin Luther King, they would kill anybody.* The muttering behind him came to an end as his black athlete friends, Bobby's protectors, drifted off to sleep. Deacon wasn't so lucky. His mind churned. He couldn't drift off.

The campaign bus droned on through the black Indiana night, past rolling fields of spring corn now waist-high in the moonlight. It was mid-April and Bobby's campaign was in full-swing, reaching for the brass ring in the Indiana primary.

The day had been a hectic one. The car in which Bobby was riding had struck and killed a dog that belonged to a little black girl. There were thousands of people waiting for him at a rally, but Bobby insisted they stop the car. He put the dog on a blanket. He put a blanket over the dog. He hugged that little girl. He told her how sorry he was and while he knew no other dog could replace her own dog, he would see that she got another dog. And tears were coming out of his eyes. Before he left, he made sure the arrangements were made, that she got another dog.

It scared Deacon to see how reckless Bobby was. In spite of what had happened to his brother, Bobby wanted to be with the people. Once a motorcycle pulled alongside their car and backfired. Pow! It was just like a rifle shot. By the time Deacon realized it wasn't, he already had one foot over the side of the car, as if he was going to jump out. He had no idea what he was going to do next.

The fire drill was, when Bobby walked through the crowds, there would be two big bodyguards in front, one on either side, and two in back. They had to squeeze him through, but they protected him with their bodies. It was strenuous work, being alert for any movement or flash from the crowds pushing and shoving all around them. And you never could tell what Bobby was going to do. Once they were walking through Hunters Point, a ghetto neighborhood in San Francisco, and

Bobby suddenly stopped and picked up a raggedy Negro boy. He looked at him, and everyone could see the hurt and shame for his country in his eyes. You ended up loving Bobby and being afraid for him at the same time.

Deacon sighed and stretched and tried to stretch his feet a few inches farther under the seat in front of him. With his big frame, he wasn't made for buses, and was barely comfortable with the entire bench seat to himself. It was past two in the morning and everybody on the bus was sleeping, even Bobby, the perpetual motion machine.

Who would win the primary in Indiana was anybody's guess.

"We shall overcome," Deacon muttered blearily to himself.

"How's that?" a voice from the aisle said, and as he looked up, Bobby swung into the seat next to him.

"Oh. . . nothin'. I was just thinkin' about Martin's end."

"Martin meant a lot to you."

"Not as much as to some. I could never follow his path of nonviolent resistance, not since college."

Bobby smiled wearily, leaning his head against the seat back. "What happened in college?"

"I marched in Orangeburg. After that, I said, 'No man will ever spit on me or set his dogs on me again. I will *kill* first!' "

"So you left the movement and went into football where you kill quarterbacks on a regular basis."

Deacon shrugged. "Exactly. It was that or commit murder."

"Who do your friends think did it? Martin, I mean."

Deacon eyed him, wondering if he dared say what was on his mind. "Who do you think killed Jack?"

Bobby was silent for a long time, his face thin and lined with old grief. "I don't know. You think you know . . . you suspect, that is, you have your suspicions . . . but in the end it turns to smoke. In the end, you have this empty hole in your life, and you don't know what to believe."

"That's where we different, Bobby. Black people *know* the FBI killed Martin. J. Edgar harassed him an' harassed him an' ol' Martin Luther wouldn't back off an' they finally got somebody to murder him. We don't need no court case for that. We're convinced."

"Whoever did it, it's a blow against democracy, that such an enormous tragedy could happen in our country." Bobby stood in the aisle, wavering with the motion of the bus.

"Not once, twice."

"That's right," Bobby agreed. "Strike two." He flashed his quick, intense smile and headed back toward his own seat.

"Don't worry, Bobby, there ain't gonna be no strike three," Deacon said quietly after his man was out of earshot. "Rosey an' me an' the boys are gonna see to it." Deacon shook his head, feeling punchy and strange for talking to himself in the dark. Still, for the rest of his life he would remember that, if he was ever wrong about something that really mattered, that was the time.

On May 7, 1968, Robert F. Kennedy won the Indiana primary. Three weeks later, he lost in Oregon to Sen. Eugene McCarthy. Still, nothing was settled, and the convention in Chicago promised to be a wide-open uproar of an affair. The primary trail wound next into California, a critical state for all the candidates. Deacon was with Bobby in northern California, but left to honor a commitment he had with Schlitz Brewing Co. for a string of appearances. Deacon talked about that time with Bill Libby. "When the campaign in California was ending, he didn't seem to need our help for a little while as much as he had. I was working for a beer company and hadn't done much for them because of the campaign. I'd agreed to begin doing appearances again when the campaign ended. I was booked for an appearance in Denver on election night and it was a commitment I felt I had to keep. I didn't want to go. I had a funny feeling about it. I wanted to stay with Bobby. But I owed something to my job, too. So I went. I was sitting in a bar delighting in the returns showing he'd won (in California) and I had just heard his victory speech. I was proud for my man, when the word came that he'd been shot.*

"I couldn't believe it. When I found how it had happened, I couldn't bear it. I think I might have prevented it. I have no illusions about myself. I am no miracle man. But I can't forget how many men we usually had surrounding him and how few were with him in the Ambassador Hotel when that madman shot him. I was usually out front of him. Maybe I'd have spotted that madman with a gun.

"I caught the first plane from Denver to L.A. Iretha met me at the airport with a change of clothes, and I flew to New York. The service was in St. Patrick's Cathedral. I stood by his body alongside Rev. Abernathy, U.N. Secretary General U Thant and Sidney Poitier. The people wept and prayed, like they were doing all across the country.

"Not being Catholic, I didn't know what to expect. At one point, people started going up to the altar, filing past where the

casket was. I thought the services were over and people were going up to pay their last respects. I left my seat and walked up the aisle. I passed Jess Unruh and saw him looking at me curiously. I got under the bright lights in front of the TV cameras and realized people were taking communion. Now I've heard it's a big sin to take communion if you're not a Catholic in good standing. Some of the nuns say you can get shot straight down to hell for it. But I figured I was this far, and as a friend of Bobby maybe the Lord could put me in for some sort of dispensation. Anyway, I kept one eye on the lady who was kneeling next to me and did everything she did. Walking back down the aisle, I didn't know if I should eat it or not. It was dissolving on my tongue, and I was real embarrassed. As I passed Jess Unruh, he was smiling at me like he understood. He probably felt there was some sort of dispensation, too. It was a moment of gentle humor that stood out in the middle of all that sadness. I like to think Bobby would have appreciated it.

"And I remember taking the sad train ride from New York to Washington D.C. with the whole country looking on and grieving, to take him to his final resting place. But most of all, when I think back on Bobby, I wish I had been there in the brief split-second that meant the difference between the life and death of the man . . . and of such a big part of the American Dream."

8

Allen's Drive

In the mid-sixties, with the rivalry between the NFL and the AFL lead-ing to a bidding war for talent, star player salaries had skyrocketed. The feeding frenzy died down for a few years with the merger of the two leagues, but soon there was a new crisis, an unrest widely spread among almost all the veteran players. By late in the decade, with the ever-increasing revenues from television, it was more and more difficult for the team owners to conceal their vastly expanded incomes. Many of the players, locked into old con-tracts, were unhappy to be playing for a small percentage of what they believed to be their true worth. Football had become big business, and the players were tired of playing for peanuts.

With the advent of the 1968 season, over six hundred veteran players went out on strike, refusing to show up for spring training. The owners voted to lock the striking players out of training camp. Dan Reeves, bowing to George Allen's wishes, allowed assistant coaches to run informal "training sessions" at some of the local parks, so the players wouldn't be too rusty when an agreement was finally signed. Allen's son Bruce remembers: "In the strike of 1968, a lot of the teams simply dismissed their players, but Dad talked the Rams into working out on their own without their coaches . . . and then he'd send me over to check up on how they were doing. Dea-con and Jack Pardee were in charge of the defense. I'd go over to whatever public park they were at, and Deacon—all 250 pounds of him—would be playing cornerback, man-to-man against Harold

Jackson, and doing a good job of it. I'd come back and tell Dad, and he'd say in that admiring, marveling way of his, 'Isn't that the most gifted player you've ever seen?' "

Deacon Jones was starting his eighth campaign in the NFL, and was in the third year of a five-year contract with a base salary of $35,000 a year for the 1968 season. His contract had perks that could more than double its value; he would get $500 for every sack, and sums in the thousands for such achievements as making the Pro Bowl, being named All-Pro, being named most valuable defensive player, and so on.

Still, Deacon was now the most popular and successful player on the Rams, as well as a growing national personality, and his salary, he felt, did not reflect the reality of his current worth on the market.

Since, at this time, owners still did not recognize player's agents, not allowing them to negotiate or even to sit in the negotiations, information on other players salaries was very limited. The old 2-4-6 rule had died out, and now blacks made up over a third of the players on some teams. But the rumors persisted that blacks throughout the league, when they could find a spot on the roster, were paid far less than whites for similar situations.

More and more Negroes were finding their way into the NFL, as owners saw ways they could use the tremendous athletic skills blacks brought to the table. Yet, there still very few in skill positions. Old ways died hard, and the belief remained that one didn't want to give a black man the ball or let him call signals. Although Deacon couldn't prove it, he saw salary disparities between blacks and whites all around the League which gave him the firm conviction that "the color of his skin was keepin' his wallet thin."

And there were issues beyond salary and race that troubled Deacon. Ever since he'd come to the National Football League, the owners' domination of the players had bothered him. The players, after all, played the game. Without them, you'd have a ball and an empty stadium. Why then couldn't they get the rights enjoyed by working people all over the country? Deacon lobbied strongly that they join one of the powerful unions. The Teamsters were interested; the NFL players would be a feather in their cap. But the majority of the players couldn't be convinced, preferring to be led by a group of inexperienced ex-players who bargained away their rights for short-term gains in a disastrous agreement, the lingering effects of which to this day have football players lagging behind athletes in baseball and basketball in compensation.

The NFL strike ended on July 15, as the players union voted to accept a pension offer. The owners called off their lockout, and drills started. Although the newspapers reported that the Rams players had voted 100 percent for the plan, several days later it was obvious that consent had not been unanimous as Jones, Snow, Grier, and Olsen failed to report to camp.

Rams management confirmed that Olsen and Snow were trying to renegotiate their contracts, and that Jones had tried to renegotiate with Dan Reeves a few months before.

The L.A. Times Bob Oates wrote on July 28, "The most important man on one of the league's strongest defensive teams—Jones was undeniably worth more than the Rams were thinking of paying him when he filed for a raise. His contract was signed more than two years ago, when neither he nor the Rams had more than a general idea of his 1968 value. Should he be bound by his 1966 signature today at the peak of an all-too-brief career? Most other young American businessmen who made 1966 deals can still make amends in 1976 if not 1986. The relevant issue is not the size of the sum Jones once agreed to but the sum pro football can now afford."

Oates continued thoughtfully, "And this, in truth, reveals the dimension of the NFL's whole financial crisis. It is mainly a crisis of misunderstanding and ineffective communication. The owners don't understand that the players consider pro football to be a quasi-public business—a community business, at least, which a) depends entirely on their talent and b) is conducted presumably in the public interests of each city."

Mal Florence reported in the same paper on August 9, "The Rams were sort of a trial case for other pro teams in their contract dispute with Jones. Football, baseball, basketball and hockey executives followed the case with interest. If the Rams relented, said one owner, and renegotiated Jones' contract, they'd be opening a can of worms for everyone."

But, with the majority of the veterans back in camp, the few striking players failed to organize within themselves. Deacon (acting on what, years later, he would admit was bad advice) refused to link his fortunes with Merlin Olsen and to negotiate together. After five days, the Rams gave an ultimatum that they wouldn't renegotiate with Olsen, and Merlin abandoned his own plan and reported to camp. Next, Elroy Hirsh was able to split off Snow, who was promised his contract would be reviewed. (It was, and he was given a raise.) Rosey Grier announced his retirement and so was out of the picture.

Deacon Jones held out longer than anybody, until he was the only Rams player still on strike. By now, Deacon's position had also hardened. For him, it was more than a question of money. He felt the players had given in too soon, just when they could have gotten *their fair share of the pie. Free agency was a player dream scoffed at by the owners. Players could not legally play for another team until they had fulfilled the terms of their contract, plus a year's option clause. Since the average pro player's career was three years, they were effectively tied to one team. Even players with longevity had to be careful or they wouldn't be picked up by another team. Deacon himself had two years left on his current contract. This meant he wouldn't be in a position to negotiate with another club until the 1971 season. Always an outspoken advocate of player's rights, Deacon was hardly a favorite of the owners, who recognized that ultimately the control over huge revenues was at stake.*

Deserted by the very players whose rights he was trying to fight for, Deacon held out as long as he dared. But, as one man against a monopoly, he finally had to face the realities of his day; if you wanted to play pro football, there was simply nowhere else to go.

Gracious in defeat, he told the reporters, "I felt the team needed me . . . that the guys depended on me. First things are first."

Dan Reeves made sure the press made no mistakes about who had won and who had lost. "David Jones has returned to the team without any changes whatsoever in the contract he signed two years ago." NFL management was firmly back in the saddle again. Deacon, the superstar, had failed with his demands. Other players could now reflect what this would mean relative to their own situations.

Doing his best to smooth the troubled waters, George Allen said, "It was an unselfish move on Jones's part. I'm pleased to have him back and now we can concentrate on football."

On September 7, in an exhibition game against San Francisco, the Rams' star defensive end was pressuring Brodie on almost every passing play, and forced the first of two fumbles leading to Rams touchdowns. Deacon Jones hadn't gotten his raise, but he was back, and with a vengeance.

Dealin' Dan

It was early June, before the strike was called, and Deacon sat alone outside Dan Reeves's office, waiting to be called into the plush inner sanctum. He'd showed up exactly at ten, and now, fifteen minutes later, had begun to fidget.

"Our meeting was for ten, wasn't it?" he asked the secretary for the third time.

"Mr. Reeves is a very busy man," she said in a frosty voice. "I will inform you when you can see him."

Deacon's advisors at the Stuart John Corporation had told him they would make him wait. Still, it wasn't easy. He shifted the batch of last season's statistics on his knees, wishing he'd brought a folder or one of those slim leather briefcases he'd seen lawyers carry. His handwritten notes, detailing his previous season's accomplishments on a yellow legal pad, suddenly seemed less impressive than they had the previous week, when he'd reviewed them with Allen. Twenty-six regular season sacks. One hundred unassisted tackles. Six postseason sacks. No defensive end in history had ever had such a season! And Coach had heartily agreed.

By this time, players in baseball had started hiring agents to get their negotiations on a more even keel. But in football, where the owners were used to being in the driver's seat, you would be fired for having an agent represent you. Dan Reeves, considered one of the enlightened owners, would actually let you bring your accountant with you for negotiation talks, but it wasn't the same thing, and Deacon, who had asked to talk about his contract, had chosen to walk in alone.

The minutes ticked by. After another half hour, a buzzer sounded on the secretary's desk. She picked up the phone, listened for a moment and then said, "Yes, Mr. Reeves." She went back to her typing, finishing the paragraph on which she was working, and turned her cold smile on Deacon.

"Mr. Reeves will see you now," she said.

Deacon unhitched himself from the soft, low armchair and made his way across the reception room to the oak-paneled door she indicated. Inside, a group of men were talking amiably. Somebody finished a joke, and they laughed in harsh little coughs, like a bunch of old crows sitting around roadside carrion.

"Come in, David, come in." Dan Reeves gestured with one hand, motioning to a straight chair sitting directly across the huge desk from him. Deacon looked around the room, recognizing Reeves's lawyer, his accountant, and three or four other people he didn't know, surrounding him in soft easy chairs and sofas. He felt alone and unprepared. He sat and waited for Reeves to make the first move.

"Now, what is this all about?" Dan asked. The smile had gone from his face, and his eyes were steely hard. Deacon tried to remember that this was a short, pudgy fellow that he could send across the room with one headslap, but that sort of gridiron logic didn't seem to apply here.

"I explained it all to Crazylegs on the phone," he said, already feeling a little defensive. "He must have told you."

"Perhaps you'd better tell me." There was no give in Reeves.

Deacon shifted uneasily, "It's about renegotiating my contract."

"You're already one of the highest-paid players on the team."

"Mr. Reeves, that old one doesn't work any more. All the players talk to each other these days." Reeves's face reddened, but he bit his lip and said nothing.

"One of the higher-paid linemen," Dan's accountant quickly added.

"My base salary was $35,000 last year. A player's active years are short, Mr. Reeves. I've got to get what I'm worth."

"Thirty-five is pretty good for a lineman," the accountant murmured, his voice clearly audible in the room.

"I'm not just any lineman!" Deacon flared. "The going rate for a player of my caliber is twice that!"

The accountant referred to his notes. "By my record, you did make nearly twice that last year, adding up all the incentives."

"My base salary should be twice that," Deacon insisted stubbornly, "before we tack on bonus money!"

Reeves affected the habit of smoking cigarettes with a long holder, not unlike the old Franklin Roosevelt mannerism. While they'd been talking, he'd been working to insert a new cigarette in his ivory holder, which he now lit. He leaned back and put his feet on the desk, beaming confidently from the wreath of smoke around his head. "I don't think, in a time when mothers all over this country are worried about their boys dying in Vietnam, and when your own people are struggling so valiantly to find jobs and work for a few dollars a week, that the press would be too sympathetic to hear you are going around whimpering that $60,000 somehow isn't enough. Hell, that's lots more than the reporters make."

"You don't have any respect for us players, when it comes to business, do you? The chicken doesn't fly with the eagle, does it? While we are out there getting our heads bashed and our bones broken, how much do you make off the team? What did you haul in last year, Mr. Reeves? A million dollars? Two million?"

"That's my business," Reeves snapped, the smile disappearing from his face.

"You think we players don't see the big numbers pouring in from your television contracts? The reporters print those numbers!"

"David," Reeves said in a soft, lecturing voice, "I'm starting to find this very tiresome. You and I and everybody in this room knows you signed a legally binding contract that runs for another three years. You have to live up to that contract, or I'll see you in court."

"Nobody knew I'd have such fantastic success."

Reeves leaned back and his eyes narrowed, "You didn't have such a great year last year."

"What?" Deacon was stunned. He waved his yellow pad in the air, "These numbers are incredible! No defensive end in history—"

Reeves raised a hand for quiet and smoothly cut him off. "Ever had so many penalties! Every week you were jumping offsides or grabbing some quarterback by the face mask. You think I can't see from up there in the stands? It was enough to make me sick!"

Deacon jumped to his feet, astounded at the turn the conversation had taken. "Those penalties happen 'cause I'm off the line faster than anybody in the league! The refs can't believe it's real. They call stuff on me they don't call on anybody else! Ask the players! Hell, ask Coach Allen!"

Reeves shrugged, looking at his lawyer. "Whether the calls are right or wrong, they stand in the books, and it makes you that much less valuable to the team."

"No defensive end ever had a year—"

The Rams owner waved him quiet. "I don't know why I even agreed to talk to you. You're in a legally binding contract. You can't play anywhere else. You have to play for me."

"Like you own me! You look on me like I'm your slave! You depreciate me year after year, like a fancy car or a house!"

"Oh, please, stop the rhetoric—you're not at a civil rights rally here, David. Legally, I do own you, at least the football rights to you. The bottom line here, you try to get out of your contract, you'll be up in Canada, or playing sandlot ball with your beer buddies."

Deacon was outraged. He shook his fist at Reeves. "I don't have to play ball for you! I own four apartments with eighty units! I'm negotiating a deal with a national chain! I've got commitments with big companies!"

Reeves raised his hands in the air in a gesture of helplessness, "See? Where'd you get all that money?"

"Mr. Reeves, it just isn't fair! You know the Rams have torn up other players' contracts when they deserved it."

"Yes, we have been honorable to our players over the years. The loyal ones. The ones who deserved it. But you come in here and hold a gun to our heads. What will you do next? Take your case to the press? Rile up our fans?"

"That's what you're afraid of, isn't it? You might lose control of—"

"I'm not afraid of anything!" Reeves had angrily jumped to his feet. He blew out an impatient breath, and slowly sat back down again. "Why am I yelling?" he asked, half to himself. "This is a clear case. I can't make you get on the field, Deacon. You could just sit out your contract. That would make you eligible to play for some other team in . . . ummm . . ." He glanced at the notes in his lawyer's hand, ". . . in 1970 or '71 . . . if anyone would want an old ballplayer then for the ridiculous salary you would no doubt be asking." Dan took a puff from his cigarette and blew the smoke in the air, "It just seems awful selfish, you letting down your team, letting down your fans, just because you want another bunch of apartment buildings!"

Deacon couldn't take it any more. He stormed out of the room, slamming the door behind him. But the loud, solid oak wood thump didn't give him any satisfaction. He had the distinct feeling there was a whole roomful of white men laughing behind his back.

Deacon reflects on Dan Reeves. "He was a little guy with a Napoleonic complex so bad he wore elevator boots so he wouldn't have to look so far up when he talked to his players. And he was also a heavy drinker. Everybody on the team knew about Dan's drinking problems, though you'll find people who will lie about it, even to this day. That's why I asked for a morning meeting, before noon, before he got to that bottle. Reeves was smart, no question about it, and he taught me some expensive lessons at that meeting.

"I guess you couldn't call him evil, he was just the guy on the other side of the line. He dealt with money, with numbers. He was a pure-blooded, cold-hearted American businessman, and he took better care of the press than his own players—he spent more money on them than he ever did on us, and they, in turn, kept fairly quiet about the way he ran the team."

Elroy "Crazylegs" Hirsh, has an entirely different recollection: "Dan Reeves was an out-and-out gentleman who cared about the Rams and tried to treat everybody fairly. He had a very bright football mind, and he went against the entire league in the forties when he hired Kenny Washington.[1] He did like to be intimately

---

1. Washington, a black of tremendous talent, played football at UCLA with Jackie Robinson. He was very popular in Los Angeles, and when Reeves wanted to move west, the Los Angeles Coliseum Commission stipulated that Washington be given a try-out. Washington became the first black NFL player in over a decade.

involved with every aspect of the football team; after all, he'd given a big part of his life to it, and knew a great deal about it. He had that right, it was his team. And he never wore elevator shoes."

"Crazylegs is a smart man," Deacon shot back, when told of Hirsh's evaluation of Reeves: "He managed to survive for years while four millionaires were scratching like tomcats for control of the Rams. He always knew what side his bread was buttered on. But in his heart, he knows Reeves first broke the color barrier because the L.A. Coliseum Commission forced him to do it. If he hadn't agreed to give Kenny a shot, they'd still be calling his team the Cleveland Rams.² Reeves was a pragmatic guy; later, he hired blacks in droves because he saw they were better players. By then, he'd been losing for over a decade. He was desperate enough for a winner to go against the wishes of the other owners."

Ex-Rams assistant coach Don Paul agrees with Hirsh that Reeves was a "good owner" and generally all-around nice guy. "Dan Reeves was a neat, clean, gentlemanly fellow. A dapper dresser, and he always smoked with that cigarette holder of his. He never interfered with us coaches on the field, and he made it possible to put the first blacks on the field."³

Ex-head coach Harland Svare also feels Deacon is too harsh on Reeves: "I don't think Reeves drank any more than the rest of us. Deacon is just bitter about a lot of things. There's the way things really were, and then there's the way he remembers them. He's the

---

2. In *Their Deeds and Dogged Faith,* p. 210, authors Rathet and Smith bear out Deacon's claim: "The key to moving West as far as Reeves was concerned was the acquisition of the Los Angeles Coliseum as a playing site. But the rival All-American Football conference was trying to lease the stadium. 'The AAFC people said we shouldn't be dealing with the NFL—they had an unwritten rule of no colored,' recalls Bill Nicholas, at the time the general manager of the Coliseum. Nicholas doesn't volunteer much more, but it appears the Coliseum commission insisted Washington be given a tryout if the commission were to offer the Rams a lease. "One of the conditions definitely was Washington trying out for the team," says Bob Snyder, the Rams' backfield coach who actually signed Washington. 'They put it in such a way, when you're battling for your life, you say sure.' Snyder frankly admits that the Rams would not have signed Washington if the team had remained in Cleveland." Rathet and Smith do point out, "It's also important to note that, while Reeves' mission was securing the Coliseum for the Rams, as opposed to breaking the NFL's color line, he did have a battle on his hands before he actually signed Washington. 'All hell broke loose [among NFL owners when word got around that Reeves intended to sign Washington],' Snyder recalls. 'There was objection to it—you can bet your butt on that. Quite a bit of objection. but despite the objections, Reeves did it.' "

3. Kenny Washington speaks out in *Their Deeds and Dogged Faith,* p.210, "Reeves had the league over a barrel," Washington said. "The Coliseum people warned the Rams that if they practiced discrimination, they couldn't use the stadium. When those NFL people began thinking about all those seats and the money they could make filling 'em, they decided my kind wasn't so bad after all."

greatest defensive end that ever was. He should take his laurels and leave it at that, but he sours everything by blowing off his mouth."

Deacon sees it differently. "Even today, I'm still one of the few who will speak out against Dan Reeves. People would have him made out as a history-maker and a nice guy, but it just isn't true. Our mighty deeds did a lot to build the greatest game the world has ever known, but the fight to get our fair share of the pie has been long and difficult.

"Back then, we players were alone; we weren't killer-business-men, and we were up against twenty-eight of the richest men in America."

In the Pressure Cooker

As the 1968 training season, shortened by the strike, finally got under way, Deacon stunned the players and outraged the owners by taking his case to the fans. Vastly popular for his slashing defensive play, Deacon's willingness to talk to sports reporters had gained him a huge reputation, and his quick mind had assured them quotable material. He was on his way to becoming more than a star player—The Deacon was becoming a pop hero and a personality in his own right. So, when he reaffirmed for the press that he wouldn't play for Los Angeles unless his salary demands were met, his comments made national news. The Rams front office felt it necessary to counter Deacon's comment, and it did so by stiffly reiterating that it would not renegotiate.

In response, Jerry Klein, Deacon's advisor, told the press, "Deacon Jones is prepared to dig in for the winter." To the chagrin of not only Dan Reeves and his staff, but management throughout the league, reporters were beginning to wonder openly why the Rams were being so stubborn. Why wouldn't they review Deacon's contract, as he seemed to have a clear case and the precedent had been set before with other players in similar situations?

Charles Maher of the *L.A. Times* thought he had the answer, and it wasn't very complimentary to Rams management:

> Setting aside the question of how much Jones might actually be worth today, and judging his case strictly by contemporary business standards, one is inclined to conclude he has a very skinny argument. The Rams have torn up other contracts, but Jones may have made a tactical error in bringing his case out in the open. On the

other hand he may have made efforts to settle it privately to no avail. The club has to capitulate in public to get him back in uniform.[4]

Over the years, the owners have shied away from this sort of publicity, because it brought to light the seamy side of the monopoly they'd been granted by the U.S. Congress and had autocratically abused over the years. But without the weight of six hundred striking veteran players behind him, Deacon's hand was weakened. When holdouts Merlin Olsen and Jack Snow made their deals and quickly returned to the fold, Deacon's fate was all but sealed. All across the country the owners united against their single remaining foe and turned up the volume in a shrill press campaign of their own.

Tex Schramm, the general manager and president of the Dallas Cowboys spoke for the owners, spelling out the dire consequences of a lawless world that would come into being if the rebel Deacon Jones got his way. "The Rams had no other course to take. The lines are clearly drawn. If you re-negotiate, you destroy the integrity of the contract. Team discipline would disintegrate, players will start to second-guess their coaching, complaining about their teammates."[5] It would be a world in chaos. A world without owners running things.

It was the second week in August, and Deacon still hadn't reported to camp. He was lying in his hot tub, reading from a stack of recent sports sections from the L.A. papers and relaxing his sore muscles. He was at his playing weight, his secret training schedule was going well at the beach, and he felt he could step into his old position at a moment's notice.

Mal Florence had written in the Sunday *Times* of July 28 that, "The absence of Jones places a burden on the entire Rams organization." Greg Schumacher, Deacon's appointed stand-in, was quoted in the same article, "I don't feel I deserve to be a starter yet. I've got a long way to go. Let's face it; no one can fill the Deacon's shoes. He's the best there is in the world. I'm just honored to back him up." Deacon sighed and set the paper on the pile next to him.

He heard Iretha come in the front door. She came to the recreation room to let out the doberman, saw the sliding door was open, and stepped on the patio. He saw she was loaded down with packages.

"Hi, Jones," she said. "Thought you'd be out yet."

"Finished early," he grunted. "Iretha, I thought we had a talk about cutting back on expenses right now."

4. Charles Maher, *Los Angeles Times*, July 23, 1968.
5. Mal Florence, *Los Angeles Times*, July 23, 1968.

Iretha pouted, "Just a little shopping with the girls."

He pointed to the showy bags. "Bullocks Wilshire. May Company. You gonna send us to the poorhouse, girl."

He saw the frown lines start on her face. He didn't like to fight with Iretha. She would either whine or shout, but in any case, nothing was ever resolved. "You gave me the money for my birthday, Jones," she said.

"I know," he said, agreeing to cut the argument off at the pass. "And it is your money. Just try not to spend too much right now. I don't know when I'm gonna get my next paycheck from the Rams . . . if I ever do."

Deacon saw the fleeting look of uncertainty in Iretha's eyes. She set the packages down on a redwood lounge chair and came over to him. "All this I read in the papers is just talk, ain't it?"

Deacon sighed, unhappy that he'd let the conversation get this far. The only thing that kept Iretha happy was money. It was the central, stabilizing influence in their relationship. She was the wife of the great Deacon Jones, and she spent his money. "There has to be money coming in, Jones," she said.

"I know that, Iretha."

"You the bread-winner, Mister Jones. I depend on you. How we gonna pay for this house, for clothes, for trips?"

"Iretha, I know all that. I'm just trying to get us our fair share. I'm tired of eatin' off the hind end of the Ram."

"You so stubborn, we gonna end up with nothin'!"

"How you figure, Iretha?" The words barely sounded from his clenched teeth.

"You jist a simple black man, up against rich white folks. You ain't gonna get nothin', Jones, nothin' but grief!"

The phone rang just as Deacon was wondering what was keeping him from hitting her. "Don't answer it!" he thundered.

"But—we don't know who it is."

"It's George Allen, for God's sake. He calls me all hours of the day and night, he calls me in the bathroom, when I'm in bed, when I'm brushing my teeth and when I'm watching television."

"George Allen is your friend, about the only friend you got left, an' when he say come back to the Rams, it be time to go!"

In the past weeks, Allen had played the difficult job of go-between, the only link remaining between Dan Reeves and Deacon, outside of what each read about the other in the newspapers. Allen was patient and unrelenting, arguing he should come back for the good of the team. When he wasn't calling, it was Eddie Meador or Jack Pardee, who called every day to say he was letting everybody down.

After the tenth ring, Deacon said, "Okay, answer it—but if it's George, I'm not here!"

She picked up the receiver, listened briefly and handed him the phone. "Don Drysdale," she said. He took the phone and stared at her. She got the message, gathering up her shopping spree and huffing back inside the house. Drysdale had put together an all-night party in honor of sports holdouts everywhere.

Deacon showed up, mainly to get away from the constant phone calls from the press, from his teammates, from Allen. The party went well at first. Everybody said nice, supportive things. But the party went on and on, and the nicer people were to him, the more alone and isolated Deacon felt. Easy for them to say "hang in there," but it was his butt on the line!

Deacon went out into the back yard and looked off into the inky black night. He was angry enough to hold off the entire world. The Rams were treating him badly and everyone knew it. But he didn't know how to answer Iretha, the enemy in his own camp. For better or worse, he had promised to support her. How could he go back on his own word?

Deacon left the party at 5:30 in the morning, and at 4:30 in the afternoon he drove to the Coliseum. His hands weren't taped and he had no thigh pads. But late in the game, Allen put him in for a few plays. The symbolic gesture complete, Deacon Jones was officially back to stay.

After the game, Deacon sat quietly in the middle of a swarm of reporters. "I thought it would serve the best interests of myself and my family to come back," he quietly told them. "I know you win with a forty-man team, but an individual can help. I thought if I returned I could boost the morale of the team and enhance our chances of winning a championship."[6]

Deacon looks back on his holdout stand. "It may have been her own self-interest, but Iretha was right. She saw right away that it's a long, hard road if a working man wants to go it alone against the bosses. She wanted no part of that.

"Maybe it was a mistake to get that far on the bad side of Dan

---

6. Mal Florence, *Los Angeles Times*, August 10, 1968.

Reeves, but I never ran my life afraid of any man. He was wrong then, and looking back, what he and the other owners did still feels wrong to me today.

"My biggest mistake—and I'll admit it right here—was when Merlin Olsen and Ed Masrey came to my house to talk about the possibilities of combining our efforts, I turned them down. Across town in the Dodgers camp, Drysdale and Koufax held out and combined their efforts and did win out. My advisors turned me against it. I guess they figured there wouldn't be room enough for two teams of lawyers if Muley and I joined forces. This is another case where, if I'd have studied and paid attention in college, maybe I could have figured it out. That's why I tell college athletes to crack the books, take plenty of courses like finance and business administration, so you'll have a clue as to how to handle your own finances."

Deacon reflects on player rights and fair compensation: "Baseball players figured it out long ago, and today even ordinary players are demanding huge sums of money. Basketball is doing well, too. By 1992 figures, in basketball your twelve players per team average over $1 million a man. In baseball, the twenty-five-man squads average nearly $500,000 a head. Football, the forty-seven-man squads average somewhere between $100,000 to $200,000 a player.

"Where it really hurts is football's pension plan. It lags far behind. It's downright criminal when you consider the average playing life of an NFL player is less than four years!

"If we can't get it in our contracts, at least the NFL Alumni Association should be sponsoring programs for the many ex-pros who are drug addicts or who have no savings and no careers. Ballplayers don't live to be very old. Many ex-players need expensive medical care because of all the knocks and shocks to their systems. NFL Alumni can't even take care of the ex-players like this who need medical treatment, much less their poor families. Travis Williams, who played for the Rams in 1971, died penniless and the chapter couldn't even raise seven thousand dollars to bury him. That really made me sick."

Dick Bass reflects on what it was like for a player to negotiate in his playing days: "It is true that, as late as 1971, the clubs still wouldn't talk to agents. When I played, agents were unheard of. The great Vince Lombardi was such a rabid company man that he cut a player who showed up with his agent. Why, you may ask, is that important? Agents make a lot of difference. Today, there is a known base salary which has been set for each position. And agents were very helpful in bringing that about, and are important in keeping the information current."

Earning Their Money

The Rams won their 1968 opener against the St. Louis Cardinals, 24-13. The Front Four had young quarterback Jim Hart running for his life and throwing prematurely for the entire game. The *L.A. Times* reported, "Lamar Lundy, in his finest hour in the last decade, joined Deacon Jones, Merlin Olsen, and Roger Brown to intimidate Hart in what was essentially a defensive victory."[7]

A defensive victory. The Fearsome Foursome, combined with George Allen's tough defensive backfield, were stamping a new strategy on the game of football. The following week, Roman Gabriel piled up touchdowns in a 45-10 rout of the Steelers. But the real story was that, with Jones, Olsen, Lundy, and Brown applying the pressure, the Steelers gained only fifty-three yards net rushing the entire game.

Traveling to Cleveland, the Rams crushed the Browns 24-6 in a game so one-sided that not once did the Browns offense get to the fifty yard line! Playing total defense, the Rams kept Cleveland quarterback Frank Ryan playing on his side of the field the entire game. In the locker room after the final whistle, Ryan told *L.A. Times* reporter Mal Florence, "The Rams rush was only half our problem. The hard part was finding a receiver."[8] The coverage by Rams deep backs Irv Cross, Clancy Williams, Eddie Meador, and Ron Smith was so tight that Ryan couldn't throw.

In the next game, which was the fourth game of the season, played at home in the Coliseum against San Francisco on October 6, the Fearsome Foursome was tested another way, with a goal-line stand. In the third quarter, with the 49ers trailing 14-7, the San Francisco team managed to bring the ball deep into Rams territory. First and goal at the Rams two. The 49ers decided to smash through with their running game, piling their big line into the Rams to wedge an opening and slamming one of their big backs into the point of attack. It was an unfortunate choice, as their first two plays gained a net one yard. On third and one, they handed Tucker the ball and ran the play at Deacon Jones, who met the big back head-on and stood him straight up, preventing the ball from crossing the goal line. With fourth and one, the 49ers elected for the field goal.

After the game, George Allen said, "That goal-line stand did it. We turned back their big backs and their big line."

7. Bob Oates, *Los Angeles Times*, September 23, 1968.
8. Mal Florence, *Los Angeles Times*, September 30, 1968.

Deacon told the press, "Dallas may have a 'multiple offense,' but we have a multiple defense. We do a lot of things out there a lot of people don't see."[9]

Traveling to Green Bay, the Rams won 16-14 on a dramatic last-minute kick by Bruce Gossett from twenty-seven yards out, gaining some small revenge for their previous year's playoff defeat at ice-coated Milwaukee Stadium. Making reference to the gloating tone of Jerry Kramer's popular book *Instant Replay,* George Allen told the press, "Jerry's book helped us win. We all read it. Now it can be called *Instant Defeat.*"[10]

Back in the Coliseum, the Rams offense spotted Atlanta fourteen points in the first quarter when they gave up an interception and a nine yard march after a fumble. The L.A. defense refused to roll over and die; instead, they decided to take matters into their own hands. They startled Atlanta quarterback Bob Berry with a surprise blitz as the Foursome—which included Greg Schumacher that day (Lamar Lundy being out with an injury) were joined by Myron Pottios, Maxie Baughan, and Jack Pardee to get to Berry six times. The Falcons never scored again as the Rams defense dominated the game. On one memorable play, Deacon collapsed his blocker backwards into the lap of the ball carrier, adding his weight to make a seven-hundred-pound stack behind the line. With this 27-14 win, George Allen's Rams were 6-0. Los Angeles had won fourteen straight league games, a string never achieved by Vince Lombardi's greatest Packers teams. The next weekend the Rams traveled to Baltimore, where disaster showed up on the field in the form of the Colts. Drowned in a sea of screaming Baltimore fans, the Rams offensive line showed confusion all afternoon, allowing five sacks of their quarterback. Gabriel, who had been sacked only four times in the entire season, couldn't get the offense going. On the field much of the game, the defense finally caved in and allowed the Colts to run for 159 yards.

After the game, George Allen earnestly told his players, "We should be ashamed to take our money this week. We didn't really earn it." The Rams' season-long problem was the Colts, who were playing almost flawless football behind the pinpoint passing of Earl Morrall, who had taken over for the injured Johnny Unitas. The Rams and the Colts were in the same division. With no wild card spots available, the Rams were suddenly thrust into a "must win" situation. From now on,

9. Mal Florence, *Los Angeles Times*, October 7, 1968.
10. Mal Florence, *Los Angeles Times*, October 14, 1968.

they were playing sudden death; any loss would put them out of the running for the title, and they had yet to play Detroit (always a bruising game), Atlanta (Van Brocklin would give his right eyetooth to beat them), San Francisco (in the mudbowl), New York, Minnesota, Chicago —and again—Baltimore. To get to the playoffs, the Rams were going to have to earn their money every week for the rest of the season.

Deacon reflects on George Allen's assessment of the loss to Baltimore. "George was right. We members of the Ram defense hadn't earned our money that week. I remember I got through to block a Lue Michaels' extra-point try in the first quarter, and I had my share of tackles. So much for the individual heroics. But our defense as a whole couldn't rise to the challenge and turn the tide from defeat to victory, and that's what they paid us for. Most days, we would have. After all, we were the mighty Fearsome Foursome, backed by the most stubborn zone defense ever invented by man. It wasn't that the ball bounced wrong, and believe me, there are days when that happens. No excuses. It was simply that we were flat on defense. In almost all the games we played during the Allen years—in, say, probably 90 percent of the games—it was our incredible defensive play that picked up the team and led us to the win. Give our offense the ball enough and deny the other team, that's what ball control is all about. But here we were, holding our own on defense, but nothing more, and the offense couldn't pick up the slack. We were unhappy with the loss, of course, stunned and angry at ourselves. But we didn't recognize the importance of the game. With the season barely half over, we would play catch-up to Baltimore the rest of the way. And, though we didn't know it at the time, with Baltimore heading for a record of 13-1 on the year, our season was already all but over for us."

The Game within the Game

After beating the Lions 10-7 in a bitter defensive duel, the Rams were 7-1 as they headed for Georgia to play hapless Atlanta (1-7). The Falcons had fired head coach Norm Hecker after losing their first three games of the season and hired fiery and unpredictable Norm Van Brocklin. In no time at all, the headstrong Dutchman was turning the team upside down in a frantic effort to find a winning combination.

The L.A. players were already working out in Atlanta when word filtered to the Rams camp that Norm was creating a special formation to handle Deacon Jones. The story was that the Falcons were going to put in another tackle at the tight end spot, a big man who would hammer Deacon from behind.

Deacon sat in the locker room, digesting the news. For a long time, he didn't say anything. Finally he called to George Menafee, the trainer who generally handled taping his arms and legs, "Mother—come here."

"What is it, Deak?"

"Mother, you hear what Van Brocklin gonna do to me Sunday?"

Menafee gave him an elfish grin. "There is a buzz going around. I was just going to look into medical supplies . . . see if we had an extralong stretcher for you."

At that moment Merlin Olsen came back from the shower room and banged around in his locker. He threw a wet towel at Deacon and chimed in, "We're callin' the Rev'rend Rosey in from L.A. to do the last rites."

"Screw that, Mother. An' screw off, Olsen. Mother, I just wonder if you brought your plaster?"

"Sure, why, you break something?"

"Yeah, his head!" Merlin chortled.

"Damn it, Muley, I ain't in the mood." Deacon stood and took the trainer by the arm. "Let us go for a little walk where we can be uninterrupted, to talk over the possibilities of how I intend to get through the perilous times between now and Monday alive and well." They walked back out on the practice field and Deacon talked for another five minutes, asking the trainer questions about a wide range of self-protective measures.

On game day, he showed up a half-hour early and had George apply extra tape to his ankles. Deacon made sure his spikes were extra short, so there was less chance they would get caught in the turf. Finally, he had the trainer alternate tape and plaster, tape and plaster on his forearms, smoothly building them up into an ordinary-looking thick tape job that had a little more heft than usual to it. The construction didn't add a lot of weight or bulk, but Deacon's arms felt hard as iron.

"Anything else I can do?" Menafee gave him his quirky grin.

"Yeah. Keep that stretcher ready for whomsoever may be in need of it." The trainer danced out of the way as Deacon practiced a brushing headslap with one of his forearms.

The man who wormed the advance information out of the Falcons got it right: From their first offensive play, Atlanta came at Deacon with two big men, a one-two punch with the first holding him while the second tried to circle and slam into him from behind. Deacon's forearms, which were hard as plaster, helped to slam away the hands of the first man, who was trying his best to get his fingers into number 75's jersey and hang on until the bag man could sneak around and do his job from the rear.

By the end of the first quarter, Deacon had been hit hard from behind three or four times. His thighs and calves ached from the pounding, his blue-and-white uniform was covered from head to toe with grass stains, and he was getting used to crawling up from the bottom of the pile, the last man to return to his position on every play. The referees were looking the other way, and not calling the crack-blocks. Clipping on the interior line, where things bunched up and accidents happened, wasn't something they gave a high priority. But Deacon knew that, at this rate, it was only a matter of time before he was seriously hurt, maybe out for the season, maybe finished for his career.

Merlin gave him a worried look. "What can I do, Deak?"

"Just get through to the quarterback. We hit him enough, maybe they'll have to back off." Double-teaming Deacon gave Merlin that much more of an opportunity to break through on his own.

"They're tryin' awful hard to get me hurt, Merlin. I think the Dutchman put out a contract."

Merlin shook his head, "Refs aren't calling anything. Somebody may have said something to somebody."

"Yeah. 'Get the Deacon,' is what they said."

"Wonder what it costs to buy a ref?"

"It's that damn Van Brocklin. Called me nigger once to my face, Muley. I been destroyin' his teams ever since."

As the Falcons broke the huddle, Merlin had time to ask, "What'll we do?"

"Stunt me this time. I want the inside."

"Risk the outside?"

"Merlin!"

Merlin nodded. The game was still early, and it was nothing out of the ordinary. They called surprise stunts at the line all the time. It was one way they made the coaches earn their salaries, with their hearts in their throats. When it worked, they were the heroes; when it didn't, hell, they were still the best defensemen in the business.

On the snap, Merlin faked his rush and then pulled back, hesitating a split second before crossing to block Deacon's man. In that micro-moment, Deacon had already slashed in front of him, angling past Merlin's man. It was hugely successful, and Deacon found himself in the backfield, bearing down on Falcons quarterback Bob Berry, who was setting up for a screen pass. Berry tried to juke to the right, but Deacon stayed with him, and, instead of tackling him, threw a tremendous headslap with one of his weighted casts. His rock-hard forearm caught the quarterback squarely in the head, and Berry went down like a ton of bricks. Deacon saw what he thought was the ball out of the corner of his eye, and dove on it. To his disappointment, it proved to be the fallen quarterback's helmet.

Even if he hadn't come away with the ball, Deacon strutted back to his side of the line, grinning to Merlin, "Wasn't that beautiful? An' he's lucky, man. If his helmet doesn't come off, his head does!"

Merlin nodded back across the line to where the Atlanta trainers were rushing out to look after their fallen Falcon. "Looks like Little Bobby Berry doesn't want to play for a while."

Deacon turned and grinned at Van Brocklin and gave him a little wave while he pretended to stretch and yawn. Berry was one of Van Brocklin's favorites. The Falcons coach had dropped promising Randy Johnson from the starting lineup in favor of Berry, who had played for him in Minnesota. Upon spotting Deacon's little gesture, the temperamental Van Brocklin looked like he would come storming out on the field, but before he could begin his charge, he was interrupted by his assistant coaches. He snarled and turned his attention back to Berry, who was having trouble figuring out what day it was and how many fingers made three.

When play finally resumed, the Falcons took after Deacon in earnest, trying to plow him into the dirt on every offensive play. About half the time, with his beefed-up arms, he was able to headslap his way out of the first hold before the second man hit him from behind. When he wasn't so lucky, his sense of timing told him when to collapse and roll into a defensive ball. As the game wore on and the double-teaming didn't seem to have its intended crippling effect, things got ugly. The second man assigned to Deacon began piling on after the play was blown dead, and Deacon started kicking. The referees still refused to blow the whistle, though by now the foul play and bad blood was obvious to both teams, the fans, and whoever was watching the telecast. Finally, after suffering one last late hit, Deacon continued kicking the man on top of him until the referees threw him out of the game.

The Rams won, 17-10, in what the press called "a squeaker over the lowly Falcons." Deacon was noted for setting up Pardee's interception, which won the game, when he jumped on Bob Berry as he attempted to ditch the ball underhand.

Nobody said anything about Van Brocklin's plan to cripple the Rams star defensive end, or about Deacon's cement forearms. Those weren't the sort of things one took to the press.

Today, Deacon remembers that game: "That's one reason why the Dutchman hated my guts. He tried to end my career, and he ended up with his favorite quarterback's head nearly knocked off. Sometimes I wonder about those refs. Easy for a player to cry 'foul,' I suppose, but the hits on me in that game were too dirty to be ignored, and the men in stripes were always looking the other way.

"That was the only game I was ever thrown out of. The last hit from behind on me was so late after the whistle was blown that I started kicking and the ref threw me out. I kicked that ugly Atlanta dog until they threw me off the field, and when they dragged me away, I was still kicking at him. Looking back, it's a good thing they did throw me out. They probably saved me from a serious injury.

"After that, we used that cement cast idea off and on for almost two years—1968 and part of 1969, before I got caught. Mother plastered my arms up whenever we figured the other guys were going to gang up on me to do me bodily harm. Certain teams, like the 49ers or the Bears, it was a given. They would do anything to win in the NFL, and I suppose still do. If you're going to stay alive, you have to take care of yourself. And there's nothing I know that's quite like a sledgehammer to the side of the head when you need to back the dogs off, to earn a little respect."

Stopping Deacon Jones

On November 17, 1968, the Rams played the 49ers to a 20-20 tie in Kezar Stadium under conditions Mal Florence of the *L.A. Times* described as "a miserable river-bottom field which chained the defensive linemen of both sides in their tracks." Once again, San Francisco had used their mudbowl to negate the slashing attack and speed of the Rams defensive line.

After the game, Merlin Olsen and Deacon Jones, speaking for the Rams players, told the press that they would urge Rams management to protest the condition of the field to commissioner Pete Rozelle. Deacon told the reporters, "It is unfair to NFL teams to play on this field. It is as bad for the 49ers as it is for the others. The field is pure dirt. You can't play football here; and I think it is up to the commissioner to legislate some minimum standards."

As usual, the 49ers tried to shrug the conditions off, claiming that, since they were equal for both teams, it didn't really matter. But it was becoming increasingly clear that, if you wanted to stop the Rams defense from overpowering you, the one proven way to do it was to gum or slick the field.

John David Crow, notorious for his earlier attempts to cripple Deacon, told the press that the 49ers had designed a new "man in motion" play to stop the Rams superstar defensive end without having to resort to the illegal "crack-back" block. Eager to put an end to the mayhem Deacon Jones was creating throughout the league, San Francisco called an unusual gathering and showed their new play to the assembled NFL scouts, billing it as a foolproof way to stop the Deacon. Unfortunately for them, they had to give it up in the actual game, as it was too muddy to truly test.

Over the years, many coaches on the various rival teams were known to pass notes on how to stop Deacon; this was an unusual case, in that San Francisco came out in the open and publicized their supposed "breakthrough." It was an unintended tribute, but the 49ers' "man in motion" play, when it finally was given its chance on dry land, was as ineffective as anything else. There had never been a defensive lineman as big, as fast, as quick, as football-smart as Deacon Jones, and it would take offensive linemen with the same reflexes and abilities to contain him. Unfortunately for Rams rivals, premier offensive linemen of this caliber were nearly nonexistent. Men with those talents became famous running backs or big tight ends.

The following week, Coach Allie Sherman's Giants came to town and once again tried the piling-on method of eliminating Deacon Jones from the game. The Rams made two monumental fumbles on punts that gave the Giants two touchdowns in the second quarter. So the Rams were losing 14-0 at halftime. The Fearsome Foursome needed to kick things into overdrive, but as the ferociously fought second half got under way, Sherman had his boys zero in on Deacon. The result was that Giants offensive tackle Willie Young found himself ejected from the game. The Rams defense came on strong, the offense slipped into high gear, and Roman Gabriel capped the Los Angeles comeback with a seventy-yard field goal drive in the last forty-one seconds to pull out the win 24-21.

After the game, Allie Sherman feigned innocence. He couldn't understand why Young was ejected from the game. "It is unusual for a player to be thrown out of a game, but I don't know what he did," he told the reporters. This was a clever ploy, and seemed to work, at least in New York City, where the press bitterly accused NFL officials of "protecting" Deacon the entire year, one New York writer claiming Willie Young's expulsion made him a "victim of the Deacon Jones Protective Society."

Deacon calmly replied. "All the man did was hit me after the whistle and call the referee a dirty name. That will get you fifteen yards and drummed out of the game in any league. The play had been over so long that everybody was getting up when he (Young) hit me. It's all in the movies. If it was a sound movie, you'd hear two very naughty words."

At this point in the season, the Rams were hanging in right behind Baltimore. They next had to play in Minnesota against the Vikings, whose front line of Carl Eller, Jim Marshall, Alan Page, and Gary Larsen (the Purple People-Eaters) was ranked with the Fearsome Foursome as the second of the top two defensive lines in the league. The Viking linebacking and secondary were also without weakness, and their fiercely competitive quarterback, Joe Kapp, was making headlines for his game-saving, last-minute, clutch pass completions. And this late in the season, the Minnesota weather would be against them. Looking forward to field conditions that might be as bad as those in Green Bay or San Francisco, Deacon told the press, "We've got to play our best game to win."

Deacon had his mind set on battling the Vikings. He had no idea he would have to climb out of a sick bed to do it.

Deacon comments on the trench warfare and many special tactics used over the years to eliminate him from the game: "Football is a great game, great enough that people shouldn't have to deny it is, at heart, a game about hitting, about taking the other guy out. Of course, today a lot of players and coaches deny the things they did because they're ashamed, or they're trying to protect their reputations with the people who buy bubble gum cards and pay big money for their autographs. With these folks, image is every-

thing, and I feel sorry for them. We were players and coaches, not saints. We did anything we could to survive, and some did anything they could get away with to win. It makes for an exciting, rich and colorful past, if you can find the few willing to talk about it.

"It is easy to see your favorite gridiron gladiators wearing their bright uniforms and bulked out in pads and helmets and to forget that, from a player's point of view, football is often about giving and receiving pain. Just remember, this isn't some computer game; those aren't electronic men down there on the field. They are real flesh and blood with muscles that ache and bones that break. One wrong move, and you're out of the game, gone for the next series, the quarter, the game, the season, the rest of your life. It's a cold-blooded game, seen from that point of view, and there's plenty that would take you out if they thought they could get away with it. It's just another thing you learn to accept. After all, I came to play the game."

The Stuff of Legends

Deacon rolled over in his bed and groaned. The light streaming in through the window in the Minnesota hotel was cold and grey. Lamar was nowhere around. Deacon decided he'd already left for the stadium. He pulled himself to a sitting position on the bed, pulling the covers around him to control the shivering, and looked around the room. A vaporizer still hissed next to his bedside, sending plumes of steam into the air, and the floor was littered with soggy clumps of Kleenex tissues. George Menifee, who'd spent the night in the chair next to his bed, filling the vaporizer every few hours and getting him aspirin and Contac cold medicine, was also gone.

Time to take stock. Deacon stood awkwardly, and almost immediately fell backwards on the bed. He lay there, cursing at the cottage-cheese flocked white ceiling. Several Rams had the flu all week, but he'd had it worst, capping off last night with a 104-degree temperature that nothing—no cold showers, penicillin, or aspirin seemed to bring down. Minnesota, he thought to himself, trying to psych himself up, the land of Norm Van Brocklin. But the crazy Dutchman had moved his act south to Atlanta, and Deacon's head felt like it was splitting open. His thoughts wandered. He was remembering how much easier it had been to get his "mad" up in the old days when the injustices of the world were so clearly defined. His head went all swimmy, and then he was thinking of his mother, stubborn Mattie Jones, and his tough, quiet father. He imagined them sitting there, silently watching him from the end of the bed. He knew that was foolish, they weren't really there, but then he imagined his mother telling him it was time to get up for work. His father didn't say anything, but there was that look in his eye like the time he'd fallen out of the orange tree.

Deacon staggered to his feet, naked except for the blanket around his shoulder, and made his way into the shower, where he twisted the faucet marked "C" and climbed in under the icy stream of water, blanket and all. Five minutes later, he emerged and scrubbed his body down with rough, dry bath towels. He slipped into a Rams sweat suit, and pulled on the long black mink coat Iretha had bought him for his birthday (with his money, he ruefully thought for the hundredth time).

Deacon swayed a little as the elevator took him down to the lobby, but he had his game face on by the time he walked out the door into the frigid Minnesota air. The doorman looked surprised to see him, even as he whistled for a cab, "Mr. Jones! We heard you weren't going to play today."

"Wishful thinking, my man. Wishful thinking," he said, passing across a crisp five-dollar bill.

The team was delighted to see him, particularly after Mother Menifee's gloomy report. Coach Allen gave Deacon a narrow-eyed appraisal. "You sure you're well enough to play?"

"We've come too far to let a little something like the flu stop us. I swear, I'd get off my death bed to play this game, Coach."

Mother took the thermometer out of his mouth and shrugged, "Temperature's down to 102."

George Allen sighed, "Well, okay." They all knew how critical this game was. With three games left, the Rams, then at 9-1-1, were still in the race for the title. But they were desperately chasing the Colts, whose single loss was to the Cleveland Browns (Who would win their Century Division with a 10-4 record). The Rams had to win here in the cold, and they'd been branded as "cold weather patsies," guys who couldn't play once things got a little chilly.

Somebody found a hanger for his mink coat, and Deacon started to get into his gear. He looked weak and shivery, but nobody said anything. "What's the field like?" he asked.

Merlin, who was double-knotting his shoes, looked up and gave him an encouraging smile. "Doesn't look like they've doctored it. It's cold and slushy, but I think our regular cleats will hold."

Deacon nodded. "First good news I've had today." He finished suiting up, pulled on his regular short-cleated shoes, and was on the field with minutes to spare. Mother brought his long Rams jacket, and he wore it on the sidelines, thrown over his shoulders when the offense was on the field. Snow fell steadily, sprinkling his shoulders and his massive afro haircut with white, and settling in a light, slushy blanket on the field.

Still, Merlin's analysis had been correct; there was enough bite in the turf that their cleats held, even on the cuts. Deacon got down into his stance and came up fast, noting with grim satisfaction that his footing was good. An evil gleam came to his eyes. Somebody was going to pay for past sins.

What followed was four quarters of nearly flawless football. The season had been one of injuries, replacements, and substitutions. Now, for the first time, Los Angeles put together sixty minutes of great offensive and defensive football. The offense, led by Roman Gabriel, scored thirty-one points. Rams receiver Wendell Tucker (from Deacon's alma mater, South Carolina State) caught three touchdown passes. And the defense, led by Deacon playing one of the greatest games of his career, smothered the Vikings, allowing only three points for the entire game. In the second quarter, with the Vikings moving the ball down to the Ram thirty-seven, quarterback Joe Kapp was cuffed by Deacon while attempting to get off a pass. He fumbled, Greg Schumacher recovered, and the Vikings never really threatened again.

Paired off against offensive tackle Doug Davis, then in his third season, Deacon played one of the most flawless, intimidating games of his All-Pro career. As Mal Florence described it, "He handled the Viking offensive linemen like they were ragbags and put relentless pressure on quarterback Joe Kapp."[11] As Bob Oates described it, "Neither flu nor snow nor gloom of night stayed Deacon Jones from his appointed rounds in Minnesota Sunday. In the snow and the rain, Jones and the nine other blockers and tacklers in George Allen's two Rams lines were the thunder and the lightning. Jones Sunday was the fastest flu-ridden tackler ever."[12]

The Rams had won with a massive and lopsided 31-3 victory over the Vikings. But the Colts, too, had won. With two games left, the Rams were 10-1-1, and the Colts were 11-1. The two teams with the best records in the NFL were scheduled to play each other in the final

11. Mal Florence, *Los Angeles Times*, December 2, 1968.
12. Bob Oates, *Los Angeles Times*, December 2, 1968.

game of the season. To be in the running for the division title, all the Rams had to do was get past the powerful, injury-ridden Chicago Bears.

Deacon remembers the aftermath of that long-ago game against the Vikings: "George Allen inspired me to get up out of bed and •*play that game. The logic of being the best, of being a winner, dictated I had to get up. And, after the game, Coach broke a long-standing rule for me. We had a no-alcohol rule on the plane, when we'd be coming back from away games. George didn't drink, and he didn't want his players and coaches getting sloppy in public. But after that game, George got Joe Sullivan to go and get me a fifth of fine cognac 'for medicinal purposes,' he said. I sat in the back of the plane all the way to Los Angeles with my black mink coat around my shoulders and my head wrapped in a towel, drinking hot tea and cognac. I pissed off some of my teammates, because I wouldn't give them any; I couldn't, because I'd promised George, and I wouldn't because it was my own personal reward. But, regardless of that, that medicine worked because by the time we touched down at LAX I'd broken my fever."*

The Shachter Snafu

The game against the Bears went badly almost from the beginning. The Rams defense was up to its usual bone-crushing efficiency, and the game should have easily been in the bag. But on series after series the offense was plagued with miscues. Tommy Mason fumbled. They missed a thirty-five yard field goal in the fourth quarter that would have given them the victory. Dick Butkus had a driving interception that ended in a Bears score. And Chicago's Clarence Childs had an eighty-eight yard kickoff run that also led to a touchdown.

It was a bitter, foul-ridden game, and the play was cruel and vicious in the trenches. The Bears would tally twelve penalties totalling one hundred and five yards and the Rams ten for one hundred and sixteen yards. It was a game controlled and ultimately decided by the officials rather than by the play on the field.

Roman Gabriel, blind-sided by Bears linebacker Jim Purnell, was knocked unconscious in the second quarter. Now near the end of the final quarter, with less than a minute left on the clock and the Rams losing by one point, Gabriel returned to attempt another of his great comebacks.

And he had his offense moving. With twenty-nine seconds left, they were already within field goal range with a first down on the Chicago thirty-two yard line. But on the next play, the officials stepped in and decided the course of the game, the Rams season, George Allen's future, and ultimately, the future of Deacon Jones. On that play, Gabriel fell back in the pocket and threw an incomplete pass to Snow. As the pass fell incomplete and the pocket collapsed around Roman, a yellow flag fluttered to the ground.

Charlie Cowan was called for holding. It wasn't the kind of call ordinarily made with the game on the line, particularly in a game where there had been nearly continuous vicious infighting and flags could have been tossed on both sides of the field on nearly every play. But tossed it was, and worse, a huge penalty was called. The ball was moved back fifteen yards from the point of infraction, which was said to have taken place six yards behind the line of scrimmage. A twenty-one yard penalty on a holding call away from the play, with the game on the line.

After the final gun, Cowan claimed furiously that both sides had been holding all day and the Bears had intimidated the officials into giving them that key call—a claim no one could prove back then, much less today, nearly thirty years later.

Terrible call or no, there was more. On an offensive holding call, yardage is lost but the down is replayed. But the referees forgot to flip back the marker card. Instead of the Rams having first down on their own forty-seven yard line, the down marker now read second down. This was a referee error of monumental proportions, the kind of thing that happens in Pop Warner League or maybe high school football. And in the tension of the moment, with every second counting and everybody concentrating on the time left in the game, nobody on the Rams bench caught the error. The Rams' coaches, intent on the clock, were not aware they had lost a down. With first down, even first down and long, Gabriel could well have gotten back within field goal range with a successful series of conservative short passes. But, with second down and long, the Rams quarterback had to play the "Hail Mary" strategy. A long toss to Wendell Tucker went incomplete. With everyone covered long on the next play, a short toss to Mason coming out of the backfield went incomplete. And finally, a desperation bomb for Harold Jackson went incomplete, on a play that the referees could easily have called defensive pass interference and yet chose to ignore. Chicago took over with five seconds to go, and the Rams didn't realize they'd been robbed until the reporters started talking about "the lost down" in the locker room. After that, the Rams filed an official protest, but Art McNally, the NFL supervisor of officials would only say, "Any further comment will have to come out of the commissioner's office."

The following Tuesday, in what sportswriter Mal Florence described as "an unprecedented public censure," Commissioner Pete Rozelle suspended the NFL officiating crew that had worked the game, admitting they "erred" in denying the Rams the down.[13] However, this did not alter the results of that critical game in any way. The game stood in the record books. Los Angeles had lost. Had the Rams won, they would have been 11-1-1, going into their final game against the Colts, who were 12-1 at the time. A Los Angeles win over Baltimore would have given the Rams the title.

Commentary detrimental to the NFL reeked from sports pages across the country, and just when it seemed that the controversy would die down, it came to light that this was the same officiating crew that had allowed the Washington Redskins to lose to Dallas on Thanksgiving Day. After that game Coach Otto Graham had told the press, "The officials stole the game from us." Rozelle fined Graham $2,500 for violating the NFL policy banning coaches and players from saying anything detrimental about officials, but Graham never retracted his comments or apologized. George Allen characteristically blamed no one else. After all, it was obvious that the Rams coaches had been intent on the clock; they were not aware they had lost a down until it was too late. Sitting in the Rams locker room deep under the cement girders of the Coliseum after the game, he talked quietly with reporters. "We have no excuses, no alibis. We've drained ourselves dry. Three years of working, and everything is down the drain. We have an axiom here that nobody can beat the Rams; the Rams lose because they beat themselves. The headline of this game is, 'Too Many Mistakes.' "

The following week the Rams narrowly missed beating Baltimore, losing 28-24 in a game that no longer mattered. The Rams ended their regular season at 10-3-1. Oddly enough, two teams won their divisions with worse records: the Browns in the Century Division with ten wins and four losses, and the Vikings in the Central Division with eight wins and six losses. The Rams sent seven players to the Pro Bowl (Roman Gabriel, Charlie Cowan, Joe Scibelli, Tom Mack, Deacon

13. Mal Florence, *Los Angeles Times*, December 10, 1968.

Jones, Merlin Olsen and Maxie Baughan), but with no wild card spots, the team wasn't even eligible for the playoffs.

George Allen, never one for the popular head-coaching hobby of schmoozing, had no plans to attend the week-long ritual of parties before the Super Bowl. He told reporters, "I feel we were as good as any team that will be playing in that game. I wouldn't want to go down there and see someone else play it." The season was down the tubes. A terrible, heart-wrenching theft from a group of men who had been driven to succeed to the best of their abilities. Worse was the bad blood that had been building between George Allen and owner Dan Reeves over the last three years. Now it came to a boiling point. In the next few weeks Allen would be fired and the team, led by an outraged and fiery Deacon Jones, would go into a massive revolt to get him back.

Deacon comments on Charlie Cowan's charge that the Bears intimidated the referees into making the call that gave Chicago the game and cost the Rams their chance at the playoffs: "At first glance, you may be inclined to dismiss such a charge. But, if you'll go back and look at the game films, you'll see that as long as Hallas was on the bench the Bears benefited from many, many questionable calls. You don't make a call like they made, not with the seconds ticking down and the game on the line. Not ever. Yet Old Man Hallas was a living legend, a physical presence in the game, and his intimidation factor with the officials was so high he was like having a twelfth player on the field. Just another reason why everybody hated him."

Rescuing George

Deacon was sitting in front of the new television set he'd bought his mother for Christmas with the warm moist wash of Central Florida air and the general hubbub of seasonal gaiety around him when the sports report came on the news with the lead story that Rams owner Dan Reeves had called his head coach George Allen on Christmas day and told him he was fired. The local sports guy was hamming it up, comparing Reeves to Old Man Scrooge, but Deacon wasn't listening any more. He was already out of his chair and half way to the front door.

"Mama," he said, "I got to go."

Mattie poked her head out of the kitchen, "Fried chicken's gonna be ready in another hour. Don't you get to playin' pool, Deacon Jones."

"No, Mama. Back to L.A.," he said impatiently.

Iretha now looked around the corner, wine glass in her hand, "What, you kidding, Jones?" The beginnings of a scowl on her face told she knew he wasn't.

Deacon didn't want a scene, he just had to go. "Iretha. George has been fired. I got to get back."

"Why? You can't do anything, honey. That be none of your business. Let the rich white folks play out their game."

Deacon gritted his teeth, remembering how gallantly Allen had treated Iretha, how Allen's wife Ettie had tried to make her feel accepted, like one of the family. He bit back the sharp things he'd been about to say. "Iretha. You got plenty of money. You stay as long as you want. I'm taking the rental car. Get another one if you want."

"No! I'm comin' wit' you!" Iretha had always considered herself above the simple folk of Eatonville. She was the wife of the great Deacon Jones.

"Okay. You got ten minutes to pack!" With that, Deacon was out the door and running for the red "Boss" Mustang he'd rented at the Orlando airport. In under a half hour, they'd said their goodbyes and Deacon had the powerful Mustang roaring past the Open Door Missionary Baptist Church and out of Eatonville. As they flashed down the dusty cutoff road that looped back to the main road, Deacon thought for a moment of the time years ago when as a young boy he'd run after the yellow Plymouth convertible and the redneck crackers who had killed the old lady with the watermelon. The more things changed, the more they stayed the same. Deacon's world was now far more complex, but injustice and human foolishness remained the same. Deacon spun the Mustang out on the highway, losing control for a moment on the side-road gravel that had spilled onto the two-lane blacktop. He was going to have to back off just a bit. No accidents now—he was needed in L.A.! The light car with the heavy V-8 engine accelerated quickly, and Deacon was soon passing every car in sight.

"Jones, why we got to go so fast?" Iretha was frightened by Deacon's attitude.

"Dan Reeves is a clever man, Iretha. He waited until we players were all out of town, back home with our families. Just like at Mississippi Valley State, when the police waited 'til everybody was off-campus for the holidays before they did their dirty work. Dirty Dan thinks by the time we get back, George is gone, everything is over, too late to do anything!"

"You can't go up against the rich white folks! I told you that in the strike, an' I was right then, an' I'm right now! You gonna get yourself thrown out of football! Where we gonna be then, Jones? Who gonna pay the bills then?"

Deacon had to resist the strong urge to let her off at the nearest bus stop. "Baby," he said through gritted teeth, "just look on George like he's our paycheck—cause that's what he is!"

Air traffic was light. Deacon had no trouble hopping a flight to Miami, and getting a first class seat to Los Angeles. As the American Airlines 707 lifted off and whined into the darkening western skies, Iretha had a few drinks and fell asleep. Deacon wandered up and down the aisles of the nearly empty plane and tried to figure out what might have happened. Nothing in the Miami papers gave a clue, but there were a few pieces of the puzzle that he knew.

Allen and Reeves had not gotten along since day one. Allen had fought for all the things that make a winner—better facilities, equipment, players. He had fought for the players, to get them more money, better playing conditions, whatever they wanted. With George, it was the team first, and he took whatever hours and money it took to get the job done. Reeves, on the other hand, fought only for control of the team. He operated on the principle that if it was good for him, then it should be done.

After the 20-20 tie in the 49ers game in the Kezar mudbowl, Allen had taken the player gripes directly to Reeves, only to have the Rams owner publicly chastise him. Reeves went directly to the press, telling them that it wasn't the coach's or the players' province to criticize stadiums of rival franchises. Allen had refused to comment to the reporters, carrying his unhappiness with him in silence. But everyone who read the sports pages in Los Angeles was aware that he'd gone to his owner for support, and Reeves hadn't backed him.

The week after that, after the Rams' last-minute win against the Giants, the Rams players had been heading for their lockers under the Coliseum when Reeves had brushed past them to talk to his head coach.

Deacon was next to Allen. They'd been congratulating each other over the triumph, when Reeves pushed through the players and came up to them. Reeves was speaking in a loud, arrogant way, and the smell of liquor was heavy on his breath.

"The turf conditions were a little better today—right, George?" Reeves asked, a silly grin plastered all over his face.

It may have been his contorted way of congratulating his head coach on a thrilling victory, but it didn't come out that way. It sounded like a taunt. Allen's face purpled, and for a moment, it looked like he was going to yell at his boss. But he managed to control his temper, and after glaring at Reeves for a moment, turned on his heel and walked away.

Reeves stuck out his hand at the departing coach. "Hey, George, don't walk away—I just wanted to congratulate you!"

But Allen's distaste of drunken conversation had kicked in, and he continued on his way.

Reeves ran after him and grabbed his shoulder. "You don't walk away from me when I'm talking to you! Nobody on this team walks away from me like that! I own this team!"

Allen spun around, his eyebrows lowered and face grim. "Dan, look—of course you own this team. Right now, you've had too much to drink. We'll talk later." Again, he turned and made his way toward the locker room.

Now it was Reeves' turn to be furious. "It's none of your business when or how much I drink!"

"That's right! It's my business to win! All of us, working together. I was convinced that you wanted a winner here, Dan. But you, you don't stick up for us!"

"When didn't I stick up for you?"

"You cave in on us all the time! The latest example, you went to the press to say it was none of our business that we had to play in a mudpit that took away our obvious team superiority. You think every member of the Rams didn't read about it in the paper? What do you think that does for our morale? You're not for this team, Dan—you're only for yourself!" And with that, Allen turned away again, leaving a furious Dan Reeves behind him. Deacon watched Reeves, afraid the man was going to run after and tackle Allen from behind. Whatever he was going to do, some of Reeves's drinking buddies talked him out of it, and they went storming off in another direction.[14]

When his plane landed at LAX, Deacon ran for the nearest news-

---

14. Mal Florence refers to this incident in his story in the *Los Angeles Times*, printed December 27, 1968 under the headline "Allen Fired; Players Threaten Revolt." Florence reported, "When Reeves entered the dressing room after the Rams 24-21 final-seconds victory over the Giants to congratulate Allen, some bitter words were exchanged. Observers said that Allen walked away from Reeves when the owner extended his hand in an appreciative gesture. Reeves then caught up with the coach, and there was a brief exchange, in the presence of a few reporters, in which Allen complained about Reeves's previous criticism of him and the players. Those who witnessed the scene said the principals departed in an ugly mood."

stand and bought the local papers. He sent Iretha on for the baggage and sat in an empty chair in one of the long corridors halfway between baggage and boarding while the overhead speakers piped in Christmas carols and the crowds hustled by heading to or from their homes for the holidays. According to the papers, plenty was happening. Reeves had told the press that Allen had been relieved of his duties because of a "personality conflict."

"George is a great coach and a fine family man," Reeves said. "It is a case of a personality conflict, perhaps, more my fault than George's."

Allen was quoted as saying, "This was probably the biggest Christmas shock of my life." Pressed further, he replayed the phone call as he remembered it. "I said, 'Merry Christmas, Dan.' He said, 'This is the end—you're fired. I didn't want to do it before Christmas.' "

The reporters, who had gotten wind of the angry conversation that took place after the Giants game, asked him about it. Allen replied simply, "I've only had six conferences with Reeves in the past two years and have seen him only once in the past seven months. After the New York game, he said to me, "How do you like the condition of the turf here?" Allen let it drop at that. It was no secret Reeves had been ill much of the 1968 season, and had spent much of his time on the East Coast. Asked what personality differences he and Reeves might have, Allen replied that his only personality clashes with Reeves came when he tried to get better training facilities for the players.

Deacon slowly turned the pages. The papers were filled with news about the Rams. Many of his teammates were already venting their ire to the press. Eddie Meador said he planned to retire. Roman Gabriel said he wanted to be reunited with George Allen at some other franchise. Charlie Cowan predicted there would be at least "twenty-eight empty spots" on the Rams roster the next year as a result of this firing. Cowan said he would not return next season, and Maxie Baughan, Jack Pardee, Deacon Jones, Tommy Mason, and Roman Gabriel all expressed the same sentiment.

"We don't want to come back and play for a loser," Cowan continued, "and Dan Reeves told some of the players he would just as soon settle for a 7-7 season."

Roman Gabriel told the press, "A personality conflict seems a minute reason for letting a man go."

Meador seconded, "I don't know if that is any kind of basis for firing a man with his record."

Merlin Olsen, as always, couched his words a bit more politically. "It's really kind of a sad thing. I've been with the Rams seven years and only the last two under Allen have been really successful. Will I retire? Wait and see."

Mal Florence noted that in the twenty-two stormy years of Rams hiring and firings (since they'd come to Los Angeles), the average tenure under Reeves was approximately three years. Allen at that point had two more years left on his five-year contract, which was estimated to pay $150,000 a year. So Allen was in prime time to be fired.

Columnist John Hall, in an article that seemed more press release for Reeves than news, took the position that, "Reeves deserves praise for standing firmly behind what he truly believes—that winning isn't the only thing, after all."[15]

Deacon read on with growing disbelief. "There have been many times when Allen's grimly all-out, no smiles, twenty-four-hours-a-day, death march approach to football has distressed Reeves." Hall went on to claim that Allen's image was protected by the Rams public relations staff, but they secretly hid their own private feelings. Under the guise of reporting "leaks," Hall accused Allen of "spying on Dallas practice sessions," and described how "genuinely disturbed" Reeves was to find Allen "really had been spying." Hall also reported that Reeves felt Allen's comments regarding the muddy conditions in Kezar "came off as a whining alibi, and that is not Dan's style." Hall went on to portray Allen as a ruthless winner. "But Reeves," he gushed, "has never liked the price you pay to play that way. It was Dan's money, Dan's courage and Dan's stamina that built the Rams." Hall ended by reporting that as the news of Allen's firing spread, one of the leading Ram scouts happily showed up at the office with a bottle of champaign.

Deacon dropped the paper to the floor with the others and balled his fists tightly together. Talk about whining! He'd never heard such loser-crap in his life!

"Now," Deacon muttered to himself, as he strode angrily down the corridor, "now they are making me mad!" He pulled a small address book from the pocket of his black mink coat, and squeezed his body into the nearest phone booth. Dan Reeves had already taken his case to the press. Time to get organized. Time for the counterattack.

Deacon hasn't changed his opinion of Dan Reeves over the years. "Dan Reeves was a self-centered little Napoleon with a huge ego.

15. John Hall, *Los Angeles Times*, December 27, 1968.

Not that Dan was stupid or foolish. It's just that his priorities were different. With Dan, owning the team came first. He liked that. It was his possession, like owning a fleet of fancy cars or a cellar full of vintage wines. His real talent was money—making it, hanging on to it, and using it to control others. Sure, he would have liked a winner, not only because he could crow about it, but because when you win, you fill the stadium and make more money. But he wasn't willing to invest all-out in the team. He ran the Rams like a middle-of-the-road business, sure to be profitable. He winced and hated it when George spent money that cut into his profits.

"George was the first coach in professional football who truly understood that you had to spend money to make money. He raised the level of play and the professional standards to what they are today, and today, admit it or not, all owners and coaches think pretty much the way he did.

"Beyond the mere spending of what it took to build a winner, George had been able to infuse us with pride, to give us the winning attitude and the winning edge. He made us winners! Dan Reeves didn't understand what George had done to us, that Coach had taken individual talent and molded us into a team dedicated to winning. Once he showed us what it meant to be a winner, anything or anybody who screwed us, who took our chances of winning away from us was going to answer for it!"

Rescuing George—Part II

The Rams players gathered at the Sheraton-West, and the angry conversations and shouting filled the air. Deacon, Maxie Baughan, Dick Bass, Eddie Meador, Charlie Cowan and Roman Gabriel all swore they would quit if the Rams didn't keep Allen. They were furious, but disorganized, and things promised to get messy. Deacon feared most that they would simply expend their rage, nothing would get done, and they would disband as unorganized, frustrated, and useless as before.

Deacon stood and held up his hands for quiet. "We are in agreement here. Why are we all yelling and fighting?"

A dozen voices spoke at once, raising all the doubts and chants he'd heard at the strike vote earlier in the year.

Again, he raised his hands for silence. "Just think on this one thing," he said. "We're all five- to ten-year veterans here in this room. We're experienced ballplayers. We've all come a long way. Dan Reeves doesn't like us, because we make more money than rookies." Here the room erupted in a chorus of boos, and Deacon again held up his hands for silence. "That's right. Think on this. The next coach Reeves hires is going to be as inexperienced as he can get away with. He's going to hire somebody he can push around, so he can show that the Rams belong to Dan Reeves. If he gets his way, this team is gone—we're all on the trading block. He'll go right back to the draft, like he always did before George. With this team, we've got a shot at the championship! How many more chances any of you going to get?" The room was silent, the men thinking about their individual chances. "Who wants to go play for the losers—to Detroit, to Atlanta, to San Francisco?" he asked. Everybody shouted "noooo!" "Okay then," he roared, "we've got one chance to be champions, and that's to get George back! We *can* do it, if we stick together! We *know* how to do it! So let's *go do it*!" The room erupted in a volley of cheers. Before their mood could change, Dick Bass and Charlie Cowen took over, forming committees and getting work schedules ironed out.

Deacon was put in charge of maintaining contact with George Allen. He started in on the first of what was to become a long series of phone conversations with Allen, whose fury at Reeves was now bolstered by offers coming in from other teams. He felt weird arguing with Coach, trying to convince him to come back. After all, a half year earlier, their situations had been reversed, with Allen calling him night and day, telling him he had to reconsider for the good of the team. But Deacon was as relentless as Allen had been and the round of calls had their effect; Coach finally promised he would "bury his pride" and talk to Reeves about coming back to the club if the opportunity presented itself.

The players' committee figured out what they were going to say and do, and then they called every reporter they knew and told them a press conference would be held the following day at the Sheraton-West.

At that conference Deacon stood in front of the bright lights with Charlie Cowan while the players publicly pledged their loyalty to their coach. It was one thing to say it verbally, but these players had signed their names on the dotted line. Charlie read the list of players who would quit if the Rams didn't keep Allen: Deacon Jones, Lamar Lundy, Maxie Baughan, Dick Bass, Charlie Cowan, Eddie Meador, and Roman Gabriel. Then there was the list of players who were considering quitting, depending on a meeting the players committee was setting up with Dan Reeves to appeal Allen's firing: Jack Pardee, Doug Woodlief, Tony Guillory, Jack Snow, Ron Smith, Claude Crabb, and Merlin Olsen.

Olsen still would not declare officially that he was quitting, but he did tell the press, "The L.A. Rams football team is not a toy to satisfy any one person or group. We have an obligation to L.A. and to southern California. Far greater things are at stake than George Allen's tenure."

No such hedging for Deacon, who made his intentions plain: "The last time you'll see number 75 play is in the Pro Bowl game if Allen doesn't come back."

After that, the days ticked by with no action other than the picket line the players set up around the Rams office on Pico Blvd. Two days later, Rams general manager Crazylegs Hirsh reiterated the management line that Reeves was a man of honor while Allen was something somewhat less. "Allen and Reeves are 110 percent individuals. Allen is 110 percent for personal goals; Reeves 110 percent for integrity. It had to happen. They were on a collision course."[16]

The picket line outside the Rams office was beginning to have a powerful effect—advanced season sales were down, down, down. Management was being hit where it hurt most, in the pocket book. One of the Rams minority stockholders, Bob Reynolds, was the first to crack the silence and raise his voice. On December 30, he was quoted in the *L.A. Times,* "It's unfortunate that Dan didn't call us" before firing Allen, he said. Reynolds didn't go on to say what the advance notice might have achieved, as Reeves had full control of all management decision-making.

The following day, pesky and irreverent columnist Jim Murray broke another kind of long silence by talking about some of the things Reeves and the Rams publicity department would rather have left in the closet. "Did Allen Lock Reeves Out of His Own House?" Murray's headline asked. "Dan Reeves . . . has a biting wit and will take a second drink. George Allen almost never smiles and has the dour outlook of a man who sees life as a series of intercepted passes." Murray went on to say that, "Allen thought Dan wanted a championship, not a team," and to note that Allen had skillfully traded his way to a winner.[17]

The days went by, but the controversy didn't calm down. Ticket sales were even reduced to a trickle, and season ticket holders were

16. *Los Angeles Times,* December 30, 1968.

17. Jim Murray, *Los Angeles Times,* December 31, 1968.

turning in their reserved seats. The message was clearly out that Dan Reeves wasn't that interested in fielding a winning team in Los Angeles. Each day saw a deluge of phone calls to the Rams office protesting Allen's firing. A citizen's committee supporting Allen was formed, and began a massive signature campaign. Twelve players in all now stood firmly by their vote of confidence, saying they would never return without their coach.

On Friday, January 3, 1969, the Rams management blinked. They sent up a trial balloon, letting it leak that if Reeves retained Allen for the following season, the Rams coach would be forced to follow certain ground rules. He would not be allowed to make promises to players without consulting management. Meanwhile, the busy little beavers in the Rams public relations department continued to batter away at Allen's reputation, leaking new rumors that questioned his integrity, and the press dutifully reported them. "It is believed there were certain irregularities in some of the trades Allen has negotiated to the betterment of the Rams. One pro football source said he was surprised to learn that he owed a club a draft choice that had already been promised to another franchise."

But the intense campaign against George Allen failed to stem the flood of public support for him, and the Reeves camp was left no alternative other than throwing in the towel. On January 7, 1969, the winningest Rams head coach ever returned like a conquering hero. Allen, who had turned down two "incredible" offers from rival teams, one in each league, said, "I'm back because my players stood up for me." (Allen told the press that one of the teams, Buffalo, had verbally offered him a large salary and 10 percent ownership of the Bills.)

Crusty and autocratic to the last, Dan Reeves refused to admit he'd crumbled under public and player pressure. "Allen's intense loyalty," he said, "and his devotion are the sole reasons" he was rehired, Reeves claimed. Reeves went on to complain that the players' attitude, though commendable, was one of the "biggest stumbling blocks" in his decision to retain Allen.

"I couldn't let the players think they were responsible for any reversal on my part," Reeves tartly lectured reporters. "As much as I admire them, football players shouldn't have any say whatever on whether a coach goes or stays."

On the other hand, the Rams' tough-minded coach made sure the press knew he'd come back on his old terms, the exact terms of his old contract, as to authority and direction. It was reported that he would now have broader authority in all areas of running the football team. Although the Rams players' committee had never actually met with Reeves, the newspapers' claimed that thirty-eight of forty players had supported their coach.

Deacon beamed contentedly when told Allen had been rehired. "He isn't the only coach who knows football . . . but he's one of the few who can coach pros." There were no words to tell the press how he really felt. It was an enormous and a monumental moment for him personally and for NFL players everywhere! *It didn't matter whether they were black or white, the slaves had risen, made their wishes known to the master, and had been successful!*

Today, Deacon remembers his part in the rehiring of George Allen as one of the most significant accomplishments of his career. "We players had been denied the basic rights other working men in America took for granted. We had a weak, foolish union with no power to protect us. Those of us who stood up for George against management could have easily been banned from football. No players in the history of the league had ever before tried anything like we did. We publicly stood up to right an obvious and grievous wrong—and we won! We paved the way; we showed it could be done."

Deacon cants his massive head, and the bittersweet smile comes to his face. "Of course, no victory is without its price. I knew it at the time. With me and the owners—Reeves personally, and NFL management as a whole—I was building up quite a score. I'd always voiced my strong opinions, and had gotten a larger and larger public following as I assumed superstar status. In 1968, I'd led the disastrous strike, and been the last holdout. Now here I was, in the thick of a player revolt that forced Reeves into an embarrassing public retreat. They never forgive and they never forget in the NFL. If you don't believe me, go back to the record books. Within a year or two after George's contract was up, those who led the move against Rams management were gone."

The "irregularity" in trading that popped into the papers as part of the attempt to bring George Allen's integrity into question may have been a reference to an incident in which the Rams coach was charged with dealing the same third- or fourth-round draft choice to two different teams, to Harland Svare when he was with the San Diego Chargers, and to somebody else.

Svare clearly remembers that incident, as he personally flew back to Rozelle's office to protest. At the official hearing, Allen steadfastly denied he'd done anything wrong until Harland pre-

sented the irrefutable proof that he had, indeed, dealt the same draft choice twice. When shown the facts, Allen immediately admitted to an honest mistake, was given a minor reprimand, and that was that. Well, not quite. The many coaches and owners in the NFL who never liked Allen do not and have never believed it was a simple mistake. Harland Svare is one of these. Reached at his health and rehabilitation center north of San Diego recently, Harland steadfastly insisted that the incident is all the proof anybody needs "to know what kind of a man George Allen really was."

In the light of the large number of trades Allen made and the complicated nature of the trades, which were often spur-of-the-moment agreements like-as-not for more than two players made over the phone with paperwork to follow, and involving third teams, draft choices, medical testing, "players to be named later", and "future draft choices," it is possible to understand how such a mistake could happen. And, since there is no pattern of trickery or foul play over Allen's great number of trades, this one incident seems less meaningful than some would perhaps make it. There is, however, one meaningful pattern—Trader George somehow managed to have consistently gotten the best of the deal in the vast majority of his many trades with these rival coaches and owners, and his spectacular success in this area did engender resentment; after all, trading players is a public business and nobody likes to be bested in the public eye.

Snake Time

The Fearsome Foursome was sitting in a little offstage room just to one side of the set of the "Steve Allen Show." At that time, Allen's show was presented live and was very popular across the country. There were a few weeks left before spring training camp, and the Foursome was relaxed, enjoying a small respite from the football wars. Lamar, who was recuperating from knee surgery, leaned back and stretched his bad leg, resting it on a well-worn coffee table.

Deacon eyed him. "How's the leg, Lamar?"

Lamar shrugged. "Too soon to tell." There was a silence between the men. Lamar finally said, "What ever happened to that band you was sinkin' all your money into?"

"WAR? I got rid of them. Lazy bums wouldn't show up for practice. I got me a new group."

Merlin, who was thumbing through a worn copy of *The Hollywood Reporter* gave him a skeptical look. "You didn't!"

Deacon nodded. "Yes, I did." Deacon didn't bother to tell them about the acting, voice, and dancing lessons. It was part of his secret training, like his daily conditioning sessions at the beach. "They're called Ray Frazier and the Shades of Madness. Got some good players, some good backup singers, too."

"Like who?" Merlin scoffed.

"Like Maxine Waters an' Julia Tillman."

"Never heard of 'em."

"Shows how much you don't know," Deacon snapped.

"Ex-Ikettes," Lamar murmured. "Sang with Ike an' Tina Turner."

"Maybe we could do another version of 'Fly in the Buttermilk,' get it right this time."

"You ain't never gonna get it right, Muley. You don't have the *beat*."

"That's a harsh thing to say to a teammate," Merlin grinned. Farm Boy had some trick up his sleeve. Deacon knew it, but he just couldn't figure out what it was. Whenever Muley was about to pull something, his voice got quiet and silky, and you couldn't say anything to rile him up. A makeup lady came by and inspected them for sweat. They allowed themselves to be damped off with dry towels, pretending like this happened every day in their lives.

"You gonna do a record, Deacon?" Lamar asked.

Deacon wasn't going to talk about it, but with Merlin pushing at him, he said more than he'd intended. "Yes, I am. I got a deal with Sundown Records, an' Sam Cooke's nephew wrote me some tunes."

Lamar whistled, "R. B. Greaves?"

"Who's R. B. Greaves?" Merlin asked.

"Wrote 'Take a Letter to Maria,' that's who."

"What did he write for you? 'Mouthin' Off at the Line'?"

"Merlin . . . " Deacon started, and then stopped. He didn't have to argue with Olsen. He turned back to Lamar. "An' Jimmy Haskell is arranging and is gonna conduct."

"What's the songs about?" Lamar had a dreamy smile on his face.

"Well, it's kinda tough to describe. The first one is called 'Lovin' a Pro.' "

"Hey, I got that one right away!" Merlin laughed.

"No. It's a sympathetic song about a professional lover."

"You mean a gigolo?"

"More like a male prostitute."

Merlin hooted and whooped, but Lamar took it more seriously. "They ain't gonna let you put something like that on the radio."

Deacon shrugged. "The other side's called 'Play the Game.' The loves and lives of a professional athlete."

And then the assistant director came and pointed them out onto the stage. They stumbled out into the bright lights and took their seats. Allen did some light-hearted chatter about football and the Foursome, and they easily tossed it around. Allen asked about Deacon's singing lessons, and Deacon replied, "I am the outstanding man at my position in football, but not in entertainment. I have the ability though, and the enthusiasm. I just need the experience."

"You like the stage? I mean, do you feel good under the bright lights?"

Deacon grinned confidently. "Well, Steve, we play in front of fifty thousand people every week."

The chatter went on for a little while, and then, with the Foursome still sitting there, Allen brought out and introduced his next guest, a slight little man he introduced as a "holy man from India." He was thin and wiry, and dressed in swaddling clothes like Gandhi. Next to the burly football players this new arrival looked frail and immaterial. While Allen talked in glowing but vague terms about the marvelous wonders the mystics of Asia could perform, the stage hands brought out a huge woven basket and placed it on the floor in front of the little man.

Deacon was beginning to sweat. He felt uncomfortable. He wasn't sure why, perhaps something he had heard, or some bit from an old Abbott and Costello movie coming back to him. Allen was now talking about the deadly cobras of India and how certain of these men were so holy that they could charm the snakes to do their bidding.

Deacon couldn't believe it. He leaned back on the sofa and tried to relax. *They wouldn't be such fools to bring a deadly snake on a show like this, would they?* But a second little man wrapped in sheets came out and with a little bow handed the first man a simple wooden flute. The mystic began to play.

Deacon's eyes widened. *Didn't the basket seem to shudder, to move just the tiniest fraction?* And then the lid fell from it and there not ten feet in front of him arose the biggest, ugliest, meanest snake he'd ever seen! The thing rose, swaying dangerously back and forth, back and forth, looking for something to sink its deadly poison fangs into. Deacon held back a cry of alarm. Didn't Allen know how much he hated snakes? A choking, gasping sound came from his throat. He somehow managed to get his feet under him, and dove over the back of the couch and was gone. *To hell with the national exposure—that was a snake, man!*

To this day, Merlin won't admit he set up the snake joke on the "Steve Allen Show." But his eyes light up and a huge grin pastes itself across his face as he tells the story: "The Fearsome Foursome was doing a guest shot on the 'Steve Allen Show,' and we'd been introduced and were sitting around on the sofa when Steve brought out his next guest, an Indian fakir with a basket. He told us there was a snake in the basket, but Deak must not have believed him and the rest of us didn't care. Anyway, there was a lot of joking around and finally the Indian took the cover off the basket and started playing some sort of reed instrument, and sure enough, here comes this big cobra out of the basket, bobbing and weaving in time to the music. Well, Deacon took one look at that thing and his eyes got real big and he disappeared right over the back end of the couch. I mean, he was gone! You can look at that footage today and you can see him do it. And he never did come back for the rest of the show."

Lamar was right about "Lovin' a Pro." Never one to shy from controversy, Deacon publicly admitted it was about the feelings of a male prostitute searching for love, and most radio stations banned it from play.

9

Two More Allen Years

The way many of the Rams players and their fans saw it, Dan Reeves, had he been allowed to fire George Allen, would have broken up their winning combination, would have traded players he felt were troublemakers, would have hired a weak coach he could mold to his will, and started all over in a brand new attempt to build a winner—just as he had five or six times during the Rams long losing streak before Allen joined the team, and just as he would again after Allen was gone. Deacon and the other veteran players who had sided with Allen realized they didn't have that many years left to play. They couldn't let Dan Reeves destroy what they had worked so hard to build together. So they'd taken the big gamble by lining up with their coach against the team ownership, and they won.

But what exactly did they win, other than sending a shudder through ownership boxes in stadiums around the league? They and the Los Angeles fans gained another two years as a winning team, as contenders for the championship. Those were Deacon's ninth and tenth campaigns, and he would never regret his decision to side with George Allen. What he personally gained from their victory over Reeves was of tremendous importance to him. Under Allen's continuing inspiration and leadership, he continued to play the intense, hard-driving brand of football that had made him a superstar. Already known as the player-image of George Allen, the totally dedicated football man, Deacon would now have two

437

more years to go for the brass ring, the championship of the world. He would never get that ring; this goal would elude him throughout his playing career. But for two years more he would still be in the hunt, and, as any ballplayer or real fan can tell you, there are few thrills in life that can compare with a drive for the title.

In the previous two years—1967 and 1968—Deacon had achieved fifty regular-season quarterback sacks (in twenty-eight games an average of nearly two a game). In those games, he'd made nearly two hundred unassisted tackles. He'd batted down over a dozen passes (a dangerous practice, because when you launch yourself up vertically to knock down a pass, you sacrifice the entire length of your outstretched body to oncoming blockers), and he had hurried rival quarterbacks at least as often as he'd sacked them. Now Deacon would continue his assault on offenses around the league, building lifetime records that have not and may never be equalled.

Whether he played in a practice scrimmage, exhibition game, or the real thing, Deacon had never learned to hit halfway. He continued to be bothered by the nagging muscle tear in the arch of his push-off foot and was now wearing a specially built shoe with a steel plate placed in the tongue to protect the injury from the malice of rival linemen. Still, he went full-out on every play, and the one question on management's mind was, how long could anybody hold up to that kind of pounding? This was the eternal question, the cold-hearted and continuing appraisal of what a player is worth on the trading block. Football, one need not be reminded, is a business run by owners for profit.

No matter that the L.A. fans idolized their Deacon, by Reeves's standards, Deacon was already prime trading bait both for his age and independent attitude. But Allen didn't think the same way, and so the star defensive end could look forward to at least two more great years with "his" team, the Rams. After that, well . . . the future would have to take care of itself.

It is enlightening to consider that, although George Allen had gained the reputation for "trading away the future," he was such an accomplished trader that the Rams were in a position to enjoy three first-round draft choices in the 1969 draft. Allen's adroit dealing was laying the future for a powerful Rams dynasty that would last through the 1970s, long after he was gone, and culminate in seven straight divisional championships under future Rams coaches Chuck Knox and Ray Malavasi.

A Question of Values

Rams football was back. The team took the field against the Buffalo Bills on a Sunday for a preseason exhibition game, and nearly seventy thousand Rams fans showed up to get a look at the 1969 version of their team. The Fearsome Foursome set out to prove intimidation was still the name of their game, and they relentlessly hounded Jack Kemp, the Bills quarterback. The Rams tore up the Bills, 50-20, and a fine time was had by all in this, the second to last tuneup game before the beginning of the regular season.

Deacon roared in to sack Kemp for a safety in the second half, at the peristyle end of the Coliseum, and a great roar went up from the crowd. He threw both his arms in the air in exaltation, and the fans roared their approval. "I love the crowd—all sixty-nine thousand of them," he told the reporters, "and I think the crowd loves me too."

Buffalo tried a five-man pass offense—sending three ends and two backs out. It was a formation that had worked well for them against other teams in the league. After the game Deacon commented, "I'd read about their five-man pass offense, but I didn't think they'd do it against us. Some teams send two or three men out, but keep the rest for blocking. When you send out five men against us, that means there is one-on-one blocking against myself, Olsen, Brown and Schumacher." Brown was now playing in the retired Rosey Grier's spot, and Greg Schumacher for the injured Lamar Lundy. "There is no way they can keep us out with this pattern. It can't be done."[1]

So much for the second half of the game; in the first half, the Bills quietly introduced a host of rookies—college running back sensation O. J. Simpson, halfback Larry Smith, tight end Bob Klein—and "Negro rookie" quarterback James Harris.[2]

On one of their first plays from scrimmage, Merlin gave Deacon the wink; the two men stunted, and Deacon found himself bearing down on Harris. Instead of slamming the young quarterback to the ground, Deacon leaped high, causing Harris to throw for an incompletion.

When he came back to the line, Merlin, who had caught the full brunt of two offensive linemen, was picking sod out of his belt. Merlin nodded, the play had been a success. Two plays later Buffalo was forced to kick.

1. Mal Florence, *Los Angeles Times*, September 7, 1969.
2. Bob Oates, *Los Angeles Times*, September 7, 1969.

Several series later they had a chance to stunt again; it was a spectacular success, and this time Deacon came roaring in on Harris from his blind side. Oddly enough, he let up at the last moment, slapping aside Harris's throwing arm and causing another incompletion.

This time, when he returned to his side of the line, Merlin frowned at him. "Deacon, what are you doing?"

"Football," Deacon replied. "We in the Coliseum. You havin' a lapse of memory?"

Merlin gritted his teeth and didn't say any more. A few plays later they stunted again, and Deacon easily slid through the blockers to slap the ball away before Harris could get his pass off. Buffalo would have to kick. As they walked off the field, Merlin pulled off his helmet and looked over at his teammate. He couldn't stand it any longer.

"*What* in the *world* are you *doing,* Deak?" he yelled.

Deacon eyed him warily. "What you talkin' about, Muley?"

"Deacon Jones, by my count, you have now missed—totally *missed* —three sacks in a row! I thought you were the mighty killer of quarterbacks! Who the hell is that out there you're protecting, *your sister?*"

By this time they'd walked past the bench, and were scooping cups of ice water out of one of the aluminum cans. While Merlin drank, he eyed Deacon, waiting for his answer.

Deacon spat and kicked the turf and finally said. "How many black quarterbacks we got in this league?"

That stunned Merlin, who wasn't really thinking along those lines. "Well, I don't know, Deak. I never stopped to count. What would that have to do with anything, anyhow?"

Deacon looked him directly in the eyes and said softly, "It got everything to do with everything, Merlin. You an' me, we out here in a little it-don't-mean-nothing tuneup game. But for Harris, this be his first game ever in the pros. An' that poor bastard has the ill fortune to be facin' the incredible and illustrious Fearsome Foursome at their finest."

"Deacon, this is *football*! Tough luck for him, that's just the way it works!"

"No, Muley," Deacon continued, the bittersweet smile coming to his lips. "There's lots more to it than you read in the newspapers."

"I don't get it! We stunt and I get buried by two men and I got the dirty uniform to prove it. It don't go in the record books, but you and I both know I earn a share of your sacks—sacks which today, for some strange reason you can't even articulate, you refuse to accomplish!" Merlin crushed his paper cup and threw it on the ground. He stood facing Deacon, hands on his hips, angrily waiting for an explanation.

"Ar-tic-u-late. That be a big word for a boy from the swamps of central Florida . . . or the pastures of Utah."

"Yeah, well, I think you owe me an explanation!"

Deacon sighed. "Merlin, try to follow the logic here. The answer to the question I asked you a moment ago is, 'one.' By my count, there is one black quarterback in the entire glorious NFL, an' his name be James Harris. After all these years, we got one. Now, if I blow him away today, if I cripple him, break his collarbone or his ribs or his throwing arm, if I smash and smack him like you know I could, there ain't gonna be *any*. You see, young James ain't learned to curl up and protect hisself yet when the wall come tumblin' down." Deacon had already spoken more than he usually did to explain his actions, but this was important to him, and he wasn't finished. "Or worse than any physical damage we might inflict, Mister Muley—you and I, between us, could destroy his confidence. Right now he's over there thinking it's his line that's at fault. But after a few quarters of playing football against us, he could believe he truly wasn't meant to play on the same field. And I'm not going to let that happen to one of the handful of Negro quarterbacks who have scratched and clawed their way this far in pro ball since the dawn of time." Deacon cocked his finger at his teammate like a pistol, and pulled the trigger. He nodded to indicate he'd had his say, and turned to walk back to the sidelines.

"You're *lettin' up on him?*" Merlin yelled after him. "I can't believe this!"

Deacon cocked a thumb at the one-sided scoreboard without bothering to look back. "Oh, yeah," he said. "Like it really matters."

Deacon still vividly remembers playing this game against the fledgling black quarterback. "I could tell James had the moves to be a good one. Out of Grambling and a strong 215 pounder, he looked like he could stand in the pocket and fire that ball with the best of them. There was no way I was going to destroy him in his first game. On the other hand, I can understand why Merlin was befuddled by my behavior. It must have seemed totally odd to him, because he knew I dedicated my life to killing quarterbacks. But Merlin wasn't thinking about the rest of me—I was also dedicated to putting an end to racial bias in pro football. I had to make sure I didn't do anything to snuff out an important young career before it got started. Was it really important? I think it was. First we proved black men could block and tackle with the best the league had to offer. Then we overcame all resistance to show we could run with the ball—and catch it. And then we proved we could be field generals. James Harris, playing the game in the pivotal years, the seventies, had a lot to do with changing attitudes about having black athletes lead their teams on the field."

The Patchwork Contenders

In their final preseason game of 1969, against the 49ers, the Rams played a magnificent first half. But the team seemed to fall apart in the second. They built a 30-0 lead, on one series sacking John Brodie four times out of five plays for a total of minus forty yards. Then they just barely managed to hang on to win 30-28. Reporters noted that there was a lack of teamwork, not the earmark of a George Allen team. Allen was experimenting with many different players, and the team had recently been plagued by a series of injuries.

With another coach this might mean a "rebuilding" year; but Allen, the man who had popularized the phrase "The future is now," went into high gear. He felt the team owed the fans more, and so he was continually introducing new faces throughout the exhibition season, in the hope of finding a solid, winning combination. He hadn't expected the rash of player injuries, but even then, refused to let them get his team down. But now Allen was going to have to get his team up because they were to play the mighty Colts in Baltimore for their season opener.

Before the game, Deacon told Mal Florence, "The Colts are going to be even better this year, because Mr. Johnny U. is back. He's the only man I fear in the game. He's the greatest quarterback of all time. The only way to beat him is to stay on top of him like we did in the 1967 game." That game had been a 34-10 Rams win. As the Rams prepared for the game, bad luck plagued them. Lamar Lundy, recovering from knee surgery, would be out for much of the season. On the Friday before their season opener, Lundy's replacement, Greg Schumacher, was sidelined. The Rams were not physically sound. Of eleven defensive positions, only Jack Pardee was in top form. Deacon Jones was still hampered by his arch injury. They took their shots and pain pills, got themselves taped, and listened to George Allen quietly explain what was expected of winners. And then they took the field in

Memorial Stadium, walking out into the roar of displeasure from sixty thousand Baltimore fans.

After the game, *Times* reporter Bob Oates wrote, "Quarterback Roman Gabriel of L.A. was ready Sunday for Baltimore. Coach George Allen and his staff were ready. The Ram offense and the defense and the special teams were ready and they came together in a superior performance to beat the NFL Champions 27-20."[3]

The Colts and the Rams were the two best teams in the NFL. Together, they had won or tied fifty of their last fifty-six starts. George Allen called it "a team victory," but Roman Gabriel summed it up best. "Now," he said, "the Colts are chasing us."

The press was still worried about the physical shape of the Rams, but the following week, they beat Atlanta 17-7. The new coach of the Falcons, Norman "Wild Man" Van Brocklin, tried a new trick against the Fearsome Foursome—he put in pro football's oldest formation, the tight T.[4] This attack was smothered by Deacon, Merlin, and the other Rams, who allowed only thirty-six net yards in the first half, and twenty-two net yards passing in the entire game. The Rams had ten sacks, five in each half—and they would have had twelve, but two were called back on questionable penalties. After the game, George Allen's eyes twinkled as he told the gathered sports writers, "Remember, gentlemen, we are prepared for *everything*."[5]

The Rams' next game, against the Saints, provided an easy victory, 36-17. New Orleans coach Tom Fears, who had been a great receiver for the Rams in their glory years in the 1950s, and who had recently moved from the Atlanta head coaching spot, continued the feud he'd begun in 1966 when he accused Allen and the Rams of dirty tricks. Perhaps still trying to influence Rams owner Dan Reeves, he told reporters, "The Rams used every trick in the book today. They knocked down our receivers and they held them at the line of scrimmage. They tackled them before the ball was there. They did it all . . . and the officials didn't do a thing except once when it was so blatant they couldn't ignore it."[6]

Deacon said, "I don't think people give us enough credit. We're a strong team. We still have a great defense and the offense is much

---

3. Bob Oates, *Los Angeles Times*, September 22, 1969.

4. The idea was that two running backs, one placed directly on each side of the quarterback, would provide additional blocking protection against the incoming Foursome.

5. Bob Oates, *Los Angeles Times*, 29 September, 1969.

6. John Weibush, *Los Angeles Times*, October 6, 1969.

improved." He went on to explain that Tom Fears's Saints weren't as saintly as he pretended. "They also changed their blocking. The tight end would be split out three to five yards. Normally I wouldn't have to worry about him. But their tackle jammed me at the line of scrimmage and then that tight end would crack back at me. Something like that can kill you."[7] Tom Fears was using the same tactic half the teams in the league had tried in an effort to get Deacon Jones out of the game, namely, the illegal crack-back block.

The following Sunday in San Francisco, Gabriel led the Rams to a 27-21 come-from-behind win against the 49ers. John Brodie had three scoring passes, and San Francisco was up 21-13 with less than twelve minutes to play. The home crowd raised a racket every time the Rams got the ball, trying to confuse them and drown out their signals. The Rams had spent the day dropping passes, fumbling, committing penalties, and making other mistakes. Now, Gabriel marched them down the field twice to score two touchdowns in the true tradition of Bob Waterfield when he led the team from behind again and again during that long-ago Rams winning era. They pulled the game out of the fire in the final minutes.

George Allen, driven by continuing team injuries to come up with something extra, was putting Deacon in on first downs as the middle guard on a five-man line to take the pass away. On these plays, Rick Cash replaced him at end. They sacked Brodie only once using this formation, but they hurried him so much that he had only one pass completion on first down the entire game.

After the game, Deacon revealed the lengths to which the officials were going to control his game. On his initial move, he generally cuffed the opposing tackle on the side of the helmet. There was nothing illegal about this. Still, the officials warned him for "excessive use of his hands." Recognizing that his only weapon against the refs was to take his case to the people, Deacon told reporters, "The refs got on me for using my hands. It must have come down from the commissioner's office. They warned me several times." Deacon went on to give an inside view of the game that's seldom been recorded. "That's part of my game. But, even though I shouldn't say this, I'm going to." The San Francisco offensive line, he said, "held me on practically every play. It was the worst grabbing I've ever seen."[8]

---

7. John Weibush, *Los Angeles Times*, October 6, 1969.
8. *Los Angeles Times*, October 13, 1969.

The argument really goes back to whether football is an offensive or a defensive game. Before Deacon Jones came to the pros, it had always been an offensive game. Now, with the zone pass defense, and with quick, fast, and big players like Deacon, defense had come to be as exciting as offense. Still, this tended to hold the scores down, and there were those who longed for the good old days.

Offensive players had always relied on illegal holding on the interior line to keep defensive players out. This holding was (and still is) hard to spot,[9] and since no ref was particularly assigned to it, the yellow flag was rarely thrown. Hence, Charlie Cowan's fury at being called for offensive holding on a critical play in the previous year's Bears game, which ended up costing the Rams a shot at the 1968 title.

Deacon, not relying on the system that gave the clear and (from his point of view, unfair) advantage to the offensive line, had perfected his headslap, a legal defensive lineman's maneuver by the rules of that time. The defensive lineman has the use of his hands. It's that simple. But Deacon's headslap, designed to reduce holding to a minimum, had shifted the balance of power on the line. With his speed and his skills, he was destroying the rest of the league, breaking through consistently to drop the quarterback or hurry the play. Now, if opposing offenses couldn't keep him out, perhaps the referees could.

By going public with his refusal to play along, Deacon brought unwanted attention to this new ploy. If, as he alleged, the call came down directly from Pete Rozelle, it didn't look good for football. Deacon was putting the entire league on notice. Since there was no rule on the books against the headslap, they were going to have to live with it until they could officially gather together, change the rules, and then figure out something to say to the fans to explain what they had done.

The Rams rolled on, making it five in a row with a 34-21 win over the Green Bay Packers. The defense led the way; the Fearsome Foursome stole the ball once outright and forced two fumbles, making thirteen straight points for the Rams.

In the first quarter, Deacon knocked the ball out of Bart Starr's hands, and Maxie Baughan got the recovery. After the game, he said, "I wanted to get that sack, and I would have got it, too, but Starr cocked his arm as if to pass and then he brought the ball down. The

---

9. One of the most common tricks is for the offensive lineman to fall back, pulling the defensive man with him by holding onto two fistfuls of his jersey. It can't easily be seen because the two men are up against each other. Once the defensive man is pulled down, the hidden hands let go.

ball was in his palm and I knew he was going to run. I just made a swipe at it—a clean one—and Maxie got the recovery."[10]

A sack. A quarterback sack. Before Deacon Jones, the maneuver was called "catching the quarterback behind the line for a loss." But Deacon himself had coined the term "sack" to describe his deeds, likening his moves to the sacking and plunder of ancient cities such as Rome and Troy. The expression caught on with announcers and sports writers, and swiftly came into universal usage.

The patchwork Rams, trained to the hilt, fueled with replacements and special plays and tactics, and motivated to win, continued to overcome the odds. They beat the Bears 9-7 on three Bruce Gossett field goals, on an overcast day in Wrigley Field. The Foursome sacked Bobby Douglass five times for fifty yards lost, and it was the first time in club history that the Rams won a game without scoring a touchdown.

The following week, the Rams offense came alive again, and the Rams went 7-0 by defeating the Falcons 38-6. Jones and Olsen made history the first half, leading a defensive charge that held Atlanta to five yards in passing and thirty-six *inches* in rushing! But the victory had its price—Maxie Baughan was injured and Joe Scibelli hurt his knee.

Next, seventy-four thousand loyal and screaming Rams fans saw their team beat the 49ers at home. Bob Oates described the scene: "The sky was a dark roof over the Coliseum but dropped only a few dashes of rain on the sellout crowd." Brodie put on an aerial show, completing twenty-five of forty-two for 356 yards—but Gabriel was even better, leading the L.A. team to a 41-30 victory. The Rams continued to be strong defensively, San Francisco's points coming more as a product of their skill than Rams' lapses. After the game, Deacon shook his head in wonderment, recalling the fifty-eight-yard pass that Brodie managed to get off to Doug Cunningham despite Deacon's savage attack. "I was all over him," exclaimed the Deacon.[11]

As their players fell by the wayside, the Rams winning streak was becoming more and more improbable. The Rams' steadfast offensive lineman, Charlie Cowan, was sidelined with an injured ankle. Myron Pottios was injured. Maxie Baughan hadn't even suited up for the game, and Joe Scibelli was out for the season. Tight end Billy Truax was hurt. In response to a question about the playing of Deacon Jones, the 49ers'

---

10. Mal Florence, *Los Angeles Times*, October 20, 1969. There is an accompanying photo which says "Sack It to Him," with the notation that the defense made thirteen straight points for the Rams.

11. Bob Oates, *Los Angeles Times*, November 10, 1969.

Ken Willard sadly reflected, "No one guy wins a game in this league or even breaks another team down." That is certainly true. But the point was, more and more of the Rams starters were falling prey to injuries.

On Sunday, November 16, 1969, history (of a sort) was made when the Rams played Philadelphia on astroturf. George Allen told his players, "Play your game as if you were playing football on the moon. You could only win two ways—blocking and tackling." And then he went out and bought some insurance—elbow pads and eighty new pairs of shoes.

The Rams defense played with unaccustomed caution, playing on the synthetic turf for the first time, and the Eagles went out to a 10-0 lead. The Rams rallied in the second half for a 23-17 victory. With the game hanging in the balance, Meador broke Allen's orders, and ran for a first down from the Rams seventeen, instead of kicking.

From the sidelines, Allen murmured, "Awfully big play."

After the game, when the reporters tried to make something out of it, Allen told them it was a prepared play, but he wouldn't have called it in that instance. No one was going to reprimand Meador, for it kept alive the drive that started the comeback that ended in the Rams longest winning streak ever—nine regular season games in a row, with a team that was bandaged and taped and stuck together, a team running on pain pills, shots, and pure guts. Pride, Coach Allen called it. And there wasn't a man on the team who didn't believe him.

There were obvious advantages to astroturf. It could lay to rest many of the charges of "doctoring the field" that had plagued the NFL over the years. Pete Rozelle came out in favor of the new playing surface, though he did not make it mandatory. Here again, the players had little or no voice in the decision. Astroturf was and remains a much harsher playing field for the players, and has led to the injury and early retirement of hundreds of athletes.

After the game, Roman Gabriel was asked about his scrambling runs, which had led the Rams to victory over the Eagles. "I paid for them though," he said as he gingerly got off a table where trainer George Menifee was taping his bruised right knee and sprained ankle. You can blame it on that astroturf. When you hit that, it's like hitting cement. They say you don't have as many injuries . . . but not that many people are using astroturf, and when they do, I think you'll have more injuries."

The Rams were typically outspoken, against the wishes of their commissioner. "That astroturf throws your timing off," said Merlin

Olsen. "You have to be cautious on it," Charlie Cowan added. And, as usual, when asked if he thought astroturf was dangerous to the players, the most outspoken of all, Deacon Jones, told reporters, "You can say that again! You tell Bill Nicholas that if he puts that stuff in the Coliseum, I'm gonna quit!"

In Punishment of Excellence

The Rams won their tenth game in a row, 24-23, with three touchdown marches against Dallas's vaunted Doomsday Defense. With only 1:02 left in the game and the Cowboys marching, the Rams defense earned the interception that saved the victory. On this key play, Deacon smashed into Danny Reeves, who was attempting a halfback pass. Deacon managed to hurry the pass, which Doug Woodlief was then able to intercept. Not since Vince Lombardi's 1962 Green Bay Packers had any team in the NFL won ten games in a row.

The following week, the Rams beat Washington 24-13. Eleven victories in a row and the Coastal Division championship went to the team that was so battered at the start of the season it was picked to come in third at best. L.A.'s signal caller, Maxie Baughan, outguessed Sonny Jurgensen at every turn. Strong-arm Sonny, who was known for the long bomb, was sacked six times and left without a touchdown until the fourth quarter. He was harassed by Deacon Jones, Merlin Olsen, Coy Bacon, Roger Brown, Diron Talbert—and Lamar Lundy, making his first appearance of the year.

Vince Lombardi, now coaching the Redskins, said, "We played our best defense of the year. We were kinda overpowered by the Rams defense."

Jurgensen talked about the game. "The Rams play pass all the time. When they get a good rush, it opens up a lot of running lanes." When asked why his team still could manage only seventy-two yards rushing, he explained that the Rams defensive line "showed us a lot of different slants and tricks, much more than we expected."

The victory gave the Rams some more laurels—in fifty years in the league, only one other club, the Chicago Bears, had ever won more than eleven consecutive games in one season. Roman Gabriel became the first NFL quarterback since the great Otto Graham to open an NFL season with eleven victories. Yet, a different game was being played on the field, this one by the officials.

Early in the game, one of the officials took Deacon aside. "You've been warned about excessive use of the hands," he said.

"What?" Deacon shouted. "What excess? What are you saying to me? I fouled someone on the last play?"

The referee pursed his lips and walked away. Deacon went back to his side of the line.

"What was that all about?" Merlin asked.

"Another ref tellin' me I can't headslap! Who the hell decides that, anyway?"

"You know who," Merlin looked skyward, where lived God and the commissioner. "You haven't exactly been a friend to the powers that be."

A few plays later, Merlin was called for jumping offsides before the snap. A marginal call at best, he was fuming when he got back to the line.

Deacon gave him a sour grin. "Somebody up there doesn't like you either, Muley. I guess they decided in their own wisdom that the L.A. defense should no longer be the killers of quarterbacks." As the game went on, the penalties piled up against the Rams, most of them so questionable that the following day the *L.A. Times* would report that the team was "harassed by a zealous crew of officials." Finally, in the fourth quarter, Deacon was called for clipping. He claimed (and the game films show) that he hit Charley Taylor from the side. That call made him see red. For years, every dirty player in the league had gotten away with clipping him. Teams had designed special crack-back blocking plays intent on crippling him. San Francisco had even held a press conference to demonstrate the "legal clipping play" that could stop the great Deacon Jones—so everybody in the league could try it. In fact in the third quarter of this game, Deacon had injured his ankle when Jerry Smith, the Redskin tight end cracked back on him while he was being jammed by the tackle. Deacon was hit from behind and later said, "He was split out about two yards [outside the tackle position]. You can't clip outside the tackle. I'm glad he only weighs 203, instead of 230. Otherwise, that might have been the end for me."

Dozens—hundreds—of clips slamming into the back of Deacon's body over the years, would-be crippling sucker punches that the referees had studiously ignored, and now he himself was called for clipping! Deacon couldn't believe it. He was so outraged, he picked up the referee's handkerchief and hurled the yellow flag to the ground in a fit of pique.

After the game, once reason returned, he sighed, "They probably should have called another penalty on me for throwing the flag. I was real upset at the time."

The papers reported that, "No one would openly criticize the officials for fear of incurring a fine from the league headquarters, but a few vets questioned some of the decisions."[12] With his public action on the field, Deacon had clearly gone as far as, or further than, had any player.

George Allen, who knew how the game was played, refused to publicly reprimand Fred Swearingen's officiating team, although the Rams were called for ten penalties totalling 108 yards. The Rams had won the game and the division title, but the damage was done. The referees had sent up a very public signal. Every upcoming opponent was alerted to the possibility that it was now open season on the Rams defense. With the referees poised, ready and willing to throw the flag on the bullies from the West Coast, couldn't tactics be employed to help them in their zealous mission? The answer would only be seven days in coming.

The following week, Rams seemed to play hesitant, flat football. Minnesota jumped out to a 14-0 lead, and the L.A. team never could catch up. George Allen, unwilling to give any clues as to specific problems, told reporters, "We lost to a better team today. We didn't play an emotional game. We didn't make one big play."

Deacon echoed his remarks. "We just didn't play Ram football. It's back to the practice field and we'll be a better team for it. They got on top and were able to stick to their game plan. We didn't stop the run like we should. It was ball control and we fell into a trap and let 'em go. Maybe we learned a lesson . . . maybe it was good it happened. We didn't take Minnesota lightly, but we weren't at our best. When we play our best, no one can stay on the same field with us."

The following week, the Lions decided to push the war against the Rams defensive line to the next logical conclusion. If the refs were looking for reasons to throw the flag on the Rams, they would give them plenty. Munson used an "erratic count" to pull the Rams offsides a total of nine times. This ploy, as George Allen said after the game, is only illegal if the officials call it, and they only called it once the entire game.[13] Sonny Jurgensen had done the same thing to the L.A. defense in Washington (ten penalties for 108 yards), but the Ram offense had been able to pick up the slack.

Munson did two abnormal things with voice inflections. He

12. *Los Angeles Times,* December 1, 1969.

13. Bob Oates, *Los Angeles Times,* December 15, 1969.

loudly accented numbers before the planned snap signal. And he moved his body on the accent. The rules allow him some movement because he is required to shift his body to shout the signals and the audible numbers in the direction of the wide receivers. What he was doing (as had Jurgensen before him) was to exaggerate these movements at the same time that he sharply called out the fake signals.[14] Deacon and others, looking down the line, saw movement, misinterpreted it, misjudged Munson's fake commands and jumped. Bob Oates of the *L.A. Times* reported, "It was cute football, on the borderline of legality, but it shouldn't have taken in a team as experienced as the Rams." Soon, the Rams were charging with caution, and Munson had more time to throw. With Gabriel unable to get the L.A. offense rolling, the Lions took them 28-0.

The following week, the Colts, taking a lesson from the Vikings, scored early and reverted to ball control—a combination of short passes and time-consuming running plays, to beat the Rams 13-7. Deacon said, "Unitas was throwing in the alley between Olsen and I and the same thing on the other side. One-two and then *bam!* There's no way you can reach him when he's throwing that quickly." He admitted ruefully, "We have allowed other people to dictate to us." After eleven victories, the Rams had been beaten three times in a row, all by teams who changed their game style to break the intense pressure of the Fearsome Foursome. With the regular season over, L.A. headed for Minnesota in an attempt to break their losing string in the playoffs, fingers crossed that the referees would let them play their game.

George Allen's son Bruce, currently working with the Raiders, said recently of the referee's reaction to Deacon's headslap. "In a way

---

14. Remember "jamming the counts," a ploy in which the defense barks their signals to confuse the opposing offensive players? A quarterback calling a fake count and using deceptive body motion is deploying an offensive trick to pull the defense across the line. Munson, as reported by Bob Oates, "encouraged the Ram front four to believe that the fake number was the snap number. They jumped off-side nine times in response to this device." Understanding tactics such as these makes watching the game more interesting—and can give one a more sympathetic understanding of the difficulties the referees face. How much motion on the part of the quarterback is too much? It's a bit like asking how much of a pitcher's motion is allowed in faking a toss to first before the umpire calls a balk. In football, it is questions such as this one which make up the "grey" area, the area of subjectivity that the refs must get straight between themselves before they call a game if they are to do a satisfactory job. In the best of all possible worlds, all games would be called exactly the same. In the real world, there are too many variables, and the inequities in playcalling within a single game and from game to game can be exasperating.

it was unfortunate. In another way, you could almost call it Dea-con's own fault. I mean, bad enough he had the most powerful left hand in football, but when he invented the double headslap and the triple headslap, he was headed for trouble. He was unstop-pable, and left offensive linemen no other option than to complain about it. Of course, that's a little bit like Muhammed Ali's oppo-nents' complaining he was too fast, or Joe Louis's opponents com-plaining he hit too hard."

Today Deacon scoffs at the way the league treated the entire question of the headslap: "Football is supposed to be about hitting. It was a totally legal move. Problem was, I learned to do it better than anybody. Everyone wasn't fast enough to do it properly—for instance, Merlin was never more than an average headslapper—but, when it worked, it brought a parity between offense and defense by reducing illegal holding. No offensive tackle wants to hang on to your jersey while you're ringing his helmet like a bell. The league was too chicken to try and outlaw it while I was playing, they knew they'd set up a howl from the fans. So they waited until the moment I retired."

About the tricky stutter-count several teams used on the Rams late in the season, Deacon has this to say: "George Allen had been accused of the same trick several times in his career, so he knew he was going to get nowhere with the refs on that one. It was all in the way they called it. Other teams brought it to the ref's attention, and he had to back off. But as long as they could get away with it, any team would continue to use it. In 1969, the refs called open season on the Rams. To my mind, they had a few conversations with themselves and with the league officials, and were keyed not to call it . . . and so our rivals got away with murder. We were able to reduce our penalties by backing off, but that was a terrible price for a pressure defense like ours to pay. Just a little thing like that, and yet it tipped the scales back in favor of the offense."

Winning One for the Vikings

The Rams gingerly took to the Minnesota field for their warm ups for the 1969 playoff game for the Western Conference championship. Deacon did a few sprints and turned to Merlin, looking surprised. "Field looks okay."

Merlin shrugged, and a huge grin spread over his face. "Maybe they want to play us straight-up."

"Maybe." The too-familiar look of worry came to Deacon easily. "Let's not take anything for granted."

The invaders from L.A. played Rams football for the entire first half, and at half-time they were leading 17-7. But Deacon's words proved prophetic. Joe Kapp, with the aid and assistance of some of the most questionable officiating ever seen in a playoff game, would bring the Vikings back with a second half rally to win 23-20. The game hinged on four official calls. As Bob Oates, writing for the *L.A. Times,* saw it, "This was a game, however, in which some of the big plays in the third and fourth quarters were made by the officials. The penalties could have been well deserved (in which case the Rams fouled themselves out of the championship) or they could have been marginal (in which case the officials took the game out of the hands of the athletes). In either event, the officials interpretation of the rules on all four plays all went against the Rams in the second half.[15]

"Bob Brown was called for clipping. According to the rules, clipping is legal from tackle to tackle. Brown is a tackle. The officials called him outside the neutral zone when he clipped, a marginal interpretation at best, particularly in a game as meaningful as this."

Brown told reporters after the game, "I don't think I've clipped five times in my entire career. I know I was in the neutral zone (the area between the tackles and one yard in front and behind the line of scrimmage), and that's legal." The game film bears out Brown's contention. The officials called clipping against the Rams when they should not have.

Oates continued, "Then there was pass interference called against Jimmy Nettles. He appeared to be going for the ball. The infraction, if any, was not flagrant—another marginal interpretation."

In the locker room after the game, George Allen told reporters, "Nettles made a great defensive play. He was going for the ball and knocked it down.

Nettles added, "I came inside of Henderson and hit the ball. I didn't touch him at all. When they dropped that flag, I had no idea what was going on." The game film here shows that, once again, the referees were clearly in error.

Next, Jack Pardee was called for "piling on," for jumping on a pile of downed players after the play was whistled dead. Washington stunted, fell, and got up; and Jack, thinking he was going for the

---

15. Bob Oates, *Los Angeles Times,* December 28, 1969.

score, tackled him. The refs felt he tackled after the play was dead, though Jack said later that the whistle went off after he was committed to his tackle. Reviewing the game, it is difficult to tell from the films, but this call is not surprising, considering that fast whistles and quick flags against the Rams seemed to be the order of the day.

Oates describes the last controversial play. "Finally, a Viking safety, when Carl Eller tackled Roman Gabriel in the Rams end zone in the fourth quarter was also a judgment call."

After the game Gabriel said, "Eller just wanted to come in. I planted myself on about the one-and-a-half yard line and that's where he hit me. But the field was slick down there and he just skidded me into the end zone." The game film seems to verify Roman's claim. The ball should have been returned to the one or two yard line, and the Rams should have retained possession. Instead, they lost two points, and had to kick to the Vikings.

The Rams led the game most of the way. They were still leading 17-7 in the fourth quarter before the referees took over. They had the ball on the Minnesota twenty when the series of calls snatched the game away from them.

Even with the referees turned against them, Deacon had one chance to pull the game out of the fire. He'd been double-teamed most of the day, yet he was in the Viking backfield on their next to last series when Kapp fumbled. But the ball bounced the other way. When asked about it, he shrugged, "The ball simply bounced among three Vikings. Also, I was behind [Coy] Bacon and my vision was cut off."

Minnesota's head coach, Bud Grant, said after the game, "The officiating was excellent—I wouldn't change a thing."

George Allen responded, "We put in an awful lot of hard work this year, and these guys just don't deserve to lose."

Allen had taken a patchwork team, weakened with injuries and replacements, all the way to the playoffs. With Allen's drive to win, any loss was bitter; how much more so then the loss of this game, lost in this way.

Deacon remembers that game. "The low level of officiating was and remains one of the biggest blights against football. With twenty-two men on the field, it is the most complicated bigtime sport. There's a lot going on in the same split seconds. In those days the refs could and did commit unforgivable acts and get away with it."

Today, Carl Eller runs several alcohol and drug rehabilitation centers in Minneapolis. For the first time, he reveals what actually happened on the play that put the game away for the Vikings. "I remember the play. We'd been behind nearly all day. Gabe ran a half-rollout to my side. I was across from Bob Brown, who was a tough man to play against, but on that play I beat him. They'd run the same play once in the first half, and so I sort-of anticipated it, which is how I got past Bob. Gabe was retreating when I caught him. He was close to the goal line. I drove him back into the end zone."

Deacon is not surprised to hear this affirmation after all these years. "Carl always was a great competitor and an upstanding human being. I would expect him to look back and tell the truth about it." Deacon continues: "The Minnesota playoff game took some of the heart out of me as a player. I'd risen to be the best in the most vicious game in the world, only to see that the officials, for whatever reasons, could snatch victory right out of our hands.

"Our next game was the runner-up bowl in Miami. We were still so furious at the loss of the Viking game that we destroyed the Cowboys. We won 31-0, shutting down Dallas and their high-powered offense for their first shutout since 1954 (212 games without a shutout). Roman Gabriel was awarded Offensive Player of the Game, and I was the Defensive Player of the Game. We sacked Craig Morton and Roger Staubach six times. But, in a way, it was all for nothing, and the great game of football was a little less great because of it."

The Smell of Honey

During this period, Deacon allowed more and more of his business affairs to be handled by Al Ross, an attorney who ran All-Pro Management. Ross handled the business affairs of several top athletes, including basketball player Rick Barry and the Vikings' Carl Eller. Once Ross took over for Deacon, the air was buzzing with their plans. Together, they were planning their own recording company, music publishing house, and show-business management team. Deacon found himself agreeing to opening his own supper club at the corner of Stocker and LaBrea in Baldwin Hills.

Deacon told Bill Libby, who was then working with Deacon on his early football biography, *Life in the Pit: The Deacon Jones Story,* "I know athletes have gone broke with restaurants and nightclubs. I'm not ignorant of it. But this is something I always wanted. With Ross, I have good advice. It will be first class, real swank. The performers I manage or record will be showcased at my own club. It will be a beautiful thing."

Al Ross was enthused. "He will be as great a show business star as he has been a sports star."

Deacon was moving up fast, perhaps too fast. He'd never paid any attention in college when they told you what to do with the money you earned. He couldn't turn to Iretha for advice; all she knew was how to spend. He'd even forgotten that old Eatonville saying his mother used to sing out around the house whenever the town gossip got on anyone for their loose wallet.

"The two things that best bring flies," Mattie would say, "are the smell of honey an' the smell of money."

Deacon thinks back to his early show business days. "Rosey Grier, Dick Bass and I were breaking new ground. We were lucky, of course—if we played in Green Bay, San Francisco, or Atlanta, we could have owned the town, but it wouldn't have been worth all that much in terms of a career in show business. We might have ended up owning a nice bar or restaurant with pictures of our career hanging on the walls, and not much else. Not that there's anything wrong with that, but I think a lot of us craved more. Pro football players are the best of the best, and they are used to the limelight and the cheer of the crowds. The entertainment industry is a natural for many of us.

"Dick Butkus and Alex Karras are examples of ballplayers from that era who were able to parlay their football careers into acting careers. But they had to come to Hollywood to do it. Hollywood or New York—those were the places. And by an act of God and the Rams, I was fortunate to play ball in the heart of ShoBiz Land. Some of the other players on the Rams, even some of my best friends, were surprised and jealous to see the intense way I went at it. After all, I was a kid from the sticks of central Florida. I shouldn't be out there using my famous mouth for quotable quotes week after week and singing and dancing on the stage when I wasn't smacking quarterbacks. But I was born for the center stage. From my point of view, I would have been a fool not to take advantage of it."

Victory by George

The Rams began the 1970 season, the fifth and final season of George Allen's contract, by winning all six of their exhibition games. Then they went on to easily win their season opener, 34-13, over Jim Hart and the St. Louis Cardinals. After their next game, which they won 19-0 over Buffalo (for the first L.A. regular season shutout in sixteen years), Bob Oates was moved to remark in the *Times,* "Allen has created one of the most predictable winning teams in the recent history of football."[16]

Allen himself said he was just glad of the win. "Over the years, some very good teams have managed to lose this kind."

The Fearsome Foursome now consisted of Coy Bacon and Diron Talbert charging from the right side and Merlin and Deacon continuing their legendary charge from the left. In the Bills game, Deacon was often *triple-blocked.* In their next game, against the San Diego Chargers, this Foursome combined to sack quarterbacks John Hadl and Marty Domres ten times as the Rams won 37-10, even though Merlin hurt his knee and could play only the first half.

John Hadl told reporters that after nine years in the NFL, he'd never seen anything like the Rams pass rush. "It's by far the best of any club we've ever played."

The day after the game, Oates reported in the *Times,* "When the Chargers see the movies, they probably will say Deacon Jones beat them. His whirlwind assaults from the outside helped Talbert and Bacon move up the middle to sack Hadl four times and Domres six times."[17]

After four years of winning football Deacon had molded himself into the player-image of Allen. Mal Florence wrote about his preparation,

> "I'd be just as high as if we were going to play UCLA next Sunday," said Deacon Jones, the Rams famed Secretary of Defense. "You can't set your sights for any one team in this league. That's absurd. You can be beaten by any team in the NFL." Although Jones was battering the Charger quarterbacks the entire afternoon, the All-Pro defensive end appeared frustrated. "You know," he said, "I've missed six sacks the last two games. I let Hadl and Domres get away from

16. Bob Oates, *Los Angeles Times,* September 28, 1970.
17. Bob Oates, *Los Angeles Times,* October 5, 1970.

me three times today. I don't know what I'm doing wrong. I think, though, that I'm leaving my feet too soon. I'm trying to bring 'em down while I'm still on the ground. What I have to do is hit them and then go 'foom'—drive right through them."[18]

For an early season game that was so one-sided, the Rams suffered an alarming number of injuries. In addition to Olsen, tight end Billy Truax, wide receiver Wendell Tucker, Alvin Haymond, Willie Ellison, and Les Josephson were all injured.

The following weekend against San Francisco, Deacon was rudely reminded of the league's antidefense posture when he was penalized with a personal foul for "headslapping." There was no official rule against the headslap, but the referees called it anyway.[19] The Rams defensive line had the feeling the refs were looking for reasons to throw the flag. Whether it was true or not, it influenced their play. With the line backing off for a split-second hesitation on every play, 49ers quarterback John Brodie had all the time he needed to win. He was able to get a quick, short pass game going (something he did very well even without help from the officials), and San Francisco took the day. Just before halftime, Deacon managed to steal the ball from 49ers back Jimmy Thomas at the San Francisco eleven, but the result was only a field goal. The outcome wasn't a rout; the 49ers scored only twenty points. But on a day when the Rams could only score six, it was enough.

In the locker room, Allen told the press, "This is probably the worst game we've played in five years. I don't want to take anything away from John Brodie or the 49ers, but we beat ourselves."

Deacon sat on the wooden bench next to his locker, wringing sweat from his dirty jersey. If Allen wasn't going to talk about the referees, he wasn't, either. Deacon accepted the fault as his own. Damn the yellow flags—the defensive lineman's job in ball-control football was to ignore all that and just keep on coming! Rather than talk in public about how quietly effective the ref's "judgment calls" could be in stopping the Rams or any other defensive football team, Deacon chose to praise the 49er quarterback. "Brodie was throwing quick-out patterns, and he only threw deep a couple of times," Deacon told the

---

18. Mal Florence, *Los Angeles Times*, October 5, 1970.

19. *Los Angeles Times,* October 12, "Jones was penalized for slapping the helmet of his blocker—sometimes this infraction is called and sometimes it is not." The headslap, which Deacon claims had always been legal, was starting to slip into a "quasi-legal" grey area, because the referees were starting to call it. The official rule banning the headslap was declared by the League the year after Deacon retired.

reporters. "He didn't have to throw the ball long because he wasn't playing from behind. I don't think I've ever gotten a passer more than twice in my career when he was going to a short pattern attack. And Brodie didn't hold the ball that long, either."

The following Sunday, the Rams got back on track with a 31-21 win over Green Bay. The game had a wild finish; in the fourth quarter, with Deacon sitting on the bench having his ankle taped, Packers quarterback Bart Starr drove his team for a comeback touchdown to tie the game at 14-14.

Were he playing for any other coach, Deacon would have been out for the rest of the day. But this was George Allen, who had taken a team of habitual losers and turned them into winners; he didn't even have to ask. Deacon had already geared his consciousness to getting back in the game. First, he took a few painful steps in the arms of the trainers.

He shook his head, "I'm goin' to need the shot."

The trainers took him behind the bench and got out the big horse-needle. The team doctor administered the shot. While his ankle froze to numb, Deacon hobbled up and down the line, testing how much weight he could put on it. One of the trainers showed up with a cup of water and a small handful of reds—amphetamines that could be counted on to boost a player over the pain, at least temporarily. Deacon gratefully gulped the pills, washing them down quickly so the bitter taste wouldn't catch back in his throat. He grimaced and tossed the paper cup behind the bench.

"Tell Coach I'm ready."

"You sure?" Mother Menifee asked.

Deacon frowned and got down in his stance. He accelerated smoothly into a full sprint.

"*Tell* him," he said.

From across the field, the Packers had been watching him test his leg; they were surprised he was coming back in. But they also thought they had a piece of information that might win them the game. Starr was informed that while Deacon could accelerate in a straight line, they didn't think he could run laterally. That's the kind of small edge that wins ball games. The Packers quarterback probed the supposed weakness, running a series of plays over his position, but the Rams star defensive end, operating on instinct and guts, managed to hold his own. After the game, Deacon gave reporters a rare inside view of the ugly side of the NFL. "The Packers were shooting for it. Forrest Gregg and John Mackey kept falling on my ankle, and sometimes they'd hit it just right."

Roman Gabriel returned from the bench, where he'd been sidelined with his own injuries, to drive his team to score a go-ahead touchdown. The Rams pulled out the victory, surviving another brutal early season game in which at one point or another Roman Gabriel, Deacon Jones, Merlin Olsen, Bob Brown, and Alvin Haymond were injured.

George Allen commented, "We kept coming back and this showed how much guts and character we have. And the fact that Gabe came back from his injuries shows you the type of leadership we have."

That Tuesday after practice, Allen held his weekly awards ceremony. Charlie Cowan won a golden jock strap for tackling a return inside the twenty—Charlie must have won 20 of those in his long and illustrious career. The morale had never been higher, as Allen handed out clock radios and stereo hi-fi's for passes caught and good runs, and running shoes for those who'd hustled. There were suits and sports outfits and golf clubs and bowling balls—all donated by loyal Ram fans or bought personally by Allen. When Allen got to Deacon, there was big television set—not only for going back in the game, but for managing to get through the line to put a mighty sack on Bart Starr. It was supposed to have been Starr's day. The Packers quarterback had been eulogized by President Nixon at a testimonial gathering on the night before the game. Deacon stood next to Allen, accepting his award while his fellows hooted and stomped their feet and cheered.

Deacon's bruised body was just beginning to come back after Sunday's pummeling. His ankle was stiff and sore, and his knee still gave him trouble. But as he stood in front of the team, he was filled with a warm glow of accomplishment. Life could really be good.

Deacon talks about the incentives for playing well. "Sack clauses were and are an important part of every lineman's contract, just as interception clauses are important for deep backs and linebackers, and completions are for quarterbacks. In the late sixties the Rams paid me $500 extra for every time I sacked the quarterback. There also was a monetary reward for forcing a fumble, things like that.

"It's no different today—players still get perks for hits. It's just that the amounts are much, much larger, and they don't call it 'hits' any more. Buddy Ryan got in trouble with the Eagles for saying something like 'put the hit on somebody.' He got reprimanded by owners and sports writers around the league, and that was a bum deal. You see, every time a player goes after the guy with the

ball, you're trying to hurt him, to kill him, to tear his head off. Bottom line, you can't train a football team any other way. What are you going to say, 'Lets go out there and ease these fellows down'? But when you say it like it is, the self-appointed moralists of the game go into a rage. They want to see it raw and brutal, but they don't want it described like it really is.

Bruce Allen remembers his father as a master motivator: "It was his idea to have a cake on Thursday after practice, to celebrate the coming victory! He loved the game of football, and that love was infectious."

Deacon agrees. "George was the best player's coach there ever was. We players always felt we were getting first-class treatment. He treated us like winners, and we responded in kind."

The Enemy Within

The Rams lost their sixth game of the 1970 season to a tough Minnesota team in the mud and the rain in Minneapolis. The L.A. offense fumbled seven times, losing possession on four of the fumbles. George Allen said, "We had the chances, the opportunities, but we just didn't take advantage of them. Sure, the weather hurt our offense. We never practice in the rain or cold. But I'm not making any excuses. You can't make that many mistakes and hope to win." The Rams defense was superb in defeat. Even with all their opponent's fumbling around, the Vikings could only manage a 13-3 win. But a loss is a loss, and the Rams tumbled into second place behind the 49ers.

The following week, the bad offensive play continued, and the Saints scored two touchdowns for a 14-0 lead in the first three minutes of the game. The Rams fought back valiantly; in the final minutes of the first half they were down by only a point, 14-13. But they seemed to stall, and New Orleans was on the march. At that point, Deacon took the game into his own hands. With the Saints in possession, second and one at the Rams thirty-five, the headslappin' Jones boy came screaming off the line to sack quarterback Edd Hargett for a ten-yard loss. The Rams' defensive spirits picked up, and on the next play, Pardee sacked Hargett again. The Saints had been driven out of field goal range and had to punt. It was the turning point in the game. After that, Roman Gabriel drove the Rams back down the field to gain a lead they never gave up. The Rams won, 30-17.

Back home in the Coliseum, with the Rams down by seven to Atlanta, defense got the ball back for one more try and Roman Gabriel passed for a touchdown with two seconds left on the clock to squeak out a 10-10 tie. It wasn't as bad as a defeat, but the Rams' hope of a title was beginning to dim as league-leading San Francisco continued its winning streak. And, to make matters worse, Deacon had injured his knee.

Against the New York Jets the following week, the Rams star defensive end could make only token appearances. He hadn't been able to practice all week, and was ineffective in the game. The Rams played what was called "their worst game in five years for Allen," and lost 31-20. "When you lose your best pass rusher, that's bound to hurt," Allen told the press.

Now two games behind the 49ers, most Rams fans began to count the team out for the season. Again, Deacon couldn't practice all week, but now he had two reasons to be out of the game. First, he had a knee injury that was more serious than anyone had thought—and then he'd had to fly to Florida to be at the bedside of his father, who was fighting a long, silent battle against cancer. It was a tense, emotional week during which Deacon had to assume leadership of the household and calm his brood of sisters, who still lived in Eatonville.

By the time he rejoined the team in Atlanta, Deacon had lost 19 pounds. He showed up two days before the game, looking drawn and tired. He didn't think he could play. He still couldn't run on the right knee, which had a deep bruise under the kneecap. The team doctor shrugged and prescribed a shot of cortisone in the knee. To everyone's amazement, the knee reacted so favorably that Deacon started against the Falcons and played his usual dominating game, slashing through the line to harass the backfield and break up his share of plays.

It was a day when the Rams defense did it all, holding Atlanta to seven points and scoring fourteen points of their own on touchdown runs by defensive end Coy Bacon and cornerback Kermit Alexander. The Rams were 6-3-1, but San Francisco lost, and so they pulled to within one game. George Allen said it all when he scrawled his favorite word across a blackboard in the locker room, "CHARACTER." Everyone smiled and looked forward to next week's game against the 49ers.

The Rams took to the gridiron against San Francisco in sunny weather, playing on a "surprisingly firm" field—and literally destroyed their opponents, to win what many called George Allen's biggest game while at Los Angeles. The teams were tied at the half, but Deacon and his friends allowed only seventy-seven total yards in the second half. Deacon grinned wolfishly as he told reporters, "The 49ers have excellent blockers. But we were dedicated to giving Brodie no time at all. We also had to be aware of their draw play with our linebackers shooting out on pass coverage."

Asked about how fit he was, he replied, "My knee held up pretty good." Pretty good, indeed. Deacon and Merlin Olsen gave Brodie no peace, breaking up his timing by hurrying him on nearly every play. Both teams were now 7-3-1. Each had beaten the other once. But the Rams had the edge and first place by virtue of outscoring the 49ers in the combination of their two games.

But then the rumors started, perhaps out of nowhere, perhaps in the heart of the Rams camp itself—whispers and speculation that Allen was leaving the Rams, that he was seriously considering offers from other clubs.

There had been gossip all year that owner Dan Reeves wasn't going to renew Allen's contract no matter how well he did. *George Allen has killed the Rams future,* the rumors went. *He's sold our future for the present.* Commenting obliquely on this whisper campaign, *Times* writer Mal Florence wrote, "It is commonly believed George Allen has put together a championship contending club by trading draft choices or marginal players for vets." Then he went on to note that the criticisms weren't exactly true. "The three superstars—Roman Gabriel, Merlin Olsen and Deacon Jones are products of the Ram draft system. Also, Charlie Cowan, Tom Mack, Joe Scibelli, Larry Smith, Diron Talbert, Jack Pardee, Clancy Williams and Eddie Meador."[20]

Now that the Rams were back in first place, the anti-Allen club quietly cranked up their campaign a notch, floating the rumor that Allen was entertaining offers elsewhere and wouldn't be coming back to the Rams.

Allen angrily spoke out. "There is no truth whatsoever. The future is *now.* My only obligation is to the players, the coaches, and the Ram fans. I love these guys." He explained he was angry because the rumors were harmful to team spirit and tended to take their eyes off the big prize—winning the championship. A day or two later, he told reporter Bob Oates, "I intend to be coaching the Rams again in 1971."

The rumor mill also declared that USC coach John McKay had already agreed to accept the Rams coaching job on the basis of a ten-year contract. When asked directly, Jack Teele, Dan Reeves's assistant, denied that there was any truth to the rumor.

20. Mal Florence, *Los Angeles Times*, October 25, 1970.

Still, with the Rams in solid contention for the title this year, somehow the question of who would coach the Rams next year was on everybody's mind. Oates commented on Reeves's failure to renew Allen's contract, which was due to expire at the end of December:

> The owner's reluctance to insure the services of a winning coach for at least one more year is unusual in a highly competitive league. Allen reasons someone on the Rams is out to sabotage him. Allen's regular season Ram record was 29-10-3 (or .744) when fired during Christmas week in 1968. Since Reeves reconsidered and rehired him, his record expanded to 47-16-4 (.746). Still, one hears the complaint, "They haven't won the big one recently."[21]

Rumor campaign or not, the Rams head coach managed to get his team ready for the next game, and the first week of George Allen's last month with the Rams began with a 34-16 roust of the New Orleans Saints. Deacon, who took three stitches in his thumb, showed how fired up the team was when he told reporters, "You've got to play every game like a championship game or, sure enough, you're going to get beat . . . The next five games will all be tough—and I say five, because I'm including the Super Bowl!"[22]

Deacon still is upset at the animosity and dissent that existed within the Rams organization: "Those same people who showed up with champagne and celebrated the last time George was fired were all still there, yipping and snapping like snarly little dogs. Dan Reeves had created a monster within his own camp, and he didn't recognize it. Over the years, he would hire weak coaches and then fire them after a year or two when they proved to be no good— then hire them back in some other capacity. Since he fired them with regularity (George was the ninth Rams head coach in 19 years), the Rams had an entire Greek chorus from old failed regimes all ready to hiss, boo, or sing at the appropriate moment.

"Since the Rams Public Relations department had close ties with the press, any innuendo, insinuation, or downright lie they could think up found its way into the papers. When they couldn't devise anything new, they would bring out the old stories about spying, and lack of character. And, since these were Reeves's old buddies, they had his ear. They constantly worked to influence him against Allen, not that Reeves needed much in that area in the first

---

21. Bob Oates, *Los Angeles Times*, December 1, 1970.
22. *Los Angeles Times*, December 7, 1970.

place, but they had to keep up the pressure. After all, they were the losers—George had us winning.

"*By now, Dan was a very sick man living in New York, with all he could do to fight cancer. He'd always tried to operate like his own general manager, but now he had to delegate more and more. Unfortunately for those who saw themselves rising in power within the organization, George Allen had taken over much of the deci-sion-making process from the very start of his tenure with the Rams. He didn't need all these hangers-on and losers telling him what to do. He was obvious about it, and this did nothing to endear the Rams head coach to his enemies in the Ram camp.*"

Give the Season to the Refs

It's always been one of the weaknesses of football. It's called "taking the game out of the players' hands." It's easy: With twenty-two men on the field, there's a lot of action to cover. All an official has to do is throw a flag for a minor infraction, and the course of football history is changed. The most common excuse for it is "keeping control of the game," and there is some element of truth here. Games can get out of hand. But this excuse for throwing the flag is an easy out, and unfor-givable in light of what it does to the game.

While fans in the stands, announcers, and reporters may howl their disagreement, players and coaches aren't allowed to disagree. They're not even supposed to publicly discuss a bad call.

What can cause a bad call? Ineptitude, bias, inability to clearly see the play, and probably personal greed. It would be naive to assume that in the entire history of football a referee had never been contacted by criminal elements (organized or disorganized) and asked to influ-ence a game. However, it is far more likely that bad calls are the result of something less melodramatic. Chances are good that poor play-call-ing is a result of one or more of the first three—ineptitude, bias, or inability to clearly see the action of the play because their line of sight is blocked by one or more players.

Refs are only human, and football is arguably the toughest game in the world to call. The men in the black-and-white-striped shirts don't hang around after a game; the final whistle blows, and they're gone, running from the wrath of the crowds who witnessed their poor work. Hence the advent of the instant replay, which, while not perfect, changed the course of many a game by righting blatant referee errors.

Historically, players and coaches try to ignore the things they can't do anything about—playing conditions, fixing the field, tricks played on them by the opposition, spying, and bad calls. But when any one of these influences the outcome of the game, a certain amount of grumbling is heard from the locker room. And occasionally, when an enormous mistake is made by the refs, a horrendous call that costs the game or even the season, the howl that goes up is heard throughout history, brought up years later when old players and diehard fans gather to talk about the game.

It happens. Ugly yellows have won games, titles, and even Super Bowls. In 1970, one terrible call changed the direction of a game, lost the season for the Rams, and probably brought down the George Allen era in Los Angeles. It happened in the second-last game of the season. It was late in the game, halfway through the fourth quarter, with the Rams trailing the Lions 21-16. Detroit was on the march when the Rams defense rose to the occasion as they had so many times in the past, forcing the Lions to punt. Alvin Haymond gathered in the ball and returned to the Ram forty-two. The Rams were surging, they had the momentum—and an official threw his yellow flag. The charge was tripping, a call so rare that it almost never happened, called against the Rams special teams' Dick Evey. Not that players, particularly offensive linemen, didn't (and don't) trip their opponents regularly. It happened so often it was part of the game, one of the reasons Deacon balled himself in the fetal position as soon as he felt himself going down.

As a frustrated Bob Oates reported in the *Times* the following day, "The official's flag cost the Rams the game and the season. The official said he'd seen Ram Dick Evey tripping a Lion. Evey had already made one block and jumped up to throw another when he was flagged."[23]

There was no talking to the referees. So, instead of retaining the ball the Rams were penalized fifteen yards. The Lions retained possession and the lead, and went on to win the game, 28-23.

The next day a disappointed George Allen was quoted in Jim Murray's column in the *L.A. Times,* "I told the team that here for the first time in five years we had 79,000 fans screaming for us. We finally had *fans,* not spectators, and they were for us and were fired up. So we were fired up, too, and had the momentum and I thought we were going to win the game. And we lost it because of the break."[24]

---

23. Bob Oates, *Los Angeles Times*, December 15, 1970.
24. Jim Murray, *Los Angeles Times*, December 15, 1970.

Deacon was less political in his remarks. The reporters flocked around him in the locker room, knowing he could be counted on to speak his mind, regardless of the NFL gag rule. As reported by Mal Florence of the *Times,* he said, "I've been in the NFL ten years. I've seen a lot of things. I've been in on a lot of plays. But I've seen only two tripping infractions called in all that time, and one was against me. It's a rare call, believe me. You could call tripping on offensive linemen all the time. When they fall down, they are always throwing their feet around."[25] Meanwhile, San Francisco won their game and regained first place. The following week, the Rams buried the New York Giants, 31-3, but their fate was in the 49ers' hands. San Francisco crushed the Oakland Raiders, and walked away with the title. As there were no wild card spots in those days, the season was over for Los Angeles. They finished in second place with a 9-4-1 record. The 49ers were 10-3-1.

Deacon reflects on that call. "Football is a tough, tough game, and it's hard to call. I don't blame the refs so much as I blame the Rams organization, not just for that call, but for all the quick yellow we'd put up with over the Allen years. We players all felt the effects of the anti-George campaign that was floated from our own management. We played hardnosed football, no different from any of the quality teams in the league. You could compare us to the Baltimore Colts, to the Packers, or to Bud Grant's Vikings. But, because of all the negative things said about Allen, we gained the reputation of being a "dirty tricks" team. Naturally, other teams picked up on it and used it against us. Rival coaches like Tom Fears were always complaining that Allen intimidated the refs, just as Halas had before him. Try as they might to stay neutral, the refs had to be sensitized to it. As successful as the Fearsome Foursome became, over the years we were always catching the quick flag. Sure, some of them were righteous calls. Call it fate, call it luck, call it misfortune, call it professional football—I believe we had more than our share of questionable calls. It's one thing if a ref takes a game from you and nothing is at stake—but we were strong contenders, and in 1968 and 1970, awful calls cost us our drives for the championship."

The ultimate skeptic, Deacon continues, "It was our own fault—we shouldn't have let our rivals get close enough to where the refs could determine the outcome."

It is easy to label Deacon a "complainer." But a, careful review

---

25. Mal Florence, *Los Angeles Times,* December 15, 1970.

of the records, the newspaper reports, and the game films of the time leaves enough room for reasonable doubt.

To put it mildly, there were a lot of football people who didn't like Allen and his tight-knit team of rough-and-tumble footballers and, even today, many are quite frank and open about it. Contacted recently, Weeb Ewbank, who head coached for twenty years, leading Baltimore in the fifties and the New York Jets in the sixties, reveals that he was no fan of Allen's. "I didn't trust him. He asked me for drills, and used them. He never gave me credit or thanks." Weeb, whose career win-loss record of 134-130 (.507) is .174 less than Allen's (118-54-5 for .681), has criticisms that range over a wide variety of topics. "He was a spender, and finally no owner would hire him." He also disagrees with Allen's philosophy of trading draft choices for proven players. "Old ball players may get you to the finals, but they can't win championships." There may be something to this. The records show Weeb won four out of five post season games, while Allen won only two out of seven. Weeb remembers Allen coming up to him one time and asking to see his Super Bowl III championship ring. "'Let me see that ring,' George said, 'I don't have one of those.'"

But Deacon scoffs, "You've got to get to the playoffs before you can play for the championship ring."

Ex-Rams and Chargers head coach Harland Svare doesn't buy any of Deacon's talk about bad playcalling. "Deacon is just bitter about a lot of things. He's one of the greatest of the great players, and he should leave it go at that. There was never any plan to 'get' George or the Rams. Every team in the league loses some games because of bad calls. That's just football. You take your lumps and you don't whine about it."

When told of these comments, Deacon just smiles. "I see the anti-George league is still intact and well after all these years."

Reeves's Revenge

Hobbled by illness and living across the country in New York, it was relatively easy for Dan Reeves to evade any questions about his plans for George Allen. And the Rams office passed the ball, asserting it was in Reeves's hands. Allen's contract would be up on December 31; as the clock ticked toward the end of the month and still no word was forthcoming, it became more and more obvious that Reeves was hanging his coach out to dry, just as he had done with Harland Svare and all the coaches before him. Speculation mounted, not whether Allen would be re-hired, but who the new coach would be. Rumored for the job were Tom Fears (ex-Rams player and ex-New Orleans Saints head coach), Ira Parseghian (highly successful Notre Dame coach), Ray Willsey (University of California coach), Ray Prochaska (Allen's offensive coach), Tom Katlin (Allen's defensive coach), and perennial candidate John McKay (USC's coach).

Allen himself was reluctant to leave. After all, he had single-mindedly devoted five years of his life to building a winning team, a championship contender. He had been tremendously successful by any standard, and he felt the Rams stood on the threshold of the Super Bowl and the championship of the world. Unwilling to give Reeves any excuse to fire him, he thoughtfully asked the press, "Why should the Rams consider anyone else?" It was a point well taken. George Allen's record since 1966 was 49-17-4. "I thought he would at least call to wish us good luck," Allen said of Reeves, talking about the last game of the season, when the team had been back East in New York to play the Giants. "But he didn't. In fact, I haven't talked to him in a year." That was how the press found out Allen was communicating to Reeves through Johnny Sanders, the Rams assistant general manager, and Jack Teele, assistant to the president.

After the San Francisco win, which briefly launched the Rams back into first place, Allen had told reporters, "I could have a job four times better if my contract isn't renewed." There were reports that Green Bay, Washington, Chicago, New Orleans, and Philadelphia all were interested.

Realistically, this time around, the veteran players on the Rams didn't expect Reeves to rehire the most winning coach they'd ever had. On December 22, Roman Gabriel said he was "almost sure" Allen wouldn't return. Deacon ground his teeth and, for once, held his tongue. He figured anything he said in Allen's favor would have a negative effect on the Rams owner.

Charles Maher, writing in the *L.A. Times*, questioned the soundness of Reeves's thinking and alluded to the whisper campaign that the Rams owner and others had carried out against Allen over the years. "It's no good to ask Dan Reeves what he's got against Allen. Reeves won't talk about it for the record . . . From here, the grounds for dismissing [Allen] look insufficient."[26]

But Reeves, who had been forced into hiring Allen and embar-

26. Charles Maher, *Los Angeles Times*, December 22, 1970.

rassed by a massive revolt from the players and fans into bringing
Allen back after firing him in late 1968, was in no mood to hire him
again, and on the final day of Allen's contract the headlines screamed
in capital letters, "ALLEN SACKED AGAIN—GROUNDS: IN-
COMPATIBILITY." The papers reported that the fifty-nine-year-old
Reeves, living in ill health in New York, had called his L.A. office
from the East Coast to say Allen's contract would not be renewed. At
the time, no new coach had been selected. Reeves told the press, "I
have no statement concerning a new head coach at this time, except to
say that I will do everything I can to provide the best possible field
leadership for our players and our fans." Reeves went on to rationalize
his own actions by explaining that Allen's "Win Now" philosophy
leaves the future unprotected.[27]

Allen, the most successful coach in Rams history, described his
telephone conversation with Reeves, the call in which the Rams owner
told him his services would no longer be needed. "It was a cold conversation, no gratitude, no appreciation. There was no thanks for what
I've done."

And so the Rams were looking for their tenth coach in the twenty-
five years since Reeves had moved the team from Cleveland. Rams
fans, more interested in winning than in Dan Reeves's personal problems, were alternately disappointed and outraged. Several ads appeared
in the L.A. newspapers protesting the move and advertising a massive
rally to be held in front of the Rams office on Pico Blvd. The anti-
George faction was going to have to move fast or they were going to
have another major revolt on their hands.

And move fast they did, announcing on Sunday, January 3, that
they had signed surprise pick Tommy Prothro, a tremendously successful college coach who had led both Oregon State and UCLA twice
to the Rose Bowl. Dan Reeves said, "We promised to try to find the
best possible man for our players and our fans. It is my conviction we
have done just that and Tommy will prove it."[28]

Further details came out the next day. Prothro, who had played
quarterback at Duke in his college days, was signed under a cloak of
secrecy in Memphis the night before club president Reeves phoned
Allen to let him go. The Rams Public Relations department revealed
that Jack Teele, acting as chief assistant to Reeves, had jetted from L.A.

---

27. "Allen Sacked Again—Grounds: Incompatibility," *Los Angeles Times*, December 31,
1970.

28. Dwight Chapin, *Los Angeles Times*, January 3, 1971.

to Memphis with a contract, registering at a Holiday Inn under the alias of "Jack Williams."[29] Operating with such cloak-and-dagger methods could be taken as an indication of the level of fear the Rams management had that their actions would bring down the wrath of the fans.

L.A. Times columnist John Hall mirrored the views of Rams management when he wrote, "There is serenity at last at the West Pico home of the Rams this morning." Hall went on to explain that the swift signing of "such a popular and respected name" as Prothro to succeed Allen "instantly defused whatever explosives might have been expected" from the demonstration planned by the former coach's supporters.[30]

In the days that followed, John Hall penned several columns in the same vein. He presented in glowing terms what he said was Prothro's football philosophy, noting "George Allen, former Rams coach, isn't the only football man with a ten-point code—a basic coaching philosophy that was once described as Allen's ten commandments."[31] Prothro's code, as presented by Hall went as follows:

1. Directing any football organization is more than a one-man job.
2. No stereotypes.
3. Balance is the prime objective on the field, in the front office, and in life.
4. Respect from the athletes is more important than affection.
5. Trades should be made by the coach.
6. A coach must accept "no" for an answer sometimes.
7. A coach should have complete confidence in the scouting department.
8. The "big play" is preferable to ball control.
9. Preparing your own team is more important than worrying about the other team.
10. No pets [private favorites].

This list would seem all well and good; yet, even on the surface, it shows two major departures from Allen's way. First, point four indicates a more authoritarian approach to the players (the method Waterfield and Svare had plied without much success), and point eight shows a major shift in football strategy. Looked at more closely, it would seem that points five and seven might contradict each other

---

29. John Hall, *Los Angeles Times*, January 4, 1971.
30. Ibid.
31. John Hall, *Los Angeles Times*, January 5, 1971.

(after all, a coach with complete confidence in his scouting department won't be the final voice in decisions on trades), while point six gives management a blanket veto over the coach. Point three can be seen as a criticism of George's dedication, which his detractors had long dismissed as fanaticism. The ten points taken together are a loosely crafted summary of the anti-George sentiments that had been whispered and served up by Reeves's cronies over the years. *George, the loner who takes too much power. George's silly slogans. Player affection for their coach is a bad thing. The owner has the right to say no. George's ball control is boring football. George had his favorites.*

So here in one fell swoop was presented a man who would right all these supposed wrongs. Hall went on to explain that Prothro had an eleventh basic principle, one that was more basic than all the rest: "The idea," he wrote, "is to win. Tommy Prothro is a winner."[32] Deacon read the article and felt bewildered. It was enough to make your head swim. *If winning was the idea, what sense did it make to fire the winningest coach the Rams ever had?* Clearly, this was the big lie. This wasn't about winning, it was about control.

In another of his columns, published in the *L.A. Times* on January 1, Hall presented Reeves's credentials: "Reeves has won five conference championships and two world titles, which is five and two more than his latest coach." But those winning years were before Reeves had complete ownership and control of the Rams; one has to question how much he personally was responsible for them. Hall also failed to note that Reeves was notorious for loading up on unneeded quarterbacks and running backs, and for dumping his picks just before they blossomed. If Reeves ever had a winning touch, he'd lost it long before the arrival of Allen. The Rams had been perennial losers through a long and dismal streak that had lasted for a decade and made them the patsies of the league and the laughing stock of Los Angeles. They hadn't won their division since 1955; finishing in fifth place in 1956; fourth in 1957; second in 1958; sixth in 1959, 1960, and 1961; seventh in 1962; sixth in 1963; fifth in 1964; and seventh in 1965. Allen came in, cleaned house, and turned things around immediately, coming in third in 1966 with an 8-6 record to give the Rams their first winning season in seven years. Allen came in first in 1967, second in 1968, first in 1969 and second in 1970, and in every year that Allen coached the Rams were strong contenders and a team to be feared.

---

32. John Hall, *Los Angeles Times*, January 5, 1971.

But Hall was more interested in slamming Allen. At one point he took Allen to task for alluding to Reeves's illness in an interview. Allen had explained that "Reeves's ill health" was one reason why he hadn't communicated with the Rams owner over the past two years, and why Reeves hadn't been so hands-on with the team. Hall intimates there is something disrespectful or even mendacious in the fact that Allen brought up this subject, as if this was a personal matter that shouldn't have been revealed by the coach. Hall himself then goes on to describe Reeves's illness as Hodgkins Disease, a form of cancer, and to discuss it in detail.[33]

The hoopla and tub-thumping from Rams management did little to discourage George Allen. John Hall, trying to build a case for the Rams owner's actions, was writing, "Nobody has ever put more heart and soul and energy into the Rams than Dan Reeves, and nobody has done as much for major league sports in Los Angeles. It was that way in 1946 and it is still that way this morning on the first day of 1971." But on that same day there were other NFL clubs who saw Reeves as foolish and vindictive, and were prepared to take advantage of his folly. The job offers came flooding in for Allen from pro teams around the country, and just seven days after being fired—while the euphoria and all the crowing over nothing was still going on among the Rams management staff—Allen was hired as the new coach and general manager of the Washington Redskins. Just as he'd lost scores of fine players in bad trades over the years, now Reeves lost the best coach the Rams ever had. Allen had built the Rams into a dynasty that would outlast Prothro's two years to rise again in 1973 under new owner Carroll Rosenbloom and new head coach Chuck Knox to dominate their division in the 1970s. Meanwhile, Allen continued to excel at that which he did best—winning. Over the next five years, he was to build the Redskins into a powerhouse, a football dynasty that lasted into the early nineties.

Once Allen was hired by the Redskins, he told the press that he had been pursued by several clubs since Reeves had fired him. He had chosen the Washington team because they had the most potential to become winners, and because they would give him the full authority to do his job.

George was asked to comment on the rumor being floated against him that he'd left Prothro with an old team on the decline. Noting

---

33. John Hall, *Los Angeles Times*, January 1, 1971.

that they had signed Bob Klein, Jim Seymour, Larry Smith, and Jack Youngblood—all first round draft choices—in the last three years, Allen said, "I don't buy that. They've been saying that for years. There's no reason why the Rams can't stay up there. They've got some good young players and some fine veterans. As I've said many times, you can play for years if you take care of yourself."[34]

Over the next five months "Trader George" proved himself again: in a string of brilliant moves, he would consummate fourteen major deals, strengthening the Redskins offense, defense, and kicking game and turning the team from a perennial loser into a winning team in his first year.

And so Dan Reeves and his crowd of old buddies committed one of the major business mistakes ever made in pro football—letting go a sure and proven winner for an unproven rookie who had never coached on the pro level, not even as the lowest assistant on the lowest rung of the ladder.

Rams management announced vaguely that Prothro had signed a "long-term contract of undisclosed length." Sportswriter Dwight Chapin wrote that most of the press was questioning if Prothro would be able to "bridge the gaps that Allen could not bridge—primarily with Reeves."[35]

While this was always an important question to ask of the Rams, nobody was asking the major one—could Tommy Prothro, so successful on the college level, do as good a job coaching pro ball? Could he coach pro ball at all?

The answer would be a resounding *no*. Prothro would head coach the Rams and the Chargers for a combined total of six seasons (plus four games of a seventh season). In charge of teams loaded with talent, after coasting the Rams to second place and an 8-5-1 record in 1971 on the strength of the house that George had built, *Prothro would never enjoy another winning season.* By way of contrast, in his twelve years head coaching the pros, *Allen never had a losing season.* The "undisclosed length" of Prothro's "long term" contract with the Rams would prove to be two years, during which he would inadvertently undo much of what Allen had built, and allow the star-studded and proven Rams to drift downward into mediocrity.

---

34. Mal Florence, "George Allen Hired as New Coach, GM of Redskins," *Los Angeles Times*, January 7, 1971.

35. Dwight Chapin, *Los Angeles Times*, January 3, 1971.

Interviewed recently by this author, prominent attorney Ed Hook-stratten, who once represented George Allen, said of him, "George was a winner, but he was strong-minded. It was his way or the highway. Nobody got to really know him, except maybe his players. Deacon, the finest defensive end ever to play in the NFL, knew him better than most. Around the league, George got the reputation of a man with an aversion to the truth. Maybe he did lie a little to his rivals. He was very crafty. What are you going to do, tell your enemies the truth?

"Privately, he was such a gentleman, but as a coach, he was a fanatic. And he was misunderstood. He was accused of dealing in voodooism, recycling old ballplayers as opposed to a system of scouting and drafting, which was the accepted way to build a ball club. George mortgaged the future to package now."

Jack Teele, who was the Rams long-time director of public relations and worked as assistant to the president during the turbulent years when Reeves and Allen were on the club, recently talked to this author about his boss: "Dan Reeves was like a father to me. He was the best football man I ever knew. He set up the scouting system that became the standard for the pros. He was the first to have school scouts, and the first to scout the small black schools. He brought in great black players like Bob Boyd, Deacon Dan Towler, Tank Younger, and Glenn Davis. Football was his life. There was probably no way the thing between him and Allen could be avoided. Allen started thinking like he was the owner, making deals and then telling us later."

George's son, Bruce Allen, talks about his father's uncanny ability to select players. "They called him Trader George, like he ran some little store out on the Navajo reservation, or traded guns and booze up the Amazon—but that was just jealousy or maybe a sort of perverted admiration. The truth is, George was a super judge of talent. I deal with players today and you see rookies who do one season and they are millionaires, they never have to play again. I can't stand a lot of them. They have money and an attitude—but no principles. Dad's way of determining if he liked a player or not was so simple you'd think other people would have thought of it before, or at least would be using it today; he would look at the stats, but that wasn't the determining factor for him. Stats are just numbers on a page, and stats can lie. George would sit down and really talk to a player. He would find out what was inside. That's why he came to understand Deacon so well. He saw that Deacon wanted to be great. Not just good, but great. So much of what he saw in Deacon was a mirror image of himself, of his own ideals."

A high-ranking Rams official who—even today, after nearly a quarter of a century—wishes to remain unnamed, talks scornfully about Allen's dealing. "Allen would do anything for the player, even things that he had no right to. When we traded for Bob Brown of the Eagles, there were things Allen promised Brown that Reeves didn't know. He promised him a car to come to the Rams! Nobody did that in those days. It was unheard of!"

Deacon shrugs, "If giving away a lousy automobile is what it takes to build a winner, why not? It's a business incentive, like giving the vice presidents of a bank or the top salesmen a company car. What's wrong with that? Hell, the players play the game—nobody's more important. But the truth is, in those days, management wanted to keep us down, to treat us like dogs . . . and even today in these enlightened times, they still would if they could!"

Deacon thinks the man he called "Coach" has not been treated fairly by history. "They're still keeping one of the very finest coaches ever to coach the game out of the Hall of Fame. George Allen! The man revolutionized football, helped bring it into the modern age. And a winner—he's got the third-best all-time win-loss average in the league! Only the great Vince Lombardi and John Madden top him. He's got a better record than all the top guys—Don Shula, Tom Landry, Chuck Knox, Weeb Ewbank. His record is better than the legendary Paul Brown or Curly Lambeau, who had a football field named after him, better than the 49ers' Bill Walsh, better even than his mentor, Pappa George Halas.

"How mean are these people? After everything he'd done for football, when George died a few years ago not a single owner except maverick Al Davis showed up to attend his funeral. Not from the Rams. Not from the Redskins. Pete Rozelle wasn't there, either."[36]

The stories about Allen's drive abound. Times writer Steve Springer talks about the time in 1974 when Allen's Redskins were beaten by the Rams in a first-round playoff game on Christmas Eve. "Nervous about talking to Allen, a young reporter tried to break the ice with small talk. 'Are you guys flying home for Christmas?" asked the reporter, coming up to Allen from behind. The coach turned, tears streaming from red eyes, and replied, "When you lose, there is no Christmas.' "[37]

Times sports writer Bob Oates uses a story to sum up Allen's

---

36. George Allen died on December 31, 1990 at the age of 72. He collapsed after returning from his daily exercise jog. At the time, Times staff writer Bob Oates, among others, called for him to be made a Hall of Famer, citing his winning record and many contributions to the game. For further information, see the front page of the Sports Section, *Los Angeles Times*, January 1, 1991.

37. Steve Springer, *Los Angeles Times*, January 1, 1991.

career. He recalls an off-season NFL meeting during Allen's first winter in Los Angeles, "Halas, addressing the NFL's club owners, stood and berated Allen at length, describing him as, among other things, a schemer and a cheater. That amused Vince Lombardi, the coach of Green Bay's five-time champions, who at the time was seated next to Dan Reeves . . . turning in Reeves' direction, Lombardi whispered loudly: 'Sounds as if you've got yourself a hell of a coach.' "[38]

---

38. Bob Oates, *Los Angeles Times*, January 1, 1991.

10

The Substitute for Winning

In a way, it was all show business. For several years, a season ticket holder who sat in the eastern end of the Coliseum had brought a big cardboard sign with him. "Secretary of Defense," it read, and whenever Deacon stopped a charge or sacked a quarterback, the sign went up. After a while, the name stuck. Jack Teele began using it in press releases and soon reporters across the country were referring to Deacon as the Secretary of Defense, the Hitman from L.A. or the Sultan of Sacks.

Meanwhile, Deacon's career in show business moved forward again when his manager, Al Ross, signed him to do a show at Lake Tahoe. Deacon Jones the football player had taken another step toward becoming Deacon Jones the celebrity.

The King's Castle

George Allen was gone, and now all Deacon could hope for was that he would be traded with him. There was a moment of hope when Allen acquired four Rams—defensive end Diron Talbert (twenty-seven years old) and veteran linebackers Maxie Baughan, Myron Pottios, and Jack Pardee.

Allen told reporters, "Talbert is one of the best ten or twelve tackles in the league. He is more desirable than Deacon Jones or Merlin Olsen because his future is ahead of him." Deacon's hopes soared when he heard that, for he knew George Allen never told the press or his rival coaches what his real intentions were.

The Rams were in a trading mood—Prothro gave away eight-year pro tight end Billy Truax (twenty-seven years old) and wide receiver Wendell Tucker to the Cowboys for the troubled wide receiver Lance Rentzel, who had pleaded guilty to the charge of indecently exposing himself to a ten-year old girl. Jack Teele assured the press, "We're not worried about his future conduct." Prothro, perhaps forgetting he was trading two for one, said, "We're losing a great one, but getting a great one."[1] The Rams also traded away veteran lineman Bob Brown, who was twenty-nine at the time. For what they gave away, they acquired (in addition to the controversial Rentzel) cornerback Kent McClougham from Oakland, halfback Travis Williams from Green Bay, tackle Harry Schuh from Oakland, and linebacker Marlin McKeever from Washington. On June 30, 1971, Prothro confided to the press, "We're stronger than we were in January."[2]

Deacon Jones didn't see it that way. From his point of view, Prothro and the Rams front office were dismantling a winner. But he waited and waited in vain for the call from Washington. There was nothing he could do about it.

It was late April when Deacon stuffed his clothes into his shiny new Cadillac and drove over to pick up his drummer. The man was sitting outside of one of Deacon's apartment complexes, where he'd been rooming free until he could get his life in order.

"What the hell is that, man?" Deacon pointed to the jumbled pile of clothes and belongings lying at the curb. "We ain't got no *truck* here."

They managed to find room for the clothes. It took a while longer to have the drums packed and shipped by parcel post. The rest of the stuff—some frayed black light posters, a red beanbag chair repaired with duct tape, three or four Hefty trash bags full of assorted junk, and two battered kitchen chairs were left on the curb.

"It'll be gone by noon," Deacon confided.

"Garbage man come by today?"

"You might say that."

Most of the band and the singers had already left, but Deacon had been waiting until the last moment, still hoping to hear Allen's summons from Washington. But the Rams weren't willing to deal him away, and so Allen signed two defensive ends from the Jets—All-Pro

---

1. John Hall, *Los Angeles Times,* May 27, 1971.
2. Bob Oates, *Los Angeles Times,* June 30, 1971.

Verlon Biggs, who had played out his option, and Jimmie Johns. Deacon had done his best for Allen, but Allen was gone and he had a new coach, a coach who was going to prove himself to everybody—players, fans and most particularly to Dan Reeves—by shuffling the deck. Time to get on with life. Time not to think about it any more.[3]

The drummer hopped in on the passenger side and Deacon pointed his big car east, driving through Pomona and Riverside, and then heading north up a long scrub-brush upgrade to the dry lands of the high desert. The drive was one long blur of yucca and sagebrush whipping by as Deacon held the pedal to the floorboards. They spent the night in Las Vegas, trying their luck at the tables, and then pushed on toward Reno the next day. They had lunch at a small coffee shop, and consulted the maps. From Reno, a two-lane blacktop led back west. At the time, Deacon hadn't been concentrating on geography. In the map, it looked easy; there was only one road into Tahoe from Reno. He settled back behind the wheel, and started down the road.

It was a half-hour before he began to get edgy. He looked over at the drummer, "You sure this is the right road, man?" Somehow, what had looked simple on the map was now beginning to bother him.

"Sure, I'm sure," the drummer said. "Only one way to Tahoe."

"You better take another hard look. We headin' into the *mountains!*"

"That be where Tahoe is, fool. In the mountains."

"No way!" Deacon pulled to the side of the road, and stared at his companion in disbelief.

"Deak, it's a *mountain* resort. *Lake Tahoe, in the beautiful High Sierras.* Ain't you never seen the brochures?"

Deacon stared at the range of hills now looming like a wall in front of him, "Hey, man—you know how to drive a car?"

"Yeah, sure."

"I was up most of last night, tryin' to hit twenty-one. If I catch a little shut-eye, you think you could take us the rest of the way?"

"Yeah, sure."

They made it with Deacon lying across the back seat, his head buried under a pile of colorful silk shirts. Once they were in Tahoe, he was all right. It was getting there that was the problem.[4]

---

3. Years later, Allen revealed to Deacon that he had tried to acquire him in a trade, but the Rams had asked for a prohibitively extensive group of players and future draft picks in return.

4. In the early nineties, Deacon was in Calgary working for the CFL Stampeders. When invited to a golf tournament, he drove west from Calgary, not realizing it would be in the heart of the Canadian Rockies. His wife Elizabeth got them there.

The first night they opened his "Soul by a Pro" review, the house was packed. Introduced as the "Fabulous Deacon Jones," and with Ray Frazier and the Shades of Madness and the three Deaconettes backing him, Deacon showed up on stage wearing a wildly colorful shirt open to his broad silver belt, and spangled pants with huge bells on the bottoms. After a few minutes of banter, he swung into his rendition of "Proud Mary." The crowd was warm and friendly. They seemed to love him.

Deacon was originally up for a one-month stint, through the end of May, but after his opening night success, the owner of The King's Castle came to him and extended for another month. Deacon happily signed, figuring that should take him right up to spring training.

A few weeks later, Prothro announced he wanted to hold a "mini-camp" before the regular spring training. Although there was no pay for attending the mini-camp and nothing in their contracts that said they had to be there, the word was Prothro expected the players to show up without exception. Deacon and many of the other veterans decided they weren't going to attend. The Rams backed down and explained to the press that thirty-seven rookies and a dozen vets were invited to the first week of camp, which was to start on Thursday, July 8. They told everyone that the rest of the veterans—including Roman Gabriel, Lance Rentzel, Merlin Olsen, and Deacon Jones—would be in the following week.

In Tahoe, Deacon developed a routine to sharpen his edge, running along the lake early in the morning, and then sleeping most of the day, waking in the evening to catch his main meal and get ready for his show. After all, he was team captain and the leader of the defense. It was great to be a singer and a performer in Tahoe, but when the season rolled around, he wanted to be ready.

One night after his show Deacon went around the lake to another club, where Bill Cosby was putting on a show. Cosby called him up on stage, Deacon moved in on a set of bongo drums, and they struck up a number together. Deacon and Cosby hit it off so well that they sang and joked around for a couple of hours. When Deacon finally headed for his bed his head was swimming with the possibilities. *Perhaps there was going to be a life for him after the gridiron!*

By the time Deacon got back to L.A., Al Ross had already lined up another gig for him. At that time, Sammy Davis Jr. was trying to revive the Coconut Grove with a series of entertainers. The review was called "Sammy Davis Presents," and Deacon agreed he would host a show on nights after home games.

Rams players who over the years had watched Deacon's second career from the sidelines were alternately amused and jealous of his new success. Rosey Grier, who had a beautiful voice, couldn't understand Deacon's popularity. Unconvinced that his former teammate had any talent worth paying the price of admission, he told writer Bill Libby, "I picked him up singing at a club once. The girls came out and did their thing. Then along came Jones. He starts out singing "Lovin' a Pro." I always watch a performer closely, trying to see what he's feelin' while he's workin'. At first the Deacon is feeling good. His face is all smiles. Then he stops smiling. His expression becomes sullen. He keeps singing for a while, then suddenly he stops. 'You in the wrong god damned key,' he says to the band. I almost fell off my chair. I went up to him later and I said, 'David, you can't do that in public. You got to fight it through.' He said, 'Rosey, you got to lose some weight.' "

Even today, his former teammates are not convinced the raw kid from central Florida was able to develop his abilities to the point where he was able to carry a tune—much less an entire show—by himself. An old rumor continues to circulate that Deacon got extended in Tahoe not for his singing ability, but because he had run up a gambling debt he had to pay off; he'd lost his shirt playing blackjack. The story goes that the casino made Deacon stay and work off his bill before it would let him go. When asked if the rumor is true, Deacon laughs, "Naw, not a word of it! If it was, I certainly wouldn't deny it! That would only add to the legend of the great Deacon Jones, held captive in the King's Castle until he had to be let go to play football! Hell, we all started out together; those boys just don't like to think I could have the kind of success on stage that I did."

The high-powered projects Deacon was developing with Al Ross proved to be high-risk as well. "At the time I had over a half-million in real estate—four buildings with over eighty units. But the problem was, they were all in South Central L.A., and collecting rent was a real problem. My brothers (older brother Judson, whom he had convinced to give up his high school coaching career and move to L.A., and younger brother Harold) and I had a real tough time going out and collecting the money in that area. The Batik Wine Company, in which I was part investor with Lou Rawls and others, went bust, too. Other projects like the recording company and the dinner club never developed. You have to understand that to make money you sometimes have to risk it. And I have never been afraid to take the risk."

The King Meets the King

Deacon was still up at the King's Castle, halfway through his engagement, when Al Ross called and asked him if he'd like to meet the King.

"I am the king," he replied automatically, "the King of Sacks."

There was a pause while Ross took it in. "No," he said finally. "I mean Elvis Presley."

Deacon held on to the phone, not saying anything, just thinking it over. He'd heard all the stories about Elvis. The singer hated blacks. It was 1971, and Elvis was at the top of his game and his songs were everywhere . . . and so were the whispers. If you were an American Negro, you knew all about the bad side of *Mister* Elvis Presley. Story was, he was born in Tupelo, Mississippi, and Deacon was more than ready to believe anything bad about the Delta rednecks. You could call that Deacon's prejudice if you want to, but he'd had reason to be nervous about those folks. The ones he'd met loved all blacks—in their place. *Step back off the sidewalk there, boy. You lookin' at me, boy? You make one mistake, boy, and you're dead meat, boy.*

"A chance to meet the King, hisself," Deacon finally replied.

"Yeah. Sure. Elvis is a big sports fan. I can set it up for next week."

A slow smile came over Deacon's face. "Yeah, sure. Set it up. I'll fly down from Tahoe and meet you."

"You sure you won't be driving?"

"Yeah, I'm sure." Deacon hung up and paced around his room. After all the dirt he'd heard on Elvis, here was a chance to scope out the guy eyeball to eyeball! If Presley was on the level, well, okay. If not, Deacon would see the true facts for himself.

The following week, Ross picked Deacon up at the Las Vegas airport in a mean black Porsche. Deacon was silent all the way over to the casino, thinking about what he was going to say. *Elvis, did you really say "The only thing a nigger can do for me is shine my shoes"?* He'd dreamed this scene a hundred times since Ross had first called him. In his daydream Elvis gives him that shy, lopsided grin of his and says, "Why, yeah, I did say that." And then, *Whop!* Deacon gives Elvis his headslap right on the sideburns, rattling his cage so bad he goes flyin' ass-over-teakettle.

Deacon had left the peaceful resistance movement behind years ago, on a chilly night in South Carolina when he was sitting in a barbed wire enclosure behind the jail in the town of Orangeburg with his suit pants torn by a dog, and his body soaked by spit and water hoses. Since then, he'd taken no truck from any man, and Elvis was just another man, somebody who had to pull his gold lamé pants on one leg at a time.

By the time they pulled up in front of the Las Vegas Hilton, Deacon had his attitude on so heavy he wasn't talking.

Ross looked over at him, "Hey, you pissed at me or something?"

"No, Al, everything's all right."

Ross shrugged and handed the car keys to the attendant. They walked around behind the gaming tables into the back, and went past the guards and all the hangers-on into Elvis's dressing room.

There he was, the King himself, standing right in front of Deacon. *At least,* Deacon reminded himself, *Elvis was the king of music. When it came to titles like that, Deacon was a king, too. He was the King of Sacks in the National Football League.*

Right then, though, Elvis didn't look very kingly. It was as if the daydream had come true. He stood looking at Deacon with that grin just the way Deacon had imagined it, and then he came right over and stuck out his hand and said, "Well, *there* you are! I was beginnin' to think you wasn't gonna come! What kinda drink can I fix you boys?"

Deacon was totally flabbergasted. As he would describe it later, he was disarmed by friendship. Elvis got them a fistful all around and before Deacon knew it he was telling the man from Tupelo how hard it was to tackle Johnny U. because of his quick trigger, and what a bitch it was chasing that little devil Tarkenton all over the field on a hot September afternoon in the Coliseum. Elvis was really loving it. You could tell, the man really loved sports. Right away, Deacon's attitude started to soften. After all, a man who loves sports can't be *all* bad.

Maybe there was a time when Elvis did say such negative things about blacks, like Deacon had heard. It was impossible to tell, because the great singer was friendly and down-to-earth and interested in what they were talking about.

Elvis poured them all another round of drinks, and they got to joking around about the Rams' chances to take it all in the upcoming season—at least, Elvis did, Deacon being serious as a heart attack when it came to who was going to win in the NFL. They must have hung out for about an hour, until Elvis's next show was about to start, and as they were leaving, Elvis invited Deacon back any time.

Deacon left feeling Elvis was a good guy. He fell silent again, pondering the meaning of things as they stood in the desert twilight outside the Hilton waiting for the man to bring Ross's Porsche around. Ross looked nervously at Deacon, but Deacon didn't say anything. He just shook his head and got in the car. Deacon guessed he finally had to admit it . . . something good had come out of Mississippi after all.

Deacon shrugs, thinking back on the time he met Elvis. "I didn't meet his ghost hitchhiking to Memphis or wandering the back yard in Graceland—this was the real thing. Yet, to this day I truly don't know how he felt about blacks. There were all these bad stories about him, yet he seemed so natural and ordinary and open. I like to think that he really wasn't that way like they say. You've got to remember, by the time I met him, he'd been away from that old muddy riverbank crowd a long time, and, if he'd ever felt Negroes were inferior, he may have grown out of it. After all, he had three backup singers who were black, and that must have meant something to him."

Ring-A-Ding-Ding

Mini-camps were one- or two-week sessions held in the heart of the off-season, generally under the pretense of "player evaluation." Tommy Prothro may have gotten the idea from college ball, where spring practice was a way of life. The practices were not covered by the player contracts and they didn't pay anything, so Deacon had turned down his invitation and decided not to go. *What am I going to learn?* he asked himself. Of those invited, only he and Bob Brown did not attend. Prothro never said publicly how he felt about that, but Bob was traded straight away, and Deacon would be gone after the season.

From the start, Prothro was determined to place his own stamp on the team, in ways both large and small. As the first week of real practice got under way, Deacon sat in the cafeteria with the other defensive linemen, joking and laughing after piling in a big dinner. There was a *ding-ding-ding* noise. Deacon looked around, surprised to see a rustle go through the dining hall as the group of men all fell silent.

"What the hell's that?" Deacon asked.

"Shhhhhhh," the player across from him whispered. "Coach Prothro has the floor."

"Has the floor? He can have the floor and the ceiling too, for all I care."

But now a dozen rookies around him had their fingers to their lips, telling Deacon to be quiet.

Prothro waited a few seconds for the hub-bub to calm down, and began to get down to the order of business. He spoke quietly, as if reading from a list at his table, and he didn't make eye contact. Deacon strained to hear what he was saying. Something about haircuts. Apparently their new coach preferred short haircuts and no beards. As if it was any of his business! Prothro droned on. Now he was talking about curfew. Deacon sat up, astounded. No curfew? Now *that* was asking for trouble! Sure, players tried to beat the curfew. It was the game they'd played ever since pro ball had been invented. But it was better a player snuck back in at three in the morning rather than not show up at all for the game the next day! Allen had always had an eleven o'clock curfew, and three bed checks throughout the night. Sure, there were fines, and sure, it was a pain in the ass, but pros were wild and burly men, and the temptations were easy and everywhere. If you were going to build a winner, you had to have some reasonable rules that everyone followed! Here was Prothro, telling everyone how to cut their hair, and then throwing away the major discipline of a curfew! *The guy didn't know what was important!*

The list went on, Prothro swiftly ticking off the items as he went. The practice hours were to start much later than they had under Allen. Again, Deacon was amazed. The Rams never learned from experience. Now they were back to the old Bob Waterfield "country club" schedule![5]

Prothro went on. As had another Ram rookie coach, Harland Svare, Prothro insisted that few veterans would be safe at their old positions. He was determined to change thirteen of the twenty-two starting positions—eight defense and five on offense. Only Jones, Olsen, and Coy Bacon might be in their old positions. *Might be.*

And still Prothro went on. Ball control and dominant defense was out, to be replaced by "big play" offense. With the trades he'd made, particularly for Lance Rentzel, the Rams would be able to sting their opponents and play exciting football.

For his next agenda items, Prothro began cutting members from the squad. Deacon blew out a deep breath and sat back angrily in his seat. Pro football was a way of life to the players, it was their source of pride, their business. *You didn't knock down a player in front of other players.* You took a player behind closed doors, where you could explain things, and where he could have his privacy.

Deacon watched the piece-by-piece destruction of the winning

---

5. Bob Oates, *Los Angeles Times,* June 30 and July 4, 1971.

combination George Allen had built over the past five years. He shouldn't have been in shock—after all, for weeks the papers had spoken of little else, building Prothro into some sort of legend before his first pro team ever took the field. But, at that moment, Deacon had never missed Allen more, or realized so deeply just what the *player's* coach had meant to the team. Allen had lifted them up, motivated them to be the best, molded them into winners. And now, here was Tommy Prothro.

The Rams Publicity Department was working overtime to sell their new man. Ram fans, if they read the sports page at all, knew Prothro loved to play bridge. He drank Cokes and smoked three to four packs of cigarettes a day. He was a "thinker" and a "technician who understood techniques." He liked to get to the office at 10:30 in the morning or later, and to stay "until the job is finished."[6]

The Rams had a new owner, Mrs. Mary Reeves, a new president, Bill Barnes, and a new coach, Tommy Prothro. Deacon saw that it was a coup for the Rams front office management, a clean sweep, a bright new day . . . for everyone but the players and the fans.

Prothro finally ended his long drone with another *ding-ding-ding,* hitting the side of his water glass with his fork.

"Okay, that's the signal," the man across the table from Deacon whispered. "We can all go now."

"What? You mean we got to sit here like children until the man ringy-dings his glass with his fork?"

"Aww, come on, man. Everybody got their own habits. Give the man a chance."

Deacon's lowering scowl took in everyone at the table. "The schedule Prothro laid out for us may be satisfactory for you rookies, but I tell you right here and now, it is not enough to make us winners."

"Yeah, sure, you think Allen was better." The rookie gave Deacon a sneer, "Allen never won nothin' here."

Deacon reached across the table. He gathered the player's shirt in his two hands and dragged him across the table until they were staring at each other, inches apart. "Maybe not, asshole. But he made us winners! And any time you want to discuss *Coach* Allen, I'll be ready!"

Deacon gave the rookie a shove; now that his anger was subsiding, he could see the rookie was little more than a wide-eyed kid. "Go on, get out of here!"

---

6. Bob Oates, *Los Angeles Times,* June 30, 1971.

The kid scrambled for the door, muttering something under his breath about has-beens and not bothering to look back. Deacon could see out of the corner of his eye two of the assistant coaches talking with Prothro and gesturing in his direction. *Great,* he thought. *All this and now I'm going to get the reputation of a troublemaker.*

Deacon talks about the coming of Tommy Prothro. "It was my sad fate to hook up with another rookie coach who had to learn his lessons all over again. Of course, Tommy never did learn the winning way. He just wasn't cut out to coach the pros. In one sense, it might have been better if I'd never met Allen. After Waterfield and Svare, I would have been able to accept Prothro's failings. But George's standards had become my standards. And here was Tommy, our new coach, putting us right back on the losing track. Oh, we still had a winning record, that first year. There was a lot of George's winning ethic ingrained in us, and that wasn't going to go away just because we changed coaches. But with all our talent, Tommy wasn't even going to be able to take us to the division championship. We weren't working hard enough, we weren't prepared, and we were making mistakes again. The real clue was when you saw the Rams blowing games to inferior teams again. We hadn't done that since before George."

Souring Relationships

Never discount the power of an NFL team's public relations department—it can make or break a coach or a player. When George Allen, who was unloved by Rams management from the start, went 3-2 in his first preseason, the team was reported as so-so and unimpressive. Allen, who hated to lose at anything and who felt the Winning Way was a habit as much as anything else, took preseason wins and losses very seriously. After that initial season, Allen's Rams teams always had successful preseason campaigns: 6-0 in 1967, 4-2 in 1968, 4-2 in 1969 and 6-0 in 1970. On the other hand, Prothro, with the kind of public relations help Allen never enjoyed, was able to play the game a little differently. In 1971, when the Prothro Rams had a 4-3 preseason with losses to Dallas, Oakland, and San Francisco, the fans were asked to forget the exhibition games, as Prothro didn't pay much attention to them. It was reported that the new coach was experimenting with rookies throughout most of the preseason. The intimation was that with the real season at hand the new Prothro Rams and the new Prothro "big play offense" would get down to the business of winning.

The wistful old black man's ditty goes, "If wishes was horses/beggars would ride, if turnips was watches/I'd wear one by my side." And in their opening game that September 19, the "new" Rams and Prothro's new way ran into their first dose of reality. The team lost to the New Orleans Saints, a team that had gone down to defeat twelve straight times since the previous November. Bob Oates wrote in the *L.A. Times* that the Rams "blew" their opener. "In the five years from 1966 through 1970 when Roman Gabriel was a winning quarterback, this was the kind of game the Rams seldom lost. For almost the first time in six years, the Rams have lost to an inferior team—and for the first time in those six years, they've lost on opening day." Oates reported that penalties and fumble calls went against the Rams repeatedly, almost monotonously, for sixty minutes.[7]

The reporters all noted that the only two bright spots for the Rams were the play of Deacon Jones (who had at least temporarily recovered from his sprained arch) and the Rams defensive line. After the game, Archie Manning was effusive in his praise; Deacon had sacked him several times, as the Rams combined for a total seven sacks in the game. Manning told the reporters gathered around him in the locker room, "I've never seen anyone react the way he does. I hope we don't run into any defense that is better than the Rams have." All this had to be like rubbing salt in Prothro's wounds; after all, he had done his best to dismantle the ball-control offense and controlling defense built by George Allen in favor of his "big play" theory of pro football.

At the same time, the Washington Redskins upset the St. Louis Cardinals 24-17 in Allen's debut as coach. From now on, to the chagrin of many of those employed in the Rams front office, the L.A. Monday morning sports pages would carry a small column ticking off Allen's wins as he turned the perennially losing Redskins into winners. As the season wore on, it would become more and more obvious that without Allen at the helm, the Rams were going nowhere.

The following week, while L.A. eked out a 20-20 tie with Atlanta (David Ray booted a forty-seven yard field goal on the final play), Allen won his second game for Washington. Already giving up on the title after two games, reporters noted that, as a whole, the L.A. performance was too uneven to figure they would make the playoffs; the

---

7. Bob Oates, *Los Angeles Times,* September 20, 1971.

team was no longer solid. The defense was vulnerable at linebacker and in a few places in the secondary. It was the kind of commentary that had been common in the Svare and Waterfield eras.

Prothro had his own spin on why victory over the habitual losers from Atlanta had eluded the Rams. It wasn't Prothro's lack of talented linebackers or defensive backs (remember the trades to Allen). Prothro blamed the loss on the man he'd come to believe was his chief dissenter on the team—Deacon Jones! After the game, Prothro told the press he hadn't wanted Deacon to refuse a penalty that preceded a twenty-five yard Atlanta field goal early in the second quarter. If Deacon had accepted the penalty, it would have pushed the Falcons back to questionable field goal range. But it would have also given them another chance to make a first down. "Deacon didn't look to the sideline for our signal," said Prothro.[8] Deacon and Coy Bacon had sacked the Falcons quarterback, Bob Berry, for a seven yard loss on third and eight at the Ram twelve. Prothro turned their brilliant play into the reason for the team's defeat. Instead of congratulating his defense on denying the Falcons a touchdown, he chose to blame their leader. As the three points gained by the field goal would have given the Rams the margin of victory (and presumably Atlanta might have missed from fifteen yards further out), Prothro reasoned that Deacon's error in judgment was responsible for the loss.

No matter how thin this line of logic, Prothro had now pinned the loss on Deacon Jones, making a public case against one of his most seasoned players, the captain of the team, and the leader of the defense. If Allen had felt that way, he wouldn't have complained to the press. He would have taken the player behind a locked door in his office so they could talk it out.

The following week, as Allen's Redskins, playing with a bunch of retread veterans known as the "Over the Hill Gang," upset mighty Dallas 20-16, Prothro's Rams hung up their first win, 17-3 over the Bears. Deacon turned in another fine performance while fighting off double-team blocking on nearly every play. But it wasn't much fun any more. Deacon knew he was risking permanent damage by shooting up his foot week after week. And for what, he asked himself. Prothro was going out of his way to blame Deacon for anything he could think of. Deacon decided he wasn't going to sacrifice his body any more. If the foot was injured, he would take himself out of the game and allow it to heal.

---

8. Bob Oates, *Los Angeles Times,* September 27, 1971.

Seven days later, while the Redskins were winning over the Oilers, the Rams beat 'the 49ers, 20-13, without the services of Roman Gabriel or Deacon Jones. Deacon, suffering from his newly resprained arch, had played in 143 consecutive games. After the game, he said, "If it had meant the difference between winning and losing, I would have gone in. But I've changed . . .maybe its because I'm a little older, and, maybe, wiser. But why should I risk the chance of knocking myself out for the season by playing in one game? Anyway, my replacement [Jack Youngblood] did a fine job."

On October 17, while Allen's "Old Geezers" knocked off the Cardinals for their fifth win in a row, the Rams defeated the Falcons 24-16. Deacon benched himself for the second straight week with his sprained arch. Merlin told reporters, "I miss Deacon Jones, but Jack Youngblood did a pretty good job."

The following week, the Rams smothered the Packers 30-13. Deacon started and played part of the first half, but benched himself again as his arch began acting up. So far, while he was on the sidelines, the Rams had continued winning; but the following week, when he was in the game, the Rams were upset 20-14 by the Dolphins and the long-bomb throwing of Bob Griese. Bob Oates wrote in the *L.A. Times,*

> Almost certainly, it was the confusion wrought by Deacon Jones's offside jump that made the touchdown [that made the difference in the game]. Jones is a veteran who should know better than to fly offside, but he hasn't played or practiced much for a month and he probably shouldn't have played at all against Miami with his bad foot. His three offside mistakes, however, almost got lost in the shuffle of 1,000 others.[9]

The following Monday night the Rams lost again, this time on national television. The Tuesday morning sports headline in the *L.A. Times* screamed, "Rams Kick It Away—And Colts Cash In, 24-17."[10] It was a game in which the Rams defense held the Colts off for most of the sixty minutes while the Rams "big play" offense sputtered. Unfortunate rookie Dave Elmendorf gave new life to the winning Colts drive twice. He ran into the punter on two occasions, giving the ball back to Baltimore both times. To many analysts that was the margin of differ-

9. Bob Oates, *Los Angeles Times,* November 1, 1971.
10. *Los Angeles Times,* November 9, 1971.

ence in the game. But the sports writers missed one bit of sideline drama. Tommy Prothro was becoming known for the gimmick play— some trick play that makes the difference and puts points on the board. George Allen, who had studied under Halas and knew every trick in the book, tended to shy away from gimmick plays. It was Allen's philosophy that no gimmick could replace hard work and practice. Trick plays were wonderful will-o'-the-wisps when they worked, but solid football won ball games. Prothro, however, felt differently; now, in a game in which he felt he couldn't trust his offense, Prothro dusted off one of his special plays. On fourth and long, he put in a play designed to spring Dave Elmendorf into the Colts backfield with a shot at blocking the kick. Elmendorf was huge and fast for his size; but as a rookie he was also awkward and relatively unskilled. The pros tended to shy away from such plays because it was too easy to rough the kicker. Kickers make wonderful actors, and tend to go down at the mere whisper of a hit. The yellow flag almost always follows. The end result is an instant turnaround in the fortunes of the game. One moment you have your opponent on the ropes, kicking the ball away; the next, he has first-down yardage and is knocking on your goal.

In this case it made even less sense because the Rams were giving the ball back to the quick-striking Colts. Elmendorf broke through on cue, crashing into the kicker and drawing the foul. Possession went back to the Colts and Johnny Unitas was only too happy to get his hands on the ball. This happened twice on fourth and long, and each time Elmendorf was penalized and the Colts drove back to score a touchdown.

Prothro's decision infuriated the veterans left on the Rams defense. No one else might have said anything, but Deacon stormed up to Prothro after the first incident and yelled, "What the hell are you doing, Prothro? You just gave away the game! When you do that, you're telling our defense you don't believe we can hold Unitas on fourth and long!"

Prothro turned away, saying nothing and pretending to be involved in his playsheets.

The second time Prothro called for the kick block play, Deacon would not be denied. He stood right in front of Prothro and yelled, "Prothro, you can't coach! You don't know how to coach! You just blew the game for us with those chicken-shit plays!"

Again, Prothro turned away as if he had better things to do. He lit up one of his ever-present cigarettes, and looked off into the distance. Deacon slammed his helmet to the ground and stalked away.

After the game, Bob Oates diplomatically wrote, "The Rams play selection did not always seem the soundest against Baltimore's assortment of zone defenses."[11]

And Tommy Prothro put the loss where he thought it belonged, on the players' backs, saying, "We played good football, but we just made some mistakes."

One thing a publicity department can't hide is the win-lose column on the Monday morning sports page, and by now the suspicion was growing that something was very wrong with the Rams.

Steve Bisheff asked a key question in the headline of his article in the *Herald Examiner*: "Is Ram Morale Stinking?"[12] But the Rams front office had managed to shift the problems from their own failures to the players. Having nothing to say about the management fiascos of the previous year, losing Allen and trading away veteran strength for wishes, hopes, and prayers, Bisheff reported that the problem might lie with the front four of the defense. He noted that young Phil Olsen was struggling, Merlin's knee blew up like a balloon after every game, and "Deacon Jones looks good but has to come out when his arch starts to bother him in the second half."

Bishoff went on to report that Lakers basketball star Wilt Chamberlain had stopped by the Rams camp to say that he would be glad to volunteer his services to the team. Prothro was reported to have replied, "Can he play defensive end?" The reaction of one Deacon Jones was not noted.

Deacon talks about breaking his string of consecutive games played at 143. "I would have gone in for George, but not for Tommy. For Allen, I was having it shot up and playing in the game, no matter what the long-term consequences. Maybe that wasn't right, but under George I felt I would give body and soul for the team. We all felt that way. I had it shot up that Thanksgiving in Detroit (1967) when Charley Bradshaw stepped on it. Game after game, I took the novocaine shot again and again, right in the top of the foot, administered by the team doctors, and the amphetamine pain pills from the trainers. But, you see, Tommy and I didn't have a good relationship. He didn't want anything to do with me. Looking back, I think he was caught between the rock and the hard place, afraid of me because of the influence I had over the players, and afraid to trade me because of what the fans would

---

11. Bob Oates, *Los Angeles Times,* November 9, 1971.
12. Steve Bisheff, *Herald Examiner,* November 11, 1971.

say. I've said it many times—there wasn't nothing I wouldn't do for Tommy, and there wasn't nothing he wouldn't do for me, and we spent the entire year of 1971 doin' nothing for each other."

As for Prothro sending in rookie Elmendorf to charge the kicker, to this day Deacon is still full of derision: "Prothro the genius gave the ball right back to the likes of Johnny Unitas and Earl Morrall. And they thankfully took it and scored on us. I told him to his face that he couldn't coach in the pros. And if you don't believe I'm right, take a look at his record. Tommy Prothro couldn't motivate a tiger out of a paper bag. He's one of the losingest coaches in pro football."

Prothro had been a success coaching college ball, and perhaps it would have been better if he had stayed there. In the pros, he head-coached two complete seasons for the Rams and four complete seasons (plus four games in a fifth season) for the San Diego Chargers. His total win-lose record for his eighty-eight games as a head coach in the NFL is thirty-five wins, fifty-one losses and two ties for a lackluster win percentage of .409.

The Big Play Rams

With eight games played in the 1971 season, the Rams were 4-3-1. The offense had scored thirty points against Green Bay and 24 against Atlanta (in their seasonal rematch). In the rest of the games they had scored twenty, twenty, twenty, seventeen, seventeen and fourteen. No matter what Prothro and the Rams Public Relations Department said, it was still defense that was pulling the team through. Prothro's big play offense was a dream rather than a reality. In fact, Allen's offense, which had been chided for being plodding, methodical, and predictable, had scored ten more points in the first eight games the year before. (At that point they were 5-2-1 and in the thick of the fight for the divisional championship.)

On Monday, November 15, the Rams defeated the Lions 21-13. Deacon didn't play, but the defense sacked Detroit quarterback Greg Landry seven times and made clutch plays that held the Lions to no touchdowns until the last three minutes.

The following week, the defense intercepted the 49ers John Brodie four times. Deacon returned to harass Brodie, and played the entire game in spite of reinjuring his arch. *L.A. Times* writer Bob Oates noted, "Bacon and Deacon Jones troubled Brodie with greater frequency as the game wore on, Jones sometimes as a middle guard with

Jack Youngblood in the lineup alternating with Phil Olsen." Perhaps with a touch of sarcasm, Oates' headline read, "Big Play Rams Enjoy Biggest Day, 17-6."[13] The big plays continued to be made by the defensive linemen left over from the Allen era.

The Rams moved on to Dallas, where they took on the Cowboys in Texas Stadium on Thanksgiving Day. The playing field was ice-hard and slippery, and the Rams line with Deacon and Coy Bacon playing injured could only apply moderate pressure to the Cowboys passing game under the deft throwing hand of Roger Staubach.

Deacon told reporters after the game, "The only way to stop a scrambler is for the linemen to rush in lanes so you can box him in. But if you do that every time, you won't get in because the offensive linemen will be on to your moves. You have to vary your charge. And Staubach hits you, when you take a chance. One time, I barely missed him."

Tommy Prothro had his own spin on the game; he blamed the players. "We simply made too many mistakes against a good team," he said.

The following week, the big-play Rams finally showed up against the hapless Saints (who would go 4-8-2 on the season). Willie Ellison racked up 247 yards and the L.A. team won 45-28. Prothro's big-play offense had finally arrived, and just in time for a showdown with George Allen's Redskins. Allen's team was 8-3-1, but L.A. had put together a respectable 7-4-1, and the game would be one of the most important ones Prothro would coach in his career. For one thing, the Rams were still in contention for the divisional title, as were the Redskins. If L.A. lost this game, the team would be knocked out of the playoffs. Worse still, Allen would gain sweet revenge for being cast aside by Rams management. Fans and sportswriters had questioned the Rams uneven performance under Prothro. Even the good old boys club was secretly snickering at the Rams front office for dismantling a winner. It was hard to fault Reeves, who had been ill and may have been influenced by his own front office into letting Allen go. This game *couldn't* end in defeat; a loss to Washington—to the loser-Redskins who had been newly energized by Allen's leadership—would forever brand the Rams front office as foolish and shortsighted.

The next day, *Times* writer Bob Oates's headline said it all: "Allen's Revenge: Skins 38, Rams 24."[14] Allen had defeated his old team, and in the process had knocked the Rams out of any hope for the playoffs. And Allen had done it the old George Halas way, with a handful of

13. Bob Oates, *Los Angeles Times,* November 22, 1971.
14. Bob Oates, *Los Angeles Times,* December 14, 1971.

Ram castoffs. Jack Pardee in particular played a brilliant game, almost single-handedly stopping several Roman Gabriel-engineered drives. Ex-Rams Myron Pottios, Richie Petitbone, and Diron Talbert each made at least one big play against their old team.

So much for the big-play Rams. It seems most of them had left with their coach.

Deacon comments on the difference between Allen and Prothro: "There were so many things George did right, yet he did them so naturally that we all took them for granted. One example comes to mind: It won him no friends with the press or the front office, but Coach insisted the team get on the plane first. And the vets got on before anybody. This meant the players would get the best seats, which meant a lot to us; after all, players are bigger and need the space, and maybe that little extra means we can rest a little more and have just that much of an edge for the game. But this meant the front office and the press got the bad seats, and so it was an unpopular decision with them. George took that on—he was a player's coach—where Tommy figured it didn't matter, and so the players usually got the worst seats. Another thing, George wouldn't let anybody have whiskey on the plane—players, coaches, nobody! You can imagine how unpopular that was! Management and sportswriters being told they had to stay dry on the team plane! These kind of perks were more important to management than winning. It's easy to see why George had no friends on the Rams except the players."

Tommy Prothro's big-play offense netted twelve fewer points on the year than had Allen's the year before (313 as opposed to 325 in 1970). And his "new" defense gave up fifty-eight more points (260 as opposed to 202 in 1970). These statistics more than any other tell how the Rams had begun to sag. In the following year, 1972, the Rams would go 6-7-1, suffering their first losing season since the Svare era. Scoring would diminish to 291 points and the team would give up 286 points. And Rams management, having had enough of Prothro, would dismiss him as quietly as possible, quickly getting rid of the coach they had proudly acclaimed two years before as "the best possible man for our players and our fans." Unfortunately, by this time Deacon was gone as well.

Happenings at the Now Grove

In 1972, Deacon knew for sure that he had crossed over from being a great athlete to a celebrity. He got offers to appear as a guest star on television series: George Peppard's "Banacek," Elizabeth Montgomery's "Bewitched," "The Brady Bunch," and "The Odd Couple." He had a continuing role on "The Odd Couple," and hit it off with the show's stars, Tony Randall and Jack Klugman, a couple of "funny, nice guys." Deacon did several skits with Tim Conway and had a successful appearance on the "Merv Griffin Show." Sonny and Cher came to his birthday party with a $20 gold piece on a solid gold necklace for a present. Deacon was a regular guest at Hugh Hefner's Playboy mansion and a regular on the local night club circuit.

Everybody wanted a piece of Deacon, to be able to say they knew the great Deacon Jones. Deacon's manager set him up with a publicity gag in Las Vegas. Deacon sat at a table at the Sands Casino Nightclub next to the stage while Jimmy Dean performed. Dean had an uptempo version of the old country-western classic "Alabama Jubilee," and when Dean began to sing it, Deacon got up and went behind stage. When Dean got to the one line in the song, "Leave the bones for Deacon Jones," Deacon stepped out into the lights. He was an imposing figure, wearing a flat black western deacon's hat and his long black mink coat. Dean was singing to the other side of the crowd. He hadn't been a party to the stunt, and didn't see him until he turned around. Dean stopped singing and gaped, and the music ground to a halt.

Deacon glared at him and grumbled, "Hey, I'm Deacon Jones—where's the bones?"

The crowd loved it. Dean recovered and waved to the band and they took off into the song again. The audience roared its approval. Deacon tried to keep his solemn look, but inside he was happy as a clam. It was almost as good as sacking Brodie or Unitas.

As part of Davis's attempt to revive the old Coconut Grove with live shows, Sammy convinced Deacon to host a show the night after every home game at the renovated Grove, which was dubbed "The Now Grove." Deacon brought Lon Fontaine on as his choreographer, and sang with his three-girl backup group, "The Deaconettes." The regulars in this group were sister-singers Maxine Waters and Julia Tilman from Ike and Tina Turner's backup group. Jimmy Haskell was Deacon's musical director, and they had a big band, between thirty and forty pieces.

The way Deacon saw it, he was a superhero footballer who wanted to entertain. Davis was tremendously encouraging; he was sold on the idea, and let Deacon run with it. They tied the show together with a "Deacon Presents" concept, where Deacon as the host would present other famous celebrities, stars and local sports personalities—and that got the show rolling. In the next months, Deacon's show featured many top guests, including Bill Cosby, Rock Hudson, Gloria Loring, and Davis, himself.

Deacon made sure the Rams were invited to his show. Anyone who wanted to come—players or management—was given complimentary tickets, and Deacon made sure to introduce them all to the audience. That year, even Tommy Prothro came to the shows. And all of Deacon's guests got *free everything.*

Deacon Jones, the swamp boy from Eatonville, would have many moments on the stage, as an actor, a celebrity and a guest speaker. He would have parts in movies (*The Norseman,* with Lee Majors; *Heaven Can Wait,* with Warren Beatty), and television. In Deacon's mind, all of that was made possible by his own hard work . . . and the generosity of one man, Sammy Davis, Jr.

Deacon remembers his teammates flocking to the Now Grove, "After a Rams home game, it was the only place to be, the place to see and to be seen. I introduced Tommy Prothro, I introduced them all. But Tommy and I were destined not to get along. The NFL is all about control; the owners control the coaches and the coaches control the players. And when the coaches can't control you, they fire you."

Dick Bass talks about Deacon the entertainer in those days. "They just loved him. It didn't matter how good Deacon sang, just so long as he slashed through that line and killed the QB next Sunday." Bass remains a staunch admirer of Deacon's flair, if not his talent. "Deacon could sell anything! When he started out, his act didn't warrant the lobby in Vegas. I saw his early show. If I had to pay, I'd want my money back. What sold it was nerve, and he had plenty of that. You have to give him credit, he had great drive to compete, to excel. He would go out and try it. And he did get better. If you saw him up in front of an audience today, you wouldn't believe it was the same man."

Jimmy Dean, contacted recently at his Appalachian retreat, clearly recollected the Alabama Jubilee incident at the Sands: "Boy, did he gave me a start! They didn't tell me anything, before-

hand. I was in the middle of my song and Lord, I turned around and here was this huge, menacing black guy towering over me! 'I'm Deacon Jones an' where's the bones?', he says, and half of me was sayin' 'Keep on singin', Jimmy,' while the other half was sayin' 'Feet, don't fail me now!' "

Hearing It Through the Grapevine

It was the last Saturday in January, 1972. Deacon was kicking back, starting to unwind from the long and frustrating season. He was at one of Roman Gabriel's weddings—Roman got married a lot—and all he wanted to do was have a few drinks with his friends and celebrate the grand occasion. But it was not to be. He was just getting into the swing of things when newsman Mario Machado came up to him and said, "Deak—I hear you've been traded."

Deacon froze in his tracks for a moment, thinking about it. He tried to shrug it off, "I don't think so, Mario. How would you know about it before I did?"

Machado just smiled a knowing newsman's smile, "You're saying you haven't been traded?"

"Not that I know. And I'd be the first to know."

"Well," Machado repeated with assurance, "be that as it may, I heard you have been."

The fun seemed to go out of the day, like the sun disappearing behind dark clouds. "Okay," Deacon said, "where am I going?"

"San Diego."

"Ohhhh. Svareland. Well . . . I hadn't heard. Nobody's talked to me, but, if it's true, thanks for passing it along."

Deacon turned from the newscaster, suddenly feeling ill. The joy of Roman's wedding was stolen from him, chased by the winds of change. He felt like the music was too loud and the crowd was moving in on him, everybody jabbering nonsense and there was no place to go. Deacon didn't want to believe it, but it would be just the sort of thing the management of the Rams would do, trade him and try to shift the responsibility around so nobody was to blame. *Let him read about it on the sports page, from one of those writers who love him so much.* That would be their style.

Deacon went outside for a breath of fresh air. He had to try and collect his thoughts. It certainly could be; the move made sense, of a sort.

Lord knows Tommy wanted him gone bad enough to make any trade. And Harland Svare, who had been the Chargers' interim coach since Sid Gillman had resigned under fire a few weeks before, was out to build his new Fearsome Foursome. Svare was aware that he and Prothro didn't see eye to eye. Svare might make a fast offer, just as he had moved quickly to get Rosey Grier from Allie Sherman. Prothro would be delighted, seeing it as his chance to be rid of the man who didn't respect him, and who, more than any other, reminded the fans of the winning ways of the last regime. The Rams front office would side with Prothro without question. After all, he was their baby and his success was their success. And they would leak it to the press, a last little bit of sweet revenge for all the times Deacon had sided with George Allen against them.

Deacon put on his game face and went back into the room. Ten minutes later, one of the guests came up to him, "Prothro's on the phone, calling for you."

Prothro's voice came out of the receiver, thin against the background noise and whoopla of the wedding celebration. Deacon heard for the second time that he'd been traded to the Chargers. He felt dry, empty, drained of feeling. He knew that this call was all he could ever expect of the Rams. Now they were legal; they could tell the world they had informed him. They wouldn't have to bother much trying to explain when or how.

"Thank you very much," Deacon said politely, and hung up.

The next day, the *Times* reported under the byline of Harley Tinkham,

> David "Deacon" Jones, the most celebrated defensive player in Rams history, was traded to the San Diego Chargers. Jones, thirty-three, an eleven-year veteran and a perennial All Pro at defensive end was traded with defensive tackle Greg Wojcik and running back Lee White for linebacker Jeff Staggs and three draft choices: the second round in 1972 and the second and third round choices in 1973.[15]

Tinkham went on to say that Jones, when asked about the trade, had responded, "I don't know yet. I haven't had a chance to think it over. I just heard it at Roman Gabriel's wedding—at his reception. That hurt me. I'm in shock."

Reporters sensed there was more to the story, and kept after Deacon over the next few days, until an article written without a byline came out a few days later. The article was titled "Bitter Over Rams

---

15. Harley Tinkham, *Times* Staff Writer, *Los Angeles Times,* January 30, 1972.

Method," and in it Deacon was quoted, "I'm not mad about being traded, but I expected to be traded like a man, not a tool." Deacon went on to explain, "I certainly thought it'd be handled better than that. I was hired in private, I expected to be fired in private. I'm responsible for a lot of their wins. The least they can do is treat me like a gentleman. What am I, just a piece of machinery or something?"[16]

Since Dan Reeves's death, the power in the Rams organization had shifted to a handful of executives in the front office. The papers reported that Deacon's trade had been negotiated by assistant general manager Johnny Sanders and head coach Tommy Prothro. At the time, Prothro was quoted as saying, "Obviously we like the trade, but I hated to part with what we did. What do you say about Deacon Jones? He is a legend in his own time and rightfully deserves the title of Secretary of Defense." Bill Barnes, the Rams president, proclaimed, "Deacon Jones is not only the greatest defensive end ever to play the game, but a fine team leader both on and off the field."[17] It was noted that the trade was consistent with the Prothro youth movement; in the 1973 draft the Rams would have ten picks in the first five rounds. So much for the managed rumor that Allen had destroyed the team's future by trading future draft picks for experience.

But all the polite civilities on the part of Rams management blew away like straw in the wind after Deacon openly told the press how he'd been informed. That made them look like inexperienced junior executives, rather than captains of the football industry. Intent on damage control, Rams public relations man Jack Teele rushed to the presses with a fourteen-point chronology that attempted to justify what had happened. Teele's points, as printed in the *Times*,[18] were:

A. The trade was finalized at noon January 29th.
B. Gabriel's wedding was scheduled for one o'clock.
C. The principals were all on the freeway then.
D. Teele drew Deacon Jones aside at the wedding as soon as he could and handed him a note.
E. The note said call Prothro immediately.
F. Teele told Jones it was important.
G. Teele returned to the Rams office, where Prothro was waiting for Jones to call.
H. Jones never called.

---

16. No byline, "Bitter Over Rams Method", *Los Angeles Times,* January 31, 1972.
17. Harley Tinkham, *Times* Staff Writer, *Los Angeles Times,* January 30, 1972.
18. No byline, "Bitter Over Rams Method," *Los Angeles Times,* January 31, 1972.

   I.   Teele concluded that Jones had forgotten to call.

   J.   Eventually Teele and Prothro decided to place the call them-
       selves.

   K.   Teele reached Jones.

   L.   Teele handed the telephone to Prothro.

   M. Prothro informed Jones.

   N.   Jones said, "Thank you very much."

There was no O, P, or Q explaining or apologizing for the leak to the press.

Even longtime Dan Reeves supporter John Hall questioned the wisdom of the deal in his *Times* column under the banner, "Is Deacon Done?" Hall wrote, "I know Deacon Jones is thirty-three, that he is hobbled by a lingering foot injury and that he had a bad season. But I didn't realize it was that bad."[19]

Deacon responded, "This is going to be one of my greatest years. I'm breathing fire. Just like a damn dragon. I'm accustomed to being the best. I feel I still am, and I'm gonna prove it."

But the Rams had done what they had done. The troublesome Deacon Jones was gone; he was history. The Rams management had chafed at the bit for five years while Dan Reeves distanced himself from the team and George Allen took over the reins of command. They had suffered while the players basked in their glory. Now, through a lucky roll of the dice they found themselves in control of the team. They knew all about public relations and what to say to the press. They had gotten rid of Allen, and found a coach more willing to listen to their ideas. In the first year of their reign no calamity had struck. True, they hadn't won the divisional title, but they'd won more games than they'd lost. Arguably, Allen could be credited with much of that. But now, Allen was gone. And, with the last powerful Allen ally traded away, the Prothro era could begin in earnest. All that remained to be seen was how good they would be at molding a football powerhouse.

Ram fans wouldn't have to wait long. By the end of the second Prothro season, they would know for sure their winning team had been sold down the river. Prothro would be ignominiously dumped by the wayside. And new management would come in from Baltimore to salvage what was left. A few years later, new Rams owner Carroll Rosenbloom told Deacon he would never have traded him. But, of course, by then it was too late.

_____

19. John Hall, *Los Angeles Times,* January 31, 1972.

Deacon still remembers hearing about his trade from a television newsman. "Some leaders of men those poor fellows turned out to be. Here they wanted to run the Rams, and they didn't even have the guts to tell me to my face what they'd done—so they leaked it to the press, the same dirty trick they'd used so many times when they wanted to smear George Allen. And, you know, no one from the Rams has ever officially sat me down and talked to me in person about it, nor have I ever received a piece of paper to that effect. Not then, and not since. I played the heart of my professional career for the Rams, and those pretenders didn't have the decency to look me in the eye and say thank you."

Jack Teele, who was head of Rams publicity at that time, did reveal that no one in the Rams front office was eager to face Deacon with the bad news. Teele claims that he was stuck with the job. Contacted recently by phone, he told me, "I was with Johnny Sanders. Nobody wanted to do the job, so I finally said, 'Aw hell, I'll go.' Deacon was legend, he was the greatest there ever was, and he changed the way defensive end was played. I had no idea how he would take being let go. I went down and told him and he said, 'You got to be kidding.' "

Deacon scoffs. "Jack's got a bad memory. That's not the way it went down at all. Once and for all, I heard about my trade from poor Mario Machado, who blurted it out at Roman's shindig, thinking I already knew all about it."

Teele did become known as the man who had done the deed; he recalls a few months later being given a spoof award for the world's dirtiest job, that of breaking the news to Deacon Jones. "It was at a dinner at the Serbian Church, one of those bawdy roasts. A guy who owns a sewer pipe company gave me the main award, a sewer pipe section. I got roasted by being presented the "The Deacon Jones Award." I was the asshole of the year for letting him go."

Deacon's response: "If Jack got an award like that, he ought to give it back, 'cause he never told me. There's a big difference between being sent to do a job and actually doing it." Teele reiterated there was no way word could have possibly gotten to Deacon before he told him, and he denied that anything had been leaked to the press.

Such reality gaps are frequent in football. In the NFL, honest memory is, apparently, as fragile a creature as ego is tenacious.

Moving South

Deacon sat in his darkened living room, brooding over his trade while the rain came down outside in brief windy gusts. Iretha was out somewhere; she always seemed to be out these days. It didn't matter, anyhow. He'd made it a practice not to talk to her about anything important. He already knew what she'd say. She'd try to persuade him that whatever meant money coming in the door was the right thing to do. *Take the money and run.*

Sometimes, when things went wrong, everything seemed to be wrong all at the same time. Deacon found himself wishing once again that he'd never married. He didn't really know what he was looking for. With Iretha, he always felt lonely. Sometimes he felt an emptiness, a sense of loss for what might have been. He usually was able to shuck those feelings off. There was always his work, his job, being the anchor of the Fearsome Foursome, the leader of the Rams.

Deacon found himself thinking about signing with the Rams just over a decade before at the airport in New Orleans. "You're a member of the Rams family," the scout had told him. Over the years since, he'd had cause to scoff at how little that meant to Rams management. Dan Reeves had taught the lesson that the players were just commodities, pieces of meat, machines that were to be depreciated and finally traded.

Yet, when you give your all to the team, when you fight and claw your way to becoming a starting member, then to becoming the most valuable player on the team, and finally to becoming so important you are considered by coaches and fans to be the franchise, even your most cynical part begins to wish the dream were a reality, that the Rams really were family. Deacon realized now that he had gradually allowed himself to be lulled into a false sense of security. He had forgotten that he could be taken away from the team—from his brothers—with one telephone call. It had happened to others, even to his mentor, George Allen. Why hadn't he seen the handwriting on the wall?

Many of the top ballplayers had consent clauses in their contracts, and if he'd thought seriously that the Rams would ever trade him, he could easily have had such a clause inserted in his contract. Deacon saw now that he'd been too proud, too sure of his status with the team, the press and the fans. *All that didn't mean diddly-squat when the front office wanted to deal you away.*

The sheets of endless rain swept across southern California, pounding against the roof and windows. Deacon paced restlessly back and forth, trying to decide what to do. Even without the matter of his loyalty to the Rams, Los Angeles had become his base of operations. He had been able to capitalize on his enormous popularity with the L.A. fans, and this was worth at least as much money as his salary. He wouldn't be able to do shows like the Now Grove. Compared to L.A., San Diego was a small market; he doubted there was much "show biz" action there.

San Diego wasn't so far away that Deacon couldn't fly up for a recording session, but it wasn't the same thing. If he went along with the trade—and he had no legal recourse to prevent it—he would be a San Diego Charger, recently with the Rams. "An ex-Ram," he muttered to himself. The taste was bitter on his lips. They could exile him, but he had spent the core of his career in L.A. and he knew that no matter where he went, in his own mind and heart he would always be a Ram.

For a moment Deacon wished once again that they'd traded him to Washington. George Allen had taken his winning ways to the Redskins, and that was the one place where Deacon felt he might transplant his loyalty, make the physical sacrifices necessary to gain his edge and then go on to give his all for a winning cause. He would do it for Allen. But Rams management wasn't going to trade him to Washington. He wondered how much of that was spite and how much was sound business sense. After all, Allen had already built a winner out of Rams cast-offs.

Deacon turned the matter over in his mind. He would be leaving town with extreme reluctance. He had business opportunities in Los Angeles. He'd become a national personality, but L.A. was his home, the place where he'd shone brightest, where he had the biggest following. If that was the way he truly felt, then why go to San Diego? After all, in his eleven years with the Rams, he had accomplished things no one had ever done in the NFL. He had established mile-high, Ruthian records for single-season sacks and lifetime sacks that would stand for at least his own lifetime, and probably long after. Why go to San Diego to become the fading star, living on past glories? Maybe it was time to pack it in, to hang up his spikes and move on to new challenges and opportunities.

Deacon smiled ruefully in the dark. He could almost hear Iretha's whining nag on that one. "But Jones, we won't be able to live. We won't have any money."

However, Svare had answered his question. He would go to San Diego because there he would be the team leader. There he could move into a player-coach role, much as Svare had held with the Giants under Allie Sherman. Svare didn't have to paint in the details; the road was clear. If Deacon wanted a chance to stay in big-time football after his playing days, this was it. They'd had their differences over the years, but Svare was a man of his word. Here was an offer made to precious few players, and to even fewer blacks. It was a chance to get on a coaching staff, a shot at management in the NFL.

Deacon paced the floor some more, but he knew he'd made up his mind. With a challenge like that in front of him, Deacon really had to go forward, to see if he could make it big on this new level. As he paced back and forth, he realized there was a second reason. He'd been cast off like an old shoe. He had something to prove: that he was still able to play the game. Rams management had made a big mistake. He had to prove it. He owed that much to his loyal fans, to the sports writers who were behind him, to those who were skeptical, and, most of all, he owed it to himself.

Thinking back, Deacon feels that the addition of a trade consent clause to his contract might have added several productive years to his career. "I was as surprised as anyone else at my being dealt away that quickly. It's just another example of how hitting the books a little more in college might have helped me. I had to learn the hard way, through experience. And those were very costly lessons."

Sweet, Sweet Revenge

Rams head coach Tommy Prothro tried to treat the game against the Chargers like an ordinary preseason game. He told reporters, "I sure hope we can win, but both we and they will be playing more important games this year."

Down in San Diego, Deacon took time off from his workout to say, "I'm not giving interviews this week. I've already done too much talking. If I don't say anything, I can't be misinterpreted. Incidentally, which one is the jugular vein?"

Charlie Cowan, following the Ram management's party line, tried to downplay the upcoming match. "I know Deak is high for this game. I also know we can get pretty emotional ourselves. But I don't see us going out just to beat Deacon Jones. I don't see this as a two-man duel between him and me. It's got to be a team thing, which is the only way I've ever played."

Svare, who had left the Rams on good terms and took pains never to burn his bridges, was caught in the middle. On the one hand, he didn't want to embarrass his old friends in Los Angeles. On the other, he very much wanted to win this game. After all, he, too, had something to prove; he had been unceremoniously dumped in favor of George Allen after the 1965 campaign. Svare told the reporters crowding around him, "We'll play our first string most of the game. It's like playing golf against your best friend."

L.A. Times writer Mal Florence summed up what he thought was the crux of the matter. "Jones, now a Charger, wants to prove to the Rams he isn't over the hill."

As it always does, the time came for the talking to end and the game to start. It was Saturday night, September 2, 1972. The Rams took the field in San Diego. Prothro had tried to downplay the significance of all the team's preseason games, as well he should; so far, the Rams had beaten Cleveland and then dropped three straight. He also very much wanted to set aside the fact that his team would be going up against ex-Ram Deacon Jones. To hear Prothro talk to the press, it was a matter of no consequence. It simply wasn't important.

Why then, did he have Deacon double-teamed on every play throughout the entire game? Why did he rotate *five different tackles* into the game against Deacon, making sure that fresh linemen were constantly going against him, play after play? Prothro used Charlie Cowan, Harry Schuw, Rich Saul, Joe Carollo, and John Williams. On double-team blocks, he alternated two tight ends—Pat Curran and Bob Christiansen—against Deacon. Deacon was used to being double-teamed, but this was like throwing the whole weight of the opposing line at him on every play.

The unusual tactics had predictable results; after the game, Prothro could crow that Deacon was unable to get a single sack. In fact, as the fourth quarter wound down, the thirty-three-year-old defensive end was close to exhaustion from playing against the constant pressure. He told reporters after the game, "As soon as I'd get used to one tackle, he'd be gone and another would come in. I'm just glad it's all over so I can concentrate on other things."

But even with the massive concentration of effort being pointed at Deacon, Prothro couldn't claim to have completely stopped him. In spite of the double-team hammering that Deacon was getting from the offensive line, he was responsible for four unassisted tackles. And, because the Rams were pouring so much energy into stopping him, other Chargers were able to break free to stop the Los Angeles attack.

Deacon may have been exhausted, but, as team captain, he never stopped encouraging his fellow Chargers. The Chargers defense, running on high octane, was able to shut down the Rams running game. And Rams quarterback Pete Beathard, playing for the injured Roman Gabriel, completed only ten of twenty-four passes and was sacked once. As a result of San Diego's "intense defense," Prothro's "big-play offense" was put out of business. Prothro, looking more and more desperate for the win, resorted to one of his gimmicks—a surprise onside kickoff. It failed.

And when it was all over, the papers reported that Deacon Jones was 1-0 over his old coach. It had to be a bitter pill for Prothro and the rest of the Rams front office. The *Times* headline read, "Jones Rouses Chargers To Hand Rams 14-13 Loss." And Bob Oates wrote, "As the new San Diego leader, Jones had his team fired up, and it won on emotion and the arm of [John] Hadl."[20]

Oates continued, "Jones is still pretty good, but no longer one-third of the defense." Considering that it took one-third of the offensive line to stop him—and that the Chargers won the game—that remark is open for some debate.

Deacon looks back and talks about some of the effects of his trade. "It definitely shortened my career as a top player. I gave my heart to the Rams, and in my own mind, I will always be a Ram. Merlin Olsen, who was only one year younger, survived the Prothro years and played through the 1976 season for L.A. And Charlie Cowan, who came the year I did, played through 1975. Once they got rid of Prothro and some in the front office, the Rams started winning again. Carroll Rosenbloom bought the team and brought in Chuck Knox, a disciplined coach who knew how to take advantage of the powerhouse George Allen had built. After that, the Rams won their division seven years in a row—but they never won the world championship.

"I sincerely believe I could have been the difference—I could have helped them get there. Not that they didn't do well without me, but with Youngblood on one end and me on the other and Olsen coming up the gut, we would have been unstoppable. It would have been the crowning point of my career, to have taken them to a Super Bowl victory. But it was not to be. And that was how—I believe—the pretenders to Reeves's throne managed to diminish George Allen's contributions to L.A. and to cheat the long-suffering Rams fans out of the winning heritage that rightfully should have been theirs."

---

20. Bob Oates, *Los Angeles Times*, September 3, 1972.

11

Big League Revenge

Fired by the Rams after the 1965 season, Harland Svare was out of NFL football for the 1966 campaigns. He signed on as defensive coordinator with the New York Giants in 1967 and 1968, until he was fired by the temperamental Allie Sherman—who blamed the defense in general and Svare in particular for the loss of an important game. In 1969, Svare went to the Redskins under Vince Lombardi, and in the team's first campaign together Lombardi coached Washington to their first winning season since 1955. But Lombardi died of cancer before the 1970 season, and when Bill Austin took over for the 1971 season the team's performance sagged again, to 6-8. Redskins president Edward Bennett Williams, tired of his team being the doormat of the league, looked around for the winningest coach available. That happened to be George Allen, recently let go by the Rams.

Svare had seen himself replaced by George Allen in 1966; now, six years later, he was again replaced, this time by a member of Allen's staff. It may have been traumatic to him, but Svare had a way of landing on his feet. He was hired in January 1971 by San Diego owner Gene Klein as the Chargers' general manager, and when head coach Sid Gilman was fired with four games remaining in the 1971 season, Svare took over that position as well.

Despite his outspoken dislike for George Allen, Svare had something in common with the man—they both believed in experienced ballplayers and were willing to trade draft choices and *younger ballplayers to get them. Harland soon traded for some of the league's more famous older players and malcontents. The way he saw it, Deacon was to be his Rosey Grier. Svare also signed on defensive end Lionel Aldridge (nine years with Green Bay), defensive tackle/end Dave Costa (nine years around the league with Oakland, Buffalo, and Denver), fullback Cid Edwards (six years with St. Louis), tight end John Mackey (eight years with Baltimore), linebacker Tim Rossovich (four years with Philadelphia)—and brilliant but erratic halfback Duane Thomas (two years with Dallas).*

But the differences between Allen and Svare's methods were perhaps more significant than the similarities. As sardonic quipper and Chargers owner Gene Klein says in his book First Down and a Billion, *"We believed that many of these players were available because they were not able to get along with the management of their former teams, rather than because of a lack of ability. Most of them were considered "free spirits," or "flakes." Their reputations were such that our defensive team was nicknamed 'Harland's Hoodlums.' " Thomas couldn't get interested in playing football, Mackey wasn't up to his former heroics, and Rossovich was plagued with injuries, but Svare got some excellent performances out of the rest of his San Diego over-the-hill gang.*

Still, winning would elude Svare with the Chargers, just as it had with Svare's Rams. In 1972, Svare believed just as much in full contact practice as he had a decade before, and his team, particularly his defensive secondary, was riddled with injuries. Svare had one other major problem: his ball-control offense, which was run under the baleful stare and sharp tongue of longtime assistant Bob Schnelker, was a bad fit with the skills of wide-open-passing quarterback John Hadl. Schnelker insisted on his way, Svare backed Schnelker, and the Chargers ended up 4-9-1 on the season.

Working for the Used Car Salesman

What kind of atmosphere was Deacon walking into? He already knew enough about Svare to believe he would never produce a winning team. But Svare had promised Deacon that he would be a team leader, and Deacon thought maybe he could parlay that into a coaching job, first as defensive line coach, a responsibility that could eventually lead to the head coaching position. With Svare's losing record, it was only a matter of time before the Chargers' owner started looking around for a replacement. And just as Svare had been waiting in the wings when Waterfield was let go, so Deacon might be in the right place at the right time, ready and waiting.

Gene Klein might not even wait as long as had Dan Reeves. Klein was not a patient man. A self-made millionaire, he'd started as a door-to-door salesman, pitching encyclopedias during the Depression. He was a businessman who, in his own words, "parlayed four used cars on a dirt lot" in the San Fernando Valley into a $1.1 billion conglomerate. Klein still counted every penny. When he reached sixty-five, Klein proudly claimed he was drawing $711 in Social Security every month. He was also in charge of banks, savings and loan companies, a big insurance company, and a movie production and distribution company, among others.

Klein claimed that he bought the Chargers expecting to apply the principles of good business management to the operation, but in *First Down and a Billion* he explained why he couldn't really succeed at that. Among Klein's excuses for the Chargers' habitual losing ways, was that the money didn't add up—that the players were paid too much and there was no way to insure success. Nonetheless, Klein held the team for nineteen years and sold it for a huge profit. In addition to profit, Klein had one other motive. In *First Down and a Billion* he says, "I think that at some point in their lives most men dream about owning a professional sports franchise. I certainly did. I thought that a pro-football team was just about the best toy anyone could ever have."[1]

So Deacon left his "home" with the Los Angeles Rams to toil for a supersalesman who had become so rich he could afford an NFL team as a grown-ups toy.

How had Harland ended up as the head coach of the Chargers? Arnold Mandell, in his book *The Nightmare Season,* recalls asking Klein that question. Klein responded that owners always want to control their teams, and he knew he could control Svare. "I first met Harland when he came into my car agency in the Valley. He was with the Rams at the time. It was 1956. He wanted an MG in the window. I took one look at him and knew he was a cherry. A cherry is what car dealers call a pushover. So I raised the price five hundred dollars more and had the contract signed in less than five minutes. When we talked about the incident several months ago, Harland didn't remember me, but I remembered him."[2]

---

1. Gene Klein and David Fisher, *First Down and a Billion,* Morrow, 1987, p. 12.
2. Ibid., p. 128.

Mandell goes on to record that Klein controlled the team with nightly phone calls and evening drinking meetings. That this arrangement didn't work any better than Dan Reeves's arrangement with his weaker coaches—Waterfield, followed by Svare, and finally Prothro—would be seen in the San Diego record.

For his part, Deacon felt he didn't have to know that much about the Svare-Klein relationship. Svare hadn't been a winner in L.A.; chances were he wasn't going to be a winner in San Diego. He left too much to chance and to subordinates like Schnelker. Svare wouldn't do the homework that George Allen had done. He wouldn't be interested in building a team around the players, the way Allen had. His tough contact scrimmages may have contributed to the string of injuries that plagued the San Diego secondary. And the open squabbling going on between quarterback John Hadl and Bob Schnelker was hurting team morale.

The 1972 season bore out Deacon's fears. Although he had a good individual year (though not great by his own standards), personally leading all the linemen on the Chargers with seventy-two tackles (thirty-nine unassisted) and had five sacks, San Diego would nonetheless go 4-9-1. Deacon played his best game against Dallas, with seven unassisted tackles and two sacks. Still, it was obvious to Deacon and practically every San Diego fan in southern California that Svare wasn't building a winning team. There were a few moments of glory. The team did tie the Raiders as George Blanda's kick failed in the closing seconds of the game, and the team beat the Colts 23-20 in a game that saw Deacon recover two Baltimore fumbles.

Playing pro football wasn't much fun for Deacon any more, even though everyone said he was a great team leader. Deacon knew in his heart that he was the captain of a team that wasn't being motivated to win. This disturbed him more than anything, for winning had been built into the very fabric of his psyche as a player. Deacon started to look forward to the days when he could move into a coaching position. Maybe, he thought, as defensive coach he might be able to counteract some of offensive coach Bob Schnelker's negativity. One thing about Harland, he certainly was loyal to his subordinates, if Schnelker was any gauge.

Personally interviewed by myself, Harland Svare today angrily denies Arnold Mandell's retelling of Gene Klein's tale of how they met: "I never bought a car from Gene, though he used to tell that story to everyone. I was a young kid from Washington the first time I met Gene. Arnie sort of missed the point: all owners want to have a good relationship with their coaches, and Gene felt he could talk to me. Gene was a bright guy, and in my years as head coach, he had some good ideas. But he had some stinkers, too, and we used to fight a lot about those."

But while Svare generally sticks up for Gene Klein, his description of the man evokes a vision of Atilla the Hun on a good day: "He could be fair when he wanted to. He was a complicated man, moral and yet very vindictive. He had lots of enemies, and he had a range of emotions. It's fair to say he was not even-minded, even-handed, or even-tempered."

To this day, Svare feels Mandell's telling of the car-buying story in his book had fatal consequences for his career as a head coach. "More than anything else, what destroyed my career in the NFL was Arnie Mandell quoting the story about how Gene first hired me . . . implying that Gene hired me because he could manipulate me; and that cost me my career in the NFL. The press picked up on it, and every day somebody would quote me something else from The Nightmare Season, until I couldn't function any more."

Deacon disagrees. "That's not what did Harland in. Losing did Harland in. Losing and losing until the fans couldn't take it any more. They know when something isn't working, and they saw Harland's offense do predictable things, year after year. The 'Sack Sven' movement became a real thing. Yet, Swede was a super-stubborn man, right to the bitter end. He backed Schnelker, even though none of the offensive players could get along with him. Schnelker was the kind of guy who would do bed checks and turn you in if you were three minutes late. He loved that kind of stuff. And he had no imagination as an offensive coach—his offense was a grind-it-out, three yards and a cloud of dust offense, everywhere he went. You'd think Harland would have gotten wise to him."

Deacon is inclined to think Klein did make the important moves behind the scenes, no matter how strongly Svare disagrees: "Everyone's interested in winning, but they all want to do it their own way. Coaching is one of those professions like writing or making movies. Everybody thinks they can do it, but great novels and really fine movies are very rare. There are a few enlightened owners, but almost all those I've had a chance to see up close like to have their own way, directly or indirectly, with the team. They'll blame the losses on the coach and the players, but it's been their fingers in the pie all along."

On Hiring Old Ballplayers

On first reflection, it seemed like Harland Svare and George Allen shared the same opinions with regard to hiring veteran ballplayers, and to some degree, this was so. Both were known to prefer experience over youth, to look down on rookies, and to seek trades rather than relying on the college draft to build their teams. But the more Deacon reflected on Svare's Chargers, the more he realized that the vital necessities were lacking.

Allen seemed to have a very strong and particular sixth sense about players. It might be described as moral radar; no one knows exactly how he did it, but Allen could take an almost instant reading on the stability, the will to win, and the fire in any player he was considering in a trade. At the same time Allen calculated a player's potential in terms of his experience and talent, he factored in this moral or character element. This major tactical element was missing from Svare's and Klein's equation as they cast about the league looking for hand-me-downs. And that makes some sense; Svare was an authoritarian coach. Players, like packaged meat, came in a variety of sizes and shapes, and could be dealt with accordingly. They were expected to be up for the games and to perform as professionals.

So, while Allen ended up with a fistful of talented and experienced players in Los Angeles, and built the famous "Over The Hill Gang" in Washington, the Chargers ended up with "Harland's Hoodlums," a rag-tag bunch of free spirits who refused to gel into a cohesive unit. It drove Deacon crazy as he tried to get a handle on his responsibilities. After all, as team captain, he felt he ought to be able to mold his players into a force to be reckoned with throughout the league. These were the type of players who responded to being treated as equals. And while he used Allen's psychology and methods as much as he could, he felt stymied at every turn by the heavy hands of Svare's assistants.

Deacon would teach through repetition and drills, working to instill a sense of pride in the men. And just when he thought he was making progress, one coach or another would destroy what he had established in one vicious yelling match, screaming at his players like they were little boys. Svare wouldn't stick up for Deacon; he let his assistants run their own shows.

Of all the misfits gathered under the Chargers' banner, the only one Deacon couldn't get through to was running back Duane Thomas. Thomas was a special case. A brilliant player, he'd been mishandled when he played for the Cowboys; traded to the Chargers, he showed up with absolutely zero motivation to play.

Of Thomas, Chargers owner Gene Klein said, "In all the years I owned the Chargers, of all the players we had, one player stands out, or, more accurately, sits out. Duane Thomas. Duane Thomas was the best football player in the world; it's just that that world was not the same one in which all the rest of us live. Thomas was the strangest human being I've ever known."[3]

Upon Thomas's arrival in San Diego, Deacon went to pick him up at the airport, only to find him walking along the center divider of the freeway, heading for the stadium. He was wearing a suit and tie and carrying a suitcase. Deacon pulled over and opened the door, and Thomas got in the car. He seemed agreeable enough. But after they parked next to the stadium, Thomas went on ahead, reached the elevator first, and, instead of holding the door for Deacon, went on alone, leaving Deacon staring at the closed elevator doors.

In a way, that incident explained Thomas more than anything to Deacon. He'd been treated as a commodity by Dallas, Landry being another of the league's "my way or the highway" coaches. With no say in how he was to play, rather than knuckle under, Thomas had turned inward and uncommunicative. A player of lesser talent would have been summarily booted out of camp, but Thomas had the magic and he knew it. Although he suited up for a practice or two, he never played in a single game for the Chargers, and was carried through the 1972 season as a hold-out.

Thomas would come up to Deacon, or whoever was trying to reason with him, put his face six inches from the offending talker, and stare. It was an unsettling routine, guaranteed to derail whatever topic was being discussed.

Gene Klein relates a similar incident. Having trouble with Thomas, who finally reported to the Chargers camp on September 19 and then promptly left again, Klein had Svare convince Thomas to meet him at an airport in Palm Springs to discuss their contract. Says Klein of his encounter with Thomas, "He stood no more than six or seven inches from me and just stared into my eyes. He didn't say a word, he just stared. I asked him a few questions. He continued staring at me. 'You got anything to say to me?' I asked again. He continued staring at me. 'Okay, if that's the way you feel,' I said, as if we'd

---

3. Gene Klein and David Fisher, *First Down and a Billion,* Morrow, 1987, p. 161.

actually had a conversation. 'That's all, go ahead back.' " Thomas left Palm Springs and the Chargers didn't see him again for two months. Then, unannounced, he showed up just before a Chargers-Cowboys game. "He dressed for the game, ran out onto the field with the team, and then sat down, cross-legged, beneath the goalposts, staring straight ahead . . . When the band started playing the national anthem, we had him half-carried, half-dragged off the field."[4] Klein and Svare finally had enough of Thomas and traded him to the only coach in the NFL who would give him a chance—George Allen. Allen was somehow able to crack the hard nut and got through to Thomas enough so that he actually took the field for the Redskins as a substitute back for the 1973 and 1974 seasons. Unfortunately, Thomas never lived up to Allen's expectations or to the great promise he'd shown as a Dallas rookie in 1970, when he'd rushed for over 800 yards, averaging 5.3 yards per carry.

To this day, Deacon still regards Duane Thomas with a sad sense of awe: "If you honestly want to understand Duane Thomas, I might suggest you read The Confessions of Nat Turner, *by William Styron. That might help a little bit. Nat Turner was the black slave who led a rebellion against the whites thirty years before the Civil War. He became more and more frustrated when he saw that his talents and rights were being abused, until he finally turned against his masters. I believe that, like Nat, Duane started out believing in something very strongly. At one time, football was a lot of fun for him. Had he begun his pro career with a player's coach like George right from the start, he'd have probably been okay. But playing football for money is a hard game, and it can suck your blood, particularly when you're playing for a hard-nosed coach, and there certainly are a lot of them around the league, even today. There was no room for the individual on Landry's Cowboys—Landry didn't listen, he talked. His players didn't have rights, they had to perform, they were cogs in the Dallas system. Thomas couldn't be like that; he had this element of free spirit, he wouldn't give in.*

"Duane wouldn't practice and he wouldn't talk. Give him any instruction at all, and he'd go into his Duane Mode. He'd get his nose next to yours and stare at your eyeballs. It was funny, in a way; Harland was scared to death of him.

"A year later, in 1974, Duane and I found ourselves in Washington, D.C., playing for the Redskins. One evening we went to

4. Gene Klein and David Fisher, *First Down and a Billion,* Morrow, 1987, p. 163.

Georgetown, intent on doing up the town. It was a rainy, miserable night, and he left his coat in my car. He wanted to go get it, so I gave him the keys. That was my mistake. Later, when Duane wanted to leave, he didn't say anything, he just left. He took off in my car and left me.

"I never really could get mad at Duane. I tried to reach out to him. See, Duane was trying to fight the entire system of pro football in his own way. He didn't realize that he was fighting a ghost. Lawsuits don't work because the owners have money enough to tie you up and delay until you die—and they'd rather spend a million bucks on lawyers than pay you $100,000 they don't think you deserve. Morality doesn't work because they just laugh at you. And Duane's quiet mode—while it was unsettling—didn't even make a dent."

Opportunity Knocks

Sunday nights after games, the Chargers held more or less informal meetings at Pernicano's Italian Restaurant. The coaches and the key players and their wives would show up and Gene Klein would preside personally or phone in his congratulations or his views on what had to be done next, depending on what had transpired on the gridiron that day.

George Pernicano owned a small piece of the team, and had several large rooms of his restaurant decorated in Chargers glory—huge pictures of players, models of the team in action, and trophies. As team captain, Deacon was much in demand, passing from table to table.

As the season wound down, with only three games to play, it was clear that the Chargers were going to end up with a losing season. Still, they had just come off wins over Kansas City and Houston, and there was an air of festivity about Pernicano's. When Deacon arrived, almost no one was there from management but Gene Klein, who was sitting alone nursing a drink at his table. Deacon deposited Iretha at another table with some of the linemen and their wives, and went over to see how things were with the boss.

Klein smiled up at him. "Been talking with Harland about you."

"Oh? Anything good?"

"Everything good," Gene said. "You've done pretty much what we've asked of you. Now what do you think about taking on an assistant coaching job with us after you hang up your spikes?"

For a moment Deacon was too stunned to speak.

"You serious?" was all he managed to blurt out.

Svare had held up the carrot from afar, hinting that Deacon might be offered such a spot, but here it was, the golden ticket being handed to him by the owner. Deacon should have been overjoyed, but for some strange reason, at that moment an image of his old college chum, Gee-Gee the Midget, flashed through his mind, Gee-Gee's lips silently mouthing the words "Careful, Davey—Don't sell out for a nickel." Deacon remembered a thousand bleak moments and a thousand times his hopes had been dashed before—the contract negotiations with Reeves that always seemed to leave him with the short end of the stick, the sad stories he'd heard about other blacks trying to make it in the NFL once their playing days were over. He wanted to be more than a figurehead or an interpreter between white coaches and black players.

Klein was looking at him, holding out his hand for confirmation, "What do you say, Deak?"

Deacon nodded. "Sounds good. But if I take this road, will I ever have a chance, somewhere down the line, at the top spot?"

The smile faded from Klein's face. He dropped his hand to the table and a sincere but troubled look came over him. "What do you mean?" he asked. Deacon knew this wasn't Gene the used car salesman. His boss could be the world's slickest when it came to closing a deal, but he could also be very conscious of moral issues. Once Klein realized something was a matter of conscience, he would never mince words.

"Well, I think I'm making it plain as a man can. Is there any chance for me? I mean, can I some day ever hope to be the head coach of the Chargers? You know, Gene, if I work my way up and I'm clearly the best man for the job?" Klein still didn't say anything, and Deacon was forced to plunge on, to try to explain himself. "Gene—if I go down this track and prove myself over time and do the job for you and I'm actually the one who deserves it, *can I get the head coaching job?*"

Klein shook his head. "No," he said, looking Deacon directly in the eye. "You can't." Klein may have joined the owner's circle, but he was one of the newer members. There was no way he would buck the old boy's club and hire a black head coach.

"No way?"

"No way."

"Then I don't want the job. You know I have to be the best at whatever I do."

Klein shrugged and waved for the waiter to bring a menu. The conversation was over.

Looking back, Deacon realizes he may have made one of the major mistakes of his career. "I can see now that my decision was short-sighted. I'd gone down to San Diego with the notion that I might become the head coach. I had reason to believe it would happen . . . after all, if Harland Svare could become a coach, why not me? Had I taken the job as offered by Gene, I could have been in the right position twenty years later when everybody finally looked around and started to notice there were no black head coaches in a game dominated by talented blacks. On the other hand, I have not found room in my life to be patient about racial inequality. I have always been grateful that Gene was honest with me."

Svare confirms that Deacon was considered for the coaching staff in San Diego. "Deacon had a chance to become a coach under me. I would have hired him. After all, I brought him to San Diego for his leadership. He had his problems; he was a heavy drinker, and I was worried about it."

Deacon remarks, "That's the pot calling the kettle black if I ever heard it. Hell, back then we were all heavy drinkers. Why am I the only one willing to admit his past sins?"

Declares Svare, "No question about it, had I continued to coach, Deacon would have ended up coaching for me."

It would have been interesting to see whether, given a second chance, Deacon would have reasoned his way into joining Svare's staff. But 1972 had been a losing year. As 1973 commenced, Svare wasn't able to turn the team around, and soon San Diego had its own Sack Svare movement. The sports writers took up the howl, the fans hooted at their head coach from the stands, and his effigy was hung in the Charger's parking lot, just as it had been in Los Angeles some years before.

And then another evil thing took shape; the local sports writers, tired of losing and hungry for reasons to explain the long dry spell, moved on to investigate and gradually spread the news of a "major" Chargers drug scandal. Singled out by the league, relatively unprotected by their own weak and ineffective union, and harried by reporters at every turn, the players' performance plummeted. The drug story, bolstered by leaks from an ongoing NFL investigation, would humiliate the players under scrutiny, applying such pressure to them as to make it nearly impossible for the team to concentrate on winning football. It was a vicious cycle, as their continuing poor performance was then blamed on the (to this day) unsubstantiated illegal drug usage. More of the drug scandal later. The point here is that Svare would soon have to give up the job of head coach. Svare would retain his position, as general

*manager, however. And he and Gene Klein would hire as their new
head coach for the 1974 season the one man Deacon would
never play ball for—Tommy Prothro.*

Bleak Season

If George Allen looked for one thing in his players, it was character;
with Harland Svare, it was intelligence. This difference in philosophy
had very real effects on the playing field. In 1973, while Allen's Redskins were 10-4 and he was well on his way to building a new dynasty,
Svare's Chargers ended up dead last in their division with a miserable
2-11-1 record.

Part of San Diego's poor showing could be blamed on injuries:
receiver Gary Garrison and seventeen-year veteran quarterback Johnny
Unitas hardly played, while rookie Dan Fouts replaced Unitas for the
season. The players' spirits sank collectively when early in the season,
without any explanation, Svare benched runner Mike Garrett. By midseason exasperated wide receiver Dave Williams, finding himself
released from the Chargers, told reporters that the team was a zoo.

Deacon felt Svare had put too much emphasis on building his
defensive line around veterans, or, more aptly, too little elsewhere.
What Svare had achieved was fine, as far as it went, but a winning
team is composed of many elements. And while the Chargers could
boast a tough defensive front, Svare hadn't built his defensive backfield
or his offensive line to the same high standards. Svare was a defensive
guy, as was George Allen. But Allen got better assistants to handle his
offense—men like Ted Marchibroda and Ray Prohaska—while Harland had the conservative Bob Schnelker. With Schnelker in charge of
the offense, San Diego was dull, plodding, and predictable. And worse,
Schnelker's personality alienated them immediately.

Concentrating on improving his leadership skills, Deacon could
see other differences between Svare and Allen. Allen was more thor-
ough and taught the theories of solid defense better to his players.
Allen knew the structure of the entire defense rather than just the line,
and by the time he was through with his players, they understood it
as well. Allen could also get more out of his players. To become champions, you need people who will perform for you and for your coaching staff. Svare wasn't a "player's coach." The players didn't like him.
Svare was too inflexible, and he wouldn't listen to new ideas when they

came from the players. The only change Deacon could see that Svare had made from his early years with the Rams was that he'd shortened the brutal two-and-a-half-hour contact scrimmages. That was something to be appreciated, particularly among the older veterans, who didn't heal as well as they had in their youth.

This is not to say that Svare wasn't a thinker, or that he wasn't interested in new ideas that might make his team a winner. In fact, Svare was more than willing to study and consider intellectual theories that might lead to better team performance on the field. While in application his theories of hiring older ballplayers didn't lead to a winning combination, he has to be given credit for attempting a path that was not well appreciated in those years and is still debated today. Svare had a quick and curious mind; more than almost any other coach of his time, Svare thought far afield from football itself in an attempt to bring success to his teams. It was this mindset that led Svare to hire a distinguished practicing psychiatrist and cochairman of psychiatry at the University of California, Arnold J. "Arnie" Mandell, as the NFL's first "football psychiatrist," and which, later in life, would lead Svare to his theories on body building and rehabilitation and to his astounding success in that profession.

The coming of Mandell seemed innocent enough. He was a quick-minded scholar with a ready smile and a sharp eye for observing the human condition. He had a good ear for dialogue and his first look at the wild and woolly world of pro football gave him some colorful imagery:

> They move in a languorously graceful stroll. Tonight they wore sandals or step-in shower clogs, torn jeans or shorts, and colorful unbuttoned short-sleeved shirts. An occasional wild hat. These working clothes contrasted dramatically with the *Playboy* fashions they sported on their nighttime excursions. They were sleek, elegant, and powerful. Their muscles rippled. Their stance and gait were arrogant and unconcerned.[5]

Of the Chargers' defense, Mandell declared,

> Harland's "dirty dozen" defensive players, especially the linemen, kept up their usual running patter—a chain of putdowns in truncated, idiosyncratic jargon. The themes were women, promiscuity,

ugliness, athletic ability and courage. They elaborated on the standard insults. "My momma can pass better than your momma" . . . "You're too goddamn little to do anything but chase people after they're gone, that's why you're a D-back" . . . "Your momma not only passes good, but she probably shaves."[6]

Mandell's firsthand impressions of the game were professional and sympathetic to the players:

> The systematic and organized work of the equipment men and trainers at the sideline was impressive. Taping, injecting local anesthetic, replacing lost rubber cleats and straps, delivering Gatorade, aspirin, antacids, salt tablets, and towels, moving with the swift efficiency of assembly-line workers in the middle of mayhem. At half time, in the locker room, the trainers and physicians were busy. Broken ribs were being X-rayed; hyperextended knees were being taped, fingers splinted, a swollen knee taped; large violaceous bruises were being poked for deeper hurts.[7]

Eight games into the season with one win, one tie, and six losses, Svare was forced to resign as head coach. He remained as general manager, and his assistant Ron Waller was assigned as the new head coach. This move brought no success, as Waller could only manage a win against five losses for the rest of the season. There had to be some reason for all these losses. Something simple, something to turn the fans' anger and frustration away from the front office, something to blame.

That something proved to be drugs. Under public and Congressional pressure, the NFL was being urged to clamp down on player use of drugs.[8] There was a strong feeling throughout the league that they had to clean their own house before someone else came in and cleaned it up for them. It wasn't a carefully thought out solution to the losing situation in San Diego. The NFL probably didn't have to think about it at all. The circumstances were there, it was handy, and it certainly took the Chargers fans' attention away from their miserable losing season. Why not go with the flow?

During 1973 the United States withdrew from Vietnam, Vice President Agnew resigned for tax evasion, and President Nixon started to

---

6. Arnold J. Mandell, M.D., *The Nightmare Season,* Random House, 1976, p. 37.

7. Ibid., pp. 19-20.

8. U.S. Congress, Senate, Proceedings: 18 June, 12,13 July, on proper and improper use of drugs by athletes. Washington, D.C.: U.S. Government Printing Office, 1973.

feel the pressure of Watergate. While frustrated members of the American Indian Movement occupied Wounded Knee in the Dakotas, the Chicago Seven conspiracy trial lumbered to an inconclusive ending. Clearly, from coast to coast there was a countermovement to what was then seen as the excesses of the 1960s—free love, free thinking, body paint and psychedelic art, mind-blowing drugs. The entire country had set about to do its house-cleaning. Could San Diego be far behind?

The situation was not as simple as it seems. There was more here than simple drug abuse. Over the years, players throughout the league had come to depend on amphetamines, which were supplied in great quantities and few controls by team trainers and physicians. They had been dispensed as a matter of course by NFL teams since as far back as the 1950s. Rob Huizenga states in his book *You're Okay, It's Just A Bruise* how astonished he was to find them still openly available in the Raiders locker room in the early eighties. "In the past, players had grabbed their medication out of a loosely supervised large jar of pills—everything from anti-inflammatories to cold meds to painkillers to sleepers. As a result, the players knew every capsule and tablet by size and color. I was surrounded by a bunch of pharmacists."[9]

Dave Meggyesy, who played outside linebacker for the St. Louis Cardinals for seven years, from 1963 to 1970, talks about the easy dispensation of drugs on the St.Louis Cardinals in the late 1960's, "Even after six years in the league, I played so fanatically that the coaches asked the team doctor to put me on tranquilizers for the games. While most guys were popping bennies to psych up for the games I was taking tranquilizers to calm down."[10] Meggyesy, who admits to using bennies [benzedrine[11]] "rarely" to get psyched up for games, comments on the short-term effects of amphetamines, "I'm not sure if bennies really help you to play better over the long run. Many players swear by them; others say they simply give you the illusion of playing well when you're not. I do know that players who use them regularly quickly become dependent on them and many begin using them even for practice. The use of bennies is on the rise among both college and

---

9. Huizenga, *You're Okay, It's Just a Bruise,* St.Martin's Griffin,1994, p.41

10. Dave Meggyesy, *Out of Their League,* Ramparts Press, 1970, pp. 113-14.

11. The three most common amphetamines are benzedrine, dexedrine and methedrine. Commonly referred to as "uppers," they are sometimes taken by the emotionally depressed to achieve euphoria and drive, or to find a release from fatigue. An opposite effect, depression of the central nervous system, is achieved with methaqualone (Quaalude), commonly called "downers" or "ludes."

professional teams—and, since bennies seem to help guys play 'better,' most coaches show little or no concern over their widespread use."[12]

A large faction of NFL veterans had relied on amphetamines to get psyched up for games and to numb pain for decades, and in the early 1970s, the San Diego Chargers were loaded with veterans. Perhaps the scandal would have passed them by, to light in some other city, but rather than promote the senseless, cold-turkey ban on amphetamines the NFL was calling for, the Chargers' team psychiatrist, Dr. Arnie Mandell, chose to install a drug control program designed to gradually ease the players away from their career-long dependency on drugs. It was a professionally designed program that had every chance of succeeding. But there was one problem: the Chargers' program involved the continued usage of amphetamines, albeit at lower and lower dosages, until the players were safely off the pills.

And that could not be, because the NFL had publically declared it should not be so. This was a big and accessible story and various news reporters swooped in like birds of prey, eager to expose and punish this example of abuse and corruption. The NFL had its own problem: the newspapers had whipped up Congress in the form of the Staggers Commission, which was set to take action if the league didn't. Professional football needed to prove to Congress and its fans throughout the country that it was serious about cleaning up what had grown to be known as "the pro football drug problem." This approach to the problem would make a lot of noise. Congress would back off. A few players' reputations would be tarnished. But it was just a bandaid, a public relations move rather than a real cure. In the early 1980s, Dr. Huizenga found unprescripted amphetamines still widely in use on the Raiders team, and players on other teams who refuse to be named claim that wide-spread use of painkillers still continues to this day. Professional football is a business. If it made economic sense, the owners, the players, the coaches, the trainers, the fans, and the League itself would have banded together years ago and cleared up painkillers and banned the numbing shots which enable players to go back out on the field. In fact, just the opposite is true. These "battlefield medications" keep players playing—that's what makes economic sense, and so everybody more or less goes along with it. Besides the "candy bottle" of pills he observed when he first came to the Raiders, Huizenga describes the tiny medical treatment room located within the Raiders'

---

12. Dave Meggyesy, *Out of Their League*, Ramparts Press, 1970, pp.104-105.

locker room, "On the side table, a host of injectibles and trays of hermetically sealed needles were piled next to knives, clips, suture materials, sterile towels, and umpteen vials of Xylocaine, Marcaine, and Decadron. On the back wall were slide-out shelves filled with aspirin-like medications, antibiotics, and cold pills. A large brown safe was pushed against the back corner. It housed potentially addictive prescription medications: bottles of Cheracol-X with codeine cough medicine, sleepers and codeine pain pills. The safe door was wide open."[13]

Ironically, back in the early seventies the league picked the Chargers to make an example of, picked the one team that was actively seeking to control the problem with team-sponsored programs and a special psychiatrist. In fact, the league used as evidence of wrong-doing the very prescriptions written by this team psychiatrist for this purpose. Eleven prescriptions made up this evidence, which was obtained in a hurried, secret, and questionable investigation. The league moved a little too fast, without thinking through their moves, and people got hurt. A handful of Chargers players found themselves fined for something that had been a practice in football as long as anybody could remember. One of those fined was Deacon Jones.

Deacon remembers Svare's last, desperate days as head coach of the Chargers. "The way the local fans felt about him, he needed bodyguards, he needed an armored car. He'd just made too many mistakes, probably the most serious of which was sticking with Bob Schnelker too long. It was a question of friendship over common sense. They'd played together, and he was too loyal.

"To this day, Harland doesn't like George Allen, because George took similar ideas and a similar program and made them work. George respected players, whereas Harland was too stubborn. I can understand that; I personally have my own stubborn streak, and it has cost me in life.

"Don't get me wrong about Harland. The man's a genius at what he does today. He understands more about fitness and the mechanics of the human body than anybody else I know. And I know this from personal experience. By fitting me with a special plate in my shoe, Harland helped me overcome my arch problem. He extended my playing days, and I'll always be grateful for that. He may not be a miracle worker, but he's maybe the next best thing. He runs a facility down there in San Diego yet today, and

13. Rob Huizenga, M.D., *You're Okay, It's Just A Bruise,* St. Martin's Griffin, 1994, p. 13.

there's a long history of hundreds of athletes like me—and ordinary people, too—he's helped to get off their backs and up and running."

Svare talks about his team psychologist. "The league had come out with a rule that you couldn't use amphetamines any more. I brought in Dr. Arnie Mandell, a local San Diego psychiatrist who knew drugs. Dr. Mandell demanded confidentiality, to gain the players' confidence, and he did prescribe amphetamines even though it was against league rules.

Judge Robert Baxley, then the lawyer who represented Dr. Mandell in some of his legal proceedings after the drug scandal broke, admitted to this writer that his client did prescribe amphetamines on a limited scale. "Dr. Mandell felt he had that right for two reasons: First, the players, many of whom had acquired genuine habits over the years (just as people who smoke cigarettes find it difficult to impossible to quit) were getting them anyway off the street and in Mexico and from players on other teams, and he'd rather he knew what they were taking. And second, under the Chargers' program, he was gradually cutting down on their doses. He had many of the younger players completely off amphetamines, and was steadily cutting down on the dosages for the rest of the players. Dr. Mandell felt that in a year or two he would have changed the players' habits, patterns which had been ingrained over their entire careers."

Of the drug scandal, Deacon says, "I should have paid more attention. The team had always provided amphetamines. They still were, no matter what the league said, only now you just had to get a prescription first . . . Harland knew what the doctor was doing—he played in the league up to the time I did, and amphetamines were just as available to the Giants as to the Rams."

Svare agrees, at least as far as to the availability: "Amphetamines were available as far back as when I played college ball for Washington State. The team doctor had them available for anybody who wanted them. We called them 'greenies.' "

Deacon adds dryly, "We couldn't afford them at the college I went to. Coming into the NFL was a new level of sophistication for me. And Harland took them when he was a Giant."

Svare does indeed admit to having taken amphetamines before playing in a Giants game, although he claims to have only taken them once. "I was so jacked up for that game I was flying. I was talking so fast no one could understand me. The thing I do remember is that after the game I was still jacked up. I couldn't go to sleep for two days." This description, quoted from Gene Klein's

For there, propped up by a stack of pillows, his own father had one of the Reverend Ike's prayer cloths draped across his eyes and forehead.

"Dad!" Deacon shouted, "You can't wear this thing! This guy's buying fancy cars and fur coats and big mansions with the money he gets from people like you!"

Deacon snatched the prayer cloth from Ishmeal's head, but in the next second, Ishmeal's clawlike hand whipped out and snatched it back. Showing surprising strength for one so far gone, Deacon's father clutched his wrist.

"You don't fool with a person's beliefs, son," he said.

Deacon nodded, and gave up the conversation. He could see Ishmeal wasn't anywhere near giving up the ghost.

As the 1973 season lumbered on, Deacon started to believe that his dad would last out the season. But then, on a Saturday in December with only three games to play, Deacon found out he was wrong. The team was in Boston, preparing for a game against the Patriots. Deacon called on a Saturday night before a Sunday game, and the word was that his dad didn't recognize anybody, but he was still fighting against the pain, struggling to live. Then Deacon got a phone call from his sister. Stubborn Ishmeal had finally given up his foothold on life. Deacon decided to play the following day's game in honor of his dad. When it was over, the team flew back to San Diego and Deacon went down home for the funeral.

There was a service at the church Ishmeal had helped to build, and Deacon spoke, giving a moving tribute to the man who had instilled in him the will to fight his way to the top. After the ceremony, the family gathered in the house Deacon had bought for his mom and dad. Deacon was now the recognized leader of the family. There was business to attend to; he wouldn't be able to leave right away. In fact, Deacon missed the next week's game against Denver. As they sat around the family table, looking back affectionately on Ishmeal's last months, Deacon mentioned the Reverend Ike's prayer cloth.

"Don't you get down on him for that," Mattie warned.

"I didn't say nothin', Mama," Deacon shrugged.

"I'm gonna tell you something about that prayer cloth. It gave your daddy the will to hang on all these months. It was the only thing he was interested in, that and how you did in the football. There's some awesome power in that prayer cloth, don't you ever doubt it."

Deacon didn't say anything about his chat with the Reverend Ike while they were having the oil changed in their white and black Silver

Clouds, or about his feelings about magic charms for money. But he thought a lot about it. And as Deacon left Eatonville, he was still pondering how it could be that a man like Reverend Ike might be doing real good for the spirit of those who believed.

Deacon remembers his father's last fight. "He was down to sixty pounds in the raw. Still, he fought like a champion. He did not want to die and he made it perfectly clear. The Eatonville Joneses always were the toughest of the clan."

Scandal

The witch hunt began during the disastrous Chargers football season of 1973, the campaign Dr. Mandell dubbed "The Nightmare Season." They weren't really very clever about it. NFL league security sent spies and plainclothes men of all shapes and sizes to go through the players' training camp rooms and the Chargers locker rooms throughout the season. The players were told by these parties, who claimed they were acting under the name of the NFL, that the entire team was the subject of an ongoing investigation.

While he heard about the raids from the other players, Deacon was never around when the investigators came raiding through. When friends like Bob Thomas or Coy Bacon, seeking guidance, asked his opinion, Deacon told them in the strongest possible language that the NFL had no legal right to search players without a warrant, and no legal right to grill players about their private lives. Although he continued to take amphetamines before games, Deacon felt confident there would be no amphetamine controversy; almost every veteran he knew in the league privately admitted to taking them, and on top of that, he was under Arnie Mandell's care as part of the team-sponsored amphetamine control program. As for marijuana usage, major segments of the American society were lighting up in those days. If that was a crime, there wouldn't be enough jails to hold everybody.

When word went out that the investigators were setting up private meetings with individual players at the Hanalea Hotel on Hotel Circle near San Diego's quaint Mexican Old Town, some of the players gathered in a small circle around Deacon.

"What you gonna do, Deak?" they asked.

"Nothin'," he replied. "I ain't gonna be there."

"They callin' 'em private conversations. They sayin' attendance is mandatory."

Deacon shook his head angrily, "Well, you can take that mandatory and shove it right up alongside the Bill of Rights. We're livin' in America, here."

When the man with the short haircut and the clipboard finally showed up and gave Deacon his specific time to attend, Deacon refused the meeting. "You have no legal bind on me," he told them. "If you think I'm guilty of something, charge me in a court of law."

The man glowered, made a few notes after Deacon's name, and walked away.

The newspapers continued to hear about the investigation, and there was much speculation as to what the charges would be and which players would be charged. Scuttlebutt had it that the investigators were after Mandell and Svare. For reasons one may only guess, owner Gene Klein was above suspicion and beyond reproach in an investigation controlled by the NFL commissioner, who was in turn hired by and responsible to the owners.

The long, difficult nightmare season went on and on, loss after loss, until it finally ended in December with the sword of the NFL investigation still hanging over the players' heads. It was not until January 29, 1974, that the *San Diego Union* broke the news with the breathless headline, "Eight Chargers Fined For Drugs." Writer Wayne Lockwood's story ran in part, "A six week investigation by the *San Diego Union* shows Chargers players are suffering from another major narcotics problem—possibly the worst in the NFL."[15]

The story went on to relate that it had been known since the "Houston Ridge" legal case that the use of amphetamines, pain killers, and anabolic steroids abounded on the team.[16] A State Board of Pharmacy medical reviewer had labeled the Chargers dressing room "Drugville USA." The paper went on to state that the new problem was "street drugs, chiefly marijuana and cocaine." The article continued, "Their recent use has involved a number of players, splitting the squad into camps of users and nonusers."

---

15. Wayne Lockwood, *San Diego Union*, January 29, 1974.

16. In 1973, former Charger defensive lineman Houston Ridge had sued and won a case against the team, claiming that muscle relaxants, pain killers and amphetamines he'd been given before a game against Miami in 1969 had contributed to a career-ending hip injury. In *First Down and a Billion*, Gene Klein states that, "The testimony given at his trial revealed that these drugs were readily available to anyone who wanted to take them, not just on the Chargers, but practically throughout pro football." [p.259]

Bryant Salter, a Chargers player representative, tried to dampen the allegations. "Anybody on the street can get street drugs, but I don't think that was the Charger's problem" in arriving at a 1-11-1 record, the worst in the history of the franchise.

Two months later, on March 3, Jack Murphy reported in the *San Diego Union* that the NFL was dragging its feet on the use of illegal drugs. He wrote that one former coach, unnamed, said that marijuana was such a problem in the 1973 season that he demanded management take action—but they wouldn't.[17] On April 16, writer Jerry Magee quoted veteran defensive tackle Dave Rowe as saying that drugs had run rampant in the NFL until 1968.[18] Drugs in sports was suddenly a hot topic, and seemingly anybody with a quotable line could have his notions printed in the *San Diego Union*; a few days later, Dr. Martin Blazina, an L.A orthopedic surgeon who worked for the Dodgers, the Lakers, the Rams and the Kings, made the news by declaring there was "drug danger in WinMania." The doctor pointed out that there is a tremendous pressure to win in sports and many people don't mind the use of drugs if it leads to a successful season. The doctor went on to state, "If the team decides to permit drugs, the doctor's role is to provide the drugs and get them into the athlete."

But all this was vague muckraking to whet the public appetite for what was to come. On April 27, the Union reported in an article by Jerry Magee that "Eight Chargers, Svare Fined In Rozelle Drug Crackdown." The eight players were portrayed as felons, with their pictures blazoned across the sports page: Bob Thomas, running back, Deacon Jones, veteran end, Coy Bacon, defensive lineman, Dave Costa, key tackle, Jerry LeVias, wide receiver, Walt Sweeney, offensive guard, Rick Redman, linebacker, and Tim Rossovich, starting linebacker. The club was fined $20,000 and commissioner Pete Rozelle slapped $40,000 in fines against Harland Svare and the eight players. Svare was fined $5,000, the most severe assessment he could be given without Rozelle going to the NFL executive committee. Svare was fined for "failure to exercise proper supervisory controls over the activities of players and others close to the club." Deacon and Tim Rossovich were fined $3,000 each. Coy Bacon, Dave Costa, and Jerry LeVias were fined $2,000 each. Rick Redman (who had been a player-coach in the 1973 season), Walt Sweeney, and Bob Thomas were fined $1,000 each.[19]

---

17. Jack Murphy, *San Diego Union,* March 3, 1974.

18. Jerry Magee, *San Diego Union,* April 16, 1974.

19. Jerry Magee, *San Diego Union,* April 27, 1974.

Magee opined that this was a sensitive maneuver on Rozelle's part, as there was no precedent for a professional sports organization being disciplined for drug usage. The new coach, Tommy Prothro, washed his hands of the affair. "I can't say much about what has happened. I was in Europe when the events seem to have taken place. All of these players are not with us now and others will be gone before we start the season.

Pete Rozelle was quoted as saying, "This disregard for NFL drug policies was first brought to our attention by reports that some Chargers players felt the situation was having an extremely adverse effect on the football team."

What drugs? What proof? What evidence? Deacon was at first stunned and then outraged to see what the NFL was apparently getting away with. Adding more fuel to the fire, Jack Murphy interviewed Harland Svare for the *San Diego Union*. "Of course," Svare said, "everybody knows we're talking about marijuana. I accept my responsibility." Svare went on to explain how he had been warned of a drug problem in the training camp at Irvine the previous July and had tried to stop it through drug education. He told how he had invited Dr. Arnold Mandell, the co-chairman of the Department of Psychiatry of the University of California at San Diego, to speak to the squad. According to the Murphy article, Mandell's speech had been misunderstood by some of the players, who thought he was condoning the use of drugs off-season, or at least displaying tolerance. Murphy also reported that later Svare, Klein, and Mandell all came to believe drugs, specifically marijuana, had ruined the team and the season.[20]

In this same story, Murphy reported that after the third game of the season, a 20-13 loss to Cincinnati, Gene Klein had roared into the locker room and accused the ballplayers of destroying the team through use of illegal drugs. Later, acting on Rozelle's advice, Klein had hired a private investigator to search out evidence. Murphy reported that Rozelle's staff had conducted fifty interviews with current Chargers and former Chargers players. Finally, in Rozelle's judgment, there was a strong case, and that was when the suspects and their attorneys were told of the fines and the probations and agreed to accept the punishments.

That's the way the story was told. But the truth is, Deacon never agreed to accept any punishment. And there were others who were equally dissatisfied: Mandell and Svare and the Chargers lawyer went

---

20. Jack Murphy, *San Diego Union,* April 27, 1974.

to New York to protest the findings. Just before the proceeding, Mandell, who was very agitated at the prospect of losing his professional standing as a doctor and educator, was asked to wait outside. The meeting didn't go as he figured; the Chargers lawyer ended up agreeing to the commissioner's demands, leaving Mandell twisting in the wind, as the pitiless expression goes.

Harland had an interesting way of looking at the situation. He told Murphy, "I was responsible for everything that went on with the San Diego Charger football team. I didn't condone it. I was not aware of the severity of the problem. I really didn't believe it. But I was responsible. I accept the discipline." Nowhere does Svare mention the Chargers amphetamine control drug program put in place by Arnie Mandell, the man he had hired.

It had been reported earlier in the *San Diego Union* that Ed Garvey, executive director of the Player's Association, had agreed with the punishments meted out to the Chargers players. But these reports proved to be in error as Garvey broke his silence by taking a hard line against the investigation, its findings, and subsequent penalties. "I do not for one minute accept in any way the findings they announced."

Pumped up by the public waves made by its series of exposes, the *San Diego Union* began running articles reviewing how it had been in the vanguard on the story throughout the past year. Stories by Jack Murphy and medical writer Peter Brown revealed on May 13, 1973 that "some Chargers had been so affected by amphetamines that they temporarily lost touch with reality."[21] On May 15, the breathless twosome revealed that Rozelle was reluctantly recognizing the possibility of a drug problem in the NFL. On May 16 and 22, they had done stories dealing with Charger attempts to reduce the flow of prescription drugs to players. And on June 28, 1973, they had noted that Rozelle was acknowledging the problem of drug abuse and instituting a program to deal with it. On September 30, 1973, *San Diego Union* editor Gene Gregston charged the NFL with footdragging and urged strong action. On October 3, they quoted quarterback John Brodie as saying the distorted values in sport had brought about the "drug crisis". On November 20, they called for stronger measures, stating NFL self-policing wasn't working. A Jack Murphy column scolded George Allen for regarding as a "distraction" the revelation by center George Burman that at least a third of his teammates used amphetamines. On

---

21. Jack Murphy and Peter Brown, *San Diego Union,* May 13, 1973.

January 29, 1974, *San Diego Union* sportswriter Wayne Lockwood wrote that his six week investigation revealed the Chargers suffered a "major narcotics problem—perhaps the worst in the NFL. On March 3, Jack Murphy revealed the NFL was investigating the Chargers, and called for prompt action. The paper's promotion had its reward when the series of articles was nominated for a Pulitzer prize. And finally, on April 26, 1974, Rozelle took action.

The following day, the pot seemed to boil over. *San Diego Union* writer Steve Bisheff took a strong moral stance against the players. "Finally, yesterday, the whole, terrible story came spilling out, appearing like some deep, ugly rash." Bisheff berated Garvey. "Garvey and the NFL Player's Association are screaming about freedom, but how much freedom can be allowed when players are caught using drugs during working hours?"[22]

The backlash from the players was inevitable. Sweeney said, "I'm appalled. I haven't used illegal drugs. I'm going to have my lawyers look into this immediately."[23] Redman told reporters, "I'm asking for a trade. I'm interested in being with an organization more competent than this one."[24]

Wide receiver Gary Garrison pointed fingers at the league investigators and the newspaper reporters, referring to the negative effect the season-long probe had on team morale. "Everybody on the club felt the heat at one time or another. No one knew who was on the list and who wasn't. It was an eerie kind of feeling."

Chargers player representative Joe Beauchamp took up the bugle in defense of the players' rights. In response to the charge that the Chargers were "the druggiest team in the NFL," Beauchamp said, "If you believe that stuff, you're very wrong. This team is no different from any other team in any sport, football, basketball, whatever."[25]

Team owner Gene Klein, eager to stay clean of any charges, went on a rampage for a leaguewide urinalysis program. He asked for required post-game drug test, saying he hoped the Players Association would agree to such tests voluntarily. If not, "I think it is time for the Congress of the United States to enact and pass legislation enforcing these tests."[26]

---

22. Steve Bisheff, *San Diego Union*, April 27, 1974.

23. *San Diego Union*, April 27, 1974.

24. *San Diego Union*, April 30, 1974.

25. Ibid.

26. Ibid.; and Gene Klein and David Fisher, *First Down and a Billion*, St.Martin's Griffin, 1987, p.260.

In the uproar that followed, the Players Association accused Rozelle of "a new vigilantism," charging that he was making up rules without consulting the players. Ed Garvey went on, "Rozelle hires a private police force to enforce these rules, determines who should be investigated and sits and listens to hearsay evidence and unsupported allegations against players. He then acts as grand jury, prosecutor, judge, jury, and appellate court. Most importantly, he can destroy a person's career by simply stating publicly that a player is guilty."[27]

Finally, the counter-wave of protests hit the press in the form of a commentary by Steve Casey, printed in the *San Diego Union*. Casey noted that good drama is not always good justice and asked if justice had been served:

> If this action is courageous and forthright, Rozelle has taken some pains to keep it a secret. To begin with, I'd like to know what the alleged drug abuse incidents were, exactly. Pete wouldn't say, his PR man wouldn't say, a team investigator wouldn't say. All are remaining mute because to get into specifics would somehow harm the players, they say.
>
> Harm the players?
>
> These 8 men have been branded as "druggies" and Pete won't even tell us what the word means. Does it mean—as that fearful word "drug abuse" conjures up—that the players slinked around sleazy sections of town looking for a connection, scored some horse and mainlined? I think not.
>
> Svare has said, "Everybody knows we're talking about marijuana," which was an interesting comment as everybody knew no such thing. If Svare is right . . . where and when did the alleged use occur?
>
> How bad is bad and how bad is worse than bad? If the NFL had solid proof that drug laws were broken, isn't there an obligation to reveal this info to authorities for prosecution?
>
> Why just the Chargers?[28]

Deacon Jones finally broke his long silence on May 18, 1974. The headline read, "Jones Denies Drug Usage," and Deacon was quoted as saying,

> I don't think that I'll play another down of pro football in San Diego, but I will play another year of football because I want to prove to the people that Deacon is a football player and not a drug addict. The only

27. Dan Foley, Copley News Service, April 30, 1974.
28. Steve Casey, *San Diego Union,* April 29, 1974.

thing I'm guilty of is being on a 2-11 team. I will not pay the $3,000 fine because I am not guilty. Anything that I have taken in the ranks of pro football was prescribed to me by the team physician.[29]

Deacon continued, criticizing Gene Klein for not supporting the team or accepting any responsibility in the affair. "It upset me that we didn't get the support of the San Diego team. If working people get in trouble, they expect the company to back them."

But talking to the press wasn't going to do much good. The damage had been done. The fine was sticking, and unless Deacon paid it, he would be prohibited from playing NFL football.

Deacon talks about Svare and Mandell's trip to New York in an effort to appeal the league ruling: "Dr. Mandell remembers the hearing as a railroad job; Gene Klein didn't even allow him to appear to defend himself and the program he'd set up for the Chargers. The owners made no fight, and my beef with Harland is that he folded his deck with Gene Klein and abandoned Arnold Mandell and the players. Instead of defending the program Dr. Mandell had set up under his authority, he washed his hands of everything."

Even today, Svare, in talking to this writer, chose to blame the League: "It was very unfair to the players. The League came down very hard. They made an example out of the San Diego Chargers. I personally got fined $5,000. Gene Klein got fined, too, as well as the ballplayers. There was no need for that. But while the problem was everywhere around the league, the investigators had prescriptions from Arnie Mandell. They were real, you could see them, they were evidence, at last they had a case."

Years later, Gene Klein seemed to absolve his head coach of much of the blame even as he took a swipe at him for being simple-minded. He said in First Down and a Billion, *"Blaming the presence of drugs in professional football on Harland Svare was like blaming toxic waste deposits on Lassie."[30] Klein went on to say that amphetamines had been handed out in locker rooms like popcorn. Beyond that, he said, half of the non-football-playing population of the United States seemed to be using tranquilizers to relax and painkillers to deal with minor aches and pains.[31]*

"Then why didn't Gene stick up for us?" Deacon wonders.

---

29. Associated Press Syndication, May 18, 1974.

30. Gene Klein and David Fisher, *First Down and a Billion,* William Morrow & Co. 1987, pp. 52, 53.

31. Ibid., p. 259.

"When the trouble came down, Gene Klein denied he knew that Dr. Mandell, the team doctor his head coach had hired, had been writing prescriptions for amphetamines. This seems unlikely, considering they had hired Mandell (who was widely known as a respected researcher in brain chemistry and the effect of drugs on behavior) to control what Gene in particular saw as a Chargers drug problem."

Mandell, faced with the prospect of a ruined reputation and his career as an eminent psychiatrist and educator shredded, took his case to the public by writing the book The Nightmare Season, which was published by Random House in 1976. The book outraged Klein, because, among other things, it portrayed him as every bit as responsible as anyone else for any alleged abuse. Recently Mandell told this writer that after reading the book an outraged Klein angrily threatened he would "get him." If that was true, the doctor didn't have long to wait. He was soon attacked on two legal fronts, which, to this day, many allege were instigated by Klein working behind the scenes. First, Mandell and Random House were sued by player Dave Williams. And second, Dr. Mandell was formally charged by the California State Medical Board with excessively prescribing drugs to football players. He was further charged by the board with "prescribing drugs without a medical indication" and with gross negligence and gross incompetence. The penalty was steep—Mandell could lose his license to practice in California, to say nothing of the damage to his reputation.

But Mandell wasn't without his resources. He was a well-known researcher and lecturer in his field. He had published hundreds of scientific papers, and was well thought of in educational and scientific circles. Unsolicited money poured in from the community and from around the country for his defense, and Mandell took on the medical board and by proxy the mighty NFL. Defended by attorney William O'Connell in the first case and Robert Baxley in the second (the latter had wrested a favorable settlement from the Chargers in the Houston Ridge case, and is currently a prominent San Diego judge). Mandell's court battles were spectacularly successful. He was totally vindicated and declared innocent on all counts.

Today, Judge Baxley makes the distinction that the NFL fines were commonly considered to have been for hearsay reports of marijuana usage, while the medical board case was for amphetamines. But Mandell was excluded from the meeting when these matters were discussed with Rozelle, and there doesn't seem to be anyone else around who is willing to talk about it. So nobody knows for sure.

And, since the player's union did not, nor did any of the

accused players take the NFL to court, it has to this day not been legally decided whether the league overstepped its authority.

Recently, this writer contacted Pete Rozelle, who stated that in those days the league was bound and determined to solve what they saw as a major drug problem, "We were attempting sanctions on drug abuse. We felt our hands were somewhat tied, because the Players Association did not want to go as far as we did. Our league security people developed information (about drug abuse in the Charger's camp)." Rozelle remembered the scandal had involved Harland Svare and Gene Klein, and that a lot had been written about it in the newspapers.

However, when asked specifically what exact information the league investigators had uncovered, Rozelle said he couldn't remember. Deacon has always questioned just what, if any, evidence the NFL had, and whether it could stand up in a court of law. It would be hard to deny that this supposed evidence, which has been kept from the public, was at the heart of the NFL's case. And yet, Rozelle could only say. "You have to understand, that was a long time ago."

When reminded that Mandell had been declared innocent of all charges and had won back his name and reputation in court actions against the league, Rozelle said carefully, "Well, yes, I do recall that was his position. . . ."

When asked if, in the light of the Mandell rulings, the NFL had ever done anything to restore the player's names and reputations, perhaps paid back their fines and come out with some sort of statement, Rozelle said once again that it was a long time ago and he couldn't "remember exactly the specifics."

When informed of Rozelle's comments, Deacon would only murmur sadly, "That's some selective memory, isn't it . . . ?"

Perhaps the final word on this sordid episode in professional football was printed, ironically, by the paper that brought it to the foreground. A year after the scandal hit the sports pages nationwide, the Union printed a small article bylined "Sports Editor, San Diego Union." This article, titled "Pro Football Fumbles The Drug Scandal," paints the NFL as the bad guy. In it, the writer scolds the NFL for failing to solve the drug problem. In a sense not intended by the writer, this is true. The league's actions forced NFL teams to squelch medical efforts to control drug abuse. The problem never did go away, and today there is much evidence that it still continues on a fairly broad scale.

George to the Rescue

It seemed unfair to Deacon. But life itself is basically unfair. How can one man be born dirt poor in central Florida while another is born with a silver spoon in his mouth in San Francisco? Life is always unfair, and Deacon knew it.

The question was, how to get on with what had to be done? Deacon had rejected the NFL fine, publically stating there was no way he was going to pay it. Rozelle's office declared that Deacon had to cough up the money or he could no longer play football. Yet the game of football had been Deacon's life for longer than he could remember. Deacon felt empty and directionless at the possibility that he would never play again. And, bottom line, Deacon couldn't just let the press brand him a druggie and railroad him out of the sport he loved. The year 1973 had been the "nightmare season" for the San Diego team, yet Deacon had stacked up decent individual statistics: sixty-seven tackles, thirty-eight unassisted, and four sacks, the kind of numbers an ordinary defensive end would have bragged about. Deacon couldn't imagine playing another season for the Chargers. There had to be some other team around the league that would be glad to have him. Klein hadn't stood behind his players when it counted; the Chargers were losers in more than the win-lose column. With Deacon there was also a disagreement over money. Deacon's contract provided for a $30,000 bonus if he went to the Pro Bowl. He was named All Pro in 1972, but Klein refused to pay the bonus. Deacon sued and eventually won, but the process was long and left more hard feelings on both sides.

The days ticked away until there were only a few weeks left until the start of spring training for the 1974 season. Deacon still hadn't paid his fine, and Rozelle still refused to grant him a hearing. Deacon finally was able to get through and speak to the commissioner on the phone. It did no good. Pete Rozelle was unrelenting; pay the fine or retire.

Under protest, the last day before spring training, Deacon sent off his check. Deacon did so in large part because a situation had developed which interested him: George Allen told him there was a spot for him on the Redskins. Tommy Prothro was eager to deal Deacon away from San Diego, so Deacon packed his bags and headed for Washington, D.C.

Over the years, those who had no use for George Allen had spun off a variety of names for him—Trader George, Ice Cream George, George of the Jungle, Green Arrow, and more—but no one could call him a loser. For Deacon, going back to Allen was easy. The Redskins had a veteran team. They were willing to make the sacrifices, and were making a serious bid for the Super Bowl. It was the brand of football Deacon Jones longed for—*winning* football.

The way would not be easy. As it says in the Bible, the spirit was willing, but the flesh was weak. The struggle to clear his name and to get away from the Chargers had taken its toll on Deacon. For the first time since 1963, Deacon showed up for training camp without his competitive edge. He struggled all spring at historic Carlyle Penn, at the Jim Thorpe school, and couldn't seem to make progress.

Deacon knew it was time to quit. He resolved that 1974 would be his last season. He just couldn't get in shape. Deacon had lost that single-mindedness that had made him a feared and terrifying "killer of quarterbacks." He had believed passionately and intensely in the sport of professional football and in himself as a terrifying leader of the pack. He had always felt that all he had to do was give his best, and the team would take care of the rest. The team was home. The team was family.

Deacon no longer believed that. He had become mixed up in the politics of big-time sports, and had been forced to face his own mortality and the sure knowledge that he was nearing the end of his great career. And, perhaps most importantly, Deacon had come to understand that he had lost his love for playing the game. The thrill of dominating on the field no longer meant what it once had.

Still, Deacon would play the season for his own pride and for *Coach*. George Allen, the master motivator, would make it fun. They would be contenders, and Deacon would bow out a winner at the end of the season.

The 1974 season started with a 13-10 win over the Giants, followed by a 17-10 loss to St. Louis, a 30-3 win over Denver, and a 28-17 loss to Cincinnati. Deacon had agreed to the role of player-coach, and evolved into a motivator and teacher for the younger players. No longer starting, Deacon played the specialist's role, going in on third down and long and rushing the passer. Not starting didn't bother Deacon; *anything for Coach*.

Getting to the championship wasn't going to be easy for the Redskins. The team was in a tough division and had a tough schedule. Allen's Over-the-Hill Gang beat the Dolphins and the Giants before falling to St. Louis in another squeaker, 23-20. They picked things up again by whipping Green Bay and Philadelphia, and so were 6-3 as they headed for an all-important game with the hated Dallas Cowboys.

The season hung in the balance, and everybody on the team knew it. With five games to go, they were going to have to play the Cowboys twice. It was the Tuesday before the Dallas game and George Allen was holding one of his pep rallies, exhorting his players to greater efforts.

"Men," he intoned dramatically, "I want to win this game so bad, I feel like going out to midfield and kicking Tom Landry's butt! What about it? I'll kick Coach Landry's butt and then you guys get out there and boot the Cowboys all over the field!"

There was the general good-natured whoop and holler from the players, and then somebody piped up from the back, "You better be careful, Coach! That Tom's in pretty good shape. Rumor is, he takes karate!"

Allen, then over sixty, had aged into a rugged Cary Grant type. He stayed in shape with a rigorous daily running and weights program. Allen's classic winner's smile lit his face from ear to ear and he waved his fists in the air like a champion, "Karate's not going to be enough for him, men! Anyone can learn to chop and sock and bust boards with their fists—but we've got the drive and the determination to win!"

The meeting broke up with a lot of ribbing and cheering, and the players headed for the locker room to suit up for practice. Allen walked quietly back to his office, thinking it over. What everyone on the team seemed to have forgotten was Allen's connection with D.C. celebrity karate expert Jhoon Rhee. Maybe there was a way all those private lessons could be used to advantage. Jhoon Rhee had a successful karate chain and was famous in the area for his philosophy of living. Like Allen, he had mottos to live by. He believed society could be made a better place if each individual followed certain basic precepts. His personal motto was

> Honesty in the heart
> Knowledge in the mind
> And strength in the body

The compact man from the Orient with the advertising slogan "Nobody bothers me" began Allen's secret intensive training.

Before the Dallas game, Allen came into the locker with three assistants wearing white outfits. Each held up a board. Allen stood there, arms crossed and with a faint smile on his lips, eyeing the first board. It said, in the big block letters Deacon knew came from Allen's own hand, "Kick Dallas Butt!!!" Allen gave a fierce cry, whirled, and cracked the first board with his foot. A roar of laughter and cheers went up from the Redskin players. The second board said, "Take This, Tom!!!" With a big shout, Allen leapt forward and cracked the second board with his left fist. The third board read, "Dallas Doesn't Bother

Us!!!" Again the Washington head coach lunged forward with a war cry. This time he lashed out with his right hand like a knife. The last board cracked and a mighty roar of approval went up from the players.

"Go get them, men!!" Allen shouted, and the Redskins surged onto the field. Nobody knew that, in all the excitement, Allen had not carried out his last strike exactly as he was supposed to. With that last karate chop, Allen had broken his hand in several places. He quickly put it in his pocket and gave his players a cheerful wave as they scrambled for the playing field.

The Redskins won their most important game of the regular season, beating Dallas 28-21. Unfortunately, Allen's custom was to congratulate the players with a hearty handshake. He grimly plunged into it, not letting on that he was hurting, and to this day, some of his own players still don't know what happened that afternoon.

Deacon remembers his own personal efforts to have the league fines lifted. "Well, I could see they had their problems, but it seemed so unfair. We players never got a hearing of our own. It was all decided without us. That wouldn't happen today. But I felt the injustice so deeply that I personally asked Pete Rozelle for my own hearing—but he was deaf and dumb to my plea."

Harland Svare is impatient with Deacon, and feels he shouldn't be digging up the past. "The scandal brought down a lot of people— you have to learn how to put those things behind you, to go on."

To which Deacon replies, "Easy for him to say. Harland stayed on with the Chargers five years as GM and then went into real estate. We players were the ones hurt by the league rulings. Remember, Gene Klein was a millionaire. For him to pay a $20,000 fine for himself and find a way to reimburse his coach was nothing. Gene would still have his team. Harland had his job. But we, the players who were named on the prescriptions and slurred as pot smokers, have to bear the sting of those unproven accusations to this day."

Deacon remembers his angry telephone conversation with Pete Rozelle. "I told him, 'I worked my way into your system. You people created our habits. You taught us all how to play with pain, how to hurt our bodies and keep on going, how to tape our sprains and broken bones, how to take novocaine and go back out there to tear people's heads off and kill quarterbacks. What you call amphetamines and I call pain pills have been sitting around on the table in every locker room in the NFL like salt tablets throughout my whole career. And now, when you're catching the heat for it, you need a few live dogs to throw to Congress and to the press.' He denied it, of course, and said I'd had plenty of warning. I told him we'd had no warning. The Chargers had validated our use of amphetamines by furnishing them to us. And amphetamines, when prescribed by a doctor, are not illegal in this country. 'So, I'm not paying.' 'Well, then,' he said, 'you're out of the league. Either you pay or you're through in this league. Pay the fine or retire.' "

Deacon continues, "Pete Rozelle wasn't going to force me out of football. I wasn't going to be Pete's scapegoat. I'd given up everything I intended for this game. The rest was not for sale. I contacted the Players Association; we players all called, and we expected them to step in and take our side in a more active way. I'd paid my dues for thirteen years, gone on strike, walked the picket lines, backed Executive Director Ed Garvey in our labor negotiations. And yet when I needed it, I got nothing, absolute zero. I had to go out and hire my own lawyer. Nobody came to my aid. And the same was true of the rest of the players. And that is one reason why, to this day, I have no respect for the players union.

"I didn't want to pay that fine. To pay it was, in a sense, a public admission of guilt. Not one writer wrote that I was paying it under protest. I wanted to sue, but I wanted to play, too, and the legal path might have taken ten years. Still, maybe I should have sued, gone tilting at windmills, one crazy player against twenty-eight of the richest men in America. I think I'd feel better today if I had."

Contacted by phone by this writer in 1993, Billy Kilmer recalls Deacon's contributions to the Redskins in 1974: "In his last year, Deacon didn't start; Ron McDole started, and was in on first downs and running plays. Deacon came in on passing situations. He was still effective. He never lost his ability to put pressure on the quarterback."

Bruce Allen adds, "Some would say that Deacon's last year was a waste, and the stats certainly seem to bear that out. But you have to look beyond the numbers. He had heart. He inspired a lot of young kids on the Redskins. They looked at Deacon's hustle and learned from him, and later on went to the Super Bowl. Guys like that are pretty rare. He meant to the Redskins what Joe Montana has done recently for the 49ers, and after that the Chiefs."

George Allen passed away several years ago. At the Allen home in Southern California, his wife Ettie showed this writer the small removable cast that he had the doctor make for him to cover his self-inflicted karate injury. Allen only wore it at home, and he never told his team. That, for him, was simply the price of leadership. Allen never let on to the players, but Ettie says he told her ruefully that, by the weakness of his handshake, "I think they know."

Jhoon Rhee and his son Chun Rhee still work on the East Coast,

*teaching their students how to live a better life through the com-
bined disciplines of mind and body. Jhoon Rhee remembers
George Allen well. "I taught him, his wife, son and daughter for a
period of two years. He and columnist Jack Anderson were both
my students. They did a demonstration together in the Capital
Arena during halftime of a tournament between Mexico City and
D.C., kicking, punching, and chopping two boards each time. I
was present when he gave his demonstration for his team, the Redskins. I remember it was a big success. But even I did not know he
broke the bones in his hand; it would be like him to say nothing,
even though it was bleeding a little. He was one with the ability to
make strong men stronger, a leader among other leaders."*

Redskin Remembrances

The Redskins beat Philadelphia and then lost by one point to Dallas
in their seasonal rematch. At 8-4 with two games to play, the Redskins
could win their division with season-ending victories over the Los
Angeles Rams and the Chicago Bears. These two wins would be coveted over all others, not only because they would bring the divisional
championship, but because of the history both Deacon and George
Allen shared with both clubs.

The Rams game was played in the Coliseum. But this was no
longer the weak Tommy Prothro Rams, and this team wasn't going to
be a pushover. The L.A. team had been sold to Carroll Rosenbloom,
who had quickly cleaned house in the front office and hired new head
coach Chuck Knox, a defensive champion much in the George Allen
mold. Knox had realized that Prothro in his two misguided years had-
n't yet had time to destroy the heart of the Rams legendary defense;
they went back to basics and were on the way to continuing the winning dynasty first built by Allen.

Allen was in a sentimental mood, and decided Deacon would start
at his old position. So, before the game, the most famous ex-Los Angeles player ever to don a uniform got up to give a motivational speech
on just how to kick Rams' butt. He spoke with the intensity of a Baptist minister, gradually picking up the beat and pace and spirit of the
congregation and moving them to a fever pitch. He finally ended with
the following exchange

"Do we want to win?"

"We want to win!," the team roared back at him.

"How badly do we want to win?!"

"We want to win b*aaad*!"

"And how bad is bad?"

"Bad is *real bad*!"

Deacon stood and raised his hand aloft, clutching his maroon and gold helmet. "Then follow me to the Super Bowl!"

With that, Deacon rushed out of the door, followed by the entire cheering, yelling, stomping Redskins football team. Unfortunately, in all the years Deacon Jones had played on the Rams, they had always suited up in the home team locker rooms on the opposite side of the Coliseum. Those locker rooms were the identical, mirror image of the locker rooms on the visitor's side, so Deacon really didn't know where he was. Instead of finding themselves charging up the tunnel and out onto the gridiron in the light of day, the players found themselves on the back side of a wrong door, bunched together in the damp darkness of the visiting team shower room.

"Whoops! Wrong door!" Deacon yelled over the sounds of his teammates milling uncertainly in the small room. He finally got things turned around and sent them back out the right way. As they came charging up on the field, Allen grinned, but he never said anything. And the Redskins, fired up and ready for action, took a healthy chunk out of the Rams, winning a close one 23-17.

Now only one remained: it was the last game of the season, the last regular season game of Deacon Jones's career as an NFL player. The Redskins went back to Washington to take on the Chicago Bears. Bruce Allen describes what happened. "It was Sonny Jurgensen's and Deacon's last year, and nearly the last game of their careers. It was in the last quarter and we'd just scored our sixth touchdown and were winning 41-0. The Bears weren't used to being shoved around and it was late in the game and getting ugly and sloppy. Of course, they were accusing us of piling it on, and maybe we were, just a little bit. Anyway, we'd just scored our final touchdown of the day when Deacon came up to my dad and said, 'I've been the back-up kicker in high school, in college, with the Rams, the Chargers, and now the Redskins. Don't you think it's time somebody let me kick one?' So Dad sent him out there to kick the extra point."

That outraged the Bears. They already were angry because they thought the Redskins were running up the score, and now, to add insult to injury, they were sending a *defensive lineman* to kick the point after.

One look at the Bears and rookie quarterback Joe Theisman, who held for the regular kicker, completely chickened out and refused to go in and hold the ball. Theisman, fresh out of Notre Dame, could see his entire career pounded into the ground by a pile of mauling Bears, and wanted no part of it. Deacon looked him in the eye and said, "The Bears may break one or two of your bones. But if you don't go out there, I'm personally gonna break every bone in your body." Theisman shrugged and reluctantly headed for the field.

On the snap, Chicago center Wally Chambers came barreling across the line, but he got called for offsides. That moved the ball five yards closer, but now it was a more awkward angle. The Chicago team called time out, the common psychological ploy so Deacon could think about it and, maybe, get a little nervous. On the next snap, the Bears line charged forward again as if the outcome of the Super Bowl was at stake. From the Redskins bench, it looked like the Bears line was offsides *en mass,* but the refs were probably tired of the whole mess and just wanted to go home, so they didn't call anything. In the face of the on-charging, snarling, roaring Bears line, Deacon just barely got the kick off. It was an ugly thing, wobbling like a drunken duck, but it hit the upright—*and went over for the score!* So the Redskins won 42-0, the Bears were outraged, and you can look it up in the record books: Deacon Jones kicks for one point-after-touchdown.

Aside from being back with a winner, there was one other joy to playing in Washington for the Redskins. Owner George Preston Marshall had sworn publicly that he'd never had a black on his team. He'd said that if he lived three thousand years, there wouldn't be any blacks in football so long as he had anything to do with it. The Redskins were the last NFL team to have no black players, until 1962 when Ron Hatcher and Bobby Mitchell became the first to play on the team. So for Deacon Jones, there was a special pride in knowing that he was on a team that had been one of the last barriers for blacks in professional football.

In the very last game of Deacon's career, the Redskins took on the Rams for the NFL East vs. West Division playoffs. Chuck Knox's revitalized Rams beat them 19-10, and so the old power that George Allen had created on the West Coast snuffed the 1974 Super Bowl hopes of the new dynasty he was building in the East.

Deacon didn't stand around on the field and meditate on his past. He didn't spend lonely moments kicking clods of mud and staring at the chalk marks and remembering the past decade of turmoil and furious action. He packed up after the game and went back to Los Angeles, which he still considered his home base.

It was on airplanes that Deacon did some of his best thinking. The last plane out of D.C. that Sunday night was nearly deserted. Sitting in the center aisle, studiously not looking out the window even though the early dusk of a December evening had faded to blackness, Deacon thought back over his career on the football field. He remembered again his decision, that long-ago night he spent soaked and shivering behind barbed wire in Orangeburg, and determined he was going to fight the system his own way. He remembered how he'd hit his first training camp like an exploding bomb of pent-up fury. How he'd learned to control and channel his anger, to become a force in the league. How he'd learned and improved and worked to become the best in the league—the best defensive end ever to play the game.

It was a lot to be proud of, Deacon supposed. But if that was so, why did he feel so empty? Why did he feel all he had accomplished was small, compared with what waited to be done? What had he really done?

The stewardess came down the aisle, handing out pillows and turning off individual overhead reading lights, and that reminded Deacon of the time early in his career when he'd made a pass at the stewardess and ended up marrying Iretha. Iretha, Iretha, Iretha . . . what was he going to do about her? It was a marriage built on sand, a marriage of necessity, a marriage of convenience. They had used each other, but there was little enough love to it, and for years now it had been a marriage in name only. Iretha would stay with him, he knew, as long as the money held out. But wasn't there any more to it than that? Now that he no longer had to concentrate 100 percent of his attention on football, it was a question he would no longer be able to ignore. Deacon Jones the football player had hung up his spikes. But what of Deacon Jones the personality? It seemed to Deacon, as he sat thinking in the darkened airplane, that he had gained a launching pad few of his people ever reached. Like Sammy Davis, Jr., Deacon had reached a place where he could touch people's hearts, where he could move them. He could be a powerful influence for his people.

Deacon had the natural wit and presence to get up in front of reporters, fans, and cameras, to delight and charm. What direction would he choose? Television and the movie business? The night club circuit? Advertising and marketing? Politics? Motivational speaking? Dangerous new worlds fluttered before Deacon's imagination, dangerous because he knew he would pour his willpower and his concentration fully into anything he did.

And it seemed to Deacon, as powerful jet engines carried him west, that the plane was winging him on to the next exciting phase in his life. Deacon felt like he'd just graduated from college. The future at that moment seemed open and full of promise. And for once Deacon forgot where he was and looked, if only briefly, out the window. Following the sun as they were, sunset still lingered. From the height of thirty thousand feet Deacon could see banks of mountainous clouds in the distance, flashed with gold and pink and purple. It seemed the image of his future, filled with excitement and the promise of things to come.

The memory of his point after brings the old bittersweet smile to Deacon's lips. "It was so fitting. I'd spent all those years after regular practice kicking in the fog and the gloom of night, and here it was a foggy, last-minute effort in the game, and there wasn't a man on the Bears who wouldn't have killed to break through to me and block that kick! And believe me, if they'd made it through, there would have been a roughing the kicker penalty—there would have been a maiming the kicker penalty! But that ugly little kick flew like the most beautiful bird, hitting the bar and hopping right over it. I made it, and it made all those years of extra effort worthwhile, like the icing on the cake. You know, my career point after completion percentage is a perfect one thousand. How many kickers in the NFL can say that?"

Deacon's leading the Redskins into the showers instead of onto the playing field is one of those embarrassing moments that people love to remember—how the greatest of the great could also mess up in truly great fashion. Deacon just smiles and shrugs his broad shoulders. "Well," he says, reminding us of what is really important, "we did win the game."

Of owner George Marshall's bigotry he is less tolerant, "Ron Hatcher saw how it was and didn't stick around. Bobby Mitchell had to accept a lot, playing there. After a while, your mind and body get tired. You can get tired of trying to prove you are a man. Yet, the worst thing a human can do is accept the abuse; it takes a little bit away from you every time. There was a big statue they'd put up of Marshall outside the stadium, and, remembering Ron and Bobby and all the blacks who'd never been allowed to play the game, I'd spit on that statue every Sunday morning when I'd walk by."

After waiting the mandatory five-year period, in 1980, David Deacon Jones was unanimously selected to the Hall of Fame on the first round, one of only a handful of players to be so honored. And he was recently selected to the NFL's 75th Anniversary All-Time Team of Greats.

Appendix

Deacon Jones's NFL Statistics

The new defensive breed, the handful of brilliant and talented professional football players led by Deacon Jones in the 1960s and 1970s, put defense on the attack. They revolutionized the game, advancing it to nearly what it is today, and in so doing made defense fun to watch and popular with the fans. Before the coming of the big, quick defensive lineman, the contributions of all defensive players were largely ignored by the NFL. While offensive statistics were uniformly published, defensive statistics were not.

In this time of spotty record-keeping of defensive play, Deacon was fortunate on two counts: First, the Los Angeles Rams enjoyed the services of excellent play-by-play transcribers, particularly Clive Grafton, for all of their home games. And second, head coach George Allen carefully preserved the individual defensive stats for the five years he coached the Rams in his yearly playbooks, which are still in the personal files maintained by his wife and son. So the bulk of Deacon's records for his years with the Rams are preserved as official team statistics.

Deacon Jones's statistics, as compiled in this book, are verified from official Los Angeles Rams team records and playbooks, San Diego Chargers team records, NFL league records, and NFL Hall of Fame records, as specifically indicated. Wherever these statistics are compiled from play-by-play records (specifically the years 1961, 1962, 1963, 1970, and 1971), Deacon's actual statistics would be higher than what has been indicated. This is because, while the Rams play-by-play records *for home games* carefully detail the defensive players responsible for sacks, tackles, and other defensive achievements, some of the *away games* do not detail them at all. In those days, the play-by-plays were the responsibility of the home team, and when the Rams went on the road, these were compiled and furnished to the Rams by the host team. While some of these on-the-road play-by-plays are excellent (for example, the Cleveland Browns and the Washington Redskins), others (such as the Chicago Bears, Detroit Lions, and Green Bay Packers) provide no details that can be used to compile defensive statistics. So, while Deacon Jones's true performance for the years where his records have been compiled from play-by-plays (1961, 1962, 1963, 1970, and 1971) might be 20 percent or more higher than recorded here, the statistics I have recorded here are based on verifiable records, not surmise. This record of Deacon Jones's achievements in the NFL as compiled and printed here presents only official statistics which are recorded, exist at this time, and can be verified by anyone who should care to do so.

On the basis of the records which do exist, the gridiron achievements of Deacon Jones are awesome; he stands head and shoulders above any other defensive end who ever played in the NFL, including those playing today. His great records, particularly the *single-season sack record, lifetime sack record, single-season solo tackle record (first for a defensive end, second for all down-linemen),* and *lifetime solo tackle record (down-line-man)* stand as far above ordinary professional football play as Babe Ruth's home run record or Joe DiMaggio's hitting streak record stand above those of their peers in baseball.

The Los Angeles Rams (now the St. Louis Rams), the team for which Deacon played the heart of his career, and the NFL as a whole should be proud of his achievements.

DEACON JONES STATISTICAL TABLES

1961 (Los Angeles Rams)*

Sacks (6 solo, 4 assist)	8**
Solo Tackles	32
Assisted Tackles	16
QB Hurries	1
Batted Balls	0
Recovered Fumbles	3***

Compiled from official Rams records, from the play-by-plays in the Rams files in Anaheim, California, on December 30, 1991, by John Klawitter, with the permission of Marshall Klein, Los Angeles Rams Vice President of Community Affairs, and the assistance of John Oswald. The 1961 sack totals have also been verified by writer and independent statistician John Turney, who is compiling lists of NFL statistics.

*The play-by-plays for four away games, October 1 at Pittsburgh, October 8 at San Francisco, November 19 at Green Bay, and November 26 at Chicago all fail to record the names of the defensive men. Therefore, Deacon's achievements in these games are lost to history.

**Solo sacks count for 1 point, assisted sacks, $\frac{1}{2}$ point.

***Deacon ran one of these back for a gain of 10 yards.

1962 (Los Angeles Rams)*

Sacks	9**
Solo Tackles	50
Batted Balls	1
Recovered Fumbles	1***
Blocked Punt	1
Blocked Field Goal	1

Compiled from official Rams records, from the play-by-plays in the Rams files in Anaheim, California, on January 8, 1992, by John Klawitter with the permission of Marshall Klein, Los Angeles Rams Vice President of Community Affairs, and John Oswald.

*The play-by-plays for five away games, September 16 at Baltimore, October 14 at Detroit, October 18 at San Francisco, December 2 in Milwaukee (Green Bay), and December 9 at Chicago fail to record the names of the defensive men responsible for making the plays. Therefore, almost all of Deacon's achievements in these games are lost to history. A notable exception was the notation in the Detroit game of October 14, where the play-by-plays record that Lions quarterback "Plum was dropped for a 15 yard loss by Jones."

**In addition to 8 solo sacks, Deacon was credited with 2 half sacks (in combination with one other tackler); by today's methods of counting sacks, he would be awarded a total of 9 sacks for the season.

***As officially recorded in Pro Football Hall of Fame in Canton, Ohio.

1963 (Los Angeles Rams)*

Sacks	4**
Solo Tackles	26
Assisted Tackles	22
Batted Balls	3***
Recovered Fumbles	1****
Blocked Kick	1 (Minnesota game)

Compiled from official Rams records, from the play-by-plays in the Rams files in Anaheim, California, on January 8, 1992, by John Klawitter with the permission of Marshall Klein, Los Angeles Rams Vice President of Community Affairs, and John Oswald. The 1963 sack totals have also been verified by writer and independent statistician John Turney, who is compiling lists of NFL statistics.

*The play-by-plays for December 15 at Baltimore fail in most instances to record the names of the defensive men responsible for making the plays. Therefore, almost all of Deacon's achievements in this game are lost to history. The statistics are also bad for the November 3 game at Minneapolis, and Deacon may have scored a sack not counted here. He may have had an assisted sack in each of the Cleveland and Detroit games (Turney gives him 2 assisted sacks in the Detroit game), and another sack in the second Chicago game, also not counted.

**One in Detroit, $1\frac{1}{2}$ in Cleveland, $\frac{1}{2}$ in Detroit (assist), $\frac{1}{2}$ in Baltimore (assist), $\frac{1}{2}$ in San Francisco (assist).

***Two knocked-down passes and one blocked field goal.

****As officially recorded in Pro Football Hall of Fame in Canton, Ohio.

1964 (Los Angeles Rams)

Sacks	22
Solo Tackles	65
Recovered Fumbles	3*

Compiled from official Rams records as reported by Rams defensive chief Tom Catlin and Rams defensive line boss LaVern Torgeson. See Bill Libby, *Life in the Pit*, Doubleday, 1970, p.111. The 1964 sack totals have also been verified by writer and independent statistician John Turney, who is compiling lists of NFL statistics.

*As officially recorded in Pro Football Hall of Fame in Canton, Ohio.

1965 (Los Angeles Rams)

Sacks	18
Solo Tackles	68
QB Hurries	29
Batted Balls	4
Recovered Fumbles	0
Safety	1

1966 (Los Angeles Rams)

Sacks	16*
Solo Tackles	93
QB Hurries	27
Forced Fumbles	2
Knockdowns/Batted Balls	10
Recovered Fumbles	1 (from NFL records)
Interceptions	1

Compiled from George Allen's files, Monday August 12, 1991, by John Klawitter in the presence of Bruce Allen, George Allen's son and Elizabeth Jones, Deacon's wife. George Allen's statistics were taken from game films, taking into account the play-by-plays. Allen was noted throughout his career for his meticulous record keeping, and his records are the Rams official statistics for those years. It should be noted that John Turney has not had the benefit of George Allen's statistics, nor has he yet had the opportunity to view the game films for those years. This is why his career sack totals, while still declaring Deacon the leader by a broad margin, are somewhat lower than those totalled in this book.

*Bill Libby lists Deacon for 19 in 1966.

1967 (Los Angeles Rams)

	Regular Season	Post-Season*		TOTAL
		Green Bay	Cleveland	
Sacks	26	0	6	32
Solo Tackles	100	4	18	122
Assisted Tackles	39	0	0	39
QB Hurries	74	3	0	77
Forced Fumbles	3	0	0	3
Knockdowns/Batted Balls	9	0	0	9
Recovered Fumbles	1 (from NFL records)		1	

*Two Post-Season Games

1968 (Los Angeles Rams)

Sacks	24
Solo Tackles	87
Assisted Tackles	23
QB Hurries	60
Forced Fumbles	6
Recovered Fumbles	0

1969 (Los Angeles Rams)*

	Regular Season	Post-Season		TOTAL
		Minnesota	Dallas	
Sacks	15	0	3	18
Solo Tackles	59	2	5	66
Assisted Tackles	55	0	0	55
QB Hurries	18	0	2	20
Knockdowns	3	0	0	3
Blocks/Interceptions	2	0	0	2
Recovered Fumbles	1 (from NFL records)			1

*During the 14 years of Deacon's career, from 1961 through 1974, the NFL played 14 games per season; today the NFL teams play 16. However, in 67 and again in 69 the Rams played 2 post-season games. Deacon's sack stats for those 4 games are indicated in the statistics after the regular season totals for 1967 and 1969.

1970 (Los Angeles Rams)*

Sacks	12
Solo Tackles	44
Assisted Tackles	16
QB Hurries	6
Recovered Fumbles	1 (from NFL records)

*The play-by-plays for one away game, November 14 at Detroit, fail to record any defensive play. Therefore, all of Deacon's achievements in that game are lost to history.

1971 (Los Angeles Rams)*

Sacks	$4\frac{1}{2}$
Solo Tackles	26
Assisted Tackles	8
QB Hurries	2
Batted Balls	3
Recovered Fumbles	0

*Deacon played hurt for almost the entire season, due to torn arch ligaments in his push-off foot. He played in only 12 games, missing the October 10 game against San Francisco at Candlestick Park and the October 17 game against the Falcons in Atlanta. He first tore the ligaments in the second game of the season, when the Falcons played in Los Angeles, and then aggravated it the next week against the Bears. The injury didn't heal until the off-season.

Compiled from official Rams records, from the play-by-plays in the Rams files in Anaheim, California on December 30, 1991, and January 8, 1992, by John Klawitter with the permission of Marshall Klein, Los Angeles Rams Vice President of Community Affairs, and John Oswald. The 1970 and 1971 sack totals have also been verified by writer and independent statistician John Turney, who is compiling lists of NFL statistics.

1972 (San Diego Chargers)*

Sacks**	6
Solo Tackles	39
Assisted Tackles	33
Recovered Fumbles	1 (from NFL records)

*Deacon led the team with a total of 72 tackles.

**In the Denver game—1, first Kansas City game—$\frac{1}{2}$, Cleveland—$\frac{1}{2}$, Miami-1, second Kansas City game—1, Dallas—2.

1973 (San Diego Chargers)*

Sacks**	5
Solo Tackles	38
Assisted Tackles	29
Recovered Fumbles	1 (stat from NFL records)

*Deacon played in 12 games.

**In the Washington game—1, First Kansas City game—$\frac{1}{2}$, Oakland—1, Atlanta—1, Cleveland—1, second Oakland game—$\frac{1}{2}$

Compiled from official San Diego Chargers statistics as supplied to John Klawitter by Pat Rogers, San Diego Chargers Public Relations Department on September 9, 1991. The 1972 and 1973 sack totals have been updated by writer and independent statistician John Turney, who is compiling lists of NFL statistics. Where Rogers gave Deacon 5 sacks for 1972 and 4_ for 1973, Turney found 6 and 5 in the play-by-plays.

1974 (Washington Redskins)*

Sacks**	3
Point After	1

*Telecast Rams-Giants game, 1992, for CBS chart totalling Deacon's sack records, including three for 1974.

**Greg Scopitoni, CBS.

Deacon Jones Career Statistics—Sacks, Solo Tackles

Sacks	$180\frac{1}{2}$ ($171\frac{1}{2}$ regular season, 9 post-season)
Solo Tackles	752 (727 regular season, 25 post-season)

Deacon Jones Career Statistics—
Recovered Fumbles, Safeties, Interceptions
(as officially recorded in the Pro Football Hall of Fame in Canton, Ohio)

Recovered Fumbles	4
Safety	2
Interceptions	1
Point After	1

Deacon Jones NFL Records

Verified by official NFL team records and statistics

NFL single-season sack leader, regular season (1967)	26
NFL single-season sack leader, regular and post-season (1967)	32
NFL career record sack leader	$180\frac{1}{2}$*
NFL career solo tackles—down lineman	752
NFL single-season solo tackles—down lineman (1967)	100**

*This total agrees with the independent research of CBS.

**Chicago Bears Center Wally Chambers surpassed this record in 1973 with 101. Deacon's record still holds for defensive ends.

Deacon Jones Special Honors

NFL All-Pro (ten times)
All-Star Pro Bowls (nine times)
NFL Most Valuable Defensive Player 1967
NFL Most Valuable Defensive Player 1968
Member, NFL Hall of Fame
Member, South Carolina Hall of Fame
Member, Florida Hall of Fame
Member, South Carolina Hall of Fame
Member, South Carolina State College Hall of Fame
"The greatest defensive end of modern football"—George Allen
"Most valuable Ram of all time"—*Los Angeles Times*
First String, All-Time Black College Athlete's Team
Starting Defensive Left End, 75th Anniversary NFL Dream Team
Vincent Lombardi Award, Boy Scouts of America

NFL Career Quarterback Sack Leaders
©Compiled by John M. Turney, all rights reserved, 1996

After years of research, John Turney has compiled a list of the top four hundred NFL sackers, everyone who has been credited with more than fifteen sacks. He has used only the strictest research standards, relying on the team play-by-plays, newspapers and game films.

Players active in 1995 are shown in **BOLD**.

Rank	Total	Name, Position, Years Played, Totals for Each Team
1.	173.5	Deacon Jones DE 1961-74, Rams (159.5), Chargers (11), Redskins (3)
2.	157.0	**Reggie White DE-DT 1985-95 Eagles (124.0), Packers (33.0)** +4.5 Showboats-USFL (23.5)
3.	150.5	Jack Youngblood DE 1971-84 Rams (150.5)
4.	148.5	Alan Page DT-DE 1967-81, Vikings (108.5), Bears (40)
5.	142.0	Lawrence Taylor OLB 1981-93 Giants (142.0)
6.	136.0	**Rickey Jackson OLB-DB 1981-95 Saints (123.0), 49ers, (13.0)**
7.	133.5	Carl Eller DE 1964-79 Vikings (130.5), Seahawks (3.0)
8.	132.5	Claude Humphrey DE 1968-74, 1976-81, Falcons (105), Eagles (2.5)
9.	130.0	Al Baker DE 1978-90, Lions (73.5), Cardinals (37.5), Browns (13.5), Vikings (5.5)
	130.0	Coy Bacon DE 1968-81, Rams (41), Chargers (23.5), Bengals (27.0), Redskins (38.5), Federals-USFL (6.5)
11.	127.0	Jim Marshall DE 1960-1979, Browns (0), Vikings (127)
12.	126.5	**Bruce Smith DE Bills (126.0)**
	126.5	Richard Dent DE 1983-95, Bears (124.5), 49ers (2.0)
14.	126.0	Cedrick Hardman DE 1970-81 49ers (111.5), Raiders (14.5), Invaders-USFL (9.0)
15	116.0	Jacob Green DE 1980-92, Seahawks (116), 49ers (0)
16.	114.0	Harvey Martin DE 1973-1983, Cowboys (114.0)
17.	112.5	Lyle Alzado DE-DT 1971-85, Broncos (64.5), Browns (24.5), Raiders (23.5)
18.	111.0	Randy White DT-LB 1975-88, Cowboys (111)
19.	109.5	Greg Townsend DE-OLB 1983-94 Raiders (107.5), Eagles (2.0)
20.	109.0	Andy Robustelli DE 1951-64 Rams (28.5), Giants (80.5)
21.	108.0	**Sean Jones DE 1984-95 Raiders (31.0), Oilers (57.5), Packers (19.5)**
	108.0	**Kevin Greene OLB-De 1985-95 Rams (72.5), Steelers (35.5)**
23.	107.5	Mark Gastineau DE 1979-88, Jets (107.5), B.C. Lions-CFL (0)
24.	106.0	Ed Jones DE 1974-78, 1980-89 Cowboys (106)
25.	105.5	**Leslie O'Neal DE-OLB 1986-95 Charges (105.5)**
26.	105.0	**Chris Doleman DE-OLB 1985-95 Vikings (88.5), Falcons (16.1)**

	105.0	Elvin Bethea DE-G 168-83 Oilers (105)
28.	103.5	Dexter Manley DE 1981-91 Redskins (97), Cardinals (0), Buccaneers (6.5), Rough Riders-CFL (0)
29.	103.0	Fred Dryer DE 1969-81 Giants (28), Rams (75)
	103.0	Jack Gregory DE 1967-79 Browns (38), Giants (65)
31.	101.0	Tommy Hart DE-LE 1968-80 49ers (92.5), Bears (7.5), Saints (1)
32.	100.0	Andre Tippett OLB 1982-88, 1990-93 Patriots (100.0)
	100.0	Ezra Johnson DE 1977-91 Packers (86), Colts (11.5), Oilers (2.5)
34.	98.5	**Pat Swilling OLB-DE 1986-95 Saints (76.5), Lions (9.0), Raiders (13.0)**
35.	97.5	**Simon Fletcher OLB-DE 1985-95 Broncos (97.5)**
36.	97.0	**Jim Jeffcoat DE-DT 1983-95 Cowboys (94.5), Bills (2.5)**
	97.0	George Andre DE 1961-73 Cowboys (97)
38.	96.5	**Charles Haley OLB-DE 1986-95 49ers (63.5), Cowboys (33.0)**
	96.5	Tony McGee DE 1971-84 Bears (5), Patriots (70.25), Redskins (21.0)
40.	96.0	George Martin DE 1975-88 Giants (96)
41.	95.5	Jethro Pugh DT 1966-78 Cowboys (96.5)
42.	95.0	Steve McMichael DT 1980-94 Patriots (0), Bears (92.5), Packers (2.5)
	95.0	Jim Katcavage DE 1956-68 Giants (95)
44.	94.5	Carl Hairston DE 1976-90 Eagles (56), Browns (37.5), Cardinals (1.0)
45.	94.0	Bob Lilly DT-DE 1961-74 Cowboys (94)
46.	93.0	**Clyde Simmons DE 1986-95 Eagles (76.0), Cardinals (17.0)**
	93.0	Fred Dean DE 1975-85 Chargers (53), 49ers (40.0)
48.	92.0	Merlin Olsen DT 1962-76 Rams (92)
49.	91.5	Howie Long DE 1981-93 Raiders (91.5)
50.	90.5	Verlon Biggs DE 1965-75 Jets (58.25), Redskins (32)
51.	87.0	John Zook DE 1969-79 Falcons (69), Cardinals (18)
52.	85.0	**Derrick Thomas OLB-DE 1989-95 Chiefs (85.0)**
53.	84.5	Eddie Edwards DE 1977-88 Bengals (84.5)
	84.5	Diron Talbert DT-DE 1968-80 Rams (19), Redskins (65.5)
55.	83.5	Leonard Marshall DE-DT 1983-94 Giants (79.5), Jets (2.0), Redskins (2.0)
56.	83.0	Charles Mann DE 1983-94 Redskins (82.0), 49ers (1.0)
57.	82.5	Lee Williams DE-DT 1984-93 Chargers (65.5), Oilers (17.0), Express-USFL (13.0)
58.	82.0	Dan Hampton DE-DT 1979-80 Bears (82.0)
	82.0	L.C. Greenwood DE 1969-81 Steelers (82)
60.	81.5	**William Fuller DE 1986-95 Oilers (59.5), Eagles (22.5), Stars-USFL (13.0)**
	81.5	Jim Osborne DT 1972-84 Bears (81.5)
62.	81.0	**Tim Harris OLB-DE 1986-95 Packers (55.0), 49ers (26.0), Eagles (0.0)**

Bibliography

"Action Highlight Films," taped sports news reports and tapes of Deacon as a motivational speaker, celebrity, motion picture star and television actor, courtesy Elizabeth Jones.

Allen, George, with Ben Olan. *Pro Football's 100 Greatest Players.* New York: Bobbs-Merrill, 1982.

Allen, George. *Strategies for Winning.* New York: McGraw-Hill, 1990.

Carruth, Gorton. *What Happened When.* New York: Harper & Row, 1989.

Chandler, Bob, and Norm Chandler Fox. *Violent Sundays.* New York: Simon & Schuster, 1984.

Dobler, Conrad, and Vic Carucci. *They Call Me Dirty.* New York: Jove, 1989.

Donovan, Pete, John Oswald, Lillian Arbenz, and Scott Jones. *The Los Angeles Rams Official 1985 Media Guide.* 1985.

Editors of Time-Life Books. *This Fabulous Century: Volume 7, 1960–1970.* Alexandria, Va.: Time-Life Books, 1970.

Gildea, William and Kenneth Turan. *The Future Is Now.* Boston: Houghton Mifflin, 1972.

Henderson, Thomas, and Peter Knobler. *Out Of Control: The Confessions of an NFL Casualty.* New York: Pocket, 1987.

Huizenga, Rob, M.D. *You're Okay, It's Just a Bruise.* New York: St. Martin's Griffin, 1994.

Kramer, Jerry, edited by Dick Schaap. *Instant Replay.* New York: New American Library, 1968.

Klein, Gene, and David Fisher. *First Down and a Billion.* New York: William Morrow, 1987.

Libby, Bill. *Life in the Pit: The Deacon Jones Story.* New York: Doubleday, 1970.

Life: 50th Anniversary Collector's Edition. New York, 1986.

Madden, John, with Dave Anderson. *Hey, Wait a Minute (I Wrote a Book!)* New York: Ballantine, 1984.

Mandell, Arnold J., M.D. *The Nightmare Season.* New York: Random House, 1976.

Meggyesy, Dave. *Out of Their League.* Forestville, Calif.: Ramparts Press, 1970.

Neft, David S., and Richare M. Cohen. *The Sports Encyclopedia/Football, Edition 9, The Modern Era, 1960–1990.* New York: St. Martin's, 1991.

The Official National Football League 1991 Record and Fact Book. New York: Workman Publishing, 1991.

"Play-By-Plays," courtesy Los Angeles Rams, 1960–1971; San Diego Chargers, 1972 and 1973; and Washington Redskins, 1974.

"Rams Playbooks," courtesy Bruce and Eddy Allen, 1966–1970.

Rathet, Mike, and Don R. Smith. *Their Deeds and Dogged Faith.* New York: Balsam Press, 1984.

Sample, Johnny. *Confessions of a Dirty Ballplayer.* New York: Dell, 1970.

Smith, Don R. *Pro Football Hall of Fame All-Time Greats.* New York: Octopus, 1988.

Turney, John M. "NFL Career Quarterback Sack Leaders," 1996.

*   *   *

Newspaper quotes of game action are from the day after the game was played—generally, but not necessarily, a Monday.

Index